The Blackwell Companion
to Modern Theology

Blackwell Companions to Religion

The Blackwell Companions to Religion series presents a collection of the most recent scholarship and knowledge about world religions. Each volume draws together newly-commissioned essays by distinguished authors in the field, and is presented in a style which is accessible to undergraduate students, as well as scholars and the interested general reader. These volumes approach the subject in a creative and forward-thinking style, providing a forum in which leading scholars in the field can make their views and research available to a wider audience.

Published

The Blackwell Companion to Judaism
Edited by Jacob Neusner and Alan J. Avery-Peck

The Blackwell Companion to Sociology of Religion
Edited by Richard K. Fenn

The Blackwell Companion to the Hebrew Bible
Edited by Leo G. Perdue

The Blackwell Companion to Postmodern Theology
Edited by Graham Ward

The Blackwell Companion to Hinduism
Edited by Gavin Flood

The Blackwell Companion to Political Theology
Edited by Peter Scott and William T. Cavanaugh

The Blackwell Companion to Protestantism
Edited by Alister E. McGrath and Darren C. Marks

The Blackwell Companion to Modern Theology
Edited by Gareth Jones

The Blackwell Companion to Christian Ethics
Edited by Stanley Hauerwas and Samuel Wells

The Blackwell Companion to Religious Ethics
Edited by William Schweiker

The Blackwell Companion to Christian Spirituality
Edited by Arthur Holder

The Blackwell Companion to the Study of Religion
Edited by Robert A. Segal

The Blackwell Companion to the Qur'ān
Edited by Andrew Rippin

The Blackwell Companion to Contemporary Islamic Thought
Edited by Ibrahim M. Abu-Rabi'

The Blackwell Companion to the Bible and Culture
Edited by John F.A. Sawyer

The Blackwell Companion to Catholicism
Edited by James J. Buckley, Frederick Christian Bauerschmidt, and Trent Pomplun

Forthcoming

The Blackwell Companion to the New Testament
Edited by David Aune

The Blackwell Companion to Eastern Christianity
Edited by Ken Parry

The Blackwell Companion to Modern Theology

Edited by

Gareth Jones

Blackwell
Publishing

BLACKWELL PUBLISHING
350 Main Street, Malden, MA 02148-5020, USA
9600 Garsington Road, Oxford OX4 2DQ, UK
550 Swanston Street, Carlton, Victoria 3053, Australia

First published 2004
First published in paperback 2007 by Blackwell Publishing Ltd

1   2007

Library of Congress Cataloging-in-Publication Data has been applied for.

ISBN 978-0-631-20685-9 (hardback)
ISBN 978-1-4051-5975-3 (paperback)

A catalogue record for this title is available from the British Library.

Set in 10 on 12.5 pt Photina
by SNP Best-set Typesetter Ltd, Hong Kong
Printed and bound in the United Kingdom
by TJ International Ltd, Padstow, Cornwall

The publisher's policy is to use permanent paper from mills that operate a sustainable forestry policy, and which has been manufactured from pulp processed using acid-free and elementary chlorine-free practices. Furthermore, the publisher ensures that the text paper and cover board used have met acceptable environmental accreditation standards.

For further information on
Blackwell Publishing, visit our website:
www.blackwellpublishing.com

Contents

Contributors

Ray Anderson is Senior Professor of Theology and Ministry at Fuller Theological Seminary in Pasadena, California. He is the author of many books and articles, the most recent including *The Shape of Practical Theology: Empowering Ministry with Theological Praxis* (2003) and *Spiritual Caregiving as Secular Sacrament: A Practical Theology for Professional Caregivers* (2003). His current research interests center on a post-theistic evangelical theology.

Richard Arrandale taught religion and theology at Christ Church University College in Canterbury, Kent, from 1997 to 2003, and he is currently pursuing a career as a freelance writer on mysticism and new age spiritualities, based in Glastonbury, UK. His publications include articles on the work of Antonin Artaud, the tensions between psychology and theology, and the interface between religion and postmodernism.

John Barton is the Oriel and Laing Professor of the Interpretation of Holy Scripture at the University of Oxford. Among his many publications are *The Spirit and the Letter* (1997) and (with John Muddiman) his edition of the *Oxford Bible Commentary* (2001). His current research interests center on a project on the nature of biblical criticism.

Stephen F. Brown is Director of the Institute of Medieval Philosophy and Theology at Boston College, Massachusetts. He is editor of five volumes of the *Opera Philosophica et Theologica* of William of Ockham, and editor of *Bonaventure: The Journey of the Mind to God* and *Aquinas, on Faith and Reason*. He is author of more than fifty articles on medieval philosophy and theology. He is currently working on an edition of Book 1 of Richard Fishacre's *Commentary on the Sentences* and collecting a number of translated medieval texts dealing with the development of theology as a scientific university discipline.

Don Browning is Alexander Campbell Professor of Religious Ethics and the Social Sciences Emeritus of the Divinity School, University of Chicago. His most recent publication is *Marriage and Modernization: Why Globalization Threatens Marriage and What to Do* *about It* (2003). He is also Director of the Religion, Culture, and Family Project located at the University of Chicago.

David B. Burrell, CSC, is Hesburgh Professor of Philosophy and Theology at the University of Notre Dame, Indiana, and author most recently of *Friendship and Ways to Truth*, as well as translator of al-Ghazali's *Faith in Divine Unity and Trust in Divine Providence*.

James M. Byrne is Associate Professor of Religious Studies at St. Michael's College, Vermont. He is the author of *God: Thoughts in an Age of Uncertainty* (2001) and *Religion and Enlightenment* (1997), together with other articles and publications. His research interests center on philosophy and modern theology.

Andrew Chester is Fellow of Selwyn College, Cambridge. He is the author of many books and articles, including work on the Pentateuchal Targums and the Letter of James. His research interests center on messianic hope and eschatology in early Judaism and Christianity.

M. Shawn Copeland is Associate Professor of Systematic Theology at Boston College, Massachusetts, and (adjunct) Associate Professor of Systematic Theology at the Institute for Black Catholic Studies, Xavier University, Louisiana. Her academic research and publications include the areas of theological and philosophical anthropology, political theology and philosophy, and embodiment, with special attention to gender and race.

Gavin D'Costa is Reader in Christian Theology and Head of the Department of Theology and Religious Studies at the University of Bristol, UK. He is a consultant to the Church of England, the Catholic Bishop's Conference, and the Vatican on issues regarding other religions. In 1998 he served as the Joseph McCarthy Visiting Professor at the Pontifical Gregorian University in Rome. Recent publications include *The Trinity and the Meeting of Religions* (2000) and *Sexing the Trinity* (2000). His research interests are in contemporary theology, theology of religions, and gender and psychoanalysis.

Patricia Daniel teaches feminism and religious studies at Christ Church University College, Canterbury, and other institutions in Kent, UK. The author of several articles on feminist theologies, she continues to research in contemporary feminism.

William Dean is Professor of Constructive Theology at the Iliff School of Theology, Denver, Colorado. Specializing in the distinctively American tradition of religious thought, his books include *American Religious Empiricism* (1986), *History Making History* (1988), *The American Spiritual Culture* (2002), and *The Religious Critic in American Culture* (1994), which received the American Academy of Religion Award for Excellence.

Dawn DeVries is John Newton Thomas Professor of Systematic Theology at Union Theological Seminary and Presbyterian School of Christian Education, Richmond, Virginia. She is currently working on a major study of Schleiermacher's dogmatic theology. She is the author of *Jesus Christ in the Preaching of Calvin and Schleiermacher* and the editor and translator of *Servant of the Word: Selected Sermons of Friedrich Schleiermacher*.

G. R. Evans is Professor of Medieval Theology and Intellectual History at the University of Cambridge. She is the author of numerous books in the fields of patristic, medieval and ecumenical history and theology, including *Philosophy and Theology in the Middle Ages* (1994), *Law and Theology in the Middle Ages* (2001), and *Anselm* (1998). She is also the author of *A Brief History of Heresy* (2003) and the editor of *The Medieval Theologians* and *The Early Christian Theologians*.

Robin Gill is Michael Ramsey Professor of Modern Theology at the University of Kent at Canterbury, UK. He is the author of some twenty books, including most recently *Changing Worlds* (2002), *The "Empty" Church Revisited* (2003), and *A Sense of Grace* (2004).

Garrett Green teaches religious studies at Connecticut College. He is the author of *Imagining God: Theology and the Religious Imagination* (1998) and *Theology, Hermeneutics, and Imagination: The Crisis of Interpretation at the End of Modernity* (2000). His current research centers on the relationship between philosophy, aesthetics, and modern theology, particularly contemporary debates about modernism and postmodernism.

John W. de Gruchy is Robert Selby Taylor Professor of Christian Studies at the University of Cape Town, South Africa. The author of many books and articles, he has recently edited the *Cambridge Companion to Bonhoeffer* (1999), as well as *Reconciliation: Restoring Justice* (2002). He remains deeply involved in the work for truth and reconciliation in South Africa, as well as continuing his long-term work on the life and thought of Dietrich Bonhoeffer.

Gareth Jones is Professor of Christian Theology and Director of the Centre for Anglican Studies, at Christ Church University College, Canterbury, UK. He was founder editor of *Reviews in Religion and Theology*, and was recently theological consultant to the House of Bishops of the Church of England. His publications include *Critical Theology* (1995) and *Christian Theology: A Brief Introduction* (1999), and his current research interests center on the role of theological reflection in the contemporary Anglican Communion.

Laurel Kearns is Associate Professor of Sociology of Religion and Environmental Studies at Drew Theological School and the Casperson School of Graduate Studies at Drew University, Madison, New Jersey. She is co-editor of the Christianity-related articles for the forthcoming *Encyclopedia of Religion and Nature* and a member of the Religion and Ecology Steering Committee for the American Academy of Religion. Her research and writing have focused on religious (predominantly Christian) ecological activism, greening the ethnography of religion, and environmental justice.

Karen Kilby is Lecturer in Systematic Theology at the University of Nottingham, UK. She has written a brief introduction to the thought of Karl Rahner, *Karl Rahner* (1997) and is about to publish a more substantial study, *Rahner: Theology and Philosophy*.

Mark Lindsay is Director of Studies at Trinity College, University of Melbourne. He has been researching the theological basis of Karl Barth's opposition to Nazism and the Holocaust, and has published a number of articles and chapters in the broad field of post-Holocaust theology.

Mark McIntosh, Associate Professor of Theology at Loyola University, Chicago, is an Episcopal priest and canon theologian to the Presiding Bishop and Primate of the Episcopal Church, USA. The author of *Mystical Theology* and other books investigating the intersection of spirituality and theology, he is also the author of the forthcoming *Blackwell Guide to Christian Theology*.

Ian Markham is the Dean of Hartford Seminary and Professor of Theology and Ethics, Hartford Seminary, Connecticut. He is the author of *Plurality and Christian Ethics* (1994), *Truth and the Reality of God* (1999), and *A Theology of Engagement* (2003). His current research centers on Christian and Hindu explanations for disagreement.

Bruce D. Marshall is Professor of Historical Theology at Southern Methodist University, Dallas, Texas, where he teaches medieval and Reformation studies, and systematic theology. He is the author of several books and articles, including *Christology in Conflict* (1987) and *Trinity and Truth* (2000). His research interests include the Trinity and Christology, philosophical issues in theology, and Judaism and Christian theology.

Charles T. Mathewes is Associate Professor of Religious Studies at the University of Virginia, where he teaches theology, ethics, and culture. He is the author of *Evil and the Augustinian Tradition* and the forthcoming *A Theology of Public Life during the World*. His research interests center on moral and political theory and Christian doctrine.

Ralph Norman is Lecturer in Historical Theology at Christ Church University College at Canterbury, Kent, UK. His monograph on the doctrine of the ascension is in preparation, and his current research interests center on the doctrine of God.

Martyn Percy is Director of the Lincoln Theological Institute based at the University of Manchester, UK, where he is also Reader in the Department of Theology and Religious Studies. His recent publications include *Salt of the Earth: Religious Resilience in a Secular Age* (2002). He is currently researching into Christianity and contemporary culture, and modern ecclesiology.

Esther D. Reed is Lecturer in Theology and Ethics at the University of St. Andrews, UK, and editor of *Studies in Christian Ethics*. She is author of *The Genesis of Ethics* (2000) and *A Theological Reading of Hegel's "Phenomenology of Spirit", with Particular Reference to its Themes of Identity, Alienation and Community* (1996). Her current research interests lie in the ethics of human rights and Protestant traditions of natural law associated with Richard Hooker, Robert Sanderson, Hugo Grotius, and more recent thinkers in this tradition.

Robert John Russell is Founder and Director of the Center for Theology and the Natural Sciences and Professor of Theology and Science in Residence, at the Graduate Theological Union, Berkeley, California. He is co-editor of the 5-volume CTNS/Vatican Observatory series on science and divine action. He is currently working on the book, *Time in Eternity: Theology and Science in Mutual Interaction*, for which he won a PCRS/Templeton Grant for research and writing on the constructive engagement of religion and science.

Carl R. Trueman is Associate Professor of Church History and Historical Theology at Westminster Theological Seminary in Philadelphia, Pennsylvania. He is author of *Luther's Legacy: Salvation and English Reformers, 1525–1556* (1997) and *The Claims of Truth: John Owen's Trinitarian Theology* (1998). His current research interests include seventeenth century Reformed Orthodoxy in relation to medieval and Renaissance thought.

John Webster is Professor of Systematic Theology at Aberdeen University, having until recently been Lady Margaret Professor of Divinity at the University of Oxford. He is the author of many books and articles on modern and systematic theology, including most recently *Holiness* (2003), and he edited the *Cambridge Companion to Barth* (2000). His research interests center on constructive Christian dogmatics and modern historical theology, with particular interest in Barth's theology in the 1920s.

Merold Westphal is Distinguished Professor of Philosophy at Fordham University in New York City. He is past president of the Hegel Society of America and of the Søren Kierkegaard Society, and has served as Executive Co-Director of the Society for Phenomenology and Existential Philosophy (SPEP). He is the author of *History and Truth in Hegel's Phenomenology* (1979), *Hegel, Freedom, and Modernity* (1992), and *Overcoming Onto-Theology* (2001), among many other publications.

Preface

What is "Modern Theology"?

Attempts to define Christian theology can be notoriously facile. One is often told that such theology is "faith seeking understanding." Alternately, it is often remarked that theology is the interpretation of doctrine, so that one regards interpretation as the business of testing and applying doctrine to the experienced life of the Church. Richard Hooker defined theology as "the science of things divine," and developing Hooker's statement is Locke's famous definition of theology, from 1698:

> Theology, which, containing the knowledge of God and his creatures, our duty to him and our fellow-creatures, and a view of our present and future state, is the comprehension of all other knowledge, directed to its true end.

Each of these definitions works quite straightforwardly, as do many others. One of the things one constantly discovers is that if Christian theology is Christian talk of God, then the fact that there are many different ways of doing that in today's world demonstrates that pluralism is inherent to any question of how to define theology. What matters then is to what extent such pluralism is true; or, better, to what extent theological ideas allow for different interpretations.

Attempts to define *modern* theology exacerbate this difficulty, for the singular reason that the concept "modernity" itself allows for no unambiguous definition. To support this argument, consider solely whether "modernity" is concerned with time, or scope. Is "modernity" a period of history, or is it a particular way of understanding? In other words, if one is attempting a first definition of modern theology, does one try to define a particular period of Christian history, with a start and an end, or does one try to define a way of thinking about Christian ideas that might be coterminous with a specific historical period, but which is intellectual rather than circumstantial?

If the former – as is often the case – then modern theology is roughly the period 1600–1980, with early modernity arguably evident in the sixteenth century, and late modernity giving way to postmodernity in the 1980s. If the latter, then modern theology "begins" when people seek to think about their faith in terms of the world in which they live, rather than the other way round. One *might* characterize this intellectual definition in relation to time – one might still trace its origin to around 1600, for example – but the essential quality is the way of thinking, rather than the historic moment when it started to occur.

These initial definitions need greater attention, however. If the governing factor is time, then questions about modernity's beginnings and ends, and hence questions about premodernity and postmodernity, become identifiable with specific historical texts and contexts, ideas and arguments. As a way of testing this argument, one can consider how it works as a way of interpreting a classic text. And, taking a text that is well beyond the usual scope of modern theology (if modernity is defined temporally), then one can legitimately ask whether or not Dante's *Divine Comedy* is a work of modern theology, and thereby whether or not modernity itself is a viable concept in interpreting a text written in 1321. On this reading, it is clearly nonsensical to argue that Dante's *Divine Comedy* is a modern text, since overwhelmingly scholarship contends that modern theology "begins" no earlier than the mid-sixteenth century. The argument is elementary: 1321 is earlier than 1550; *quod erat demonstrandum*.

If modernity is defined in terms of scope, however, the situation becomes much more complex. Considering the same, unusual example, Dante's *Divine Comedy*, one now has to ask whether or not the text itself betrays what one might call a modern theological understanding of the relationship between God and the world, and then whether or not this betrayal is deliberate or accidental; i.e., intended by Dante, or not. If Dante intended to write a text that demonstrates a modern understanding of the relationship between God and the world, then his *Divine Comedy* is a work of modern theology, whether or not it was written in 1321.

Such an exercise requires that one first decide what criteria one considers fundamental to one's definition of modernity. That argument, however, is itself circular, because: What comes first, a modern understanding, or criteria of the modern? Or, stated more clearly: What possible criteria for defining modernity can one identify, that do not arise naturally from the texts that were written in modern times? One recognizes the problem: criteria of interpretation that are alien to the texts to be interpreted are often worse than useless.

All of this becomes quickly and unnecessarily baffling, almost as if the sheer difficulty of defining the way Christians speak of God is not in itself sufficiently difficult. For the sake of argument, therefore, this *Companion* grants that questions of historical contingency – *time* – are secondary to questions of critical thinking – *scope* – and that consequently modern theology is to be defined in terms of how we consider the problems that arise when theologians attempt to understand the relationship between God and the world. Here we can make a first assertion that governs the philosophy of this volume: *modern* theology begins when theologians look beyond the Church for answers to their questions.

Such an argument allows one to focus upon certain key texts, individuals, themes, and arguments, whilst not covering others. To some extent it is arbitrary, of course: decisions about inclusion and exclusion generally are. Modern theology has a manageable shape, however, one that has been recognized and studied for several generations, and one that remains largely normative for how one understands much Christian reflection in the eighteenth to twentieth centuries. It is characterized by questions of engagement with philosophy, society, science, and culture, and populated – if that is the right term – by such figures as Kant, Hegel, Schleiermacher, Barth, and Rahner. It is a period when certain ways of interpreting Christian ideas arrived at new definitions of history and eschatology, for example, or the central doctrines of the Christian faith. And it was – is – a period when new challenges arose to make people think about their faith with renewed urgency. As indicated, however, one key intellectual idea characterizes these attempts: people start to look beyond the Church for answers to their questions.

Dante's *Divine Comedy*

Naturally enough, therefore, the vast majority of texts and ideas that will be considered in this volume come from the period when people started looking beyond the Church for answers to their questions, after approximately 1700. To find a way into a more nuanced definition, however, one may reconsider Dante's *Divine Comedy* at this point, making a distinction between medieval and modern theologies that is informative. The traditional way to understand Dante's poem is to view it as a reflection upon the tension between philosophy and theology, personified in the figures of Virgil and Dante respectively. On this reading philosophy leads the pilgrim – Dante – into a sequence of reflections and encounters, principally with the consequences of moral failings. This process is characterized by a high degree of openness, so that for Virgil reason is given free rein to address the questions humanity faces in understanding itself morally.

This process, however, is very limited: it can lead Dante through Hell and into Purgatory, for example, but it cannot cross the boundary of Purgatory, into Heaven itself. Why? Because Heaven is the realm of God and the Church, and only faith – and faith-thinking, or theology – can find its way in that world. Heaven is *closed*; and it "opens" only to the eyes of faith, not to those of reason. Virgil, therefore, is literally incapable of guiding Dante into Heaven, because he cannot "see" Heaven, a reality that afflicts him and which characterizes his state in Limbo, as Dante describes in the *Purgatorio* of the *Divine Comedy*:

> I am Virgil; and for no other crime
> Than not having faith, I lost heaven . . .
> (*Purgatorio* VII. 7–8)[1]

On this reading, Dante's *Divine Comedy* is a work of medieval theology because medieval theology is characterized by an emphasis upon a closed universe, ordered by God and intelligible solely to God. Philosophy, it is true, pushes toward openness, so that one might argue that certain forms of scholastic theology in the fourteenth and fifteenth centuries find their center in the debate over the proper limits of reason, and the extent to which they can play any role in theological reflection. That tension – between closure and openness, faith and reason – is central to Dante, as I have argued; but it is also central to the greater world of medieval and scholastic theologies. And, for Dante at least, it is a tension that can only be resolved in favor of closure, because God's world is the *locus* of God's being, and God's being is not open to human thought.

There is at least one other way to read Dante, however, and it is what I have characterized as the modern reading of the *Divine Comedy*. On this reading the tension between philosophy and theology is not antagonistic, and cannot be characterized in terms of a juxtaposition of openness and closure. Rather, the subject matter of both philosophy and theology is the same, namely, human being. The sole difference, admittedly a significant one, is that philosophy and theology approach this subject matter from different perspectives, and with different presuppositions; or, stated more clearly, they give different answers to the same questions.

One of the clearest examples of this process at work in twentieth-century thought was in the relationship between the philosopher Martin Heidegger and the theologian Rudolf Bultmann. For both Heidegger and Bultmann the proper subject matter of reflection was human being, something which both men thought was best intelligible in terms of existentialist analysis. As Bultmann readily acknowledged, Heidegger's historical phenomenological analysis of the conditions of possibility of authentic existence is as useful for theology as it is for philosophy. Why? Because human being is evidently human existence, and as such requires understanding prior to asking more fundamental – transcendental – questions of it. As Bultmann wrote in his 1925 essay "What does it mean to speak about God?": "Before one can speak of God, one must first be able to speak of man."

Once that analysis had been achieved, Heidegger and Bultmann undoubtedly wanted to go in different directions, the former toward the non-religious category Being, the latter towards God and an understanding of human existence before God: *coram deo*, as Bultmann knew it from his Lutheran tradition. For the sake of our question about *modernity*, however, this distinction is irrelevant. What matters is that both Heidegger and Bultmann agree on the fundamental questions *and* some of their answers. Or, to state it in terms of Dante's *Divine Comedy*: Virgil and Dante are able to travel the same road, because they both understand the same road map. And that road map, though it ultimately comes from God – as Virgil well knows – is *our* road map, for better or for worse, and as such we have to understand it by any moral and intellectual means possible.

I think this model offers a very important way of thinking about modern theology. The idea of terrain that can be mapped has been used to speak both of divine action – in the form of God's revelation in Christ – and of human responses to that divine action. In both senses the key idea is that there is something that can be known, and something that can be said about what is known, that has distinct limits or boundaries. One is mapping something with a clear "shape," in other words, a clear shape that permits an accurate rendition. Such an idea characterizes quite a lot of biblical or doctrinal interpretation in Church history, actually, albeit in a fairly crude manner.

The model that informs this volume is somewhat different, however. Instead of a single map for a single terrain, therefore, this volume allows that the terrain of God's relationship with the world looks different when seen from different perspectives, and that consequently different maps will be appropriate for different people in different situations. The old question about maps, therefore – are they accurate? – is replaced by a new one: are they useful? Or better: Do they have value and meaning? Do they represent the world and God's relationship with it as it is viewed by certain people in certain places? Returning to Dante and Virgil, it becomes not so much a question of identifying *the* route through Hell and Purgatory, as *their* route through Hell and Purgatory. It is a huge difference, one that clearly indicates the shift toward a modern concern with peoples' contextualized perspectives and interpretations.

For what it is worth, I do not think Dante's *Divine Comedy* really allows such a thoroughgoing modern reading; it *is* a medieval text from the fourteenth century, and it does present a closed world in which all questions are resolved by heavenly answers. That does not mean, however, that the modern reading has no virtues, and that looking at Christian history and its texts from the modern perspective is pointless. It is after all the basic premise of hermeneutic theory that meaning can be *translated* from context to context, generated by the interaction between text and interpreter. The modern reading of Dante's *Divine Comedy*, therefore, is just that: a reading. As such it merits understanding not simply because it might be historically significant – and for better or worse, modern theology is a massive dimension of the history of Christian reflection – but also because it sheds light on the original, which is God's relationship with the world, and Christian witness to the many dimensions of God's presence and absence.

A "Companion to Modern Theology," consequently, is not simply a companion to a particular period of Christian history, or a particular set of figures, ideas, and challenges. It is also a companion to a way of thinking through the main principles and values of Christianity, its relevance for the world as well as the Church, and the great contributions all kinds of intellectual reflection make to the life of faith seeking understanding. As indicated, the point of such a volume is to provide a road map, with certain important routes through the terrain of modern theology, the general shape of that discipline and, perhaps most importantly, how it works as a line of inquiry. Or better: how it works as *lines* of inquiry, for one of the most valuable insights students can have is that there are many different ways of understanding modern theology, and a lot of them are plausible accounts of the subjects under discussion. Good students will realize this fact, and good textbooks will help them appreciate it.

The Structure of this Book

What the reader should expect to find in this book, therefore, is a series of essays that build up a thorough, composite picture of modern theology in terms of its major themes and issues, figures and movements. To use again the image of the road map, the book should work as a series of indications by which one can navigate the subject matter. And since there can be, by definition, no one road map that is absolutely perfect – no one account of modern theology that is complete and unchallengeable – so the student has to work with the material in these essays, using them to provoke thoughts and arguments and their own lines of inquiry that will take them more deeply into modern theology's pertinent questions.

As importantly, then, the student should also be clear about what she will *not* find in this textbook. She will not find objective accounts of important names, events, and ideas, as if these can be presented separately from their intellectual and socio-historical contexts. She will not find texts that can be filleted, rather as one fillets a fish, in order to arrive at the "basic facts" that can then be utilized in an essay or assignment. There *are* textbooks like that, some of them very successful, but they tend to deaden argument, rather than encourage it. If modern theology is something worth studying, if it offers ideas and arguments that are worth studying, then it must be because it stimulates people to have their own thoughts about the basic themes and beliefs of Christianity, and the ways in which people talk about those themes and beliefs. Modern theology *must* stimulate thought and argument: that is the basic premise that has guided the creation of this book and its constituent chapters.

What Does the Book Look Like in Detail, Therefore?

After this Preface has set out some basic points about the scope of the volume in general, Part I introduces readers to the essential perspectives and engagements that have shaped the development of modern theology, and consequently the way in which modern theological questions are still interpreted. Robin Gill's opening chapter, "The Practice of Faith," highlights the creative tensions between how one looks at the interpretation of faith and the practical questions that lead on to questions of moral and cultural relevance. Gill leads the reader through some of these tensions, using a close reading of certain biblical passages to illustrate the points he wants to make to challenge the reader to think again about faith and practice, not as an end in itself, but as a challenge to all responsible theological reflection. Part of this debate is inevitably about the authority of the Bible, and in his chapter "Biblical Studies" John Barton offers a lucid account of how the interpretation of the Bible has been shaped by modern thought, and also how biblical interpretation has itself influenced the development of modern theology.

Taken together, therefore, the essays by Gill and Barton address one of the most natural of all starting points for modern theology, which should make readers think about how they want to assess questions of origin and authority in modern theology in general. The chapters by David B. Burrell and Charles Mathewes, on philosophy and culture respectively, take up similar challenges, but consider quite different subjects. As well as the important points Burrell and Mathewes make about philosophy and culture in their essays, what is also significant is the way in which they demonstrate that philosophical reflection is inherently cultural, and cultural reflection is inherently philosophical. Philosophy and culture can be considered together, as faith and the Bible can be considered together, each pair challenging the reader to reconsider some basic assumptions about the character of modern theology.

The remaining essays in the first section also work in similar ways. Thus, the chapters by Don Browning and Ray Anderson, on social theory and theological anthropology respectively, work together to build up a sense of the way in which modern theology's engagement with these disciplines has altered how we understand Christian claims about the ways in which people live together. Again, the chapter on history by William Dean offers sustained readings of the deep structures of abiding intellectual questions for modern theology, bringing together many of the previous questions in Part I, but centered now on specific hermeneutic problems.

Taken as a whole, therefore, Part I should stimulate the reader to look at modern theology's relations with these lines of inquiry with fresh eyes. The nine essays of Parts II and III continue this approach, dividing into two main groups, one considering the central doctrines of the Christian faith, the other the principal periods of Christian history that modern theology is charged to interpret. The chapters by G. R. Evans and Morwenna Ludlow on patristics, Stephen Brown on the medieval Church, Carl Trueman on the Reformation, and Garrett Green on modernity, all look afresh at the interpretive challenges students face when they consider the issues for modern theology raised by these doctrines and historical periods. The chapters by Bruce Marshall on the Trinity, John Webster on the incarnation, Esther Reed on redemption, Andrew Chester on eschatology, and Gavin D'Costa on Church and sacraments, build up an image of the major doctrinal "building blocks," the taught ideas that modern theology then interprets.

Student should not, I repeat, expect to find "complete" and "factual" accounts of these doctrines and periods in these nine essays though. There are original and sophisticated considerations with significant claims to authority and sound judgment. Their real significance for this book as a whole, however, lies in their ability to continue the process begun in Part I: i.e. drawing students into the ways in which modern theology functions as a series of intellectual arguments and models. To use an oft-cited example from the way in which language works, the first sixteen essays in this book offer a provocative and original take on the grammar and syntax of modern theology, revealing the ways in which it communicates in order to help students themselves to understand better the challenges they face when they want to think about this subject.

If Parts I–III offer the grammar and syntax of modern theology, then it is fair to say that Part IV provides a series of chapters that consider the figures who create the significant vocabulary of the discipline. Certain of these essays, for example my own on Kant, Merold Westphal's on Hegel, and Dawn DeVries's on Schleiermacher, look at figures who, though long dead, can fairly claim to be the progenitors of modern theology in particular, and indeed modern thought in general. Similarly, the remaining chapters in this part, Mark Lindsay on Barth, Karen Kilby on Rahner, John de Gruchy on Bonhoeffer, James Byrne on Bultmann and Tillich, and Mark McIntosh on von Balthasar, all consider some of the great figures of twentieth-century theology. Discerning readers will immediately recognize that this list is not exclusive! There is no place, apparently, for Emil Brunner or Adolf von Harnack, nor for the liberation and feminist theologians who are so important for very recent theology. Nor, indeed, are there any figures other than dead white males in Part IV, which requires some explanation, perhaps.

The answer to this query is two-fold. First, the eight chapters in Part IV address highly significant figures: no one would wish to omit any of them. Again, each of these essays brings into its discussion some of the other figures that one might argue characterize modern theology, so that, for example, Harnack and Brunner are present in these treatments, even if they do not feature in chapter headings. The rationale for Part IV apart, however, my second reason for structuring the book in this way and with these chapters is pedagogic: it has to do with how I want people to read Part V as well as Part IV. It has to do with understanding the great figures and ideas of more recent theology as explicit *challenges* to the ways in which we interpret modern theology, rather than offering further chapters about figures who might be viewed, however unfortunately, "in isolation." To some extent that is inevitable with individuals like Kant and Hegel. It is not inevitable with feminism and race, however, and these enormous challenges and indeed responsibilities should never be treated as simply "figures" or "ideas" alongside other, perhaps far older and historic, figures and ideas.

The eight essays in Part V therefore take up this theme of challenge and responsibility, so that the pieces by Ian Markham on Christianity and other religions, Martyn Percy on economics and social justice, Patricia Daniel on feminism, Ralph Norman on the rediscovery of mysticism, Laurel Kearns on ecology, Richard Arrandale on drama, film and postmodernity, Shawn Copeland on race, and Robert John Russell and Kirk Wegter-McNelly on science, all resonate with this approach to their subjects. This list of eight challenges and responsibilities is not exhaustive, of course; no one would claim that, least of all the contributors, who have achieved astonishingly focused and pertinent treatments of their subjects. They are indicative, however, of the range of challenges and responsibilities that modern theology has faced and continues to face.

By the end of these thirty-two chapters readers will have a thorough knowledge of a very wide spectrum of material relevant to modern theology. They will also have a considerable palette of different ways to approach modern theology, and they will even have a sense of where modern theology has come from and, as importantly, where it is going. They will then have a sense – or many senses! – of how a textbook like this one relates to Graham Ward's admirable one on postmodern theologies, *The Postmodern God*.[2] Remember the point about structure: modern theology is composite, and so is its interpretation. For those with energy and interest, therefore, these essays have bibliographical references and notes that continue these interpretations, leading the reader further into the complexities and subtleties of modern theological reflection.

That, in the final analysis, is what this textbook has been designed to achieve. Modern theology, unlike say postmodern theologies, permits an emphasis on methodology, on *how* to think through intellectual problems as critically as possible. That is not an accident: modern theology has often been closely related to notions of critical *education*, so that modern theology's pedagogic influences can often be mirrored by an emphasis upon how today's students might yet engage with its ideas and figures in order to learn how to think more clearly about the Christian faith.

Modern theology is also about collisions and tensions, however: collisions and tensions between ideas and individuals, as well as between the challenges and responsibilities that Christianity now faces and will continue to face in the foreseeable future. If this textbook has been put together, and its chapters written, with this critical model in mind, it is because one of the best ways to handle those challenges and responsibilities, the *business* of thinking and thereby owning modern theology's concerns, is still to reflect critically on modern theology's subject matter. Critical reflection is about intelligent engagement, and the student who remembers that point will not go far wrong in navigating the complexities of modern theology with the help of these thirty-two guides.

It remains to thank many people for their help and guidance in bringing this volume to publication. Reading through these essays again and again, I have always been impressed by their authors' integrity and commitment, not to mention sheer knowledge and understanding. I am similarly hugely grateful for the work of Valery Rose and her team of copy-editors. Rebecca Harkin, senior commissioning editor in theology at Blackwell Publishing, has marshalled everything beautifully. Last but not least, my wife, Nicky, has been the epitome of love and support in this enerprise as in everything in life and work.

Notes

1 Dante Alighieri, *The Divine Comedy*, trans. C. H. Sisson (Oxford: Oxford University Press, 1993), p. 225.
2 Graham Ward, *The Postmodern God* (Oxford: Blackwell, 1997).

PART I
Theology and . . .

CHAPTER 1
The Practice of Faith

Robin Gill

Within relatively homogeneous communities theology is typically understood as a scholarly activity undertaken by people of faith for others who share the same faith within a context of communal religious practice. Scholastic theology in medieval Europe would have been understood in this way. Anselm's celebrated depiction of theology as "faith seeking understanding" was written in the context of a society in which "faith," "religion," and "Catholicism" were all one and the same thing for his readers. In traditional Islamic societies today this is often still the dominant understanding of theology, as it remains among many communities of orthodox Jews, traditionalist Roman Catholics and Eastern Orthodox, and amongst fundamentalist Protestants. However, since the introduction of modern forms of theological scholarship over the last 150 years, especially within university-based theology in the West, the relationship between faith, religious practice, and theology has become far more ambiguous. It can no longer be assumed that all of those studying, or indeed all of those teaching, academic theology share either the same faith or a common pattern of religious practice. A comparative rather than confessional approach to academic theology also ensures that a variety of contrasting faith positions and religious practices are analyzed critically. The theological pluralism of the academy now typically reflects the cultural pluralism of Western society at large. Yet even within this pluralistic context the role of faith and practice does not disappear.

In what follows I will look at the complex relationship between faith, practice, and theology that is apparent in different areas within academic theology in the West. To illustrate this relationship I will suggest how a single biblical story – Luke's story of the healing of ten lepers – might be studied in each of these different areas. In the Revised Standard Version (RSV) of Luke 17 this story reads as follows:

(11) On the way to Jerusalem [Jesus] was passing along between Samaria and Galilee. (12) And as he entered a village, he was met by ten lepers, who stood at a distance (13) and lifted up their voices and said, "Jesus, Master, have mercy on us." (14) When he saw them

he said to them, "Go and show yourselves to the priests." And as they went they were cleansed. (15) Then one of them, when he saw that he was healed, turned back, praising God with a loud voice; (16) and he fell on his face at Jesus' feet, giving him thanks. Now he was a Samaritan. (17) Then Jesus said, "Were not ten cleansed? Where are the nine? (18) Was no one found to return and give praise to God except this foreigner?" (19) And he said to him, "Rise and go your way; your faith has made you well."

Faith and Biblical Studies

It might be supposed that nobody would spend her life studying Christian Scriptures unless she was personally committed to those Scriptures and believed that they contained the key to salvation. Yet, in practice, there is as much tension here as in any other area of theology or religious studies in the Western academy. Many biblical scholars do indeed approach their subject from a perspective of faith and religious practice, but some do not. And even those who do, hold many different opinions on the authority of Scripture for their faith and religious practice. Pluralism and tension abound in this area of academic theology today.

At some levels this is hardly surprising. There are many technical aspects of biblical studies, such as the linguistic, source and textual areas, which require considerable skills but not faith as such. So, just as classical scholars can often derive pleasure and satisfaction from studying texts that are at variance with their own beliefs and commitments, it is not difficult to see how some secular scholars can approach biblical texts in a similar way. In both contexts there are intellectual challenges and puzzles that can fully engage the imaginations of those with the appropriate skills, but without involving any existential commitment on their part. Establishing the chronological order of the Synoptic Gospels say, arguing in detail for or against the existence of Q, or recovering the most reliable Greek test of the New Testament, are not activities in themselves that require Christian faith. It might even be argued that such study sharpens skills that can then be applied to other more pragmatic areas of life. Ironically such an argument was used at the beginning of the twentieth century for the training of Anglican ordinands: typically they (and many other intellectuals) were required to study classics rather than theology as their training for ministry. Perhaps there was even a presumption that studying a work such as Plato's *Republic* (a particular favorite for that generation) improved the minds of ordinands rather more than studying the Bible.

By the middle of the twentieth century Anglican ordination training had changed very considerably. Now it was assumed, and not just by Anglican evangelicals, that a rigorous study of biblical exegesis was an essential part of ordination training. Yet, after a century of biblical criticism, the dominant assumption was that biblical exegesis must be conducted in a critical context – especially that of historical criticism. Nonetheless, biblical exegesis for Anglican ordinands of all descriptions was a confessional activity. It was studied to inform the future teaching and preaching ministry of these ordinands, who themselves constituted the majority of those studying theology at English universities (in Scotland there was a very similar pattern of male, Presbyterian ordinands forming the majority of those studying theology at Edinburgh, Glasgow, St. Andrews or Aberdeen).

However, today the Western academy is radically transformed. In Britain (as elsewhere in Europe and North America) a majority of those studying theology in university are neither male nor ordinands and are not necessarily Anglicans (or, in Scotland, Presbyterians) at all; and biblical interpretation has assumed at least as large a role as biblical exegesis in the syllabus. As a result this syllabus can no longer presume that the function of biblical studies is to inform the teaching and preaching of (male) Anglican or Presbyterian ordinands. Such a confessional function has been replaced with a more comparative function. The syllabus in Biblical Studies is now more likely to require students to become familiar with different and contrasting patterns of hermeneutics. Biblical interpretation requires an awareness that across time and across different contemporary cultures (diachronically and synchronically) biblical texts are understood, interpreted and appropriated very differently. Pluralism and comparative critical study have once again entered the discipline. Biblical interpretation involves the exploration of different and sometimes contradictory faith communities as they have sought to use the Bible.

Illustration

The story of ten lepers, in Luke's Gospel, can be studied without reference to faith at all. At the levels of textual scholarship and translation, the opening verse contains a number of possibilities. The RSV opts for "between Samaria and Galilee," but another possibility is "through the midst of Samaria and Galilee." Both the Greek text and the English translations of it have a number of possibilities, all of which struggle to make sense of the rather vague geography in the story. Some scholars have suggested that the problem here may go back to Luke himself and that he probably had a rather confused idea of inland boundaries. Other scholars have looked carefully at the language of the story, detecting in, for example, the next verse, Greek words that are typical of Luke's style of writing. Again this story can be studied from a perspective of Synoptic scholarship. It is found only in Luke, and uniquely it involves a simultaneous healing of ten people from the same disease, yet the final phrase "your faith has made you well" links it clearly to other Synoptic healing stories (Mark 5:24, Matthew 9:22, Luke 8:48, and Mark 10:52, Luke 18:42).

Biblical interpretation would suggest another way of approaching this story. Rather than being concerned to establish the original Greek text or to examine the story in relation to other stories in the Synoptic Gospels, biblical interpretation would be more concerned to understand the different ways it has been understood by various faith communities across time and across different contemporary cultures. Some might look at the various ways the story has been portrayed in art or in literature. Others might look at the role it has played in sermons in different ages. Others again might look at the different ways it has been received in modern Western countries with no direct experience of leprosy, compared with, say, parts of Africa where it is still endemic.

Faith and Systematic Theology

Those who study academic theology in the West will encounter the work of historical and present-day systematic theology from a variety of contrasting, and sometimes competing, traditions. They will need, for example, to be as familiar with the writings of Thomas Aquinas as with those of Martin Luther and John Calvin. They will need to study, say, both Karl Barth and Karl Rahner. As with any other arts- or social science-based subject, it is usually considered to be inadequate to study the ideas of any single author without being able to relate those ideas critically to the competing ideas of others. Comparative, critical study is as important to systematic theology within the academy as it is to philosophy or to sociology. All three subjects can, of course, be taught in a confessional manner. At times Marxist sociology and various brands of philosophy have been taught in this way. However, the dominant approach within the Western academy is, either to discourage such confessional teaching, or to counter it with teaching using alternative confessional bases. Whether a critical and relatively detached approach is adopted, or a multi-confessional approach, the student of academic theology is inevitably confronted with a self-consciously pluralistic subject.

This has a number of implications for the relationship between faith and systematic theology:

1   Systematic theology becomes a form of history of ideas or sociology of knowledge. By juxtaposing competing understandings of theology, systematic theology becomes less the systematic exploration of the tenets of faith than a critical comparison of competing understandings of faith. Indeed, few of those who teach systematic theology within the modern academy have themselves written, or will ever write, a systematic theology. Rather they are scholars who have specialized in studying the written systematic theologies of past and present theologians. They may seek to trace the provenance of these ideas, as a history-of-ideas approach does in a variety of disciplines (and most notably within philosophy). Or they may seek additional connections between these changing ideas and changes within society at large, as the sociology of knowledge attempts to do. Yet both of these approaches have a strong tendency to locate faith in a comparative and critical context . . . it is the faith of others that is typically studied as much as one's own faith.

2   Systematic theology thus becomes more a comparative than a confessional form of study. Even if someone who teaches or studies theology has a strong commitment to faith and religious practice (as of course many, but not all, do), the very discipline in its modern form encourages critical comparison rather than confession. If ideas from competing theological traditions are studied in a scholarly manner in the modern academy, then they do need to be approached with a degree of sympathy. If they are dismissed too early, on some confessional basis, then their significance is likely to be overlooked. The careful comparison of divergent views sits uncomfortably with a mono-confessional and apologetic approach to theology.

3   The very process of modern academic theology makes it difficult to sustain an unquestioning faith. There is a clear difference between those people of faith who

have never heard their faith seriously challenged and those who retain their faith in the context of a pluralistic and critical academy. This remains the case even when the content of the two faiths appears to be identical. For example, people from these two contexts may have a similar belief in a personal God. Yet those in the pluralistic context are aware that this belief is challenged by many other people on a variety of grounds, whereas those in the first context do not. The faith of those in the pluralistic context is no longer an unquestioning faith: it is a faith held in contrast to (and sometimes in defiance of) others in society.

It would, though, be a mistake to assume from this that faith has little to do with systematic theology in the modern academy. Many, perhaps most, of those who actually write a systematic theology in the first place do have an explicit faith commitment located within a specific community of religious practice. It is clearly incumbent, then, on those studying a particular systematic theology to seek to understand that faith commitment – whether they share that commitment themselves or not. Again, many (but not all) students of systematic theology are drawn into the discipline precisely because they have a sense of "faith seeking understanding." Just as many students of philosophy or the social sciences have a personal interest in their subject, so do many students of systematic theology. More than that, some people come to systematic theology because they are convinced that a mature faith needs a comparative and critical assessment. Systematic theology thus allows them to compare and contrast their own faith with that of others and, in the process, to refine and nuance their faith.

Illustration

The story of ten lepers in Luke's Gospel suggests a number of issues for a comparative and critical approach to Systematic theology. To take just two, there is the issue of miracles and their significance and there is the role of faith in the story. Both of these issues tend to divide theologians in ways that are fascinating for students today.

There has been much discussion within theology about the meaning and coherence of the concept of "miracle" (albeit the term itself is not used within this story), especially following David Hume's provocative definition of a miracle as "a violation of the laws of nature." In the fast developing literature on science and religion it is often argued that such a definition now appears anachronistic in a context of post-Newtonian physics. Physicists today are far less likely to talk about fixed "laws of nature" than they might have been in the past. As a result some theologians argue that those who dismiss the miraculous element in stories such as that of the ten lepers are simply the products of outdated philosophy of the Enlightenment. Others remain skeptical but argue that the story still has theological significance even without primitive notions of the miraculous. Much depends here upon the different understanding of God's "actions" in the world and upon how far Christians in the modern world can sustain a world-view thoroughly at odds with prevailing culture.

Within the story the role of faith is clearly important. Yet there is an ambiguity here that has puzzled and divided theologians. The normal expectation within healing stories in the Synoptic Gospels is that faith necessarily precedes healing. So, for example, in the story of the woman with a hemorrhage (Mark 5:34, Matthew 9:22, Luke 8:48), she too is told that "your faith has made you well." But in the story of the ten lepers only one of the lepers is told this, when all ten had been healed. Why is he alone told this? One explanation is that all ten had faith and were therefore healed, but only one was specifically commended because he gave thanks. A more conservative explanation is that the tenth differed because he alone was "saved": the others were healed of their leprosy but not actually "saved." Neither explanation is particularly satisfactory (the second, for example, does not account for why this story uses the phrase "your faith has made you well" in a different way from other stories). Yet the two explanations do suggest very different traditions of theology behind them.

Faith and Religious Studies

A further process of refinement is possible for those who are prepared to compare and contrast their own faith with that of non-Christian religious traditions. Sometimes termed comparative theology (rather than what was once termed "comparative religion"), Christian theology is set within a broader context of, say, Jewish theology or Islamic theology, in an attempt to identify and perhaps evaluate points of convergence and divergence.

Such an approach is not without its critics. Some, following Karl Barth, would reject it on the grounds that Christianity is not "a religion." The uniqueness of Christian faith means that it is always mistaken to compare it with any other so-called "faith," whether this faith is a secular form of "faith" or one drawn from one or other of the world religions. On this understanding Christian faith is wholly incomparable, so any attempt at such comparison inevitably involves serious distortion. Christian faith is based solely upon the Word of God made known uniquely in Jesus Christ, not upon some shared religious experience common to humanity or upon some knowledge of God derived independently of Jesus Christ.

In contrast, some within the academic discipline of religious studies argue that comparative theology is mistaken because it is too fideistic. They argue that Religious Studies differs from comparative theology in that it is "value-free" and independent of any faith commitment. So, whereas comparative theology, or traditional theology in any form, is viewed primarily in confessional terms, "religious studies" is seen as a detached, scientific discipline concerned with describing and analyzing religious phenomena without any existential commitment to them. The very term "religious studies" rather than "comparative religion" is often preferred for this reason: the latter is considered to be too value-laden and judgmental. On this understanding, theology in any form is a discipline suitable particularly for those training for ministry within churches, whereas religious studies is a discipline more suitable for those training to be teachers in a non-confessional setting. Or, to express this differently, theology aims to promote and refine faith whereas religious studies seeks rather to promote greater knowledge and discernment about religious issues. Theology is thus a fideistic discipline suitable for ministers, whereas religious studies is a detached discipline suitable for diplomats or civil servants.

It is not too difficult to show that both of these criticisms hardly match the disciplines of theology and religious studies as they are now typically taught and studied in Western academies. In their different ways they present caricatures of both theology and religious studies.

In the light of the understanding of systematic theology already outlined it is difficult to maintain the sharp contrast between theology and religious studies in the second criticism. It is simply not the case that in the West academic theology is invariably a confessional discipline taught in faith to people who share that faith. Even those training for ordained ministry in many mainline denominations will be expected to study a wide variety of approaches to theology which they do not personally share. It is also misleading to imagine that all of those studying religious studies in the Western academy have no prior religious commitments and approach their subject in a detached rather than fideistic manner. On the contrary, many are likely to engage in religious studies precisely because of their existential interests and concerns. It is quite possible for those, say, with defined Christian commitments themselves to wish to relate these commitments to those within religious traditions outside Christianity. Some distinguished Jewish and Islamic scholars have chosen to study Christian theology for similar reasons. A desire to study differing religious traditions does not in itself exclude a commitment to a particular tradition. Indeed, on analogy with the study of art or music, those who study a particular subject might typically be expected to have a strong attachment to at least some aspects of that subject. Religious studies, in practice, often has a balance of faith and critical detachment very similar to theology as it is typically taught and studied today in the Western academy.

The first criticism, based upon the dogmatic claim that Christian theology is wholly incomparable, ignores the considerable body of scholarship that has been concerned to analyze the Jewish, Roman and Greek roots of Christian theology. It also ignores the family relationship of Christianity to Islam and the fact that the Koran itself contains sacred traditions about Jesus Christ. The relationship between Judaism and Christianity has received particular attention in the Western academy. In part this has been stimulated by the growing awareness that some forms of Christianity have acted historically as bearers of anti-Judaism and may even have contributed to the culture of European anti-Semitism that made possible the horrors of the Jewish Holocaust. However, it has also been stimulated by Jewish and Christian theologians reading each others' works and sometimes training and studying together. Such study reveals how much early Christianity derived from Judaism and that they still share many theological precepts today.

Some scholars have also studied the extent to which early Christianity borrowed concepts more widely from the Mediterranean world. For example, the New Testament scholar Wayne Meeks has argued at length that the Pauline virtues have much in common with contemporary Graeco-Roman virtues. Or, to take a later example, Augustine in the fourth century consciously borrowed from Cicero in his understanding of both natural law and just war theory. In turn, Aquinas was later to borrow directly from the newly rediscovered ideas of Aristotle (preserved, ironically, by Islamic scholars) in writing his own systematic theology.

None of this contradicts the distinctiveness or uniqueness of Christian theology, or specifically its central focus upon Jesus Christ, yet it does question the claim that Christian theology is wholly incomparable. On the basis of this considerable amount of modern scholarship, there do seem to be solid grounds for the claim instead that Christian faith does have a clear relationship with other forms of theistic faith outside Christianity.

But what about those forms of faith that are not theistic? Theologians again soon divide on this question. Some, like Hans Küng, argue that on global issues such as international peace or the environment there are points of contact across many different forms of religious faith – whether theistic or not – and that such issues require us urgently to recognize these. However, others remain unconvinced, arguing that attempts to supply a comprehensive definition of "religious faith" have been remarkably unsuccessful. Whatever the outcome of this debate, it is difficult to maintain convincingly that Christian faith, let alone Christian practice, is wholly incomparable. Both systematic theology and religious studies in the Western academy have a similar tension or paradox. On the one hand, those who study and teach in these areas still show considerable evidence of faith and religious practice. Yet, on the other, they also seem to value critical detachment.

Illustration

The story of the ten lepers in Luke's Gospel explicitly involves the healing of a religious "alien" ("Now he was a Samaritan"), who alone is praised by Jesus. There are interesting points of contact here with the reports of the praise Jesus gives to two other "aliens," the Centurion (Luke 7:9, Matthew 8:10) and the Canaanite woman (Matthew 15:28). Those who have argued against the Barthian position in religious studies have tended to use this as evidence. They have also pointed to evidence gained from a comparative study of healing/miracle stories in other religions, in both the ancient and modern worlds.

This raises a very crucial issue within comparative theology, namely, what if anything is distinctive about Jesus within the Synoptic Gospels. Specifically in relation to healing stories, there are clearly many parallels with other "healers" past and present. There is even evidence of this within Luke's own story in the command "Go and show yourselves to the priests." It is a feature of a number of healing stories (e.g. Mark 1:40–5) that Jewish cultic ritual is part of healing.

So what is distinctively "Christian" about the healing stories in the Synoptic Gospels? Some have argued that it is the specific link that Jesus makes between healing and the apocalyptic Kingdom of God that is most distinctive. So the next two verses after this story in Luke reinforce the point that "The Kingdom of God is in the midst of you" (Luke 17:20–1). More dramatically still is the earlier saying of Jesus in Luke's Gospel that "if it is by the finger of God that I cast out demons, then the Kingdom of God has come upon you" (Luke 11:20). A comparative study of such sayings in the context of healing can help to see both continuities between early Christianity and other religious traditions and points of distinctiveness.

Faith and Church History

The changed constituency of the Western academy has also had a radical effect upon the teaching of Church history. In a mono-confessional context Church history is typically interpreted in the light of particular denominations. Anglicans pay particular attention to Anglican divines such as Hooker, Presbyterians to Knox, Methodists to Wesley, and so forth. Church history is thus focused upon those people or events considered most significant to that faith community. More polemically, this focus is sometimes portrayed as the path of "orthodoxy" to be contrasted with the errors propagated by other Christians. As a result Church history in such mono-confessional contexts constitutes an important feature of identity, reinforcing boundaries between faithful Christians and others.

Yet in a pluralist environment Church history becomes more complicated. It is not, of course, value free: particular people and events are still selected for discussion and others are not; those selected are given different amounts of time and consideration; and the perspectives of different historians inevitably shape their interpretations of the significance of these people and events. Once it is conceded that selection and interpretation are inextricably involved in any study of history, and especially in any study of Church history, then absolute detachment is no more possible (or perhaps even desirable) here than it is in religious studies. Even within the pluralist context of the Western academy today, faith, or rather a multiplicity of faiths, is still a part of Church history.

However, the multiplicity of faiths involved in Church history today does entail a greater attention than in the past to divergent branches of Christianity set in a variety of cultures. Any serious study of Church history within the modern academy pays attention not simply to Western Christianity but also to Christianity in non-Western countries. The history of Christian missions, for example, is not simply relegated to a separate discipline of mission studies, but is part of a global account of Christian history. In addition, sociological studies of new religious movements, cults and sects in both Western and non-Western countries form a part of this global account. And, within accounts of early Christianity, previously discredited movements such as that of Gnosticism are treated with a new seriousness. Christian history is depicted less as the history of the successful "orthodox" and more as a varied and pluriform family of interrelated movements arising from the New Testament.

Illustration

Attention to the history of attitudes toward leprosy in Christian history has been particularly helpful. There is now widespread agreement that the term "leprosy" was applied in the ancient world to a variety of skin complaints and disfigurements, rather than just to the disease of leprosy in the modern sense. Within Leviticus, for example, the concern about leprosy is more to do with ritual pollution than with contagion (it was "soiling" rather than "catchy"). As a result of this distinction, some translations of the New Testament now prefer to substitute a reference to "skin complaints" for the term "leprosy" in stories such as that of the ten "lepers" in Luke.

Despite the Synoptic Gospel stories about Jesus healing and even touching "lepers" (Mark 1:41), a fear of leprosy remained within the medieval Church. This fear even helped to shape church buildings, with the aim of reducing contact between lepers and non-lepers. Through narrow slanted windows lepers were allowed to view the central actions of the Mass without polluting other members of the congregation.

Leprosy was also given particular attention within more recent Christian missions. Before the invention of modern drugs, the isolation and sometimes courageous care of lepers by medical missionaries was often cited by Victorians as evidence of deep Christian faith. In postcolonial studies such missionary work tends to be viewed more circumspectly. Motives other than pure Christian altruism are detected by some as underlying many "heroic" missionary endeavors.

Faith and Moral Theology

Very similar changes can also be found in moral theology/Christian ethics (distinctions between "morality" and "ethics" tend to be rather contrived: in origin the first derives from Latin and the second from Greek). A changing constituency within the Western academy, allied to a shift towards hermeneutics, has radically changed the discipline. However, in this instance, the current dominance of virtue ethics presents a particularly intricate intertwining of faith, practice, and theology – an intertwining which I believe characterizes applied theology in general.

A generation ago, when university theological students were predominantly young, male ordinands, Christian ethics (if it was taught at all in Britain) was distinctly more confessional in character than it is today. Classic Anglican moral theologians of the first half of the twentieth century, such as Kenneth Kirk and Robert Mortimer (both later to become bishops), presented a mixture of ethical/theological analysis and advice on pastoral practice in their books. They could assume that their audience of ordinands shared the same faith and religious practices as themselves and were looking to be guided about how they should respond to ethical issues once they were themselves ordained. Similarly, Roman Catholic moral theologians of the time, or Church of Scotland practical theologians north of the Border, also mixed analysis and pastoral advice in their work, and simply assumed that they wrote from faith to faith within their respective communities. As a result Roman Catholic moral theologians of this period largely ignored Luther and Calvin, just as Scottish practical theologians paid little attention to Aquinas. Christian ethics at the time was predominantly confessional, both in its scope and in its approach. That is, it was written from within particular denominations, by people of particular faith traditions, to fellow believers.

Within the Western academy such an approach would be less likely to commend itself today. An approach to Christian ethics that simply bypassed one of the major traditions would usually be judged to be inadequate. Roman Catholic theologians have now entered the mainstream of the Western academy and, in the process, have ensured that the natural law tradition is taken seriously even within formerly Presbyterian or Anglican faculties. In turn, these Roman Catholic theologians have taken seriously the biblical scholarship generated by generations of Reformed and Anglican theologians. This two-way process has ensured that Christian ethics is now more genuinely ecumenical than it typically was a generation ago. Scholars across denominations and across different faith traditions mutually read each other's works. They may still disagree with each other – ecumenical dialog does not guarantee consensus – but they are less likely than hitherto simply to ignore each other.

This shift within the academic study of Christian ethics entails changes similar to those already noted in other areas of theology: critical comparison tends to replace a mono-confessional approach; pluralism rather than consensus predominates; and a degree of academic detachment becomes evident. There is no need to rehearse these points again within this new context.

However, there is one point that is new here. A multi-confessional approach to Christian ethics soon reveals that there are incommensurable moral differences between Christians. Of course, there always were real moral differences between Christians within particular denominations. Nevertheless, as long as Christian ethics was conducted separately by denominations, each might maintain the hope that their internal moral differences could in time be resolved. The doctrine of the "consensus of the faithful" reinforced this hope. But once Christian ethics is studied in a multi-confessional and ecumenical context, then it soon becomes apparent that such differences are in reality incommensurable. For example, there is no way finally to resolve crucial differences between denominations about when full human life begins or when, if ever, it is legitimate to end human life. As a result, bioethics and just-war ethics have both faced differences between Christians, which a comparative, critical approach to Christian ethics can help us better to understand but not to resolve. More than that, such an approach has revealed that there are sometimes stronger connections on particular moral issues between Christians and their secular counterparts than there are between opposing Christians.

The current debates about stem cell research or physician-assisted suicide demonstrate this clearly. Supporters and opponents of stem cell research using embryos created by cell nuclear replacement can be found amongst both Christians and secularists. Within particular denominations it can, of course, be maintained that only one side represents "orthodoxy" from a Christian perspective. Traditionalist Roman Catholics have indeed held this view, condemning such stem cell research as contrary to natural law and to the gospel. Yet across denominations such claims to "orthodoxy" soon appear tendentious where there is no agreement about when full human life begins, or indeed whether an embryo created by cell nuclear replacement constitutes a potential human being at all.

Even physician-assisted suicide, which is rejected by most denominations, is not condemned by all theologians. The latter tend to argue that it is too readily concluded from the doctrines of creation and resurrection that physician-assisted suicide is wrong. In contrast, they maintain that a belief that there is a life beyond this life might actually encourage Christians to believe that there is no need to cling to this life. My point is not to side here with either position but merely to suggest that a critical comparative approach to Christian ethics soon reveals incommensurable differences of faith and practice between Christians on moral issues.

Given this, a shift away from ethical decision-making within academic Christian ethics and toward virtue ethics is hardly surprising. As a result of this shift, recent Christian ethics has rediscovered new links with systematic theology and, ironically, with sociology. Within virtue ethics the focus is upon virtuous character and upon those communities that nurture and shape character. We are the products less of rational, individualistic moral decisions made from one situation to another than of ways of living shaped by tradition and community. As Christians our moral lives and characters are shaped by the faith and practice of worshipping communities and the traditions that they carry over the centuries. Such an understanding of Christian ethics places it firmly within the broader context of applied or practical theology.

Illustration

The story of the ten lepers in Luke's Gospel contains a number of explicit virtues. At the outset there is the plea to Jesus by the lepers themselves: "Jesus, Master, have mercy on us." A regular feature of healing stories in the Synoptic Gospels is either a plea for mercy, to which Jesus responds (e.g. by blind Bartimaeus in Mark 10:47, Luke 18:37), or Jesus showing compassion to someone who is vulnerable (e.g. to the widow of Nairn in Luke 7:13). A number of Christian ethicists have followed Augustine in arguing that "love," or perhaps better "compassion," is at the heart of Christian ethics. There are, however, distinct differences between those ethicists who argue that love/compassion is always personalist or individualistic and those who believe that it can be communitarian and be translated into norms.

At the end of the story of the ten lepers is thanksgiving. For most commentators this is a straightforward expression of gratitude, which they see as instructive for Christian moral behavior. A belief in divine grace should encourage people to be grateful. Yet some have argued that understood within the social context of the Middle East, gratitude in the story is a form of submission and closure: the one who has been healed acknowledges Jesus as the source of the healing and concludes their relationship. Expressing gratitude is, then, the end of a relationship not the beginning of one.

Faith and Applied Theology

Applied or practical theology within the Western academy is the discipline especially concerned with this interaction between faith and practice. Sometimes this relationship is envisaged as faith shaping practice, sometimes as practice shaping faith, and sometimes as an interaction of the two. Applied theology within the modern academy has a similar comparative, critical role to that of systematic theology as well as having clear links to secular disciplines such as sociology. A discipline that was once considered to be an appendix to systematic and biblical theology within the academy has now become a central player in understanding the tension or, perhaps better, interaction between faith and practice evident in all of the other areas of theology. It is also a discipline that has made considerable use of the social sciences to understand this interaction more fully.

Applied theology a generation ago often consisted of little more than practical advice to ordinands. A teacher with considerable experience of ordained ministry would teach young ordinands how they should conduct funeral services, how they should preach, how they should conduct pastoral visiting, or similar related tasks. Having studied biblical and systematic theology in the academy, the applied or practical theologian was the person responsible for teaching ordinands the practicalities of ordained ministry. In the Church of Scotland applied theologians typically taught within a university, but often had been university chaplains or highly regarded parish ministers first. In the Church of England "pastoral theology" (as it was usually termed) was more typically taught within a seminary, albeit by priests with pastoral experience similar to that of their counterparts in Scotland.

However well intended this model of applied theology, it faced serious difficulties. The parish experience of those teaching applied theology for any length of time, whether in the university or in a seminary, inevitably became more distant. So, just as trainee teachers frequently resent being told how to teach children by those who no longer teach them themselves, ordinands were often suspicious of the advice they were being given by former parish ministers, however experienced they had once been. Again, models of professional formation from disciplines such as medicine, suggested that the proper place for practical training was not in an academy but in the context of the job itself. Critical placements alongside reflexive practitioners were more likely to generate good professional formation.

Once the profile of those studying theology within the academy also changed it was soon clear that this "hints and tips for ordinands" approach to applied theology was no longer appropriate. The pluralism of present-day students within the Western academy, noted already in all other areas of theology, has also had a radical impact upon academic applied theology. The discipline still maintained a central focus upon faith and practice, but it could no longer assume any shared faith or practice among theological students. The relationship between divergent, and sometimes conflicting, patterns of Christian faith and practice now became the primary subject matter of applied theology within the academy.

The concept of "praxis" is sometimes used within applied theology to denote this new understanding. Initially taken from Marxist studies, it suggests that behavior is given priority over theory, but that there remains a two-way process between the two. In a more traditional understanding of religious practice it was often assumed that faith takes priority over practice. Christian faith thus sets the template for Christian practice. Within theological studies it was frequently assumed that the primary task of theology was to establish an adequate faith based upon a careful study of the Bible and Christian tradition. Once that had been achieved then issues of practice could be addressed. In a similar way it was often assumed in philosophy that the primary task was to produce clarity of thought and theory before any practical problems could be adequately addressed. Marxist studies reversed this understanding, arguing that what people actually do and how they behave should be the starting point of analysis. On this approach, practice is given priority and theory is, in the first place, the attempt to understand practice. Once theory is adequately grounded in an analysis of present-day practice then it too can shape future practice.

By no means all applied theologians give explicit credence to Marxism (although some liberation theologians certainly do), but they do typically work from this approach based upon praxis. In the relationship between faith and practice they give far more attention to practice than most other theologians do. Those working within applied liturgical studies often argue that it is worship that shapes doctrine and in turn is shaped by doctrine. Those working within Christian ethics argue that it is Christian communities that mold Christian character, which, in turn, shapes the ethical decision-making of individuals. Those working within Christian education argue that Christian formation within families, churches and, perhaps, within schools, is crucial for nurturing faith, and that this faith, once nurtured, should then inform Christian formation. In each of these areas within applied theology there is a priority given to practice, as well as an awareness of a continuing interaction between practice and faith. And in each of these areas the social sciences assume an important role.

Naturally an extensive use of social sciences within any area of theology is likely to generate suspicions of relativism and reductionism. A suspicion of relativism is raised here, as it is in other areas of theology, by the increasing pluralism of those teaching and studying applied theology. And a suspicion of reductionism is generated by the fear that extensive use of social sciences will soon eliminate transcendence altogether. Churches and church practices will soon, so it is feared, be reduced to the purely secular. For example, a use of organizational or business theory to understand churches will simply reduce them to nothing more than secular organizations or (worse still) businesses.

This is surely a profound misunderstanding of both applied theology and the social sciences. To explain or understand churches or religious practice in social-scientific terms is not in itself to explain them away. There manifestly are, for example, financial and economic features of institutional churches: they have budgets, they raise income and they spend money. All of these features can be compared with the similar activities of secular organizations and, if they are to be achieved effectively and efficiently, might benefit from such comparison. But to assume from this that institutional churches are "nothing but" financial/economic institutions would be an obvious exaggeration. Similarly, church leadership does have points in common with other forms of secular leadership. Yet studying it in this way does not of itself imply that it is *only* to be understood in this way. A judicious use of social science within applied theology is perfectly compatible with a commitment to transcendence.

At the heart of applied theology, then, is a concern for faith, practice, and theology. Even if the relationship between these three has become more complex and varied within the Western academy today, a concern to study and better to understand their relationship remains.

Illustration

The story of the ten lepers in Luke's Gospel makes important links between faith and practice that have wider implications for society at large. The explicit connection between the final "your faith has made you well" and the healing has already been noted (albeit with some ambiguity). However, there is also an implicit connection with a notion of "care" that has been highly influential within the caring professions. Within this healing story, as in many other, an initial plea for "mercy" is met with an immediate response from Jesus. Compassion or love is typically accompanied by action and even by a call to "show yourselves to the priest." This closely fits the claim of liberation theology that praxis is crucial.

Again, applied theologians are likely to see an implicit concern for the vulnerable and oppressed within this story. A strong feature of the early healing stories in Mark's Gospel is that they involve Jesus deliberately flouting traditional Jewish attitudes toward impurity and Sabbath-keeping in order to heal those who are sick. Applied theologians themselves soon divide, though, on whether they see such healing in terms primarily of challenging and changing social conventions or whether they see it rather in terms of personal and individual acts.

Finally there is a deep and ongoing division among different Christian communities about the implications of the Synoptic healing stories for health care today. The most radical position is taken by groups such as Christian Scientists and some conservative evangelical groups who argue for "covenanted healing" – according to which God has covenanted to heal all those who are prayed for in faith. Taken literally such theological positions make conventional modern medicine (even for diseases such as leprosy in its modern sense) irrelevant or even sinful. In contrast, other Christians effectively believe with Luther that "the day of miracles is past" and that all disease should be treated by modern medicine alone. Between these two positions are some who argue that religious faith can still be relevant (even complementary) to modern medicine. They might even cite leprosy in the ancient sense – often involving psychosomatic skin complaints and a strong sense of pollution – as an obvious example.

Bibliography

Barton, J. ed. 2001. *The Cambridge Companion to Biblical Interpretation.* Cambridge: Cambridge University Press.

Ford, D. and Hardy, D. eds. 1989. *The Modern Theologians.* Oxford: Basil Blackwell.

Gill, R. ed. 1995. *Readings in Modern Theology.* London: SPCK.

Gill, R. ed. 2001. *The Cambridge Companion to Christian Ethics.* Cambridge: Cambridge University Press.

Gunton, C. ed. 1997. *The Cambridge Companion to Christian Doctrine.* Cambridge: Cambridge University Press.

Hodgson, P. and King, R. eds. 1985. *Readings in Christian Theology.* Philadelphia, PA: Fortress Press; London: SPCK.

Loades, A. ed. 1990. *Feminist Theology.* London: SPCK.

McGrath, A. E. ed. 1995. *The Christian Theology Reader.* Oxford: Blackwell.

Rowland, C. ed. 2001. *The Cambridge Companion to Liberation Theology.* Cambridge: Cambridge University Press.

Woodward, J. and Pattison, S. eds. 2000. *The Blackwell Reader in Pastoral and Practical Theology.* Oxford: Blackwell.

CHAPTER 2
Biblical Studies

John Barton

The Bible and the Critics

In the years after World War II there was a widespread consensus about the Bible. Methods of scholarly study were generally agreed, and for both Old and New Testaments there were models of the text's historical development and religious importance that provided a groundplan all students needed to learn and appropriate. Biblical studies had been an ecumenical success story, too, giving the Protestant churches many insights on which all could agree. They also facilitated dialogue with the Catholic Church, whose scholars had been allowed by Pope Pius XII's encyclical *Divino Afflante Spiritu* of 1943 to engage in critical biblical study alongside their Protestant colleagues. The Second Vatican Council also gave a massive impetus to critical study of the Bible.

In the last twenty years or so there has been a major shift in biblical studies. Consensus even about method has broken down, and the field is now a battleground of conflicting approaches, with no agreed conclusions any longer. This can be exhilarating, but it can give the observer a sense of disorientation. Against the background of "postmodernism" there is now a feeling that anything goes in the study of the Bible.

This can intensify a popular feeling among believing Christians and Jews that biblical scholars are the enemies of faith. In fact, most biblical scholars the world over are religious believers themselves, though not always of a very orthodox kind. Nearly all are Christians, but in recent years biblical study has also been practiced more among Jewish scholars. Traditionally, study of Scripture in Judaism followed well-worn paths of rabbinic exegesis, and did not engage with "critical" issues, but this is changing today. Only in very recent years have agnostics and even atheists come to take an interest in the Bible, partly because of the turn to "literary" and sociological interpretations which will be discussed below. But a religious motivation for biblical study is still the predominant one. This does not mean, however, that the conclusions to which biblical scholars come are always religiously very palatable.

For most people who study the Bible the concern remains, as it has always been, to yield results that are helpful and informative for religious believers. Until the last couple of decades this was achieved through what is usually called "the historical-critical method" – not really a *method*, more a series of questions that one can put to the text, a particular style of interrogating it. In itself this is not a theological approach, and it can be and is applied to many types of literature besides the Bible; but most scholars used to be convinced that no theological assessment of Scripture could afford to bypass it.

"Introduction"

The most basic operation of biblical criticism as traditionally practiced by professional scholars is known, technically, as "Introduction" (*Einleitung* in German). This amounts to asking about the origins of the text one is studying: When was Genesis written? Who wrote the Gospels? Where did the book of Job originate? Even in dealing with works recent by comparison with the biblical books (such as the plays of Shakespeare) such questions can be very difficult to answer. When the material is as old as some of the Bible, it is not surprising that there is enough uncertainty to make "Introduction" a full-time occupation for some scholars. It is important to notice that books called *Introduction to the Old/New Testament* tend to be about these issues, rather than being "introductions" in the everyday sense of the word – though in the English-speaking world there is some confusion over this, and both types of book will be found with such titles.

Questions of "introduction" are one area where extra-biblical sources are particularly useful. In the course of the twentieth century huge numbers of texts from Egypt, Mesopotamia, and Syria–Palestine were found by archeologists, and these have contributed materially to filling in the background to the production of the texts that make up the Bible. Over the last fifty years the Dead Sea Scrolls have been a special focus of interest, throwing considerable light on Judaism at the time of Jesus, and so making the context of the New Testament far clearer than it has ever been before. The study of patristic and rabbinic texts has also been an important source of information about the making of the Bible; for although their authors often did not know any more than we do about how the biblical books were composed, they provide invaluable information about the early reception of these books, from which it is sometimes possible to reconstruct how they came into being in the first place.

Source criticism

The attempt to ask questions of "introduction" about many biblical books, however, uncovers confusing data. Many books of the Old Testament, in particular, contain passages that seem to be older than others in the same book, or that are duplicates of narratives found elsewhere. A notorious example is the "wife–sister" stories found in similar forms in Genesis 12, 20, and 26, where one of the patriarchs passes off his wife as his sister to avoid being killed by a foreign ruler who wants her for his harem. Else-where, different versions of a story seem to be interwoven – see, for example, the Flood story in Genesis 6–9, where in its finished form the account is highly confusing. (How many animals entered the ark? How long did the Flood last?) This led eighteenth- and nineteenth-century scholars to postulate underlying documents or "sources" from which many books of the Bible, but especially the Pentateuch, were composed.

Source criticism of the Pentateuch reached its classic formulation at the end of the nineteenth century in the work of Julius Wellhausen (1844–1918). According to his analysis, there were originally four sources from which the Pentateuch was composed. These are conventionally know as J, E, D, and P, coming respectively from the ninth, eighth, seventh, and sixth (or fifth) centuries BCE (see G. Davies 2001). Important theological consequences follow from this: one is that Israelite monotheism, which is far more evident in the later than in the earlier of the sources, developed gradually over time, rather than having been part of an early "deposit" of faith given to Moses. Another is that the complex sacrificial and purity system that had come to character-ize Judaism by New Testament times did not appear until after the Babylonian exile of the sixth century: it, too, had no early roots. These conclusions scandalized (and con-tinue to scandalize) some orthodox Jews and conservative Christians, but they have been widely accepted in the scholarly community for over a century.

In the English-speaking world, acceptance of the Wellhausen hypothesis came about through the work of the Scottish scholar William Robertson Smith (1846–94) and an Oxford Professor of Hebrew, Samuel Rolles Driver (1846–1914). Subsequent scholars refined and revised Wellhausen's analysis. Especially in the German-speaking world work on this continues, with highly sophisticated theories about the composition of the Old Testament books. In the "historical" books, for example – those running from Joshua to Kings – a widely accepted theory postulates many sources and several layers of editorial work, with sigla such as DtrG, DtrP, and DtrN used freely in the scholarly literature. To the non-specialist reader, they impart an air of mystery, but are a short-hand way of signaling the composite character of these books, which tell a continuous story but one that is far from straightforward in its literary origins.

The Gospels are also a case where source criticism continues to be a lively scene. Most scholars think that the authors of Matthew and Luke (whoever they were) used Mark's Gospel, long recognized by most as the earliest. Many believe that the other material which Matthew and Luke share comes from a now lost document consisting mainly of sayings of Jesus, conventionally termed Q (from German *Quelle*, "source"). Literature on this hypothetical entity runs into many thousands of books and articles, and it remains debated whether it really ever existed at all (see Tuckett 1996). If it did not, then Matthew must have had access to Luke, or vice versa – simpler hypotheses but with their own problems because of the different ways in which the same material is used in the two Gospels. John's Gospel is seen by some as based on the other three, to form what Clement of Alexandria in ancient times called a "spiritual" Gospel, but by others as quite independent of them and resting on its own complicated prehistory of many sources. Just as Old Testament source criticism is important because it helps us to reconstruct how religious thought and practice developed in ancient Israel, so source analysis of the Gospels has always had at its heart the hope of getting access to the authentic sayings of Jesus and the truth about his life and deeds. It belongs to the "quest of the historical Jesus," which has passed through several phases since the eighteenth century.

One of the heirs of this quest is the American "Jesus Seminar," in which scholars meet to discuss the authenticity of sayings of Jesus recorded in the Gospels, and actually express their conclusions through a vote. This strikes many as somewhat "reductionist" – as though such questions could be decided democratically – but its findings are influential for many scholars. The search for what can be known with reasonable certainty about Jesus and his first followers remains of intense interest to many both inside and outside the churches (cf. Crossan 1991, Sanders 1987), and in recent years has become important also to a Jewish constituency, which often claims that the real Jesus was a much more centrally Jewish figure that Christian apologetic has made him. The work of Geza Vermes, a pioneer in Scrolls research, has been central here (see Vermes 2000). Such claims can only be substantiated or confuted through serious source-critical work on the Gospels.

Form criticism

The Bible is a written document, but much of it must rest on oral tradition. Jesus, like Socrates or the prophets of the Old Testament, probably did not write down any of his own teaching. We possess it only in Greek translation from the hands of later writers, who must ultimately have relied on traditions passed down by his disciples. Even the stories about him probably depend on originally oral transmission within the early churches, and were not written down till some time later than their occurrence. We could say the same about many Old Testament texts. The books of the prophets presumably rest on the work of the prophets' disciples, who collected oral material and ordered it (in ways that still baffle its readers); and the Psalms were probably meant for recitation or singing, and may well have existed for many years before anyone wrote them down.

In the mid-twentieth century, influential biblical scholars thought a lot could be known about the original contexts in which such material was used orally, and the discipline of form criticism developed in an attempt to systematize approaches to originally oral material – partly under the influence of similar studies in the field of Norse and Middle Eastern studies. In the case of the Gospels, the leading form critic was Rudolf Bultmann (1884–1976), who tried to establish the various types into which the Gospel stories fell: pronouncement stories designed to end in an aphorism, miracle stories whose climax was the crowd's acclamation of Jesus, and so on (see Bultmann 1963). In Old Testament studies, Sigmund Mowinckel (1884–1996) paid particular attention to the Psalms, arguing in a series of studies that they could best be understood as texts intended for recitation at various Israelite festivals. He reconstructed these on the basis of his classification of psalm-types, and with the help of comparative material from other ancient Near Eastern cultures (see Mowinckel 1962).

Form criticism has fallen on rather hard times in recent biblical scholarship. There is a widespread feeling that earlier form critics were over-confident in their ability to reconstruct the occasions on which particular types of saying or narrative were used in the early church, or the religious contexts in which texts such as the Psalms were recited. Ordinary believers always thought form-critical work on the Gospels excessively skeptical in its effects, attributing too much importance to the early church context in which stories were allegedly shaped, and too little to the likelihood of their really going back to Jesus himself. Furthermore, recent interest in narrative material in both Testaments has tended to concentrate on its written form, and has returned to an older skepticism about the possibility of getting back behind the present form of the text (thus Wellhausen believed the sources in the Pentateuch rested on folk memory, but thought the task of rediscovering this tradition completely impossible). Narrative material tends now to be studied for its literary skill, not for its underlying oral roots. And in the case of the Psalms, Mowinckel's work is widely recognized as plausible but, in the end, entirely hypothetical. New interests in the Psalter have emerged, chiefly that of its final composition or *redaction*. This brings us to the next topic.

Redaction criticism

"Redaction" is a technical term much used in biblical studies to refer to the process of editing which gave us the finished form of most of our biblical books – assuming that they are made up of pre-existing sources, as implied by source criticism. The redactor, like the authors of the original sources, is normally anonymous, but it may be possible to discover quite a lot about this person by studying how the underlying material has been reshaped in turning it into a finished book. In the 1970s and 1980s it was redaction criticism, the study of the biblical redactors, that many thought promised most in biblical studies. It is probably the predominant approach in many German theology faculties. If source critics study the underlying materials in the biblical books, and form critics explain how they developed over the years in preaching, teaching, and worship, redaction critics have the task of explaining the intentions of those who assembled the material to make our existing books. These people, after all, are the nearest thing most biblical books have to an "author." Matthew, Mark, Luke, and John, whether or not they were really called by those names, are the people from whose hands we now receive the Bible, and their work consisted very largely of putting together material that already existed in written or oral form (cf. Bornkamm, Barth, and Held 1982).

In Old Testament studies it was widely felt that redaction criticism was more "constructive" than the other methods we have examined so far, because it put back together what the other "criticisms" had taken apart. Source critics had discovered, for example, that the book of Isaiah consisted of three originally discrete sections (1–39, 40–55, 56–66) coming from three different periods (and each in itself already composite). But redaction critics began to be interested in how the book finally came together to make the finished whole we now encounter when we open a Bible (cf. Conrad 1991). This was widely felt to be a worthy aim, which overcame the rather "negative" effect of earlier types of criticism. In the case of the Gospels, a redaction-critical approach was interested in the distinctive theology of each Gospel as a work in its own right, not simply as the repository of older tradition. It noticed, for example, that it is Luke that contains much of the teaching of Jesus on God's mercy toward humankind – the parables of the Prodigal Son and the Good Samaritan – and Matthew who talks most of the Last Judgment, including most of the references to "wailing and gnashing of teeth." Instead of treating the Gospels as a uniform quarry for stories and sayings of Jesus, redaction critics saw each Gospel as having its own distinctive profile.

Redaction criticism had an important influence on all the churches through a new Sunday lectionary compiled in the aftermath of the Second Vatican Council, in the Catholic Church, but in due course adopted, with a few modifications, by many churches world-wide as the *Revised Common Lectionary (RCL)*. Here each Gospel is read through in order week by week and so heard as a whole in its own right, rather than as in the old system where passages were selected from different Gospels: thus there is a year of Matthew, a year of Mark, a year of Luke (John is mostly read in Lent and Eastertide each year). In the original Catholic version, Old Testament passages were chosen to match the Gospel reading for the day, but even that is modified in the *RCL* so that for much of the year Old Testament passages also are read in order. This is done to respect the books from which they are taken as texts in their own right, rather than treating them as collections of useful extracts.

Thus redaction criticism has been widely seen as a return to the kind of respect for the Bible that the more "destructive" work of source and form critics had called in question. As we shall see in surveying more recent trends, there has been a widespread feeling that biblical criticism had become over-critical and unhelpful to most Bible readers, who are, after all, interested in the Bible as a book of faith rather than out of antiquarian concerns. The high value placed by many on redaction criticism is perhaps symptomatic of that feeling.

A turn to theology

The feeling that biblical criticism was somehow insufficiently reverent toward what is, for Jews and Christians, a sacred text has not been felt only by people outside the academic world of biblical studies: it is felt also by some biblical scholars themselves, and always has been. Wellhausen gave up his chair in Theology because he felt that he was making his students less fit for service as Lutheran pastors. Consequently there have been periodic attempts to "reintegrate" biblical studies into theology, or to "give the Bible back to the Church."

In the 1940s and 1950s this happened throughout the world of biblical studies in what is commonly known as the "Biblical Theology Movement." This was a primarily North American phenomenon, but one which had ripples in British and even in German scholarship. Biblical Theologians (in this technical sense) were not only interested in the theological ideas in the text (as the discipline of biblical theology has always been) but were concerned for the text's *normativity* for the Church. They tended to argue that in the Bible there were particular ways of seeing the world – often, they suggested, enshrined in the peculiarities of biblical Hebrew and Greek – which we needed to recapture. "Fragmenting" the text by practicing source or form criticism was beside the point. What was needed was to hear its whole witness to God. In the 1970s and 1980s redaction criticism, as just outlined, was felt by some to have the same reintegrative potential. But it was in the late 1970s that a movement began which has been particularly important in raising the theological profile of the biblical text, under the slogan "The Canonical Approach."

This movement owes its origins to the Yale Old Testament scholar Brevard S. Childs. Childs has argued in many publications for what he calls a canonical approach to biblical study (see especially Childs 1970 and 1979). This means taking seriously the fact that the Bible is not simply a random collection of ancient texts – a kind of anthology of Jewish and Christian writings – but functions as the Scriptures of the Christian Church (and, in the case of the Old Testament, of Judaism). He believes accordingly that far more attention ought to be paid to making scriptural interpretation "confessional," that is, religiously committed. Historical biblical criticism has been, according to him, studiedly neutral. It has appealed to criteria meant to be acceptable whether or not one has faith. This means that it has deliberately ignored the fact that these texts function as the "canon" for faith communities. Some way needs to be found of expounding them "as Scripture" rather than in this determinedly "secular" way, and so of helping the Church to appropriate them as a divine word. This necessitates looking first at the "final form" of the text, rather than rooting around in its origins and sources.

By no means everyone in the world of biblical studies is convinced by this, but it has brought about a major shift in the kinds of questions that many scholars ask of the biblical text. Redaction criticism, which seemed originally quite radical, and constructive in refocusing people's minds on the finished form of biblical texts, now looks rather tame and timid. "Canonical" critics insist on seeing not just (say) Isaiah as one book again, but the whole Bible as a single work. They expound it not from a standpoint of supposed scholarly "objectivity," but with a deliberate commitment to its religious authority.

The sea-change this implies may be put as follows. Older biblical criticism was often (indeed, usually) practiced by scholars who did have a high commitment to the inspiration and authority of the Bible. But they thought the proper way to study it was first to analyze it critically in the ways described above, and only then to move on to questions of its religious significance. This was true of Protestant and Catholic scholars alike. The newer movement denies that this is desirable; indeed, it tends to argue that it is actually impossible. Once you begin by studying the text "neutrally," you have sold the pass; and you are then faced with the problem of how to reunite the "neutral" text with a religiously committed application of it. But the problem is of your own making! You should never have divorced the text from questions of faith in the first place. The religious claims of the text ought never to be bracketed out, not even procedurally, for that concedes the case of skeptics who do not think these texts are special. For a Christian they are special, and they need special types of interpretation, a "special hermeneutic" as it would traditionally have been called. "General hermeneutics" – interpretative principles applicable to any text whatever – are simply inadequate when it comes to the Bible.

Brevard Childs has followers in Britain, especially Walter Moberly in Durham (see Moberly 2000), Francis Watson in Aberdeen (Watson 1994), and Christopher Seitz in St. Andrews (Seitz 1998), all of whom in different ways have tried to apply his ideas to the interpretation of both Old and New Testaments. They would all argue that it is imperative for scholars to read the biblical text from a committed position. But they would go further than this, and say that the supposed neutrality of biblical criticism was always an illusion anyway. For biblical criticism derives from the Enlightenment, and the Enlightenment had a built-in bias against the religious claims of the Bible or, indeed, of any text. Scholars thought they were being detached and neutral when in fact they were approaching the text rationalistically, with a bias against divine inspiration and authority and in favor of naturalistic explanation. This point of view, which may be called in some ways a return to (or rapprochement with) conservative Christian views of the nature of biblical criticism, is making considerable headway in the world of biblical studies at the moment.

"Advocacy" readings

The belief that every reader of the Bible has a commitment, even when pretending or trying to be neutral, has led to an attempt to discover what the commitments of respected scholars of the past actually were. It has been easy to show that many were very much the product of their class, time, and political persuasion. Certain scholars have been particularly skillful in uncovering the hidden bias of much traditional "objective" scholarship – indeed, there is now a genre of writing known as "metacommentary" that seeks to do this. Outstanding exponents are David Clines at Sheffield (see Clines 1995), and Yvonne Sherwood at Glasgow (see Sherwood 2000).

But linked with this acute perception of the failings of past (and some present) scholars there is often a sense that, since everyone is bound to have a bias – a commitment – the important thing is to make it a good and wholesome one. A commitment to human liberation is widely regarded as just such a wholesome commitment, whether it be to political liberation for those oppressed by unjust societal structures, or to the liberation of women from social oppression by men and the systems men have created. Feminists and liberation theologians have sought to replace the conservative or "liberal" readings of the Bible common in the past with readings based on a liberation perspective. A case in point would be Gustavo Gutiérrez's study of the book of Job (Gutiérrez 1987), and much of the work being done by Christopher Rowland (Rowland and Corner 1990). Especially in the USA, feminist readings of both the Old and the New Testament now abound. There is a whole series of feminist *Companions to the Bible* published by the Sheffield Academic Press (an important source of innovative publishing in biblical studies), edited by the Israeli scholar Athalya Brenner, who teaches in both Israel and the Netherlands.

The newer literary criticism

At the same time as scholars have been advocating readings of the Bible with more commitment – either religious or social – there has also been another turn in biblical studies, which contributes to the sense of ferment in this now very variegated field. This other turn is in a literary direction. "The Bible as Literature" used to be regarded by serious biblical scholars as a dilettante interest, and some students of literature (C. S. Lewis would be an obvious example) agreed, seeing it as an attempt to water down the Bible's religious claim. In any case it tended, in the English-speaking world, to be short-hand for praising the Authorized Version, rather than engaging with biblical criticism. But since the 1980s, secular literary critics have begun to take the Bible in its original languages seriously as great world literature. One of the first was Frank Kermode with *The Genesis of Secrecy* (1979), a sophisticated study of Mark's Gospel in the light of par-allels in English literature, especially in the work of James Joyce. He and Robert Alter, a (Jewish) professor of comparative literature in California, joined forces to produce *The Literary Guide to the Bible* (1987), in which each biblical book is analyzed in a literary, rather than a theological or conventionally "critical," way. Some of the authors use the techniques of structuralism, which enjoyed a brief vogue in biblical studies in the 1970s, but most engage in what literary critics normally call a "close reading," often with some similarities to redaction criticism.

In Britain the Department of Biblical Studies at Sheffield has been crucial in pro-moting literary approaches to the Bible. In its publications one often sees that a concern for literary aspects of the biblical text can coexist with, and complement, a religious commitment of a "canonical" or "advocacy" kind. For many students of the Bible a lit-erary reading of the "final form" of the biblical text joins hands with the holistic style of interpretation required by a canonical approach. Evangelical scholars in particular are often attracted by both types of study, which seem to reverse the apparently destruc-tive tendency of the older biblical criticism. It is very likely that all these "post-critical" developments will continue to feed into the now very complex world of biblical studies.

Old Testament Studies Today

Many of the movements discussed above apply in equal measure to both Old and New Testament studies, but there are also some developments specific to each.

The Old Testament as Scripture

The Old Testament has never been unproblematic as the Scriptures of the Church, because it represents the literature of Israel before Christ, and remains the holy book of Judaism. There have been many movements in the Church frankly hostile to retain-ing the Old Testament. Marcion in the ancient Church represented this tendency; in the nineteenth century it was espoused by Adolf von Harnack; and in the twentieth, Rudolf Bultmann's position comes close to regarding the Old Testament as superannuated – useful at best as a record of how inadequate life is without Christ. But in the twentieth century there were also movements strongly affirming the place of the Old Testament in the Christian scheme of things.

This can be seen in the two greatest Theologies of the Old Testament, written respec-tively before and after World War II, those of Walter Eichrodt and Gerhard von Rad.

The Biblical Theology Movement, mentioned above, was also influential in the English-speaking world in rehabilitating the Old Testament. It often argued that the New Testament itself could only be understood if read with "Hebrew" categories of thought in mind. The figures of George Ernest Wright in the USA (see Wright 1952) and Alan Richardson in Britain (see Richardson 1950) were important in this Movement. Thus a considerable rearguard action was fought against any desire to remove the Old Testament from effective Christian Scripture. The tendency of church lectionaries (especially the *Revised Common Lectionary*) to include more Old Testament readings is also a factor here.

Nevertheless the 1970s and 1980s saw a renewed feeling among some scholars that the Old Testament was being sold short: that it had turned into the object of an essentially antiquarian investigation, with a huge concentration on historical, archeological, and linguistic matters, and little emphasis on its place in the Church. This is the background of Brevard Childs's "canonical approach," described above. Childs argued that, beyond historical criticism – which had its proper place – Christians need to regain a sense of being addressed by the Old Testament as their Scriptures. This implied reading the text as a coherent whole in its present form.

Childs's work has revolutionized the questions people are willing to ask about the Old Testament in an academic context. It no longer seems odd for a scholar to ask what God is saying to the Church through this or that Old Testament passage, where earlier generations of critics might have been more likely to see this as a "devotional" question outside the proper sphere of academic study. People speak of the need to "reclaim" the Old Testament for the Church from the grip of purely academic study. Much support for Childs has come from his own Reformed tradition. It often goes hand in hand with an attachment to Barthian theology, for Barth always maintained that biblical interpretation was properly to be done within the Church, not hived off into an area of "academic" specialization. Childs has been severely criticized, most notably by James Barr, for threatening to undo the centuries of patient critical work on the text (cf. Barr 1983, 1999). But his proposals have struck a chord with many in the churches.

The history of interpretation

The idea that the Old Testament text should be read as a coherent whole is often linked with the argument that that is how it used to be read before the historical critics came along. Accordingly there has been a massive revival of interest in "pre-critical" reading of the Old Testament, in rabbinic, patristic, and Reformation writers. Childs himself gave considerable impetus to this movement by writing a long commentary on Exodus in which he presented not merely a critical reading dealing with the traditional concerns of source, form, and redaction critics, but also much information about interpretations in traditional Judaism and Christianity – with excerpts from the rabbis, the Fathers, and the Reformers.

It so happens that an interest in the history of the reception of texts is a growing concern in the wider literary world. People nowadays write about how Shakespeare (for example) was read, and how his plays were performed, in the seventeenth, eighteenth, or nineteenth centuries. Childs's theological program thus chimes in with leading secular movements of literary criticism. By no means all those interested in the text's reception are "canonical critics"; some are themselves "secular" students of the Bible as literature, who simply find the effects the text has had on generations of readers more interesting and important than the quest for its supposed "original" meaning. But there is no doubt that the theological and literary concerns complement each other well in the present climate of thought. An important influence on the more secular interest in reception history has been the work of Hans-Georg Gadamer. His idea that one never approaches a text "cold" but always with a "pre-understanding" was influential in earlier times on such biblical scholars as von Rad. The history of interpretation is a rapidly burgeoning area of study in Old Testament scholarship.

New historical criticism

While these theological programs have been making the running for some, historical work on the Old Testament has not stood still. Archeological excavation in the Middle East continues apace, and still contributes much to our knowledge of the biblical text. At the same time, however, there is an important revisionist movement at work in Old Testament studies at the moment, represented in Britain by Philip R. Davies and Keith W. Whitelam in Sheffield (see P. R. Davies 1992, Whitelam 1996), and on the Continent by Niels Peter Lemche and Thomas L. Thompson (an American) in Copenhagen (see Thompson 1999, Lemche 1998). For these writers, the historical study of ancient Israel has until very recently been far too focused on the biblical text. A classic example would be John Bright's *A History of Israel* (Bright 1960), studied by several generations of theological students and still in active use today. Bright draws a great deal on "external" evidence (archeology in particular), but he follows the Old Testament's own presentation of the history of Israel very closely. The impression is given that the Bible got it all more or less right: Abraham, for example, may not have done exactly what Genesis reports, but he was a real historical person who lived in roughly the period implied by the Bible. The general shape of Israel's history as the Old Testament describes it is seen as confirmed by both textual and archeological study.

All this is now up for discussion. The newer historians of Israel think that modern scholars have been far too easily taken in by the ideological bias of the biblical account, which is strongly pro-Israel and talks as though Israel was a major player on the world stage, rather than a tiny backwater. They argue indeed that "Israel" itself is a theological construction which owes more to the thought of the community after the exile (in the fifth or fourth centuries, or even later) than to any historical reality in earlier times: it is an ideal "people of God" rather than a socio-political reality that actually existed on the ground. The patriarchs are largely figures of fiction (just as Wellhausen thought!); the kings of Israel and Judah are made in the likeness of later Persian or even Hellenistic rulers; even the scale of the exile to Babylon has been grossly exaggerated in the interests of those who returned, who wanted to portray themselves as the "true" core of the nation. The history of the indigenous population of Canaan, whom Whitelam refers to provocatively as "Palestinians," has been unfairly neglected or vilified.

Late datings

Hand in hand with this revisionism about the history of Israel goes a tendency to re-date the Old Testament sources to a much later period than most scholars have previously thought plausible. Even the apparently "annalistic" material in Kings – which for most historians represents the bedrock in the history of Israel – does not really come from the time of the Hebrew monarchy in the ninth to seventh centuries BCE, but from a much later time. Some even place it in the Hellenistic period, in the third or even second century BCE. This implies that it is the purest fiction. Not only does this undermine our confidence in the texts as an accurate portrayal of Israel's history; it also changes our ideas of how theological thought developed in the Old Testament period, for it leaves us (among other things) knowing nothing at all about the great prophets, the supposed fount of so much that is distinctive in the Old Testament. Their books, like the histories, become evidence for the thinking in the last couple of centuries BCE, and throw no light whatever on earlier times.

Most scholars probably find these newer movements exaggerated. While acknowledging that we have sometimes been too gullible when reading the Old Testament, they doubt whether the complex Old Testament text was really made from whole cloth in so late a period, and prefer to think that it does rest on a great deal of genuine historical reminiscence, and on some written sources, however fragmentary. Though it is true that Israelite writers had an ideological stance of their own and were no more "neutral" historians than are we who study them, they were not simply inventing a nation. Israel emerges as sufficiently distinctive for us to be obliged to think that something like it actually existed. Nevertheless, new historical movements have brought about another major shift in the questions people are prepared to put to the Old Testament, and their challenge will not go away.

New Testament Studies Today

Historical criticism

The methods of historical criticism continue to be practiced by New Testament scholars, just as by their colleagues in Old Testament studies. But the results are often quite different from those familiar in the scholarship of thirty or forty years ago. Source criticism of the Gospels, for example, no longer operates uniformly with the old assumption that the Synoptic Gospels are composed from four sources (Mark, Q, M, and L – the latter two representing the material unique, respectively, to Matthew and Luke). The very existence of Q is being called in question by many, at the same time as the Q "industry" continues to produce full-scale studies of this hypothetical source. The possibility that one or other of Matthew and Luke read the other's work – derided by critics in the earlier twentieth century – is now regarded by many as a serious option. Meanwhile the independence of John, part of the whole basis for speaking of "Synoptic Gospels" by contradistinction from the Fourth Gospel, is no longer accepted by all (see the discussion in Brown 1979). Even such bizarre ideas (bizarre by older standards) as that Luke used John are no longer unthinkable for all, though they would represent clearly minority positions. And John itself is widely seen as composite, the putting together of sources or strata just as diverse as those used by the Synoptists.

Form criticism is also no longer in the ascendant. The normal form-critical supposition, worked out in detail by Rudolf Bultmann and a host of followers, was that each pericope in the Gospels had an independent existence as a story told liturgically in the early Church. Only much later were all these pericopae honed down into their present form, and eventually strung along a narrative thread by the evangelists. But this is under attack from two sides. On the one hand there are literary critics of the Gospels who think that the evangelists themselves favored the pericope-by-pericope method of telling the story of Jesus, not because the units already existed but because that was how they naturally wrote. On the other are conservative voices urging that the stories may have been written down much earlier than used to be thought, and that they may even represent eye-witness testimony simply copied into the Gospels as we now have them (cf. Gerhardsson 1979).

Redaction criticism, similarly, is put under strain by newer ways of seeing the Gospels. Redaction critics depended for their life-blood on source and form criticism, for to study the Gospels' redaction is to study what the redactor has made of previously existing materials – whether these are seen as earlier written sources or as independent units transmitted orally over a long period of time. By comparing the (reconstructed) original contents of sources or small "forms" with the finished Gospel one could then, it was supposed, see the interests the evangelist himself had and how he had shaped the material he had inherited. One problem with this was always that we had no independent access to the evangelist's sources: they had to be reconstructed from the very finished product we would later go on to study, a process clearly prone to circularity! But in any case people have come to think that there may have been an element of oversophistication in much redaction-critical work. Can we really be so sure that we can identify the particular features of Mark's Christology, say, enough to distinguish it plainly from Matthew's or even John's? Maybe we are asking the material to yield more answers than it is adapted to do.

Thus at the same time as historical criticism of the Gospels has continued, scholars have become much more tentative in their commitment to its results. There is a certain wariness in New Testament studies today, not unlike the effect of challenges by historical minimalists in Old Testament studies. It is not that the questions historical critics ask are unreasonable, or that we should not like to have answers to them; it is simply a feeling that in many cases answers may not really be available.

The final form of the text

All this has driven some New Testament specialists, like their Old Testament colleagues though perhaps for partly different reasons, in the direction of paying more attention to the Gospels as they present themselves to us now: in their "final form." This results in a literary turn, away from historical inquiry and toward reader-response criticism and narrative criticism. We may ask what the text says to a receptive reader (and indeed what it has said in the past to such readers – here too, reception history has its part to play). And we also ask how the text works on us: by what literary mechanisms it conveys the effects it does. This may be an (historical) interest in the writer and his techniques, but more commonly now it consists of asking about the text's own structures, the "intention of the work" (in Umberto Eco's phrase). People now sometimes say they are interested not in the meaning *behind* the text (as traditional historical critics are thought to have been) but in the meaning *in front of* the text, that is, in its interplay with its readers. This places Gospel study firmly in the world of contemporary literary studies. Some feel, however, that this is also a way of restoring theological value to biblical study, for it is very much in the interchange between reader and text that the text comes to speak to the modern believer, who is interested in what it *means* rather than in what it *meant* (to use terminology developed by Krister Stendahl).

Social science and the New Testament

Even in asking what a text meant, however, there is more than meets the eye. Traditional critics have asked about the meanings of texts as if they were purely exercises in communicating theological ideas, rather like a kind of treatise or essay. But this can easily overlook the social dimension of the text: who was meant to read it, and how were they to encounter it in the first place? And what must have been their situation – social, political, ethical – if this was an appropriate text for them to receive? It is in the case of the letters of Paul that these questions have come most to the fore, and it has proved necessary to delve into the social history of the earliest Christian communities in ways that would traditionally have been associated more with the study of the classical than of the New Testament world. But we have come to see that these two worlds are really one. The early Christian writings cannot be understood without a picture of the social conditions in which they made sense, and that inevitably involves trying to piece together – sometimes from the very texts being studied – some account of what it was like to belong to a Christian group in Corinth or Ephesus or Rome. Particularly valuable here has been the work of Wayne Meeks (Meeks 1983; cf. Theissen 1990).

But it is not as though there is no external evidence to help in these inquiries. The Mediterranean world of the New Testament period is rich in inscriptional and literary remains; and for the Jewish context there is the immense contribution being made by the Dead Sea Scrolls. To some extent New Testament scholars are forever re-examining the same old texts, the very brief compass of the New Testament; but they do so in a scholarly context greatly changed by the discovery of the Dead Sea Scrolls and other caches of documents testifying to the complex culture in which the New Testament came to be.

A return to historical inquiry

The new sociological interest in the New Testament background represents, in a way, a return to the centrality of historical concerns, though in a new mode, prompted by the different emphases of historians today as against those of their predecessors in the mid-twentieth century. Historical criticism, however changed, is certainly not dead in New Testament studies. This is evident from the renewed interest in the "historical Jesus," as attested in the Jesus Seminar (already mentioned above) and the work of scholars with quite other concerns, such as Gerd Theissen: the result is a lively debate between those who see Jesus as having been essentially a teacher of "wisdom" in the manner of the Cynics and those who retain an older image of him as an eschatological prophet (see Crossan 1991).

But Paul also has been the subject of a major shift in interpretation which is concerned (to some extent in a traditional way) with his theological teaching. Through the work of E. P. Sanders above all, Paul's teaching on the Jewish law has been extensively re-evaluated, and the distorting lens of Lutheran interpretation (as Sanders sees it) removed, so that his relation to contemporary Judaism is made much clearer (see Sanders 1977).

In the study of both the Gospels and Paul, therefore, there is plenty of historical work still to do. The demise of historical criticism has been much exaggerated. Nevertheless, the world of biblical studies is now far more pluriform than it was a generation age, and historical concerns take their place no longer as the one dominant discipline, but as one among a whole variety of competing interests.

References

Alter, R. and Kermode, F. 1987. *The Literary Guide to the Bible*. London: Collins.

Barr, J. 1983. *Holy Scripture: Canon, Authority, Criticism*. Oxford: Oxford University Press.

Barr, J. 1999. *The Concept of Biblical Theology: An Old Testament Perspective*. London: SCM Press.

Barton, J. 1996. *Reading the Old Testament: Method in Biblical Study*, 2nd edn. London: Darton, Longman & Todd.

Barton, J. 1998. *The Cambridge Companion to Biblical Interpretation*. Cambridge: Cambridge University Press.

Bornkamm, G., Barth, G., and Held, H. J. 1982. *Tradition and Interpretation in Matthew*. London: SCM Press.

Bright, J. 1960. *A History of Israel*. London: SCM Press.

Brown, R. E. 1979. *The Community of the Beloved Disciple*. London: Geoffrey Chapman.

Bultmann, R. 1963. *The History of the Synoptic Tradition*. Oxford: Basil Blackwell.

Childs, B. S. 1970. *Biblical Theology in Crisis*. Philadelphia, PA: Westminster.

Childs, B. S. 1979. *Introduction to the Old Testament as Scripture*. London: SCM Press.

Clines, D. J. A. 1995. *Interested Parties: The Ideology of Writers and Readers of the Hebrew Bible*. Sheffield: Sheffield Academic Press.

Conrad, E. W. 1991. *Reading Isaiah*. Minneapolis, MN: Fortress Press.

Crossan, J. D. 1991. *The Historical Jesus: The Life of a Mediterranean Jewish Peasant*. Edinburgh: T. & T. Clark.

Davies, G. 2001. "Introduction to the Pentateuch," *The Oxford Bible Commentary*, ed. J. Barton and J. Muddiman. Oxford: Oxford University Press, pp. 12–38.

Davies, P. R. 1992. *In Search of "Ancient Israel."* Sheffield: JSOT Press.

Gerhardsson, B. 1979. *The Origins of the Gospel Tradition*. Philadelphia, PA: Fortress Press.

Gutiérrez, G. 1987. *On Job: God-Talk and the Suffering of the Innocent*. Maryknoll, NY: Orbis.

Kermode, F. 1979. *The Genesis of Secrecy: On the Interpretation of Narrative.* Cambridge, MA: Harvard University Press.

Lemche, N.-P. 1998. *The Israelites in History and Tradition.* London: SPCK.

Meeks, W. 1983. *The First Urban Christians: The Social World of the Apostle Paul.* New Haven, CT and London: Yale University Press.

Moberly, R. W. L. 2000. *The Bible, Theology and Faith: A Study of Abraham and Jesus.* Cambridge: Cambridge University Press.

Mowinckel, S. 1962. *The Psalms in Israel's Worship.* Oxford: Basil Blackwell.

Richardson, A. 1950. *A Theological Word Book of the Bible.* London: SCM Press.

Rowland, C. C. and Corner, M. 1990. *Liberating Exegesis: The Challenge of Liberation Theology to Biblical Studies.* London: SPCK.

Sanders, E. P. 1977. *Paul and Palestinian Judaism: A Comparison of Patterns of Religion.* London: SCM Press.

Sanders, E. P. 1987. *Jesus and Judaism.* London: SCM Press.

Seitz, C. 1998. *World without End: The Old Testament as Abiding Theological Witness.* Grand Rapids, MI: Eerdmans.

Sherwood, Y. 2000. *A Biblical Text and its Afterlives: The Survival of Jonah in Western Culture.* Cambridge: Cambridge University Press.

Theissen, G. 1990. *The Social Setting of Pauline Christianity: Essays on Corinth.* Edinburgh: T. & T. Clark.

Thompson, T. L. 1999. *The Bible in History: How Writers Create a Past.* London: Jonathan Cape.

Tuckett, C. M. 1996. *Q and the History of Early Christianity.* Edinburgh: T. & T. Clark.

Vermes, G. 2000. *Jesus the Jew,* 2nd edn. London: SCM Press.

Watson, F. 1994. *Text, Church, and World: Biblical Interpretation in Theological Perspective.* Edinburgh: T. & T. Clark.

Whitelam, K. W. 1996. *The Invention of Ancient Israel: The Silencing of Palestinian History.* London: Routledge.

Wright, G. E. 1952. *God Who Acts: Biblical Theology as Recital.* London: SCM Press.

CHAPTER 3
Philosophy

David B. Burrell

These reflections intend to explore the range of relationships obtaining between theology and other disciplines, or less stringently put, between faith and culture. Yet astute readers will immediately perceive that the terms themselves are far richer and more fluid once we begin to detach them from their conventional role of naming established academic disciplines. Or put more constructively, the perennial vigor of those very disciplines attests to the fact that they are always reaching beyond settled modes of discourse to discover new approaches to their subject. In short, a discipline like theology is constantly transforming itself, and the key to that transformation lies in the way in which the very terms it must employ inevitably carry considerable cultural freight. So it should prove illuminating if we let the word "philosophy" in the title stand for ways of understanding which the current cultural milieu considers acceptable. So in Aquinas's time, the commanding way in which the writings of Aristotle had broken open new ways of understanding, constrained Aquinas to open his *Summa theologiae* by asking whether theology could be a *scientia*, that is, a mode of knowing. The way in which he proceeded to answer that question would open up avenues hitherto unsuspected by Aristotelians, as we shall see, yet more significant for our purposes is the way he put the question. For if theology could not be considered to be a form of knowledge, then faith would at most be a matter of the heart and not of the mind, whereas for Aquinas it had to address both if it were to be a fully human perfection.[1]

Faith indeed provides the initial principles proper to theology, as rational reflection on the data of our senses provides the first principles of philosophy, and therein lies the mark distinguishing one from the other. Yet we could also address the main topic by asking what relation theology bears to faith, for the conception we have of theology will depend a great deal on the ways we have seen those initial principles of faith being elaborated into a theology. Presuming that the principles of faith come from revelation, and so differ categorically from the deliverances of our senses, are they treated as *given* there, much as some empiricists were wont to treat "sense-data" as *given*, so generating what philosophers like Wilfrid Sellars were later to caricature as "the myth of the given"? Or does the use of reason to inquire into the meaning of revelation issue in a dramatic to and fro of interpretation, which we call theology, so that this mode of inquiry becomes a quest for understanding not unlike continuing rational reflection on our sense experience? I shall indeed argue that a picture like this latter one best reflects the work of the great spirits who have shaped the discipline of theology, and who have given us the working definition of "faith seeking understanding." I shall also show how theology executed in this way belies the conjunction of the title of this part of the book, "Theology and . . ." with our title, "Philosophy," which suggests that we are faced with two adequately distinct endeavors.

But it were best not to jump to such a conclusion, but to begin with what the title does indeed suggest: that theology is one thing and philosophy another. And the time-honored way of marking the difference is by whether one employs data (or premises) from revelation or not: philosophy does not do so while theology must, for that is what sets it apart. A simple enough distinction, certainly, yet difficulties begin when we note the recurrent presumption that what supplies the paradigm for understanding is philosophy, so that whatever we might claim to "know by faith" must pass that bar. This presumption is often implicit, but what lends it credence is the original contention that knowing-by-faith *adds something* to what we have come to call "knowing." Now if that is so, how can we assess whether or not knowing-by-faith is properly a form of knowledge? That is, how can we determine whether or not what theology asserts is true? Notice how easily this conundrum is generated by the image of faith as something *added*, or better, the deliverances of revelation as *adding* something to knowing *tout court*. For what is added must then measure up to that to which it has been added. Yet such an image has been congenial to both sides of the faith/reason debate; it has long represented a time-honored way to distinguish these two disciplines. As we shall see, however, everything turns on the way in which the "additive" image is employed. Without critical attention to actual practice, the additive image will reinforce the implication of the original conjunction: that these are two separate things, each originally and necessarily quite extrinsic to the other. But how else can it be taken?

It may help to place this apparently intractable issue in two contexts which in fact envelop it. Think first of Aristotle's own reflections on knowing (or *epistémê*) in his Posterior Analytics, and how those explicit methodological prescriptions are often quite at variance with his own practice. In fact, Aquinas will later note that his rules for constituting bona fide knowledge can only characterize a constructed science like geometry. So explicit pictures of procedures for relating bodies of knowing, or even rules for constituting knowledge itself, can often shipwreck on actual practice. Another more theological context would be the vexed history of the relation of *natural* to *supernatural* orders. Is the latter something added to nature, with the resulting picture of a universe constructed of two stories, which theologians must then busy themselves relating to each other? This is the baroque picture which Henri de Lubac succeeded in dismantling, so opening the way for that mode of theology which animated Vatican II.[2] A similar mindset among Thomists of the time divided Aquinas's treatment of God into two parts: *de Deo uno* and *de Deo trino*, with that which treats of God's oneness proceeding in a philosophical mode, while theology enters only when triunity is at issue. Aquinas does indeed divide his treatment of God into two parts, but the division is pedagogical rather than ideological; moreover, the entire treatment takes place in his *Summa theologiae (ST)*, and only after he confirms its title as a work of theology by explicitly showing how theology can be a mode of knowing, a *scientia*.

So one begins to feel the need for a critical way of appropriating the time-honored distinction between philosophy and theology. Let us look more closely at the combinations and permutations which result when we factor in the implicit presumption that philosophy sets the norm. Two diametrically opposite inferences can result, as can happen, for example, when one either reads Aquinas that way, and so hears him saying that knowing-by-faith exalts knowledge properly speaking, or reads a modern rationalist like Freud, and thereby finds it redundant. Moreover, one could go on to ask the Aquinas so figured: how will knowing-by-faith exalt ordinary knowing? And the answer could be at least two-fold, reflecting two very disparate views of transcendence. The first response would be closer to Aquinas but arrived at only by re-configuring the distinction in a more critical fashion: knowing-by-faith can enrich or fulfill human understanding; while the second would construe knowing-by-faith as allowing us to escape the limitations of human understanding and of human life – a view of transcendence roundly (and rightly) criticized by many an ancient or contemporary thinker. And the charges of redundancy can be understood quite differently as well: as Freud does, that faith not only adds nothing cognitive but even retards critical acumen to keep believers in an infantile relation to reality; or as new age folks might claim for "spirituality," that what the humdrum world finds redundant is actually ecstasy for the initiated.

Another set of responses is generated when the additive picture is left intact and believers undertake to reverse the presumptive normativity of reason, embodied in philosophy, to replace it assertively by theology. Then it would be faith which sets the norm, and does so precisely to make up the deficiencies of reason. While this strategy more properly captures the Reformers than medievals like Aquinas, traces of it can be found in him as well. In both cases, the deficiency of reason can either be *de facto*, given the extreme difficulty in adjudicating issues surrounding divinity; or *de jure*, reflecting different views of the effects of original sin on human understanding. The logical difficulties which such a strategy elicits, as displayed in Karl Barth's increasingly self-critical elaboration of it, point to the incoherence of any merely additive picture: the very terms required to articulate the norm of faith must be taken from reason. So it becomes increasingly clear how pointless it is to try to identify the norm in theological matters either with faith or with reason; both must be operative, and theologians can be ranked by the way their work displays this mutual normativity.

Such will be my contention, in any case, and it should prove the more persuasive if the arguments for it display that rhetorical structure which properly befits theological inquiry. That is, arguments purporting to establish the mutual normativity proper to theology can only proceed indirectly, by noting how a mode of argumentation which rests on reason alone cannot adequately articulate its subject. The subject here is the understanding proper to human beings, which cannot but be curiously open-ended. In the global terms we have been using to this point, one can propose that philosophy points beyond itself in such a way that theology fulfills it, or correlatively, that philosophy cannot ground itself, so that philosophical reflection "begins and ends in wonder"

– as Aristotle noted in an uncharacteristically rhapsodic passage initiating his *Metaphysics*. Wonder offers an opening for revelation, which theology will proceed to elaborate precisely to thematize the wonder itself, for if a revelation cannot be seen to be doing just that then it can be dismissed as redundant. So it is the very picture of the sufficiency of reason to express the human condition which theology must use reason to undermine, in a way proper to it and best described as rhetorical. Interestingly enough, it is this very mode of argument which Aquinas displays at the opening of his *Summa Theologiae*, in the second question, often mistaken as offering five "proofs" for God's existence. Following Aquinas's own explicit comments, all responsible commentators have recognized that these cannot be proper demonstrations, but many have attempted to make them probative in some other sense. Yet the careful way in which he structures them presents them as argument-forms which show how we might put to the test (and in that sense, probe [*probari*]) any attempt to offer a complete explanation of the universe and its order. If we can be brought to see how our attempts to do just that continue to fail, then we might be able to open our minds (and eventually our hearts as well) to that One "whom we call God."

Aquinas's Approach to Mutual Clarification

The upshot of "turning around" (the Hebrew metaphor rendered *metanoia* in the New Testament) the usual presumption that "philosophy" sets the norm is to discover that the understanding available to us needs to be completed, fulfilled. But how? By adding something to it, some additional propositions, perhaps? Were that the case, as it appears to be for many philosophers of religion, there would be no mode of understanding proper to knowing-by-faith, nor would the additive picture require any critical appropriation. Aquinas offers another way of identifying what might be added: images from revelation to supplement what the world supplies to our senses, plus a perspicacity by way of divine light which enhances our capacity to perceive the import of these "God-given images" (*ST* 1.12.13). No divinely proffered propositions here, for propositions are of human making; rather, multivalent images awaiting our probing and elaboration. Just as what the world affords our senses causes us to wonder, so these images offer a yet more ample field for wonder. Alternatively, and this is John Henry Newman's tactic, what if the actual use of reason always involved faith of some sort? If that were the case, then the faith corresponding to a purported divine revelation would not be totally foreign to us, even though it would clearly be of a different order than the native trust which animates anything we do. Yet a revelation which could offer the best help in articulating that native trust would thereby flesh out and enrich our operative understanding, and notably our understanding of the very reaches of human understanding. One clear presumption of this argument is a robust realism: that there is something to know. The issue then becomes: how can we best know it?

Yet does not Aquinas also say that faith adds propositions as well? In an especially prescient response to the query whether God's triunity can be attained by reason without the benefit of revelation, he gives reasons why that could never be the case, reasons which reinforce his keen appreciation of just how "negative" is the knowledge that creatures can have of the creator (*ST* 1.32.1). In brief, accustomed as we are to tracing causal pathways in seeking explanations of any sort, it is quite another thing to try to trace the way to a cause of being, to the "universal cause of all existence" (*ST* 1.45.2). Even armed as he was with Aristotle's rich phenomenology of "four causes," it is problematic which one of these, if any, could answer to the "cause of being." So even should we stretch human reason to arrive there, with the help of intervening thinkers like Plotinus (relayed to him by pseudo-Dionysius), we could know little or nothing about that One, since it would completely escape Aristotle's mode of defining things, as Moses Maimonides had so clearly shown.[3] So *a fortiori*, the very inner life of God, revealed in the person of Jesus, and so intimated in the Christian scriptures but articulated within that community only after four centuries of struggle with diverse formulations, could hardly be proposed as a proper object for rational inquiry. Yet Aquinas goes on to note that once revealed and formulated, such a revelation can serve as a powerful corrective to apparently inevitable errors regarding the relation of the "cause of being" to beings: namely, that it could only be an impersonal and necessary emanation. This quite unexpected response (in the context of showing how God's triunity surpassed the powers of reason [*ST* 1.32.1.3]) unveils the deeper roots of Aquinas's own treatment of creation, wherein the inner-divine processions of Word and of Spirit serve as the eternal exemplars of an utterly free action on God's part: free because it was a fully intentional activity of expression (Word) and of ecstatic love (Spirit).[4]

What emboldened Aquinas to identify what had been the prevailing philosophical picture of the origin of all things – impersonal and necessary emanation – as an "error"? Precisely what had come to be revealed to him, through a revelation formulated in a tradition, about the creator. It was this revelation-tradition which allowed him to put to question the only account which philosophers until that time had deemed creditable.[5] Besides being used to gain critical purchase on alternative accounts, the same tradition had also built these hard-won propositions into theological account in its own right. In our time we have distinguished these two efforts, dividing them into philosophical and systematic theology, yet as we have seen, Aquinas engaged in both efforts with equal grace. Indeed, properly executed, one informs the other, and the result can be called "mutual clarification," in a phrase which captures the way Gilles Emery has characterized Aquinas's method in theological inquiry (Emery 1995:285–341). If this account offers a both accurate and attractive picture of properly theological inquiry, note how it formulates nicely the mutual normativity of faith and of reason, so leading us away from that "foundational" model of knowing which had insisted on a clear separation of theology from philosophy, while presuming that "philosophy" provided the norm by which any purported assertion had to be assessed.

Bernard Lonergan regularly contrasted these alternatives as the "need for certitude" versus the "quest for understanding," identifying what philosophers call "foundationalism" with the need for certitude.[6] Another look at Descartes' *Discourse on Method* as expressing a deep-seated *need* for certitude helps to underscore the import of this contrast, especially when one notes what different dimensions of the human psyche are reflected by needs rather than by quests. The quest for understanding formulates Augustine's classical definition of theology as "faith seeking understanding" in an idiom which alludes as well to Aristotle's intellectual virtues, thereby reminding us that understanding *in divinis* will always involve growth in understanding. This idiom also alludes to the fact that faith is ever a journey, and that the propositions which attempt to formulate "articles of faith" are at best guideposts along that way, which opens as a way to wisdom for those intent upon the quest. In that aspiration to wisdom, of course, reason needs all the help it can get, so pressing the quest for understanding to serve the journey of faith affords philosophy its medieval distinction of being the "handmaid of theology." We have seen how critical a role creation, and indeed the proper account of creation, plays in this synthesis, so it will not be surprising to note how the subsequent drive to "liberate" philosophy to an autonomous status involved disregarding the link to a creator. Indeed, the dramatic movement inherent in modernity did more than effect a return to Aristotle's insouciance about the question of origins, for it presented itself as a post-medieval alternative to a created universe.[7] The key to the "mutual clarification" which philosophy and theology can provide for each other lies in articulating creation.

To mention the shared goal of wisdom returns us to the etymology of the term "philosophy" – something easily forgotten when either of our key terms are identified via current academic disciplines. Rendering "philosophy" as Socrates presented it, as the desire for wisdom rather than its achievement or possession, reminds us that both disciplines are fated never to achieve their goal. Indeed, that is the reason why Clement of Alexandria explicitly pre-empted the classical name "philosophy" for Christian theology, calling it the "true philosophy." Here again the testimony of a rich tradition reminds us that distinctions cannot be separations, and that each one needs the other. Indeed, we have been correcting the additive picture all along to show at once how the very formulations of theology require continual assistance from reason, and how the presence of revelation can release philosophy, regarded as a particular way of using intellectual skills, to serve its animating purpose of a search for wisdom by questing for understanding. Using Aquinas as a paradigmatic thinker, the additive picture has been enhanced, if not replaced, by one of "mutual clarification." Other theologians will offer parallel testimony, corroborating the mutuality inherent in those disciplines which were presented at the outset of this inquiry as separate and so needing to be linked. In fact, the linkage is already present, even though often implicit, in the conceptual care with which theologians must proceed in their rarefied atmosphere, as well as in the original faith which must be present to animate any philosophical inquiry, once one has discarded a foundational picture of rational inquiry.

Augustine and the Part that Practice Plays

Just as those who thought themselves modern could not escape being post-medieval, so we are fated to be postmodern once we reject a foundational account of inquiry. Yet the way beyond rejection to a constructive account has already been suggested by alluding to Newman's *Grammar of Assent*, composed as a direct riposte to modernist conceptions of philosophical inquiry in their heyday.[8] The strategy of mutual clarification outlined here has been structured by Alasdair MacIntyre's elaboration of Newman's prescient suggestions into a general account of inquiry as invariably "tradition-directed."[9] His observations prove particularly enlightening for theological inquiry and its internal relation to a tradition focused on articulating revelation. If the actual use of reason to pursue a substantive inquiry inevitably presupposes something akin to faith (which Alvin Plantinga characterizes as "basic beliefs"), then a tradition like that of Christian theology offers abundant illustration of this path of mutual clarification, for it has found it opportune from the beginning to mine Hellenic modes of thought to elaborate its key doctrines of divine incarnation and triunity.[10] Indeed, it now appears that the medieval understanding of philosophy as a handmaid of a yet richer under-standing may suggest a way to liberate philosophical skills from the pretensions of com-plete comprehension to their proper role of facilitating human understanding. What is at stake here is a conception of philosophy which is not inflated, which answers to its originating impulse of wonder while retaining a properly self-critical edge. The work of Pierre Hadot may well show us a way of coming to a renewed appreciation of those dimensions, for his unveiling of the critical role which "spiritual exercises" played in ancient philosophy suggests a context within which to place the modern notion of "propositional attitudes" in order to bring out some features of understanding which that conception can easily overlook.[11]

That context is, of course, that of intellectual virtues. It can perhaps best be illus-trated by invoking another thinker in the Christian tradition who should prove enlight-ening in his own way: Aurelius Augustine. Readers of the *Confessions* steeped in modernity find it odd when, in his struggle for intellectual clarification detailed in the seventh book, he feels it necessary to decide between Platonism and Christianity. Why can't he think of himself as a Christian Platonist; certainly many have done just that? Yet Pierre Hadot's familiarity with the demands which ancient philosophy makes on philosophers themselves reminds us that they could only see this mode of thinking as involving the entirety of a person's relation to the universe, and so comprehending not just a "set of beliefs" but a way of life as well: a way of life embodied in a set of prac-tices which embraces one's life and forms one's attitudes. Now this is precisely what Christian liturgical formation is intended to do: introduce us into a world which should become more and more an alternative to the world in which we live; indeed, into the "kingdom of God." If the Platonism of his time pretended, as philosophies tend to do, to offer a complete comprehension of the universe, then it would come replete with practices as well, and some of these would inevitably clash with the mystagogy of Christian initiation. That is, at least, a plausible reconstruction of what faced Augustine. What is more telling for us is the need to reconstruct our own conception of philosophy to appreciate his dilemma, yet that reconstruction may bring us closer to an authentic understanding of the role of philosophy in human existence than its modernist frame of a set of beliefs (or "propositional attitudes").[12]

Yet more constructively, however: can we mine this same thinker for a positive con-ception of the mutual clarification which reason and faith can bring to one another? The answer is contained in an attentive reading of the *Confessions* themselves, for the final word is not one of opposition, but one which reshapes the Plotinian directions which initially gave him a way of entering the world of spirit as the domain of mind and of mind's internal good, God. That reshaping will follow the form of the incarnation of the Word made flesh, to bring human beings into a tensive relation between time and eternity, flesh and spirit, precisely there where Platonists tend to oppose them.[13] What allowed him so to reconceive philosophy and its role was the fresh context that revelation provided, an illumination which the *Confessions* puts in disarmingly simple terms: "the mystery of the Word made flesh I had not begun to guess. . . . None of this is in the Platonist books" (7:xix, xxi). He would not even be able to "guess" such a mystery, of course; nor indeed can we, for that very thought exceeds our imagination for what is possible – even when imagination for what is possible is the very thing on which philosophy has long prided itself! These final chapters of Book 7 of the *Confessions* offer a paradigm instance of "faith seeking understanding," the celebrated formula of Augustine's which animated the work of medieval philosophical theologians, beginning with Anselm.

Book 7 documents the discovery of the idiom which Augustine needed to find a proper way of conceptualizing God, not as another being among beings, but as the "life of the life of my soul" or the wisdom which grants wisdom to the wise – in short, the source of all that is, and hence should never be thought of as standing over against anything that is.[14] It was probably the *Enneads* of Plotinus which offered him this idiom, and chapter 16 notes why it recommended itself: "I asked myself why I approved of the beauty of bodies, whether celestial or terrestrial, and what justification I had for giving an unqualified judgment on mutable things. . . . In the course of this inquiry why I made such value judgments as I was making, I found the unchangeable and authentic eternity of truth to transcend my mutable mind" (7:xvi).[15] The text goes on to describe how he appropriated that idiom for his own quest:

> And so step by step I ascended from bodies to the soul which perceives through the body, and from there to its inward forces . . . [and] from there again I ascended to the power of reasoning to which is attributed the power of judging deliverances of the bodily senses. This power, which in myself I found to be mutable, raised itself to the level of its own intelligence, and . . . at that point it had no hesitation in declaring that the unchangeable is preferable to the changeable, since unless it could somehow know this, there would be no certainty in preferring it to the mutable. So in the flash of a trembling glance it attained to that which is. At that moment I saw your "invisible nature understood through the things which are made" (Rom 1:20). (7:xvi)

It should be clear how intimately this description relies on the neoplatonic structure of the mind's capacity to return to its origin, yet equally clear how that logic now actively structures Augustine's own search for the truth. The description is just that: an account of language put to use and becoming a trusted tool for discovery. This is indeed faith seeking understanding, by utilizing a mode of understanding made available to it, yet pressing it on to hitherto unsuspected reaches. The final citation from scripture indicates what animates that extension and potential transformation of the original idiom: this is reason at the service of an understanding offered by revelation and available through faith – indeed, otherwise unimaginable, yet one which human beings need to articulate by using all the resources available to us.

Kierkegaard's Way of Contextualizing Reason

If our earlier guides can be classed as "premodern," our final mentor managed to presage much that is "postmodern," as well as to share with Newman an admiration which Wittgenstein reserved for few thinkers, and these two alone among theological minds. Søren Kierkegaard exploited pseudonyms in order to be able to dramatize the diverse postures which religious persons can (and often should) assume toward the faith which continues to beckon them. For while a faith tradition can lay claim to our allegiance, we can only respond in kind by way of critical reflection, which must at once scrutinize what the tradition offers as well as let that tradition challenge currently touted norms of rationality. Kierkegaard displayed his appreciation of this call for "mutual clarification" by creating within himself and his readers enough space for reflection on the deliverances of faith and of reason, in order to show how each could indeed illuminate the other. The pseudonym most apt to display the inner reciprocal relation between faith and reason (or theology and philosophy) is that of Anti-Climacus in *Sickness unto Death*.[16] For it is conceived by way of contrast to that of Climacus in the more directly philosophical *Concluding Unscientific Postscript*, so that the work can be "edifying," and thereby stand on the very threshold of a properly religious work. Anti-Climacus anticipates the work of Pierre Hadot by reminding us that a philosophy which leads beyond itself will require of its adherents as well as its novices a set of practices designed to "build up" in them the appropriate responses to the calls they have heard, and so facilitate their hearing yet others, while the interaction between practices and reflection will help us discern the authenticity of the calls.

The rhetorical structure of the work is designed to dethrone the reigning conception of philosophy, that of Hegel's "system," and to do so by displaying an alternative which will alone be capable of leading one to what the Enlightenment sought: "the individual." He names the sickness which structures this inquiry "despair," and by "despair" he means the recurring and often acute sense of privation which we cannot help but feel in being unable to attain "that unique individual" which we are called to become. The human ideal opened up by the Reformation and endorsed in an autonomous fashion by the Enlightenment is in fact unattainable, yet we human beings regularly mask that fact from ourselves by countless distractions (as Pascal remarked), while philosophers do so in a more elaborate way by constructing "systems" in the image of Hegel. Yet the claim to an autonomous philosophy which would supersede the older medieval faith is issued in a mode of discourse so abstract that it bypasses the very goal of that endeavor: to make of oneself "an individual." The polemical portions of this work (not to be attributed, *tout court*, to Kierkegaard himself) will engage us with a prose redolent of "the system," thereby showing us how "tolerably well" he knows it, yet designed to display how wide of the mark it will carry us. The mark, again, is a conception of the human person able both to delineate our specificity as well as lead us to realize it individually. The conception to which we are introduced is that of *relating*, borrowed from the medieval articulation of spirit as what is able to "relate to all things" (itself cribbed from the opening lines of Aristotle's *Metaphysics*) and of the earlier Cappadocian attempt to articulate the triunity of God by identifying the "persons" of the divine trinity as "subsistent relations."

This conception, introduced by a definition which takes the form of a conceit but which formulates precisely the specificity of human beings by accentuating the gerundive form, "relating," is opposed to that of a *synthesis*, by which he can distinguish himself from a favorite ploy of Hegel's. Yet he also implicitly targets Aristotle's definition of human beings as "rational animals," thereby showing his own modernity while trenchantly criticizing its current icon. Indeed, this gesture reminds us of an aporia in Aristotle's work: if living things, indeed human beings especially, and notably Socrates, serve as paradigms for his decisive category of *substance*, he nonetheless fails to bring out how humans transcend that very category in the very act of defining it. This, of course, is what Hegel showed so well, and in that sense Kierkegaard is building on him while rejecting the omnivorous instincts of his philosophical legacy. So we are not "a relation" but "a relating," which accentuates how our very being is already an activity, and also how as a *relating* it is a "being towards." (Aquinas had noted how the very "to-be" [*esse*] of creatures is "to-be-related" [*ST* 1.45.3].) Yet the transcendence proper to rational creatures which allows them to fulfill their destiny (or reject it) is also present in this very "being-related" as an inner exigency. That is to say, Kierkegaard adopts a classical view of freedom as a "hunger for the good," steadfastly refusing the modern reduction of freedom to aimless choice, or the mere "ability to do otherwise," with its roots in Scotus. This sets the stage for his evocative use of "despair," which captures a range of attitudes linked to the experience of a *privation*, that is, something which ought to be present yet is not.

It is this "category" of *despair* which signals our awareness of being spirit, that is, of being-related in the very constitution of our being. Yet such an awareness must be "everywhere dialectical," as he puts it, executing what Hegel proposed as the heart of an authentically philosophical logic better than even Hegel knew how to do. That is, most of us find ourselves living lives of "quiet desperation" because we are indeed "in despair" but remain oblivious of the fact, save for a nagging sense of "not being there" or of "not being able to get through," which becomes his operative sense for *despair*. Get through to what? Kierkegaard's answer reveals how much his view of human being and of human freedom is rooted in Plato's inner quest for "the good," yet the path he takes reveals the power of this dialectical logic. It is in fact a dialectic of *consciousness*, of degrees of awareness of one's own state of inner alienation from one's proper good. The stages move from the common one of endemic lack of awareness to an acute awareness (which is close to our poignant use of "despair") and on to the demonic despair of refusing any remedy for our situation, which Anti-Climacus cannily likens to a manuscript error which takes on a life of its own to challenge the writer by insisting that it "will not be corrected." Short of demonic despair, there is but one way out of the acute awareness of having "missed the mark," and that lies in our being able to name the good from which we have alienated ourselves as the God who reveals a forgiving face in Jesus, thereby calling us to faith via repentance. This dynamic retains accents of his Lutheran formation and also displays the finest lineaments of Dante's sensibility, by showing just how redundant is forensic judgment when our own inner orientation suffices to foreshadow the way we must go. We are unable to overcome despair ourselves, yet it will evaporate once the relating finds itself "rooted in the power which constitutes it," a point where the definition of *self* transmutes into that of *faith*.

What Kierkegaard helps readers to do, in *Sickness unto Death*, is to appropriate Hegel's dialectic in a way that allows it both to reveal and to serve a profoundly human movement to faith in the "power which constitutes" us, namely, the creator who is also our redeemer. So Kierkegaard's own faith perspective directs him to a novel use of Hegel's acute philosophical tools, and one which displays Hegel's acuity far better than the "system" which had captured him for later generations, and threatened to undermine authentic Christian faith by making it subservient to a sovereign and omnivorous reason. In short, Kierkegaard succeeds in turning the tables on the pretenses of "philosophy" by utilizing those very philosophical skills to show how it can best fulfill its own aims by serving an innately human movement to faith. The operative premise, of course, is that we are in fact creatures of this God, which this work does not set out to prove since its peculiar pseudonym had identified the author as one on the way to faith. Indeed, Anti-Climacus is teetering on its very threshold, open to exploring how a key premise like the free creation of the universe might illuminate a philosophical, indeed a proto-psychological, picture of humanity. So if Kierkegaard's clearly pseudonymous works make him appear to be an "irrationalist" to philosophers, that should alert us to the polemical steps he felt it necessary to take in the face of a reason captured by "rationalism." This mediating work, however, utilizes the attentuated pseudonym of "Anti-Climacus" to show how reason and faith can collaborate in illuminating what it means to be human in a far more searching way than the current rationalist paradigm allowed. Once again, a properly rhetorical use of reason, employed to show how Christian faith can illuminate the darker reaches of the human spirit, offers a fresh paradigm for self-understanding.

Theology and Philosophy

The way in which the respective disciplines of philosophy and theology relate to each other is clearly a function of one's conception of reason and of faith. This selection of examples ranging over the Christian tradition has shown us how culture-bound such conceptions can be, and so should help us to correct the preconceptions we might bring to such a discussion. Moreover, having the perspective we do on modernist conceptions of the endemic opposition between the two should open us to appreciate those who saw them as more complementary than opposed. An historical-systematic approach to the tradition can help us to mine it for conceptions and distinctions which our age may have obscured. In this way we will not only be alerted to our own preconceptions, but can also work to correct them in the light of a richer range of mentors. That very exercise should allow us to appreciate traditions as vehicles for reflection rather than repositories of opinions, and so free us to pursue our own inquiry in a more self-critical and promising spirit.

Notes

1   For an astute presentation of Aquinas, see Mark Jordan's contribution to Kretzmann and Stump (1993:232–51), entitled: "Theology and Philosophy," as well as Jenkins (1997).

2   See his celebrated *Surnaturel*, translated as *The Mystery of the Supernatural* (De Lubac 1967).

3   For an illuminating historical account of Aquinas's debt to pseudo-Dionysius (and through him to neo-Platonism), see Booth (1985), and for a more systematic treatment, see Rudi te Velde (1995). For Aquinas's relation to Maimonides and others, see my "Aquinas and Islamic and Jewish Thinkers," in Kretzmann and Stump (1993:60–84).

4   For a detailed study of this correlation between "processions" and creation, see Emery (1995), or a fine review and summary of the argument by Houser (1996:493–7).

5   My *Knowing the Unknowable God* (Burrell 1986) details the way in which Aquinas assimilated the work of Avicenna and of Maimonides to forge his alternative account.

6   Lonergan's seminal work *Insight* has recently been republished as part of his collected works by the University of Toronto Press (1997).

7   Michael Buckley's *At the Origins of Modern Atheism* (1987) offers an illuminating contemporary complement to De Lubac's *Drama of Atheist Humanism* (1949).

8   Consult, preferably, Nicholas Lash's edition of Newman's *An Essay in Aid of a Grammar of Assent* (1979) for its illuminating introduction.

9   These views are elaborated successively in *Whose Justice? Which Rationality?* (MacIntyre 1988), and *Three Rival Versions of Moral Enquiry* (MacIntyre 1990).

10 A good beginning for Plantinga's work is his essay "Reason and Belief in God," in Plantinga and Wolsterstorff (1983).

11 Pierre Hadot's original work, *Exercises spirituels et philosophie antique*, 2nd edn. (1987) is now out of print, but an excellent summary of his thought is available in his *Qu'est-ce que la philosophie antique?* (1995) and a superb collection of his articles has been translated and presented by Davidson (1995).

12 It would be fascinating to ask whether "philosophy" so conceived would be vulnerable to the critique which Richard Rorty reserves for what he takes it to be, following the modern Cartesian paradigm.

13 For an enlightening view of Augustine reversing neoplatonic tendencies, see John Cavadini, "Time and Ascent in *Confessions* XI" (1993:171–85). For another essay on the intrinsically narrative character of his thought, see Wetzel (1992).

14 For an illuminating discussion of the linguistic-conceptual apparatus indispensable to articulating God as "distinct from" creation, yet in a way which forbids us to think of God as something else in the universe, see Tanner (1988); and for a lucid presentation of "the distinction" of creator from creation as decisive for Christian theology, see Sokolowski (1981).

15 For a discussion of Augustine's sources, see Henry Chadwick's translation (which I shall use throughout) of the *Confessions* (1991:xix).

16 An English translation by Howard and Edna Hong, with extensive critical apparatus, was published by Princeton University Press in 1980; a later translation by Alastair Hannay was published by Penguin in 1989.

References

Augustine, St. 1991. *Confessions*, trans. H. Chadwick. Oxford: Oxford University Press.

Booth, E. 1985. *Aristotelian Aporetic Ontology in Islamic and Christian Writers.* Cambridge: Cambridge University Press.

Buckley, M. 1987. *At the Origins of Modern Atheism*. New Haven, CT: Yale University Press.

Burrell, D. B. 1986. *Knowing the Unknowable God*. Notre Dame, IN: University of Notre Dame Press.

Burrell, D. B. 1993. "Aquinas and Islamic and Jewish Thinkers," in *Cambridge Companion to Aquinas*, eds. N. Kretzmann and E. Stump. New York: Cambridge University Press.

Cavadini, J. 1993. "Time and Ascent in *Confessions* XI," in *Collectanea Augustiniana 2: Presbyter Factus Sum*, eds. J. Lienhard, E. Muller, and R. Teske. New York: Peter Lang, pp. 171–85.

Davidson, A. 1995. *Philosophy as a Way of Life*. Oxford: Blackwell.

De Lubac, H. 1949. *Drama of Atheist Humanism*. London: Sheed and Ward.

De Lubac, H. 1967. *The Mystery of the Supernatural*. New York: Herder & Herder.

Emery, G. 1995. *La Trinité Créatrice*. Paris: Vrin.

Hadot, P. 1995. *Qu'est-ce que la philosophie?* Paris: Gallimard.

Houser, R. E. 1996. "Review of Gilles Emery's *La Trinité Créatrice*." *Thomist* 60:493–7.

Jenkins, J. 1997. *Knowledge and Faith in Thomas Aquinas*. New York: Cambridge University Press.

Jordan, M. 1993. "Theology and Philosophy," in *Cambridge Companion to Aquinas*, eds. N. Kretzmann and E. Stump. New York: Cambridge University Press, pp. 232–51.

Kretzmann, N. and Stump, E. eds. 1993. *Cambridge Companion to Aquinas*. New York: Cambridge University Press.

Lienhard, J., Muller, E., and Teske, R. eds. 1993. *Collectanea Augustiniana 2: Presbyter Factus Sum*. New York: Peter Lang.

Lonergan, B. 1997. *Insight*. Toronto: University of Toronto Press.

MacIntyre, A. 1988. *Whose Justice? Which Rationality?* Notre Dame, IN: University of Notre Dame Press.

MacIntyre, A. 1990. *Three Rival Versions of Moral Enquiry*. Notre Dame, IN: University of Notre Dame Press.

Newman, J. H. 1979. *An Essay in Aid of a Grammar of Assent*, ed. N. Lash. Notre Dame, IN: University of Notre Dame Press.

Plantinga, A. 1983. "Reason and Belief in God," in *Faith and Rationality*, eds. A. Plantinga and N. Wolsterstorff. Grand Rapids, MI: Eerdmans.

Plantinga, A. and Wolsterstorff, N. eds. 1983. *Faith and Rationality*. Grand Rapids, MI: Eerdmans.

Sokolowski, R. 1981. *God of Faith and Reason*. Notre Dame, IN: University of Notre Dame Press.

Tanner, K. 1988. *God and Creation in Christian Theology*. Oxford: Basil Blackwell.

te Velde, R. 1995. *Participation and Substantiality in Thomas Aquinas*. Leiden: Brill.

Wetzel, J. 1992. *Augustine and the Limits of Virtue*. Cambridge: Cambridge University Press.

CHAPTER 4

Culture

Charles T. Mathewes

The concept of culture is simultaneously perilous and promising for theological reflection, and for the same reasons. Until fairly recently, however, modern theologians understood "culture" unproblematically to signify the setting of theological inquiry, a setting which can itself be the subject of such theological inquiry. "Theology" and "culture" operated on different levels, and theologians interpreted cultural phenomena; Paul Tillich, for example, famously analyzed post-impressionist paintings as expressing broader cultural disaffections with inherited understandings and representations of nature, disaffections which he connected with a nascent recognition that technology has helped us forget the primordial "conditionedness" of all existence.

Recent work on "culture" has made things more murky, because it has shown how almost all human activity can be understood as "cultured" in a way that highlights the contingency and fragility of the particular formations of human social existence within which we live, move, and have our being. This new understanding should trouble theology. Of course, there are many bad reasons why academic theologians might resist understanding their work as "cultural" – fears of losing authority, and the concomitant expansion of who can challenge theologians (and how they can be challenged) – but there are also *prima facie* good reasons for suspicion – in particular, concerns about whether convictions that seem fundamental to theology (apparently trans-cultural convictions about God and Christ, for example) can survive encounter with the concept of "culture." The encounter between theology and recent understandings of culture is thus more complex than a simple affirmation or negation; it involves mutual critique.

The intellectual projects gathered under the description "theology and culture" have ancestors in older theological conundrums, but the term "culture" appears only in modernity. Only recently have theologians begun to appreciate the term's complexity and historical contingency. This chapter seeks to aid this appreciation. After recounting in the first section the concept of culture's historical development and detailing its present complexity, it argues in the second section that, while modern theology has long struggled with the concept of "culture," several recent theologians offer useful guidance in its theological application. We will find that culture is more theologically central, both as peril and as promise, than one might have thought.

The Concept of Culture

"Culture" is not a natural kind, like silver or dandelions or trout; nor is it an intentionally fabricated artifact, like Walkmans™ (which require trademarks) or Napalm, or the Chicago Bulls. Like "religion," it lies somewhere in between these two – more malleable (because dependent on human use) than the first, but less consequent upon explicit human decision than the second. The concept of culture is itself a cultural artifact, which came into being only in the eighteenth century. Before then, entirely different conceptual schemes informed what now gets collected under the concept of "culture." We can narrate the development of "culture," thereby highlighting some of its latent tensions and complexities. This is meant not as an adequate historical narrative, but rather as a useful heuristic device; it transforms culture from something obvious into something "denaturalized and suspended before our eyes as an object of scrutiny" (Masuzawa 1998:91). This history is thus primarily a way to see "culture's " complexity.[1]

History of the concept of culture

The concept of culture emerges from many sources, three of which are particularly important. First, eighteenth-century debates in France and England, concerning the character of human development and the purpose of education, resulted in the idea of the "cultured person." These debates were sparked by anxieties about identity, particularly in the face of threats from populations mobilized by industrialization – both directly revolutionary threats posed by the new working class, and the indirect but no less impressive threat of the newly empowered and enriched middle class, who imperiled the aristocracy's control over society (and who indeed fulfilled that threat in the twentieth century). New means of discrimination were required, on both a class and an individual level, and what we can call the "classist" concept of culture arose to meet this need. (Later thinkers such as Matthew Arnold and T. S. Eliot build on this concept.) "Culture" came into initial use as a marker of refinement and, of necessity, social class; the "cultured person" was the civilized and sophisticated person. Significantly, because of the very conditions that caused its birth, the modern concept of culture is profoundly secular, and indeed possesses an anti-theological orientation: as Raymond Williams has pointed out, " 'Culture' was then at once the secularization and the liberalization of earlier metaphysical forms" (Williams 1977:15). The concept of "culture" thus offers an (at least initially) non-theological locus of value and significance for human beings.

Later thinkers, particularly the German Romantics, gave culture an explicitly political valence when they conceptualized linguistically distinct societies as distinct national "cultures," using the term to mark national identity. This development had benefits, particularly the pressure it immediately put on the "classicist" notions with which the concept was initially burdened, eventually expanding the concept of culture to include "folk" cultures. But it also created problems, especially its implicit assumption that cultures are essentially primordial and homogeneous wholes – entailing an "esthetic holism" in regard to cultures, and ascribing to them a monolithic identity-conferring power over their participants (Tanner 1997:10). This understandable attention to cultural homogeneity arose from attempts to conceptualize Romantics' nostalgia for what they thought was being lost. The awareness of massive social transformations, and the increasing realization of human historicity, made thinkers sensitive to the separateness of social structures (as if we had inhabited an ice-floe we thought was solid earth, but which one day separated itself from the continent and began to drift into the sea). This transformation focused attention on questions of cultural integrity, and on the "authentic" and the "genuine" in contrast to the "artificial" and "merely conventional." Intellectuals imagined culture as the organic expression of a people's racial character, the "outward" correlate of their inner essence, thereby legitimating general disquiet about the replacement of this cultural inheritance with the fabricated products of mass-production industry.

The concept of culture not only developed from reflection at home; it also developed from ethnographic reflections, in particular reflections about how to understand human differences along lines that are neither developmentally triumphalist nor essentially racial or climatological. This source drew on Romanticism's aggressive defense of the old folkways in the face of an increasingly pervasive industrialization, and its perceived corrosive effects on tradition. But it went beyond earlier formulations' emphases on culture as value-constituting, person-determining, and authentic, to include recognition of the *contingency* of human structures. "Contingency" here does not mean *arbitrariness*, or a straightforward social contractualism or voluntarism, where everything is (or ought to be) the object of explicit (even potentially explicit) assent; it means rather to highlight the fact that cultures (and thus people) are decisively different, which is due not to essential divergences in "race" or nature, but to thoroughly accidental differences of climate, geography, history, and above all the influence (or inheritance) of the innumerable choices and decisions humans have made over millennia about all the questions of how to live life, the minutiae as well as the momentous (insofar as we can specify such decisions as one or the other).

If recognition of culture's inclusion of all sorts of (indeed, all) human interactions, was the result of historical imagination, the recognition of the contingency of culture awaited the encounter of European intellectuals with radically different cultures. In a way, paradoxically, we can say that the appreciation of culture's breadth was a consequence of reflection on the historical depth of specific cultures "native" to Europe, while the appreciation of culture's depth – or rather, its "shallowness" – arose from reflection on the global breadth of human cultures. "Cultural evolutionists" such as E. B. Tylor understood human diversity to represent different stages of development, undermining thereby the Romantics' insistence on cultural homogeneity; furthermore, they assumed "implicit forms of contexualism and functionalism" which "suggest a non-evaluative relativism" (Tanner 1997:19). Anthropologists brought all of these elements into a practically (if provisionally) applicable concept, affirming that "the human intellect is conditioned from the very start, not by some ahistorical Kantian set of categories or structural principles, but by the concepts, values, and worldview of the particular culture in which human beings begin to think" (1997:24). This account culminates in the work of Clifford Geertz, which depicts culture as the self-spun "webs of significance" that humans inhabit (Geertz 1973:5). (However, Geertz's work in some ways strains against this vision as well.)

Our concept of culture possesses the inheritance of these very diverse sources. But recent cultural theory has added more complexity to this mix by charting how the concept of culture "deconstructs" itself – how it conceals some very powerful dynamic tensions. For our purposes the most important of these tensions are those between the concept's implication of universality and locality, value and relativism, and determinism and contingency. This semantic over-determination of the concept of culture provides it with an enormous, indeed perilous, flexibility. Its complexity compels any application of the concept to emphasize some of its aspects and implicitly de-emphasize others. Even so, these dynamics interrelate to give "culture" the semantic and epistemological vitality, and volatility, that it, for good and ill, possesses.

Elements of the concept of culture

Universality and locality   The tension between "culture" as the universal value-creator for human beings, and also varying over time and space in significant ways, makes the concept crucial for discussions of relativism. This manifests itself in an oscillation between the "universality" and the "locality" of cultures. Culture is "a human universal," but in a complex way. First of all, it is "universal" across all human beings, but it is so only by being manifest in manifold diverse forms. Secondly, it is not just universal in the sense of something all humans share, but also by being *pervasive*; culture saturates all aspects of our lives, and there is no part of us quarantined from its influence. The phrase "cultural contingencies" reveals the third way in which culture's universality is complex: while formally culture is necessary for human development, the actual forms "culture" takes are due to innumerable minute and apparently wholly contingent and accidental decisions made by many people.

Until quite recently, twentieth-century anthropology emphasized the relativity of cultures rather than the universality of culture; anthropologists have focused more on the material differences among cultures than on the formal commonality among all of them as "cultures."[2] This has had a salutary effect on the ethnocentrism that seems so powerful a temptation for the human mind ("Western" and otherwise). But this project of noting "local knowledge" is not wholly innocent of an intellectual prehistory that orients it in important ways. It should be understood against the backdrop of a larger framework of disaffection present in modern Western intellectual discourse, disaffection regarding precisely that "modern Western intellectual discourse." More specifically, the anthropological ethnography that has dominated twentieth-century anthropology has been largely in the service of reinforcing those anxieties, deriving from the Romantics, about the (corrosive) effects of modernization and the loss of tradition on "organic" cultures, and anxieties about the effects of global capitalism on human flourishing.

This intellectual agenda has caused anthropology, consciously or not, to valorize those cultural structures present at – or better, present the instant before – the moment in which contact was made with them by Westerners (hopefully Western anthropologists, who would, if well trained, at least attempt not to contaminate the natives). This not only leads to anthropologists possessing a curiously romantic, not to say nostalgic, attitude to local cultures, as well as setting themselves the impossible task of trying to observe what by definition they cannot observe without altering it by being present to observe it (in a way interestingly similar to quantum physics' "Uncertainty Principle"); it also presumes a curiously quasi-aesthetic approach to cultures, in which it is possible to ask about the "authenticity" and/or "inauthenticity" of certain cultural developments. This "authenticity" paradigm is reinforced by tendencies (especially in cultural linguistics) to classify (and implicitly valorize) the diverse human cultures in ways significantly similar to the phylogeny of natural kinds such as apes, ants, and lichens. Ironically, attention to the relativity and locality of distinct cultures often supports the very instrumentalization of those "local cultures" – their utilization as pawns in games played by Western intellectuals regarding the reality of relativism and the meaning of modernity, games in which non-Western "others" are used, like clubs, to batter the heads of one's intellectual opponents.[3]

The anthropological consensus on both "culture" and "modernity," which underlies this "authenticity" paradigm , has come under severe criticism in the last several decades. Specifically, criticisms have been leveled against what now appear to be the consensus's untenably rigorous demands for cultural homogeneity, even purity: Why, critics ask, cannot cultures change dramatically and still remain themselves? Why must they remain static, "prehistorical," to be genuine (see Fabian 1983)? Indeed, "the demand for cultural consistency," on which much earlier modernist cultural thought was predicated, with its interest in the "authentic" and genuine as the true representatives of culture, "seems almost an esthetic demand" (Tanner 1997:44). When we turn the concept of culture reflexively upon ourselves and our history, the whole paradigm of cultural authenticity seems more tied up with contingent capitalist demands for precious and scarce goods ("marvelous possessions") than it is with any actual theoretical necessity. Indeed, the notion of authenticity seems spurious as soon as one reflects on the West's own history of perpetual self-(re-)fashioning; as Marshall Sahlins suggests, "the West owes its own sense of cultural superiority to an invention of the past so flagrant it should make European natives blush to call other peoples culturally counterfeit" (Sahlins 1993:7).

This critique has attacked not only the presumed understanding of "culture," but also the connected understanding of "modernity," specifically the presumption that modernity is (unlike all other humanly fabricated realities) an essentially seamless, monolithic reality, to which all cultures must conform, and so lose their distinct localness in favor of a more Western localness (or for some earlier visions, the total *un*-localness) of modernity. In fact, recent thinkers reflecting on the effects of globalization on "modernization" have argued that no monolithic modernization account is adequate for our understanding of *any* culture, including Western ones (cf. Appadurai 1996). As Bernard Yack has argued, the very idea of "modernity" seems fetishistic, a crystalization of otherwise amorphous and free-floating discontents; the question of authenticity arises in reaction to it via the "residual" categories of "local" or "organic" cultures which are opposed to this "modern" specter in our thought (Yack 1997:50).

These criticisms of "culture" and "modernity" have compelled dramatic changes in what cultural inquiry is understood to be. Again, as Sahlins puts it, "the days are over for an ethnography that was the archaeology of the living, searching under the disturbed topsoil of modernity for the traces of a pristine and 'primitive' existence" (Sahlins 1993:25). Furthermore, they have reopened the Pandora's box of conceptual tensions latent in the concept of culture (or rather, they have allowed us openly to acknowledge that the tensions have been there throughout this century's struggles with the concept of culture). Specifically they have highlighted two other tensions that cultural theorists are increasingly stressing (as opposed to the "universal/local" tension) – namely, the tension between contingency and determination, and that between conflict and consensus. We must next unpack these tensions.

Contingency and determination   Once we accept that cultures can change before our eyes, and still remain identifiably themselves, we can understand the complex co-presence in cultures of contingency and determination. Cultures' "contingency" means that they did not have to develop this way, that a present cultural configuration results from millions of minuscule decisions by agents who only rarely knew what they were doing. This contingency can be both exhilarating and dizzying, or vertigo-inducing; as Stanley Cavell has written, it forbids us any extra-accidental skeleton of reasons which fix it firmly to the earth:

> That on the whole we do [share a cultural consensus] is a matter of our sharing routes of interest and feeling, modes of response, sense of humor and of significance and of fulfillment, of what is outrageous, of what is similar to what else, what a rebuke, what forgiveness, of when an utterance is an assertion, when an appeal, when an explanation – all the whirl of organism Wittgenstein calls "forms of life." Human speech and activity, sanity and community, rest upon nothing more, but nothing less, than this. It is a vision as simple as it is difficult, and as difficult as it is (and because it is) terrifying.   (Cavell 1969:52)

If it is simply "accidents all the way down," one may feel simultaneously the excitement of having things be "up to us," and yet the terror of knowing that *we* are not "up to us." It is the contingency of cultures, and the perennially lurking relativism of this claim, that has occupied the attention of most recent thought on culture. Such scholars attend to this contingency as a crucial (though admittedly in some ways profoundly unsatisfactory) explanatory principle, making it their task to understand "how things got this way" by charting the manifold accidents that led to the status quo (insofar as it is very *status* at all). This has led to an altogether commendable attention to change and the "historicity" of cultures, a renewed emphasis on the fact that they are always *in via*, never complete and thus always (in some significant sense) up for grabs.

Alongside this emphasis on the contingency of cultures, however, is a recognition of the degree to which we are determined by our cultural conditions. This can lead to a feeling of anomie, a despairing paralysis and relativism, and a sense that one is trapped in the culture without escape (and can lead to quasi-gnostic attempts to escape this condition by knowledge, such as that proposed by Richard Rorty). (Indeed, as Mark Edmundson has recently suggested, much recent cultural theory, while emphasizing the contingency of cultural formations, has at a much deeper level succumbed to a despair about the possibilities of genuine transformation, and accepts a curiously dualistic, "gothic" conception of power which forbids any hope [Edmundson 1997]. On this view, cultural contingency is merely the surface manifestation of a deeper determinism in human existence.)

Conflict and consensus   Culture's simultaneous contingency and yet determination reflect the recent appreciation of cultures' dynamic character, the fact that both conflict and consensus are equally essential to a culture's survival. While earlier theories pictured culture as a homogeneous and stable framework – which functions to absorb change without disturbing the fundamental structures of society – more recent theorists have argued that conflict is central to cultural existence as a means of sustaining the necessary full complexity of cultural systems.[4] As Stephen Greenwalt argues, culture is now understood to be fluid, a "structure of improvisation" that is not found in any static constellation of values but rather in the constant flux of a "general symbolic economy" which is marked by the "*exchange* of material goods, ideas, and – through institutions like enslavement, adoption, or marriage – people" (Greenwalt 1990:229–30). Culture is not an altogether settled and unquestioned deposit, that which "goes without saying" in a society; rather, it is equally in what gets said, and in the form in which those debates happen. Culture is as much the debates that tie the centripedal forces of culture together as it is the different forces themselves.[5]

Still, even as "cultural identity becomes . . . a hybrid, relational affair, something that lives between as much as within cultures," there is the possibility for talking of culture as an organized whole – "Whether or not culture is a common focus of *agreement*, culture binds people together as a common focus for *engagement*" (Tanner 1997:57–8). The very fact of conflict becomes a sign of, and a further reinforcement of, an underlying consensus about what is worth arguing over, and how such an argument can proceed. This does not mean, of course, that all arguments are irresolvable, static oppositions with pre-set constraints, intellectual variants of trench warfare; but arguments must happen on a common ground, however vaguely defined such a common ground is. Nor must this consensus be total or absolute; there is no fixity in stability, but some things must be stable for others to be debatable. Understood thusly, "culture" is not so much a collection of things or a systemic structure as *a process* – a disputatious, ongoing, and always complex (and even contradictory) process of self- and societal definition and control. The importance of debate and conflict in culture entails that *power* is an inescapable factor in culture, and that "culture" and "politics" are not unrelated terms. (We will return, briefly, to theorists' anxieties about "power" later.)[6]

The recognition of the integral role conflict plays within consensus (and vice versa) – what we may call the "culturedness" of conflict – expands the scope of what may, and indeed *must*, be plausibly studied as "cultural" in interesting ways. Since conflict is part of the cultural consensus, and indeed embodies that consensus, it is possible to see those resistances to some cultural structure or system as themselves plausibly cultural as well, and indeed this makes understanding the whole scope of a culture, including all of its opponents, a prerequisite for understanding any part of it. This recognition warrants inquiry into "low" culture as much as "high" culture, not to mention "material," "mass," "pop" and "popular" culture, and projects focused on these sorts of culture are increasingly taken with theoretical seriousness (see McDannell 1995).

In sum, "culture" is an exceedingly intricate concept, helpful for studying a bewildering diversity of human phenomena. By managing to encompass all these diverse elements, "culture" serves as the human science's Swiss Army knife. But recent cultural theory has recognized the ambiguities latent in "culture's" very conceptual flexibility. These theorists insist that cultures are not "closed systems," and argue that the idea of "*a* culture" is only heuristically useful, for actual cultures are complexly interrelated, intermeshed, incomplete, conflictual and fluid things (Tanner 1997:53–6). The basic problem is not that *cultures* are messy or unruly; rather the problem lies in the *concept* of culture itself, for its very flexibility ensures its pervasiveness in human existence. In its extreme moments, culture seems to claim that nothing is untouched by "culture," and so nothing is not "cultural," not the product of human relations. Culture is hence especially vexing for theologians, who want to insist on the openness of human experience to what lies beyond human fabrication (see Milbank 1997:2).

The Theology of Culture

Theologians have employed the concept of culture from its beginnings; indeed its development was partially shaped by theological interests. Typically they understand "culture" to mean "world," or possibly the meaning-structures of the world, and assume that it unproblematically illuminates the sphere of human existence, and they attempt to relate theological concerns – which *prima facie* are not simply human – to our existence in culture. But the concept's full complexity and ambiguity has, until recently, been only partially apprehended by theologians, and so has caused innumerable problems. There are more things in "culture" than are dreamt of in most theologies.

From Schleiermacher to Barth

The history of the engagement between theological inquiry and the concept of "culture" should begin with Schleiermacher's attempt, at the end of the eighteenth century, to engage those he called the "cultured despisers of religion" in an argument about the cultural necessity of religion. His understanding of culture was crucially Romantic: cultures are homogeneous and hegemonic – or at least can be heuristically so understood. Fully "cultured" individuals participate in the paradigmatically religious experience of unity with the cosmos which – though it is the essential experience from which all "positive" religions take their start – is manifest in radically particular explicit forms, as determined by individuals' cultural and historical setting. While Schleiermacher employed different strategies for his apologetic (in his *Speeches on Religion*, 1799) and dogmatic (in his *Glaubenslehre*, 1821–2) theological projects, his account of theology's relation to its cultural setting remained fundamentally stable. In general, the theologian details a perspicuous presentation of a culture's expressions of its religious faith, in order to show their interrelations, thereby deepening the community's expressed piety.[7]

Today Schleiermacher is criticized most often for not being cultural enough, particularly in his overly de-historicized transcendental account of religious experience (see Proudfoot 1985); ironically, however, such criticisms speak to how much his approach to theology convinced theologians to begin from local experiences of faith. But in fact his thought is if anything *too* cultural, too fixed on the determining power of cultures over individuals, to permit much genuine theological creativity to function. Theology does not offer culture an external critique, but rather an internal organization (which may entail some accidental critique); it cannot speak prophetically to some cultural configuration, or highlight its radical contingency.[8]

As the nineteenth century wore on and Romantic disaffection with industrializing societies became accommodated in the structures of feeling and intellect (simultaneously institutionalized in certain structures of resistance to it, such as universities, and also nostalgized as charming stodgy technophobia), the critical leverage of Schleiermacher's apologetics was lost, and his dogmatic analysis of religion within determinate cultural forms increasingly anchored all theology. This was reinforced by the increasing sophistication of historiography: the German "history of religions" school increasingly confirmed the deep connections between an era's intellectual achievements and its cultural and historical conditions, and its lessons were appropriated in constructive theological work, so that later nineteenth-century theology, culminating in Ernst Troeltsch, emphasized culture's determination of theology (see Troeltsch [1923], 1979). (Troeltsch's work so emphasized this determination that it attracted the epithet *Kulturprotestantismus*, "culture Protestantism.") The disastrous end of this mode came in the German intellectuals' infamous declaration (in August 1914) of their support for the German Reich in World War I, along with its ugly echo in the "German Christians" of the Nazi era.[9]

It was Troeltsch's sense of culture's determinative power over theology that the so-called "Dialectical" theologians rejected by claiming that theology possesses a source transcending all cultural structures, either via the transcendental/existential conditions of human subjectivity (as in Bultmann) or, more famously, via the absolutely other and transcendent Word of God (as in Barth). Such theologians acknowledged the cultural determination of "religion" as a human construct (thus Barth's famous delight in Feuerbach, and his treatment of him as the greatest "liberal" theologian); but they thought theology was not about a culture's religion, but rather about the Word of God, which negated the cultural codes of the day, and created the grounds for its own reception. For the "Dialectical" theologians, at least in their extreme formulations, holding a theological discussion of culture is not something theologians can do; it is only something they can *report*, as having already been done, and announced, by the Living God. Theology always works against the cultural status quo of the time.

While the "Dialectical" theologians' approach to the question of theology and culture was a profound and well-warranted corrective to the earlier and more sanguine

Kulturprotestantismus, it was limited largely to negations of the cultural and theological givens of the time. Once this negation had had its desired effect, there was little that the "Dialectical" theologians, *qua* theologians, could say. Not only could they not offer more positive guidance – that was, after all, to be found in the Word of God – but also, because they eschewed altogether the positive voice, they could not even detail how the Word of God works in order to help us inhabit our cultural situation. The "radically other" God was so other that it seemed hard to see God's positive relevance to our lives. If Barth was right in saying, against Schleiermacher, that one cannot say "God" just by shouting "man," it could equally be said against the early Barth that one cannot say "God" just by shouting "no."[10]

From Tillich to today

Paul Tillich realized this limitation of "Dialectical" theology, and from his disaffection he developed a position that attempted to incorporate these theologians' critiques of the cultural situation alongside (or within) an affirmation of cultural energies as attempting to express the "depth dimension" present in all human experience. The point of Tillich's project, the first to be generally known as "theology of culture," was fundamentally diagnostic: it sought to help culture understand and respond to its real longings. Building upon a cultural ontology which proposed that religion is the "substance" of culture, culture the "form" of religion, Tillich developed a quite complex picture of humans as culturally determined, yet equally culturally creative – though that creativity emerges from their encounters with the "depth dimension" of their lives. Furthermore, his "method of correlation" sought to identify and articulate the latent hopes, anxieties and understandings of a "culture" which may be most usefully engaged by theological inquiry, in order to reveal the religious condition of that culture. The Tillichian theologian of culture has both diagnostic and prescriptive tasks: she must first uncover the complex theonomous energies of the culture, and then explain how the culture might better (more directly, more authentically) draw upon those energies. Thus the project, while it had a means of recognizing the idolatrous and even demonic in cultural formations (remember that the young Tillich was a "religious socialist," just as Barth was interested in socialism before World War I), was most fundamentally *therapeutic*, interested in recognizing affiliations between Christian faith and the "secular culture" of modernity, even as those affiliations were distortions and/or outright perversions of the Gospel message.

Tillich's work has been quite influential in both Protestant and Catholic circles.[11] When coupled with a Geertzian understanding of culture as a meaning-system, it offers a powerful tool for a theological reading of culture. His insistence that there is always a theonomous depth dimension to any culture, even if the culture seeks to suppress it, provides a powerful rhetorical device for cultural critique. But Tillich's thought is vexed by several problems of its own, which we can call the problems of elitism, intellectualism, and collaborationism. The elitism and intellectualism are interconnected; he conceives of culture largely along the lines of "high culture," ignoring what scholars today call popular culture, and this exclusive focus on high-cultural artifacts makes him see culture as quintessentially expressed in sophisticated intellectual activity, and largely ignore its relationship to material economic conditions. Still, these criticisms are contingent to Tillich's explicit formulations, not inherent in the deep structure of the program itself (see Cobb 1995). More essential are the attitudes that lead critics to accuse the program of collaborationism. Many criticize its tendency to make Christian language serve cultural self-interpretation; they argue that Tillich reinterprets the basic symbols of Christian faith so that they lose their doctrinal detail and dilute the language's specificity. (Thus Tillich never developed a doctrine of God, particularly in regard to Trinity and Pneumatology.) "Tillichians" might reply that this descent into vagueness is not a one-way street, but is rather the first consequence of the initial "defrosting," so to speak, of the deep existential meaning of theological concepts, a meaning locked inside the doctrinal formulae by centuries of dogmatic deep freezing; once the symbols' energies are liberated, they will become dynamic once again.

But this response does not meet the second form of the collaborationist critique, which argues that the deepest problem with Tillich's account is not so much with its theology as with its understanding of culture, and the profundity of the critique that a Tillichian program can launch against its cultural setting. Like the theology of Schleiermacher, Tillich's "theology of culture" understands itself as inescapably lodged within its cultural setting, and so must be ultimately interested in cultural therapy; he does not want to critique culture, but to make it more authentically itself. Thus this position still relies on the idea of an integrated complete culture, and on the idea of critique as internal critique. But recent cultural theory suggests that, if there are no autonomous cultures, then more is available than this – in particular, there is no need to conceive of culture as a monolithic, entirely determining power; the fractiousness and complexity of culture make available to us significant resources for critique not available when we think of culture as a homogeneous, hegemonic, autonomous whole.

H. Richard Niebuhr offers an alternative form of theological–cultural analysis, most explicitly in his (in)famous typology (in *Christ and Culture*) of "Christ against Culture," "Christ of Culture," "Christ above Culture," "Christ and Culture in paradox," and "Christ transforming Culture." Niebuhr's proposal is often misunderstood as essentially descriptive, though it most basically serves a normative project. *Christ and Culture* revises Troeltsch's program in a Barthian direction, both by emphasizing its essentially normative purpose (thereby resisting Troetsch's scientism), and by transcending Troeltsch's vague normative proposal, especially his dissatisfyingly amorphous account of the "religious *a priori*." The ruckus surrounding this typology has obscured its purpose, for while Niebuhr seeks to acknowledge the value of other standpoints, his position, confessionally within the last "Christ the transformer of culture" type, unapologetically (though charitably) interprets the other types from this perspective. Thus, Niebuhr's own proposal is better appreciated through his concepts of "radical monotheism" and "responsibility," which ground his understanding of the connection between theology and culture; "Radical monotheists" accept the relativity of all cultural situations by understanding their lives as responses to the absolutely sovereign God. Niebuhr's ethico-cultural proposal is famously underdeveloped, and intentionally so; in this amorphousness he followed Barth in resisting our pre-judgments of the Word of God in particular settings, thereby vexing our expectation of (and hope for) some algorithm whereby we can merely input our situation and receive in return (as output) the right thing to do. If, as Niebuhr believes (with Barth), God calls us to freedom, the theologian must refuse our longing to remain enslaved.

Niebuhr thinks we need neither a radically external critique, such as Barth proposes, nor a sheerly internal one, such as Tillich supposes; there is ground for a middle way, as his account of "relativity" attempts to suggest. But his thought was hindered from further specificity, not only intentionally, but also by his understanding of culture; what restrained him from further specificity was his inability to understand culture as other than a monolithic, unitary, enframing power. H. Richard Niebuhr intuited that this was a problem, but he could not conceive of how to resolve it.

This vagueness has been the target of severe criticisms by recent thinkers. Foremost here is John Howard Yoder, who critiques the theological attitude toward culture articulated by Tillich, and suggested by Niebuhr.[12] For him that attitude gains tactical advantages for Christian faith, but at the cost of strategic catastrophe: namely, the co-optation of theological language into the cultural status quo. Yoder therefore rejects the sympathetic interpretive orientations of Tillich and Niebuhr toward the "larger" secular culture, arguing instead for the priority of the Church, which only indirectly speaks to the culture. Like Barth, he insists that the theologian's engagement with culture should not come at the cost of domesticating the theological message. This position is clearly not "correlationist," in Tillich's sense (though its appeals to the Gospel's strangeness resonate with the strangeness humans feel at the factitious world as a whole), nor is it Niebuhr's "Christ transforming Culture" stance (or if it is, the meaning of "transformation" is significantly different). Indeed, for Yoder, both Niebuhr and Tillich err by being too intertwined with culture, and hence betray the distinctiveness of the Christian Gospel. In part this is due to their understanding of "culture"; Yoder thinks Niebuhr pictures culture as an autonomous monolith, legitimating a laxism and a "low estimate of the power of evil" (Stassen, Yeager, and Yoder 1996:89) therein; even worse, Niebuhr's theological vision was too vague to offer any critical leverage, because "[t]he name 'God' has become a cipher for Niebuhr's rejecting any *concrete* value claims superior to our selves" (1996:284 n. 140). As an alternative to these views, Yoder offers a theology that is ecclesially and biblically anchored in the very particular, concrete, incarnated vision of Jesus and the Church that is expressed in the biblical narratives.

The disaffections expressed by Yoder are given a more positive formulation by George Lindbeck in his *The Nature of Doctrine*. For Lindbeck, religions are kinds of cultures, and they provide a "medium that shapes the entirety of life and thought. . . . Like a culture or language, it is a communal phenomenon that shapes the subjectivities of individuals rather than being primarily a manifestation of those subjectivities" (Lindbeck 1984:33). Lindbeck makes a special effort to avoid the original interiority (and necessary individualism) of earlier accounts, arguing instead that "[a] religion is above all an external word . . . that molds and shapes the self and its world, rather than an expression or thematization of a preexisting self" (1984:34). Theology, in this vision, provides a conceptual articulation of this language, its "grammar." (This is not a simply descriptive enterprise, but can actually be creative, as the scope of "intratextuality" continually changes to include new concerns and surrender merely antiquarian interests;

1984:115.) Theology, then, is a sort of autobiographical ethnography, a vision of how a particular "culture" – namely, the Christian one – understands itself and its world.

All these accounts offer valuable lessons and potential pitfalls. Tillichian and Niebuhrian approaches permit (indeed, require) a theological openness to what appear to be non-Christian cultural phenomena; but they are vulnerable to accusations that they lack any determinate content of genuine "Christianness," because they do not offer much in the way of general guidelines about how to protect the Christian message from perversion by collaboration with non-Christian interests. Yoder is acutely aware of this, but his zeal to avoid it drives him toward the opposite peril: by organizing his account around concerns about purity, he causes the term "Christian" to take on a fundamentally oppositional role to some other vision. It gets defined not by being one thing, but rather by *not* being another. The danger here is not that Christians might derive cultural identity from theological premises; the danger is that the identity Christians accept would be determined by the context in which they operate. Christians, that is, would be seeing their faith through others' eyes, and not their own.

The basic problem with all of these attempts to relate theology and culture lies in the concept of culture that they all employ, a concept that assumes a fundamental integrity to culture. Yoder identifies this in Niebuhr (and a similar flaw is visible in Tillich); but the problem equally troubles Yoder's position, for he assumes, not that the secular culture is homogeneous (it is legion), but that the idea of *the* Christian culture is plausible. But, as we saw in this chapter's first section, the concept of culture, properly employed, dismisses the criterion of "authenticity" in cultural development, and therefore resists the idea of wholly distinct ontological realities called "cultures" – the very idea all of these theologians rely on, whether in interpreting the context to which the Christian message speaks (as in Niebuhr and Tillich), or in interpreting the community within which that message gains its determinate sense (as in Yoder and Lindbeck). The next section suggests that two recent proposals help us transcend these difficulties.

The current situation

As the first section argued, the concept of "culture" is an artifact – inescapable, pervasive, and, like all human artifacts, ambiguous; it obscures certain insights at the same time that it highlights others. In particular, the entire intellectual bestiary within which "culture" has its place stands in a curious relationship to theological discourse, because it exists partially as a quasi-theological term, disputing earlier, more theologically accommodating vocabularies. Pre-modern theologies offer no correlate for "culture"; they did not use an equivalent concept to understand their world. Indeed the concept replaces earlier terms with both negative and positive theological valuations – negative ones, because "culture" suggests the "human" world, which is often for theologians conceived of as a profane anti-Christian Babylon; positive ones, because it identifies genuine "cultured" values (of maturity, sophistication, and authenticity, among others) as well as an inescapable framework of all human existence. To affirm "culture" risks affirming the authentic value of a construction that seems purely (and therefore perversely) human; but to condemn "culture" risks not only demonizing some human groups, but also implicitly sanctifying ourselves.[13] So the term's conceptual complexity troubles any straightforward use.

Furthermore, the concept of culture tends to dominate other concepts, and to act as the master concept in whose terms all others must be understood. When we recall that "culture" partly replaces earlier theological frameworks, the concept's tendencies toward omnipresence and omnipotence – and cultural theorists' pretentions to omniscience – may not seem so strange. The problem is that "culture" often operates with an under-scrutinized concept of power: all is cultural, and so all seems to be more of the same. As Emerson said, "use what language we will, we can never say anything but what we are."[14] Thus the concept of culture can be simultaneously enabling and paralyzing: while it "de-naturalizes" human realities – revealing their bare contingency – it can tend equally to deflate our will to alter cultural configurations, by insisting that our response to those realities is just as "contaminated" by culture – and, presumably, by injustice – as those initial realities.

This worry drives recent "postmodern" cultural theory, particularly in its fundamentally iconoclastic (what it calls "ironic") disposition, and its ideal of total "critique" (see Yack 1986). But "critique" here merely replaces "culture" with itself as the master concept. Hence academic cultural analysis remains tragically partial, trapped in bare reiterations of sterile critiques, without allowing any more positive proposal about how we ought to respond to our implication in the cultural structures of our day. While some think the problem lies in the refusal of academics to affirm any real good, in fact the problem is those critics' blanket affirmation of one unquestioned good – namely, the good of critique. The critique of culture is finally inert, because it attaches no purpose to critique outside of critique itself. Hence, the exchange of the concept of "culture" with the wholly negative concept of "critique" is no real advance.

Is there a way to use the concept without allowing it hegemony? This question can be asked in a more theologically illuminating way: Can we use the concept of culture without treating it as a stand-in for a necessary, hence divinized (or, as for many cultural theorists, demonic) status quo? This essay does not mean to give comfort to those promoting further cultural "secularization." Quite the contrary; as theologians have long known, iconoclasm can be idolatrous (see Schweiker 1990). Here theologians offer more than diagnosis, and can use the concept of culture in a way unavailable to those ignorant of the history of Christian thought – by admitting our drive to integrity and unity, while simultaneously refusing to affix that drive to the concept of "culture." While recent cultural theory offers little help in this task, certain theological resources can, by emphasizing the relativity of all things "beneath" (or "within") the sovereignty of God. Of course, modern theologians blundered into problems by ignoring the "cultured-ness" of "culture" – by taking its conceptualizations as common knowledge – and hence accepting its imposition of a false choice of "otherworldliness" or "collaborationism" in relating the Christian message to cultural realities. But recent conceptualizations of theology and culture, most especially those of John Milbank and Kathryn Tanner, offer a way beyond this stalemate; they both use "culture" but do not submit to it, accepting its recognition of human creativity while still insisting that that creativity signifies the human's freedom and openness to something surpassing preexistent human realities – that is, God.

In several books John Milbank has elaborated a provocative and promising response to the received view of culture. In *Theology and Social Theory*, he critiqued modern social theory as built upon an either "heretical" or "pagan" theological project of "naturalizing the supernatural," and proposed replacing those theories with an Augustinian and Blondelian project seeking to "supernaturalize the natural" (Milbank 1990:209). More recently, in *The Word Made Strange*, he argued that culture, especially the linguistic formations that mediate it, is always already theological, waiting to be transfigured and thereby "made strange" yet again. This does not entail giving the cultural status quo a theological *imprimatur*; on the contrary, in a way surprisingly like Schleiermacher (though admittedly with important material differences), he shows how the "cultured despisers" are precisely un-cultured insofar as they are despisers of the Christian *logos*. He proposes a "gothic" account of culture, in which "every act of association, every act of economic exchange, involves a mutual judgment about what is right, true and beautiful, about the order we are to have in common," and that order is "a kind of 'sublimed' micro/macrocosmic relation" (Milbank 1997:279, 280) between individuals, society, and God.

If Milbank builds his account out of Christology (via the doctrine of the *logos*), Kathryn Tanner develops a similar account out of Pneumatology (Tanner 1997). For her, recent cultural theory's emphasis on the cross-fertilization of various cultural forms and forces helps us see that all participants in any culture participate in the cultural activity of creating and sustaining cultural meaning, and that no form of culture is wholly autonomous or completely quarantined from any other, but instead that all forms (i.e. both "high" and "low" culture) are mutually interrelated. Drawing a parallel between cultural production and theological reflection, Tanner argues that theology should understand itself as an essentially *formal* activity, which "twists" cultural sign-systems in order to make the Christian gospel apprehensively apprehensible by the culture. This emphasis on the formality of theology, seemingly so Troeltschian, actually builds on a material (and very Barthian) claim about the sovereign freedom of God (and in particular the Holy Spirit) over the human status quo. For Tanner, cultural theory's realization of the contingency of human configurations is merely a way of emphasizing the relativism of human structures before the absolute freedom of God.[15]

Conclusion

The concept of culture, as the recent theoretical attention to it demonstrates, provides an ambiguously useful tool for understanding human existence. While the concept can illuminate and critique theological practices and their social settings, it can equally vex theology's insistence on the openness of human experience to "the other" and "the new". What the most promising recent proposals offer us, however, is a way of seeing in culture itself – in its manifestations and its dynamics – that very otherness and newness that we thought we had to seek somewhere "outside" it.

A number of interesting and important questions (for example, about consumerism, "mass," "pop," and "popular" culture) have been ignored here, only for reasons of space. Nonetheless, we can say that theology's engagement with culture – with both "theology" and "culture" understood in their "catholic" universally inclusive sense – is not a *superadditum* to some core theological project. As theology is most fundamentally about mediating otherness, some form of theological engagement with culture is already internal to theology. Theology begins from the realization that otherness – and particularly the otherness of God – is at the heart of human selfhood. Anxieties about the mutual contamination of culture and theology reveal here nothing less than our sinfulness, our lack of being the fully worldly beings we are supposed to be. Hence, alongside Milbank's Christological theology of culture and Tanner's Pneumatological one, one might construct a Patrological theology of culture: If God the Father is the Creator and Sustainer of the universe, we must insist that theological discourse – discourse about God – is the most profoundly cultural discourse one can find. In the end, the worry will have never been that theology could be "too cultural," but that it might be, because of wholly human failings, not cultural enough.

Notes

1   As the footnotes only partially show, much of this narrative is drawn from Williams (1983) and Tanner (1997). I want to finesse the question of agency in this historical sketch. The development of the concept of culture was due to individual human agents; but much of that development was accidental and can only be identified in retrospect. This raises broader questions about the nature of historiography that I will not address here. See Bernstein (1994).
2   See Sperber (1985), esp. Essay 1, "Interpretive Ethnography and Theoretical Anthropology".
3   The best recent work on this is Moody-Adams (1997).
4   Though the Frankfurt School of social thought foreshadows cultural theory.
5   And as with these debates, much of the most creative cultural work occurs where the debates are liveliest, on the margins and in the liminal spaces. See Homi Bhabha (1994).
6   On the curiously underdeveloped concept of "power" typically employed here, see Hjort (1993).
7   Cf. Schleiermacher (1928), Propositions 15–19.
8   This is connected to Schleiermacher's distinction between religion and ethics, and his refusal of what we would call a Christian social ethic.
9   Recently, however, they have arisen again in an interestingly different context, through concerns about what is often called "civil religion," particularly in the United States. See Bellah et al. (1985); for a recent non-American discussion, see Shanks (1995).
10 Barth himself realized this, and in later work suggested that God's alienness to culture is an alienness identical to our own alienness to ourselves, a view he pursued most courageously in his famous late essay "The Humanity of God." See his *The Humanity of God* (1978). McCormack (1995) tries to acquit the early Barth but in fact rather ends up indicting his later work as well. Recent deconstructionist thought can be seen as following the early Barth; see Webb (1993).
11 For Protestant thought, see Scharlemann (1990). For Catholic thought, see Tracy (1981). One can locate some of the more theological work of George Steiner in this tradition as well; cf. his *Real Presences* (1989).
12 Stanley Hauerwas is another important thinker here; but Yoder best exemplifies this view.

13   Today, this sort of ethnically-cleansed "identity politics" is just another style of cultural engagement; perhaps, indeed, the most common style. See Hughes (1993).

14   From "Experience," in *Selections from Ralph Waldo Emerson* (1957), p. 271.

15   One wonders, however, whether Tanner's work underspecifies the concept of "conflict"; is conflict *empty*, about nothing but itself, or is it about the overflowingness of God? Tanner's work might be usefully augmented by some of what Milbank has said regarding the differing Kantian and Thomistic views of the relation between human experience and what lies "beyond" it; indeed, a critique of the cultural theorists' overtly Nietzschean view of conflict might help here.

References

Appadurai, A. 1996. *Modernity at Large: Cultural Dimensions of Globalization.* Minneapolis, MN: University of Minnesota Press.

Barth, K. 1978. *The Humanity of God,* trans. T. Weiser. Atlanta, GA: John Knox.

Bellah, R. N. et al. 1985. *Habits of the Heart: Individualism and Commitment in American Life.* Berkeley, CA: University of California Press.

Bernstein, M. A., 1994. *Foregone Conclusions: Against Apocalyptic History.* Berkeley, CA: University of California Press.

Bhabha, H. 1994. *The Location of Culture.* New York: Routledge.

Cavell, S. 1969. "The Availability of Wittgenstein's Later Philosophy," in *Must We Mean What We Say? A Book of Essays.* New York: Cambridge University Press, pp. 44–72.

Cobb, K. 1995. "Reconsidering the Status of Popular Culture in Tillich's Theology of Culture," *Journal of the American Academy of Religion* LXIII (1) (Spring): 53–84.

Edmundson, M. 1997. *Nightmare on Main Street.* Cambridge, MA: Harvard University Press.

Emerson, R. W. 1957. "Experience," in *Selections from Ralph Waldo Emerson,* ed. S. E. Whicher. Boston, MA: Houghton Mifflin.

Fabian, J. 1983. *Time and the Other: How Anthropology Makes its Object.* New York: Columbia University Press.

Geertz, C. 1973. *The Interpretation of Cultures.* New York: Basic Books.

Greenwalt, S. 1990. "Culture," in *Critical Terms for Literary Study,* eds. F. Lentricchia and T. McLaughlin. Chicago, IL: Chicago University Press, pp. 229–30.

Hjort, M. 1993. *The Strategy of Letters.* Cambridge, MA: Harvard University Press.

Hughes, R. 1993. *Culture of Complaint: The Fraying of America.* New York: Oxford University Press.

Lindbeck, G. 1984. *The Nature of Doctrine: Religion and Theology in a Postliberal Age.* Philadelphia, PA: Westminster Press.

McCormack, B. L. 1995. *Karl Barth's Critically Realistic Dialectical Theology: Its Genesis and Development, 1909–1936.* Oxford: Clarendon Press.

McDannell, C. 1995. *Material Christianity: Religion and Popular Culture in America.* New Haven, CT: Yale University Press.

Masuzawa, T. 1998. "Culture," in *Critical Terms for Religious Studies,* ed. M. C. Taylor. Chicago, IL: University of Chicago Press, pp. 70–93.

Milbank, J. 1990. *Theology and Social Theory.* Oxford: Basil Blackwell.

Milbank, J. 1997. *The Word Made Strange: Theology, Language, Culture.* Oxford: Blackwell.

Moody-Adams, M. 1997. *Fieldwork in Familiar Places: Morality, Culture, and Philosophy.* Cambridge, MA: Harvard University Press.

Niebuhr, H. 1951. *Christ and Culture.* New York: Harper.

Proudfoot, W. 1985. *Religious Experience*. Berkeley, CA: University of California Press.

Sahlins, M. 1993. "Goodbye to *Tristes Tropes*: Ethnography in the Context of Modern World History," *Journal of Modern History* 65(1) (March): 1–25.

Scharlemann, R. 1990. "Transcendental and Poietic Imagination in a Theology of Culture," in *Morphologies of Faith: Essays in Religion and Culture in Honor of Nathan A. Scott, Jr.*, eds. M. Gerhart and A. C. Yu. Atlanta, GA: Scholars' Press, pp. 109–22.

Schleiermacher, F. 1928. *The Christian Faith*, eds. H. R. MacKintosh and J. S. Stewart. Edinburgh: T. & T. Clark.

Schweiker, W. 1990. *Mimetic Reflections: A Study in Hermeneutics, Theology, and Ethics*. New York: Fordham University Press.

Shanks, A. 1995. *Civil Society, Civil Religion*. Oxford: Blackwell.

Sperber, D. 1985. *On Anthropological Knowledge*. New York: Cambridge University Press.

Stassen, G. H., Yeager, D. M., and Yoder, J. H. 1996. *Authentic Transformation: A New Vision of Christ and Culture*. Nashville, TN: Abingdon Press.

Steiner, G. 1989. *Real Presences*. Chicago, IL: University of Chicago Press.

Tanner, K. 1997. *Theories of Culture: A New Agenda for Theology*. Minneapolis, MN: Fortress Press.

Taylor, M. C. ed. 1998. *Critical Terms for Religious Studies*. Chicago, IL: University of Chicago Press.

Tracy, D. 1981. *The Analogical Imagination: Christian Theology and the Culture of Pluralism*. New York: Crossroad.

Troeltsch, E. 1979. *Christian Thought: Its History and Application*, ed. Baron F. von Hügel. London: University of London Press [1923]; reprinted Westport, CT: Hyperion Press.

Webb, S. 1993. *Blessed Excess: Religion and the Hyperbolic Imagination*. Albany, NY: State University of New York Press.

Williams, R. 1977. *Marxism and Literature*. New York: Oxford University Press.

Williams, R. 1983. *Culture and Society, 1750–1950*. New York: Columbia University Press.

Yack, B. 1986. *The Longing for Total Revolution: Philosophic Sources of Social Discontent from Rousseau to Marx and Nietzsche*. Princeton, NJ: Princeton University Press.

Yack, B. 1997. *The Fetishism of Modernities: Epochal Self-Consciousness in Contemporary Social and Political Thought*. Notre Dame, IN: University of Notre Dame Press.

CHAPTER 5
Social Theory

Don Browning

Why should Christian theology be interested in social theory? To answer this question, some definitions need to be advanced.

Theology is often defined as systematic reflection on the truth and relevance of the Christian faith. The Christian faith not only claims to speak a truth decisive for one's ultimate salvation, it also holds that it contains definitive insights into the nature of ethical living and the good society. For this reason, Christian theology is concerned not only about doctrine or true belief but also about the practical ordering of individual and group life. Edward Farley believes that theology is fundamentally a *habitus* in which the search for knowledge of God and an existential way of life are one and the same (Farley 1983).

Such claims suggest that the Christian faith contains assumptions about the nature and possibilities of individual and social action. Early Christianity, generally thought to be the normative source of Christian theology, did not systematically elaborate these assumptions, but succeeding generations of theologians often tried to do this. The notable illustrations would be the theories of action and society found in the Platonism of Augustine and the Aristotelianism of Thomas Aquinas. The differentiation of institutions in modern societies from control by religion has made it impossible for Christian theology to regulate directly secular social life.[1] Nonetheless, theology still has the obligation of relating its view of life to the processes and events of contemporary society, even if this must now be done persuasively and dialogically and not by the force of tradition alone. To do this, theology itself must make use of implicit or explicit theories about the nature of individual action and social processes in modern societies.

On the other hand, modern societies have generated a variety of theories in the academic disciplines of sociology, political science, economics, and psychology that have claimed to be more or less comprehensive accounts of how modern societies function. Marx, Freud, Weber, Durkheim, Talcott Parsons, Jürgen Habermas, Niklas Luhmann, Anthony Giddens, and economic theorists such as Gary Becker and Richard Posner have developed such relatively complete theories. Theology, especially in its more practical forms, has in recent years both used and critiqued these various theories. Latin American liberation theology employed, although generally revised, insights from both Weber and Marx but tended to reject structural–functionalist views represented by social theorists such as Talcott Parsons.[2] Political theologians Johann Baptist Metz and Helmut Peukert both rely on, yet critique, the thought of Habermas as do American theologians Francis Fiorenza, Paul Lakeland, and Gary Simpson (Metz 1980, Peukert 1984, Lakeland 1990, Fiorenza 1992a, b, Simpson 2002). German theologian Michael Welker turns to the thought of sociologist Niklas Luhmann, as does his American co-author William Schweiker (Schweiker and Welker forthcoming).

But how are decisions made as to which style of social theory constitutes a fruitful partner for theology? The answer goes something like this: the best social theory from the standpoint of theology is one that seems to account for the nature of social processes and social change but is complete enough to also provide for the possibility of religion, especially the kind of religion Christianity appears to be. Theologians should not, and on the whole do not, turn to social theory to prove Christianity. Furthermore, theologians do not derive their core normative ideas from social theory. They primarily gain an understanding of certain features of contemporary life that helps them communicate (or mediate) their theological ideas more accurately and practically to present-day society.

But this is not the only motivation. In using social theory, theologians almost always enter into dialog with it, interpret it, critique it, pick and choose from its various insights, and often show that a particular theory has limitations or contradictions that it cannot solve without turning to theology. The dialogical use of social theory by theology is often quite complex; at the same time as the theologian gains insights from a particular theory, she or he may also realize that this same theory puts hard questions to Christianity and its role in human life. In using the theory, theology may at the same time have to defend itself from the theory's criticism of Christianity, as theologians using Marx and Freud have done repeatedly. Finally, the use of social theory by theologians sometimes has apologetic functions; it strengthens theology's capacity to communicate and answer the tough questions that social theory often puts to theology.

Theology and *Phronēsis*

Over the last several decades, there has been a rebirth of what is commonly called "practical philosophy." This turn in philosophy has had important implications for theology, social theory, and the more discrete social sciences such as sociology, psychology, political science, and economics. It is associated with the hermeneutic philosophy of Hans-Georg Gadamer and Paul Ricoeur, the ordinary language analysis of Wittgenstein and Peter Winch, the discourse ethics of Jürgen Habermas, and American pragmatism – especially the recent work of Richard Rorty and Richard Bernstein (Rorty 1979, Ricoeur 1981a, Gadamer [1960] 1982, Habermas 1990).[3]

The convergence of these different schools of thought has brought the Greek terms *praxis* (practice) and *phronēsis* (practical wisdom, or practical reason) into prominence in much of contemporary philosophy. The elevation of these terms has revived the ancient view of human beings as practical actors trying first of all to determine what they should do to order their lives together. This at first glance might appear to be a trivial claim. It becomes more important, however, when placed against two other dominant views of humans celebrated in the late nineteenth and twentieth centuries. These are the views of humans as primarily technical or economic creatures (built around the idea of *techne*, or technical reason) or as pursuers of scientific knowledge (built around the concept of *theoria*, or theoretical reason). These last two views of humans, and their associated understandings of human rationality, have gone hand-in-hand with what sociologists call the modernization process. Modernization, since the writings of the great German sociologist Max Weber, has been understood as a strategy of life in which technical reason has been increasingly applied to the enhancement of life satisfactions and the ordering of society (Weber 1958). Technical reason generally has been defined as the use of a certain kind of means–end thinking to solve life problems, i.e., the use of the most efficient and powerful means possible to realize ends that are themselves assumed but not critically evaluated. Technical reason, within the context of modernity, has had an alliance with theoretical reason or science. Science increasingly has provided the knowledge needed by technical reason to accomplish its goals. Many contemporary social theorists believe that in late modernity, science or theoretical reason has been captured and indeed corrupted by technical reason and the cultural goal of controlling nature and society for the increase of individual satisfactions.

The push by practical philosophy to make *phronēsis*, or practical wisdom, the center of our image of humans is not designed to vanquish either *techne* or *theoria*. It is, rather, to locate them within *phronēsis*. *Phronēsis*, as practical and moral reasoning about the good individual and social life, is presented in these philosophies as more fundamental than either of the other two forms of human reason. Humans need both technical and theoretical reason, but these must be guided by practical reason. Increasingly, technical and theoretical reason are understood as abstractions from the concreteness of *phronēsis*. This means that, in real life, technical and theoretical reason should be situated within the more inclusive framework of practical reason and either wittingly or unwittingly be guided by it. We cannot order individual and social action, as foundationalist philosophies have advocated, by inductively or deductively moving the full task of determining our individual and social ethics from science or technology upward.[4] The central human activity is practical reason; science and technology must find their rightful places, and their rightful contributions, in relationship to practical ethical reflection and action designed to regulate individual and social life.

Phronēsis in Gadamer, Ricoeur, and Bernstein

Ordering the relation between practical, theoretical, and technical reason is only a small part of social theory. It is, nonetheless, an important beginning point. And, as I said above, it has important implications for defining the nature of both theology and social theory. It means that both, when fully and properly viewed, should be seen as forms of practical reflection and action. When this is acknowledged, theology and social theory have certain overlaps or analogies that give them an affinity, although certainly not an identity.

This assertion will be clearer if we ask, what exactly is *phronēsis* or practical reason? How does it work? What are its sources? There are many answers to these questions. I will discuss two classic alternatives that both find their roots in Aristotle. One view says practical reason is strictly a process of reasoning about the means to certain ends that are themselves assumed. Aristotle's famous illustration went like this: "I want to drink, says appetite; this is drink, says sense or imagination or mind; straightway I drink."[5] Note that in this example, thirst and the identification of drink are assumed and reasoning is mainly about the best means to appropriate the beverage – "straightway I drink." This is an expression of technical reason and some philosophers have basically identified practical reason *with* technical rationality – with calculations about efficiency in the sense found in this illustration. This is thought to have been the view of the philosopher David Hume (Dahl 1984:14, 23–34). It is also the view of human reason undergirding much of the more functionally oriented and rational-choice social theories of our day – those views that see human action as primarily a matter of calculating prudential means to attaining material satisfactions such as food, water, sex, wealth, and reproduction for individuals in society.[6]

But Aristotle had a broader theory of practical reason. Aristotelian scholar Norman Dahl argues that this view sees *phronēsis* as evaluating the ends of action as well as the means. This, according to Dahl, is reason asking not only "what do I want?" but also "what do I *really* want?" and "what would it be morally good to want?" This is reason evaluating the norms and ideals of action as well as the means of action. This second view of practical reason is the one that has been rehabilitated by the turn to practical philosophy, and the one thought to be so useful for gaining the most complete understanding of individual and social action.

This is where the thought of Hans-Georg Gadamer, Paul Ricoeur, and Richard Bernstein has been so useful in reorienting social theory and the more discrete social sciences. They have helped re-establish an understanding of how practical reason avails itself of the norms and ideals that guide and evaluate social practices. It is argued that the sketch of practical reason that I am about to present is a more adequate account of how free individuals and groups act, deliberate, and reshape their social life than accounts that build on more functional or technical accounts of *phronēsis*.

We must begin with Gadamer, a German philosopher whose writings over the last half of the twentieth century had a massive influence on social theory, theology, and the specific social sciences. His major work was *Truth and Method* (1960). The core of his thought was his argument for the close relation between understanding (*verstehen*) and *phronēsis*. Understanding something – a text, another person, another society, or event – is for him a form of practical activity. Why? Because one always begins the understanding process out of a particular history and a particular set of concerns and questions shaped by that history. Those who claim that theoretical reason is and should be the dominant human activity have seen understanding as an act of cognitive objectivity. They have seen it as a matter of pushing aside or suppressing one's questions and the history that shaped them and then apprehending the object of knowledge independently of these tradition-formed practical concerns. Once, according to this view, objective understanding is accomplished, then one can apply this objective knowledge to the various practical concerns of life. It is a matter of moving from *theory to practice*, from theory to application. But Gadamer, significantly influenced by the older German philosopher Martin Heidegger, said no. A concern with application shapes understanding from the beginning. In developing his argument, Gadamer invokes Aristotle as a model:

> To conclude, if we relate Aristotle's description of the ethical phenomenon and especially of the virtue of moral knowledge to our own investigation, we find that Aristotle's analysis is in fact a kind of model of the problems of hermeneutics. We, too, determined that application is neither a subsequent nor a merely occasional part of the phenomenon of understanding, but co-determines it as a whole from the beginning. (Gadamer 1982:289)

The idea that a concern with application co-determines understanding from the beginning is a hard concept to grasp. Twentieth-century people have been so educated to believe that understanding requires objectivity that to hear Gadamer say otherwise seems wrong. But it becomes clearer when we read his argument that understanding should be understood as "conversation" or "dialogue" where one understands another in light of one's own beginning point – one's history, social experience, and the questions and concerns that flow from them (Gadamer 1982:330–3). We understand texts and other communications by contrasting and comparing them to our own historically shaped practices, perspectives, and questions. Remove these from the understanding process and we lose our point of reference.

Hence, Gadamer rehabilitated the role of prejudices (to be understood in the sense of pre-judgments shaped by one's traditions) in the understanding process. He rejected the Enlightenment, positivistic, and scientistic idea that we should suppress our pre-judgments in order to understand something (Gadamer 1982:235–53). To fully comprehend, however, the role of pre-judgment in understanding, it is also important to grasp Gadamer's two concepts of effective history and classics. For Gadamer, the past is not simply a dead event that happened long ago. The past lives on in tradition, culture, and institutions, to shape the contemporary experience of societies and individuals (1982:267). Persons and groups may not be very conscious of how this is so, but in a variety of silent ways, the past lives on in present experience. When we attempt to understand some text, event, or monument of the past, we do so from a stance of having been already influenced by that which we are now trying to understand. When interpreting the past, the distinction between subject and object (the interpreting subject and the object to be understood) is blurred; we already know to some extent the thing that we are attempting to understand more deeply. This is especially true when we attempt to understand the classics of the traditions that shape us. These classics – whether they be religious or philosophical texts or works of art – have already subtly shaped us before we attempt to consciously understand them more deeply (1982:253–8). This is how we should conceive of understanding as a conversation or dialogue; we generally already have a point of contact or analogy with that which we are coming to understand.

This is especially true when we try to understand the religious and philosophical classics of the past that constitute a pervasive source of our ideals and to which we repeatedly return for clarification and renewal. When social action runs into a conflict or impasse about the norms and ideals that should guide us, we ask: what ideals are already a part of us, do we understand them correctly, and are they true? This creates the understanding process – the dialog or conversation between our present experience and the classics that time and time again our culture has returned to, to clarify where it is going. Since present experience is always changing and since we are always confronted with new challenges, each time we return to our classics to clarify our ideals, we create a new "fusion of horizons" – a somewhat new structure of meaning – between our contemporary questions and these classics (1982:273). Hence, individual and social action, when it is free and undistorted, moves in a **circle** from present situations and their crises backward to the clarification of goals and ideals – the understanding of classics – to a return once again to present situations for renewed and better defined guiding ideals. It is a practice–theory–practice movement – not a process of moving from theory to practice. Because interpretation and understanding as practical activities are so central to this view, it can conveniently be called a hermeneutic theory of social action built on a hermeneutic circle.

Hermeneutic Views of Theology and Social Theory

If all social action basically has a hermeneutic character in which *phronēsis* and *verstehen* come together, what distinguishes Christian theology from social theory? Both would be seen as types of practical understanding. But their difference would be this: theology is a view of social action that explicitly finds its classics (its norms and ideals) in what it considers to be the revelatory power of the story of creation, fall, and redemption recorded in the Hebrew and Christian scriptures. Social theory as an exercise in *verstehen* also would need some way of locating its classics, but it might not necessarily use the Christian classics. Nonetheless, because of the pervasive presence and influence of Christian classics in Western culture, various social theories may implicitly use them in the horizon of their conceptuality as unacknowledged sources of norms and ideals.

Examples of either Judaism or Christianity – or both – functioning to shape the normative horizon or background assumptions of various social theories are not difficult to find. Some commentators have argued that even though Marx saw religion as a source of ideology often justifying capitalist exploitation, from another perspective Jewish utopian visions of the kingdom of God in this world indirectly animated his vision of the just society (Miranda 1974:229–49). It can be argued that Freud's view of the importance of the restraints of the superego – although he held that they should now become conscious and rational rather than unconscious and blind – stemmed from his continuing appreciation of Moses as a law-giver to the Jews (Rieff 1979:281–3). Max Weber's theory of how Protestantism – specifically his interpretation of Luther's concept of vocation (*Beruf*) and Calvin's doctrine of predestination – shaped an economic ethic for Western societies, was probably more than a value-neutral explanatory conception (Weber 1958:181–3). It may, as well, have reflected his unconscious appreciation for his own Protestant heritage mediated through his mother (Gerth and Wright Mills 1958:5–7, 28–31). And finally, the neoclassical economics of Milton Friedman and Gary Becker, which holds all social action to be motivated by calculations of costs and benefits to individual satisfactions, may have deeper background beliefs than the theory itself acknowledges. Economist Donald McCloskey has argued that neoclassical economics is actually fed by an implicit narrative about the meaning of life that builds on the Protestant ethic of hard work, rational action, and saving for the future (McCloskey 1990:135–40).

If many examples of contemporary social theory contain background beliefs that are open to Christian and Jewish theological visions or narratives, what does that say about the relation of social theory to theology? Does this, for example, make social theory a kind of theology? Not quite. But it does suggest that a categorical distinction between social theory and theology may be difficult to argue for convincingly. Theology *self-consciously* and *explicitly* interprets and defends Judeo-Christian visions and narratives about life and society. If prominent examples of social theory hazily and vaguely make use of these same visions and narratives, it does not mean that social theory is theology, but it does suggest that it is difficult for social theory to orient itself to accounts of social action without itself implicitly relying on some kind of vision of the ultimate context of human experience. Furthermore, it points to a non-scientific aspect of much of contemporary social theory over which it does not have full control, partially because it may not even fully acknowledge its presence. On this point, theology appears more honest and forthright than much of social theory. Theology openly acknowledges, interprets, and defends its ultimate vision and the narratives that convey it.

Secular social theory may fail to make explicit these visions and fail to advance any kind of ordered defense of them. Yet they influence and tilt the views of individual and social action nonetheless. John Milbank in his *Theology and Social Theory* (1990) analyzes the horizon and hidden assumptions of several kinds of social theory – Durkheim, Weber, Marx, Parsons as well as the entire field of postmodernism – and finds, not so much an implicit Christian vision or ontology, but an ancient pagan ontology of violence and power (Milbank 1990:278–325). In *Religious Thought and the Modern Psychologies* (1987), I made a similar analysis of the major schools of contemporary psychology – Freud, Skinner, Jung, the humanistic psychologies, Erikson, Kohut – and found that they all contained deep metaphors about the nature of the ultimate context of experience, metaphors that function analogously to religious visions (Browning 1987). Metaphors of life and death (Freud), of ultimate harmony (Jung and humanistic psychology), of care (Erikson and, strangely enough, Skinner), or of purposeful design (the later Kohut) all pointed to visions of the way the world at its heart really is. These visions shaped the deep existential attitudes of these respective psychologies toward either trust, joy, solicitude, distrust, or despair. Yet, these psychologies give no account of these deep quasi-religious assumptions. Sociologist Peter Berger, in his popular *A Rumor of Angels*, argued that officially the social sciences relativize if not completely undercut all religious claims; implicitly, however, "signals of transcendence" (rumors of angels) shine through these disciplines and practical thought time and again (Berger 1969:61–94). If we were to take Milbank seriously, the signals of transcendence in the secular social sciences are more likely to be rumors of devils or forces of violence.

The difficulty social theory has in gaining autonomy from implicit or explicit religious visions may not be a shortcoming. They may be inevitable and therefore should be handled positively. Rather than fighting against them, denying them, and failing to acknowledge the various ways they are detectable in the background beliefs of various social theories, some scholars argue that social theory should acknowledge and use these religious visions directly in its work. This might be the implication of Gadamer in his admonition to use the pre-judgments of one's effective history in the process of understanding as dialog. Since religion was so significantly a part of the traditions that shape us, pre-judgments about the nature and value of the ultimate context of experience plausibly would make up a great deal of our effective history. Hence, it might follow that to understand something necessarily occurs against the background of our inherited religious visions of the good and true.

In light of this insight, some social theorists have tried to develop accounts of human action large enough to incorporate directly many of the insights of Gadamer. The British social theorist Anthony Giddens is certainly a leading example of one who both absorbs and critiques Gadamer (Giddens 1977).[7] But Giddens has not gone as far in this direction as the American sociologist Robert Bellah and his team in their successful *Habits of the Heart: Individualism and Commitment in American Life* (Bellah et al. 1985). In this book, the Bellah team tried to assess the status of individualism and commitment in contemporary North American life. They concluded that individualism, especially in the middle classes, had the upper hand and that the struggle to develop a language of commitment was itself impoverished. These authors argued that it was impossible for sociologists to investigate individualism and commitment in the United States without interpreting contemporary life there in light of the classics that shaped the American vision in the first place. These formative influences were the biblical tradition with its emphasis on covenant, and the republican tradition with its stress on representative democracy. In the beginning, these two traditions kept the balance between individualism and commitment, but in subsequent generations, the demise of the biblical tradition has allowed individualism – both utilitarian and expressive individualism – to gain ground and go increasingly unchecked (1985:27, 32–5).

A complete review of their position is not the purpose of this discussion. I mention it to illustrate their indebtedness to Gadamer and their explicit use of religion within social theory. In an appendix to the book titled "Social Science as Public Philosophy," Bellah makes the following Gadamerian statement:

> It is precisely the boundary between the social sciences and the humanities that social science as public philosophy most wants to open up. Social science is not a disembodied cognitive enterprise. It is a tradition, or set of traditions, deeply rooted in the philosophical and humanistic (and, to more than a small extent, the religious) history of the West. Social science makes assumptions about the nature of persons, the nature of society, and the relation between persons and society. It also, whether it admits it or not, makes assumptions about good persons and a good society and considers how far these conceptions are embodied in our actual society. Becoming conscious of the cultural roots of these assumptions would remind the social scientist that these assumptions are contestable and that the

choice of assumptions involves controversies that lie deep in the history of Western thought. Social science as public philosophy would make the philosophical conversation concerning these matters its own.   (Bellah et al. 1985:301)

Gadamer's concepts of tradition, classics, effective history, and understanding as dialog are implicit in this quote. Tradition constitutes the source of our effective history, even the effective history of the social theorist. Philosophical, humanistic, and even religious sources – classics – give that tradition its special shape. This constitutes Bellah's justi-fication for using the classic covenant and republican traditions as frameworks for understanding the tensions between individualism and commitment in American life. Finally, the entire inquiry is a historically situated dialog. In one place these authors specifically acknowledge the influence of Gadamer when they write:

Hans-Georg Gadamer has provided us with valuable guidance in our understanding of our work as always involving a dialog with the tradition out of which we come. He reminds us also that our conversation with contemporaries or predecessors is never closed on itself but is always *about something*.   (Bellah et al. 1985:330)

Several observations about Bellah's position are relevant. First, social theory, in this view, becomes a somewhat more systematic and disciplined version of good common sense; both are expressions of *phronēsis*. Second, the distinction between theology and social theory all but collapses. Since social theory needs a positive place for classics, both religious and philosophical, Western religious ideals have a rightful role to play directly in the understanding process that constitutes social science and social theory. Third, Bellah's position gets close to grounding social theory in an explicitly religious beginning point. The covenant tradition, for example, is simply assumed; it is a begin-ning point, indeed a confessional beginning point; but now in Bellah's work it is inserted into social theory, not just Christian theology.

In making this move, Bellah gets close to doing in sociology and social theory what John Milbank calls for when he seems to suggest that Western social science should ground itself in the view of society that Augustine set forth in his City of God (Milbank 1990:380–434). He argues that Augustine developed a theory of society based on ecclesiology. But to call it theory, he insists, would do violence to its narrative and per-formative character. First of all, Augustine narrated a description of the practices and rituals of the early *ecclesia* as a community of peace. As a community of peace, it told a counter-history and counter-narrative to the vision of life as honor, excellence, dom-ination, and control characteristic of pagan life. The peaceful practices of the Church were founded on a vision of a peaceful and loving God revealed through Christ; peace in the pagan context was grounded on political control and violence perpetrated by the *Civitas terra* (the earthly city) (1990:380–5). When theology reflects on this performa-tive narrative of ecclesial practice, it gives rise to a speculative ontology of peace – one that can provide a framework for a "Christian sociology" (1990:380). Milbank continues:

Talk of a "Christian sociology" or of "theology as a social science" is not, therefore, as silly as talk of Christian mathematics (I suspend judgement here) precisely because there can be no sociology in the sense of a universal "rational" account of the "social" character of all societies, and Christian sociology is distinctive simply because it explicates, and adopts the vantage point of, a distinct society, the church.   (Milbank 1990:380–1)

The idea of a Christian sociology based on a narrative and reflective ontology of peace is close, as I indicated above, to Bellah's belief that sociology must actively employ cultural classics in its interpretative process, including the classics of faith. However, both points of view contain fresh insights that beg for clarification. Should all of sociology become explicitly religious, perhaps even Christian, because of the prominence of Christian effective history in the cultural narrative of the West?

I don't think either Milbank or Bellah go that far. I read Milbank's message as one addressed primarily to the Church and to theology in its confessional mode. Christian theology, he is arguing, has implications for sociology and social theory; it should be willing to review and critique all allegedly secular perspectives to expose their illusory claims to a value-free rationality and to uncover their implicit deep narratives and ontologies, many of which contradict Christian ontologies and do so arbitrarily and uncritically. Bellah is more ambitious; he wants sociology and other aspects of social theory to expand and take responsibility for reason's dependence on the religious dimensions of its effective history.

Both views, however, fail to realize fully the complexities of their proposals. Both are correct in showing that the social sciences to not rest on a foundation of universal reason. Both are helpful in showing the importance of history and tradition for the exercise of reason, even in the social sciences. However, to be convincing in its critical dialog with the so-called secular social sciences, theology would have to go beyond Milbank's belief that it can do this by simply "re-narrating" the Christian story and thereby make manifest its ontology of peace. Theology would have to go beyond confession or witness in ways that Milbank resists.

Without this additional move, Habermas's criticism of Gadamer's defense of tradition would also apply to a Christian sociology (Giddens 1977).[8] Tradition, although certainly the source of effective history and the assumptive background of all practical thought, can also be a conveyor of ideology, distortions in power, and inequality. Indeed, even classics that are full of wisdom may still be embedded (because of the eras or circumstances in which they were conceived) in distortions that need identification, criticism, and some cleansing. In order to understand the classics and take them seriously and introduce them into public discourse, their insights must be tested by various additional moral and metaphysical analyses. The Milbankian would have to show, to use a phrase of Richard Bernstein's, that there are "good reasons" to think that a Christian ontology of peace enjoys more plausibility than alternative narratives and ontologies about the ultimate context of experience (Bernstein 1983:223–31).

In other words, theology as Christian sociology would have to gain some degree of "distanciation" – to borrow a term from Paul Ricoeur – from its own narrative matrix (Ricoeur 1981c:131–44). This would be no naïve positivistic flight into objectivity; but it would need to go beyond speculation as a second-order elaboration of the Christian narrative. A Christian sociology must be willing to enter into dialog with alternative perspectives, hear criticisms, and make public replies. It would entail developing some

brand of metaphysics. It would have to become apologetic if it were to enter into critical dialog with the culture and sustain this dialog.

If Milbank's proposal for theology as Christian sociology is aimed primarily at the
Church, then it at least has plausibility. But to be truly effective it would need to go
beyond a strictly confessional approach. To meet criticism from others, especially at the
metaphysical level, is no small matter, and one I will not address directly in this chapter.
But I will recommend the writings of Schubert Ogden, John Cobb, David Tracy, and
Franklin Gamwell as examples of theologians who are trying to accomplish a critical
conversation between theology and social theory, even going so far as to address basic
metaphysical questions (Cobb 1965, Ogden 1966, Tracy 1975, Gamwell 1990).

In the case of Bellah, it is hard to interpret the full implications of his proposal. When
Bellah suggests that "social science as public philosophy would make the philosophical
conversation" concerning its effective history and its deep assumptions "its own," he
seems to be suggesting a new superdiscipline that would subsume the explanatory
social sciences to moral philosophy and even theology. But the idea that social science
would make this conversation "its own" suggests that any such superdiscipline would
not only confess its basic religio-cultural assumptions, narratives, and ontologies, it
would try to *critically defend* its choices. This is precisely what Bellah and his team do
not do in *Habits of the Heart* and their follow-up book, *The Good Society* (1991). Bellah
and company never try to defend critically why covenant theology is superior to other
perspectives for grounding the relation between individualism and commitment; they
simply show it was a classic resource in American history. Some of the same metaphysical and moral philosophical tasks that Milbank faces would also need to be confronted by Bellah were such a superdiscipline to be attempted.

In conclusion, both Milbank and Bellah develop interesting proposals about the
relation of theology to social theory. They are addressed, as I read them, to slightly different audiences. Both have merit. But both entail more demanding interdisciplinary
and critical programs than either fully acknowledges. In the meantime, it is better to
acknowledge that no clear boundary between social theory and Christian theology can
be easily drawn. This means that dialog and mutual critique between their respective
implicit and explicit deep narratives and ontologies should be fruitful and entirely justified. This is true for a variety of reasons, but most especially to keep social theory and
the discrete social sciences from becoming the new crypto-theologies of our day.

The More Specific Contributions of Social Theory

Even though social theory relies on deep narratives and ontologies that bring it close
to theology, theology's interest in social theory has more to do with its capacity to
explain certain social processes. By this I mean social theory's ability to locate certain
psychological, social-systemic, economic, and cultural conditions that shape, although
seldom completely determine, individual and social action. Some social scientists
present these conditions as irresistible. They develop what I would call "hard" theories
of explanation; the forces and processes they identify are presented in deterministic
terms. This was certainly the case with Marx's theory of the determining power of the

practices of material production. These practices of production doubtless shape thought and feeling, and give rise to ideologies that defend those who most profit from these practices. As useful as his theory is, it is widely conceded that Marx overstated his case. Much of social theory informed by the model of *phronēsis*, as presented above, depicts individuals and communities as coping with such forces with degrees of freedom, and sometimes quite creatively.

Nonetheless, the material and social-systemic conditions shaping social action need to be understood by any socially responsible theology. Hermeneutic theorist Paul Ricoeur has gone beyond Gadamer in locating explanation, and the cognitive distancing that it requires, as a submoment within a larger view of understanding as dialog and conversation (Ricoeur 1981d:145–64). Hence, the search for causal patterns need not totally undermine a fuller view of social action and social theory based on *phronēsis*, understanding, and the role of both freedom and tradition that these concepts entail.

There are two sets of explanatory concepts of particular importance to contemporary practical or public theologies: (1) *modernization and globalization* and (2) *differentiation and division of labor*. There are certainly other important concepts, but these will serve to illustrate how theology is using social theory.

The idea of *modernization* is closely related to the concept of technical reason discussed at the beginning of the chapter. Since Max Weber, modernization has been seen by social theorists as the application of technical reason to progressively wider aspects of life. It is a social process that first emerged in the industrial West but gradually spread to other parts of the world, thereby suggesting a kind of world dominance by Western countries and their values. Jürgen Habermas distinguishes between technical rationality, or "purposive rationality" (his preferred term), applied to markets, and technical reason, applied to bureaucratic control (Habermas 1987:209, 332–42). Capitalism is the primary example of the first and socialism, especially Soviet-style communism, was the primary example of the second. Both forms of technical reason disrupt what Habermas calls the "lifeworld" – the immediate face-to-face practical dialog of individuals and small communities in their exercise of *phronēsis* (1987:121–6).

The spread of bureaucratic forms of technical reason in socialist countries creates dependency of individuals on governments and leads them to turn away from family and neighbor and sources of help and creative dialog. The spread of market forms of technical reason absorbs more and more people into the cost–benefit and efficiency-dominated logics of the business world. Notice the move of men from farms and crafts to the wage economy in the nineteenth century, followed in Western countries by a similar move of most women from home to paid employment in the twentieth century. Now most adults in Western market-driven countries are in the competitive, efficiency-driven systems of the market economy. Theorists as different as Habermas, the sociologist Alan Wolfe, and the rational-choice economist Gary Becker believe that, increasingly, individuals are thinking about intimate relations, marriage, and parenting in cost–benefit terms (Wolfe 1989:51–60; Becker 1991). And increasingly they are wondering if the costs exceed the benefits, hence the decline in birth and marriage rates and the increase of divorce in most Western societies.

If this is so, modernization has enormous implications for any practical or public theology wishing to address the modern world. Should Christian theology be for or against the modernization process? Many theorists believe that modernization will be destructive of communities and, finally, the democratic process itself unless strong pockets of voluntary organizations or civil society can emerge to resist its spread. Religion – especially churches – is one of the major sources of civil society; hence, theology's task is not so much a matter of suppressing technical reason and its benefits as developing strong counter-ideologies and counter-communities where a more religiously based *phronēsis* can work to limit and confine its expansion. This would entail developing powerful theological grounds for asserting that persons must be treated as ends and never as means, in spite of technical reason's tendency to reduce all of life to means. Various theological strategies are at work to do just this – some rooted in the Reformed covenant theology such as the work of Max Stackhouse, Mary Stewart van Leeuwen, and John Witte, Jr., some in liberation theology and its theory of base communities, and some in the classic Catholic theory of subsidiarity and its idea that governments and market should support, and not override, the agency and initiative of individuals, families, and local groups (Van Leeuwen 1990, Carr and Van Leeuwen 1997, Stackhouse 1997, Witte 1997).

There is much discussion today in the social sciences about the phenomenon of *globalization*. It is closely associated with modernization but also distinguished from it.[9] For instance, modernization, even in older social science discussions, was depicted as a kind of globalizing process. It was depicted as spreading from northern European countries and the US to the rest of the world; sooner or later the entire globe would be industrial, technically educated, and democratic in the Western style. More recent definitions of globalization absorb but recontextualize modernization theory. Electronic communication has made it possible for technical rationality, information, and cultural images to flow from east to west, south to north. In addition, certain features of modernization seem to work as well in more authoritarian governments like the People's Republic of China or Singapore as they do in the democratic West, thereby suggesting a possible decoupling of modernization from democracy and from the political polities of Europe and the US.

However this discussion might go, globalization presents a new challenge to theology. Theology, often thought of as addressing certain specific national and cultural contexts, may now need to address, critique, and help guide abstract globalizing systemic processes that cut across national and cultural boundaries.

Differentiation and division of labor are distinguishable yet closely related additional concepts relevant to a practical and public theology. The concept of division of labor is ancient but became quite central in the writings of Marx. The concept hypothesizes an archaic simple society where most individuals and families were deeply involved in all the tasks of life required to survive – cooking, building, hunting and growing, exchange, religious ritual, and the political ordering of the group, however elemental that might have been. Gradually, the theory goes, societies discovered the efficiency that comes with specialization; this was the social strategy of allowing some people to concentrate on one activity while depending on diverse specialists for other important functions. As societies matured, these specializations became hardened, autonomous from one another, and even alienated. Specializations can compete and dominate each other; those specializations producing private property and capital can, for instance, dominate workers (Marx 1978:160–1). Specialists themselves can become separated from the rest of life. Marx believed that the classless society following the world communist revolution would lessen the division of labor and the alienation and domination that it had brought (1978:197).

Division of labor leads to the *differentiation* of social institutions. Before the division of labor became highly developed, some social theorists believe, religion and family (in the sense of clan or tribe) controlled much of the social order. As the division of labor increased, specialists organized themselves institutionally; law, medicine, business, education, government, and religious institutions became relatively autonomous from one another, developed their own logics and power bases, and were more and more independent of older centers of control and guidance such as religion and family. The reverse was also true: religion, and family, became less and less influential in these increasingly autonomous sectors of society, leading some commentators to proclaim their increasing irrelevance.[10] This is one way to explain the so-called secularization process.

This description of contemporary social processes has credibility even if certain details are still a matter of dispute. However, religion is not necessarily disappearing in all Western societies where this differentiation process, and its associated secularizing tendencies, are quite advanced. Institutional religion is under siege in many countries of Western Europe but not all modern societies. Individual religious interest (the concern with "spirituality") and even religious institutions are relatively important in the US, Spain, Italy, Northern Ireland and Eire, and much of Central and South America. But the issue is, do religious institutions in even these countries have a sustained influence on other parts of society – law, education, business, politics? If they don't, then religion has lost much of its power even where it is still fairly visible.

Practical and political theologies in confronting this state of affairs have gravitated toward dialogical models of social influence. There is today no Constantinian synthesis between church and state as once existed in medieval Europe, where religion could easily dictate to the rest of society. Cultural Protestantism has lost much of its power in the United States. Established churches such as the Church of England still exist and enjoy some privileges, but their actual social influence must be earned and not taken for granted.

This has given rise to a variety of practical strategies on the part of theology. The one I have been implicitly pointing to in this chapter is often called the "critical correlational" view of theology, and in addition to Tracy, Ogden, and Gamwell, this perspective is also associated with the names of William Schweiker, Thomas Groome, James Fowler, myself and others (Groome 1980, Fowler 1983, 1987, Browning 1983, 1991, Schweiker 1995). This view locates theology firmly in the hermeneutic process as described above. In its more practical manifestations, this perspective brings questions stemming from contemporary experience and our effective histories to the classics of the Christian faith and then returns to address specific arenas of life. This view believes that all theology, as does all thought, begins with confession, i.e., begins with how the theologian has been shaped by tradition prior to the beginning of critical reflection.

But the critical correlational view also believes that the Christian faith contains within it hints of metaphysical and moral truths which, although always first presented wrapped in a confessional narrative, can be given sufficient philosophical clarity to enter into dialog and mutual criticism with the different spheres of society. Hence, this view of the relation of theology to social theory goes beyond the confessionalism of both Bellah and Milbank. If theology is to avoid the two-fold pitfall of either subordinating social theory to theology through confessional fiat or becoming a mere tool of social theory, it must be willing to take on a critical and apologetic agenda.

Notes

1   For a basic discussion of the process of differentiation, see Talcott Parsons (1968:318).
2   For a discussion about the use and revision of Marx in liberation theology, see Gutiérrez (1990:214–25). See also Gutiérrez (1973) and Segundo (1976).
3   For an application of Wittgenstein's ordinary language analysis to the philosophy of the social sciences, see Winch (1958), Habermas (1990), and Rorty (1979).
4   For two important critiques of foundationalism, see Rorty (1979) and Bernstein (1983).
5   For a discussion of Hume's view of practical reason see its similarity to this first Aristotelian view; see Dahl (1984:26–9).
6   For a discussion of social science as technical reason in Hume's sense, see Bellah (1983). For a rational-choice view of social action, see Becker (1976).
7   For a secondary discussion of Giddens's use and critique of Gadamer, see Craib (1992:25).
8   Since Habermas's critiques of Gadamer's traditionalism and potential for ideological distortion is strewn throughout his early writings, I refer the reader to an excellent secondary resource. See Paul Ricoeur, "Hermeneutics and the Critique of Ideology," in Ricoeur 1981a:63–100.
9   The leading theorist of globalization is Roland Robertson (1992). Other important works are Peter Beyer (1994), and Saskia Sassen (1998).
10 For symposia that investigate the embattled character of both religion and family in modern societies, see D'Antonio and Aldous (1983) and Thomas (1988).

References

Becker, G. 1976. *The Economic Approach to Human Behavior.* Chicago, IL: University of Chicago Press.

Becker, G. 1991. *A Treatise on the Family.* Cambridge, MA: Harvard University Press.

Bellah, R. 1983, "Social Science as Practical Reason," in *Ethics, Social Sciences, and Policy Analysis,* ed. D. Callahan. New York: Plenum Press.

Bellah, R. et al. 1985. *Habits of the Heart: Individualism and Commitment in American Life.* New York: Harper and Row.

Berger, P. 1969. *A Rumor of Angels.* New York: Doubleday.

Bernstein, R. 1983. *Beyond Objectivism and Relativism.* Philadelphia, PA: University of Pennsylvania Press.

Beyer, P. 1994. *Religion and Globalization.* London: Sage.

Browning, D. ed. 1983. *Practical Theology.* San Francisco, CA: Harper and Row.

Browning, D. 1987. *Religious Thought and the Modern Psychologies.* Minneapolis, MN: Fortress Press.

Browning, D. 1991. *A Fundamental Practical Theology.* Minneapolis, MN: Fortress Press.

Browning, D. and Fiorenza, F. eds. 1991. *Habermas, Modernity, and Public Theology.* New York: Crossroad.

Callahan, D. ed. 1983. *Ethics, Social Sciences, and Policy Analysis.* New York: Plenum Press.

Carr, A. and Van Leeuwen, M. S. 1997. *Feminism, Religion, and the Family.* Louisville, KY: Westminster/John Knox Press.

Cobb, J. 1965. *A Christian Natural Theology.* Philadelphia, PA: Westminster Press.

Craib, I. 1992. *Anthony Giddens.* London: Routledge.

Dahl, N. O. 1984. *Practical Reason, Aristotle, and Weakness of the Will.* Minneapolis, MN: University of Minnesota Press.

D'Antonio, W. and Aldous, J. 1983. *Families and Religions: Conflict and Change in Modern Society.* Beverly Hills, CA: Sage.

Farley, E. 1983. *Theologia.* Minneapolis, MN: Fortress Press.

Fiorenza, F. S. 1992a. "Introduction: a Critical Reception for a Practical Public Theology," in *Habermas, Modernity, and Public Theology*, eds. D. Browning and F. Fiorenza. New York: Crossroad, pp. 1–19.

Fiorenza, F. S. 1992b. "The Church as a Community of Interpretation: Political Theology between Discourse Ethics and Hermeneutical Reconstruction," in *Habermas, Modernity, and Public Theology*, eds. D. Browning and F. Fiorenza. New York: Crossroad, pp. 66–91.

Fowler, J. 1983. "Practical Theology and the Shaping of Christian Lives," in *Practical Theology*, ed. D. Browning. San Francisco, CA: Harper and Row, pp. 148–66.

Fowler, J. 1987. *Faith Development and Pastoral Care.* Philadelphia, PA: Fortress Press.

Gadamer, H.-G. 1982. *Truth and Method.* New York: Crossroad.

Gamwell, F. 1990. *The Divine Good.* New York: Harper and Row.

Gerth, H. H. and Wright Mills, C. 1958. "Introduction: the Man and his Work," in *From Max Weber.* New York: Oxford University Press.

Giddens, A. 1977. *Studies in Social and Political Theory.* London: Hutchinson.

Groome, T. 1980. *Christian Religious Education.* New York: Harper and Row.

Gutiérrez, G. 1973. *A Theology of Liberation.* Maryknoll, NY: Orbis Books.

Gutiérrez, G. 1990. "Theology and Social Sciences," in *Liberation Theology at the Crossroads: Democracy and Revolution*, ed. P. Sigmund. Oxford: Oxford University Press.

Habermas, J. 1987. *The Theory of Communicative Action*, vol. II. Boston, MA: Beacon Press.

Habermas, J. 1990. *Moral Consciousness and Communicative Action.* Cambridge, MA: MIT Press.

Lakeland, P. 1990. *Theology and Critical Theory: The Discourse of the Church.* Nashville, TN: Abingdon Press.

McCloskey, D. 1990. *If You're So Smart: The Narrative of Economic Expertise.* Chicago, IL: University of Chicago Press.

Marx, K. 1978. "The German Ideology," in *Marx–Engels Reader*, ed. R. Tucker. New York: W. W. Norton.

Metz, J. B. 1980. *Faith in History and Society.* New York: Crossroad.

Milbank, J. 1990. *Theology and Social Theory: Beyond Secular Reason.* Oxford: Basil Blackwell.

Miranda, J. 1974. *Marx and the Bible.* Maryknoll, NY: Orbis Press.

Ogden, S. 1966. *The Reality of God.* New York: Harper and Row.

Parsons, T. 1968. *The Structure of Social Action*, vol. 1. New York: Free Press.

Peukert, H. 1984. *Science, Action, and Fundamental Theology.* Cambridge, MA: MIT Press.

Ricoeur, P. 1981a. *Hermeneutics and the Human Sciences.* Cambridge: Cambridge University Press.

Ricoeur, P. 1981b. "Hermeneutics and the Critique of Ideology," in P. Ricoeur, *Hermeneutics and the Human Sciences.* Cambridge: Cambridge University Press, pp. 63–100.

Ricoeur, P. 1981c. "The Hermeneutical Function of Distanciation," in P. Ricoeur, *Hermeneutics and the Human Sciences.* Cambridge: Cambridge University Press, pp. 131–44.

Ricoeur, P. 1981d. "What is a Text? Explanation and Understanding," in P. Ricoeur, *Hermeneutics and the Human Sciences*. Cambridge: Cambridge University Press, pp. 145–64.

Rieff, P. 1979. *Freud: The Mind of the Moralist*. Chicago, IL: University of Chicago Press.

Robertson, R. 1992. *Globalization: Social Theory and Global Culture*. London: Sage.

Rorty, R. 1979. *Philosophy and the Mirror of Nature*. Princeton, NJ: Princeton University Press.

Sassen, S. 1998. *Globalization and its Discontents*. New York: New Press.

Schweiker, W. 1995. *Responsibility and Christian Ethics*. Cambridge: Cambridge University Press.

Schweiker, W. and Welker, M. forthcoming. *Beyond the Crisis of Western Christianity*. Valley Forge, PA: Trinity International Press.

Segundo, J. 1976. *The Liberation of Theology*. Maryknoll, NY: Orbis Books.

Sigmund, P. ed. 1990. *Liberation Theology at the Crossroads: Democracy and Revolution*. Oxford: Oxford University Press.

Simpson, G. 2002. *Critical Social Theory*. Minneapolis, MN: Fortress Press.

Stackhouse, M. 1997. *Covenant and Commitment: Faith, Family, and Economic Life*. Louisville, KY: Westminster/John Knox Press.

Thomas, D. 1988. *The Religion and Family Connection: Social Science Perspectives*. Provo, UT: Religious Studies Center.

Tracy, D. 1975. *Blessed Rage for Order*. Minneapolis, MN: Seabury Press.

Van Leeuwen, M. S. 1990. *Gender and Grace*. Downers Grove, IL: Intervarsity Press.

Weber, M. 1958. *The Protestant Ethic and the Spirit of Capitalism* [1904–5]. New York: Charles Scribner's Sons.

Winch, P. 1958. *The Idea of a Social Science and its Relation to Philosophy*. London: Routledge and Kegan Paul.

Witte, J., Jr. 1997. *From Sacrament to Contract: Marriage, Religion, and Law in the Western Tradition*. Louisville, KY: Westminster/John Knox Press.

Wolfe, A. 1989. *Whose Keeper? Social Science and Moral Obligation*. Berkeley, CA: University of California Press.

CHAPTER 6
Theological Anthropology

Ray Anderson

"Who knows whether the human spirit goes upward and the spirit of animals goes downward to the earth?" (Ecclesiastes 3:21). Who knows indeed! In former times, we might account for such ignorance by attributing it to lack of scientific knowledge and philosophical precision. But how should we now account for the fact that some form of the same question tantalizes our scientists and torments our philosophers? Even the terms "spirit" and "soul" remain ambiguous as used in contemporary thought, with "soul" generally used to designate the metaphysical aspect of the human person in such a way that "spirit" is included. This implies a dualism between a physical and non-physical entity residing in each person which cries out for some explanation in light of recent studies regarding the effect of the brain upon personality characteristics.

Modern science suggests that there is no manifestation of the human personality that is not produced through the brain even though the brain may not be the effective cause. What is it that really makes humans unique amidst all of the creatures of the world if we can now transplant vital organs from animals into humans? What and where is the human soul if we can account for personal and spiritual attributes of the self as manifestations of physical and electrical interactions of the brain? Recent research has suggested that some persons appear to have distinctive brain patterns which might account for their propensity toward religious feelings and belief. If the human brain is considered the source of even our deepest spiritual and personal attributes, what has become of the soul?

Has the concept of a human soul disappeared in the presence of molecular biology, clinical psychology, and computer-driven brain scans? Is the disappearance of the soul a consequence of our world "come of age" or is it we who are lost and our souls doing the searching? Perhaps one indication that humans have a soul is that they appear to be the only creatures on earth that are thinking about it! (Ray S. Anderson 1998). Thomas Moore expresses this malaise dramatically:

> The great malady of the twentieth century, implicated in all of our troubles and affecting us individually and socially, is "loss of soul." When soul is neglected, it doesn't just go away;

it appears symptomatically in obsessions, addictions, violence, and loss of meaning. Our temptation is to isolate these symptoms or to try to eradicate them one by one; but the root problem is that we have lost our wisdom about the soul, even our interest in it.   (Moore 1992:xi)

Whether we call it spirit or soul, the question remains: what is it that makes humans both precious and perverse? What gives rise to our deepest religious insights but can also plunge us into the depths of guilt and despair? In our primitive condition did we once have a soul that has now disappeared in the presence of molecular biologists, clinical psychologists, and computer-driven brain scans?

These are questions which theological anthropology seeks to answer by examining the biblical account of the creation, from the dust of the ground, of humans who also bear the imprint of the divine image and likeness (Genesis 1:26–7). We will look first of all at some of the biblical terms and concepts which contribute toward a biblical anthropology, especially with regard to the issue of what it means to say that humans have a "soul."

Biblical Anthropology: a Review and Discussion

The Hebrew word *nephesh*, translated as "soul" or "life," is often coupled with other, more concrete words, especially with *basar* (flesh) and *lev*, *levav* (heart). The Hebrew has no distinct word for "body" as does the Greek (*soma*). *Nephesh* is often used in parallel with *basar* (flesh), never in contrast. The terms are not used as a natural contrast such as "body and soul," but are often virtually synonymous, being two ways of referring to the self in both its physical and non-physical existence. (Ray S. Anderson 1982:209, Hill 1984:100).

Ruach (spirit), unlike *basar* (flesh), is never used as a practical synonym for *nephesh*, but is frequently employed in contrast to the *nephesh*. Non-human creatures (animals) also were created as "living souls" (Genesis 1:20, 21, 24). The Bible even speaks of the "spirit" (*ruach*) of beasts (Ecclesiastes 3:21). Humans are differentiated from the animals not because they have "soul and spirit" (*nephesh* and *ruach*), but rather because of the special orientation of the human soul/spirit life in relation to God.

Whereas *nephesh* means "life," *ruach* means "vigorous life," or an inspired life. God will often take away the spirit from a person and give another spirit, for better or for worse (I Samuel 10:6, 16:13, 14). In particular, God will give his own spirit to a chosen person and even be asked to bestow it upon one who seeks it (Psalms 51:10–12).

Heart (*lev*) commonly signifies the seat of intelligence, cunning, good or wicked thoughts, pride, humility, joy, but never compassion, tenderness, or intense feeling. The Israelites expressed feeling through terms relating to the bowels, or entrails, not the heart. Consequently, when Jesus rebuked his disciples for hardness of heart, it was their lack of insight, or sheer stupidity, he referred to, not their callousness and lack of feeling. The heart is the center of the subjective self. It does not constitute a third dimension of the self alongside the body and soul, but is the core of the self as personal being.

When Moses directed that a census be taken of the Israelites (Exodus 30:11), it was the number of "souls" (*nephesh*) that was to be counted, never the number of spirits (*ruach*). More than one spirit can be within a person, but only one soul. While soul and spirit may be distinguished from one another (Hebrews 4:12), this is said to be a discernment made by the Word of God, not by human self-reflection.

Those whom Paul describes as "fleshly" (*sarkikos*) are also "soulish" (*psychikos*). Paul never used the body and the soul as contrasts for the spiritual and the unspiritual, or for the mortal and the immortal, as did the Greeks. Instead, he used these terms to designate qualities of life expressed through both the physical and non-physical life. "Spirit" and "spiritual" signify a divine quality of life, received as a gift from God and having a share in God's Spirit. "Flesh" and "carnal" do not signify merely a natural or physical quality of life but a corrupt, self-centered and mortal kind of life. It is not human nature that is the enemy of the spirit, but distortion or corruption of that human nature.

When we introduce the concept of "spirit," are we then committed to a three-fold division of the person into body, soul and spirit? This question was debated by early church theologians and the view that we are continues to be held by some today.

Those who hold to this three-part division are called "trichotomists," while those who view the human being as essentially "body and soul" are called "dichotomists." The early Church was confronted with these issues in the christological debate with Apollinaris of Laodocea in the fourth century. Influenced by Platonic dualism, which posited a gulf between the worlds of body and spirit (*nous*), Apollinaris became convinced that the soul performed the function of mediating between these two poles. The soul was thus not understood as either purely physical or mental. This trichotomist view was condemned at the Fourth Council of Constantinople in 869–79 CE.[1]

Despite this, some continue to hold to a three-fold division of the human self due to the New Testament use of these terms. Hebrews 4:12, for example, speaks of a "dividing of soul and spirit," and Paul prays for the preservation of "spirit and soul and body" (I Thessalonians 5:23). In other passages, however, soul and spirit are used as synonyms of the self as a unity. Luke records Mary's song as expressing this when she says, "My soul magnifies the Lord, and my spirit rejoices in God my Savior" (Luke 1:46–7). Here it is clear that there is a single subject which is expressed alike in the terms "soul" and "spirit" (Barth 1960).

While persons have "spirit" as the basis of their individual and personal spiritual life, theologian Karl Barth (1960:354) says that this does not constitute a "third entity" alongside body and soul. "Man has spirit, as one who is possessed by it. Although it belongs to the constitution of man, it is not, like soul and body and as a third thing alongside them, a moment of his constitution as such. It belongs to his constitution in so far as it is its superior, determining and limiting basis."

Scripture never says "soul" where only "spirit" can be meant, but it often says "spirit" where "soul" is meant. From this we can conclude that the constitution of a person as soul and body cannot be fully described without thinking first of the spirit as its essential core.

The human spirit is unique in its orientation of the body/soul unity toward God in a special relationship determined by God. The whole person is expressed in the spirit, since the spirit is the principle and power of life in its relation to God.

Theologian Helmut Thielicke (1984:446) says that the function of spirit as essential to the life and power of the person is consistently depicted in the Bible as that of a life force that issues out of the "heart," or the inner life of the person. One cannot cut away the life of the spirit as a "religious appendix" that serves no necessary function. "This means that the spirit must be distinguished from the soul or psyche, it must not be psychologically or psychopathologically derived from the psyche."

Spirituality, therefore, is at the core of our human nature as personal beings, endowed with spiritual life, expressed in a unity of body and soul. Spiritual self-identity, as used theologically and in biblical terms, is contingent upon the Spirit of God both as to its formation and as to its growth.

If a biblical anthropology is determinative for a Christian view of the human self, then a strict dualism between body and soul as well as a trichotomy between body, soul and spirit can be rejected. What is distinctive about human beings is not that they have a "soul" which animals do not possess, nor that they have a "spirit" which other creatures do not possess, but as "besouled body" and "embodied soul," the "spirit" of that existence is opened toward God in a unique way as the source of life. The whole of human life, body and soul, is thus oriented toward a destiny beyond mortal or natural life. It is this orientation which constitutes the spiritual life of the self. At the same time, this orientation is contingent upon a spiritual reality which is external to the self but which approaches, and summons a response from, the self. What interests the Bible, says Barth (1960:409), is a person's perception with regard to encounter and relation with God. It is this and not autonomous rationality, which marks humans off from the animals and the rest of creation.

The human "soul," as contrasted with the soulish life of animals, represents the whole person as a physical, personal and spiritual being, especially the inner core of an individual's life as created and upheld by God. The uniqueness of human persons as contrasted with non-human creatures is solely due to the encounter, relation, and destiny of humans contingent upon relation with the Spirit of God as the source of earthly life and the possibility of eternal life.

In continuing to use the word "soul" as referring to this inner core of the self, theological anthropology refers to the personal and spiritual dimension of the person. Soul is the life of the person, says Barth (1960:370). "To call man [sic] 'soul' is simply to say in the first place that he is the life which is essentially necessary for his body." Thus, the phrase "body and soul" is not intended to suggest that the soul is something which is merely "in" the body, or separate from the body, but the whole person with both an interior and an exterior life in the world.

The role of theological anthropology is to speak to the deeper yearnings and struggles of human existence as much as to bring to those existential human concerns a Word from God. Despite the ambiguity of the biblical terms which refer to a human soul or spirit, an indissoluble core of meaning persists in the biblical material, which points to the inner core of the whole person, including the body. It is in this sense that theological anthropology speaks of the "soul" as referring to the entirety of the self as personal, spiritual being.

How do we acquire a soul?

How does each newborn infant acquire a human soul as opposed to a merely creaturely soul? Medieval theologians alternated between two views on this question. "Traducionists" held that the soul originated in the act of conception. A "soul seed" (in contrast to a "body seed") detached from the soul of the parents to become the independent soul of the child. "Creationists," on the other hand, held that each person's "soul" was implanted at the moment of conception by a divine act, an immediate creation *ex nihilo* (Ray S. Anderson 1982:42f). Through the sexual act, the parents create the proper physiological conditions for the existence of a human being, but they are only secondary agents in the process. Regarding this debate, Barth (1960:573) has suggested that none of these theories lead us one step forward with regard to the origin of the human.

The most that we can say is that a human person begins as any other creature, in a biological process which entails fertilization and cell division. However, even in that process, the resulting life form carries the form of the human, even in its prenatal stage. Once conceived in a human womb, the embryo is essentially human, dependent only upon sufficient bio-chemical support to come to birth as a human person. At the same time, biological life is a necessary but insufficient condition to be human. The human self is contingent upon something more than biological life (*bios*) in order to have vital human life (*zoe*). In the New Testament, *zoe* refers to a person's life made abundantly full, and this life is inseparable from Jesus Christ as the source of life (cf. John 10:10; I Timothy 6:11, 12, 19).

From this brief discussion we can conclude that the biblical terms soul and spirit are primarily functional rather than denoting discrete substances or entities. As such, while there are some distinctive patterns of use, the words used by the Bible to denote aspects of human life are not analytical and precise in a philosophical or semantic sense. Nonetheless, without the use of the word "soul" as a deep metaphor of that which makes each human life personal and unique, we would lose semantic contact with the essence of what it is to be a person created in the divine image and likeness.

Is the soul immortal?

The word "soul" (*nephesh*) is never used to refer to something external to a person. The "soul" refers to either the whole person, or some aspect of the person, such as what we would call thoughts, feelings, energy, spirituality, the subjective viewpoint, mind, personality, psychology, or breath. The soul could never exist outside of a person. Death affects the soul as well as the body, says Barth (1960:370). "The ostensibly all-powerful soul becomes completely impotent in death because it becomes bodiless."

When the Bible says that a person's soul departed, it could be translated as "the person's life departed," or "she died" (Genesis 35:18).

The Old Testament theologian Hans Walter Wolff (1974:20) says that the soul (*nephesh*) of a person is "never given the meaning of an indestructible core of being, in contradistinction to the physical life, and even capable of living when cut off from that life." Where there is mention of a "departing" of the soul from a person (Genesis 35:18), or its "return" (Lamentations 1:11), the basic idea is that of a ceasing or restoration of breathing.

The concept of an immortal soul is thus without clear biblical support. The saying of Jesus in Matthew 10:28 should not be construed as teaching the immortality of the soul: "Do not fear those who kill the body but cannot kill the soul; rather fear him who can destroy both soul and body in hell." This does not say that the soul cannot be killed, Barth reminds us, "but only that no man can kill it, while God has the power to cause both soul and body to pass away and be destroyed in the nether world. Hence we do not have here a doctrine of the immortality of the soul" (1960:379).

Humans are not described in Scripture as having a different earthly origin than animals, but as having their origination, as *human* creatures, qualitatively marked off from that of non-human creatures by the endowment of the divine image.

The Image and Likeness of God

In the biblical account of creation it is a personal relation with God that distinguishes the human from all other creatures. As such, humans are endowed with a unique quality of personhood as the primary content of the "image and likeness of God" (Genesis 1:26–7, 5:1, 9:6).[2]

While the references to this divine image and likeness are rare in the Bible, the theme runs throughout Scripture (cf. Psalm 8:5; Hebrews 2:5–9). Humans are of "more value" than earth creatures (Matthew 6:26, 10:31, 12:9–12; Luke 12:24), and are the object of God's special concern (Hebrews 2:14–18).[3]

The image and likeness of God (Genesis 1:26–7) can be understood as a capacity for relationship with the self, others, and God in a knowing way, and an openness to a future which provides hope and meaning to life (Ray S. Anderson 1982:215–26; see also Saucy 1993:17–52). The physical body itself is not held to be in the image of God, such that God has some aspect corresponding to the physical body of humans. Human beings as "embodied souls" and "besouled bodies" are in the image of God as upheld by the Spirit of God which attends and summons forth the human spirit (Barth 1960:350ff).

In the second creation account the divine image is not possessed by the single individual: "it is not good that the man should be alone" (Genesis 2:18). Only when the man and the woman exist as complementary forms of human being is there a sense of completeness: "This at last is bone of my bones and flesh of my flesh" (Genesis 2:23). From this passage, some contemporary theologians view this image and likeness more in relational terms than as a static attribute or rational/spiritual capacity. It is in relationship with other persons as well as with God that the divine image is expressed (Berkouwer 1962:8ff, 179, Barth 1960:196). This "ecological" relation between the physical and the non-physical aspects of the human self, and of one human with another, is positively determined by this divine endowment and is subject to disorder and destructiveness when humans fall out of God's grace through sin.

The effect of sin on the image

In the biblical account, the original humans are depicted as being in a state of innocence, under divine command and preservation, though subject to temptation. Sin emerged as an act of self-determination in disobedience to the divine command (Genesis 3). The holistic and relational nature of the soul/body unity as depicted in Scripture is also reflected in the effects of sin.

The effects of sin produced disunity and disorder at the physical, social, psychological, and spiritual core of human life such that the original unity of personal well being as embodied soul and besouled body became disrupted and subject to dissolution and death. The image of God as social, spiritual and moral health was corrupted and became the source of pride, jealousy, hatred, and violence against others. The ecology of human life in terms of relationship with the earth, with other humans, and with God was thrown out of balance so that injustice, oppression, poverty, and war permeated all of human society.

The theological concept of a "fall from grace" as the source of human disorder, disease, violence, and death, is first of all a fatal spiritual "death" which affected every aspect of human life. As a result, humans experience shame, confusion, guilt, and alienation from God as well as distrust of each other. Physical death, while not occurring instantly as a result of sin, became an inevitable consequence of the spiritual separation from God, as both body and soul have no immortality apart from the Spirit of God. Sin did not result in the loss of immortality as an intrinsic characteristic of the soul, but rather, made the human as a body/soul unity subject to the natural mortality of creaturely life.[4]

A Christian view of the human is rooted in this biblical portrayal of the origin and destiny of persons as bearing the divine image, as objects of divine love and grace, and of infinite value, despite the inveterate tendencies toward evil and violence found in every culture. The solidarity of all persons as bound together in a common humanity despite differences of race, religion, sexual orientation, and culture is a concept derived out of the New Testament construct of the Adam–Christ relation. For the Apostle Paul, the figure of Adam stands as the bond of all humanity in a common origin and a common fate. But this is not a universal principle accessible to general knowledge. It is only through the person of Jesus Christ that Paul can say that "even as one man's trespass led to condemnation for all men, so one man's act of righteousness leads to acquittal and life for all men" (Romans 5:18).

Paul attributes cosmic and anthropological significance to the incarnation of God in the person of Jesus, "descended from David according to the flesh and designated Son of God in power according to the Spirit of holiness by his resurrection from the dead" (Romans 1:3). Paul's vision of humanity is first of all through Christ and then back to Adam. In the relation of Christ to Adam, all humans are bound into a solidarity of life under God's election and promise, and thus all are bound up in the solidarity of sin. Sin is not attributable to biological, racial, or cultural forms of humanity. Rather, sin is a disruption of the core social paradigm for humanity found in every race, culture, and nation. Because the consequence of sin is death, it is death that is the basic human dilemma, not merely sin. Thus Paul says, "If, because of one man's trespass, death reigned through that one man, much more will those who receive the abundance of grace and the free gift of righteousness reign in life through the one man Jesus Christ" (Romans 5:17). True humanity is now found in Christ who has conquered death, so that all humans who die because of Adam's sin can now find their humanity restored in being related to Christ.

In a theological anthropology, human nature is not defined ultimately by tracing back humanity to its origin, nor by explaining humanity in terms of its existence under the conditions of sin. Rather, human nature is creaturely life experienced as personal, social, sexual, and spiritual life under divine determination, judgment, and promise. In a theological anthropology, sin is understood as a failure to live humanly in every area of social, personal, sexual, and spiritual life. Therefore, salvation from sin is also to be experienced as the recovery of true humanity in each of these aspects of life. The tendency of some to view salvation as "saving souls" without regard to the total life of the person as a physical, social, and psychological being is more of a Greek concept than a Christian one. From the perspective of theological anthropology, salvation touches each area of a person's embodied life, though not with equal effect short of the resurrection of the body.

The Concept of Self

The concept of the self in modern philosophy can be traced back as far as Descartes (1596–1650), who introduced the concept of the self as a spiritual substance. Locke (1632–1704) disputed this concept of Descartes's and suggested that the existence of the self depends on consciousness of oneself continuing in the present the same as in the past. This self is the seat of personal identity as distinct from the soul or spiritual substance. Hume (1711–76) found it impossible to intuit a permanent self by an analysis of consciousness. The self only had subjective validity as an inference drawn from experience, though he admitted that the self was always more than the experience of the self at any one time. Kant (1724–1804) restricted the status of the self to the phenomenal realm of experience. where the self is something which persons are called upon to realize and bring into existence through response to duty and freedom. In this conscious ethical action, the true self comes to know itself. Fichte (1762–1814), followed by Hegel (1770–1831), developed an ideal concept of the self through a dialectical process by which an absolute subject emerges which guarantees the unity of the self in the face of the antithetical principles of existence. William James (1842–1910) suggested a psychological approach to the self as the functional center of the person who is known by others as this person, and thus who knows himself or herself through these many "social selves." Psychology, concluded James, has little use for a concept of the self as an entity.

Modern psychology at first tended to reject a concept of the self as inaccessible to empirical study and thus not formalizable in psychological theories. The banishment of the self was most pronounced in the work of Skinner (1953) and the development of behaviorism. At the same time, in the more recent work in the neo-Freudian analytic school of ego psychology represented by the British object-relations psychology, there is renewed interest in the self (Guntrip 1971). This is also true in the so-called third-force psychologies: humanistic psychology, existential psychology, and phenomenology. In these movements the self is considered not only as driven by urges or outside stimuli, but moved by meanings and values.

Social psychologists gave attention to self-conception variables in their theories about interpersonal attraction and conformity behaviors, but with little concern for the concept of a self lying behind the socially formed identity of the person. Theorists and researchers have thus far considered the self almost entirely as a phenomenon of self-consciousness. Rogers (1961) was one of the first clinicians to attempt extensive research on self-conceptions and described the self as an organized con-figuration of perceptions which are admissible to awareness. While there is continued interest in the phenomenon of the self in both philosophical and psychological literature, there is little agreement as to the existence of a self beyond the variables of self-perception.

Moral philosophers and ethicists are generally committed to the concept of a self that has continuity over time as a basis for attributing moral responsibility. Many assert that it is illogical to hold a person morally responsible for an act unless that act is freely performed by the person. In this respect, Kant at least provided a basis for considering the self as a moral agent accountable to the categorical imperative of willing the good as an ethical duty for all persons in all situations. Macmurray (1957) argued that self-hood is derivative of personal agency in positive interaction with other persons.

The being of the self thus precedes its "self-identity" as a psychologically conditioned aspect. Theologically, one might say that the image of God as constitutive of the self is more than the "religious" aspect of the self. It is the entire self, both in its being and in its becoming.

Biblical views of the self

The Bible rarely uses the word "self" in the sense of self–life. In the New Testament, the major instance is the phrase "deny yourself" (Matthew 16:24; Mark 8:34; Luke 9:23). These three passages refer to the same incident, in which Jesus reminds his disciples that, like him in his own devotion to the service of God, they too must be willing to turn away from the kind of self-preoccupation that leads to loss of life, but invest themselves in daily commitment to God's sovereign will and thus "gain their life." The "old self" (Romans 6:6; sometimes called "flesh" by Paul, Romans 7:18) is devoted to self-interest, while the "new self" (Ephesians 4:24; Colossians 3:10; sometimes spoken of as being "raised with Christ," Ephesians 2:5–6) is devoted to self-fulfillment and realization of one's deepest longings and eternal joy through the indwelling Holy Spirit. In the vocabulary of the New Testament, "self" can mean negatively the egocentric self–life, but it can also mean positively the person's soul or spirit, which is of inestimable value both to God and, therefore, to oneself (Clark 1990:309–17). We are to love God with all of our heart, soul, strength, and mind, and "our neighbor as ourselves" (Matthew 22:39).

Christian faith requires the concept of the self in much the same way as does moral philosophy. God is viewed as the judge of all humankind, who holds persons responsible for their actions. The continued identity of the self as originally created by God, fallen into sin, restored through divine forgiveness based on the atonement of Christ, and destined to inherit eternal life through resurrection, is essential to Christian faith. Created in the image of God, who is considered to be the quintessence of personal being, humans are held to be inherently personal. Violation of this personal being unique to each individual carries with it severe consequences in the biblical literature (cf. Genesis 9:6; Matthew 18:6).

The continuity of self-identity through death and resurrection

"If mortals die, will they live again?" is a question older than Job (14:14), but asked by every new generation. Not content with vague, impersonal generalities, Job persisted: "After my skin has been thus destroyed, then in my flesh I shall see God . . . and my eyes shall behold, and not another" (19:27).

The concept of resurrection may not have been clear in the mind of Job, but he clearly expresses the desire that his very own self (soul) would survive the destruction of his flesh so that he, in his body, should stand before God. It is his own self-identity – and *not another* – that must survive, not merely as an extension of his present life, but that he could finally confront God. It was not death itself that tormented Job, but the loss of God's presence and affirmation.

The majority of persons who believe in some form of life after death assume the existence of some form of a non-physical personal entity that survives, whether it is called soul or spirit. Biblical revelation supports the belief that personal self-identity continues after death, but that this is solely due to God's sovereign determination, not due to an immortal soul or mind residing in the human person. What is at stake is not only the belief that there is life after death, but whether or not that life is due to something resident in human nature or whether it is due to God's power and Spirit. The Bible views death as the end of human life in its totality, except for the sovereign power and determination of God; only through the death and resurrection of Jesus Christ do we have assurance of our own resurrection and continuing identity following death.

We must admit that the Bible does not provide an answer as to how personal self-identity continues through the death and resurrection process in such a way that it is the very *same* person who dies with a corruptible body and is raised with an incorruptible body, as Paul seems to indicate is the case. Paul's argument in I Corinthians 15 rests on the fact that the same Christ who died was raised again; and if this is true, then those who die "in Christ" will also be raised. The testimony of the disciples to the fact that it was the same Jesus that died who presented himself to them alive supports Paul's argument, even though he probably only had access to this information through their oral report. The written report which came after Paul's death confirms this truth (cf. John 20:19–29).

Where Scripture does affirm the stability and continuity of the self through death and resurrection, the basis is not the existence of an indestructible soul but the guarantee of the Spirit of God (II Corinthians 5:5). The assurance that self-identity will survive death is not based on some non-physical aspect of the person but on the bond between the risen Jesus Christ and the believer through the Holy Spirit. "If the Spirit of him who raised Jesus from the dead dwells in you, he who raised Christ from the dead will give life to your mortal bodies also through his Spirit that dwells in you" (Romans 8:11; cf. I Thessalonians 4:13–15).

Ethical Issues

Critical ethical issues relating to conception as well as to termination of life are first of all questions as to what constitutes human life. A theological anthropology is the underlying moral basis for ethical rules for living and dying. We are to "love our neighbors as ourselves" (Matthew 22:39). The unborn, though not yet persons in the full sense, are "neighbors" in the human sense and thus can claim a moral demand upon the living for the preservation of their life within the limits of human possibility. Physical life has intrinsic and relative value as possibility, though it does not constitute an absolute value. The absolute value of human life is upheld by God through the frailties, torments, and trauma of life on this earth.

Even as it could be a violation of the value of human life to be forced to live merely at the biological level, so it would be a violation of the value of human life to be forced to live in a role structure (economic, social, or political) which has as a consequence the deprivation of life as a gift, to be with and for the other in a relationship of parity and reciprocity. "Human rights" are thus grounded in the ecological construct of humanity itself, not in an abstract principle mediated through self-determination; the other person has a right to my responsible action in upholding her own humanity, but not the right to kill me for failing in this responsibility. The "right" to be free from a person or persons who diminish my own quality of life is qualified by my need of persons to uphold the gift of life which constitutes my humanity.

A theological anthropology is the positive moral basis for the liberation of human sexuality from degradation, oppression, and exploitation; in Christ, "there is neither Jew nor Greek, slave nor free, male nor female," for in Christ all are one (Galatians 3:28). Human personhood is male and female, male or female, equally and mutually human, a polarity and community of personal being manifest through biological sexual differentiation, but under the promise of freedom from such limitations through life beyond death.

Because our humanity is under divine determination, judgment, and redemption – from Adam to Christ – a Christian vision of the human is liberating, hopeful, and therapeutic. In life beyond death through the new humanity of Jesus Christ, there will no longer be "mourning, nor crying, nor pain" (Revelations 21:4). The final vision of humanity is more human than human imagination or experience can picture.

Notes

1 For a discussion of the history of doctrine with regard to the trichotomy and dichotomy controversy, see Barth (1960:355).
2 "For Man to be created in the likeness of God's image can only mean that on him, too, personhood is bestowed as the definitive characteristic of his nature. . . . This quality of personhood shapes the totality of his psycho-physical existence; it is this which comprises the essentially human, and distinguishes him from all other creatures" (W. Eichrodt 1975:126).
3 Eichrodt reflects on Psalm 8:4 as follows:"Ultimately therefore it is a spiritual factor which determines the value Man sets upon himself, namely his consciousness of partnership with God, a privilege of which no other creation is considered worthy" (Eichrodt 1975:120–1).
4 For a discussion of the concept of human mortality see my book, *Theology, Death and Dying* (Oxford: Basil Blackwell, 1986), pp. 37–63.

References

Anderson, H. 1994. "The Recovery of Soul," in *The Treasure of Earthen Vessels – Explorations in Theological Anthropology*, eds. B. H. Childs and D. W. Waanders. Louisville, KY: Westminster/John Knox Press, pp. 208–23.

Anderson, Ray S. 1982. *On Being Human: Essays in Theological Anthropology*. Grand Rapids, MI: Eerdmans.

Anderson, Ray S. 1995. *Self Care: A Theology of Personal Wholeness and Spiritual Healing*. Wheaton: Victor Books.

Anderson, Ray S. 1998. "On Being Human: the Spiritual Saga of a Creaturely Soul," in *Whatever Became of the Soul? Theological and Scientific Portraits of Human Nature*, ed. Nancey Murphy and Warren Brown. Minneapolis, MN: Fortress Press.

Ashbrook, J. 1991. "Soul: its Meaning and its Making," *Journal of Pastoral Care* 45 (2) Summer: 159–68.

Barth, K. 1959. *Church Dogmatics*, vol. III, part 1. Edinburgh: T. & T. Clark.

Barth, K. 1960. *Church Dogmatics*, vol. III, part 2. Edinburgh: T. & T. Clark.

Becker, E. 1973. *The Denial of Death*. New York: Macmillan, Free Press.

Berkouwer, G. C. 1962. *Man: The Image of God*. Grand Rapids, MI: Eerdmans.

Bonhoeffer, D. 1963. *The Communion of Saints*. New York: Harper and Row.

Brunner, E. 1975. *Man in Revolt*. Philadelphia, PA: Westminster Press.

Bube, R. 1972. "Other Options?" *Journal of the American Scientific Affiliation* 24 (March).

Capps, D. 1994. "The Soul as the 'Coreness' of the Self," in *The Treasure of Earthen Vessels: Explorations in Theological Anthropology*, eds. B. H. Childs and D. W. Waanders. Louisville, KY: Westminster/John Knox Press, pp. 82–104.

Castell, A. 1957. *The Self in Philosophy*. New York: Macmillan.

Clark, D. K. 1990. "Interpreting the Biblical Words for the Self," *Journal of Psychology and Theology* 18 (4), La Mirada, CA, pp. 309–17.

Cooper, J. W. 1989. *Body, Soul, & Life Everlasting: Biblical Anthropology and the Monism–Dualism Debate*. Grand Rapids, MI: Eerdmans.

Corrington, R. S. 1986. *Nature's Self: Our Journey from Origin to Spirit*. Lanham, MD: Rowman and Littlefield.

Eichrodt, W. 1975. *Theology of the Old Testament*, vol. 2. Philadelphia, PA: Westminster Press.

Elmore, V. O. 1986. *Man as God's Creation*. Nashville, TN: Broadman Press.

Farley, E. 1984. "Toward a Contemporary Theology of Human Being," in *Images of Man*, eds. J. William Angell and E. Pendleton Banks. Macon, GA: Mercer University Press.

Fichtner, J. 1978. *Man the Image of God: A Christian Anthropology*. New York: Alba House.

Gorman, M. 1967. "The Self," in *New Catholic Encyclopedia*, vol. XIII. San Francisco, CA: Catholic University of America Press, 1967.

Guntrip, H. 1971. *Psychoanalytic Theory, Therapy, and the Self*. New York: Basic Books.

Hill, E. 1984. *Being Human: A Biblical Perspective*. London: Geoffrey Chapman.

James, W. 1890. *Principles of Psychology*, vol. 1. New York: Holt.

Jewett, P. K. 1975. *Man as Male and Female*. Grand Rapids, MI: Eerdmans.

Laver, E. and Mlecko, J. eds. 1982. *A Christian Understanding of the Human Person: Basic Readings*. New York: Paulist Press.

Lee, B. ed. 1982. *Psychological Theories of the Self*. New York and London: Plenum Press.

McFadyen, A. I. 1990. *The Call to Personhood: A Christian Theory of the Individual in Social Relationships*. Cambridge: Cambridge University Press.

Macmurray, J. 1957. *The Self as Agent*. London: Faber and Faber.

Macquarrie, J. 1983. *In Search of Humanity: A Theological and Philosophical Approach*. New York: Crossroad.

Moltmann, J. 1974. *Man: Christian Anthropology in the Conflicts of the Present*. Philadelphia, PA: Fortress Press.

Moltmann, J. 1985. *God in Creation: A New Theology of Creation and the Spirit of God*. San Francisco, CA: Harper and Row.

Moore, T. 1992. *Care of the Soul: A Guide for Cultivating Depth and Sacredness in Everyday Life*. New York: Harper Collins.

Pannenberg, W. 1985. *Anthropology in Theological Perspective*, trans. Matthew J. O'Connell. Philadelphia, PA: Westminster Press.

Porteous, N. W. 1962. "The Nature of Man in the Old Testament," in *The Interpreter's Dictionary of the Bible*, vol. III, ed. G. A. Buttrick. New York: Abingdon Press.

Reichmann, J. B., SJ. 1985. *Philosophy of the Human Person*. Chicago, IL: Loyola University Press.

Rogers, C. 1961. *On Becoming a Person*. Boston, MA: Houghton Mifflin.

Saucy, R. L. 1993. "Theology of Human Nature," in *Christian Perspectives on Being Human: A Multidisciplinary Approach to Integration*, eds. J. P. Moreland and D. M. Ciocchi. Grand Rapids, MI: Baker Book House, pp. 17–52.

Skinner, B. F. 1953. *Science and Human Behavior*. New York: Macmillan.

Suls, J. ed. 1982. *Psychological Perspectives on the Self*, vol. 1. Hillsdale, NJ: Lawrence Erlbaum.

Thielicke, H. 1984. *Being Human . . . Becoming Human*. New York: Doubleday.

Torrance, T. F. 1985. *Theology and Science at the Frontiers of Knowledge*. Edinburgh: Scottish Academic Press.

Wolff, H. W. 1974. *Anthropology of the Old Testament*. Philadelphia, PA: Fortress Press.

CHAPTER 7

History

William Dean

In Western thought there are two principal theories of history, which I will call "the witness theory of history" and "the participant theory of history." The first makes the historian an observer of the past, and the second makes the historian an improviser on the past, who not only observes but creatively shapes the past.

They focus on history, not on some ideal world beyond history. They refer to contingent, unrepeatable, spatial, and temporal events in order to explain why societies and their meanings change, rather than to eternal things to explain why societies should become what they ideally are.

When the witness and participant theories of history turn to religion, they both see religion as historical and claim that God is known primarily in the events of history.

The choices between the witness and participant theories of history have greatly affected the development of religion in the West. The witness theory has prevailed (at least in Christianity), but the participant theory of history, like a dog at the heels, has continued to challenge the witness theory.

I will comment informally on the unfolding story of the contrast between these two theories as it anticipated and then guided the history of Christianity; but initially, I should warn that my discussion is limited. I leave out rationalistic and mystical accounts of religion, on the grounds that – no matter how popular they are today – they refer primarily to permanent ideals located beyond historical flux, and thus do not belong in a discussion of theories of history. When I discuss history I discuss what it has meant to various *civilizations* (Hebrew, classical, modern, postmodern), rather than to what it has meant to individuals. I accept the Dutch historian Johan Huizinga's definition of history as "the intellectual form in which a civilization renders account to itself of its past" (Huizinga 1963:9). Also, I discuss *theories* of history, people's ideas of the nature and consequences of historical change. I include enough historical evidence to define and relate those theories, but not enough to justify either theory.[1]

The Witness Theory of History and the Participant Theory of History

According to the witness theory of history, the person who is a religious historian and a believer is a witness, a person who receives historical evidence and religious truth. First, as historian, he or she examines rigorously and judiciously a body of historical evidence. Secondly, as a believer, he or she sees that evidence as a metaphor for spiritual realities that lie beyond history, including the God who lies beyond history. The obligation of the historian and the believer is to be a good witness to how changes in historical evidence explain changes in the knowledge of spiritual realities.

According to the participant theory of history, the historian and believer is not only a recipient of historical evidence and its truths but also a participant, a person who actively shapes, or interprets, historical evidence and religious truth. The historian attempts to be not only passive but also active, particularly when making judgments about history. The believer unapologetically intervenes in historical events, revising the past to make it more responsive to present religious needs.

The differences between these two theories of history should not be exaggerated. To be a witness of history is not to be an indifferent spectator of history, but to resonate personally with the truths as they speak through the evidence. Also, witnesses of history are never so passive that they escape entirely the need actively to interpret history in ways it has never before been interpreted. To be a participant in history is not to make history whatever one wants it to be, but to recognize that the past permits only some, not any, interpretations, and that to step beyond the bounds of what the evidence permits is to turn history into fantasy.

The two theories have different origins and outcomes. The witness theory of history can be traced at least to the Greeks, perhaps beyond the Greeks. It is exemplified by some classical Greek thinkers, especially historians, but not by Greeks such as Homer, for whom history is more about myths than about actual events. The witness theory has shaped fifteen hundred years of classical theology and has led to the modern academic discipline of history. The participant theory of history can be traced to the authors of the Hebrew Bible. It has been neglected, at least until recently, by historians and theologians; but many people who are not scholars have favored it, as though intuitively. It appears to be newly viable in the academic world, especially for post-modern scholars.

It is tempting to tag these two kinds of history: "History for the Hellenes" and "History for the Hebrews."[2] Taken too seriously, the tags could encourage people to make all Greeks alike and all Hebrews alike, setting up a simple-minded distinction between Athens and Jerusalem. But, reckless as they are, these labels properly personalize the rivalry between the two theories and suggest why the theories thrive in some periods and not in others. The witness theory is properly associated with the rationalistic side of the classical Greek character, and thrives in times when people are confident enough to believe they can understand history, perhaps even objectively, if they just listen critically. The participant theory of history is properly associated with the Hebrew preference for the concrete and the avoidance of the abstract, and thrives in times when people have diminished confidence in their rational abilities and believe that the meaning of history is uncertain, as it is for many today.

History for the Hellenes and History for the Hebrews

For Herodotus (484–424 BCE) and Thucydides (460–399 BCE) history was, more than anything else, a body of evidence about the past, and the purpose of the historians was to help others to use that evidence. To witness to this evidence was not to be totally passive, but to be active enough to discover what is objectively the case. Herodotus wrote, he said, so "that men's actions may not in time be forgotten nor things great and wonderful, accomplished whether by Greeks or barbarians, go without report" (1958, vol. 1:1). Thucydides disparaged "the vulgar," who are careless "in the investigation of truth, accepting readily the first story that comes to hand." He, however, could "rest satisfied with having proceeded upon the clearest data, and having arrived at conclusions as exact as can be expected in matters of such antiquity" (1959:230). Admittedly, both Herodotus and Thucydides mixed their witness with strong interpretations; in their histories both consistently favored the Greeks; Herodotus included legends he knew were apocryphal; and Thucydides invented speeches for his long-dead heroes. Nevertheless, their high seriousness about memory and objectivity makes them witnessing historians.

For the Hebrew historians – the writers of the Pentateuch, the histories, and the prophetic literature – history was not primarily a body of evidence, but was an interaction, a creative interaction in which both they and their God participated. They assumed that God decided how to address the Israelites in particular times and places, and they assumed that their own reading of God's largely mysterious will was more like a construction than a rational inquiry seeking the objective truth. Although never making the point abstractly, they seem, nevertheless, to have assumed that both God and the believer participated in the continuous making and re-making of the truth.

Because the Greek historians tended to believe that they must weigh conflicting interpretations, seek the most reliable account, respect accuracy, and aspire even to objectivity, they can be credited with having introduced what became the modern academic standards for writing history.

Like the Greeks, the Hebrew historians were anxious to get history right; they worried, for example, that they might be misled by false prophets. But they were not preoccupied with technical criteria for determining what was the most reliable account of an event. They were more interested in the religious attentiveness of the historian and they allowed conflicting accounts to stand unevaluated and side by side in their scriptures – something that would astound most modern historians.

The Greeks, said Arnaldo Momigliano, "liked history, but never made it the foundation of their lives." The Greek historians' inquiry could be dispassionate partly because it did not determine the meaning of their lives. They found their religious meanings in rhetorical schools, mystery cults, or philosophies, none of which depended directly on historical evidence. Plato, for example, believed that the search for truth had to begin in history, but that history itself contained nothing fundamentally important. History was little more than a window to truths on the other side of history, to universal truths unaffected by time and place and circumstance; whereas for the Hebrews, Momigliano says, "history and religion were one" (Momigliano 1990:20). The divine lived in, not beyond, history. History told of a people's spiritual and physical negotiations with the divine and of how people's spiritual and physical existence depended on these negotiations.

Because what was most important was manifest only in history, narratives were important for both Greek and Hebrew historians. Because they are chronological, narratives can represent temporal activities the way pure ideas, which characteristically represent non-temporal things, cannot. But for the Greeks the narrative tended to be a metaphor referring to a non-narrative reality behind history. For the Hebrews the narrative was not a metaphor for truths beyond history, but a representation of historical realities themselves. For the Hebrews, history is as deep as it gets; it is history all the way down.

The sequels to these ancient beginnings of historiography are confusing. By the middle of the fourth century BCE, the Jews began to lose interest in writing history and in finding meaning within historical process. They based their religious lives on the historical Torah, but made its meaning as fixed as the Greeks' eternal truths. The witness theory of history was adopted by the Romans, sustained at a theoretical level by the Christian ecclesiastical historians and theologians, and then brought into the modern era, where it remained the standard way to understand history. Nevertheless, popular Judaism and Christianity kept alive a participant theory of history, and that theory is now seriously challenging the witness theory of history.

The Participant Theory of History and the Ancient Hebrews

For the early Hebrews, the truth about God was known in traditions, and traditions were shaped in history. The Hebrews saw tradition as an expression of God's will in the past, but it was not frozen, forever the same. Clearly, tradition was not truth in its own right, but an instrument for understanding how God's will addressed problems in Israel's history. But as Israel's problems changed, so did God's will. Thus, tradition expressed God's changing will for past and, finally, even for present situations. But for tradition to speak to the present, it had to be reconstructed, and this reconstruction required the participation of the historian.

Thus, the Hebrews emphasized changes in God's will and they emphasized the believer's role in those changes. This emphasis on the change in God's will and on the believer's contribution to that change was unmatched by anything in the Greek world. The difference between the Hebrew emphasis on change and the Greek lack of emphasis may have arisen because the Hebrew world was theologically different from the Greek world. The Hebrews believed in one God, not many, and for this same God to address new problems, it had to speak or be heard in new ways. Getting new truth from the same God was less of an issue for the Greeks, who had many Gods, able to address in more or less typical and consistent ways a variety of problems. The Hebrews had no choice but to make the will of God historical (or situation-specific) and to make their interpretation of that will different in each new situation.

This emphasis on change and interpretation can be illustrated by a look at the changing meanings of the Torah (the law of the Hebrews, given in the Pentateuch, the first five books of the Christian Old Testament and the Hebrew Bible). Old Testament historian Martin Noth argues that Pentateuchal law did not express the fixed will of a fixed God, but the will of God for a particular situation. That law was affected, for example, by the new political and social situation at the time of the settlement in the land of Canaan. Also, Hebrew settlers constructively shaped their Covenant with God, distinguishing their religious life from that of the surrounding Canaanites. It is not an exaggeration to say that the settlers and their God conspired to create laws and that, later, the law, as part of the settled past, went on to create in new ways their own creators (God and the Hebrews). Thus, Noth argues that originally the laws were not absolute, but relative to particular historical situations. They "presupposed a particular state of affairs, as laws normally do in human history," he said (Noth 1966:104). Similarly, Gerhard von Rad has argued that each generation was presented with a new historical situation and "with the ever-identical and yet ever-new task of understanding itself as Israel." Israel allowed its literature, in a kind of "law of theological dialectic," to add strangely contradictory accounts of its past. At each juncture, von Rad said, Israel acted largely in continuity, but also partly in discontinuity with its past (von Rad 1962, vol. 1: v, vi, 119).

However, as the Bible grew, the laws moved from being situation-specific, or "historical," to becoming non-historical. In the post-exilic period, the laws became simply "the law," no longer community- or situation-responsive, but fixed and eternal. Now, says Noth, " 'The law' became an *absolute entity*, valid without respect to precedent, time or history; based on itself, binding simply because it existed as law, because it was of divine origin and authority" (Noth 1966:86; italics are Noth's). Or, as Momigliano says, the law became "the Torah," and for Hellenistic Jews, "There is no earlier and no later in the Torah" (Momigliano 1990:23). The laws arose from history but they became fixed metaphors for a God whose will had become, in effect, independent of history.

Whereas earlier, Douglas Knight said, Israel's "tradition process" presupposed that not only Israel's law but its general religious meanings were revised to fit new social situations, and that the people played an indispensable role in that revision, Knight gets at the participatory, tradition-creating process by connecting changes in religious tradition to changes in the revelation of God. First, past tradition provides the framework in terms of which past revelation is understood and present revelation can occur. Secondly, because traditions fit specific situations and because situations are constantly changing, new renditions of the tradition must be made, and, thus, new revelations occur. Thirdly, the new revelations are channeled to the future by a continuity among traditions through time. Of course, none of this implies that revelation is "progressive." (What would progress mean, how would it be even measured, without some fixed standard of meaning, which the tradition process itself makes impossible?) But Knight says that, while not progressive, the tradition process, nevertheless, "creates new meaning" (Knight 1977:169).

Thus, the Hebrews took their religious identity, not from beyond history, but from within history. It was history that provided both the old traditions and the new, incongruous situations that required new interpretations leading to revised traditions. The new interpretations also were contingent and decisional – in effect, historical. Past revelations were always outrun; new traditions gave new knowledge of God; and, for these reasons, the God of the future was necessarily unknown.

This traditioning process was sustained, at least partially, in the activities of Jesus and in the early Church. The Jews lived under the domination of the Roman Empire, hoped for the restoration of a political kingdom or the arrival of an eschatological kingdom, and yearned for a viable faith appropriate to these new expectations. Once again, the historical context provided new questions that for some were answered by Jesus as the Christ.

History for the Hebrews can be characterized as a participant theory of history. The person who is historian and believer, the situation, and God conspired together so that old traditions and truths could be revised to answer new problems. None of this is to deny that history has structure, unity or aims, but it affirms that they arise in and are altered as a result of historical participation. Even God is seen as a historical partici-pant, one who makes promises, fulfills promises, reacts in anger, and makes judgments, working within continuities of tradition and breaking continuities of tradition.

To overlook the importance of this historical process, particularly in the modern era, is, von Rad caustically suggests, just what can be expected from the "high-handed methods of pneumatic theology" (von Rad 1955:3) – theology that witnesses to spiri-tual or ideal truths rather than participates fully in ever-changing historical events and meanings.

The Witness Theory of History and Classical Christian Theology

Basing their work only partly on the Old Testament, the third- and fourth-century founders of Christian historiography introduced the leading edge of just that "pneu-matic theology." While history was the study of evidence of historical events, this evi-dence was seen as a metaphor, not for the events of history but for realities located beyond history. As a historian, one witnessed to that evidence, and as a believer, one witnessed to its metaphorical meaning.

Eusebius of Caesarea (265–339 or 340 CE), who founded Christian ecclesiastical history, and Augustine of Hippo (354–430, CE), who founded classical Christian theol-ogy, came closer to following Herodotus, who saw history as evidence and metaphor, than to the ancient Hebrews, for whom history was a result of interactive participa-tion. As heirs of the Hebrew emphasis on history, these early classical Christian thinkers insisted on historical study and were sharply critical of those who neglected the Scriptures, which for them were the historical locus of revelation. But as occupants of a Hellenistic culture and as heirs to Stoic and neo-Platonic traditions of thought (Eusebius was a disciple of Origin; Augustine, a neo-Platonist), they were imbued with a philosophy that allowed them (1) to separate spiritual realities from material realities, and (2) to locate spiritual realities outside and above history and to confine material realities to history. Accordingly, while historical events were to be known, the impor-tant truth was to be found in things unseen, things beyond history.

In his *Ecclesiastical History*, Eusebius is the witness to evidence, carefully portraying the history of the Church from its beginnings until the time of his writing (324 or 325). He was, he said, "the first to undertake this present project" of ecclesiastical history. Seeking to "escape error and danger," he read those who have left "faint traces, in which in their several ways they have bequeathed to us particular accounts of the times through which they passed." He had "plucked, as it were, from meadows of literature suitable passages from these authors of long ago" (1954:3–4).

As a believer he was witness to the Word, embodied in its greatest clarity by Jesus. Eusebius examined historical evidence of the Church and then treated that evidence as a metaphor for the workings of the Word, seeing church leaders as "the ambassadors of the divine word," just as the great prophets and apostles were the "vessels" of the Word (1954:3, 4, 9, 37). Old Testament laws, for example, were not new responses to new situations, but only particular representations of the universal and eternal Word. And the criterion for the success or failure of the Church's life was not the creativity of its response to new situations, but the consistency of its replication of the one eternal Word.

Eusebius, like most classical Greeks, never made history itself the source for the religious life; for Eusebius history and religion were not one. The true source of religion lay outside history, as it did for the Greek historians. It lay in the Word as it was manifest in the Scriptures, just as, for the classical Greeks, the source lay in the truths offered by rhetorical schools, mystery cults, and philosophies.

Just as the Hellenistic Jews made the truth of the Torah ahistorical and eternal, Eusebius and his Christian successors made the Word ahistorical and eternal. In each case, the historian and the believer witnessed to history, both as evidence and as metaphor. For both the Hellenistic Jews and Hellenistic Christians, care for evidence was of vital importance, for it was the metaphorical medium for the contemporary religious person. But for both, the vital question was: To what extent does history represent something beyond history?

Just as the Hellenistic Jews treasured the original law, Eusebius treasured the life and sayings of Jesus and the early Church, for in these original instances the Word was most perfectly manifest. Consistency with Jesus and the early Church became the working criterion of ecclesiastical success and the standard for Christian ecclesiastical historians. "In no other history," says Momigliano, "does precedent mean so much as in ecclesiastical history" (Momigliano 1990:136).

Less than two centuries after Eusebius's *Ecclesiastical History*, written in 324 or 325, church history went into eclipse. The historian's technical study of history was gradually replaced by the theologian's philosophy of history. The transition was smooth, for the theologians also supported a witness theory of history, but with greater philosophical self-consciousness. A standard theology corresponding with that theory was established, and predominate until the twentieth century – as can be illustrated by brief comments on how history was treated by Augustine of Hippo, Martin Luther, Thomas Aquinas, and the twentieth-century theologian Paul Tillich.

Both Augustine (354–430) and Luther (1483–1546) recognized, to put it in Augustine's words, that "whatever evidence we have of past times in that which is called history helps us a great deal in the understanding of sacred books, even if we learned it outside of the Church as a part of our childhood education" (Augustine 1958:63). Both Augustine and Luther trusted reason and observation as ways to understand what for Augustine was the City of Man or for Luther was the earthly kingdom. But history was important because it was an instrument of God's eternal will, a will that cannot be contained in history itself. Thus, according to Augustine, the sack of Rome seen as mere historical evidence is just so much activity; when seen from faith, it became a metaphor for the essential meaning of life apart from faith.

This duality between material history and ahistorical truth is particularly clear in Augustine's "On Nature and Grace," where Augustine debates Pelagius, and in Luther's *On the Bondage of the Will*, where Luther debates Erasmus. In important respects, these debates were debates between the witness theory of history and the participant theory of history. According to Augustine and Luther, Pelagius and Erasmus were wrong in believing that people could contribute to their salvation. Pelagius and Erasmus did not understand that history is instructive only when it is seen to reflect a reality beyond history, the will of God. History is so devoid of contingency and decision, and God's control of history is so complete, that both Augustine and Luther were driven to introduce a theory of predestination. For both Augustine and Luther, history is the arena, not for human accomplishment, but for faithful witness to God's eternal grace as it operates through history from beyond history. The failing of Pelagius and Erasmus was that they did not make historical salvation totally dependent on God's unchanging will. They allowed history to be somewhat dependent on human initiative.

When Augustine and Luther deny the efficacy of human decisions and acts, they make impossible the Hebrew historiography, the participant theory of history. History for the Hebrews must assume a measure of human freedom: the freedom to reinterpret an earlier tradition, adjusting it to a new historical situation; thereby, the freedom partially to alter a community's relation to God; and thereby, the freedom to participate actively in the salvation process. But for Augustine and Luther, salvation in history is the expression of an eternal and irresistible divine force. Traditions and relations cannot be reinterpreted, certainly not by free acts of human participation. The only appropriate initial response to God's will is to witness it, helplessly. Augustine reached this truth as a Platonist, Luther as a nominalist (who treated ideas as names of things rather than as manifestations of universal truths). Nevertheless, for both Augustine and Luther history was utterly dependent on the creating and redeeming will of God.

Thomas Aquinas (1224–74) adopted a different approach, one that came closer than Augustine's and Luther's to a participant theory of history. For him, the universal truths that manifest God's will do reside in history, rather than beyond history. Natural knowledge can be understood through a combination of sense experience, memory, and reason, as they relate to history. Revealed knowledge comes from the basically historical locus of events recorded in Scripture. In addition, God is currently active in history, giving the world its final, formal, efficient, and material causes (Aquinas 1975:86–104). Unlike Augustine and Luther, Thomas assumed that humans are able to carry history in directions that God had not intended. All of this would seem to allow human decision, also active in history, the power to interact with a historical God and to affect the course of history and salvation.

However, for Aquinas God's influence on history is necessary and incontrovertible. Thus, though Aquinas acknowledges that humans are free to affect history, the question of how freedom is to be exercised is rendered mute. God is self-caused, necessary, eternal, immutable, and omnipotent, and therefore unaffected by history. And because God's influence is ubiquitous and irresistible, there is no way (unless it be mysterious) in which human freedom could be effective. In the final analysis, Thomas believed that human initiative could not affect salvation, as the participant theory of history had suggested it could.

Paul Tillich (1886–1965), a German theologian who emigrated to America, is often seen as a modern successor to Augustine and Luther and for good reason, especially with regard to the interpretation of history. For Tillich, history is finite and is known through a rigorous examination of finite events. History becomes theologically significant only when faith "transfers historical truth into the dimension of the truth of faith" (Tillich 1957:86), allowing history to refer to the infinite and, therefore, to what is non-historical. Thus, "historical revelation is not revelation *in* history but *through* history" (Tillich 1951:120; emphasis as in original). History can be the finite, symbolic medium through which the Ultimate becomes manifest. Accordingly, the Christ can be known to finite minds only through symbols in finite history. Thus, for Christianity, the Christ is symbolized in Jesus. To interpret finite, historical events as the activity of God is to reduce the infinite to the finite and to create an idol. For the same reasons, it is idolatrous to presume that finite human initiative can affect the infinite God.

Tillich followed the romantic and idealistic traditions of modern Europe, particularly F. W. Schelling's nineteenth-century idealism, rather than Augustine's fifth-century Platonism. In his theory of history, Tillich did not deviate significantly from Friedrich Schleiermacher (1768–1834), also a philosophical idealist. Tillich's modern idealism led him to a witness theory of history, bringing him closer to the classical Greeks than to the biblical Hebrews.

Finally, it should be noted that Tillich is no anachronistic stranger to twentieth-century theology. In his understanding of history, he represents the most important group of twentieth-century theologians, who might be called "old historicists." Reinhold Niebuhr, Wolfhart Pannenberg, Langdon Gilkey, and Roger Shinn, for example, proved themselves to be *historicists* when they denied classical and Reformation theology's divine determinism and acknowledged that history is indeterminate, deeply ambiguous, and capable of generating new forms of religious meaning. They intended also to separate themselves from most Greek philosophers and historians, sometimes (and largely inaccurately) claiming the Greeks were ahistorical because they thought history was cyclical, or recurrent. Nevertheless, they were *old* historicists because they retained a belief in the timeless validity and universal applicability of Gospel truth and a belief that historical behavior should be religiously assessed only by reference to a truth that transcends history. Like Tillich, they had the believer seeing a dimension of reality unknown to the pure historian. They were and are critical and balanced historians for whom secular history is both evidence of the finite past and a medium for ultimate meaning; but they directed their faith beyond history rather than to history and the historical activity of humans.

The Revival of the Participant Theory of History

Meanwhile, as over the centuries the witness view of history reigned in academic historiography and theology, for ordinary religious people the skies hung very low indeed, low enough for the Gods to be affected by history, as well as to affect history. Whether negotiating with God through prayer, ritual exercises, or moral behaviors, participants in popular Christianity tended to believe that they had real influence on the ultimate meaning of historical events. History was an arena in which people could interact effectively with God, Jesus, Mary, the angels, and the saints. In the twentieth century the trust in the effects of human participation was most evident in evangelical and fundamentalist sects and in the practices of the more literalistic laity in orthodox denominations. They kept alive the participant theory of history, even though its supernaturalism contradicted the naturalism of the rising scientific world view. When the theologians and church leaders rejected popular Christianity for its crudeness, they also ceded – unwittingly, it seems – the dominant biblical view of history to the popular Christianity they criticized.

Gradually, this underground participant theory of history gained currency in learned circles, beginning, most obviously, with the philosophy of history of Georg Wilhelm Friedrich Hegel (1770–1813). For Hegel, history does not point beyond itself to an ahistorical (Platonic, idealistic) realm of pure ideas, but contains all that is real and important. There is an implicit purpose or Spirit in the world, and it works in and through the particularities of historical activity as they dialectically unfold, converting mere possibilities into settled historical events. People should participate in that unfolding; to see themselves as merely witnesses to history is to miss the real action.

Although Hegel took a giant step toward a modern, participant view of history, his *Lectures on the Philosophy of World History* claimed both too much and too little for history. For example, he claimed too much for history when he identified the Absolute Spirit, as it operates in a nation, with the actual historical spirit of that nation. In doing this, he put the actions of at least one state beyond the independent judgment of God or of the prophet, thereby paving the way for the religious nationalism that was later embodied in twentieth-century fascism. Ironically in his effort to emphasize history, he put history beyond the judgment of the participants in history. On the other hand, Hegel claimed too little for history, making it the passive instrument of a coercive dialectical logic. He denatured history by denying, in effect, just those arbitrary, accidental, free decisions of people or of God that were the genius of the Hebrew participant view of history (Hegel 1975:103, 28).

The strengths and weaknesses of Hegel's historicism were seen by Ernst Troeltsch (1865–1923) when in 1902 he announced that the "new world" was developing "an unreservedly historical view of human affairs." He turned to the "historico-critical" theories of Schleiermacher and Hegel as the only serious acknowledgments of the importance of historicity in religion, but then noted that when they made Christianity the historical husk of the Absolute kernel, they effectively absolutized one religion, making it independent of particular historical circumstances (Troeltsch 1971:45, 71–2). He went on to claim that "Christianity has . . . no historical uniformity, but displays a different character in every age." It is relative to "an immeasurable, incomparable profusion of always-new, unique, and hence individual tendencies" (Troeltsch 1957:43–4).

But then, in lectures written just before he died in 1923, Troeltsch worried that to abandon the Absolute entirely would make religions "simply illusions or the products of human vanity." Without explaining how he knew, he asserted that all religions "are products of the impulse towards absolute objective truth," that they all share "a common ground in the Divine Spirit" (1957:61). Presciently, he objected to those extremes of the participant theory of history that would lead American historian Carl Becker ten years later to title his most famous speech: "Every Man his Own Historian." Troeltsch's limits to historicity and his unexplained trust in faith's access to the Absolute were to appear in the historical relativism of H. Richard Niebuhr and Gordon Kaufman, both of whom acknowledged their dependence on Troeltsch.

The fullest modern expression of the participant view of history, and of history for the Hebrews, is the "socio-historical method" of the "Chicago School" of theology. Among major developments in the history of modern Western religious historiography, it was the most neglected, even though it used the popular radical empiricism, pragmatism, and metaphysical naturalism of William James and John Dewey and the progressivism and relativism of contemporary American historians. The Chicago School was neglected partly because its sociological approach to history, although resembling Emile Durkheim's, was ahead of its time, too American, and too mundane for most religious scholars.

The major Chicago School theorists, all faculty of the Divinity School of the University of Chicago, were Gerald Birney Smith (1868–1929), Shailer Mathews (1863–1941), and Shirley Jackson Case (1872–1947). One effect of their sociological approach was their willingness to abandon Troeltsch's search for the One behind the Many and to take the religious risk Troeltsch was unwilling to take – not only relativizing religious truth, even that of Christianity, but refusing subsequently to connect religion to the Absolute. Shailer Mathews believed there were many Christianities, each relative to a social context, none representative of an essential Christianity. "My studies," he said, "have convinced me that Christianity was the religion of people who called themselves Christian; that is to say, who believed themselves loyal to Jesus Christ, but that there was no static body of truth which was a continuum to be accepted or rejected or modified" (Mathews 1969:180). Mathews and the Chicago School theologians treated religious creeds and institutions functionally, much as John Dewey would in his 1934 *A Common Faith*. Religious institutions and creeds arose in response to the mismatch between a community's working theological heritage and the new religious needs implicit in a new social environment, and they invented a new harmony between traditions and the changing environment. This invention created new theological truth – hence, the Chicago School named its work "constructive theology." Clearly, the historian and believer is a participant in history, believing his or her construction would help shape future history.

For Case and Mathews, the New Testament and the early Church were constructive responses to religious crises. For Mathews, the major changes in Christian Theology (such as theories of atonement or of concepts of God) were, phase by phase, specific and creative responses to social or political problems in the course of Western social history. Smith reached the same conclusions through focusing on cultural rather than social and political history.

More than any previous movement in Christian thought, the Chicago School grounded theology in history. Historiography, rather than metaphysics or an authoritative heritage, was the foundation and justification for their theologies. Their distinctiveness led to their isolation, and they fought back. They claimed that fundamentalists and European neo-Reformation theologians – especially Kierkegaard and Barth – were ahistorical thinkers, bent on recovering pure New Testament beliefs and hauling them into the present, even though the present was immersed in problems quite unlike those implicit in the first century. Case turned and fought not only the conservatives, but liberal idealists like Paul Tillich. Despite the idealists' efforts to put doctrines in "forms acceptable to modern modes of thinking," he wrote, they wanted to retain a residue of eternally valid dogma and to discard the rest. They failed to understand that historical context changed the content, as well as the form, of all religious thought, eliminating any substantial continuity. Case went so far as to claim that such obviously false arguments invited the rise of fundamentalism and crisis theology (Case 1933:66–7).

For the Chicago School, then, past and present history was and is a function of participation. Past history was immensely important – not as a standard to be emulated – but as a record of the active interaction between past traditions, past circumstances, and the historical imagination. This interaction was creative activity, in that religious thought had continually to be actively revised to meet the new religious needs that arose in each historical era. Admittedly, this experimental construction carried the risk that theologies could be wrong and fail to work in the new environment – a risk that witness theorists of history sought to avoid by validating theology through reference to something beyond the flux of history.

The Chicago School's battle with the fundamentalists and idealists was costly, for it exposed its Achilles' heel, its tendency always to sell the continuities of tradition to the demands of the present and to see each transaction as one more step in a progress toward higher truth. Ironically, they became "presentists," making their present scientific and democratic belief the criterion for all past belief – the exact converse of Christian thinkers from Eusebius to Barth, who were "pastists," making Christian origins the criterion for all that followed. This presentism seemed to contradict the Chicago School's own claim that each historical act was *sui generis*, creative in its own right, and not subject to any fixed standard – not even the standard taken out of the present.

Finally, as the brutality and despair of the twentieth century mounted, the optimism implicit in the Chicago School's progressivism would look historically naïve, even to the remnants of the later Chicago School: the optimism fell out of sync with a world that was increasingly pessimistic.

New Tales of Two Historiographies

Current history is itself affecting the contest between the witness theory of history and the participant theory of history. As has been implied, most twentieth-century theologians felt they had no choice but to look for God partly beyond history, on the grounds that nothing sacred could be fully manifest within their own violent century. But also, in this most secular century ever, other theologians, as well as most philosophers and scientists, argued that truths beyond history were indefensible and implausible, so that, if there is meaning at all, it must be found through human participation in social and national history themselves.

With a grim realism, Karl Barth in Europe and Reinhold Niebuhr in the United States attacked claims that human participation can save history from the evil in which it is enmeshed, and saw themselves standing with Reformation theologians, recommending a contrite witness to a grace from beyond history. Although Niebuhr refused to analyze the nature of the God beyond history, as classical theologians had, his belief in the existence of such a God offered him religious security and freed him to treat history primarily as a laboratory for human sin. Barth and Niebuhr maintained that people who believed human participation could fundamentally enhance history were either proud, hopelessly superficial, or bluffing, claiming to have a wisdom they did not have. The view of Barth and Niebuhr was so persuasive that, by mid-century, not only progressive liberals and the Chicago School theologians, but all academic advocates of the participant theory of history had lost prominence, leaving Christian theology to the orthodox or neo-orthodox, who saw themselves as theologians whose primary source was the Bible.

In the last three decades of the twentieth century, however, postmodern theologians gained a hearing. Ironically, though chastised for their departure from the historic faith, they advanced a biblical view of history – one far closer to the participant view of history than that of the classical theologians. European and American theologians began to suggest that those who claimed to be in touch with a world beyond history were themselves bluffing. Deprived of a realm beyond history, they argued, people have no choice but to accept history and, literally, to make history.

At the turn of the millennium, it appears that in Europe and America a combination of intellectual currents has washed away the assurance that history is rooted in a world beyond history. Whether the skeptical existentialism of Nietzsche and Martin Heidegger, the linguistic relativism of Ludwig Wittgenstein, the hermeneutical suspicion of Jacques Derrida and Michel Foucault, or the neo-pragmatism of Willard Quine and Richard Rorty, claims to see through history to something fixed and stable seemed to verge on the comic.

Feminist and Black theologians joined the chorus, showing that so-called history-transcending theological claims, though wanting to be unwarped by historical bias, were exactly that. Left with almost no precedents, they tended unapologetically to construct theological truths that gave greater meaning to women and people of color.

In addition, after decades of neglect, William James, John Dewey, and Alfred North Whitehead began to have unanticipated influences on those American theologians who were interested in a historicism but still influenced by pragmatism and "radical empiricism."

Out of these various developments a "new historicism" arose, one that superseded the "old historicism." Because they were not only affected by history but confined to history, the new historicists in theology and the philosophy of religion felt they had no alternative but either to abandon religion or to locate it entirely within a historical world that was their last, best hope. With little recognition that they echoed history for the Hebrews or the historicism of the Chicago School, religious scholars began to argue that religious truths were generated out of the interaction between historical imagination and religious heritages. They struggled to reconceive a role for historical tradition,[3] to say specifically how religious reality can rise on the tide of historical interpretations,[4] and to develop a concept of God.[5]

At the beginning of the twenty-first century these and other struggles between theories of history could be described by reference to Reinhold Niebuhr's 1949 *Faith and History*. In the "Preface" Niebuhr carves out a space for his own work on history – a space between those prewar optimists who made historical development itself redemptive and those postwar pessimists who despaired of any redemption. Niebuhr rejects both, correcting historical pessimism with biblical faith and historical optimism with a gospel that looks beyond history to something "the same yesterday, today and forever" (1949:vii–viii). Niebuhr and others were heard, and their listeners were not satisfied with what they heard. By the century's end, after the Cold War and in the vacuum that followed, the pessimists had grown stronger, claiming to be even more intimate with the indifferent power and the moral ambiguities of history. They seemed to suggest that history will never be responsive to truths from beyond history (the witness theory of history), and that history will never, even with God, carry the seeds of redemption (the participant theory of history).

In the decades to come, theories of history may rotate around the question of whether this new pessimism about history is warranted. If it is not warranted, then history may be redemptive after all, as the participant theorists say, or it may be a metaphor for extra-historical truth, as the witness theorists say.

But if that new pessimism is warranted, then those who oppose it will have little choice but to participate in history militantly, until it is no longer warranted.

Notes

1   John Van Seters focuses on genres when he compares Greek and Israelitic theories of history in his *In Search of History* (1983). His focus on genres allows him to see similarities between the two theories of history.
2   Admittedly, "the Hebrews" is, technically, a designation for one of the small and early groups that were to become the Israelites, so that the identification between "the Hebrews" and the people of the Hebrew Bible, or Old Testament people, is technically wrong. But other terms, such as "Israelites" or "Jews," refer to these peoples at some but not all periods in their history and are just as technically wrong.
3   For example, see Brown (1994).
4   For example, see Dean (1988).
5   For example, see Kaufman (1993).

References

Aquinas, T. 1975. *Summa Contra Gentiles*, book I, trans. A. C. Pegis. Notre Dame, IN: University of Notre Dame Press.

Augustine, St. 1958. *On Christian Doctrine*, trans. D. W. Robertson, Jr. New York: Liberal Arts Press.

Augustine, St. 1992. "On Nature and Grace," in *St. Augustine: Four Anti-Pelagian Writings*, trans. John A. Mourant and William J. Collinge. Washington, DC: Catholic University of America Press.

Brown, D. 1994. *The Boundaries of Our Habitation*. Albany, NY: State University of New York Press.

Case, S. J. 1933. "Whither Historicism?" in *The Process of Religion: Essays in Honor of Dean Shailer Mathews*, ed. M. H. Krumbine. New York: Macmillan.

Dean, W. 1988. *History Making History: The New Historicism in American Religious Thought*. Albany, NY: State University of New York Press.

Eusebius. 1954. *The Ecclesiastical History and the Martyrs of Palestine*, vol. 1, trans. H. J. Lawlor and J. E. L. Oulton. London: SPCK.

Hegel, G.W. F. 1975. "Introduction: Reason in History," in *Lectures on the Philosophy of World History*, trans. H. B. Nisbet. New York: Cambridge University Press.

Herodotus. 1958. *The Histories of Herodotus*, 2 vols., trans. Harry Carter. New York: Heritage Press.

Huizinga, J. 1963. "A Definition of the Concept of History," in *Philosophy and History: Essays Presented to Ernst Cassirer*, eds. R. Klibansky and H. J. Paton. New York: Harper and Row.

Kaufman, G. 1993. *In Face of Mystery*. Cambridge, MA: Harvard University Press.

Knight, D. 1977. "Revelation through Tradition," in *Tradition and Theology in the Old Testament*, ed. D. A. Knight. Philadelphia, PA: Fortress Press.

Luther, M. 1979. *The Bondage of the Will*, trans. Henry Cole. Grand Rapids, MI: Baker Book House.

Mathews, S. 1969. "Theology as Group Belief," in *Contemporary American Theology: Theological Autobiographies*, 2nd series, ed. V. Ferm. Freeport, NY: Books for Libraries Press.

Momigliano, A. 1990. *The Classical Foundations of Modern Historiography*. Berkeley, CA: University of California Press.

Niebuhr, R. 1949. *Faith and History: A Comparison of Christian and Modern Views of History*. New York: Charles Scribner's Sons.

Noth, M. 1966. "The Laws in the Pentateuch: their Assumptions and Meaning," in M. Noth, *The Laws in the Pentateuch and Other Studies*. Philadelphia, PA: Fortress Press.

Thucydides. 1959. "History of the Peloponnesian War," trans. R. Crawley, in *The Greek Historians*, ed. M. I. Finley. New York: Viking Press.

Tillich, P. 1951. *Systematic Theology*, vol. 1. Chicago, IL: University of Chicago Press.

Tillich, P. 1957. *Dynamics of Faith*. New York: Harper.

Troeltsch, E. 1971. *The Absoluteness of Christianity and the History of Religions*. Richmond, VA: John Knox Press.

van Seters, J. 1983. *In Search of History: Historiography in the Ancient World and the Origins of Biblical History*. New Haven, CT: Yale University Press.

von Rad, G. 1955. "The Form-Critical Problem of the Hexateuch," in G. von Rad, *The Problem of the Hexateuch and Other Essays*. New York: McGraw-Hill.

von Rad, G. 1962. *Old Testament Theology*, 2 vols. New York: Harper.

PART II

History

CHAPTER 8

Patristics

G. R. Evans and Morwenna Ludlow

Introduction

"Patristics" is the study of a period which begins as the first generation of Jesus's followers passed away and the "apostolic age" ended, and which merges at the other end into the Middle Ages. The authors who wrote in these centuries have come to be known as "the Fathers." They have acquired a special authority, and the history of their era, with its significant texts and its definitive moments (such as the early ecumenical Councils, the framing of the Niceno-Constantinopolitan Creed, the emergence of a ministerial structure) has become the resource to which theologians have had resort for authoritative answers to a number of questions about faith and order.

But the identification of such a period is itself not uncontroversial. First, it assumes that "earlier is better," that the place to look for the right answers is the primitive Church, as close to the time of Christ as possible, and that there has been no "development" since (to use John Henry Newman's expression) on which equal reliance ought to be placed, or which can usefully modify the presumptions of those early days. Secondly, there is the question of the parameters of the period, when it can be deemed to end, and what aspects of the Christian life of the time can be taken to be normative for Christians of later generations.

The Beginning of the Idea of "the Fathers"

The idea of working in a tradition, of having been handed a body of thought and belief, was present right from the start of written theology: Irenaeus (c.130–c.200) was aware that the Gnostics share the same Scriptures; but they used the inherited rule of faith to assess and condemn their interpretation of them. However, most scholars now agree that this rule of faith was *not* a written source, not a proto-creed, but a body of belief which Irenaeus, for example, felt free to express in various different ways, brief and more extensive. The term "Father" for Christian forebears (i.e. those who passed on the rule of faith) was already current in Irenaeus's time.

Christian authors, *scriptores ecclesiastici*, were early aware that they were writing in a "tradition," in the Christian sense of a "handing on," of a body of thought and belief. In the period we are concerned with, the canon of Scripture was largely settled. It was not in dispute that there existed a body of texts which had been inspired by God himself and which were therefore the Word of God. There was still room for disagreement about the status of some of the apocryphal materials. Jerome was still considering that question at the end of the fourth century.

The meaning of "inspired" prompted some discussion. Early Christians believed that the Septuagint was an inspired translation of the Old Testament. The iconography of the four evangelists in the West shows them writing at the dictation of a dove, representing the Holy Spirit, which has its beak in their ears. The implication was strong that the Holy Spirit spoke the Word directly to the various authors of the books of the Bible, who simply wrote it down. The Old Testament prophets too could be thought to be inspired. In his *Prologue* to his reflections on the Psalms, which were paraphrased in the twelfth century by Peter Lombard and recast again about 1230, Cassiodorus gave definitions to help his readers "know where they were" with prophets. *Inspiratio*, it was suggested, involved direct input from the Holy Spirit. A mere dream or vision was not strictly "inspiration" (Torrell 1977:5).

Jerome encountered a further ramification of this assumption when he translated the Bible into the improved Latin version which won universal acceptance as the Vulgate. Was the translator himself inspired? Jerome was sure he himself was not, and said so, but the readers and commentators of the Middle Ages consistently took his Latin version to be "the Word." They analyzed every turn of phrase exactly as they would have done if God had spoken into the ears of the evangelists and prophets in Jerome's Latin.

Was there a category of specially authoritative authors who were not in the canon but who could be relied on more than the others? This happened naturally without there being necessarily any "theory" about it at first. There were various theologians whose writings had had enormous influence, even if they were not directly cited as authoritative works, or works of a "Father." A good example is Origen, of whose works selections were made into a kind of textbook by Basil of Caesarea and Gregory of Nazianzus in the latter half of the fourth century.

Maurice Wiles suggests that a change happened in the fifth century (Wiles 1979:47–8). In the Trinitarian controversies all parties claimed they were interpreting Scripture in a manner true to the rule of faith; in the Christological controversies both sides claimed also to be correctly interpreting the non-scriptural but written formula or "creed" of Nicaea and they tried to show that the works of earlier writers conformed to their views. In order to "prove" what the written, post-scriptural tradition was, they constructed dossiers of texts, which were described as being of "the holy Fathers." Each party appealed to roughly the same authors, but selected and interpreted the material to give weight to its own case. Lists of accepted authoritative authors became less consistent in later centuries, but the idea that there were such authors persisted.

It was not usual at first to speak of "Fathers" at all except with reference to the *patres* of the Old Testament, the patriarchs. Augustine may have been the first to apply the word "Father" to a writer who was not a bishop, when he used it of Jerome. The formula of Chalcedon was described as being "in agreement with the holy Fathers." "Fathers" gradually began to seem an appropriate term for the ancient, senior, most respected Christian authors. It carried with it the assumption that there had been at least two great ages of writing about the Christian faith, that of the composition of the books which found their way into the canon of Scripture and a later but still special age when writings of high authority came into being, possessing a reliability and an authority which could not be matched by the writings of more recent authors. If that was so, when did that age end? Or did it perhaps continue, with a few latter-day "Fathers" still holding a distinct place in the scheme of things at the divine behest? Some twelfth-century collections contain extracts from Anselm of Canterbury, Bernard of Clairvaux, Hugh of St Victor, who have found a natural place alongside Augustine and Gregory the Great.

Once there was an idea of "the Fathers," later authors could be envisaged as *patrum vestigia sequentes*, "following in the footsteps of the Fathers" (Robert Grosseteste 1986, III.i.30, p. 132). Were certain individuals down the ages favored with divine assistance in their thinking, even much later than the earliest period of the Church? This question was never really determined in any systematic way. Yet by the late twelfth and thirteenth centuries there was a developing sense that some authors were respectable because they belonged to a former age whereas contemporaries were fair game for challenge or disagreement (*antiqui et moderni*).

A series of names emerged, who eventually formed the loose group known as "the Fathers," ending roughly with Bede in the West. We can begin to trace this evolution and its accompanying debate about "standing" more systematically by looking at what happened to the tradition Jerome (d. 420) began with his *De viris illustribus*. Jerome wrote the *De viris illustribus*, in which he listed the Christian authors who might be read by inquirers who wished to know who to trust for interpretation of Scripture, for moral guidance and for theological opinion. Gennadius of Marseilles (late fifth century) continued Jerome's work with about a hundred extra names, taken mainly from the fifth century, drawn from both Eastern and Western halves of the Empire.

The *Decretum Gelasianum*, "*on books to be received and books not to be received*," was usually held, in the Middle Ages, to have been a *decretum* of Pope Gelasius (492–6), and that gave it "authority" on the subject of "authoritativeness." It begins with a list of books of the Old and New Testaments which it identifies as those "on which the Catholic Church was founded (*fundata est*) by the grace of God" (*Das Decretum Gelasianum de libris recipiendis et non recipiendis* 1912, ch. 3). It includes (chapter 4) a list of writings whose use the Church does not prohibit. There are also references to works of Gregory of Nazianzus, Basil, Athanasius, John of Constantinople, Theophilus Alexandrinus, Cyril of Alexandria, Hilary of Poitiers, Ambrose, Augustine, Jerome, Prosper of Aquitaine, *gesta* of the martyrs and *vitae patrum*, Rufinus, Origen, Eusebius of Caesarea, Orosius, Sedulis, Iuvencus. There is a chapter on those works which are not to be received because they contain heretical teachings.

This text became the touchstone or reference-point for the trustworthiness and Christian standing of early authors, at least in the West. The idea of bringing the list up to date proved attractive from time to time (*Das Decretum Gelasianum de libris recipiendis et non recipiendis* 1912:66ff.). The *Libri Carolini*, to which we shall come in a moment, already tend to prefer Western authorities such as Ambrose, Jerome, Augustine, Hilary, or Gregory the Great, and they keep on the whole to the Gelasian list. Sigebert of Gembloux (b. c.1030 in Belgium) wrote a latter-day *De viris Illustribus* in the late eleventh century, consciously bringing to his own time what Jerome and Gennadius had done (vaingloriously placing his own works at some length, at the end).

Medieval Patristic Collections

One way of knowing when an author has "arrived" at patristic status in medieval eyes is to see what company he keeps in collections of extracts. Conversely, a development which strongly encouraged later writers to look for "authority" in the writings of their predecessors was the habit of extracting from the texts short portions which could be quoted to support a particular viewpoint. Collections of such useful extracts were commonplace in the Carolingian period and beyond. The methodology remained in use throughout the Middle Ages. It kept a range of authors in play. But it unavoidably led to the breaking up into small pieces of what may have been an extended argument in the original.

Earlier Greek Christian and Byzantine *catenae* survive from the fifth century, many of which were published in the late nineteenth to twentieth centuries. Examples are: Procopius of Gaza (c.475 to c.538) on Ecclesiastes, containing excerpts from Origen, Gregory Thaumaturgos, Dionysius of Alexandria, Gregory of Nyssa, Didymus Alexandrinus, Evagrius, Nilus, and others (*Corpus Christianorum Series Graeca* [hereafter *CCSG*] 4), the *Collectio Coisliniana* (*CCSG* 15), and the *Catena Siniatica* on Genesis and Exodus (*CCSG* 2).

It was in about 700 that "patristic texts" began to be seen in canonical collections in the West, for example, in the *Collectio Hibernensis*. The *Libri Carolini* is a useful example of a collaborative enterprise. The Second Nicene Council of 787 had restored the Byzantine East to an iconophile position. This change, and with it the apparent ending of the iconoclastic controversy, was welcomed by Pope Hadrian. A copy of the proceedings of the Council (in Latin) came to the court of Charlemagne. The Emperor was unaware of the Papal approval of what had been agreed, and he set about having a rejoinder drawn up, on the assumption that the East was still in the wrong. This exercise of "amassing headings against the synod," *capitulare adversus synodum*, was formally orchestrated by Theodulph, still in ignorance of papal approval, as a critique of the Council. Politically misconceived though it turned out the enterprise was, it had the value of causing Carolingian scholars to think out their position on the use of authorities. The *Libri Carolini* make the point that the Holy Spirit is not now given in the measure in which he was given in apostolic times: *secundum apostolicae mensurae gratiam* (IV.20).

The ninth-century Sedulius Scottus's *Collectaneum miscellaneum* is a collection of excerpts of biblical, patristic, classical materials, including ready-made *florilegia*, which it has been suggested were copied out perhaps as an *aide-mémoire* rather than as a teaching aid. He speaks with respect of the "wisdom of the Greeks," as "like multicoloured precious stones," which he has brought together with care and effort (Sedulius Scottus

1988:3). Burchard of Worms has a significant proportion of patristic texts (247 out of 1,785). Ivo of Chartres speaks of *orthodoxi patres* (*Patrologia Latina* 161.47), including *popes*, *councils* and *scriptores ecclesiastici*. Gratian includes a good deal of patristic material (on the authority perhaps of Gelasius's list *De libris legendis et reiiciendis*). So our writers are often used in extracted form with no expectation that the user will go back and read the whole book.

This system of collecting extracts largely provided the materials for the *Glossa ordinaria*, the standard commentary on the Bible, which was brought finally into being in the twelfth century, on the basis of work stretching back several centuries. For certain books of the Bible a single patristic commentator tended to be dominant. For example, Gregory the Great is naturally very important on the book of Job, because of his much-read *Moralia*. The seventh-century Irish monk Lathchen abbreviated Gregory's thoughts on Job in his *Egloga* and that formed a "work" in its own right, but one with a different purpose (Lathchen 1969:145).

The same habit of working from collections of extracts underlies the *Sentences* (*sententiae*, or opinions) of Peter Lombard, which became the standard theological textbook from the thirteenth century. It prompted Thomas Aquinas as late as the thirteenth century to put together a "Catena Aurea," a "golden chain" of quotations on the Gospels.

The monastic custody of the early Christian literary tradition was a very different affair in East and West. To the Benedictines of the West we owe the survival of many copies of ancient secular and Christian texts which might otherwise have been lost; their attitude was one of stewardship. In the East, "Athonite monasticism . . . has nothing to do with human culture and learning, and it consequently takes no part in education. . . . *Vana curiositas?* Study would only involve fierce struggles with Satan and the possibility of losing [one's] faith" (Amand de Mendieta 1961:25). Nevertheless, manuscript collections did survive unread. Indeed, it has been suggested that there are still to be found, in the collections of manuscripts on Mount Athos which have survived the depredations of centuries during which many have been removed or destroyed, "unknown or almost unknown theological treatises, homilies, exegetical commentaries or ascetic works of the Greek Fathers and other ecclesiastical writers" (Amand de Mendieta 1961:35).

From Erasmus to Migne

At the beginning of the sixteenth century, Erasmus already displayed some of the instincts we see again in the nineteenth century. He recognized the importance of establishing reliable texts of the Fathers. In the early 1500s he was exploring the works of Origen, conscious that Origen had been branded a heretic, but drawn to a number of his ideas. He tells John Colet in a letter (181) of 1504, that he has read a good part of Origen's works and he believes that he has profited. His interest lay not only in the Greek Fathers, to which his own increasing command of Greek was giving him access, but in the Latins who had long been routinely available. Editorial work on Jerome (1516), Cyprian (1520), Arnobius (1522), Hilary (1523), Irenaeus (1526), Ambrose

(1537), eleven volumes on Augustine, and after he moved to Freiburg, on Lactantius (1529), Chrysostom (1530), and Basil (1532), brought him back to Origen shortly before he died.

Quotations from the Fathers by Luther and Calvin make it clear that respect for the Fathers did not die away altogether in sixteenth-century reforming circles with the call to *sola scriptura*. Calvin cites Augustine 204 times in the *Institutes*, Gregory the Great and Ambrose more than 20 times each and Chrysostom 36 times. At the Council of Trent both sides marshaled Augustine and other Fathers in argument.

There is a still-useful body of editions of patristic texts and discussion of their place in the Christian scheme of things, deriving from the work of sixteenth- and seventeenth-century and later scholars. Francisco Torres, one of the "Fathers" of the Council of Trent, took an interest in the patristic *fontes*. Jacques Sirmond (1559–1651) was the Jesuit editor of a range of patristic texts. These supplemented and improved the early printed books, which had included printings of a number of patristic texts.

The Maurists, the Benedictine monks of St Maur, were, from the 1670s, engaged upon the production of texts. J. Mabillon (1632–1707) brought the study of paleography into the edition of texts. D. de Montfaucon (1655–1741) produced editions of Athanasius, Chrysostom, and some of Origen. L. d'Achery and F. Aubert are other notable names in this endeavor. English scholars of the seventeenth century who took an interest in the Greek Fathers include Henry Savile (who edited Chrysostom), Lancelot Andrews, John Cosin, Patrick Young, James Ussher, Richard Montague, William Laud, and even two Puritan chaplains to Oliver Cromwell, Peter Sterry and Jeremiah White. The group known as the "Cambridge Platonists" included Benjamin Whichcote, Henry More, Ralph Cudworth, and John Smith. They returned to the confidence that as rational creatures, human beings could enjoy the vision of God by an exercise in the "purification" of their reason.

In the nineteenth century, J. P. Migne, a priest turned Paris publisher, produced the *Patrologia Latina* series (1844–55) and the *Patrologia Graeca* (1857–66). The first series went up to the early thirteenth century (the pontificate of Innocent III); the second to the fifteenth century, with a Latin translation alongside the Greek text. Migne's *Patrologia* preserved some texts (e.g. those of the Maurists) which were lost in the French Revolution. He left scholars in patristic and medieval Greek and Latin studies lastingly in his debt. The texts were extremely varied in standard; some were reprints of the Maurist editions, or of early printed editions. Migne did not hesitate to reprint some existing editions without critical revision. The indexing was uncertain. Few texts were reliable editorially and there was much misattribution. But the texts were there, conveniently assembled and available in most academic libraries, the essential foundation for worldwide patristic studies which had hitherto been lacking because of the limited availability of the early printed texts.

"Patristics": the Forming of a Discipline

The Oxford Movement of the mid-nineteenth century was the starting point of modern patristics in England. John Henry Newman became excited as a young man by the history of Arianism. His *The Arians of the Fourth Century*, first published in 1833, grappled not only with the source-texts (abundantly available to him in Oxford in early printed books), but with the underlying questions of genre and authoritativeness. He does not yet see patristics as a discipline in its own right; he describes Arianism (Newman 1876:2) as a period which "especially invites the attention of the student in ecclesiastical history." He speaks of "ancient writers" (1876:3) as readily as of "the Fathers."

Both in their scholarly editions (e.g. Pusey's of Cyril of Alexandria and Newman's of Athanasius) and in their conviction of the theological usefulness of the period, members of the Oxford Movement were keen to gain the writings a wider audience, through projects such as *A Library of the Fathers*, which was planned in 1836. In the 1830s Newman was seeking to popularize the patristic background in colorful accounts in the *British Magazine* (Newman 1835a:662–8; 1835b:41–8, 158–65, 277–84). Other translations appeared in the wake of this: an SPCK popular edition (*The Fathers for English Readers*, late nineteenth century) and most importantly the two large series *Ante-Nicene Writers* and *A Select Library of Nicene and Post-Nicene Fathers*. J. B. Lightfoot's *The Apostolic Fathers* (1869ff.) provided a translation of *Clement of Rome*, the *Ignatian Epistles* and the *Epistle of Polycarp*.

Owen Chadwick speaks of the respect of the Oxford Movement for the tradition of the ancient and undivided Church (Chadwick 1990:30), but it is apparent that toward the end of his long life Newman had got beyond that in the sophisticated understanding of what was appropriate in the treatment and handling of patristic texts. In the 1881 edition of his translation of the *Select Treatises of St. Athanasius in Controversy with the Arians* Newman wrote reflectively about his assumptions of this period:

> In some quarters an over-estimation prevailed of the early Christian writers, as if they had an authority so special, and a position so like that of a court of final appeal, that those who had a title to handle their writings were but few. . . . Things are much altered since 1836–1845. I yield to no-one still in special devotion to those centuries of the Catholic Church which the holy Fathers represent; but I see no difficulty at this day in a writer proposing to himself a free translation of their treatises, if he makes an open profession of what he is doing.   (Newman 1881:vi)

"Théologie, tendant la main de l'histoire" was the description of the Archbishop of Malines in his introductory remarks to the first issue of the *Revue d'Histoire Ecclésiastique* 1 (1900). Theology needed to incorporate critical method, historical method, philosophical method. Patristics, like theology at large, had become an interdisciplinary subject, which means that it crossed traditional disciplinary boundaries. It was not classics. It was not history. It was not philosophy. But it participated in each of these areas of intellectual endeavor, and others.

It was also conspicuously a common endeavor of a community of scholarship. Among the correspondence preserved in the Bodleian Library are exchanges between the scholars who (we can now see) were forming this modern discipline of theology. The *Journal of Theological Studies* (*JTS*), begun in 1899, brought together at its launching many of the leading theological scholars of Oxford and Cambridge, who met and talked and exchanged papers, using the *JTS*, as H. B. Swete put it in his introductory statement to the first issue, as "a regular organ of communication between students whose lives are spent at the universities and elsewhere, in the pursuit of scientific theology" (Swete 1899:1). The Committee of Direction included the two Regius Professors of Divinity from Oxford and Cambridge (Inge and Swete); the two Regius Professors of Hebrew (Driver and Kirkpatrick); Lock (Dean Ireland Professor at Oxford); Moberly (Pastoral Theology, Oxford); Ryle, the Hulsean Professor at Cambridge; and Stanton, the Ely Professor at Cambridge; with J. Armitage Robinson, formerly the Norrisian Professor of Divinity at Cambridge, and Robertson, the principal of Kings College London. All except Turner were clerics. And indeed some contributors did make the *Journal* their commonplace-book. The editor, C. H. Turner, included nine of his own pieces in Volume I; others too appear several times in the early volumes.

Turner remarked in his "History and Use of the Creeds" for the Church Historical Society that although he was not a liturgiologist, he had had scholarly friends to whom he had been "fortunate in being able to appeal" (Turner 1910:5). F. C. Burkitt "rendered into English" the *Hymn of Bardaisan* in 1899, noting that "it was first edited in the great series of Apocryphal Acts published in 1871 by the late Dr. William Wright," but that it had been republished with "a fresh translation" a year ago "by my friend Professor Bevan, of Cambridge." This community of friendship (and rivalry) is evident in the surviving correspondence of scholars, asking one another questions about their research, sending one another drafts for comment, engaging in informal "peer-review." C. H. Turner wrote to Alexander Souter on January 8, 1906, "I don't agree with you . . . but I have, in deference to your view, whittled down 'surely' into 'I think'" (Bodleian Library, MS Eng. Lett. C615). C. H. Milne wrote to Alexander Souter on March 10, 1929, "Many thanks for your 'review' of my paper. It will be of the utmost value to me when I attack the subject again," and on September 3, 1931, "I hear that in a review of C. H. Turner's book you are very eulogistically referred to in *The Times Literary Supplement*."

The contrast of "culture" in the sense of national "scholarly characteristics" is also visible. The Benedictine G. Morin was an assiduous correspondent with Oxford theologians and the contrast of his flowery and exuberant style with theirs is obvious.

As a new Honours subject in Oxford from 1870, Theology had to distinguish itself from the existing ones, and that principally meant establishing that patristic texts needed a treatment of a different kind from that which they would receive if they were secular Greek or Latin classics. However, the recognition that Patristics is distinct from Classics was slow to come. While the *Patristic Greek Lexikon* was beginning its lengthy progress from the germ of the idea in 1906, a ninth edition of the Greek dictionary of Liddell and Scott was planned. H. S. Jones recognized in his Preface that it was no longer satisfactory to include haphazard entries labeled "Byzantine" or otherwise recognized not to be classical Greek usage, when it was now apparent that the field of such usages was vast and could not be casually "sampled" in this way. As late as 1927, James Mountford at Cornell wrote to Alexander Souter to thank him for a copy of his "Earliest Latin Commentaries." He comments that, "The book is a further demonstration that the field of scholarship is not to be bounded by the death of Juvenal to Tacitus. Unhappily, there is still a large number of Latinists whose interests extend only from

Lucretius to Lucan and who cannot believe that any good purpose is served by over-stepping those limits" (Bodleian Library, MS Eng. Lett. C611).

One of the difficulties was that the natural chronological endpoint for the Eastern authors was not the same as that for the West. The history of Latin Christian writing after the end of the ancient world did not run parallel with that of Greek Christian writing. The need for work on Christian Latin obtruded itself in various connections. For example, C. H. Turner wrote to Alexander Souter on January 4, 1906: "I forgot to ask yesterday whether you have any further references for 'rector' in the technical sense of a Christian ruler or bishop in Ambrosiaster" (Bodleian Library, MS Eng. Lett. C615). On May 29, 1919, W. M. Ramsay wrote to C. H. Turner: "I have been working a little at some names in your Latin Nicene lists. Have you any view as to the time when the translations into different languages were made? Do they represent translations made at the time, or shortly after the Council was held, or were they made at some later day? He believes they date from close to 325. They are therefore an extremely valuable authority" (Bodleian Library, MS Eng. Lett. C617).

On May 3, 1928, Christine Mohrmann, one of the pioneers who made the history of Christian Latin a study in its own right, wrote to Alexander Souter. He was begin-ning his period as Professor of New Testament Greek at Oxford, but his lasting interest was in the Latin tradition. She told him that she was "at work on a linguistic study of the language of Augustine," and she asked for "a few practical hints in the matter." In 1947 she was co-editing the new journal *Vigiliae Christianae: A Review of Early Christian Life and Language*, the first paper of whose first issue is her "Le latin commun et le latin des chrétiens" (Mohrmann 1947). She drew together there a variety of evidences that Christian Latin is "une langue spéciale" in the sense that there is a functional differ-ence between it and secular late classical Latin. She points to Augustine's conscious-ness that new words were being formed. He gives the example of *salvare* and *salvator*, formed from *salus*, and he comments: "The grammarians do not ask whether it is Latin, but the Christians enquire how far it is true": *nec quaerant grammatici quam sit latinum, sed Christiani quam verum* (1947:4; and Augustine, *Sermon* 299.6).

Modern Patristics

Von Harnack

In his *History of Dogma*, Adolf von Harnack (1851–1930) emphasized that the disci-pline of the history of dogma distinguished itself from that of church history by its nar-rower subject matter, and differed from systematic theology in refusing to see dogmas as timeless truths: "the business of the history of dogma is, in the first place, to ascer-tain the origin of Dogmas (or Dogma), and then secondly, to describe their development (their variations)" (von Harnack 1897:1). He developed a notion of development in which writers from Augustine onwards "disclosed a new conception of Christianity, but at the same time appropriated the old dogmas" (von Harnack 1897:8), recognizing some continuity but denying that the Roman Catholic Church and her doctrines con-stituted a natural and necessary outgrowth from the early Church and stressing that

"Protestantism must . . . under all circumstances be recognised as a new thing" (von Harnack 1897:9, n.2). The idea that dogma unfolds itself was dismissed as "unscientific" and von Harnack famously declared that "dogma has its history in the individual living man and nowhere else" (von Harnack 1897:12). Consequently, the scholar must attend to the context in which dogmas originated and developed, taking into account the influence of Scripture and tradition (both doctrine and "blind custom"); the liturgical and institutional life of the Church; prevailing intellectual, religious, political, social, and moral trends; the needs both for logical consistency and for coherence of belief within the Church; and the Church's need to reject error (von Harnack 1897:12).

Although it can easily be argued that von Harnack failed to live up to this method himself, and that some of these ideas entered modern patristics by other routes, this contextualizing and historical approach has colored all patristic research since. However, he is influential not just for his method, but for his conclusions reached by it. First, he claimed that the development of dogma in the early Church represented a process of Hellenization, as Christian beliefs came to be expressed, explained, and justified with Greek concepts. Secondly, in his lectures on *The Essence of Christianity* (delivered in Berlin between 1899 and 1900) von Harnack drew some more strictly theological conclusions from his research. Like previous church historians, he located authority in an original unified state; his novelty, however, was to draw a clear dividing line between "the gospel" and "dogma," seeing the former as the true "essence of Christianity" and defining it in moral–religious terms as Jesus's message of the fatherhood of God, the value of each human and the ethical obligations that spring from those truths. Dogma, then, represents a falling-away from this central religious truth, and Hellenistic modes of thought were the form this falling-away first took. Thus by moving patristics away from the use of early Christian literature as "proof texts" toward a more critical approach whilst still asking about the essence of Christianity, von Harnack raised the question which has pursued it for the hundred years since: what is the relation between patristics and theology?

Finally, through works on writers like Marcion (1924), von Harnack promoted the historical study of writers on the fringes of the Christian tradition and emphasized the importance of establishing reliable texts, since most marginal or heretical writers were lost and fragments from them were quoted only by their opponents. This interest was carried on by von Harnack's successor at Berlin, Hans Lietzmann (1875–1942), whose work on Apollinaris of Laodicea (Lietzmann 1904) greatly facilitated the study of the Christological controversies by its attempt to distinguish genuine and spurious Apollinarian texts. He also produced the notable *History of the Early Church* (4 volumes, 1932–44).

Duchesne

Von Harnack's work was most positively received among Protestants, although more so by academics than by the Lutheran Church, with which von Harnack had a somewhat uneasy relationship. However, some Catholic historians used the same methods in order to challenge his conclusions. Thus, the Frenchman Louis Duchesne

(1843–1922) insisted on the necessity of rescuing church history from the current inadequate and narrow approach, yet criticized von Harnack for neglecting "everything which is rite, hierarchy, sacrament, popular devotion" (Duchesne 1892:403). Duchesne did not abandon the early church texts used by the seminarians' textbooks, but he approached them more critically and complemented them with the use of the new archeological and epigraphical techniques being used by secular historians (an advance on von Harnack's approach, which was almost exclusively textual).

Duchesne was a devout and loyal priest; yet he inevitably raised the hackles of his fellow Roman Catholics, particularly since he challenged some dearly held myths about the southern French sees, which were popularly supposed to have apostolic foundations. This opposition had its effect on his career: having been elected to the Chair of church history at the prestigious Institut Catholique in Paris in 1877, he resigned in 1885, after adverse reaction to his lectures on the history of doctrine. He carried on his work at the École Supérieur des Lettres and, from 1895, the French School at Rome. However, his effort to establish church history as a scientific enterprise earned Duchesne the respect of the secular French academic establishment at a period when Catholicism had a far from comfortable position in France, and he was elected a member of the Académie française in 1910. By 1963 Duchesne's *Histoire ancienne de l'Église* was being cited by the future Cardinal Daniélou as "still useful" – a comment which speaks both for the quality and durability of Duchesne's scholarship as well as for the Church's changed attitude to his historical method.

The "ressourcement": de Lubac and Daniélou

The Roman Catholic movement known as "modernism" questioned further the relation between history and the Church. By emphasizing how much the Church had changed, the modernists gave the impression that no particular historical instantiation was important, that all Church doctrines, forms, and customs were merely useful pointers to (or outgrowths of) a subjective and interior experience. They challenged the contemporary neo-scholastic orthodoxy, which eschewed modern historical techniques and tended to use the past as a kind of source-book to prove the correctness of the Roman Church's current dogmas and constitution. Although the modernists were few in number, they startled Rome and were condemned by Pius X, most famously in his encyclical *Pascendi* in 1907, which summed up their errors as "historicism," "immanentism," and "agnosticism."

The gulf between modernism and neo-scholasticism formed the theological backdrop for the most important development within Roman Catholicism from the point of view of patristic studies: the *ressourcement* and the interconnected development of the so-called *nouvelle théologie*. The political and social background was no less important: theologians of all denominations felt a need for reassessment and renewal after the experiences of World War I and this combined with the end of a long period during which anti-clericalism had dominated France. In the 1930s many theologians returned from exiled monastic communities with a desire to renew Roman Catholic theology in a mode which took seriously not only modern historical and philosophical developments but also a sophisticated theological reflection upon them. A vital part of this movement was a return to the sources (a *ressourcement*) of Christian life and faith – both biblical and patristic – investigating them through historical research and using them to renew current theology. Historical studies of the Bible and of early Church doctrine, liturgy, and ecclesiology became interconnected and the new research was conducted in an ecumenical spirit: these Roman Catholics emphasized that the early Church was – historically speaking – the root of *all* modern denominations and not just the church of Rome (whilst admittedly often still emphasizing typically Roman elements in the tradition). This spirit of scholarship and renewal had an important impact on the Second Vatican Council, at which several prominent *ressourcement* scholars, including de Lubac and Daniélou, were *periti*.

The examples of de Lubac and Daniélou illustrate well the development of Roman Catholic patristic studies in this period. The first publication of the Jesuit Henri de Lubac (1896–1991) was an analysis of the biblical exegesis of the third-century Origen of Alexandria (de Lubac 1950); his most famous historical work (de Lubac 1998) studied exegesis in the medieval period. Even those of his works which claim not to be historical reveal de Lubac's dependence on the thought of the early Church. In the introduction to *Catholicism* he declared:

> If the quotations are numerous . . . it is because I wanted to [draw] on the treasures, so little utilised, in the patristic writings. This is not to overlook in a frenzy of archaism the precisions and developments in theology which have been made since their time, nor do I take over in their entirety all the ideas they offer us: I seek only to understand them and to listen to what they have to tell us. . . . The greater becomes one's familiarity with this immense army of witnesses . . . the keener is one's realisation of how deep is the unity in which all these meet together.   (De Lubac 1988:19–20)

As Professor of Theology at Lyons from 1934, de Lubac taught two other influential scholars during their training as Jesuits: the Frenchman Jean Daniélou (1905–74) and the Swiss Hans Urs von Balthasar (1905–88; he left the order in 1950). Although most of Daniélou's important work was in patristics, and most of von Balthasar's in systematic theology, both men, like de Lubac, illustrate the integration of historical and theological reflection together with a desire to communicate with the contemporary world, which characterized *nouvelle théologie*. In the field of patristics, von Balthasar published two detailed, albeit highly individual, monographs on Maximus the Confessor (von Balthasar 1941) and on Gregory of Nyssa (von Balthasar 1995) plus articles on Origen (von Balthasar 1957). Daniélou's first work was an enormously influential study of the spiritual theology of Gregory of Nyssa, an author to whom he returned frequently in his career (Daniélou 1944); this was followed by studies of Origen (Daniélou 1955) and Philo of Alexandria (Daniélou 1958), surveys of various aspects of the early Church such as liturgy, sacraments, and use of the Bible, and large-scale histories of early Christian doctrine and church history.

The choice of these subjects indicates a strong interest in the Greek Fathers. Writers like Gregory and Origen appealed because of their use of contemporary philosophy, their attention to Scripture, and their belief that true piety lies in the transformation of the soul. Furthermore, the Greek Fathers' theology helped resolve one of the tensions between neo-scholasticism and modernism. While both depended in different ways on a distinction between nature and grace, the Greek Fathers and the new Catholic writers questioned it. They emphasized that God worked throughout the whole of human history (facilitating ecumenical dialogue and conversation with other religions), and they focused on the spiritual as opposed to the purely doctrinal or liturgical aspects of Christianity.

De Lubac and Daniélou were also instrumental in introducing patristic writers to a wider non-academic audience with their more popular works, and their writings indicate two issues of increasing concern to patristics: the study of premodern hermeneutics and of the influence of Judaism on early Christianity.

Ecumenism and patristics

The great divisions of the Church occurred in the Middle Ages (the Schism of 1054 between East and West) and at the end of the Middle Ages (the divisions of the Reformation). When modern ecumenism began in earnest with the Second Vatican Council, the patristic texts had the attraction of providing authoritative guidance on the common faith of the undivided Church. This encouraged the churches meeting in bilateral or multilateral dialogues to make extensive use of scholars with specialist patristic knowledge among their numbers.

Patristics and other disciplines

In the latter half of the twentieth century, much more interest was paid to archeological evidence and much more such evidence relating to early Christianity became available, especially in North Africa. It is particularly useful in helping the historian map the geographic spread of Christianity in the first few centuries. It has provided evidence about early Christian life and belief where extant literary sources are very rare (e.g. Britain), or for heretical writers and groups whose texts were not preserved (e.g. Montanists and Donatists). It can also illuminate artistic and liturgical developments, which are poorly reflected in texts, if at all (Frend 1997:29ff.).

Though the archeologist can be unsympathetic to the concerns of the student of the texts, one major subset of archeological discovery has been the unearthing of new texts. Of great importance to the study of patristics has been the study of the finds at Nag Hammadi in Upper Egypt. The texts, which are probably late fourth-century copies of works written in the second century, are important because they provide concrete evidence of the beliefs of the gnostic groups on the fringes of Christianity, which were attacked by writers like Irenaeus – although any mapping of the specific views he cites directly onto the Nag Hammadi texts is very difficult.

Although the texts were discovered accidentally by a local man in 1945, the complexity of preparing them for publication meant that they did not make a real impact on patristic studies until the 1970s. A provisional translation appeared in 1977 and a photographic facsimile was produced in the same period, but definitive editions are still being produced (some in the series *Nag Hammadi Studies*). The study of other papyrus finds, for example those at Oxyrhynchus, helps scholars fill out the picture of early Christian society by studying texts like letters and various sorts of church documents. Use of archeological evidence has stimulated a growing trend for the study of early Christianity, in particular geographic centers such as Alexandria, Syria, Antioch, and Caesarea. This research has further emphasized the diversity among early Christians and, in particular, it has become clear that not only Hellenistic culture but also that of diaspora Judaism affected the beliefs and practices of early Christian communities in very different ways.

In the twentieth and twenty-first centuries, patristic scholars have become more sympathetic to the methods of the social sciences: current studies of the early Church often use categories like culture, society, class, hierarchy, and gender in order to interpret the historical evidence. They have also benefited from developments in the study of rhetoric and late Platonism. In their awareness of similarities which cut across the whole world of late antiquity, patristic scholars have become closer than ever to classicists, especially in the United States: see, for example, the work of Peter Brown (Brown 1988) and Elizabeth Clark (Clark 1992).

Establishing the texts and creating the scholarly apparatus

The first series of modern scholarly editions of patristic texts was the Vienna Corpus (*Corpus Scriptorum Ecclesiasticorum Latinorum*), begun in 1866. Von Harnack, with O. von Gebhardt, founded the series *Texte und Untersuchungen zur Geschichte der altchristlichen Literatur* (1882–); he also initiated the Commission on the Church Fathers at Berlin, which produced editions of the early Greek Fathers, *Die griechischen christlichen Schriftsteller der ersten drei Jahrhunderte* (1897–). In 1942 de Lubac and Daniélou established the series *Sources Chrétiennes*, which provided new editions of patristic texts with a parallel French translation. By the year 2000 the series had run to over 450 volumes. In the German-speaking world the increasingly strong influence of German classical philologists on patristics studies facilitated the production of such editions as Werner Jaeger's series of works by Gregory of Nyssa. The latter half of the twentieth century saw the appearance of the important *Corpus Christianorum* editions, with series of Greek, Latin, and medieval works.

New theological works are very rarely found on ancient papyrus; occasionally they emerge through the discovery of Byzantine or medieval manuscript copies (for example, the texts and translations of some newly discovered letters by Augustine of Hippo were published in the 1980s, and of some of his sermons in the 1990s). Some patristic texts which were no longer extant in Greek have been recovered through the careful study of their Syriac translations: this process began at the beginning of the twentieth century but has gathered pace in recent years. Texts rescued in this way include, for example, works by Evagrius of Pontus, whose importance for the history of monasticism has only recently been fully appreciated.

Dictionaries and study-aids

The *Patristic Greek Lexikon* was begun on a suggestion made by the Central Society for Sacred Study in 1906 at the time when H. B. Swete was the Warden of the Society (Lampe 1961:iii). Within three years eighty clergy and others had been found who were sufficiently interested in patristic studies to be willing to be included in a list of searchers. C. H. Turner was writing to Alexander Souter on March 1, 1916 with a progress report and a request. "Our scheme" for the *Lexikon* is, he says, "rapidly taking shape. I wonder if you could help us with the section of Greek words used in the Latin Fathers – we have as yet no collection of these, and I think they should clearly come in" (Bodleian Library, MS Eng. Lett. C615). The prospective searchers were to be allocated portions of the *Patrologia Graeca* of J. P. Migne, from which they would collect material for the *Lexikon* on slips. (The flavor of this task is captured in correspondence on another task. On June 12, 1933, C. H. Milne was writing to Alexander Souter about his collection of "a goodly number of Hilary quotations" from the Gospels. "I have now completed those from Matthew. They consist of 759 slips, and are ready to be dispatched. I retain them until (not without some degree of satisfaction!), I can show you the pile.") For the *Lexikon*, a Committee of Direction was formed and in 1915 an editor was appointed. He was Darwell Stone, then Principal of Pusey House, and he was to serve until his death in 1941.

After 1941, the Committee, which was by then chaired by N. P. Williams, and from 1943 by R. H. Lightfoot, appointed F. L. Cross to be the new editor. He was then the Librarian of Pusey House, and later Lady Margaret Professor of Divinity at the University of Oxford. The editor who brought the project to completion in 1961 was G. W. H. Lampe. The *Patristic Greek Lexikon* in the end covered the period from Clement of Rome at the end of the first century to Theodore of Studium.

The Preface to the *Patristic Greek Lexikon* reflected the policy decision which had been arrived at by 1965, to make the object of the work "the provision of as full a treatment as possible of all words of special theological or ecclesiastical significance" and the listing of words in the Fathers which do not appear in Liddell and Scott or which are "but poorly attested there" (Lampe 1961:iv).

The *Thesaurus Linguae Latinae* was conceived as an attempt to include in one word-list the Christian with the secular Latin tradition up to the sixth century. However, even if it seemed acceptable in England at first to base the *Patristic Greek Lexikon* on Migne it was apparent elsewhere that Migne would not do as a basis for a dictionary, where it was essential that the words listed as contained in a given text or context be accurate. When the *Thesaurus Linguae Latinae* was planned it was realized that first it would be necessary to create reliable editions of the writers whose "words" were to be included. This was the beginning of the Vienna Corpus, under the guidance of Johannes Vahlen (Hanslik 1966:71–4).

Journals and conferences

In 1951 the enormous four-yearly Oxford Patristic Conferences began, drawing hundreds of patristic scholars from all over the world, with their proceedings published in an expanding batch of *Studia Patristica* volumes, at first in the series *Texte und Unter-suchungen zur Geschichte der Altchristlichen Literatur* (Berlin) and then by the Pergamon Press, then by Cistercian Publications, and then Peeters, Leuven.

The four volumes of the Proceedings of the Third Conference, of 1959, begin with an introductory essay by A. Mandouze; he takes the patristic age to be the "golden age" of Christian writing (*aetas aurea scriptorum ecclesiasticorum*). He celebrates the range patristics now embraces as reflected in the sections into which papers are divided by the Conference and its Proceedings: *editiones, critica, philologica, biblica, judaica, historica, liturgica, iuridica, theologica, philosophica, monastica, ascetica* (Mandouze 1961). Some major individual patristic writers now have their own conference series.

The vitality and scope of patristic studies is also demonstrated by the current exis-tence of over half a dozen journals specifically dedicated to the discipline, besides others which frequently publish articles on the early Church.

Conclusion

In 1905, Darwell Stone, the Librarian of Pusey House, who was to be editor of the *Patristic Greek Lexikon*, published his reflections in *The Conditions of Church Life in the First Six Centuries* (Stone 1905). He discusses baptism, confirmation, and the eucharist, against a background of citation of the texts ("there is evidence in the *Canons of Hippolytus* and in the writings of Tertullian and Cyprian of the celebration of the Eucharist in connexion with special events and days" (Stone 1905:15). He considers the evidence that the invocation of saints "was widespread, tolerated, and approved by Fathers of acknowledged eminence" from the fourth century at least (Stone 1905:25).

A century later, patristics as a discipline sees itself less and less as having a primary duty to establish orthodoxy. Von Harnack's view eventually won the day, but for some decades theologians of the *ressourcement* saw the Fathers as a source for renewing the Church, and it was common for Anglican scholars to accept the historical–critical inter-pretation of Scripture, but to look to the patristic period as the definitive expression of doctrine. The continued application of the historical–critical method to patristic texts also has undermined that confidence, however. Consequently, patristics has come more and more to be the study of *all* forms of early Christianity (a development reinforced by the facts that it is increasingly studied in secular institutions, often by non-believers, and that common with any academic discipline, the longer it is established the more its range has expanded as scholars search for topics not previously studied).

Another effect of the application of historical–critical methods – not least in estab-lishing texts of marginal writers – has been to show that many people labeled heretics were not as heretical as once thought, even by quite conservative standards. This process began at the beginning of the twentieth century with the reassessment of Nestorius and Apollinarius (by J. F. Bethune-Baker 1908 and C. Raven 1923, respec-tively); one of the dominant issues since the 1970s has been a similar debate regard-ing Arianism (initiated by R. Gregg and D. Groh's *Early Arianism: A View of Salvation* 1981). Even the gnostics have been re-examined, in particular by feminist scholars such as Elaine Pagels and Rosemary Ruether.

Opinions now seem to differ as to whether the patristic period is especially important because it takes the student back to Christianity's beginnings or whether it is to be placed straightforwardly side by side with other periods as fruitful and instructive in the same way as they are. Those who hold the former view less commonly insist that the earliest Church was the purest church, although they do often have ecumenical reasons for studying a period before the Church was officially divided: the implication is that Christians should begin from beliefs which were once shared by all. Others may not themselves hold the "older is better" view, but seek to recover aspects of that period which are all too often either missed or misunderstood by those who do hold that opinion. Thus feminists like Rosemary Ruether do not claim that the patterns of early Christianity should be definitive – because they were patriarchal – but they never-theless study women who succeeded in making their voices heard. Others, like Kari Elisabeth Børresen, examine tensions within the Church Fathers' anthropology which complicate the understanding of their view of women. Historical scholarship has made it clear that certain patriarchal theological and structural patterns which grew up in the patristic era remained entrenched precisely because later generations regarded the Fathers' writings as peculiarly authoritative.

Those who deny the era of the Fathers any special authority are not claiming that it cannot inform theological reflection in any way – rather, that patristic thought is to be set beside that from later ages. Systematic theologians show no signs of ceasing to use patristic material as a source; some scholars, such as Maurice Wiles and Rowan Williams have spent much of their careers moving between patristics and theology. Frances Young has asked whether the dissatisfaction with purely historical analysis, and interest in modern literary theory which has challenged biblical scholars, will lead patristic scholars toward a reading of their sources which is more theological (Young 1997:433–4). Consequently, although some patristic scholars have suggested that the future of the discipline will mean "less theology, more history" (Clark 1986:3), and although there will always be ample space for a more strictly historical approach, it seems likely that in fact more history will simply mean more theology.

References

Altaner, B. 1960. *Patrology*. Freiburg: Herder.

Amand de Mendieta, E. 1961. "Mount Athos and Greek Patristic Editions," *Studia Patristica* III: 23–37.

Apostolic Fathers. 1869ff. trans. J. B. Lightfoot (a translation of *Clement of Rome*, the *Ignatian Epistles*, and the *Epistle of Polycarp*). London: Macmillan.

Aquinas, T. 1952. *Catena Aurea in Quatuor Evangelia*, ed. P. Angelici Guarienti. Rome: Marietti.

Backus, I. 1997. *The Reception of the Church Fathers in the West: From the Carolingians to the Maurists*. Leiden: Brill.

Bethune-Baker, J. F. 1908. *Nestorius and his Teaching*. Cambridge: Cambridge University Press.

Brown, P. 1988. *The Body and Society*. New York: Columbia University Press.

Chadwick. O. 1990. *The Spirit of the Oxford Movement*. Cambridge: Cambridge University Press.

Clark, E. 1986. "The State and Future of Historical Theology: Patristic Studies," in E. Clark, *Ascetic Piety and Women's Faith*. Lampeter: Edward Mellen.

Clark, E. 1992. *The Origenist Controversy: The Cultural Construction of an Early Christian Debate.* Princeton, NJ: Princeton University Press.

Daniélou, J. trans. 1942. *Grégoire de Nysse, La Vie de Moïse. Sources chrétiennes* I. Paris: Éditions du Cerf (reissued with Greek text, 1955).

Daniélou, J. 1944. *Platonisme et théologie mystique: doctrine spirituelle de saint Grégoire de Nysse.* Paris: Aubier, Éditions Montaigne.

Daniélou, J. 1955. *Origen.* London/New York: 1955 [original French edition, 1948].

Daniélou, J. 1958. *Philon d'Alexandrie.* Paris: A. Fayard.

Daniélou, J. 1964. *A History of Early Christian Doctrine before the Council of Nicaea,* vol. 1: *The Theology of Jewish Christianity;* vol. 2: *Gospel Message and Hellenistic Culture;* vol. 3: *The Origins of Latin Christianity.* London: Darton, Longman and Todd [original French edition, 1958].

Daniélou, J. and Marrou, H. 1964. *The Christian Centuries: A New History of the Catholic Church,* vol. 1: *The First Six Hundred Years.* London: Darton, Longman and Todd [original French edition, 1963].

Das Decretum Gelasianum de libris recipiendis et non recipiendis. 1912. ed. E. von Dobschütz, in *Texte und Untersuchungen* 8(4). Leipzig: Hinrichs.

De Lubac, H. 1950. *Histoire et Esprit. L'intelligence de l'Écriture d'après Origène.* Paris: Aubier.

De Lubac, H. 1988. *Catholicism: Christ and the Common Destiny of Man.* San Francisco, CA: Ignatius Press [original French edition, 1938].

De Lubac, H. 1998. *Medieval Exegesis.* Grand Rapids, MI/Edinburgh: W. B. Eerdmans/T. & T. Clark [original French edition, 1959–64].

De Lubac, H. and Doutreleau, L. eds. 1944. *Homélies sur la Genèse. Sources chrétiennes* 7. Paris: Éditions du Cerf.

De Lubac, H. and Fortier P. eds. 1947. *Homélies sur l'Exode. Sources chrétiennes* 16. Paris: Éditions du Cerf.

Duchesne, L. 1892. *Bulletin Critique* XII.

Duchesne, L. 1914. *Early History of the Christian Church from its Foundation to the End of the Fifth Century.* London: Murray [original French edition, 1906–10].

Frend, W. H. C. 1997. "Archaeology, the Ally of Patristics," *Studia Patristica* XXIX.

Gregg, R. and Groh, D. 1981. *Early Arianism: A View of Salvation.* London: SCM Press.

Grosseteste, R. 1986. *De Cessatione Legalium,* eds. R. C. Dales and E. B. King. Oxford: Oxford University Press.

Hanslik, R. 1966. "To the Hundredth Anniversary of CSEL," *Studia Patristica* VII.

Jaeger, W. 1947. Review of the series *The Ancient Christian Writers: Vigiliae Chritiana,* 1.

Lampe, G. W. H. ed. 1961. Preface to *A Patristic Greek Lexikon.* Oxford: Clarendon Press.

Lathchen. 1969. *Egloga.* ed. M. Adraian. *Corpus Christianorum Series Latina* 145.

Libri carolini. 1997. *MGH Legum,* sectio III, *Concilia II, Supplementum,* ed. H. Bastgen; *MGH Concilia II,* eds. A. Freeman and P. Meyvaert. Hanover: Hannsche.

Lietzmann, H. 1904. *Apollinarius von Laodicea und seine Schule.* Tübingen: J. C. B. Mohr.

Lietzmann, H. 1993. *A History of the Early Church.* Cambridge: James Clarke [original German edition, 1932–44].

Mandouze, A. 1961. "Mesure et démesure de la Patristique," in *Studia Patristica,* ed. F. L. Cross, published as *Texte und Untersuchungen zur Geschichte der altchristlichen Literatur* 78.

Mohrmann, C. 1947. "Le latin commun et le latin des chrétiens," *Vigiliae Christianae* I, pp. 1–12.

Müller, G. ed. 1977–98. *Theologische Realenzyklopädie.* Berlin: Walter de Gruyter.

Nag Hammadi Codices. 1972–84. *The Facsimile Edition of the Nag Hammadi Codices.* Leiden: Brill.

Newman, J. H. 1835a. *The British Magazine* 7.

Newman, J. H. 1835b. *The British Magazine* 8.

Newman, J. H. 1876. *The Arians of the Fourth Century.* London: Basil Montague Pickering.

Newman, J. H. 1881. *Select Treatises of St. Athanasius in Controversy with the Arians*. Oxford: J. & J. Parker.

Patrides, C. A. ed. 1980. *The Cambridge Platonists*. Cambridge: Cambridge University Press.

Raven, C. 1923. *Apollinarianism: An Essay on the Christology of the Early Church*. Cambridge: Cambridge University Press.

Robinson, J. M. ed. 1977. *The Nag Hammadi Library in English*. Leiden: Brill.

Sanday, W. 1903. "Contentio veritatis," *Journal of Theological Studies* IV:1–16.

Sedulius Scottus. 1988. *Collectaneum miscellaneum*, ed. D. Simpson, *Corpus Christianorum Continuatio Mediaevalis* 67.

Stone, D. 1905. *The Conditions of Church Life in the First Six Centuries*. London: SPCK/Church Historical Society.

Swete, H. B. 1899. Introductory statement to *Journal of Theological Studies* I.

Torrell, J.-P. 1977. "Théorie de la prophétie et philosophie de la connaissance aux environs de 1230," *Spicilegium Sacrum Lovaniense* 40.

Turner, C. H. 1910. *The History and Use of Creeds and Anathemas in the Early Centuries of the Church*. London: SPCK/Church Historical Society.

Von Balthasar, H. U. 1941. *Kosmische Liturgie. Das Weltbild Maximus des Bekenners*. Einsiedeln: Johannes-Verlag.

Von Balthasar, H. U. 1957. *Parole et Mystère chez Origène*. Paris: Éditions du Cerf (containing essays originally published 1936 and 1937).

Von Balthasar, H. U. 1995. *Presence and Thought: An Essay on the Religious Philosophy of Gregory of Nyssa*. San Francisco, CA: Ignatius Press [original French edition, 1942].

Von Harnack, A. 1897–1910. *History of Dogma*. London: Williams & Norgate.

Von Harnack, A. 1901. *The Essence of Christianity*. London: Theological Translation Library.

Wiles, M. F. 1979. "The Patristic Appeal to Tradition," in M. F. Wiles, *Explorations in Theology* 4. London: SCM Press.

Young, F. 1997. "From Suspicion and Sociology to Spirituality: On Method, Hermeneutics and Appropriation with Respect to Patristic Material," in *Studia Patristica* XXIX. Leuven: Peeters.

Reference works

Oxford Dictionary of the Christian Church. 1997. 3rd edn., eds. F. L. Cross and E. A. Livingstone. Oxford: Oxford University Press [original edition, 1957].

A Patristic Greek Lexikon. 1961. ed. G. W. H. Lampe. Oxford: Clarendon Press.

Thesaurus Linguae Latinae. 1900. Leipzig: Teubner.

Series

Ante-Nicene Writers: Translations of the Fathers down to AD325. 1867–72. eds. A. Roberts and J. Donaldson. Edinburgh: T. & T. Clark.

Corpus Christianorum. Turnhout: Brepols; Leuven: University Press.
  Series Apocryphum 1983–
  Series Graeca 1977–
  Series Latina 1954–
  Continuatio mediaevalis 1971–

Corpus Scriptorum Ecclesiasticorum Latinorum. 1866– . Vienna: Österreichischen Akademie der Wissenschaften.

Gregorii Nysseni Opera. 1958– . founding editor, W. Jaeger. Leiden: Brill.

Die griechischen christlichen Schriftsteller der ersten drei Jahrhunderte. 1897– . founding editor, A. von Harnack. Leipzig: J. C. Hinrichs; later, Berlin: Akademie-Verlag.

A Library of the Fathers of the Holy Catholic Church, anterior to the division of the east and west, translated by members of the English church. 1843–61. eds. E. B. Pusey, J. Keble, J. H. Newman, C. Marriot. Oxford: J. & J. Parker; London: F. & J. Rivington.

Nag Hammadi Studies. 1975– . eds. Martin Kraemer, James M. Robinson, Frederik Wisse et al. Leiden: Brill.

Nicene and Post-Nicene Fathers of the Christian Church. 1890–1900. eds. P. Schaff and H. Wace. Edinburgh: T. & T. Clark.

Sources Chrétiennes. 1942– . Paris.

Texte und Untersuchungen zur Geschichte der altchristlichen Literatur. 1882– . founding editor, A. von Harnack. Leipzig: J. C. Hinrichs; later, Berlin: Akademie-Verlag.

Journals

Journal of Early Christian Studies, 1993– . Baltimore, MD.

Journal of Theological Studies, 1899– . London, Oxford.

Patristic and Byzantine Review, 1981– . Kingston, NY.

Patristica Sorbonensia, 1957– . Paris.

Patristische Texte und Studien, 1963– . Berlin.

Recherches augustiniennes, 1958– . Paris.

Recherches de science religieuse, 1910– . Paris.

Second Century, 1981– . Abilene.

St. Vladimir's Theological Quarterly, 1957– . Tuckahoe, NY.

Vigiliae Christianae, 1947– . Amsterdam.

Zeitschrift für antikes Christentum, 1997– . Berlin.

CHAPTER 9

Medieval Theology

Stephen F. Brown

"Theology" is not a biblical word. It is a Greek word, a pagan word, and because of the variety of pagan religious beliefs, it is also an equivocal word. As a pagan expression providing an equivocal view of the gods, the term "theology" did not enter the world of the Christian West easily. The pagan Roman philosopher Varro (d. 27 BCE) inherited from the Greek tradition the complex or equivocal understanding of the Greek meanings of "theology." He spoke of three types: (1) the theology of the poets, which beautifully portrayed the polytheistic world of human imagination; (2) the theology of the philosophers, Plato and Aristotle, who presented reason's explanation of the world and its events; and (3) the most influential form of theology, civil theology, with its portrait of the gods who ruled the beliefs, aspirations, and activities of the ordinary citizens of the city.

None of these portraits fits the triune Christian God. The Christian Tertullian (d. c.220), in his *Ad nationes*, reported Varro's depiction of the gods and rebutted each of its three forms, wanting to have nothing to do with what the Greeks and Romans called "theology." Augustine (d. 430), too, was aware of Varro's three-fold portrait of the gods. In Book VI of *The City of God* he examined each type in detail and rejected each of these forms of theology. He discovered, however, other pagan writers, the Platonists, whom he considered to have come closer to the truth. On the philosophical level, they represented God as transcending the soul, and their depiction of Him as superior to the world and human souls, and as the source of the incorporeal light that could lead men and women to human fulfillment, made Augustine more sympathetic to this form of "theology." Their depiction of a loftier god inspired Augustine to call such people *Dei cognitores* rather than *theologi*, thus separating them from the devotees of the types of gods described by Varro. Augustine's choice of language shows that the term *theologi* in the fifth-century West was still a pejorative noun, linked as it was to the gods of the poets, philosophers, and emperors.

Peter Abelard (d. 1142), many centuries later, is credited with bringing the term "theology" into the medieval Latin vocabulary. This is not because we have Abelardian works entitled *Theologia Christiana* or *Theologia Summi boni*, for these titles are later inventions. The manuscripts of Abelard have simply the *incipits* or opening words of his treatises. Yet, it is Abelard himself who speaks of a collection of questions concerning various areas of Christian teaching, and he calls this collection "our theology": "The solution to these proposed questions we reserve for examination in our theology." Still, even among Peter's disciples, *theologia* limited itself to the study of the triune God, and *beneficia* was the term used to describe discussions of Christ and the sacraments. "Theology" was, thus, not a term indicating the study of all areas of Christian belief.

Bernard of Clairvaux (d. 1153) mocked Abelard's *theologia*. He declared that Peter's approach to divine revelation was *stultilogia* (foolishness). It turned the reading of the Bible into a source-book for questions to manifest superior debating prowess. In Abelard's approach, as Bernard read it, the spiritual and contemplative reading of the Scriptures was set aside. In Bernard's view, Abelard's "theology" was less a study of God and more a study of man's study of God. It stressed argument over conviction. We thus have a split in the way in which theology was pursued. Some study of the Scriptures was done for affective reasons: it led people to a deeper sense and feeling for God; the other approach was pursued because of a search for a better understanding of the truths of the faith, and aimed at distinguishing truth from error or heresy. Affective or monastic theology could describe the former; aspective or theoretical theology could name the latter.

The medieval debate over truth and error, although having its roots in Patristic efforts to defend and lead people to the Christian faith, thus seems to have begun in Abelard's *Theologia Christiana*. In this work, Peter Abelard defined faith as "the judgment of things not seen." Bernard of Clairvaux saw this as a distortion of Paul's declaration that "faith is the argument of things not seen." Faith is primary. It is the ground for the acceptance of the realities presented by revelation. Such overwhelming realities are not justified by human judgment. Faith is a gift from God, not the result of human conclusions. Abelard, in fact, did not deny the primacy or certitude of faith. When he said that faith is "a judgment of things not seen," he did not intend either of the meanings that Bernard gave to his statement, namely, that "faith is either opinion or each believer can choose or judge which of the truths he wishes to affirm." Peter, rather, underscored the difference between "comprehend" (*comprehendere*), "know experientially" (*cognoscere*), and "understand" (*intelligere*). Only God comprehends the divine reality that is Himself. The angels and the blessed in heaven know experientially the realities of the faith. In this life, we can neither comprehend nor know experientially faith's realities. Still, we can get some understanding of the objects of faith. Faith is an invitation to search. It excites in us an inquiry that hopefully will beget in us a deeper understanding of the realities we believe in. Despite his attempts at understanding, faith is, for Peter, primary and is the necessary condition for such understanding. In terms of the Vulgate version of Isaiah 7:9, which he employs: "Unless you believe, you shall not understand."

When Abelard's opponents brought forth the text of Gregory the Great, that "faith has no merit if it is based on evidence," he answered that such an interpretation goes against the very practice of Gregory and many of the other Fathers of the Church. They used arguments against those who attacked the faith, and through argumentation they also attempted to bring about a clearer understanding of the chief mysteries of the Trinity and Incarnation. Gregory's text, then, should be understood as a prohibition against the claim for experiential knowledge (*cognitio*), not a charge against Isaiah's invitation to understanding (*intelligentia*).

The term "theology," although employed at times by Abelard, really became current only in the thirteenth century, in the setting of the newly formed universities. There, at first, the preparatory curriculum for those who were to study Scripture followed the seven liberal arts: the trivium (grammar, rhetoric, and dialectic) and the quadrivium (arithmetic, geometry, astronomy, and music). Quite quickly, in the thirteenth century, that curriculum changed when many more of the works of Aristotle became available in Latin translations and expanded the area called "dialectic." Since the time of Boethius (d. 524) some of Aristotle's logical works were available in competent Latin forms, and with solid commentaries. In the twelfth and thirteenth centuries the rest of his logical works and all of his more philosophical works became available. For our present consideration, the *Physics* and *Metaphysics* were most important. In different ways, they dealt with divine things. Aristotle himself speaks of his first philosophy or metaphysics as a philosophical rather than a mythical or political *theologia*. In the new efforts of the Christian universities, it was Aristotle's challenge that forced theologians to show the superiority of the Christian revelation concerning God and his providence. It was in this arena that "theology" was developed as a distinct discipline, and as superior to Aristotle's first philosophy or *theologia*. As we will see, this was not an easy task.

Theology Viewed as an Organized Collection of Questions

Peter Abelard's teacher, Anselm of Laon (d. 1117), made one of the first medieval attempts at gathering questions that moved the study of the Scriptures from textual exegesis into a systematic whole. His organizational plan was based on the model of John Scottus Eriugena, a translator and commentator on Dionysius the Areopagyte's works: Creation, the Fall of angels and men, the necessity of Redemption, Redemption, and the Sacraments. His collection of questions followed this order. Later collectors of questions arising from the Scriptures might organize them according to different models: Peter Lombard (d. 1160) took as his model the division presented by St. Augustine in *De doctrina Christiana*: the study of Scripture is about things and signs. Robert Grosseteste's (d. 1253), in *Hexaëmeron*, unified his theology through Christ, whose divine nature united Him with the divine persons and whose human nature made Him one with all creatures. Grosseteste's goal was thus a Christocentric approach to the unification of the Scripture message.

The most well-organized and influential Augustinian collection of such questions must be attributed to Peter Lombard's *Sentences*. Many of those whose works have come down to us as *summae* (i.e. *summae quaestionum*, or collections of questions) in the twelfth and early thirteenth centuries are in fact following the lead of Lombard's work. It is easy, then, to understand why Alexander of Hales chose the *Sentences* of Lombard as an official textbook to supplement the study of the Scriptures themselves in the third decade of the thirteenth century. In effect, Lombard's work was already functioning in that way.

However, Lombard's *Sentences* was not the sole supplement to studying Scripture itself. Peter Comestor (d. 1180) had written a *Historia scholastica* (1169–73) that brought an historical, rather than a logical, order to the Scripture message. He realized that the Bible itself was a complicated collection of works: "a forest" through which Christians had to find their way. His *Historia*, a Bible history that provided, with the help of the Fathers of the Church and profane historians, a map through the forest, was also an alternate way of studying the Scripture message.

As the universities developed in the thirteenth century, then, there were three alternatives for studying the Scriptural message: the Bible itself, the *Historia scholastica*, and the *Sentences*, or *Summae quaestionum*, that followed more or less the *Sentences* of Lombard.

The study of the Bible always held the primary place in the curriculum. It could, however, take place in any of the three aforementioned ways. Even when they studied the Bible itself, some medievals preferred to get an over-view of the whole of both the Old and New Testaments; others preferred to look at a specific work of the Old Testament and then contrast it with the enhancing viewpoint of a New Testament work. As they stepped somewhat beyond the biblical text itself, some favored the unified historical view provided by Peter Comestor's *Historia scholastica*. As the university developed its alternative to Aristotle's philosophical wisdom, the *Sentences* of Lombard, or collection of questions according to a logical ordering principle, became the more dominant way of studying the revelation found in the Scriptures. Yet, it is important to realize that each of these different approaches was in reality a different manner of studying the biblical message. God's revelation, as understood by the Christian Church, not as presented by heretical exponents, remained central to all forms of medieval theological study.

The tensions concerning different ways of studying Scripture are well illustrated in the *Summa aurea* of William of Auxerre. There, William raises the question of whether the Fathers of the Church, especially Augustine and Gregory the Great, were not weakening the authority of Scripture when they sought arguments to support the faith. Doesn't faith stand on its own terms? Why does it need rational arguments? In the 1220s William gives the answer that justifies and has justified "theology" since the time of the Fathers of the Church. He quotes St. Augustine's *On the Trinity*: I do not approve of all knowledge, since some of it is pursued out of pure vanity or without purpose, but I do approve "of that knowledge by which our most wholesome faith, which leads to true fulfillment, is begotten, nourished, defended and strengthened." This citation from St. Augustine summarizes the justification for medieval developments in theology: rational argument is needed for begetting, nourishing, defending, and strengthening the faith. And, as we have already seen, in the case of Abelard, Gregory the Great's warning that "faith loses its merit when it has evidence supporting it" is only applicable when a person resists belief unless there is evidence that is the sole justifying ground for acceptance. Faith is the primary motive or ground for assenting to the indubitable truth of revelation. By faith, our minds are expanded to a fuller capacity. We submit, through faith, to a mind higher than our own, who reveals a reality beyond any produced by our own will or reason.

The Competition with Aristotle

The greatest Christian Latin writer of the West was undoubtedly St. Augustine. His influence is overwhelming: Hugh of St. Victor (d. c.1141), the author of a *Collection of Sentences* (*summa sententiarum*) and *On the Sacraments of the Christian Faith* (*De sacramentis fidei Christianae*), through his many citations from the Bishop of Hippo established himself as "the second Augustine." The numerous citations of Augustine in Lombard's *Sentences* could easily make him a worthy candidate for the same title. Augustine is, beyond doubt, the most influential Patristic authority among medieval writers. Despite Augustine's formidable presence, there would be a challenge to the organization he gave to the divine mysteries and especially to the neo-Platonic influences on his reflections. He lived in a world that was ruled intellectually by Stoic and neo-Platonic philosophers. His criticism of the Stoic form of neo-Platonist thought, in Book XIX of *The City of God*, is masterful in its ridicule of a man-centered reality. There he redefined "justice" as "the tranquillity of order." His new order had God, not man, at the apex. Man's search for "peace" could only be found when man realized that he was a creature of God, not a self-made man. It could only be established when men submitted themselves to the divine order, not an order constructed by their own thought or fancy.

Augustine's model of Christian thinking earned respect for a millennium, and even beyond. Yet, Christian theologians encountered a new challenge in the late twelfth and the thirteenth centuries. A new voice was in the air: Aristotle's voice. It was supported in different ways by his early Greek commentators, Themistius and Alexander of Aphrodisias, and the Arabian Avempace, who presented a very metaphysical and lofty Aristotle. But it was also advanced by an Averroes who approached a more physically anchored Aristotle who only spoke of a divine being to the degree that he was a cause manifested through his effects.

The preparatory curriculum had changed. The Arts faculty that studied the traditional seven liberal arts only did so in a nominal way. The Arts curriculum at the University of Paris by 1255 had changed to a philosophy curriculum: the older "dialectics" section of the seven liberal arts squeezed out the other subjects and had slowly introduced the other works of Aristotle in their place. This was the new preparation for the study of Scripture – the Aristotelian philosophy curriculum. It challenged the very structure and nature of the Scripture or theology faculty. If Aristotle in his philosophical writings could offer a proof for a Prime Mover or god, could the Christians inspired by the Scriptures offer a more solid proof? In short, could theology be as solid a science as Aristotle's *theologia*, or did it fall short of any scientific measure?

At the University of Paris, the Franciscan Odo Rigaud (d. 1275), citing Aristotle's very terms (*dignitates*, *suppositiones*, and *conclusiones*) describing scientific procedure, attempted to show the similarity between the scientific method of Aristotle and that of a scientific theology. Shortly thereafter, the new precision is most evident in the *Commentary on the Sentences* of St. Bonaventure (d. 1274). It is important to note that in some of his works Bonaventure uses a more traditional neo-Platonic and Augustinan approach to studying reality as portrayed by the Scriptures. However, in his university responsibilities of lecturing on the *Sentences* of Peter Lombard, he adjusts his method to the challenge of Aristotle's works. First of all, he divides his prologue to the work into four parts that explicitly parallel the four causes of Aristotle, studying the material, formal, final, and efficient causes proposed by the Philosopher. If you compare Bonaventure's Prologue to the *Sentences* with the *Summa* attributed to his Franciscan predecessor at Paris, Alexander of Hales, you will find striking differences between the two on almost all considerations of the various causes. If we look at the efficient cause, we can note that for Alexander, the author of a *Summa* or the *Sentences* is God (since they treat of God's revelation), whereas for Bonaventure, the author of the *Sentences* is Peter Lombard. Bonaventure justifies his position by distinguishing between a scribe, a compiler, a commentator, and an author. An author differs from the others: he writes his own words and joins them to the words of others, as does a commentator. The difference between an author and a commentator, however, is this: an author's own words form the principal part of the work, whereas the words of others are added for the sake of confirmation.

Likewise, in dealing with the formal cause, or way of proceeding, of the *Sentences*, there will be a distinct variation in the theological study of the Scriptures between the two men. For Alexander, following Augustine, any study of God, the cause of causes, is wisdom. Even Aristotle's study of the cause of causes, the Prime Mover, is wisdom, though less properly, since it concerns itself with the cause of causes as a form of knowledge following the way of art and reasoning. This is not wisdom properly and principally speaking, which is the wisdom of the Scriptures "that perfects the soul according to affection by moving the believer toward the good through principles of fear and love." Alexander, again following Augustine, affirms that science, in contrast to wisdom, is the study of caused beings. Furthermore, it perfects our knowledge in accord with truth. If we would schematize Alexander's view of the kinds of knowledge we can obtain in our studies, we would say that there is: (1) Christian Theology: wisdom as wisdom – the study of God which leads us to the love of God; (2) First Philosophy: wisdom as science – the study of the cause of causes which deepens our knowledge of the first cause; and (3) the Sciences – science as science – knowledge of caused things, including those that also are consequent, though not first, causes. Bonaventure looks to the end or purpose of studying the *Sentences* of Lombard. Since that purpose is to promote the faith, it follows an investigative approach that is effective in advancing the faith. Such a rational pursuit as that found in the *Sentences* is not about belief as such; the theology of the *Sentences* is "about belief as something to be understood." According to Bonaventure, this kind of investigative procedure is necessary to advance the faith for three types of men: "for some are opposed to the faith, some are weak in faith, and some are strong in faith." The questioning approach of the *Sentences* provides arguments and analogies helpful in the defense of the faith against those who challenge it. Secondly, the investigative approach helps those who are weak in the faith, by presenting arguments supporting the faith. If heretics and other attackers were to give arguments and there were none to show the Catholic positions, befuddled believers would not continue to believe. So far, Bonaventure seems to follow closely Augustine's declaration at the beginning of *On the Trinity*, chapter XIV, supporting the kind of study "by which that most wholesome faith that leads to true blessedness is begotten, nourished,

defended and strengthened." Yet, Bonaventure still has his third group of people to consider: those strong in the faith. For this group, the study associated with the *Sentences*
is effective in bringing the intellectual pleasure of understanding. The nature of the
believer's soul is to understand what it believes. As Bonaventure has already said: the
theology of the *Sentences* is "about belief as something to be understood." In terms of
Alexander's categories, Bonaventure has altered the scheme a bit: there is now also a
Christian Theology that is wisdom as science. He may in many works, such as *The
Journey of the Mind to God*, *The Triple Way*, and *The Tree of Life*, pursue wisdom as
wisdom; but he has also made room in his *Commentary on the Sentences*, *Disputed Questions on the Trinity*, *Disputed Questions on the Knowledge of Christ*, that is, his more properly university classroom works, for a more scientific approach of an Aristotelian type
in studying God's revelation. Similar variations can be found in the treatments that
other masters approve for the considerations of the material and final causes of *Summae*
and the *Sentences*.

The most explicit attempt at setting up the analogy between philosophical study and
theological study, however, is found at the beginning of the very first question of *The
Summa of Theology* (*Summa Theologiae*) of Thomas Aquinas (d. 1274). For clarification
purposes he first, and quite surprisingly, asks: "Whether, besides the philosophical disciplines, any further teaching is required?" In other words: Is reason sufficient in itself
in man's pursuit of fulfillment? He answers that for man to obtain salvation it is necessary to have a teaching revealed by God. He explains why:

> For the truth about God, such as reason can know it, would only be known by a few, and
> that after a long time, and with the admixture of many errors; whereas man's whole
> salvation, which is in God, depends upon the knowledge of this truth.

This is true of the knowledge of God such as reason can know Him. A revelation is *a
fortiori* necessary for the truths that are only knowable through divine revelation, such
as God as triune, and the Incarnation of the Son of God. So far, Aquinas is showing the
limitations of philosophy and of the Philosopher, Aristotle. In the second article of the
first question of the *Summa*, he shows, however, the strong presence of Aristotle in his
conception of theology. There he asks if the study of sacred teaching can be a science.
He answers:

> We must bear in mind that there are two kinds of sciences. There are some which proceed
> from principles known by the natural light of the intellect, such as arithmetic and geom-
> etry and the like. There are also some which proceed from principles known by the light of
> a higher science: thus the science of optics proceeds from principles established by geom-
> etry, and music from principles established by arithmetic. So it is that sacred doctrine is a
> science because it proceeds from principles made known by the light of a higher science,
> namely, the science of God and the blessed. Hence, just as music accepts on authority the
> principles taught by the arithmetician, so sacred doctrine accepts the principles revealed
> by God.

This distinction concerning the different kinds of sciences, along with examples of
optics and music as subalternated sciences, comes from Aristotle's chief treatise on

scientific knowledge, the *Posterior Analytics*. For Thomas, Aristotle's subalternated, but nonetheless legitimate, sciences justify the claim that theology is a subalternated science. Like Aristotle's subalternated sciences, which do not have the direct evidence that would make them sciences in their own right, theology also lacks direct evidence that would make it a science on its own. Yet theology, like optics and music, is based on the evidence that exists for those who know directly the divine realities revealed in the Scriptures, namely God and the blessed. It even has a greater claim to being a subalternated science than optics and music do: it is based on divine authority, which neither deceives nor can be deceived, whereas optics and music are based on human authority, which is subject to deception.

The first principles employed in theological deductions of further truths are premises accepted on faith. In fact, Thomas considers the first principles of theology to be the articles of the Creed, and the very word "Creed" derives from *credere*, which means "to believe" or "to accept on faith." How can theology be a science if it is based on faith? Are not faith and science opposed to one another? Does not Aquinas himself say that you can not have faith and science about the same thing? The answer to these queries requires a number of clarifications. First of all, proper science is based on evidence and is not compatible with faith. Subalternated science is based on authority, and the authority itself – not the one who accepts on faith the declarations of the authority – has evidence. Next, however, in his *Commentary on the "De Trinitate" of Boethius*, we can see Thomas's effort to make his claim of a parallel between the method of theology and the method of philosophy even stronger, and he does so by focusing on first principles that in neither discipline can be proved. In the case of theology, first principles or the articles of the Creed are accepted because God has revealed them. As first principles, they can be accepted only because the First Truth, God, who has both knowledge and veracity, guarantees them. This does not mean that they are blindly believed. Reason does not abandon the first principles of the Christian faith:

> They are also defended against those who attack them, as the Philosopher argues against those who deny principles. Moreover they are clarified by certain analogies, just as the principles that are naturally known are made evident by induction but not proved by demonstrative reasoning.

Once again, the procedures of Aristotle, now concerning first principles, are employed in a parallel way in Thomas's manner of pursuing theology. Yet, this is only the prologue to the actual practice of doing theology, where much more of Aristotle's actual philosophy, and not just his method of proceeding, will be brought up for consideration and judgment. Aristotle's total corpus played a significant role in the formation of Aquinas's philosophical–theological synthesis.

Differing Verdicts on the "Aristotelianization" of Theology

The two strongest critics of Aquinas's claims concerning the scientific nature of theology were Henry of Ghent (d. 1293) and Godfrey of Fontaines (d. c.1309). Henry criticized Aquinas from an Augustinian perspective. This does not mean that Henry neglected Aristotle. Indeed, he knew him exceptionally well and this is most evident in his criticism of Aquinas's claim that theology is a subalternated science, a science subalternated to the knowledge that God and the blessed have of the divine, and a knowledge revealed by God through his prophets and evangelists. What it does mean is that Henry tells you exactly what Aristotle meant by subalternated science and how his theory of subalternation is not applicable to the God of the Scriptures.

Henry analyzes in detail the meaning of subalternation and studies each of the examples of subalternation that Aristotle provides in his *Posterior Analytics*. He attempts to show that they do not fit the case of Christian theology. The essential characteristic of Aristotle's discussion of subalternation according to Henry is that the subalternating science presents the *why* (*scientia propter quid*) of that of which the subalternated science presents the *that* (*scientia quia*). Knowledge of the *why* of something, according to Aristotle, is attained by reasoning. God, however, does not reason. So, it cannot be the case that God's knowledge is superior to man's knowledge because He reasons about the *why* of things, while we humans only know the *that* of reality. In brief, from Henry's perspective, Aristotle's theory of subalternation follows a human model that does not fit the divine way of knowing. It is not applicable to the actuality of the triune God's knowledge and its relationship to the truth He has revealed to us.

Godfrey of Fontaines criticizes Aquinas from an Aristotelian viewpoint. He is strongly critical of Aquinas, with whom he generally has great sympathies. In the present case, however, where he evaluates Thomas's theory of the subalternation of theology, he distinguishes acutely between the certitude of evidence (found in philosophy) and the certitude of belief or conviction (found in those who accept the Scriptures as God's revealed word). He then argues:

> To say, therefore, that the principles of theology are only believed and not known or understood, and thus possessing only the certitude of conviction, still produce scientific certitude in the conclusions drawn from them is to say that the conclusions are better known than the principles, namely, that the conclusions have the twofold certitude of evidence and conviction while the principles have only the latter one. Now this is to say contradictory things and it harms on a large scale theology and its teachers to propose such fictitious claims concerning it to those entering upon its study.

Both Henry and Godfrey disagree with Thomas Aquinas's theory of the subalternation of university theology to the knowledge of God and the blessed. If both fight against Aquinas, they fight even more against one another. Henry begins the battle against Godfrey by affirming the implications of the latter's critique of Aquinas:

> It is an absolutely startling thing that in every other university faculty the teachers attempt to praise their science to the extent that this is possible. It is only certain theologians, who in order that they might seem to praise philosophy, put down theology, asserting that it is not a science and that the true things that we believe cannot really be made intelligible in the present life. Such people shut off for themselves any road toward knowing and understanding the truths of the faith, and they fill others with despair of coming to understand them. This is an extremely pernicious approach and it is harmful to the Church and a dangerous position.

Godfrey's position itself at this stage of his explanation is quite limited. It centers mainly on how a theologian and a simple believer differ in their faith. Both believe and accept the truths of the faith because of their belief. If there is any difference between the two types of believer then it consists in the theologian's superior knowledge of the Scriptures: he can tell you the Scriptural warrants for affirming the Trinity of persons, or the Incarnation of the Son of God, or the divine production of creatures. The theologian's knowledge is a science of the Scriptures (*scientia sacrae Scripturae*).

For Henry, Godfrey's portrait of the theologian is too weak. Godfrey, according to Henry, makes theology a science of texts, not a science of the realities of which the Scriptures speak. Henry claims that some theologians receive extra help from God to understand the realities of which the Scriptures speak. This special light, according to Henry, is a middle light (*lumen medium*) between the light of faith and the light of glory. Certainly, it presupposes the light of faith, but it also permits a theologian to go beyond simple faith to some understanding of its mysteries. It does not provide the kind of evidence that we can anticipate in the light of glory, but it does give some evidence of the realities in which we believe. We can sense the presence of this middle light in Augustine, Hugh of Saint-Victor, and many other theologians. They do not simply cite Scriptural texts; they manifest a certain grasp of the realities of the faith. No one reading their works could fail to see that they are talking about the triune God, not just about Scriptural texts.

Godfrey, perhaps in response to Henry's critique, will return to a theology that attempts to gain some knowledge of the realities of the faith. Nonetheless, he continues to stress that theology is based on faith, not on evidence. He will search for analogies to bring some understanding of the mysteries of faith, but he always underscores the fact that theologians have a science of the faith (*scientia fidei*). If we measure our knowledge according to evidence, then philosophy is superior to theology. If we measure it in terms of certitude, then theology is superior to philosophy, since our theological knowledge depends on God, who can neither deceive nor be deceived, whereas our natural knowledge can at times go astray. Yet, by the very fact that we search for examples and analogies taken from philosophical experience, we admit the superiority of evidence found in our natural knowledge – we use it to go from the known (natural objects) to the unknown (revealed objects of faith).

Henry has a very different theory of knowledge. For him, God is the first thing known and it is in light of divine illumination that we know creatures as creatures and not just as objects that are unexplainably present before us. God is not the first reality we know explicitly, but when we examine what we do know and examine it deeply, we realize that we could know nothing without the assistance of the divine light. It is parallel to the case of our seeing. We assume that we first know the varied colored things that appear to our senses. Only later do we realize that without the light of the sun, we would be able to see nothing. We are not first conscious of the light, but we realize later that we could see nothing without it. *A fortiori* is it the case with the objects of faith for the theologian: he would see nothing divine if it were not for the middle light. And just as we are not aware of the light of faith, but we do believe because of it, so we are not aware of the middle light of theological understanding, but it is by its assistance that theologians come to understand the realities or mysteries of the faith. Henry, then, is more protective of mystical experiences and special graces than Godfrey ever would be. Certainly, the latter would admit that revelation is a special grace, but he tends to limit the actuality of such special graces to Scriptural revelation. He places strong question marks over claims for special lights for theologians. Thus, he accuses Henry of a certain haughtiness and presumption. For sure, he is convinced that neither he nor many other theologians have such a special middle light between the lights of faith and glory. For Godfrey, theology is hard intellectual work.

The Development of a New Accent

At the beginning of the fourteenth century, the Dominican Durandus of Saint-Pourçain assigned three meanings to the word "theology." "Theology" could be a synonym for "Scripture." In this sense of the word, the accent was on the content of revelation. This meaning of "theology" well fitted the uses of Alexander of Hales and his contemporaries, who all considered theology in its various forms simply as varied expressions of the word of God.

Theology's second meaning in Durandus's catalog expresses the character principally accentuated by St. Thomas and Godfrey. It focuses on the scientific character of theology, which centers on the manner in which conclusions legitimately flow from and are anchored in the premises that support them. It is what we might call deductive theology, and is well based, among other supports, on Aristotle's distinction between "science" (*episteme*) and "intuition" or "intellect" (*nous*). *Nous* is immediate insight or an illumination into the source or cause of an effect. "Science" is mediate or arrives through reflection. It starts with "insights" or "first principles" and moves on to conclusions that flow from these principles or premises. Durandus tells us that in his era, the beginning of the fourteenth century, this is the principal meaning of "theology." Theology begins with the articles of the faith as principles and then derives further, more explicit, truths as conclusions. It is a "lasting quality of the soul by means of which it deduces further things from the articles of the faith and the sayings of Sacred Scripture in the way that conclusions are deduced from principles."

The third meaning of "theology" focuses on the principles or premises with which deductive theology begins. We noted already that Thomas Aquinas identified the first principles of theology as the articles of the faith. In doing so, he differed significantly from the meaning that William of Auxerre gave to first principles. William gave his attention to the knower or believer and what he first came to know. For him, the principles of theology were the things that first struck those who heard the Gospels preached: that Christ was poor, that he was meek and humble, etc. For Aquinas, the first principles are on a different level. They are the truths that are first in the order of importance. That Christ is the Son of God is not more true than that he was poor; but it is more important in the order of teaching or in the order of a fuller understanding of the mystery of Christ. The third meaning of "theology" concentrates on the principles or premises of theology rather than on the conclusions drawn from the principles. It is presented by Durandus as the type of theology that is "a lasting quality of the soul by means of which the faith and those things handed down in sacred Scripture are defended and clarified by using principles that we know better." It follows the pattern of Aquinas's *Commentary on the "De Trinitate" of Boethius*, where the focus is on the principles or articles of the faith taken on their own terms rather than on the principles taken as premises for deriving other new knowledge.

A Franciscan theologian from the second decade of the fourteenth century, Peter Aureoli (d. 1322), became the great defender at Paris of the third, and less common, form of theology. He did not speak of "theology" in terms of "science," but rather in terms of "wisdom." And he interpreted "wisdom," according to Book VI of Aristotle's *Nicomachean Ethics*, as a combination of "science" and "insight" or "intellect." Peter Aureoli thus distinguished the deductive or scientific approach to theology from the declarative or premise-oriented theology that focused on the first principles or fundamental starting points of theology. His theology primarily concentrated on the premises or articles of the faith in themselves and not on the principles as premises for further conclusions. Remember that Aquinas, in his *Commentary on the "De Trinitate" of Boethius*, had said that Aristotle defended his first principles by showing that to deny them led to self-contradiction, and that he attempted to give analogies or examples that would confirm first principles. This is what Peter Aureoli considered the primary task of the theologian: to explain key theological terms, and to defend the articles of the faith against heretics, and to find suitable analogies to confirm these articles. He was not primarily interested in extending the domain of Christian theology; he was principally concerned with finding ways of nourishing the faith of believers and confirming the main articles of the faith. These articles of the faith thus became the center of attention. Explaining the terms connected with a trinitarian God or with a divine Mediator was one of the principal chores of the theologian. Another task was to develop the facility to answer the challenges of heretical thinkers concerning these truths. A further challenge was to discover the most suitable examples or analogies to illustrate as adequately as possible the faith content of the Church's belief or creed concerning the Trinity or Incarnation.

Aureoli defended this declarative approach to the study of theology by appealing to St. Augustine and claiming that his *De Trinitate* was a sure illustration of the clarification of theological terms, of the separation of true doctrine from heretical teachings, and of the search for sturdier analogies of the mystery of the triune God. In following the example of Augustine, the theologian develops a habit that is distinct from the habit of faith. It is a declarative habit, not a faith habit – which the theologian has in common with all believers.

In the 1340s Gregory of Rimini commented on the *Sentences* of Lombard at Paris and opposed the declarative theology of Peter Aureoli. According to Gregory, a theologian does not principally search for analogies drawn from the natural world. He does not principally go to other sciences, or other teachings, or to probable propositions. His principal effort is to understand the Scriptures. He advances the knowledge of the faith by extending its explicit domain. Theology is deductive. It draws out what follows necessarily from the truths contained formally in Sacred Scripture. The theologian's ability is not really distinct from that of the simple believer. He principally develops a faith habit. The difference is that his faith habit is one that holds more explicitly what the ordinary believer holds implicitly. All believers accept whatever God has revealed; a theologian is able to make explicit what most believers hold implicitly because of their trust in the First Truth who is the guarantee of the Christian faith. In his advice to Peter Aureoli and declarative theologians, Gregory instructs them to go back to Augustine and reread his texts. They have gotten it all wrong:

> But it is established that every such element of knowledge either is expressly contained in Sacred Scripture or is deducible from what is contained there. Otherwise, the Scriptures would not suffice for our salvation and for the defense of our faith, etc. Yet, Augustine, in the last chapter of Book II of *On Christian Teaching* tells us that the Scriptures do suffice, when he says: "Whatever a man might learn outside of Scripture, if it is harmful, it is condemned in the Sacred Writings; if it is useful, then it is already found there."

In short, theology is primarily about faith. Dependence on other sources is accidental, not essential or primary. As believers, we do not accept something as true because of a probable argument supporting it; we accept it because it is divinely revealed. Theologians have as their main task to manifest what is divinely revealed, not to search for non-essential arguments to bolster the faith.

A Necessary Marriage

Although Peter Aureoli and Gregory of Rimini had their followers, many theologians saw the need for both approaches to theology. Peter of Candia, who lectured on the *Sentences* of Lombard at Paris in 1378–80, criticized both authors to the degree that they stressed only one side of the theological challenge. For Peter of Candia both approaches were necessary and legitimate. We can consider the divine revelation as containing explicit truths or we can consider it as providing principles that can be further understood by being made more explicit. We cannot think of declarative and deductive theology as though they are two distinct opposed theologies. We should rather speak of them as two legitimate and necessary theological habits or abilities that should be developed by all well-balanced theologians. All the truths of the faith are not explicitly contained in the Scriptures: that is why the Fathers of the Church and the Councils had to make them explicit. In doing so, they practiced deductive theology. Still, not all doctrines are clear in themselves. At times, when dealing with the Trinity, words such as "person," "nature," and "substance" need to be defined. Distortions coming from heretical teachings need to be corrected. And even though we accept God's revelation because of the gift of faith, still arguments confirm and strengthen our faith. Faith is fundamental. We do not accept revealed truths because of the arguments presented. Yet, the arguments are not useless. That is why St. Augustine encouraged his readers to pursue "that knowledge by which our most wholesome faith, which leads to true happiness, is begotten, nourished, defended and strengthened." Faith is a gift or grace, but it is also begotten by good example, by preaching, by argument, and many other human efforts. God can give his gifts through human instruments. As Aquinas put it: "science begets and nourishes faith by way of external persuasion . . . but the chief proper cause of faith is that which moves man inwardly to assent." God uses human instruments, such as preachers and teachers, to beget, nourish, defend, and strengthen faith.

Yet, such instruments are not sufficient on their own to produce faith. If they were, then every competent preacher would be effective in leading his listeners to affirm the faith and every able teacher would be successful in his efforts to defend and strengthen the faith. Theology in none of its forms provides the evidence for the assent of faith. The affirmations to revealed truth are based on the gift of faith. Peter of Candia poses his question concerning the nature of theology in these precise terms: "Does the intellect of human beings here in this world acquire through theological study evident knowledge of revealed truths?" And his formal answer is: "Through theological study only declarative and faith-extending habits are developed, and through these developed abilities no evident knowledge of the articles of the faith is acquired." This statement well summarizes the efforts of medieval theologians to explain what they hoped to attain in their classes of theology.

CHAPTER 10

Reformation

Carl R. Trueman

Introduction

The most cataclysmic theological changes in the West between those precipitated by the Aristotelian renaissance of the twelfth century and those surrounding the Enlightenment of the late seventeenth and eighteenth centuries center on the period of history known as the Reformation, which, allowing for the arbitrary nature of clear-cut periodization of history, ran from c.1500 to c.1650. Of course, the Reformation was not only – or, some would argue, even primarily – a theological event. It embraced a whole complex of social, economic, and political movements and changes which fundamentally transformed the nature of European society;[1] nevertheless, the theological dimension of the period cannot be ignored, for to do so would, on a historical level, involve a basic misunderstanding of how individuals and societies thought of themselves in relation to each other, to the world around them, and to God; and, on a theological level, one cannot even begin to understand the nature of the Church situation today without some grasp of the issues which served as the means of dividing the Western Church into its Roman Catholic and Protestant halves.[2]

The amount of scholarship on Reformation theology is vast – and the amount of theological literature, books, and pamphlets, which the Reformers and their opponents produced via the relatively recent invention of the printing press, is scarcely less impressive in volume. As a result, an article such as this is necessarily selective, almost to the point of absurdity; however, in order to give the reader some basic orientation within the field, I shall focus on four key areas: the Lutheran doctrine of justification; the Christology which underlay this doctrine and which served to separate the Lutheran and Reformed confessions; and some comments on the nature of theological development within Protestant theology in the late sixteenth and early seventeenth centuries. Issues relating to matters such as authority, tradition, and Church, while arguably just as important as those to be discussed, cannot be dealt with adequately alongside these and so will be left to one side, as will discussion of those figures and movements which stood outside of the mainstream magisterial Reformation, such as the anabaptists.

The Lutheran Doctrine of Justification

One of the key elements of Reformation theology which distinguished it from the theology of the medieval period was its emphasis on the priority of the assurance of salvation in the Christian life. This is not to argue, of course, that the medievals had no interest in being certain of God's favor. The immediate theological background of Martin Luther himself was the so-called *via moderna*, the "modern way," associated with theologians such as Gabriel Biel (c.1415–95).[3] Put simply, this tradition understood salvation as being made possible through a gracious *pactum* ("pact") which God had made with human beings. In this *pactum* God had willed that the grace would be given to those who did their best (*facienti quod in se est, Deus gratiam non denegat* – literally: "To the one who does what is in him, God does not deny grace"). On the surface, this would appear to provide a cast-iron means of establishing whether one is in a state of grace or not: one simply does one's best and draws the inevitable conclusion. Nevertheless, a problem arises in establishing exactly how one knows one has done one's best, and certainly, in the experience of Luther it was the case that the harder he worked at being a faithful Christian, the more he realized how far short of "doing his best" he actually fell. The result for Luther, then, was not assurance of salvation but despair, and it was this despair that provided the personal dynamic for Luther's Reformation theology, a theology driven by the need to answer the simple yet crucial question, "Where can I find a gracious God?"

In a passage whose chronology and details have been hotly disputed by scholars over the years, Luther described how his experiences as a young monk and scholar led to his so-called "Reformation breakthrough." His experience focused on Romans 1:17, particularly the reference to "the justice of God":

> I hated this work "the justice of God" which by the use and usage of the doctors I was taught to understand philosophically in terms of the so-called formal or active justice with which God is just and punishes sinners and the unrighteous. For, however irreproachably I lived as a monk, I felt myself before God to be a sinner with a most unquiet conscience, nor could I be confident that I had pleased him with my satisfaction. . . . At last, God being merciful . . . I noticed the context of the words, namely, "The justice of God is revealed in it; as it is written, the just shall live by faith." Then and there, I began to understand the justice of God as that by which the righteous man lives by the gift of God, namely, by faith, and this sentence "The justice of God is revealed in the gospel" to be that passive justice with which the merciful God justifies us by faith as it is written: "The just shall live by faith."[4]

The passage contains all the ingredients outlined above: the initial belief that it is human efforts that provide the immediate cause of God's graciousness to the individual; the increasingly desperate attempts to please God through works of self-righteousness; the ultimate failure of this approach to answer the question of how God can be gracious to the sinner; and the new understanding of Romans 1:17 which, as Luther says further on, "opened the gates of paradise."

What Luther is claiming here is that the antidote to the agonies of conscience to which he was subjected because of his own failure to meet God's exacting standards of righteousness was his discovery that the justice of God was not something by which

God punished human beings, but something by which he himself made them righteous – in other words, the realization that salvation did not depend upon what he did for God but upon what God did for him. Such a position is, of course, hardly radical and points merely to an anti-Pelagian understanding of salvation which roots all saving activity in the initiative and continuing work of God. Where Luther develops the Christian tradition in a more radical way is in his understanding of in what precisely this divine justification of sinners consists.

Fundamental to this is that which later scholarship has come to characterize as the law–gospel dialectic. Luther operated with an understanding of humanity that saw its basic sin as being that of self-justification. This was manifested in any number of ways. At the Heidelberg Disputation of 1518, Luther referred to those whom he called "theologians of glory."[5] A thinly veiled attack on both the medieval schoolmen and contemporary Catholic theologians, this name was used to describe those Luther regarded as attempting to create God in their own image by building up a picture of God and his attributes which reflected their own human expectation of who God should be and what he should expect from human beings. The result was a God who bears a striking resemblance to sinful humanity. As an alternative, Luther proposed a "theology of the cross" – a theology which begins at the point at which God himself has chosen to reveal himself. According to Luther, this point is the cross, where all human expectations of who God is and how he acts are completely overturned – he sows his strength through his weakness, his glory through his humiliation, his love through his wrath poured out on the Son.[6]

This "theology of the cross" is not just a point of theological epistemology or methodology, but something with profound soteriological implications. For Luther, the way one comes to know this revealed God is not by simply exchanging one set of premises or data for another, the analogy of being for the analogy of the cross, but by exerting faith – and faith is the gift of God. This ties in with Luther's whole doctrine of justification by faith and with the dialectic between the law and the gospel. The problem is that sinful human beings are always trying to create God in their own image and always trying to please him through their own efforts, rather than approaching God as he has given himself to be approached by them. Within this context, the Law, with its demands that the individual perform perfect acts of righteousness, demonstrates that humans cannot please God by their own efforts (e.g. WA 40:482.22–483.11). As a result, they are driven to despair of themselves and thus to look to Christ where God's salvation is to be found. As Luther declares in his *Lectures on Galatians*:

> When the Law urges you, despairing of your own works, to seek help and solace in Christ, then that is indeed its proper use: thus, through the gospel, it serves justification. This is the best and most perfect use of the Law.   (WA 40:490.22–4)

The Law, then, is that which points to the impossibility of human self-justification and which starts the process of overturning natural human expectations of who God is and what he expects. It is only when this process of despair has been experienced that the believer then turns to Christ and, grasping him through faith, is justified through Christ's righteousness:

> It must be noted here that these three things, faith, Christ, and acceptance, are linked. Faith grasps Christ and holds him present, as a ring incloses a gem. Whoever is found with such faith, having grasped Christ within their heart, him will God declare righteous. This is the means and basis by which we obtain remission of sins and righteousness. "Because you believe in me" says God "and by faith have grasped Christ whom I have given to you to be your Justifier and Saviour, therefore you are righteous." Thus, God accepts or accounts righteous only on account of Christ in whom you believe.   (WA 40:233.16–24)

A number of observations are in order at this point. First, it is important to understand that the basis of the believer's righteousness, indeed, the only righteousness which the believer possesses, is that of Christ. This is not *imparted* to the believer in some kind of intrinsic way which renders the believer more holy than previously and which would point to an understanding of justification as a process – such an idea would represent precisely the kind of medieval Catholic tradition, stemming from Augustine, which Luther had found so inadequate in terms of his own experience and which he found contradicted by Paul's teaching in Romans. Instead, the righteousness is imputed to the believer – it remains extrinsic but is accounted to the believer, and it is this which constitutes the basis of his justification – God's declaration that believers *are* righteous on account of Christ not *being made righteous* through some process of sanctification.[7]

This fundamental objectivity to justification is, however, balanced by a subjective pole in Luther's thinking – the righteousness of Christ is not imputed to individuals solely on the basis of Christ's incarnation, death, and resurrection. Instead, it needs to be appropriated by the individual through faith. Faith effects a union between the believer and Christ that leads to a "joyful exchange" of sins for righteousness – Christ takes the believer's sins and the believer receives Christ's righteousness. In a particularly striking passage in *The Freedom of a Christian*, Luther uses one of his favorite analogies, that of bride and bridegroom, to press home this point:

> Faith joins the soul with Christ as a bride is joined to her bridegroom. . . . Thus the soul which believes can boast of and glory in whatever Christ possesses as though it were its own . . . and whatever the soul possesses, Christ claims as his own. . . . Christ is full of grace, life, salvation. The soul is full of sins, death, damnation. Let faith come between them and Christ will have the sins, death and damnation, while the soul will have grace, life, and salvation.   (WA 7:54.31–55.36)

This, then, is justification by faith – believers, despairing of their own righteousness, turn to Christ in faith and find that a joyful exchange of their sins for Christ's righteousness takes place.

Two questions obviously arise at this point. The first is that of good works: where do they fit into the grand scheme of things, if the righteousness of justification always remains extrinsic? The answer Luther gave is straightforward: they are not a cause of justification but an effect of it. It is because believers realize what Christ has done for them that they then respond by loving God with all their hearts and souls and minds, and their neighbors as themselves. There is, of course, much debate about the nature of Luther's ethical teaching and the precise nature of good works, but two things stand out: first, they play no role in justification; and, secondly, they are based upon the believer's assurance of God's favor. In both these respects, Luther's thinking – and, indeed, much of the Reformation after him – represents a fundamental break with medieval teaching, which both stressed the need for good works in justification (though works based upon God's grace, variously understood) and denied the possibility of assurance of salvation to all but the elite few who had had a direct revelation of their elect status from God himself.[8]

The second question is: is faith itself not a good work? Indeed, so important are the implications of this question that they form an important part of what was perhaps Luther's greatest theological work, *The Bondage of the Will*, which was itself almost a line-by-line refutation of Erasmus of Rotterdam's work, *Diatribe on Free Will*. The work is too long and complex to do it justice here, but suffice it to say that Luther developed a rigorous and arguably deterministic doctrine of double predestination based not on human impotence after the Fall but upon the very nature of God and his knowledge of creation, which served to underscore the fact that faith itself was a gift of God given only to those whom he had chosen, and not the result of any human initiative or autonomous response to God's offer of salvation. If this predestinarian note was somewhat muted in much of his other writings, it is yet arguable that the abandonment of such a position would have required a significant modification of his understanding of human nature and of the nature and origin of faith.[9]

Assurance, Christology, and Eucharist

Luther's search for the gracious God led him, as we noted above, to the cross at Calvary. It was there, in the broken body of the incarnate God hanging upon the cross, that Luther found the God of grace for whom he had been looking. Underlying this notion was an understanding of Christ's person which had radical implications for the whole of his theology, particularly, as history was to demonstrate, for his understanding of the eucharist.

Parallel to the distinction between law and gospel was a distinction in Luther's theology between God hidden and God revealed. God hidden was the awesome and terrible God of judgment and of death. For a human being to approach the hidden God was tantamount to suicide – one could expect nothing from such a God but hell and destruction. The revealed God, however, was the God of grace and mercy – those who approached God where and how he had revealed himself and given himself to be known, would find him gracious and merciful, the God of gospel love. This emphasis gives Luther's theology a profound christocentricity – it is in the incarnate Christ that we find God as he has given himself to us, as he reveals himself to us.[10] Thus, in answer to the pressing question, "Where can I find the gracious God?" the reply resounds "In Christ and in Christ alone." The dramatic impact of this upon Luther's Christology is that he refuses to countenance any kind of gracious encounter between human beings and God which does not involve Christ, and that not simply as the second person of the Trinity, but as the incarnate person as well. It is in the humanity of Christ that the believer finds God revealed as gracious, and to seek an encounter with God outside of that humanity is to seek the hidden God of judgment, not the revealed God of grace. Put simply, the result is that wherever we today find the gracious God, there we also find the gracious God's humanity as well.

In terms of Reformation history, the immediate and devastating consequence of this view was a breach between the Lutheran and Reformed churches over the nature of the eucharist, a breach formalized by the failure to reach agreement on the issue at the Colloquy of Marburg in 1529, where the principal protagonists were Luther himself and the Zurich pastor and churchman Huldrych Zwingli.[11] While agreeing on $14\frac{1}{2}$ out of 15 points for discussion, they failed to agree on the significance of the eucharist.[12] Zwingli argued for a symbolic presence of Christ in the eucharist, partly on the grounds that Christ's body was circumscribed by the normal physical dimensions of a human body, and that this had ascended to heaven where he would remain until the second coming. The key words "This is my body" could not, therefore, have anything other than a primarily symbolic meaning.

For Luther, this effectively turned the eucharist into a disaster area – if the humanity of Christ was not present but God was there in some way, then it must be the hidden God of judgment, and the eucharist is thus a means of judgment and damnation not of grace. Instead, Luther saw no reason to take the words of institution at anything other than face value: Christ said it was his body – therefore, it must be his body. The metaphysical problems involved in tying the bread and the flesh together in the same space did not worry him; for Luther, it was simply necessary to accept by faith that Christ's humanity, in some deep and mysterious way, was there in the bread and that, as in the word, so in the eucharist the poor sinner found the gracious God.

In assessing the breach between Luther and Zwingli at Marburg, it is tempting to see the issue as somewhat trivial given the large amount of common ground between the two men – a debate over an admittedly difficult, though somewhat peripheral, piece of exegesis. Indeed, the debate at Marburg tended to focus almost entirely on the issue of exegesis at the expense of the underlying doctrinal concerns, with Zwingli arguing that, as a literal interpretation of other sayings of Christ, such as "I am the door," made no sense, one was under no obligation to pursue such literalism with regard to the words of institution. Luther's response was simply to assert that non-literal interpretation could be used when no other approach offered cogent results, but the literal way should always be preferred. In the case of the eucharist, he argued, the literal approach did not result in any absurdity. In arguing this, of course, he merely begged the question of the criteria by which something is judged absurd, and thus pointed to the real points of dispute between the Reformed and the Lutherans: those of Christology and soteriology. It was ultimately the differing understandings of these two areas which provided the criteria by which each side judged the exegesis of the other to be absurd.

To interpret the debate in purely exegetical terms, then, is to underestimate the theological issues at stake. While it is true that the debates at Marburg hardly went beyond points of exegesis and the hurling of insults, the underlying questions, those of soteriology and Christology, are fundamentally important, and neither Luther nor Zwingli could really have come to any meaningful agreement at Marburg without a distinct modification, if not abandonment, of key theological points. It is these issues which were the real source of doctrinal, and hence ecclesiastical, division, and it was debates about these questions which were to dominate the subsequent debates between the two branches of mainstream Protestantism.

Lutheran and Reformed Theology: a Christological Comparison

Unlike Lutheranism, Reformed theology did not look to one single individual as its symbolic theological fountainhead. Instead, its origins and development lay with a number of highly significant theologians, of whom Huldrych Zwingli, Martin Bucer, and Johannes Oecolampadius are probably the most significant of the first generation. In subsequent years, John Calvin, Heinrich Bullinger, Peter Martyr Vermigli, Theodore Beza, Jerome Zanchius, Amandus Polanus, Franciscus Junius, and William Perkins also had significant impact.[13] Of all of these men, John Calvin was without doubt the most significant, giving rise to the unfortunate characterization of Reformed theology as "Calvinism," a term which hides the pluriform roots of the movement and gives Calvin a role in Reformed theology analogous to that of Luther in Lutheranism – a role which, for all his pre-eminence as *primus inter pares*, Calvin never actually played.[14]

The key to understanding Reformed theology as a separate movement with Protestantism is to understand that which distinguishes it from its main rival, Lutheranism. While there are a variety of differences between the two movements, historically they are distinguished, as we have noted, by differing views of the eucharist. It is this that caused the fundamental breach between the two traditions and which was thus ultimately responsible for their separate confessional histories and identities. Beneath the difference on the eucharist lie two entirely different christologies: the Lutheran Christology involves a complete union of the Logos with the human nature, to the extent that the properties of the divine nature, such as omnipresence, are communicated to the human nature with the result that where the divinity is, there is the humanity also. In arguing for this, the Lutherans safeguarded their doctrine of salvation which, as we have seen, depended upon the ubiquity of Christ's humanity. Reformed Christology, however, denies this, arguing that while the human nature of Christ is grasped by the Logos and the two natures are truly united in one person, the Logos continues to have an existence outside of the human nature of Christ even after the incarnation.[15] To put the matter in terms of the communication of properties from one nature to the other, for the Lutherans the communication takes place between the natures, while for the Reformed the communication takes place in the person, with both natures retaining their distinctive properties. The Reformed teaching, known to posterity as the *extra calvinisticum*, marks off Reformed Christology, and indeed, Reformed theology as a whole, from that of the Lutheran churches.

Neither side was prepared to give significant ground to the other: for the Lutherans, Reformed Christology, with its willingness to distinguish so clearly between the divine and the human presence of Christ, smacked of Nestorianism; for the Reformed, the Lutheran emphasis upon the communication of properties between the natures seemed to disrupt the reality of Christ's humanity and pointed towards an Apollinarian Christology involving a confusion of the two natures.

The difference in Christology emerged very clearly in the formal treatments of Christ's life and ministry within the theologies of the two movements. Both groups used the motif of humiliation and exaltation to describe the life of Christ in theological terms. This approach was adopted in order to underline the historical movement of Christ's life and work in order to avoid an overly abstract or metaphysical approach to incarnation which missed, or underemphasized, the underlying saving purpose of Christ in history. Thus, there was a common concern behind both Lutheran and Reformed approaches. It is there, however, that much of the similarity both begins and ends.

For the Lutherans, the humiliation of Christ began at his incarnation when the Logos took flesh and the attributes of divinity were communicated directly from the divine nature to the human nature.[16] It is important, however, to note that this humiliation is not a necessary part of the incarnation. Stooping to take human flesh was indeed an act of great condescension on God's part, but it is not this in which Christ's humiliation consists. After all, Christ is now exalted, but the incarnational union still continues. Instead, the humiliation consists in the voluntary and temporary surrender of the full powers of divinity by Christ so that he might suffer and die for the life of the world. The subject of this humiliation is the human nature as it is in union with the divine. The communication of properties between the natures means that, if Christ is to suffer and die for the world, then there must be a voluntary suspension of these divine attributes on the part of the human nature during Christ's earthly ministry. This surrender starts in the womb of the Virgin Mary and continues to his death on the cross. It is then that the exaltation of Christ begins.

In Lutheran theology, the exaltation of Christ began historically with his return from the dead in the grave followed by his literal descent into Hell (involving a literal reading of the (in)famously difficult clause in the Apostles' Creed), his resurrection, his ascension to heaven, and his current session at the right hand of the Father. Theologically, this involves the resumption of the plenary exercise of divine power which had been surrendered in the humiliation. In line with the teaching on humiliation, the divine nature is not the active subject of exaltation, but the human nature as it is united with the divine in the person of the mediator.

For the Reformed, the issue of humiliation and exaltation was somewhat different because of the different understanding of the nature of the communication of properties.[17] Because the divine attributes were not communicated to the human nature, the human nature could not voluntarily surrender use of them. As a result, the Reformed, while not regarding the incarnation itself as the humiliation (on the grounds, as the Lutherans, that it continues into the eschaton), located the humiliation in the hiding of divine glory and the submissive will to the Father that is involved both in the moment of incarnation and in Christ's subsequent life and ministry. The Logos is not, of course, diminished by the incarnation, and so, strictly speaking, the state of humiliation was restricted by the Reformed to the ministry of Christ on earth, up to and including his death on the cross.

As well as the key difference in the understanding of humiliation generated by the different understandings of the communication of properties, the Reformed also disagreed with Lutherans regarding the state of exaltation. Instead of starting it with the descent into Hell, understood literally, the Reformed read this clause of the Apostles' Creed as a symbolic statement concerning the terrible nature of Christ's experience on the cross and in the grave, and thus start the exaltation with the resurrection. More significant still is their understanding of the session of Christ at the right hand of the Father: the Lutherans, in line with their understanding of the direct communication of properties, regarded this as referring to Christ's omnipresence; the Reformed, in line with their adherence to the *extra calvinisticum*, understood Christ's body as locally present in heaven, only to return to earth at the second coming. Thus, once again, the Christological discussion leads in at least one way to questions relating to Christ's presence in the eucharist.

In assessing Reformation theology and the debates which shaped the progress of Protestantism in the two centuries after Luther's initial call for reform, it is important to see that it is Christology, as it relates to issues of salvation, revelation, assurance, and sacraments, that holds center stage. It is this that provides a fundamental point of continuity between Reformation Protestantism and its post-Reformation, pre-Enlightenment, development. It is to this development that we now turn.

Post-Reformation Developments

After the initial period of Reformation activity in the first half of the sixteenth century, the Lutheran and Reformed set about consolidating the political and theological gains made by the earlier Reformers. What is interesting about this period is not simply the continued conflict between the three major confessional traditions in the West, Roman Catholic, Lutheran, and Reformed, but also the fact that within each of these groups themselves similar controversial issues arose. This is perhaps not surprising, given the fact that all three confessions were, to an extent, in dialogue with the basic Augustinian trajectory of theology which had shaped Western theological discussion for a thousand years. Thus, the same issues about the nature and relationship of God's grace to human freedom and salvation arose for all three groups: the Catholics witnessed controversy between the Jansenists and the Molinists, with the former holding to an anti-Pelagian, the latter a semi-Pelagian understanding of grace; the Lutherans divided quickly after Luther's death into the Philippists, followers of Melanchthon and his moderate approach to predestination, and the Gnesio-Lutherans, who regarded themselves as preserving the authentic voice of their master on this issue;[18] and the Reformed founded a group later called the Arminians, after a controversial Leiden professor, Jacob Arminius, breaking with strict predestinarianism and drawing on the arguments of the Molinists to achieve the conceptual changes necessary.[19] The picture, then, very soon became far more complex even than the breach at Marburg had suggested.

The development of Reformed and Lutheran theology in the 150 years after the initial blasts of Luther and Zwingli against the papacy has been a source of much scholarly controversy, much of it focusing on whether that which developed in the late sixteenth and seventeenth centuries represents a legitimate development or a fundamental deviation from the theology of the early Reformers. There is not space here to analyze or assess the argument for and against the so-called "discontinuity thesis," which regards later Protestant Orthodoxy, that consolidated, confessional voice which developed in the later sixteenth century within both traditions, as a basic betrayal of the early Reformation.[20] Instead, it will be useful simply to outline a number of issues which must be taken into account in any scholarly assessment of the question.

First, it is important to note that Reformation theology itself is not a total break with the theological past. When, for example, one looks at the relationship of Luther to his mentors in the *via moderna*, one can see points both of continuity and of discontinuity. On the one hand, his notion of justification by the imputed righteousness of Christ marks him off from Gabriel Biel, with his emphasis upon the intrinsic righteousness of the believer as the basis for justification. On the other hand, when one realizes that Biel's understanding of their righteousness is set within the *pactum* framework which allows inferior works to be accounted as meritorious, one finds an emphasis upon the priority of God's will and decision in salvation which arguably carries over into Luther. Furthermore, in arguing for an anti-Pelagian understanding of salvation, Luther places himself within a tradition which goes back through the Middle Ages to the early Church Fathers. Again, if Luther does innovate in *The Bondage of the Will*, such innovation takes place *within* an established anti-Pelagian trajectory of theology. None of the mainstream Reformers regarded themselves as innovators and all were concerned to maintain a dialogue with the past.

Given, then, the complexity of the relationship between Reformation and pre-Reformation theology, it is clear that any approach to the field which ignores this, opting for simple black-and-white models of analysis, is doomed to produce a distorted picture of the theological developments which took place at the hands of Luther, Zwingli, and company. Following on from this, if it is illegitimate to analyze Reformation theology in abstraction from the wider Western tradition, how much more so is it to remove that theology which built upon it from that same tradition? One must beware, then, any approach to the question of the development of post-Reformation Lutheranism and Reformed theology which attempts to explain it solely in terms of what was done between 1517 and 1559. The larger diachronic context is of crucial importance.

A second important point to remember when approaching post-Reformation Protestantism is the need to set the phenomenon within the wider cultural, social, and political contexts. Much has been made by some scholars of the reappearance in Protestant theology of the elaborate structure and language (often Aristotelian in origin) of medieval scholasticism, and this has been interpreted as a sign of the increasing "rationalism" of Protestant theology on the eve of the Enlightenment. Certainly, when one compares Calvin's *Institutes* with Francis Turretin's *Institutes of Elenctic Theology*, the linguistic and methodological differences are striking. Nevertheless, before blaming the change on a sinister internal principle driving Protestant theology towards rationalism, it is worthwhile asking whether there are any other reasons that may account for the change. First, it must be noted that over one hundred years separates the two works – and there can be little historical basis for assuming that two works separated by such a period of time should automatically resemble each other in terms of language and approach.[21]

Thirdly, the issue of genre must be addressed: Calvin wrote, as he tells us, to provide a handbook to accompany his commentaries, a theological source-book which allowed him to avoid long topical *excursus* during his commentaries; Turretin, however, was producing a textbook of theology which addressed topics in a way that made them easy to teach and to interrelate in the classroom, and which addressed positions of opponents in a clear and helpful manner. In other words, to compare the respective *Institutes* of Calvin and Turretin in terms of form is about as useful as comparing apples and oranges. What we have is two different types of theological production, intended to achieve two different pedagogic purposes.

Fourthly, the fact that Turretin and others returned to using the language and structures of medieval scholastic theology does not mean either that they abandoned the Reformation theology of their ancestors or that they regressed to some kind of arid, rationalistic approach to theology. In fact, what happened historically in the years after the start of the Reformation was the movement of Protestant theology from the church into the academy, with the result that theologians found it both necessary and useful to take on board the established structures and language of contemporary educational culture. This culture was not restricted to one confessional tradition but embodied a European phenomenon – all theologians of the sixteenth and seventeenth centuries, whether Roman Catholic, Lutheran, or Reformed, partook of a curriculum which in terms of its basic structure and scholastic/Aristotelian language exhibited a reasonable level of consistency across the board. Thus, we find remarkable similarities in approach between, say, Turretin's *Institutes* and the *Methodus Theologiae* of Richard Baxter, not because there was a similarly remarkable coincidence of content – Turretin was "High Orthodox," presenting a thoroughgoing Reformed confessionalism, while Baxter was more eclectic and had significant leanings towards Arminianism – but because both adopted and adapted the current structural and linguistic culture to their own purposes. In each case, argument proceeds by working under the broad headings of scholastic theology: prolegomena, doctrine of God, etc., using the tried and tested method of asking questions, presenting the case for and against, and a resolution of the issue. This reflected the pedagogic procedures of the classroom, not some sinister inner rationalism working itself out – and, one has to say, to anyone who has read works using this method, whether medieval, Renaissance, or post-Reformation, it does seem to have been a remarkably good way of exploring any given issue.[22]

In light of this, the key question concerning post-Reformation theology is not whether it used modes of discourse that were typical of the intellectual culture of its day, nor whether it used the same language as the early Reformers – of course it did – but *how* it used such modes and language, and what it expressed through them. This leads to the fifth factor which must be taken into account: the increasing complexity of the polemical context. In the above discussion concerning the Christological differences between the Lutherans and the Reformed, it was clear that what began ostensibly as a debate over exegesis of passages relevant to the eucharist gradually brought to the surface distinct differences over the very person of Christ himself, particularly in terms of how the two natures of Christ related to each other in the incarnation. The result was that a theological vocabulary of an increasingly technical and complex nature was needed in order to achieve the level of precision demanded by the nature of the debates in which the two sides were engaged. For example, to return to the central point at issue between Lutheran and Reformed, that of the communication of properties in the incarnation, the Lutherans came to distinguish the communication into three *genera* (Mueller 1934:272–86). The first, the *genus idiomaticum*, refers to the predication of the attributes of both natures to the one person of the mediator: e.g. Jesus Christ, the one human being, suffers and dies. The purpose of this is to emphasize the unity of the person over the alleged Nestorianism of the Reformed. The second, the *genus maiestaticum*, refers to the hypostatic relationship of the human nature of Christ within the union. The human nature is only constituted as a person in the context of the union (it is, in itself, *anhypostatic*, to use the patristic phrase of Leontius of Byzantium). This genus also refers to the transfer of properties within the person between the divine nature and the human nature and accounts for the ubiquity of Christ's flesh. Thirdly, the *genus apotelesmaticum* emphasizes the fact that nothing is done by either nature of the Mediator without the full communion and cooperation of the other. Of these three, the Reformed obviously rejected the second genus, the *maiestaticum*, as this crystalized the point of disagreement between the two confessions, and tended only to adhere to the first, the *idiomaticum*, which they tended to understand only as referring to a verbal peculiarity and not, as the Lutherans, as referring to the real attribution of both sets of properties to the person who really bears them.

What is important to grasp about this apparent hair-splitting is that this increased technicality in no way disrupted the original intention of the earlier debates – that of establishing the relationship between the two natures in order to guarantee the ubiquity of Christ's flesh – nor did it place later Lutheran thought in a position of fundamental discontinuity with the past: it is, rather, an indicator of the requirements of contemporary polemical theology and of the need to provide a clear definition of what prevents the Lutherans from being Reformed. What it actually did was to bring into much sharper focus the very points which had been at issue all along. It is thus not enough to point to change in language or increases in technical precision and complexity in themselves as indicating fundamental changes in theological direction: the purpose to which that language is being put is the real point at issue. It is these factors – diachronic and synchronic contexts, genre, and the use, not the type, made of particular structures of argument and language – which must provide the basic framework for interpreting the development of Reformation theology in the post-Reformation period. When this is done, as it has been, the result is that the Lutheran and Reformed orthodoxy of the late sixteenth and seventeenth centuries can be seen as part of the ongoing Western tradition and not as a fundamental break with that tradition.

The Significance of Reformation Theology

Despite the many differences between Reformation theology and the medieval background with which it so consciously disagreed, it seems increasingly evident to scholars that it is not to be understood as the fundamental break with the past that an earlier generation of polemicists considered it to be. There may be great disagreements over issues of authority, exegesis, grace, justification, sacraments, and ecclesiology between the Reformers and their Catholic predecessors and contemporaries, but there was also much they had in common: a desire to stand in continuity with the Church Fathers, particularly Augustine; in many cases, a basic anti-Pelagianism; and a fundamental adherence to Western trinitarianism and the basic structures of Catholic Christology. In terms, therefore, of its basic concerns and the kinds of theological questions being asked, Reformation theology is not a wholesale break with the earlier tradition but a debate within that ongoing tradition. This is not to underestimate the differences – it is still, *pace* much ecumenical writing, difficult to square Luther's teaching on justification with the Council of Trent's declarations on this issue[23] – but to point out that the kind of theology being pursued by both medievals and Reformers in terms of its basic ontological and theological structures, emphases, and concerns, exhibits strong points of continuity. It was only with the rise of the Enlightenment, with its emphasis upon the priority of subjective epistemology and upon human autonomy, that this kind of theology gave way to something radically different. Seen in this light, it is arguable that the Reformation is not the intellectual watershed of Western religious thought that it is sometimes made out to be: it had profound ecclesiastical implications; but it did not change the nature of the theological game in the way that the work of Aristotle did in the twelfth century or Descartes and, even more so, Kant was to do in the Enlightenment. It thus stands between the two great philosophical shifts in the Western world – the Aristotelian Renaissance and the Enlightenment – not as a fundamental change in theology as a whole but as a significant change of direction *within* the established Western Augustinian tradition.

Notes

1   For a good historical discussion of the Reformation, see Cameron (1991).

2   A good introduction to the theological issues is McGrath (1993).

3   For a discussion of Biel's thought, see Oberman (1983).

4   Quoted in the Introduction to Martin Luther, *Lectures on Romans* (1961:xxxvi–xxxvii). The original text is in *D. Martin Luthers Werke: Kritische Gesamtausgabe*, 63 vols. (Weimar, 1883–1987) (hereafter *WA*), 54:179–87.

5   For an English translation of the theses at the Heidelberg Disputation, see Dillenberger (1961:500–3).

6   The true theologian is one who, according to Thesis 20, "perceives what is visible of God, God's 'backside', by beholding the sufferings and the cross" (Dillenberger 1961:502).

7   For a history of justification from the early Church to the present day, see McGrath (1986).

8   Luther's basic position on the relationship of justification to good works is expounded in the 1520 treatise *The Freedom of a Christian*, which can be found translated in Dillenberger (1961:42–85).

9   The best English translation of this work is that by Packer and Johnston, *The Bondage of the Will* (1957).

10   See, for example, Packer and Johnston (1957:169–71).

11   On the thought of Zwingli, see Stephens (1986).

12   For Luther's principal writings on the eucharist, see *Luther's Works*, 55 vols. (St. Louis/Philadelphia, 1958–86), vols. 35–8. Of particular interest in his controversy with the papacy is "The Babylonian Captivity of the Church" in vol. 36; his principal writings against Zwingli can be found in vols. 37–8, the latter of which contains various accounts of the

Marburg Colloquy written from both Lutheran and Zwinglian perspectives. For Zwingli on the eucharist, see Pipkin (1985, vol. 2).

13   The literature on Reformed theology is vast. For a good guide to its developments, see Muller, *Post-Reformation Reformed Dogmatics* (1986–). See also the essays in Trueman and Clark (1999) and Assett and Dekker (2001).

14   The best introduction to Calvin's life and thought remains Wendel (1963).

15   See Calvin (1960, vol. 2:13.4). For good discussions of Reformed Christology, particularly in terms of continuity/discontinuity with patristic and medieval precedents, see Willis (1966); also Oberman (1992b:234–58).

16   For good Lutheran discussions of humiliation and exaltation, see Elert (1962:236ff.); Mueller (1934:287ff.); Schmid (1961:376–81).

17   A classic statement of the Reformed tradition can be found in the *Synopsis Purioris Theologiae* (often known as the Leiden Synopsis), disputations 27 and 28. See the edition by Bavinck (1881:262–81). Perhaps a more accessible, though somewhat eclectic survey, can be found in Heppe (1950:488–509).

18   On post-Reformation Lutheranism, see Preus (1970–2).

19   On Arminius's life, see Bangs (1971); on his theology, see Muller (1991); on his use of Molinism, see Dekker (1996:337–52).

20   The most succinct statement of this position is that of Basil Hall, "Calvin against the Calvinists" in (1966:19–37). Other scholars associated with variations on this theme are T. F. Torrance, J. B. Torrance, Brian Armstrong, and Ernst Bizer.

21   On the issue of Aristotelian language, see Trueman (1998:34–44).

22   On scholasticism as method, not content, see Weisheipl (2003), "Scholastic Method," in *The New Catholic Encyclopedia* 12:1145–6.

23   For a brave but ultimately unconvincing attempt to do this, see Küng (1964).

References

Asselt, W. J. van, and Dekker, E. eds. 2001. *Reformation and Scholasticism: An Ecumenical Enterprise*. Grand Rapids, MI: Baker.

Bangs, C. 1971. *Arminius: A Study in the Dutch Reformation*. Nashville, TN: Abingdon Press.

Bavinck, H. ed. 1881. *Synopsis Purioris Theologiae*. Leiden: Donner.

Calvin, J. 1960. *Institutes of the Christian Religion*, ed. J. T. McNeill, 2 vols. Philadelphia, PA: Fortress Press.

Cameron, E. 1991. *The European Reformation*. Oxford: Oxford University Press.

Dekker, E. 1996. "Was Arminius a Molinist?" *Sixteenth Century Journal* 27:337–52.

Dillenberger, J. ed. 1961. *Martin Luther*. Garden City, NY: Anchor.

Duffield, G. E. 1966. *John Calvin*. Grand Rapids, MI: Eerdmans.

Elert, W. 1962. *The Structure of Lutheranism*, trans. W. A. Hansen. St. Louis, MO: Concordia.

Hall, B. 1966. "Calvin against the Calvinists," in *John Calvin*, ed. G. E. Duffield. Grand Rapids, MI: Eerdmans.

Heppe, H. 1950. *Reformed Dogmatics*, trans. G. T. Thomson. Grand Rapids, MI: Baker.

Küng, H. 1964. *Justification*. Philadelphia, PA: Westminster.

Luther, M. 1958–86. *Luther's Works*. Philadelphia, PA: Westminster.

Luther, M. 1961. *Lectures on Romans*, trans. W. Pauck. London: SCM Press.

McGrath, A. E. 1986. *Iustitia Dei*, 2 vols. Cambridge: Cambridge University Press.

McGrath, A. E. 1993. *Reformation Thought: An Introduction*, 2nd edn. Oxford: Blackwell.

Mueller, J. T. 1934. *Christian Dogmatics*. St. Louis: MO: Concordia.

Muller, R. A. 1986–2004. *Post-Reformation Reformed Dogmatics*, 4 vols. Grand Rapids, MI: Baker.

Muller, R. A. 1991. *God, Creation, and Providence in the Thought of Jacob Arminius*. Grand Rapids, MI: Baker.

Oberman, H. A. 1983. *The Harvest of Medieval Theology: Gabriel Biel and Late Medieval Nominalism*. Durham: Labyrinth.

Oberman, H. A. 1992a. *The Dawn of the Reformation*. Edinburgh: T. & T. Clark.

Oberman, H. A. 1992b. "The 'Extra' Dimension in the Theology of Calvin," in H. A. Oberman, *The Dawn of the Reformation*. Edinburgh: T. & T. Clark.

Packer, J. I. and Johnston, O. R. 1957. *The Bondage of the Will*. Cambridge: Cambridge University Press.

Pipkin, H. W. ed. 1985. *Selected Writings of Huldrych Zwingli*, 2 vols. Allison Park, PA: Pickwick.

Preus, R. D. 1970–2. *The Theology of Post-Reformation Lutheranism*, 2 vols. St. Louis MO: Concordia.

Schmid, H. 1961. *The Doctrinal Theology of the Evangelical Lutheran Church*, trans. C. A. Hay and H. E. Jacobs. Minneapolis, MN: Augsburg.

Stephens, W. P. 1986. *The Theology of Huldrych Zwingli*. Oxford: Oxford University Press.

Trueman, C. R. 1998. *The Claims of Truth: John Owen's Trinitarian Theology*. Carlisle: Paternoster.

Trueman, C. R. and Clark, R. S. eds. 1999. *Protestant Scholasticism: Essays in Reassessment*. Carlisle: Paternoster.

Weisheipl, J. A. 2003. "Scholastic Method," in *The New Catholic Encyclopedia*, vol. 12, pp. 1145–6.

Wendel, F. 1963. *Calvin: The Origins and Development of his Religious Thought*, trans. P. Mairet. London: Fontana.

Willis, E. D. 1966. *Calvin's Catholic Christology*. Leiden: Brill.

CHAPTER 11
Modernity

Garrett Green

Any attempt to understand the relationship between theology and modernity involves the interpreter in a fundamental ambiguity from the outset, for the two are by no means independently identifiable quantities but rather are interlinked in a complex history. Such, at any rate, is the case for the tradition of modern Christian theology, which will be our primary concern here. From one perspective modernity itself might plausibly be interpreted as the product of Western Christian culture, springing from sources in Renaissance and Reformation Europe that blossomed into maturity in the Enlightenment of the seventeenth and eighteenth centuries. But if that is the case, how do we account for the radically anti-Christian character of some of the most important writings of that very Enlightenment, not to mention its aftermath in the secular thought of the nineteenth and twentieth centuries? One of the most dramatic and influential of those later thinkers, Friedrich Nietzsche, argued explicitly that both were in fact true: modernity is the inevitable outcome of Christianity and is at the same time its dissolution. The event that he calls "the death of God" does not result from the assault of some external enemy on the fortress of Christian theology; rather, it is the ironic outcome of Christian belief itself – what he calls its morality. "What it was that really triumphed over the Christian god," Nietzsche writes, was "Christian morality itself, the concept of truthfulness that was understood ever more rigorously . . . translated and sublimated into a scientific conscience, into intellectual cleanliness at any price." The history of Christian thought on this account is the history of its progressive dissolution: "After Christian truthfulness has drawn one inference after another, it must end by drawing its *most striking inference*, its inference *against* itself" (Nietzsche 1967:161, 1974:307).[1] One need not share Nietzsche's jaundiced view of Christianity in order to agree with him that the seeds of secular modernity are contained within its history.

The term *modern* is one of those unavoidable but elusive terms we employ in order to organize the vast and complex flow of historical time into manageable chunks, and to identify the broad patterns that enable us to distinguish one age from another. Since the seventeenth century in Europe, the word *modern* has become the favored designation for our own time in contradistinction to the *ancient* and *medieval* periods. It had been used in a variety of ways in the history of Western culture, beginning as early as the fifth century CE, when Latin Christians called their new age *modernus* to distinguish it from pagan antiquity. Recent historians have variously associated the origins of modernity with the European Renaissance, the Protestant Reformation, or the Enlightenment. In our present context – the relationship of theology and modernity – the most useful point at which to locate the beginnings of modernity is in seventeenth-century Europe. It was during this period that a new sensibility and new cultural forms first emerged that were no longer based on ecclesiastical authority or religious tradition. These emerging modern ideas and institutions, however, were not simply anti-religious; rather, they represent an attempt to ground religion itself in a new way, to build culture on a new and modern foundation and to know God and to justify belief in him without recourse to the authoritarianism of the previous age. The twentieth-century theologian and martyr Dietrich Bonhoeffer, writing from a prison cell in the waning days of the Third Reich, seized upon a phrase from the seventeenth-century philosopher and statesman Hugo Grotius to capture the essential feature of modernity: *etsi deus non daretur*, to be modern is to live one's life, to do one's thinking, and to organize society "as if there were no God." For Bonhoeffer this motto came to represent *die mündiggewordene Welt*, the modern world that has "come of age," the era of cultural adulthood when we no longer seek the solace and support of traditional authority but strive to live in a this-worldly (secular) manner, relying on our own resources as human beings.

The Origins of Modernity

Dating modernity from the seventeenth century implies that the Protestant Reformation – the most plausible alternative candidate for the origin of the modern world – is essentially premodern, still part of the Middle Ages. The clearest way to state the relationship is to say that the Reformation of the sixteenth century created the preconditions for a modernity that first emerged on the stage of history a century later. Or, expressed in different metaphor, modernity was conceived in the Reformation but born in the Enlightenment. Protestantism represents the fracturing of the "one holy order" that had held the imagination of Western European civilization in thrall throughout the Middle Ages. That ideal unity, of course, was never fully realized in practice; yet its powerful hold over the medieval imagination is one of the defining characteristics of premodern Christian civilization. By its rejection, in both theory and practice, of the unitary authority of the Roman Church, the revolt of the Protestants brought to an end the ideal of an ecclesiastically centered civilization of Christian peoples. The immediate political consequence was the Thirty Years War (1618–1648), in which Catholic and Protestant forces, marching under the banners of competing religious absolutes, wreaked havoc over much of Europe and left Germany, in particular, in physical and cultural ruins. A similar lesson about the consequences of confessional strife was meanwhile being learned in Britain as the forces of a Puritan Protestantism succeeded in breaking the hold of the old ecclesiastical–political order. The fact that the traditional institutions of Church and State were restored did not erase the rift in the hearts and minds of the Anglo-Saxon cultural elite, many of whom assumed leadership in the emerging modern world. The concrete symbol of the end of the old order and the new religious and political pluralism in Europe was the formula at the heart of the Peace of Westphalia (1648) that put an end to the wars of religion: *cuius regio eius religio*. Henceforth every principality would worship according to the religious convictions of its prince. This new order ought not to be confused with freedom of religion, which still lay in the future. Rather, it legitimated a system of juxtaposed "absolutes" in which rival claimants to ultimate authority coexisted side by side: unmistakable evidence that the era of religious uniformity had passed into history.

A good way to conceptualize the radical disjuncture between the modern world and its ancient and medieval predecessors is to start at the level of world-view in the most concrete sense of the term: the picture of the world that every age carries in its imagination, and which functions as a means of physical, psychological, and religious orientation. Historians and philosophers have long associated the "Copernican Revolution" (the label was coined by the modern philosopher Immanuel Kant) with the origins of modernity and its break with the past. To understand why it was revolutionary, one must look at the image of the world that it displaced, which can be called the Aristotelian–Christian world-view.[2] As the name suggests, this picture of the world originated in Greek antiquity, specifically in the philosophy of Aristotle, and was subsequently elaborated in the astronomy of Ptolemy (second-century CE). It was appropriated by Christian thinkers early in the Church's history and served as the common assumption of Christian civilization until it was dislodged in early modernity by the heliocentric schema of Copernicus and his successors. In the Aristotelian–Ptolemaic world-view the earth was located in the center of a finite universe and enclosed within the concentric spherical shells of the seven planets (the Moon, Mercury, Venus, the Sun, Mars, Jupiter, Saturn), which were in turn enclosed by the sphere of the fixed stars. From Aristotle on, a sharp distinction was made between the heavens, the realm of perfection and harmony, and the "sublunary" region including the earth, characterized by corruption and change. Aristotle thought of God, the prime mover who imparted motion to the universe, as surrounding it nonspatially. In the Christianized version of this world-view the invisible heaven was conceived spatially as identical with, or beyond, the outermost firmament. This heaven, the abode of angels and saints, was counterposed to its opposite, hell, located in the center of the earth at the point of farthest remove from God. The ascension of Christ, as well as the blessed, was accordingly thought of as an upward movement through the lower heavens to the highest heaven beyond the spheres.

The Aristotelian–Christian world-view was thus far more than an astronomical theory, comprising the stage or framework for the whole divine–human drama of creation and redemption. For just this reason, its replacement by the new Copernican picture of the heavens was a "revolutionary" event for theology as well as astronomy. On the one hand, it represented the displacement of man from the center of the universe. (As the Old Cardinal in Bertolt Brecht's play *Galileo*, puts it: "Mr. Galilei transfers mankind from the center of the universe to somewhere on the outskirts. Mr. Galilei is therefore an enemy of mankind.") The other side of the coin, however, is that the new world-view has been discovered by human reason, so that in a different and more important sense, man is more than ever at the center of things: the old *geocentric* world has been replaced by the modern *anthropocentric* world. The old Aristotelian–Christian world-view persisted in the Catholic theology of the Counter-Reformation, but its hold gradually loosened in the new Protestant theologies, especially among Lutherans. Lutheran orthodoxy, following Luther himself, ceased to think of heavenly glory in spatio-temporal terms at all; even Christ's ascension took spatial form only until he disappeared into the clouds, and then only for the sake of the disciples' limited understanding. This doctrine was attacked by Reformed theologians, who as late as the early eighteenth century were still opposing the teachings of Copernicus as unbiblical. The original appearance of Copernicus's *De revolutionibus orbium coelestium* was due to a Lutheran theologian and reformer of Nürnberg, Andreas Osiander, who first published it in 1543 together with his own preface. Despite this promising start, however, the Lutheran universities were among the slowest to adopt the new Copernican theory, primarily because of the opposition of Luther's leading associate, Philipp Melanchthon, who attacked it on scientific grounds in his textbook on physics.

The theological revolution represented by the destruction of the old Aristotelian–Christian world-view is epitomized in an exchange that allegedly took place between the Emperor Napoleon and the modern astronomer Laplace. To the monarch's pious query, "Where is God in your system of the universe?" the scientist reportedly retorted, "Sire, we have no need of that hypothesis!" The papal astronomer in Brecht's play *Galileo*, after learning of Galileo's discoveries, makes the comment, "Now it's for the theologians to set the heavens right again" – which can be taken as a motto for the task of modern theology.

The modern world that appeared on the scene in the course of the seventeenth century – the Treaty of Westphalia in 1648 makes a useful symbolic date of birth – can be seen as the outcome of three factors, two negative and one positive.

The first was the new awareness of plurality that was the unintended legacy of the Reformation. The result of the Thirty Years War was to legitimize confessional multiplicity and to provide it with a constitutional basis. Henceforth Lutheran, Reformed, and Roman Catholic Christians – each claiming supreme religious authority – were forced to coexist in mutual proximity and animosity, a situation that spoke louder to the European peoples than the voices of their several theologians and creeds. The lesson inevitably drawn by many from this arrangement was the skeptical one that none of the confessions had a monopoly on the truth, and this realization undermined the authority of the churches and eventually the doctrines they taught. The classic statement of this modern attitude toward religious doctrines is expressed in the play *Nathan the Wise*, by the eighteenth-century German poet and philosopher G. E. Lessing (1729–81). His parable of the three rings epitomizes the twin attitudes of the Enlightenment toward religion: tolerance, along with an underlying skepticism about religious orthodoxy.

A second factor in the birth of modernity is closely related to the first: a growing weariness over religious wars and persecution. Not only had confessional division undermined the authority of religious institutions, but it had also eventuated in mutual hatred and violence. The wars of religion had awakened a deep yearning for unity and peace, the very qualities once guaranteed by religion but now seemingly destroyed by confessional strife. And the happy exception of the Netherlands also seemed to offer a lesson: tolerance pays. Here was a nation that permitted religious freedom and was thriving economically!

In addition to the negative incentives of competing ultimate authorities and religious warfare, emerging modernity was given positive encouragement by a third factor, the rise of what was then called the "new science" and has come down to us as *modern* science. The full impact of the change that had been heralded by Copernicus was brought home in the work of Galileo (1564–1642), who produced actual evidence for the heliocentric theory, firmly linking celestial with terrestrial reality. Using the new-fangled technology of the telescope, he was able to demonstrate that the same principles applied "up there" as "down here." It is surely no accident that the most notorious clash between the official church and modern science was occasioned by Galileo's discoveries, which brought into stark contrast the incompatible paradigms of the old world picture and the new. The new science reached its culmination in the work of a man born the same year that Galileo died, Isaac Newton (1642–1727), whose *Philosophiæ Naturalis Principia Mathematica* first exhibited the new world-view in all its glory. It appeared as a vast cosmic machine in which space and time are the infinite and uniform containers of material bodies, which move according to universal laws. The most powerful feature of the Newtonian theory was its contention that those laws are written in the language of mathematics, and are thus universally applicable and knowable in principle by all men on the basis of their natural endowments. Newton was also prepared to say where God was located in his system – namely, external to it as its creator, who had originally set it in motion and now intervened only occasionally in order to make minor adjustments to the mechanism. It was not long, however, before even this weakened notion of divine providence withered away, leaving the "watchmaker" God of the Deists.

Paralleling the new science was an equally revolutionary shift in philosophy. The thinker usually acknowledged to be the founder of *modern* philosophy, René Descartes (1596–1650), likewise belongs to seventeenth-century Europe. The essence of the revolution he brought about is the concept of methodological doubt. (Brecht's Galileo: "The millennium of faith is ended, said I, this is the millennium of doubt.") But Cartesian doubt is not an indication of unbelief but rather a doubting for the sake of certainty. By making doubt the first principle of philosophy, Descartes intended not to undermine religion but rather to set it on a new and secure foundation. The method bears a striking resemblance to the science of this day, to which he was also a notable contributor. His thought experiment rests on a simple premise: if one employs doubt as a kind of epistemological acid to dissolve away all doubtful propositions, one will be left with the indubitable core of experience, which Descartes expressed in that most famous of philosophical utterances, *cogito ergo sum* ("I think, therefore I am"). The sheer awareness of my own existence, he is saying, I can by no means doubt away. And this survivor of doubt, this *cogito*, then becomes the foundation for a new philosophical program, in which the philosopher is able to establish even belief in God with new certitude. Beyond the question of whether the Cartesian method is plausible, however, is the new "metaphysical" quandary in which it leaves philosophy. For Descartes was forced to acknowledge two "substances," two kinds of fundamental reality, which he called *res cogitans* ("thinking substance") and *res extensa* ("extended substance"). This situation leads to the infamous "Cartesian dualism" of mind and matter, much lamented by modern philosophers because it apparently leaves the thinking subject isolated from the world of material objects. Descartes' achievement, on the other hand, is considerable, for he has provided an answer to the question of Laplace by finding a place in the modern world for God, a secure place within the human subject. Less successful is his attempt to relate God to the external world machine of modern science, for he was the first thinker to compare the creator to a fine watchmaker, who plays a necessary role in the origin of the world but then has no apparent job to do in its ongoing history.

Enlightenment: the Religion of Reason

Proposals to ground religion, not on the specific claims of one historic tradition or another but rather on universal reason, found a ready audience among Europeans wearied by a century of confessional strife. The analogy with science was powerfully suggestive: just as there is a *natural science* based on universal mathematical laws that are transparent to reason, might there not be a *natural religion* likewise knowable by all without regard to time, place, or historical tradition? As the seventeenth century unfolded, a number of thinkers answered this question in the affirmative. An early example appears in the work of Edward, Lord Herbert of Cherbury (1583–1648), a veteran of the Thirty Years War and brother of the poet George Herbert. Seeking a common basis for religion that could be acknowledged by all human beings, Lord Herbert concluded from his study of ancient and modern religion that God had endowed his human creatures with certain Common Notions (*notitiae communes*) that are sufficient to ground the essentials of religious faith in all times and places. There are five such innate ideas, he contended: (1) that God exists, and (2) ought to be worshiped, (3) that virtuous living is the best way to honor God, (4) that all people abhor evil, and (5) that there will be rewards and punishments after death. This teaching, put forth in his book *De veritate* (1624), has earned him the label "Father of Deism," a movement that ignited a religious controversy that was to dominate England for the next century and more.

The Deist Controversy sprang from the tension between a universal *natural* religion and the specific teachings of the historical traditions, called *positive* religions by the Enlightenment rationalists.[3] Even if philosophers like Descartes or Herbert of Cherbury could succeed in making room for a kind of general theism, the specific claims of Christian (and by implication, other) revelation would still need to be brought into harmony with the world-view of modernity. This question focused attention on the Bible, whose meaning and status has been one of the most persistent and controversial issues of modern theology. In seventeenth- and eighteenth-century Britain this issue divided religious rationalists into two camps: rational supernaturalists, who acknowledged the importance of reason but affirmed the necessity of revelation as well, and the Deists, who either rejected revelation outright or reduced it to a mere accommodation to the masses of the same rational religion obtainable by philosophers through reason. The position of those who argued for the necessity of revelation is epitomized by the philosopher John Locke (1632–1704), widely known for his empiricism and for his contributions to modern theories of toleration and individual liberty, but also the author of the classic work of rational supernaturalism, *The Reasonableness of Christianity* (1695). The book's argument presupposes Locke's tripartite distinction among propositions "above, contrary and according to reason." The latter two cases present no difficulties, since any claim that is contrary to reason is false on its face while claims shown to be in accord with reason are obviously true. The heart of Locke's argument for Christianity, however, is that it teaches essential revealed truths that are *above* reason, and thus neither contradicted nor supported by it. Primary among them is Jesus's claim to be the Messiah. Locke argues that we are justified in accepting this central Christian doctrine "above reason," since it is warranted externally by the fact that Jesus fulfilled prophecies and performed miracles. Such "outward signs" confirm the reasonableness of Christianity.

Locke's opponents, who came to be called Deists, denied the possibility of suprarational truth and insisted accordingly that genuine religion be purged of all mystery. The two most important Deists were John Toland (1670–1722), author of *Christianity Not Mysterious* (1696), and Matthew Tindal (1655–1733), the Oxford scholar who in 1730 published *Christianity as Old as the Creation*, destined to become known as the "Deists' Bible." Toland's subtitle tells it all: . . . *a Treatise Shewing, That there is nothing in the Gospel Contrary to Reason, Nor Above it: And that no Christian Doctrine can be properly call'd a Mystery.* Christian revelation, he argues, can be shown to agree in all its essentials with natural religion (for which no revelation is necessary). "What is once reveal'd," he maintains, "we must as well understand as any other Matter in the World, *Revelation* being only of use to enform us, whilst the Evidence of its Subject perswades us" (Toland 1969:146). Revealed and natural religion thus differ only in form and not in content. Deism culminates in Tindal's claim that, since biblical revelation merely recapitulates natural religion, Christianity is "as old as the creation." Once again the subtitle gives the gist: . . . *the Gospel, a Republication of the Religion of Nature.* The warrants for believing the propositions of Christianity are thus not external, as in Locke, but internal: "there can be no other Distinction between Morality and Religion, than that the former is acting according to the Reason of Things consider'd in themselves; the other, acting according to the same Reason of Things consider'd as the Will of God" – a distinction that effectively reduces religion to morality and later provides Kant with his definition of religion (Tindal 1967:298).[4] Joseph Butler (1692–1752) wrote the most telling rejoinder to the Deists in *The Analogy of Religion* (1736), in which he argues that nature is not nearly so uniform and rationally accessible as the proponents of natural religion assume but is, rather, as ambiguous and recalcitrant as revelation. But this argument proved to be a two-edged sword, for though it convinced some to accept revealed mystery it provoked others – like David Hume – to reject both Deism and rational supernaturalism.

The philosophy of Hume (1711–76) marks the end of an era in religious thought, for his devastating attacks on miracles and the fulfillment of prophecy undermined the external warrants on which the rational supernaturalists based their case. But his equally compelling critique of the argument from design, the favorite prop of the Deists, represented the end of their appeal as well. The effect of this double assault was to undermine the common assumption of both sides, the rationality of religious belief. Hume thus drives a wedge between faith and reason, challenging his contemporaries either to acknowledge that religion is based on a wholly irrational faith (a position he claimed not to oppose) or to abandon it altogether. His challenge was heard in far-off Königsberg, where Kant credited Hume with awakening him from his "dogmatic slumbers."

Before turning to the culmination of the Enlightenment in the thought of Immanuel Kant, we need to look briefly at the quite different situation that obtained in France. The French Enlightenment differed from its British and German counterparts primarily because the relationship of modernity to the past was fundamentally different in France. King Louis XIV (1643–1715) set out to unify the French nation and culture under the banner of the Counter-Reformation, which entailed the suppression of Protestantism by force, most dramatically in the destruction of the Huguenots through exile, repression, and conversion. The French state remained the dutiful servant of the Roman Church until the Revolution of 1789. This situation helps to explain why even so bitter an enemy of the Church as Voltaire, on his deathbed confessed to a priest and issued a written apology. (Under prevailing law, bodies of those who died refusing the sacramental ministry of the Catholic Church were to be dragged naked through the streets and thrown unburied on the dump; and despite his confession, Voltaire narrowly escaped this fate when he died two months later.) The French *philosophes*, though they borrowed arguments from the English Deists, were thus far more outspoken in their rejection of superstition and religious persecution. The epitome of the French Enlightenment, Voltaire (1694–1778; born François Marie Arouet), often sought to disguise his true views, but he was evidently a Deist, who relied on the argument from design and appealed to the analogy of the watchmaker God. But he reserved the most scathing of his rapier prose for attacking the Church, delighting in the motto *écrasez l'infâme* ("crush the infamous thing"). Voltaire was the mentor and inspiration for a group of younger French intellectuals who called themselves "the philosophers" and came to typify the Enlightenment in France. The most visible fruit of their work was the *Encyclopedia* (*Encyclopédie, ou Dictionnaire raisonné des sciences, des arts et des métiers*, 28 volumes, 1751–72), under the editorship of Jean d'Alembert (1717–83) and Denis Diderot (1713–84), which was marked by a militant atheism and materialism. Thus under Louis XIV both the Church and unbelief paradoxically flourished (Hirsch 1949, vol. 3:60).

Beyond Enlightenment: Kant

The thinker who offered the most famous definition of Enlightenment,[5] Immanuel Kant (1724–1804), also marks its culmination and is thus the one most responsible for bringing it to an end and ushering in a new era in the relationship of theology and modernity. His critical philosophy is the watershed of modern thought, the prism through which the earlier lines of modernity are gathered up and refracted in new patterns that set the course of religious thought for the coming century – and beyond. Kant is the quintessential modern thinker, the one whose contribution is so definitive that without taking him into account no adequate understanding of theology and modernity is possible. He is the author of two interrelated revolutions in modern thought, one philosophical and the other theological. In the former role Kant takes up where Hume had left off, extending and systematizing the critique of natural theology; in the latter he lays the foundation for a whole new way of doing theology – one that sets the pattern for the liberal theologies of the next two centuries. He announces his intentions in the preface to the *Critique of Pure Reason*: "I have . . . found it necessary," he writes, "to deny *knowledge*, in order to make room for *faith*" (Kant 1965).

The first, or philosophical, task ("to deny *knowledge*") Kant carries out in his *Critique of Pure Reason* by proposing a bold new model of reason as inherently active, not simply the receptive *tabula rasa* of earlier empiricists such as Locke. But neither does Kant take the other extreme, exemplified by rationalists like Herbert of Cherbury, who see reason itself as a source of knowledge. His middle way he calls *critical*, proposing that reason works "synthetically" to produce knowledge by applying *a priori* rational concepts to data supplied by the senses *a posteriori*. "Critique" is his name for the philosophical analysis of experience that seeks to factor out the implicit *a priori* concepts by which we organize and categorize sense data in order to synthesize knowledge. As far as theology is concerned, the results of this analysis are largely negative, for we can in principle have no knowledge of transcendent *noumena* such as God but only of the *phenomena* that appear to our senses. On the other hand, we not only can but must conceive of God, a concept that Kant calls "the Ideal of Pure Reason." So we are left at the end of the First Critique with not an atheism but an agnosticism, in which we are unable to have knowledge of that which we must necessarily conceive.

But Kant's project for reconstructing theology is not yet complete, for in the second volume of his critical philosophy, the *Critique of Practical Reason*, he carries out his constructive theological task ("to make room for *faith*"). Here it is essential to note that it is *knowledge*, not *reason*, that he has excluded from theology. Although he is convinced that we can have no *theoretical knowledge* of God, he argues in the Second Critique that we can nevertheless have a *practical faith*, and that this faith is *rational*. Indeed, it is not too much to say that rational faith in God is not optional but necessary. Our moral experience, our conscience, Kant is saying, *demands* the reality of the objects of religious belief – freedom, immortality, and God (Kant calls these the "postulates of pure practical reason"). Do we therefore have knowledge of these objects? No (for all the reasons given in the First Critique). Is it rational to accept them? Yes – moreover, it is irrational not to do so (for all the reasons given in the Second Critique)! Kant spells out this rational theology in *Religion within the Limits of Reason Alone* (1793), which is simultaneously a brief for what he calls "pure rational faith" and an apologetic argument for the Christian religion as the one that most nearly exemplifies that ideal. For the same reason, however, the book also contains a polemical rejection of the "positivity" of Christianity – meaning all of its concrete historical specificity – so that in the end little is left of the historic faith of the Church except an abstract shell of rationalized ethics.

Kant's solution to the problem of theology and modernity can be seen in retrospect as a powerful model that has been repeated in numerous variations in the liberal theologies and philosophies of religion in the nineteenth and twentieth centuries. In each case the religious thinker first identifies one aspect of human experience (practical reason in Kant's case), which is at the same time both the definitively human characteristic and the essence of religion. A case can then be made for the truth of the Christian religion, understood to be one expression or symbolic embodiment (typically the highest or best) of the essential *humanum*, which is also the religious *a priori*. The price for such accommodation of Christianity to modernity, however, comes high; for the "positive" elements of the gospel – those concrete particulars that have historically counted as essential features of the faith – must be sacrificed to the universally human and religious aspects. Religious thought of the nineteenth and twentieth centuries can be read as a dialectic in which successive variations on Kant's program compete with one another, punctuated periodically by forceful attempts to reject the liberal model and return theology to its orthodox roots.

The Nineteenth Century: Romanticism, Idealism, and Their Critics

The most influential of those variations comes from the other figure most often credited with setting the course of liberal theology, Friedrich Schleiermacher (1768–1834) who, unlike Kant, was a theologian and churchman. Typically called the "father of modern Protestant theology," he was raised in a pietistic home and came of age as part of the early Romantic movement in Germany. His two major accomplishments, both concerned with the relation of theology to modernity, are associated with two quite different books. In 1799, while a part of the circle of young Romantic poets and philosophers, he published *On Religion: Speeches to Its Cultured Despisers*, in which he proposed a radically new view of religion as an immediate (pre-reflective) relation to the *Universum* or All that manifests itself in feeling – which he called the "feeling of absolute [or utter] dependence." This religious intuition is available to every human being; but in sharp contrast to the natural religion of the Enlightenment and to Kant's ethical religion, it is located in neither the intellect nor the will but in the affections. This universal experience of religion is to be distinguished from all the specific historical religions, including Christianity, yet at the same time it is the essential root of them all. In keeping with this view of religion, the *Speeches* are rhetorical and apologetic in style, seeking to evoke ("conjure") that spirit of religion in the hearts of his skeptical fellow Romantics, the "cultured despisers" of his subtitle.

Two decades later, as a professor in the newly founded Humboldt University of Berlin, Schleiermacher published a work of a very different style, his theological magnum opus titled *The Christian Faith* and known informally as the *Glaubenslehre* or "doctrine of faith." Despite the stylistic shift, *The Christian Faith* can be seen as Schleiermacher's attempt to interpret the doctrines of Christianity in accordance with the new concept of religion developed in the *Speeches*. In a lengthy introduction he classifies Christianity in relation to the other major religions of the world, from which it is differentiated by relating its experience of religion specifically to "the redemption accomplished in Jesus of Nazareth." Christian doctrines, on Schleiermacher's terms, are not metaphysical descriptions of supernatural reality but rather, verbal accounts of the uniquely Christian religious experience. This revolutionary turn in modern theology means that for the followers of Schleiermacher doctrines are descriptive not of God but of faith, or religious experience – though these theologians remain convinced that such theology is still *indirectly* descriptive of God.

Along with Kant and Schleiermacher, the third towering figure from this fertile period in German thought, G. W. F. Hegel (1770–1831), gave a different but equally influential twist to the relationship of theology and modernity. A colleague and critic of Schleiermacher at the University of Berlin, Hegel represents the culmination of German Idealism, a movement that has its roots in Kant's practical philosophy, and which J. G. Fichte (1762–1814) and F. W. J. Schelling (1775–1854) developed into full-blown Idealist systems. By rejecting Kant's notion of a *Ding an sich* – the "thing in itself," which has reality apart from our knowledge of it – they argued in effect that all reason is practical reason, since it constructs its objects of knowledge, which can thus be accounted for without recourse to an ineffable and paradoxical *Ding an sich*. This move dissolves the dichotomy of subject and object into a concept of the absolute ego (*das Ich*, the "I" or self), which the Idealists identify as the first principle of philosophy. In Hegel's mature system, the culmination of German Idealism, ultimate reality is interpreted as the dialectical unfolding of God, or Absolute Spirit, through history in a process that is at the same time God's self-revelation and self-realization. To understand Hegel's view of theology and modernity, it is necessary to look at the final stages of this historical dialectic, which Hegel calls Absolute Spirit and distinguishes into the three domains of art, religion, and philosophy. Each of these, as a form of Absolute Spirit, contains the entire truth as its *content*; but only in the final transformation (*Aufhebung*) of art and religion into pure philosophy does the truth attain its perfect *form*. Art expresses the truth in sensuous forms; in religion, the next stage, the truth is expressed in ideas, but they take shape in imagination – sensuous images that represent the truth metaphorically or symbolically. Only at the pinnacle of the system does the truth achieve its purified expression in the pure translucent Concept, in which all traces of sensuality are left behind. Viewed from the perspective of Hegel's philosophy of religion, Spirit manifests itself in a history of different religious forms culminating in the Absolute Religion, which Hegel identifies with Christianity. By working out this vast and intricate system, Hegel sought to do for modernity what Thomas Aquinas had done for the medieval world: to produce a "modern synthesis" that would reconcile the truth of historic Christianity with the thought forms of the modern world. Not many subsequent thinkers are convinced that he succeeded, yet nearly all have been influenced by his way of thinking. And the immediate successors of Hegel, disagreeing about the meaning and significance of his philosophy, took modern religious thought in important new directions.

The Hermeneutics of Suspicion and the Problem of History

Some of Hegel's immediate followers, who became known as the Hegelian Right, believed that his Idealist system had indeed achieved the reconciliation of Christian truth and modernity; but their influence was short-lived. Far more important in the long run were those on the other side of the split, the so-called Young Hegelians on the Left, of whom three are especially crucial for later religious thought.

Ludwig Feuerbach (1804–1872) has been called "Hegel's Fate," since he begins from the Hegelian system, learns from it how to think dialectically, but then inverts the whole enterprise into an historical materialism that denies rather than justifies the truth claims of Christian theology. In *The Essence of Christianity* (1841), his best-known work, Feuerbach reduces theology to anthropology, arguing that religion is based on an illusory reversal of subject and object in which the essential attributes of humanity are projected onto an imaginary divine subject. Like Hegel, he sees the incarnation of Christ as the decisive historical turning point; but he inverts its meaning, interpreting it as the moment in which the projected attributes of "God" are reclaimed by alienated humanity. Feuerbach thus develops a "theological" atheism that does not attack theology from without but turns its own implicit logic against it. In his later work, Feuerbach leaves Hegel behind entirely and develops a critique of religion as a misinterpretation of the forces of nature by an illusory imagination.

Feuerbach's early dialectical critique of religion was politicized by Karl Marx (1818–83), who interprets religious projection not simply as a theoretical error but rather as the practical means by which the economically dominant classes have kept the dissatisfaction of the oppressed classes in check by diverting their energies to unrealistic otherworldly goals. He too claims to have inverted Hegel's system – not, as is sometimes reported, by "turning Hegel on his head" but rather by finding the Idealist Hegel already standing on his head and returning him to a firm footing on the earth. Like Feuerbach, Marx learns to think dialectically from Hegel but then uses the method to produce the opposite outcome: what Marx calls dialectical materialism, a philosophy that offers the key to history and the motivation for the oppressed classes to rise up and transform social reality. Religion is thus at the same time crucially important to the historical process and wholly negative in its effects, the opiate that drugs the oppressed into harmless dreams of another world, the flowers that disguise the true nature of the economic chains that bind them. Religious critique is therefore the opening wedge in the original Marxist program for socio-political transformation. There have been others – especially the Liberation Theologians of the twentieth century – who have nevertheless believed that a modified Marxist analysis is a useful tool that can be employed on behalf of theology. There are signs, however, now that the great political empire that claimed Marx as its prophet has faded from the stage of history, that the influence of his thought, whether positive or negative, is waning as the new century unfolds.

The kind of critical thought exemplified by Feuerbach and Marx has come to be called the hermeneutics of suspicion, and it constitutes one of the most powerful intellectual and moral factors in religious thought since the middle of the nineteenth century. The other thinkers most commonly associated with this movement are Nietzsche and Freud, but others in the past century and a half might also be usefully understood as practitioners of hermeneutical suspicion. An example is the third major figure among the Young Hegelians, David Friedrich Strauss (1808–74), who can be thought of as the originator of the historical critique of Christianity. After studying theology, Strauss came under the influence of Hegel. He taught philosophy briefly before publishing his *Life of Jesus* (1835), which became one of the most influential and controversial books in modern religious thought, among not only scholars but also the general public. Strauss is responsible for introducing a new interpretive key into biblical scholarship, which he called mythological criticism, intended as a mediating position between rationalistic interpretation (which took miracle stories to be either misinterpretations of scientifically explainable events or deliberate frauds), on the one hand, and orthodox interpretation (which assumed that the gospels present wholly reliable eye-witness accounts of supernatural occurrences), on the other. Strauss thus undercuts the common assumption of both sides, that the biblical account provides factual information about the real Jesus. He was convinced that whatever facts could be established are insufficient to give us a Jesus worthy of religious faith. Strauss does not maintain that the individual authors fictionalized the facts, but rather that the biblical narratives are the product of an unconscious myth-building power of the early Christian community, by which it expressed the truth it apprehended in the form of its stories about Jesus. The storm of protest in response to the book ended Strauss's academic career and unleashed a public controversy not only in Germany but also in Britain after *The Life of Jesus* appeared in a translation by the novelist George Eliot, who was also responsible for the English version of Feuerbach's *Essence of Christianity*.

The controversy about Strauss's Jesus represents the most dramatic chapter in the struggle over one of the major issues of theology and modernity, the problem of the historical reliability of the Bible. The issue first emerged in the eighteenth century when G. E. Lessing published posthumous fragments by the radical Deist Hermann Samuel Reimarus challenging the historical truth of central biblical narratives. After Strauss the arguments generally focused on attempts to distinguish myth from history, with liberals typically arguing that the biblical writers presented their ideas in the form of mythical stories, and conservatives insisting on the factual accuracy of the texts. A new chapter in the battle over faith and history unfolded in the twentieth century after Rudolf Bultmann (1884–1976) proposed that scripture be *demythologized* by means of what he called "existential interpretation," a method heavily influenced by the early thought of the philosopher Martin Heidegger. Bultmann believed that his approach made it possible to distinguish the essential message of the New Testament proclamation (*kerygma*) from the mythic form in which it was expressed by the ancient authors. His opponents, especially Karl Barth (1886–1968), charged that demythologization distorts the essential message of Scripture, which cannot be isolated from the historical narrative in which it is embedded.

Dissenting Voices in Modern Theology

Before leaving the nineteenth century behind it is important to remember that not all Christian thinkers followed the path of accommodation to modernity blazed by Kant, Schleiermacher, and Hegel. There were, first, those representatives of traditional orthodoxy who tried their best to remain staunchly unaffected by modern ideas. In addition to Catholic traditionalists, this group includes various restoration movements among European Protestants; but of all the attempts to restore the Church to its historical confessions none was more influential than the Princeton Theology, which flourished for more than a century at Princeton Theological Seminary. The leading theologians of this movement, especially Charles Hodge (1797–1878) and his successor, Benjamin Warfield (1851–1921), combined a doctrine of direct verbal inspiration of Scripture with a commitment to conservative Calvinist confessionalism. Although they saw themselves as simply re-stating orthodox doctrine, they were in fact modern thinkers in their stress on the use of reason and their insistence that theology is a science in the modern sense of the term. The Princeton theologians also defended Christian orthodoxy against modern secular and scientific ideas, especially Darwin's theory of evolution. Their struggle with liberal theologians led in the early twentieth century to the Fundamentalist–Modernist controversy, which split the Presbyterians and some other mainline churches into separate liberal and fundamentalist or evangelical denominations.

Not all those who rejected theological accommodation to modernity, however, were confessional restorationists. Two towering figures from the second half of the nineteenth century – Søren Kierkegaard (1813–55) and Friedrich Nietzsche (1844–1900) – though in some ways direct opposites, offer powerful critiques of Enlightenment and Idealist rationalism while attacking modern acculturated Christendom, which they see as incompatible with New Testament Christianity. And both are masters of irony and indirection, deliberately making it difficult to pin down their precise positions.

Kierkegaard, reacting strongly against the Hegelianism of the leaders of the new Danish People's Church founded after the revolution of 1848, employed irony and a complex pattern of pseudonymous writings to challenge the bourgeois Christianity of his times with the strangeness of the New Testament gospel. He ridicules and parodies the systems of the Hegelians while using Socrates as a foil for presenting the radicality of true Christian faith, which he sees as discontinuous with rational argument, a "scandal" that can only be appropriated by means of a subjective "leap." His influence was not felt beyond Denmark until the twentieth century, when his writings began to appear in German and English.

Nietzsche is equally scathing in his rejection of modern bourgeois society and religion, but his alternative is not Christian faith, against which he hurls vehement arguments. No phrase better epitomizes the modern challenge to theology than the "death of God," Nietzsche's name for the defining experience of modernity. His attitude towards Christianity is complicated, however, for he occasionally expresses sympathy for genuine Christians, and his rather contradictory view of Jesus seems sometimes to want to separate him from the vengeful "Christianity" created in his name by his disciples and St. Paul. On the one hand, Nietzsche can be seen as the heir to the atheism of the Enlightenment (Voltaire was one of his heroes); but on the other hand he is the prophet of postmodernism, who seems to reject all objectivity, leaving us with an unresolved interplay of competing interpretations.

Catholic Theology and Modernity

So far the drama of theology and modernity appears as a largely Protestant story. One reason, of course, is the role played by the Protestant Reformation in the emergence of the modern world. Another reason is the historical fact that the earliest confrontations between emerging modernity and traditional theology occurred in Protestant countries, especially Germany and Great Britain. But the historical connection between Protestant Christianity and modernity by no means implies that the story should be of interest only to Protestants, for the issues that they first encountered and to which they responded came eventually to confront other religious communities as well: Jews as they gradually emerged from the ghettos of Europe, starting in the eighteenth century, and Roman Catholics beginning in the nineteenth century. By the twentieth century, the globalization of European and North American culture meant that all of the world's religious traditions faced similar challenges. Although each religious community obviously comes to terms with modernity in its own way, there are nevertheless significant parallels among them, and the experiences of European Protestants from the seventeenth to the nineteenth centuries are therefore instructive for others as well.

Roman Catholic theology remained largely insulated from the winds of secular modernity until the early nineteenth century, when revulsion in France against the excesses of the Revolution combined with the spirit of the rising Romantic movement to produce the Catholic Traditionalism of such figures as the Viscomte de Chateaubriand (1768–1848), Joseph de Maistre (1753–1821), Félicité de Lamennais (1782–1854), and Louis Bautain (1796–1867). Meanwhile in Germany a newly founded Catholic theological college became in 1817 the Catholic Faculty of the University of Tübingen, which already had an ancient and distinguished Protestant Faculty. This unique situation, a century and a half before the ecumenical movement of the late twentieth century, led to the formation of the Catholic Tübingen School under the leadership of J. S. Drey (1777–1853) and J. A. Möhler (1796–1838). Encouraged by the association with their Protestant colleagues, these Tübingen Catholics began to respond to the modern ideas of Kant, Schleiermacher, and Hegel. Although their early works were largely indebted to the Romantic movement, they remained wary of Schleiermacher's "feeling of absolute dependence," and through study of the Church Fathers and later Catholic tradition they developed a new, more dynamic understanding of the Church and its doctrine.

Hopes that the new theology might lead the way to a revitalization of the Catholic Church were dashed by the wave of revolutions that swept across Europe in 1848. Pope Pius IX, who had begun as a theological progressive, was forced to flee Rome and leave power to the revolutionaries until he was rescued by French troops. His reaction was swift and dramatic, leading to what has been termed the Fortress Mentality that was to characterize the Roman Church for more than a century. The Roman hierarchy came to see the Church as a citadel to defend the faithful against the forces of modernity; and as the secular authority of the Church decreased, its claims to spiritual supremacy increased as though in compensation. The retrenchment reached a climax in the Vatican Council of 1870–1, the first since the Reformation, which redoubled the Roman Church's rejection of everything Protestant and modern, and proclaimed the doctrine of the Pope's infallible teaching authority on matters of faith and morals.

One further development in Catholic theology in the nineteenth century deserves to be mentioned – one that had consequences for both Roman Catholics and Anglicans. The Tractarian or Oxford Movement originated in the Church of England in the 1830s in response to political developments, and rapidly captured the attention of the public, especially after the appearance in 1841 of the famous Tract 90 by John Henry Newman (1801–90), the most important theologian associated with the movement. The Tractarians sought to re-establish the authority of the Church, reverse the trend toward rationalism in religion, and renew a sense of religious mystery and "reserve." Several of its leaders were outspoken in their rejection of Protestant ideas and influences, a tendency that appeared to be confirmed by Newman's dramatic defection to the Roman Church in 1845. The Oxford Movement, though shaken, nevertheless continued to influence not only Anglicans but also other denominations at home and abroad. Meanwhile Newman continued his influence, now as a Roman Catholic theologian and eventually as a cardinal. Of his many significant writings, the one most noteworthy for the relationship of theology and modernity is his *Essay on the Development of Christian Doctrine*, written while he was still an Anglican but which he later reaffirmed; it played a major role in the ongoing Roman Catholic debate about history and doctrinal change.

The Twentieth Century and Beyond

Most of the issues affecting theology and modernity that had been raised since the seventeenth century continued to challenge thinkers in the twentieth century. Since those developments are treated in detail elsewhere in this volume, all that remains for us is to indicate in a few broad strokes the range of alternatives and to diagnose our situation as a new century unfolds.

   The opening years of the twentieth century appear in retrospect as a kind of coda to the nineteenth, the calm before the storm that was about to break over Europe. Protestant Liberal Theology was in the ascendancy, led by Albrecht Ritchl (1822–89), Wilhelm Herrmann (1846–1922), and Adolf von Harnack (1851–1930), whose 1900 Berlin lectures on the "Essence of Christianity"[6] epitomized the movement. They also drew the fire of Alfred Loisy (1857–1940), leader of the Catholic Modernists, whose attempt to break down the walls of the Fortress Mentality in Rome was quashed by papal condemnations in 1907.

   The mood changed, and with it theology, after the First World War (1914–18). The Dialectical Theology of Karl Barth and his associates, inspired by Kierkegaard among others, attacked the "culture Protestantism" of Harnack and the Liberals and began a new era in Protestant theology. Over the next two decades, controversies between Barth and Bultmann, then Barth and Emil Brunner, brought the unity of the original group to an end and sowed the seeds of the various theological options that were to dominate theology in the coming decades. Bultmann and Paul Tillich (1886–1965), each in his own way, appropriated existentialist philosophy in order to bridge the gap between Christian faith and modernity. The most important work of Protestant theology in the twentieth century, Barth's monumental *Church Dogmatics*, began to appear in the early 1930s, just as a second great crisis overwhelmed the nations of Europe and eventually much of the world. One could argue that the great challenge of modernity was posed in the twentieth century not by new philosophies or even by science but rather by Adolf

Hitler and the Holocaust. Most of the theologians who set the course of theology in the first half of the century were affected, often in fundamental ways, by the encounter with National Socialism and the crisis it represented for theology.

The latter half of the twentieth century is more difficult to characterize (perhaps for lack of sufficient hindsight), but the Second Vatican Council (1962–5) was surely the defining event for Roman Catholic theology, as the Fortress Mentality of the Tridentine Church gave way to the *aggiornamento* of Pope John XXIII. The council also helped to launch the ecumenical movement, which has deeply affected Christian theology of all types. At about the same time a different theological response to modernity appeared in the various politically focused theological movements from the 1960s onward: Liberation Theology, first in Latin America and later elsewhere; Black Theology; and Feminist Theologies of several kinds.

The Postmodern Question: the End of Modernity?

At the start of a new century and a new millennium, one of the questions that theologians, along with many other intellectuals, are asking is whether the increasing influence of "postmodern" thought represents the end of the modern era and the advent of a new age. Though it is surely too soon to know for certain, most commentators seem to agree that postmodernity is best understood as the latest chapter in the ongoing history of modernity, now spread from Europe to virtually the entire world. Whatever the labels one chooses, it is evident that something basic has changed about how (post)moderns think about their world. Fewer and fewer thinkers are prepared to accept what would once have been the bedrock of modernity, the assumption that there are enduring standards of rationality inherent in human experience that transcend differences of time, place, and culture. Antifoundationalism in philosophy has spread rapidly to theology, and the pressing issues now have to do less with the alleged undermining of religion by science and more with the threat of relativism. Throughout the modern era there have periodically been voices of protest against the assumption that a common rationality can provide a foundation for theology – for example, in the Counter-Enlightenment of J. G. Hamann, F. H. Jacobi, and J. G. Herder in the eighteenth century; in Kierkegaard in the nineteenth century; and in Karl Barth in the twentieth. In the past, such figures have often been labeled "irrationalists" or dismissed by critics as merely "confessional." In the postmodern environment of contemporary theology, such criticisms are less persuasive, and these thinkers are being read with renewed attention. The generation of theologians that once dismissed Barth as "neo-orthodox" is giving way to younger scholars who see in Barth's refusal to accommodate Christian theology to the requirements of an earlier "modernity" a possible model for revitalizing theology in a postmodern environment.

Meanwhile, the great problems of theology and modernity will continue to challenge religious thinkers of the twenty-first century: the relationship of religious faith to modern science, the historical particularity of the Bible, the authority of Scripture, the proper use of philosophy in theology, the truth of Christianity in a religiously pluralistic world – and many others, whose shape we can only begin to imagine.

Notes

1 For an analysis of Nietzsche's interpretation of Christianity and a Christian theological interpretation of it, see my book *Theology, Hermeneutics, and Imagination* (2000: chs. 5 and 8).
2 The following account of the Aristotelian–Christian world picture is based on Emanuel
   Hirsch (1949:113–28).
3 For an explanation of the concept of positivity and the distinction between positive and
   natural religion, see Green (2000:26–30).
4 According to Kant, "Religion is (subjectively regarded) the cognition of all our duties *as* divine
   commands" (Kant 1956:153; emphasis as in original); cf. Kant (1960:142).
5 "*Enlightenment is man's emergence from his self-incurred immaturity. Immaturity* is the inability
   to use one's own understanding without the guidance of another. This immaturity is *self-
   incurred* if its cause is not lack of understanding, but lack of resolution and courage to use
   it without the guidance of another. The motto of enlightenment is therefore: *Sapere aude!*
   ['Dare to be wise!']. Have courage to use your *own* understanding!" (Immanuel Kant, "An
   Answer to the Question: 'What is Enlightenment?'") (1991:54).
6 They are published in English as *What is Christianity?* (Von Harnack 1957).

References

Green, G. 2000. *Theology, Hermeneutics, and Imagination: The Crisis of Interpretation at the End of
   Modernity.* Cambridge: Cambridge University Press.
Hirsch, E. 1949. *Geschichte der neuern evangelischen Theologie,* vol. 3. Gütersloh: C. Bertelsmann.
Kant, I. 1956. *Die Religion innerhalb der Grenzen der blossen Vernunft,* ed. K. Vorländer, Philosophis-
   che Bibliothek, vol. XLV. Hamburg: Felix Meiner.
Kant, I. 1960. *Religion within the Limits of Reason Alone,* trans. T. M. Greene and H. H. Hudson.
   New York: Harper.
Kant, I. 1965. *Critique of Pure Reason,* trans. N. Kemp Smith. New York: St. Martin's Press.
Kant, I. 1991. "An Answer to the Question: 'What is Enlightenment?'," in *Kant: Political Writings,*
   ed. H. Reiss, trans. H. B. Nisbet, 2nd rev. edn. Cambridge: Cambridge University Press.
Nietzsche, F. 1967. *On the Genealogy of Morals, and Ecce Homo,* trans. W. Kaufmann and R. J.
   Hollingdale. New York: Random House.
Nietzsche, F. 1974. *The Gay Science,* trans. W. Kaufmann. New York: Random House.
Tindal, M. 1967. *Christianity as Old as the Creation,* ed. G. Gawlick. London, 1730; facsimile
   reprint, Stuttgart-Bad Cannstatt: Friedrich Fromann Verlag.
Toland, J. 1969. *Christianity not Mysterious.* London, 1696; facsimile reprint, Stuttgart-Bad
   Cannstatt: Friedrich Fromann Verlag.
Von Harnack, A. 1957. *What is Christianity?* New York: Harper and Row.

PART III
Themes

CHAPTER 12
Trinity

Bruce D. Marshall

The Trinity: Two Classic Modern Approaches

In 1831 Friedrich Schleiermacher published the second, extensively revised, edition of *The Christian Faith*, destined to be among the most influential works in modern Protestant theology. He concluded the new version as he had the first, with a brief but penetrating analysis and criticism of the doctrine of the Trinity.

Schleiermacher argues that the traditional Christian doctrine of the Trinity – the teaching that the one God is eternally three distinct persons, Father, Son, and Holy Spirit – does not in fact belong among the essential elements of Christian teaching. To be sure, the doctrine takes off from a sound intuition about redemption through Christ and its communication by the church. Jesus Christ can be the redeemer, and the church can be the bearer of his redemption to the world, only if God's own being is genuinely present both in Christ himself and in the "common spirit" of the church. The Christian belief in redemption requires, therefore, the "equation of what is divine in each of these unions [of God to Christ and to the church] with that in the other, and also of both with the divine essence in itself." In this two-fold equation (*Gleichstellung*) consists "what is essential in the doctrine of the Trinity," and for this reason conceptual means must be located to make the equation "as definitely as possible" (Schleiermacher 1976:all from §170, 1; cf. 172, 1).[1]

As Schleiermacher sees it, however, the traditional doctrine of the Trinity goes well beyond this salutary intuition. It posits in "the highest being" an eternal distinction of "the Son" and "the Holy Spirit" from one another and from "the Father" whose divinity they bring into the world. This eternal distinction supposedly forms the basis of God's temporal presence in Christ and in the church, but obtains in God independently of these two temporal modes of divine presence. Thus originates, in Schleiermacher's view, "that duality" characteristic of classical Christian trinitarianism: "unity of essence and Trinity of persons" (§170, 2).

The notion of an eternal distinction of persons in God lacks, however, any basis in the religious experience of Christians, from which all genuinely Christian doctrines must finally spring (see §170, 2–3; 172, 3). We know God only as we are experientially related to him in various ways, and these relations give us no basis for speculation about the being of God in himself, independently of the varieties of his presence to us in time (see §172, 1; also 170, postscript). Even if they did it would make no difference to the content of the Christian's redemptive experience of God in Christ; the supposition of an eternal divine Trinity would be irrelevant even if we had some way of knowing that it was true (see §170, 3).

To this Schleiermacher adds a rigorous appraisal of the conceptual coherence of the traditional doctrine (§171). Classical trinitarianism succeeds in making intelligible neither the equality of the three persons with one another (§171, 2) nor the identity of the three with the divine essence (§171, 3) – not for want of trying, but because neither can be thought consistently in the first place. Of course it may be that the New Testament so clearly supports the traditional church teaching that we have no choice but to try formulating what this teaching drives at in new and more coherent ways. But it is at least worth asking – here Schleiermacher does no more – whether the biblical evidence might be better interpreted, and the intelligibility of Christian teaching better preserved, by articulating Christian faith's awareness of God's three-fold presence in the world in a conceptual idiom more like ancient Sabellianism than Athanasian trinitarianism (§172, 3).

A generation later another theologian published a quite different trinitarian theology which, while now virtually unread, was once as influential in its own orbit as Schleiermacher's was in his. Though like Schleiermacher a native German speaker, Johann Baptist Franzelin otherwise inhabited a quite different theological world. An Austrian Catholic, longtime professor of dogmatic theology at the Gregorianum (the Jesuit college in Rome), influential defender of papal infallibility at Vatican I, and later Cardinal, Franzelin issued the first edition of *The Triune God* in 1869.[2] As with all of his dogmatic treatises, he sought in his treatment of the Trinity to combine a textually rigorous attention to the authoritative bases of traditional Christian teaching (Scripture, the councils, and the Church Fathers East and West) with a renewed appreciation of medieval and Renaissance scholasticism, above all the teaching of Thomas Aquinas. While he never cites Schleiermacher, Franzelin vigorously defends all of the trinitarian claims upon which Schleiermacher sought to cast doubt.

As Franzelin sees it, Scripture explicitly teaches the church's traditional doctrine of the Trinity. In particular Matthew 28:19, John 10:30, 1:1, and 16:13–15 establish that Father, Son, and Spirit are three distinct persons and at the same time the one God (Franzelin 1895:15–30; cf. Schleiermacher's dismissal of trinitarian readings of John in §170, 2). Since Matthew 28:19 is a baptismal formula, by which "all who have embraced the faith are initiated and gathered into the church," it also displays the centrality of the doctrine of the Trinity for Christian faith: in it "Christ the Lord has brought together a compendium of the doctrine and faith to be professed concerning God who is one in nature, but three persons" (1895:15).

For Franzelin the Council of Nicaea (325) already makes explicit the uniform teaching of the church that this distinction of persons belongs to God eternally, without prejudice to God's unity of nature (a unity in number, and not simply in kind) (see 1895:110–14). This teaching poses a difficult, but not insoluble, conceptual problem. On the one hand, grasping the coherence of belief in the Trinity requires taking the divine unity – a teaching not only revealed by God but accessible to reason (see 1895:115) – as basic, and thereby requires taking the dogmatic treatise *de Deo uno* as the "foundation" for reflection on the Trinity (1895:3); on the other hand, it requires just the sort of "speculation" that Schleiermacher rejects – reflection on the eternal relations of the divine persons to one another, apart from any action they may undertake toward us. Here Franzelin develops a version of the Augustinian and Thomistic idea that the persons are distinct in virtue of certain relations to one another, while these relations are in the end identical with the one divine essence, and so with the one God. As such they are "subsistent" relations, and thereby genuinely constitutive of distinct persons who just are the one God (see 1895:307–38).

Franzelin treats in detail the relations of the divine persons to us as well as their relations to one another. Here in particular he makes much of a distinction between what applies to the divine persons "internally" (*interne, ad intra*, or, occasionally, *immanente*), and so would be true of them even if they had created no world, and what applies to them "externally" (*externe* or *ad extra*), as a result of their actions in the world they have made (see, for example, 1895:190–1, 587–8). He devotes the last section of the treatise to a discussion of the question, long debated in Catholic theology, of whether the action of the Holy Spirit in time (his "mission" from the Son and the Father) creates a relationship with believers which is unique to the Spirit himself (see 1895:571–600). Arguing that this would compromise the divine unity, Franzelin answers in the negative (a response hotly contested by some, and defended by others), though he thinks that we need not have any such unique relation to the Spirit in order to be sure that he is a person eternally distinct from the other two – in order, that is, to know that the one God is the Trinity.

Theologians commonly claim that the century just past, especially in its later stages, has seen a profound renewal of trinitarian theology. This intended renewal aims, in effect, to rescue Christian thought about the Trinity from Schleiermacher and Franzelin alike. Despite their apparent opposition to one another, each is now often assumed to embody a position (whether or not explicitly associated with his name) which distorts the most basic concerns of Christian faith in the Trinity, and ruinously renders the triune God irrelevant to both Christian life and Christian theology. In fact contemporary trinitarian opinion sometimes suggests that a theologian like Franzelin – and the Western scholastic tradition he seeks to represent – arrives by implication at a position quite like the one Schleiermacher explicitly advocates. While Schleiermacher apparently denies outright that the God whom we come to know in Christ and the church can really be a Trinity of persons, Franzelin insists that God really is the Trinity, but starts out and develops his trinitarian theology in a way which effectively denies that we could ever come to know this Trinity in Christ and the church: the God whom we actually encounter in the economy of salvation might as well not be triune.

To characterize an enterprise as a "renewal" suggests two related thoughts: novelty and quality. Renewal (as opposed to invention or discovery) involves, to be sure, only relative novelty. Current trinitarian reflection usually claims novelty in comparison with at least the relatively recent past, but also argues that the present renewal turns on a fresh appreciation of more ancient trinitarian views. Fresh ideas only make for renewal (as opposed to demolition) when they are good ones. So present trinitarian theology naturally also claims that the relatively new ideas it brings are improvements – often radical ones – over the views it intends to replace.

Trinitarian theology at the beginning of the twenty-first century thus tends to involve both historical judgments about its own relationship with Christian thought prior to the onset of the putative renewal, and normative judgments about the merits of the ideas upon which the renewal is based. Identifying some of the leading ideas in recent trinitarian theology will enable a brief assessment, as to both novelty and quality, of the suggestion that there has lately been a trinitarian renewal.

Six Characteristic Theses of Recent Trinitarian Theology

On the Protestant side the proposed trinitarian renewal may be traced especially to Karl Barth.[3] On the Catholic side Karl Rahner has been especially influential (Rahner 1997). Barth and Rahner can therefore serve as useful points of orientation for a characterization of recent trinitarian theology. To be sure, trinitarian theology has become an increasingly ecumenical enterprise, engaged with a largely common set of problems and assumptions, and very much including Eastern Orthodox theology. The following six theses are thus offered as a brief typology of claims widely made in the current trinitarian debate. Despite their differences in substance and style, Wolfhart Pannenberg, Jürgen Moltmann, Walter Kasper, Robert Jenson, and Catherine LaCugna – to name only some of the more prominent figures in recent trinitarian theology – all advocate versions of most of the following claims. Naturally these theses have been developed in a variety of different ways, and they represent the view of no one theologian in particular.

(1)   The Trinity is the most essential, basic, or (at times) distinctive Christian doctrine. Christian identity, both communal and individual, thus depends upon the doctrine of the Trinity. Barth makes this point by saying that the distinctive character of the revelation attested in Scripture directs us first of all to the doctrine of the Trinity (see I/1:296), Rahner by saying that the Trinity is "the primordial mystery of Christianity," and as such, a mystery which bears on the total reality of our salvation (1997:21).

(a)   As a corollary to (1), trinitarian theologies now regularly argue that the doctrine has to have deep connections with ordinary Christian life as a whole. Since the Trinity is the most basic Christian teaching, its essential contents must be accessible to every believer. Should profession of faith in the triune God fail to make traceable differences in the way the Christian community and its members preach, pray, teach, and console, then the profession itself is faulty; it somehow lacks the content proper to trinitarian teaching. Conversely, notions about the Trinity which lack a discernible connection with ordinary Christian life (including much of the technical material of traditional trinitarian theology) have no relevance to the doctrine of the Trinity, though they may perhaps be of interest to theologians. So for Rahner theologians have an obligation "to understand and present the doctrine of the Trinity in such a way that it becomes a reality in the concrete religious life of the Christian" (1997:10; on the insignificance of various technical debates see 1997:47–8, 80–1).[4]

(2) The doctrine of the Trinity is the Christian way of identifying God. In order adequately to pick out or locate the one true God, and to distinguish him from other candidates for divinity and divine worship, we have to be able to locate the Father, the Son, and the Holy Spirit, and to distinguish them both from each other and from everything else. The presence and action of Father, Son, and Spirit in human history and (for some theologians) in the depths of human subjectivity enable us to identify them. The doctrine of the Trinity thus serves not to label a perhaps insoluble conceptual puzzle, but to specify what Christians are talking about when they speak of "God." Barth puts the point programmatically: "The doctrine of the Trinity aims to answer the question: *who* is God?" and so "fundamentally distinguishes the Christian doctrine of God as Christian" (I/1:301).[5]

To this thesis two corollaries are typically joined.

(a) We can only identify the Father, the Son, and the Spirit once Jesus has appeared on the scene. What he does and suffers enables us to pick him out as the Father's Son, who receives and gives the Spirit. Some apprehension of God may be available prior to or apart from acquaintance with Jesus's life, death, and resurrection, though about the extent and nature of such apprehension dispute arises. In any case we lack access to actions or characteristics sufficient to distinguish any of the three from each other and from ourselves until these identifying features are displayed by Jesus's interrelations with the other two.

(b) Father, Son, and Spirit must be identified together if we are to identify them at all. Though we cannot pick out any of the three without reference to Jesus, we cannot grasp any one of the three in his personal uniqueness or individuality without also being able to locate the other two; identification of any one, we could say, implies identification of the others. Rahner's remark suggests both (2a) and (2b): "We know about the Trinity because the Word of the Father has entered our history and has given us his Spirit" (1997:48).

(3) The "economic" Trinity and the "immanent" Trinity are the same. This claim can be put in various ways: God in his saving action "for us" is the same as (or identical with) God "in himself," the Trinity *ad extra* is the same as the Trinity *ad intra*, and so forth. By various conceptual means, advocates of this thesis want to make at least the claim that in God, the Trinity we encounter in time goes all the way down. Just as God is the Father, the Son, and the Spirit in the creative and saving arrangement (or "economy") he has actually brought about, so also he is the Father, the Son, and the Spirit "immanently" or "antecedently in himself" (as Barth sometimes puts the point; see I/1:428, 466, 479–80).

Rahner regards (3) as the "basic assumption" (*Grundaxiom*) which must be followed by any trinitarian theology hoping to uphold (1) and (2). In his well-known formulation, "The 'economic' Trinity is the 'immanent' Trinity, and conversely" (1997:22). But Barth is equally firm: "The reality of God which meets us in revelation is precisely his reality in all the depths of eternity," so that "everything we say about the so-called immanent Trinity" is simply "the indispensable presupposition of the economic Trinity" (I/1:479).

(a) Although the immanent Trinity is the same as the economic (since, as Rahner stresses, the axiom which identifies the two is reversible), we *know* the immanent Trinity only from what happens in the economy of salvation – above all from the passion and resurrection of Jesus and the pentecostal outpouring of the Spirit. That the one God is to be identified as Father, Son, and Spirit (cf. 2) is not primarily a revealed doctrine *about* God, but belongs to our encounter *with* God through the presence and action of the Father, Jesus, and the Spirit. Did our access to the triune God at any point depend solely on holding true some authoritative statements about the Trinity (such as the scriptural passages analyzed by Franzelin), then the doctrine of the Trinity would cease to mark out the basic mystery of salvation which affects our whole life (cf. [1a]). It would mean that "we ourselves really have nothing to do with the mystery of the Trinity, except that we know something 'about' it through revelation" (Rahner 1997:14). The immanent Trinity has to be, and can only be, "read off" the economic (see Barth, I/1:480).

(4) Father, Son, and Spirit are genuine *persons*, agents who address and interact with one another in love and mutual knowledge. So we meet with them in the economy of salvation: the Father commands the Son Jesus, and the Son implores, but also obeys, the Father (see Mark 14:32–41 and parallels); Jesus the Son breathes the Spirit upon the apostles in the upper room (John 20:22–3); the same Spirit "drives" (Mark 1:12) or "leads" (Matthew 4:1, Luke 4:1) the Son into the wilderness to be tempted by the devil. Since the three are personal agents in the economy, they must (as [3] requires) be interacting persons all the way down, in their "immanent" life together.

Here much recent trinitarian theology parts company with Barth and Rahner. Fearing tritheism, these two reject the idea that there are three "individuals," "personalities," "egos" (Barth, I/1:350–1), "consciousnesses" or "centers of action" (Rahner 1997:43) in God, and so hesitate to characterize as "persons" the three who are the one God (see Barth, I/1:355–61; Rahner 1997:42–5, 103–15). Though neither rejects trinitarian application of the concept "person" outright, each thinks the matter – especially the unity of God – better served by an alternative (Barth's "mode of being," Rahner's "distinct mode of subsistence"). For this both have been widely criticized for failing to appreciate the implications of their own commitment to theses (1) to (3), by holding on to modalist leftovers which keep them from a sufficiently bold affirmation of the differences and interactions among the three, "immanent" as well as "economic."

(a) Father, Son, and Spirit are irreducibly distinct personal agents in their interaction not only with one another, but with us. The divine actions of creation and salvation therefore establish a relationship with creatures unique to each of the divine persons. Neither creation nor salvation is the work simply of the one God, but both are the work of the three persons in their uniqueness and distinction from one another. On this Rahner vigorously insists, especially regarding unique relations of Christ and the Holy Spirit with believers in grace (see 1997:26–7, 34–8). Barth does as well, at least in his later theology.[6] Hence the charge that both are inconsistent in their misgivings about (4).

(b)   Both (4) and (4a) suggest that trinitarian theology ought to exhibit a robustly "personalist" character, in contrast to "essentialist" approaches which take knowledge of the one divine essence (however attained) as the basis for assertions about the distinctions and relations among the persons and with us. Here trinitarian theology across the board has felt the influence of recent Eastern Orthodox views.[7]

(c)   The unity of the three should be conceived primarily as intimate interpersonal "communion," rather than supposing that what makes the three one God is chiefly their common possession of (numerically) the same essence. This goes together with a preference for thinking about the unity of the triune God "socially" rather than "psychologically" (for Rahner's own doubts about the "psychological analogy," despite his reservations regarding [4], see 1997:115–20).

(5)   The doctrine of the Trinity should suffuse the whole of Christian theology. Every topic should bear a distinctively trinitarian stamp – not only the theology of the incarnation and of Jesus's passion and resurrection, but of creation, grace, the sacraments, the last things, and so forth. Unless we can show what difference it makes to the treatment of an issue that God is triune, the Trinity becomes a theologically isolated and perhaps non-functional doctrine, even when it is elaborated in great detail. With that (1) and (2) are forgone (see Rahner 1997:12–15).[8]

(a)   In order to uphold (5), trinitarian reflection, and indeed the whole enterprise of Christian theology, needs to "start" in the right place: with the three persons whose interactions and differences from one another are displayed for us by the economy of salvation. If theology "starts" from the one God, the divine essence, or the attributes of God, the doctrine of the Trinity will inevitably cease to function properly in the larger system of theological topics, and it may become impossible coherently to maintain that the one God is the Trinity in the first place.

So Rahner faults Thomas Aquinas, and subsequent scholasticism even more, for "separating" theological discussion of "the one God" from discussion of "the triune God," and then treating them in that sequence. This procedure "must give rise to the impression" of "a Trinity which is absolutely closed in on itself" and "from which we are excluded" – starting with "the one God" must, in other words, entail the denial of most of theses (1) to (4) (1997:18; see 1997:15–21, 45–6, 82–3). Similarly, Barth worries that failing to present the Trinity at the outset "really contradicts the highly important statements which must be made about . . . the comprehensive significance of the doctrine of the Trinity" (I/1:301). These remarks suggest that a faulty order of presentation logically prevents theology from making needful assertions about the Trinity. Both writers sometimes indicate, however, that the problem may be more pedagogical than substantive (see Rahner 1997:20; Barth, I/1:303).

(6)   All of the foregoing points are best made, or perhaps only makeable at all, by recourse to "the" Eastern or Greek approach to (or "model of") the Trinity, rather than to "the" Western or Latin one. Eastern trinitarian theology has the merit of "starting" with the economic Trinity of persons (or, as Rahner argues, with the person of the Father in particular), rather than with "an a-trinitarian treatise on 'the one God'" (1997:18) or with the divine essence and attributes. It treats the Trinity from the outset as a mystery of salvation, refuses to separate the immanent from the economic Trinity, and advances to a grasp of the divine unity on the basis of the economically enacted distinctions among the persons. In all this, Eastern theology rightly follows Scripture. Western trinitarian theology lacks all of these virtues, and usually fails to avoid precisely those trinitarian demerits which the Eastern tradition correctly rejects. A contemporary renewal of trinitarian theology should therefore repair to the formative figures of Eastern theology, especially the Cappadocians. Rahner promotes this historical thesis, with occasional reservations (see 1997:15–21, 58–61, 83–4). Barth does not, and especially in his treatment of the *Filioque* prefers Western antecedents to Eastern ones (see I/1:473–89). In this, however, most subsequent trinitarian theology has not followed him.

The thesis itself has a definite historical location. A century ago the French Jesuit Théodore de Régnon first gave wide currency to the idea that two clearly identifiable traditions of trinitarian theology largely oppose one another.[9] The Greek tradition stems primarily from the Cappadocians, the Latin or "scholastic" from Augustine. The difference between the two lies above all in the decision of the Latin scholastics to start, following Augustine, with the one divine essence, while the Cappadocians begin with the Trinity of persons; this difference colors the two traditions down to the present day.[10] Though trinitarian theologians now rarely take this historical thesis directly from de Régnon, the commonplace assumption embodied in (6) apparently stems from him, and not from more recent Eastern Orthodox theology.[11] The notion of opposed "Eastern" and "Western" trinitarian traditions seems to be itself originally a Western idea.

A Trinitarian Renewal?

Here we can offer only a brief consideration of the merits of these characteristic theses of recent trinitarian theology, and of the suggestion that they constitute needed novelties, at least in the West. The first three theses will receive the most attention.

The importance of identifying the Trinity

Surely (1) lacks the novelty sometimes attributed to it (leaving aside its corollary for the moment). Nor need we go back so far as the Greek Fathers to retrieve the thesis. Thus

Thomas Aquinas: "The Christian faith consists above all (*principaliter*) in the confession of the Holy Trinity, and it glories especially in the cross of our Lord Jesus Christ." [12] But this claim seems well attested even in the Latin manualist darkness from which Rahner and others seek to deliver trinitarian theology. As we have observed, Franzelin takes Scripture's trinitarian baptismal formula to be the church's "compendium of the doctrine and faith to be professed concerning God." Or consider the Roman theologian Riccardo Tabarelli, professor at the Lateran a generation after Franzelin: "The mystery of the Trinity is not only the distinctive summit (*caput*) of Christian revelation, but the basic teaching of the whole of Christianity and the essence of the gospel" (Tabarelli 1964:9).

Protestant theologians endorse (1) with equal insistence – not only the reformers and scholastics of the sixteenth and seventeenth centuries, but many in the nineteenth century as well. Thus the Lutheran Isaak August Dorner, like the Catholic Franzelin, makes much of the trinitarian significance of the Matthean baptismal formula, and takes belief in the Trinity as basic to Christian identity.[13] Though he follows Schleiermacher in supposing that the distinctive experience of Christian faith must be the final source and guarantee of Christian doctrine, Dorner insists against his predecessor that such faith requires a robust affirmation of the divine Trinity: "the objective existence of eternal distinctions in God is the necessary presupposition for personal communion with God through Christ in faith" (Dorner 1883, §31, 1:414). In this he does not regard himself as a voice crying in the wilderness, but as perfecting a trinitarian renewal (though he does not call it that) already underway since the middle of his century, which has successfully reversed a fatal neglect of the Trinity in several earlier generations of Protestant theology.[14]

We might also take these affirmations of the centrality of the Trinity for Christian faith to suggest the basic claim made in (2): in order to pick out the one God, we have to pick out the persons of the Trinity. On the ability to identify God largely depends the sort of relationship it is possible to have with God – including, for example, whether one can successfully direct worship to the one true God and not, idolatrously, to something else. That the doctrine of the Trinity gives the distinctively Christian way of "identifying" God is, to be sure, a relatively recent way of putting the claim embodied in (2), which even contemporary advocates of (2) do not always employ.[15] In fact this thesis is probably more novel in formulation than in substance, and is arguably among the most characteristic claims of trinitarian theology, traditional or contemporary.[16]

It comes, however, in weaker and stronger versions, each of which poses problems. A weaker version claims that we need to be able to locate the persons of the Trinity in order to identify the one God *fully*, while a stronger version claims that we need to be able to locate the persons of the Trinity in order to identify the one God *at all*. By allowing that God can be identified to some extent without reference to the persons of the Trinity, a weaker version seems to require that picking out the persons of the Trinity logically (and perhaps psychologically) supplements this preliminary identification of the one God (since the converse cannot be the case: we cannot, presumably, identify the persons of the Trinity without also identifying the one God, so the latter could never be added on to the former, only the former to the latter). This suggests that belief in the one God has to enjoy a centrality among Christian convictions which belief in the

Trinity lacks, and so pries (2) loose from (1). Puzzlement also arises as to *how* we could identify the one God without picking out the persons of the Trinity. Merely believing, correctly enough, that there is (for example) a single omnipotent being does not guarantee that we will actually assign this omnipotence to its true bearer – that we will succeed in identifying the subject of this omnipotence. To solve this problem by going further, and saying that we can identify the one God as a personal agent without reference to the Trinity, suggests that we can locate a divine person without identifying any of the persons who are the one God. This, however, may not be compatible with belief in the Trinity at all.

The stronger version avoids just these problems by simply excluding the possibility that those who (for whatever reason) fail to spot the persons of the Trinity can succeed in picking out God in the first place; (2a) and (2b) tend to reinforce this point, and so to support a stronger version of the thesis. But Christians seem to have good reasons not to confine to themselves the capacity to locate God. We need not enter into the debate about the possibility of natural theology to find relevant cases. As texts like Romans 11:28–9 indicate, the God whom Christians locate has permanently elected Abraham's carnal descendants to be his own people, which seems to require that they – that is, the Jewish people to the end of time – have the capacity to identify and worship the God who has elected them. But of course Israel does not identify God by reference to the persons of the Trinity. Apart from whether another religious community might be able to locate the one God, the logic of Christian worship itself poses a problem here. Christians claim in any case to worship the God of Israel, yet supposing this God to be the same as the Trinity, or as any one of the three persons, apparently leads to various kinds of incoherence.[17]

It should not be assumed that traditional versions of (2) accept only a weak form of the thesis, and that the stronger form is a modern innovation. Aquinas argues that "among those things which we hold true about God by faith, it is singular to Christian faith that we confess the Trinity of persons in the unity of the divine essence. For under this profession we are sealed by Christ in baptism." To be sure, some of what Christians hold true by faith may be shared with Jews and Muslims, for example the conviction that God is one. Therefore "in order to indicate the unique and singular teaching of the Christian faith, our discussion of the faith has not been entitled 'on God,' but 'on the Trinity.'"[18] It might be supposed that Thomas means to "start" with the one God, known also by Jews and Muslims, and then supplement this preliminary apprehension of God by reference to the persons of the Trinity. But on their face these comments might equally be taken to suggest that belief in a single God is not by itself sufficient to locate this God and enable one, for example, to succeed in worshipping him. For that we need "the singular teaching of the Christian faith." Whether Aquinas holds a weaker or stronger form of (2) depends, among other things, on the extent to which he thinks we need to have distinctively Christian convictions in order to have true beliefs about God in the first place.[19] Whether a weaker or stronger form of the thesis is more plausible likewise depends in part on how this question ought to be answered.

Presumably few trinitarian theologians ancient or modern would quarrel with the corollary that the doctrine of the Trinity ought to shape everyday Christian practice and belief in deep and discernible ways (cf. 1a). After all, as Aquinas and Franzelin observe, the doctrine is the heart of every Christian's baptismal faith. Whether it can be laid at the door of trinitarian *theology* "that Christians, for all their orthodox confession of the Trinity, are virtually mere 'monotheists' in their religious existence," is in any case open to doubt (Rahner 1997:10). Vast socio-historical triumphs and disasters are not likely to have been wrought by events that went on in the heads of theologians long dead. Even supposing that traditional Western trinitarian theology suffers from deep errors (like putting its discussion of "the one God" before "the Trinity") and needlessly arcane preoccupations (like whether mode of origin or relation is person-constituting in God), such theological misconceptions would be unlikely to keep the doctrine of the Trinity from mattering to Christians.

But the idea that such a profound deformation of Christianity has occurred at all seems implausible, at least if (1) and (2) are right. If this doctrine really is the most essential Christian teaching, and articulates the most basic Christian beliefs about who God is, how could Christians be generally ignorant of it or indifferent to it? If there actually are communities whose identity turns on (1) and (2), then their members must generally know *how* to be trinitarian in their identification of God and their everyday religious life, even if they lack much explicit knowledge *about* the doctrine of the Trinity. Of course it is almost always worthwhile to try to make implicit knowledge more explicit, not least to head off possible distortions of communal belief and practice. But this should not be confused with restoring trinitarian conviction to the church, as though it were not even implicit, and had to be put there by theologians. To worry that the doctrine of the Trinity might become irrelevant to Christian life suggests that the doctrine is in fact no more than an abstruse conceptual puzzle, and not the most basic Christian teaching: (1a) thus seems incoherent with the claim about the indispensable role of the doctrine to which it is supposed to be the corollary.

Economic and immanent

Whether the "economic Trinity" and the "immanent Trinity" are identical, as (3) proposes, depends on what these terms refer to – more precisely, on whether they refer to the same thing.[20] Unfortunately defenses of (3) display a confusing welter of assumptions about the referents of these terms. Some accounts suggest that "the economic Trinity" refers to the actions of the divine persons *ad extra* or "externally," while "the immanent Trinity" refers to the relations (and perhaps also actions) among the divine persons *ad intra* or "internally." This has the disadvantage of requiring that we already know what is "external" and "internal" to the Trinity, which the distinction between the "economic" and "immanent" Trinity itself is supposed to tell us. Along similar lines Rahner suggests that "the economic Trinity" refers to God's "three concrete ways of being given," while "the immanent Trinity" refers to the same God's "three relative concrete ways of existing" (1997:74). This too simply relabels the problem, since we now need to know how to distinguish divine ways of being given from divine ways of existing. Rahner makes a more informative suggestion when he proposes that "the immanent Trinity" refers to three divine persons who are "in God, setting aside his free self-communication" (1997:101). Presuming that God's "free self-communication" refers to the economic Trinity, (3) would then be the claim that the Father, Son, and Spirit with whom we meet in the economy of salvation are identical with the Father, Son, and Spirit "aside" from the economy of salvation.

This too can be taken in different ways. It might mean that even if the Father, the Son, and the Spirit had created no world or undertaken no saving economy for us, they would still be the same three *persons*, the same triune God, whom we encounter in time. This seems plausible enough, and apparently supports the conviction, which often motivates (3), that all the way down God is the Trinity of persons with whom we become acquainted in the doings and sufferings of Israel, Jesus, and the church. But taken this way (3) hardly seems novel, or indeed a claim which anyone ever thought to deny. No one, that is, has suggested that there are *six* divine persons, three of whom we meet in the economy and, hidden behind these, three others who comprise a shadowy "immanent" Trinity.[21] In Aquinas's austere but far-reaching formulation, the missions of the divine persons (the "economy of salvation," roughly) always "*include* an eternal procession, and add to it a temporal effect," namely that "a divine person . . . exists in the creature in a new way" (Aquinas, *Summa theologiae*, I, 43, 2, ad 3 and c; my emphasis). Since for Aquinas the divine persons have their personal uniqueness or identity in virtue of the relations of origin to which the "eternal processions" give rise, this observation implies that we become acquainted by way of the "temporal missions" with exactly the same three persons who are eternally the one God, and who would be the one God even if there were no economy of creation and salvation.

Recent trinitarian theologies often, however, seem to take (3) in a much stronger way. Not only are Father, Son, and Spirit the same persons in the economy as they would be "aside" from it, they are the same *in every respect* (or at least in every respect pertinent to salvation). The three have, in other words, exactly the same features or attributes "immanently" as they do "economically." So Barth, for example, argues that "God is the one whom he is in his works." Of course "he is also the same one in himself, before and after and above his works," so that "he is who he is even without them." But nonetheless "he is also in himself none other than precisely the one whom he is in his works" (II/1:260). This might simply be an insistent version of the weaker claim that the divine three are the same persons in their works as they would be "even without them," but Barth can lean toward the much stronger claim. The very being of God, he argues, is an "act," a "deed," and an "occurrence" (*Geschehen*), and "the content of this occurrence consists in the fact that the Word of God became flesh and that his Spirit is poured out on all flesh" (II/1:267).

This suggests that the Son and the Spirit have the very same features in virtue of their (and the Father's) "works" (like being flesh and being poured out) as they have in virtue of their divine being, "even without" these works. But this is incoherent. The works themselves, once undertaken, are features of the divine persons, and result in the possession by the persons of various characteristics (like being incarnate or being poured out on all flesh). If they did not undertake the works, then they would not have the features or characteristics which depend on undertaking the works.

We can generalize the point. The very idea of the divine persons "aside" from the economy requires that there be some difference between the three persons in the economy and these three persons not in the economy. Otherwise the immanent Trinity would be indiscernible from the economic, and so the idea of the Trinity "aside" from the economy would be void. But the strong version of (3) is just the claim that Father, Son, and Spirit have all the same features "aside" from the economy as they possess on account of the economy. The three divine persons cannot both have and not have all the same features "aside" from the economy as they possess on account of it. The imma-nent Trinity cannot, in other words, be both identical with and discernible from the economic. It thus seems impossible to maintain the strong version of (3), which wants to take it as an unqualified identity statement.

Theologies seeking trinitarian renewal sometimes iron out the incoherence in the strong version of (3) by arguing that the immanent Trinity really is indiscernible from the economic. There just is no "outside" to the economy of salvation, no feature any divine person would have even if the three had created and redeemed no world (e.g. Jenson 1982:103–48). In this maximalist version of (3), the persons of the Trinity apparently cannot avoid having precisely those features which belong to them in the temporal economy of salvation: the Word cannot avoid being incarnate as Mary's first-born and crucified son, the Spirit cannot avoid being outpoured in Jerusalem at Pente-cost, and so forth. On this view, after all, there is no situation "aside" from the economy by reference to which these could be features which the persons of the Trinity have *acquired*, but which these same persons might also not have acquired.

This is a consistent position, but for well-established theological reasons an implau-sible one. As a whole and at every point, the economy of creation and salvation is a gift of the triune God to creatures. Only a free being can give a gift to another. A God who could not help enacting the incarnational and pentecostal economy of salvation nar-rated in Scripture would not undertake it freely, and so could not give it to creatures as a gift. The traditional insistence that the divine persons need not have the features they freely acquire in the temporal economy – that the immanent Trinity is *not* in every respect identical with the economic – stems not from a merely speculative interest in preserving God's freedom, but from the deep conviction of Christian faith that the saving work of the Trinity is wholly an act of free grace. For this reason theologians who want to take (3) as an unqualified identity statement usually, if inconsistently, assume that there nonetheless has to be a situation outside any economy of creation and redemption from which the divine persons may freely undertake the history of salvation which actually comes to pass.

As to novelty, most of the claims embodied in (3) and (3a) were already current in the nineteenth century, in much the same terms Rahner, Barth, and their followers would later use. Thus Dorner: "The economic Trinity . . . leads back to immanent dis-tinctions in God himself, all the more so because in the world of revelation we have to do not merely with a teaching of truths, but with the true *being* of God in the world, with God's actions, indeed with his self-communication (*Selbstmittheilung*)" (Dorner 1883, §29, 2:370; cf. pp. 351–2, 363–4, 416–17n.2). Indeed, the strong and, espe-cially, the maximalist versions of (3) find a clear precedent in Schleiermacher, despite their often vehement repudiation of him. Though he does not use the terms "economic" and "immanent" to talk about the Trinity, Schleiermacher departs from traditional trinitarian views for the same reason that the strong and maximalist versions of (3) do. Christian theology ought to equate in every respect – "as definitely as possible" – the being of God "in itself" with the being of God in Christ and the church (1976, §170, 1). Traditional understandings of the Trinity fail to do this because they posit in "the highest being" an eternal distinction of persons "independently" of God's being in Christ and the church (§170, 2). To be sure, on other grounds Schleiermacher cannot regard either Jesus Christ or the spirit which animates the church as really God, or as divine persons in their own right. But granted the assumption that Christ and the Spirit are true God, strong and maximalist defenses of (3) hew closely to the logic by which Schleiermacher identifies the immanent with the economic being of God.

Talk of an "economic Trinity" and an "immanent Trinity" which are identical with one another apparently disguises diverse claims, which turn out to be either uncontroversial, incoherent, or implausible; (3) might therefore be dropped as more confusing than helpful. In any case Christian faith in a triune God who fully but freely enters space and time demands of theology an account of who these persons are which does not rely on the features they acquire in the economy in order to distinguish and relate them (though the temporal actions of the persons may of course have a role in our *knowledge* about these distinctions and relations). Though often dismissed as irrelevant or misguided by advocates of the strong and maximalist versions of (3), traditional "treatises on the Trinity" have sought to provide just this sort of account.

Feminist theologies sometimes reject the doctrine of the Trinity as irretrievably patriarchal. Those which do not, and instead join in the trinitarian renewal, usually advocate strong or maximalist versions of (3). At the same time they tend to deny that the masculine elements in the scriptural and ecclesial rendering of God's temporal acts (a person of the Trinity becoming incarnate as a male; Jesus's address to the one who sent him as "Father") really belong to the economy of salvation in a constitutive way. As a result these elements also fail to inform us about the being or inner life of God on display in the economy (see Johnson 1992:191–223, LaCugna 1991). This last suggestion appears more coherent with a weak version of (3) than with the stronger ones feminist theologies more often support, since a weak version allows that there be features the divine persons possess in virtue of their temporal acts, even features quite central to the economy, which they would otherwise not have. But even a weak version of (3) will run up against limits on the extent to which it can prescind from the particular features of the temporal economy which actually comes to pass (by taking them, for example, as a collection of symbols of the divine mystery for which others might equally well be substituted). Past a point, it will no longer be possible to suppose that this particular economy lets us in on the very being and life of God – that in it we encounter the divine persons themselves in their temporal acts, and so can still read the immanent Trinity off the economic. Where that point lies is another, and in connection with feminist concerns much debated, question.

Moreover, even on the weak and uncontroversial version of (3), the claim (3a) that the immanent Trinity can *only* be "read off" the economic poses problems of its own. This suggestion often stems from the worry that unless the temporal actions of Father, Son, and Spirit are a sufficient basis for grasping who they are (even apart from any possible economy of creation and salvation), the persons of the Trinity will remain inaccessible to us. Apart from the economy we lack evidence for grasping who the divine persons are, and need the economy to make good the deficit. The problem, though, is that the scripturally narrated economy of salvation gives us *too much* evidence about how to distinguish and relate the Father, the Son, and the Spirit, and we need some way to narrow the field.

This is perhaps clearest when it comes to the relation between the Son and the Spirit. As recent trinitarian theologies have often observed, the New Testament depicts not only actions by the incarnate Son Jesus of which the Spirit is the term (the Son breathes the Spirit upon the apostles, sends the Spirit to them, and so forth), but also actions of the Spirit of which the Son is the term (the Spirit drives Jesus into the wilderness, incites him to preach good news to the poor, is the power who raises him, and so forth). How are we to "read off" from this a conclusion about what makes the Son and the Spirit the unique individuals they are? One influential suggestion has been that divine persons can be sent only by those from whom they originate, and that their personal uniqueness derives from these relations of origin (cf. Aquinas, *Summa theologiae*, I, 43, 1). Since the Father sends the Son and both send the Spirit, we can "read off" from these economic data that the Son originates from the Father, and the Holy Spirit originates from both the Father and the Son. Given the distinct location of each person in this order of origin, we can discern what makes each one the unique individual he is. But while the New Testament never says exactly that the Spirit "sends" the Son, it clearly makes the Son the term of the Spirit's action (like "leading" into the wilderness). From this the traditional principles allow us to infer that the Spirit originates from the Father, and the Son originates from both the Father and the Spirit.[22]

Thus we can read off from the economy both that the Spirit originates from the Son, and that the Son originates from the Spirit. But these look like contradictories, so one of them has to be false. "To originate from" implies "to depend totally for one's being upon." If the Spirit depends totally for his being upon the Son, as the Son does upon the Father, the Son cannot also depend totally for his being upon the Spirit. The Son cannot depend totally for his being on one who, as originating from him, cannot be unless he is. The same goes, *mutatis mutandis*, if the Son depends totally for his being upon the Spirit. Thus if we are to "read" the economic data in a way which yields a coherent set of results regarding the relations of origin among the divine persons, we need guidance which the economic data do not themselves provide – perhaps from some sort of authoritative teaching *about* what makes each person the unique individual he is.[23]

Where to start?

The question of where trinitarian theology should "start" (cf. 5a) connects many of the issues raised by theses (4) to (6). The difference between "personalist" and "essentialist" views of the Trinity (cf. 4) consists in, or results from, different theological starting points; whether or not a trinitarian identification of God adequately informs the whole of Christian theology (cf. 5) turns on whether theology starts with the persons or the essence; in the distinction between personalist and essentialist approaches to the Trinity, and thereby in different starting points, the basic difference between the "Eastern" and "Western" trinitarian traditions is held to consist (cf. 6). The plausibility

of much of theses (4) to (6) therefore hangs on whether the *content* of a trinitarian theology depends in any important way on where it starts.

Probably the clearest notion of a starting point in theology (or any other verbal
enterprise) is that of the first item in the order of *presentation* – where the book starts.
Schleiermacher advocates with particular force the idea that the content of Christian
theology, or at least the possibility of grasping the content correctly, depends on the
right sequence of topics. For just this reason he argues that the doctrine of the Trinity
has to come *last* in the order of presentation, so as to avoid the false impression that
"acceptance of the doctrine of the Trinity is the condition without which one cannot
believe in redemption and the founding of the Kingdom of God by the divine in Christ
and the Holy Spirit" (1976, §172, 3). More recent trinitarian theology often accepts
this claim about the difference the order of presentation makes, and uses it to insist
that, on the contrary, the (economic) Trinity has to come first.

Presumably any trinitarian theology needs to offer an account of how the three
interacting persons with whom we meet in the economy of creation and salvation are
one God. It needs to indicate, in other words, how it is *consistent* to suppose both that
the Father, the Son, and the Spirit who make themselves available to us in time are irreducibly distinct from one another, and also that they are, whether taken together or
one by one, irreducibly not distinct from the one God. To the accomplishment of this
basic trinitarian task the order of presentation makes no difference at all. Where one
statement comes in a sequence of statements simply has nothing to do with its consistency (or inconsistency) with other statements in the sequence. And of course the
sequence can include any statement at all; a sequence of statements places no logical
or conceptual constraints on what the next statement will be (though this statement
may be inconsistent with earlier ones). The order of presentation simply has nothing
to do with what can get said in a trinitarian theology, and with whether what gets said
is coherent.

Nor does the order of presentation have anything to do with the content and coherence of a theology as a whole, and in particular with whether a robust awareness of
the Trinity informs other theological topics. A scholastic theologian like Aquinas is
sometimes faulted for saying relatively little about the temporal actions of the divine
persons in his questions about the Trinity in the first part of the *Summa theologiae*;
together with the order of presentation (where discussion of the one divine essence precedes that of the persons), this leaves the impression that "everything about God which
is important for us has already been said in the treatise on the one God" (Rahner
1997:17). It may simply be, however, that the scholastics generally do not think that
questions about the processions, relations, and so forth in God are the place to look for
a trinitarian account of, say, creation, the image of God in humans, or our deifying participation in the life of God.[24] Here too one need not go back to the medievals. Having
begun his presentation with "the one God," a manualist like Tabarelli nonetheless
observes that the Trinity is "the basis of all the mysteries which are revealed in the
gospel . . . from the doctrine of the Trinity the other mysteries of Christ borrow their
light, and are contained in it as their common bond" (Tabarelli 1964:9).

The worry about where to start in trinitarian theology might be reframed as a claim
about the order of *justification*. What happens among the divine persons in the economy

of salvation has to serve as the epistemic basis not only for assertions about the divine persons "in themselves" (cf. 3a and 4b), but for the assertion that they are one God or share a single divine essence. When it takes (3) in this way, recent trinitarian theology apparently reverses Franzelin's insistence that one always has to have the unity of the divine nature "before one's eyes" in order to grasp the personal distinctions properly (Franzelin 1895:3), but accepts his assumption that the coherence of the two claims depends on which one is taken as epistemically basic.

In this sense, the claim that we have to "start" with the divine persons amounts to saying that the unity of God has to be, and can only be, *inferred* with logical necessity from the distinctions and relations among the divine persons displayed in the economy of salvation. Unless this strong claim can be made out (and defenders of a personalist starting point have not tried to go this far), it will suffice for trinitarian theology to show that the personal distinctions and the unity of God are consistent with one another.[25] To this end it will make no difference whether one proceeds in "personalist" fashion by trying to exhibit the consistency of the divine unity with the personal distinctions, or in "essentialist" fashion by trying to exhibit the consistency of the personal distinctions with the divine unity.

None of this implies that the *content* of trinitarian proposals might not fail to cohere with the most basic convictions of Christian faith about the Trinity. Thus Rahner, for example, worries that Franzelin's refusal to attribute to the Holy Spirit a relationship to us which the Son and the Father lack reduces trinitarian faith to "mere monotheism." For his part Franzelin worries that ascribing to the Spirit such a relationship is compatible only with tritheism. Whether the coherence of the Christian conviction that the one God is the Trinity really depends on the answer to this warmly debated question is perhaps open to doubt. In any case, showing that a particular theological claim about the Trinity fails to square with the most basic elements of trinitarian faith calls for more than a verdict about where the disputed claim starts. It requires a demonstration that the claim is logically incompatible with any coherent way of maintaining that the three persons are the one God.

Of course decisions about how to proceed in presenting and justifying trinitarian claims may have pedagogical significance, even if the content and coherence of those claims fails to depend on such decisions. Here the rule is to start in the place most helpful to understanding, and not to insist on beginning the same way every time. The philosopher W. V. Quine says somewhere that asking where you should start in philosophy is like asking where you should start in Ohio: it depends on where you are and where you want to go. Surely the same holds for trinitarian theology. Arriving at a coherent account of the Trinity depends on setting out from your present location, whatever that may happen to be, and finding a route (there will no doubt be several) which will allow you to move from that point of departure toward your goal.

To the extent that it depends on the notion of opposed starting points, (6) also turns out not to be very informative: if there are important differences in content between trinitarian theologies written in Greek and those written in Latin, these cannot depend on where each "starts." To be sure, recent trinitarian theologies differ widely on (6). Some decline to play off Eastern against Western views, and draw freely from both.[26]

But historical research into the connections and contrasts between Greek and Latin trinitarian theology, unbound by de Régnon's assumption that these constitute two disparate traditions, has only begun to bear fruit.[27]

The main casualty of (6) is no doubt the long scholastic tradition of reflection on the Trinity. Stretching roughly from Anselm into the eighteenth century on both the Protestant and Catholic sides, scholasticism takes earlier texts like Augustine's *De Trinitate* as points of departure for critical analysis (not as sets of conclusions to be repeated), and argues with considerable conceptual rigor over many of the options currently proposed as solutions to trinitarian problems. Thesis (6) has repeatedly assured trinitarian theologians that they would find in this whole complex tradition of inquiry only essentialist misery, and therefore could safely leave it behind.

We have observed that when it comes to novelty, some common claims of recent trinitarian theology seem less to get beyond Schleiermacher and Franzelin than to oscillate between them, depending on the point at issue. Even apart from questions about the plausibility of these claims, under the influence of (6) the assumption that something new has happened is yet more problematic. When guided by this thesis, the past century's reflection on the Trinity arguably embodies not so much the renewal as the eclipse of trinitarian theology as an ongoing tradition of inquiry.

Notes

1   References to Schleiermacher (1976) will be by paragraph (§) and section number in the text. I will cite English translations where they are available, but have freely modified them in light of the original-language texts (references to which may be found in each of the cited translations).

2   J. B. Franzelin, *Tractatus de Deo Trino secundum personas* (references in the text are from the 4th edition of 1895).

3   Karl Barth, *Church Dogmatics* (1956–75). References will be by volume and part number in the text. In some respects Barth thought of himself as "renewing" trinitarian theology less than do many who rely on and develop his views.

4   For an insistent version of (1a), see LaCugna (1991).

5   For a vigorous version of (2), see Jenson (1982, 1997).

6   Though he continues to prefer "mode of being" to "person," Barth's treatment of reconciliation makes much of the voluntary interaction of the Father and the Son on our behalf, and thereby of their differences as agents (e.g., in his account of Jesus's obedience to the Father's command, which is not only "economic" [IV/1:198] but "belongs to the inner life of God," entails a genuine immanent "subordination" of the Son to the Father, and requires a "dynamic" rather than "static" way of thinking about the divine unity [IV/1:201–2; see IV/1:192–210]).

7   Especially that of John Zizioulas (1985).

8   For an energetically trinitarian account of Jesus's passion and resurrection, which Rahner himself does not undertake, see Hans Urs von Balthasar, *Mysterium Paschale* (1993). For a different one see Jürgen Moltmann, *The Trinity and the Kingdom* (1981:21–96).

9   In his *Études de théologie positive sur la Sainte Trinité*, 4 vols. (1892–8). Rahner explicitly follows de Régnon on this point. See *Theological Investigations*, vol. 1 (1961:146).

10 See de Régnon's summary in *Études*, vol. 1:428–35.

11   In his influential *The Mystical Theology of the Eastern Church*, for example, Vladimir Lossky draws from de Régnon not only the historical thesis (1957:57–8), which he uses more polemically than his source, but many of his trinitarian citations of the Greek Fathers. As Michel Barnes has observed, the English translation obscures the extent of Lossky's dependence by dropping most of the references to de Régnon in the notes of the French original (Barnes 1995a:51–79). Cf. Lossky, *Essai sur la théologie mystique de l'église d'orient* (1944:43–64).

12   *De Rationibus Fidei*, prooem (no. 949), Raymund Verardo (1954:253). Cf. also Aquinas, *Summa theologiae*, II–II, 174, 6, c: "The whole faith of the church is founded on the revelation made to the apostles concerning faith in the unity and trinity [of God]." Since Aquinas is (together with Augustine) perhaps the theologian whose unhappy influence is assumed to create the most pressing need for trinitarian renewal, he will serve as a useful counterpoint in the evaluation of the present theses.

13   "Early on the doctrine of the Trinity," especially in its baptismal role, "was the holy sign which distinguished Christians from all non-Christians" (Dorner 1883, §29, 1:363; cf. also pp. 349–52).

14   Cf. the discussion in Dorner (1883, §30b:397–412). I am grateful to Lewis Ayres for pointing out this passage to me.

15   Walter Kasper and Wolfhart Pannenberg, for example, take locating what Christians are talking about when they speak of "Father," "Son," and "Holy Spirit" as a basic problem in the doctrine of God, though they do not describe this as the question of how to "identify" God. See Kasper (1984:133–229); Pannenberg (1991:259–80, 300–36).

16   For an argument in support of (1), and of a version of (2), based on Christian eucharistic practice, see Marshall (2000a:17–49).

17   On these issues see my essays, "The Jewish People and Christian Theology" (Marshall 1997:81–100), and "Do Christians Worship the God of Israel?" (Marshall 2000b:231–64). The latter argues that only a weak version of (2) is compatible with a non-supersessionist understanding of the Church's relationship to the Jewish people.

18   *Expositio Primae Decretalis* I (no. 1139), Verardo (1954:418b). The "discussion" to which Aquinas refers here is his own, in the first part of the *Expositio*.

19   On this see my essay, "Faith and Reason Revisited: Aquinas and Luther on Deciding What is True" (Marshall 1999:1–48).

20   On this see also Marshall (2000a:263–5).

21   Though Barth's odd remarks about the triune God making a "copy" (*Nachbild*) of himself in the world do give one pause. Cf. III/2:218–19.

22   As, e.g., Thomas Weinandy argues in *The Father's Spirit of Sonship* (1995), though he usually speaks of the Son originating "in" rather than "from" the Spirit (but cf. p. 70, in note 31).

23   In part to execute a pre-emptive strike against the *Filioque*, modern Orthodox theologians sometimes reject (3a) entirely: the identity-constituting characteristics of the persons cannot be "read off" their temporal actions at all. But this too makes for puzzles. If there need be *no* coordination between the relations among the persons which their temporal actions display and what makes each the unique individual he is, then we have to admit the possibility of a temporal economy in which, say, the Spirit could send the Father to be incarnate of the Virgin Mary, and could then breathe the Son upon the world through the risen Father. This Augustine and the Western scholastic tradition have uniformly denied (see, e.g., Aquinas, *Summa theologiae*, I, 43, 4), which is not to say (with some strong and all maximal versions of [3]) that the temporal economy which actually comes to pass is the *only* one the triune God could undertake.

24   Each of these topics in Aquinas and other medieval theologians has been the subject of a
     substantial recent study: Gilles Emery, *La trinité créatrice* (1995); D. Juvenal Merriell, *To the
     Image of the Trinity* (1990); Luc-Thomas Somme, *Fils adoptifs de Dieu par Jésus Christ* (1997).
25   We cannot decide here whether the converse claim has actually been advocated in the tra-
     dition, namely that the personal distinctions must be derived from the unity of essence. In
     any case, after the condemnation at the Fourth Lateran Council (1215) of the proposition
     that the divine essence or nature "generates" (attributed, whether or not correctly, to
     Joachim of Fiore), the scholastic tradition explicitly rejects any idea of deriving the persons
     from the essence. In fact Thomas Aquinas apparently puts the *Summa theologiae*'s discus-
     sion of the personal distinctions after the questions about the divine essence precisely as an
     aid to avoiding this idea. Even the fullest understanding of the divine essence cannot by itself
     yield any knowledge of the divine persons, which requires a grasp of the relations of oppo-
     sition among them. On this see Schmidbaur (1995).
26   See, e.g., the trinitarian sections in vols. 3 and 5 of von Balthasar's *Theo-Drama* (1992,
     1998), and Yves Congar, *I Believe in the Holy Spirit* (1983), especially vol. 3.
27   Cf. André de Halleux (1990:215–68); Michel Barnes (1995b:237–50); Gilles Emery
     (2000:521–63); Lewis Ayres (2000:39–82).

References

Aquinas, T. 1948–52. *Summa theologiae*, ed. Peter Caramello, 4 vols. Turin and Rome: Marietti.
Aquinas, T. 1954a. *De Rationibus Fidei*, in Verardo (1954:253–68).
Aquinas, T. 1954b. *Expositio Primae Decretalis* in Verardo (1954:417–26).
Ayres, L. 2000. "'Remember that you are Catholic' (*sermon* 52, 2): Augustine on the Unity of
    the Triune God," *Journal of Early Christian Studies* 8:39–82.
Barnes, M. 1995a. "De Régnon Reconsidered," *Augustinian Studies* 26:51–79.
Barnes, M. 1995b. "Augustine in Contemporary Trinitarian Theology," *Theological Studies*
    56:237–50.
Barth, K. 1956–75. *Church Dogmatics*, trans. G. Bromily et al. Edinburgh: T. & T. Clark.
Buckley, J. J. and Yeago, D. eds. 2000. *Knowing the Triune God.* Grand Rapids, MI: Eerdmans.
Congar, Y. 1983. *I Believe in the Holy Spirit*, trans. D. Smith. London: Geoffrey Chapman.
De Halleux, A. 1990. "Personnalisme ou essentialisme trinitaire chez les pères cappadociens?"
    Patrologie et oecuménisme. Leuven: Peters.
De Régnon, T. 1892–8. *Études de théologie positive sur la Sainte Trinité*, 4 vols. Paris: Victor Retaux
    et Fils.
Dorner, I. A. 1883. *A System of Christian Doctrine*, vol. 1, trans. A. Cave. Edinburgh: T. & T. Clark.
Emery, G. 1995. *La Trinité créatrice.* Paris: J. Vrin.
Emery, G. 2000. "Essentialisme or Personalism in the Treatise on God in St. Thomas Aquinas?"
    The Thomist 64(4):521–63.
Franzelin, J. B. 1895. *Tractatus de Deo Trino secundum personas*, 4th edn. Rome: Ex Typographia
    Polyglotta.
Gunton, C. ed. 1997. *The Cambridge Companion to Christian Doctrine.* Cambridge: Cambridge Uni-
    versity Press.
Jenson, R. W. 1982. *The Triune Identity.* Philadelphia, PA: Fortress Press.
Jenson, R. W. 1997. *Systematic Theology*, vol. 1: *The Triune God.* New York: Oxford University Press.
Johnson, E. 1992. *She Who Is.* New York: Crossroad.
Kasper, W. 1984. *The God of Jesus Christ*, trans. M. J. O'Connell. New York: Crossroad.

LaCugna, C. M. 1991. *God for Us: The Trinity and Christian Life.* San Francisco, CA: HarperCollins.

Lossky, V. 1944. *Essai sur la théologie de l'église d'orient.* Paris: Aubier.

Lossky, V. 1957. *The Mystical Theology of the Eastern Church.* London: James Clarke.

Marshall, B. D. 1997. "The Jewish People and Christian Theology," in *The Cambridge Companion to Christian Doctrine*, ed. C. Gunton. Cambridge: Cambridge University Press, pp. 81–100.

Marshall, B. D. 1999. "Faith and Reason Revisited: Aquinas and Luther on Deciding What is True," *The Thomist* 63(1):1–48.

Marshall, B. D. 2000a. *Trinity and Truth.* Cambridge: Cambridge University Press.

Marshall, B. D. 2000b. "Do Christians Worship the God of Israel?" in *Knowing the Triune God*, eds. J. J. Buckley and D. Yeago. Grand Rapids, MI: Eerdmans, pp. 231–64.

Merriel, D. J. 1990. *To the Image of the Trinity.* Toronto: Pontifical Institute of Medieval Studies.

Moltmann, J. 1981. *The Trinity and the Kingdom*, trans. M. Kohl. San Francisco, CA: Harper & Row.

Pannenberg, W. 1991. *Systematic Theology*, vol. 1, trans. G. Bromily. Grand Rapids, MI: Eerdmans.

Rahner, K. 1961. *Theological Investigations*, vol. 1, trans. C. Ernst. London: Darton, Longman & Todd.

Rahner, K. 1997. *The Trinity* [1967], 2nd edn., trans. J. Donceel. New York: Crossroad.

Schleiermacher, F. 1976. *The Christian Faith*, trans. H. R. Mackintosh and J. S. Stewart. Philadelphia, PA: Fortress Press.

Schmidbaur, H. C. 1995. *Personarum Trinitas: Die trinitarische Gotteslehre des heiligen Thomas von Aquin.* St. Ottilien: Eos Verlag.

Somme, L. -T. 1997. *Fils adoptifs de Dieu par Jésus Christ.* Paris: J. Vrin.

Tabarelli, R. 1964. *De SS. Trinitate*, ed. C. Fabro. Rome: Pontifica Universitas Lateranensis.

Verardo, R. ed. 1954. *S. Thomae Aquinatis Opuscula Theologica*, vol. 1. Turin and Rome: Marietti.

Von Balthasar, H. U. 1992, 1998. *Theo-Drama*, vols. 3 and 5, trans. G. Harrison. San Francisco, CA: Ignatius Press.

Von Balthasar, H. U. 1993. *Mysterium Paschale*, trans. Aiden Nichols. Grand Rapids, MI: Eerdmans.

Weinandy, T. 1995. *The Father's Spirit of Sonship.* Edinburgh: T. & T. Clark.

Zizioulas, J. 1985. *Being as Communion.* New York: SVS Press.

CHAPTER 13

Incarnation

John Webster

The doctrine of the incarnation is an attempt at conceptual expansion of the church's confession that Jesus Christ is Lord. It is humble, delighted, repentant, and joyful repetition at the level of theological concepts, of the primary affirmation of the church: that the church's Lord, Jesus, is the incomparably comprehensive context of all creaturely being, knowing and acting, because in and as him God is with humankind in free, creative, and saving love. Theological talk of the incarnation of God in Jesus Christ is thus the orderly intellectual exposition of the divine self-exposition; it is a constructive (and therefore critical) attempt to trace the movement of the being and act of God the Son who takes flesh.

To write in such terms is to invite the reproach that confession and critical inquiry have been fatally confused. But theology would be wise not to rise too swiftly or with too much determination to protest against the reproach. Partly this is because the charge of "foolishness" is a permanent accompaniment for any authentically Christian theology which is serious about struggling against sin in the intellectual realm: the reproach identifies that the question of the regeneration of the mind can never be laid aside in the way in which theology responds to its critics. Partly, again, theology's reluctance to make a response of the kind for which its critics might hope is a function of the fact that theology is a positive science, that is, a mode of intellectual activity ordered towards a given reality of a particular character. Theology cannot establish on transcendental grounds the conditions of possibility of its object, neither to itself nor to its critics. To attempt to do so would be to adopt a perverse stance towards the object, one which would, indeed, be almost a willful rejection of that object and its claim. For that object – God incarnate, the Word made flesh – is not one more matter for the free play of intellectual judgment. Rather, the object is itself judge, wholly and originally; and perhaps *the* test of the authenticity of any theology of incarnation will be whether it emerges from that judgment or prefers, instead, to establish an independent colony of the mind from which to make raids on the church's confession.

This chapter proceeds in three stages. First, it gives a more extensive account of the task of a doctrine of the incarnation along the lines just indicated; second, it identifies some characteristic features of modern Christian thought which have impeded unanxious pursuit of that task; and third, it offers a dogmatic expansion of the Christian confession which tries to display its intellectual and spiritual architecture. We proceed, that is, from orientation to archeology and thence to exposition.

Orientation

Construals of who Jesus Christ is and construals of the nature of the Christological task are mutually reinforcing. Thus, for example, from the end of the eighteenth century the method of Protestant Christology was dominated by deep and sustained engagement with the historical records about Jesus; but the plausibility of the historical methods used to pursue that engagement derived not only from the general prestige of historical science in German and (slightly later) English intellectual culture, but also from the humanist and moralistic interpretations of Jesus which found classic expression in Kant's religious writings. The critical and sometimes apologetic use of historical inquiry both drew upon and confirmed theological convictions about Jesus. However, formal and material concerns rarely exist in equilibrium; much more often, precedence is given to either the formal or the material. Mainstream modern Christology, especially when it acknowledges an obligation to its wider intellectual environment, characteristically gives a measure of priority to the formal conditions for public speech about Jesus. The reason for this is that the intellectual world in which modern Christology was decisively shaped (Germany at the turn of the nineteenth century) was much preoccupied with the effects upon religious claims of philosophical idealism and the disciplines of historical inquiry to which idealism was closely akin. To put matters very crudely: religious claims about Jesus were subordinate to universally valid processes of intellectual inquiry considered to have greater authority than the merely domestic doctrine of the church. Those universally valid processes of inquiry were, of course, by no means religiously neutral; in the case of Christology, as we shall see, they usually involved an assumption that Jesus is not a presently active figure but simply a figure from the past, available only through historical report. But the effect of their acceptance was that the domestic doctrine of the church was not trusted to have sufficient authority to determine the formal means by which investigation into Jesus Christ might properly be undertaken.

The hegemony of the formal has rarely been overthrown by explicit refutation, which often ends in a methodological tangle. The most persuasive attempts to operate by a different set of rules – amongst Protestants, Barth's Christological metaphysics; amongst Roman Catholics, von Balthasar's Christological dramatics – have not waited upon formal permission to proceed but simply set about the descriptive Christological task, demonstrating in actual use the priority of material claims over formal requirements. Though what follows advocates the priority of substantive doctrine, it nevertheless begins by drawing attention to some of the formal or methodological consequences for Christology of the material content of the church's claim. That material content can be summed up thus: *The doctrine of the incarnation is an attempt at conceptual expansion of the church's confession that Jesus Christ is Lord.*

The doctrine is concerned with *the church's confession that Jesus Christ is Lord.* Because the doctrine of the incarnation is an attempt at a conceptual expansion of the church's confession, it starts from a given. It is neither an arbitrary nor a constructive exercise, but the following of a reality which precedes and incloses its activity. That which is given to Christology is, however, more closely defined not as an intellectual or spiritual *positum,* a received piece of tradition or authoritative Christian experience. What is given is the personal, communicative self-presence of Jesus Christ, in and as whom the creative, redemptive and perfecting work of God, willed by the Father and brought to realization by the Holy Spirit, are enacted. *He* is the given; in his inalienable and unique subjectivity, he is the supreme conditioning factor in all creaturely occurrence and therefore the supreme conditioning factor in all thought and speech about himself. Because he is Lord, he can only be thought of as Lord; if he is not thought of as Lord, and with the rational deference which is due to him as Lord, then he is not thought of at all. As Lord, he is the incomparably comprehensive context of all creaturely being, knowing and acting. The ontological ground of Christology is he himself; similarly, the epistemological ground of Christology – the condition under which true knowledge of this reality is possible – is he himself, for he is the agent through whom knowledge of himself is realized. Because Jesus Christ is Lord, comprehending all other contexts but comprehended by none, thought about him must follow the particular path indicated by his self-presenting reality.

Two images, both taken from Bonhoeffer's Berlin Christology lectures of 1933, reinforce the point. The first is that Christology is the "center of its own space" (Bonhoeffer 1978:28). That is to say, the intellectual activity of theology does not transcend the reality of Jesus Christ but is transcended by it; his reality incloses theology, rather than the other way round. Accordingly, thinking about Jesus Christ cannot be classificatory, a matter of assigning him a place in an existing order of objects, whether material or spiritual. Rather, he is that in terms of which all other reality is to be mapped. The second image reinforces the first by suggesting that Christology is concerned, not with spontaneous human utterance about Jesus Christ but with a divine "Counter-Logos": "When the Counter-Logos appears in history, no longer as an idea but as 'Word' become flesh, there is no longer any possibility of assimilating him into the existing order of the human logos" (1978:30). Such a Counter-Logos shapes Christology in a profound way, most of all by repudiating any idea that theological talk about Jesus Christ is a pure initiative: it is, rather, that which *must* be said because the church and its theology have already been *spoken to,* arrested, and in a very important sense, *silenced* by Jesus Christ who is God's Word, the free and lordly utterance of God. "The incarnation of the Word is the great 'Thus saith the Lord' to which theology can only give the assent that it has heard and understood it" (Barth 1958:59). And so: "Teaching about Christ begins in silence" (Bonhoeffer 1978:27).

The point of both those images could be stated more formally by saying that for Christian faith and theology, the church's confession of the lordship of Jesus Christ the incarnate Word is analytic not synthetic. That confession indicates a reality which cannot be broken down into more primitive elements or deduced from some higher vantage point, and so it works from an assumption which "is a genuine and proper assumption, in so far as it cannot be over-topped by any other, and therefore suspended on, and even disputed by, a higher assumption" (Barth 1956:131). Christology deals with that which grounds all things and therefore cannot itself be grounded. "Christology deals with the revelation of God as a mystery" (ibid.). Because according to the confession Jesus Christ is divine, he is that than which nothing greater can be conceived; theology, therefore, may not operate as if it were competent or permitted to occupy a position prior to, independent of or outside his reality. The office of theological reason is to follow the direction in which the divine reality beckons as it sets itself before us; that is theology's discipleship to revelation. And so, the *ratio cognoscendi* for a theological account of the incarnation is the sheer active, self-bestowing majesty of the Word made flesh. A number of consequences follow from this.

First, the doctrine of the incarnation is an exercise of retrospective rather than constructive or poetic reason. That is, it seeks to draw attention to that which has taken place, that which has already announced itself and made itself a matter for confession; it is not a matter of engaging in a struggle to establish the conditions under which an event of incarnation might be considered a possible object of confession. The rule for theological (indeed, for all) reasoning is: thought follows reality, because possibility follows actuality. The incarnation is thus that *from which* theology moves, rather than that *toward which* it moves. The incarnation is a *perfectum*, an achieved reality which guides theological thinking by ordering thinking toward itself. Such language – guiding, ordering – is inescapably personal, once again reminding us that what generates the theology of the incarnation is the active self-present reality of Jesus Christ, who *is*, independent of and inexhaustibly prior to any representation of him that might be made.

Secondly, therefore, the doctrine of the incarnation is only in a very limited sense a "valuation" of Jesus Christ. Talk of Jesus Christ as the Word made flesh is not to be thought of as a mythological expression of the religious or moral value which Christians find in him or place upon him as an object of regard or worship. Naturally, of course, all theological language, however objective in orientation and however much it may reach beyond itself, is also an expression of the speaker: to deny this would be docetic. But what is of critical importance is that *in* this self-expressive, "worldly" character, theological language about Jesus Christ should genuinely *refer*, genuinely – if confusedly and certainly inadequately – point beyond itself to that by which it is confronted. Where such reference fails, and language about Jesus Christ is no longer properly ostensive, then theology becomes merely a nominalist expression of religious feeling, contingently attached to the name of Jesus. But a doctrine of the incarnation must properly operate in a quite different fashion: it must be an acknowledgment of the inherent transcendent goodness, beauty, and truth of Jesus Christ the Word made flesh; it cannot be an arbitrary conferral of value or dignity. In the end, this is because of the nature of the reality with which Christology concerns itself. Jesus Christ is Lord; lordship which is conferred is a contradiction in terms. To speak theologically of the Word made flesh is thus not to predicate an honorific title of Christ, or to assign him a place in a Christian world of values, even if it be the highest place. It is to confess him to be the one Lord Jesus Christ, the only begotten Son of God. Theology is not competent to make any other judgment.

Thirdly, the sphere of the doctrine of the incarnation is the church. Much of the disrepair of the doctrine of the incarnation in modernity stems from the assumption that the doctrine can be transplanted out of its natural habitat – the practices of Christian faith – and nevertheless continue to flourish. This transplanting occurs very often when the doctrine of the incarnation is approached as a matter for apologetics, defended by the deployment of historical evidences, by the reasoning of philosophical theism, or by a theory of religious symbol. All such strategies are characteristically underdetermined by the *content* of the doctrine, assuming that it can be defended by showing its compatibility with a generic theory of what is ultimate. The cost, however, is that the "churchly" character of the theology of the incarnation – its inseparability from the worship, witness and holiness of the church – is laid aside. Crucially, theology thereby loses sight of the all-important word which stands before and brackets the confession of the one Lord Jesus Christ: *Credo*, I believe. The sphere of the *Credo* is the sphere of the church; and as conceptual expansion of the *Credo*, the doctrine of the incarnation cannot aspire to leave behind the domestic culture of the Christian community.

Fourthly, however, that "domestic culture" is not to be envisaged as a happily stable set of ecclesial practices "containing" Jesus Christ or, perhaps, embodying in its life the same divine reality of which he is the supreme incarnation. (Anglican Christology of the later nineteenth and twentieth centuries sometimes fostered this impression.) To think in such terms is to confuse incarnation and immanence, and thereby radically to misconstrue what it means to say that the church is the sphere in which the doctrine of the incarnation is to be located. The church is not the institutional container of the incarnation; it is, rather, that sphere of human life and fellowship which is besieged by, permanently under attack from, the Word made flesh. One of the most striking features of Bonhoeffer's *Christology* fragments is his insistence that Jesus Christ is a question posed *to* the church, that the church is relentlessly interrogated by the fact that at the heart of its life is the presence of the incarnate one, who cannot be assimilated into or clothed by a form of religious life (Bonhoeffer 1978:301, Torrance 1965:117–27). The consequences of this for theological procedure are immense. It means that – not only for spirituality but for theology, too – "There are only two ways possible of encountering Jesus: man must die or he must put Jesus to death" (Bonhoeffer 1978:35). To speak thus risks seeming indulgent, even histrionic. But it is soberly to draw attention to something close to the heart of an authentic doctrine of the incarnation, namely that the function of any such doctrine is in part to keep the church alert to two realities: the sheer critical force of the one who is confessed, and the pervasive temptation to use concepts for the purposes of idolatrous control.

To sum up so far: the doctrine of the incarnation is oriented to the core element of the church's confession, namely that Jesus Christ is Lord, the one who as Lord himself sets the conditions under which he comes to be known and acknowledged as such. Theological talk of incarnation is an act of retrospection rather than *poiesis*; of acknowledgment rather than valuation; of the church rather than universal reason; of being interrogated by, rather than of interrogating the personal reality which is the matter of the church's attestation.

Next, and more briefly, the task of the doctrine of the incarnation is *conceptual expansion* of the church's confession. The expansion takes the form of appeal to and refashioning of a small number of ontological categories, chief among them being *substance, person and nature*.

A long and authoritative tradition in modern Christology has held that the conceptual idiom in which the doctrine of the incarnation found classic expression is a declension from authentic Christian engagement with Jesus. That tradition – of which the most authoritative popular example is Harnack's *What Is Christianity?*, but whose presiding genius is Ritschl – was given renewed energy by theological existentialism, and found a more recent voice in liberal Anglican revisionary histories of patristic Christology from the last third of the twentieth century. These diverse figures were in their different ways and for different reasons all agreed on one central point: that the "metaphysical" conceptuality of the doctrine of the incarnation was an unsuitable vehicle for articulating the ethico-religious concerns which ought to lie at the center of theological talk about Jesus Christ. This conviction was backed up in a variety of ways: by reading the Christology of the New Testament in "functional" rather than "ontological" terms; by critical doctrinal history of the patristic developments, claiming that ontology was an infection caught from the cultural context of Christian faith; by an emphasis upon the saving work of Christ "for me" over the technicalities of his person; and by a commitment to Christian existence as the foundational reality around which "objective" doctrines have to be arranged and by which they are to be criticized.

It must readily be admitted that there is a debased form of Christology which is "abstract" in the sense that it accords priority to concepts such that the personal history of Jesus's life, death and resurrection comes to seem almost a symbolization of an idea. No part of Christian theology – least of all theological talk about God in the flesh – should fail to avoid that. Nevertheless, the wholesale rejection of concepts in Christology is untenable on a number of grounds. First, it tends to read the concepts of which the doctrine of the incarnation makes use as belonging more to descriptive than to analytical metaphysics, whereas in their Christological employment the concepts are more concerned with the relations between substances than the nature of substances. Description and analysis, obviously, cannot be kept entirely distinct. But when the categories used to give an account of the incarnation are read only descriptively, then they can threaten to become little more than a bizarre piece of metaphysical psychology – as, for example, when the term "person" is construed as "personality" (cf. Williams 1976:253–60).

Secondly, it is of the utmost importance to emphasize that the *use* of concepts may modify, or even radically transform, their habitual range of reference. As we shall see in looking at some of the basic concepts used in incarnational theology, what is most interesting about them is not their pre-history but their modification when they are bent to serve the purpose of articulating the Christian confession. Liberal Protestant Christology frequently underplayed the element of transformation, in order to maximize the gap between credal Christology and the religion of Jesus, and to minimize the differences between credal Christology and its intellectual environment. But it could only do so by overlooking the intellectually innovative and culturally dislocated character of patristic Christology.

Thirdly, the retention of conceptual language in giving an account of Jesus Christ is a *conditio sine qua non* for the rejection of subjectivism in Christology. Ontological concepts, above all, the concept of "substance," resist the debasement of Christology to spirituality, and so function as an essential element of theological realism. Christology which does not spell out the ontological dimensions of the person of Jesus Christ in rela-tion to God finds it very difficult to resist the pull of subjectivism and moralism, and quickly turns Jesus into a mythological condensation of the religious and ethical com-mitments of the believing self. The use of ontology is thus a way of ensuring that the identity of Jesus is not subject to the vagaries of religious use, and that what faith con-fesses is who Jesus indissolubly *is*.

Lastly, the doctrine of the incarnation is an *attempt* at conceptual expansion of the church's confession that Jesus Christ is Lord. Like all Christian doctrine, the doctrine of the incarnation is caught between the necessity of concepts and the fact that they are not naturally fitting. What is required in this situation is not the rejection of concepts but their sanctification. Responsible thought and speech simply could not proceed without some kind of conceptual equipment; what is needed is, therefore, the conver-sion of concepts. Thought and speech about Jesus Christ are thought and speech annexed by his self-exposition. They are the exercise of "dethroned and distraught reason" (Bonhoeffer 1978:30). But though they are not fitting, they are made fitting, sanctified, in service to the communicative presence of Christ, even though they always stand on the threshold of breakdown, in the midst of the crisis of the fact of their own unsuitability for the task they have to perform. That task is to enable rational grasp of the character and scope of the church's confession. The concepts of Christology are not an improvement upon the confession. They do not provide a better warranted, or a more conceptually stable and precise, mode of expression – in fact, they are always frail and ill-adapted. Nor are Christological concepts speculative, in the sense of being an attempt to identify transcendental metaphysical conditions from which a doctrine of incarnation might be deduced. Rather, they have the modest task of ordering and arranging the church's thought and speech about Jesus Christ in such a way as to display its shapeliness, coherence, and explanatory power. Concepts do not add to the confession, but work both from it and back toward it, starting from that which is well known in the sphere of faith and church, and returning to that sphere having under-taken their task. But concepts can only do this if the theologian deploys them with a sense that they are permanently on the brink of dissolution, always aware of their own impossibility, and never, therefore, any more than an *attempt*.

In such an attempt, it is the task of Christian theology to construct concepts which are *appropriate* to the matter of the incarnation, and to ensure their appropriate use. Concepts and their use are to be judged appropriate, first, if they are sufficiently trans-parent and delicate to enable apprehension of that which they indicate – the reality of Jesus Christ. Concepts must not obscure, and certainly not dominate, that reality, but should be subservient to it. Secondly, concepts and their use are to be judged appropri-ate if they resist the temptation to replace the primary modes of speech in which the church's confession of Christ is expressed: homological, kerygmatic, doxological, and aretological language and, above all, the prophetic and apostolic language of Scripture. If it is true that "the root of dogma is the confession of Christ" (Schlink 1967:34), then the conceptual matter of dogma needs to be self-effacing, such that dogma will adopt a *rhetoric of indication*. That is, its rhetoric – its language and concepts, its patterns of argument, its "voice" – will be such that it is a testifying to the matter of incarnation. Its rhetoric will therefore be deliberately minimalist, unelaborate, unfinished, shy of exhaustive explanation, above all, governed by the scriptual witness in which it finds its beginning and end.

Archaeology

Modernity is commonly reputed to have laid in ruins the account of Christological reason just outlined. It did not, in fact, do so; it simply installed in the centers of greatest intellectual prestige (the research universities) one contingent version of instrumental reason to which most Protestant and, later, some Roman Catholic theologies found themselves hard put to respond by anything other than concessions. The failure to respond and the readiness to make concessions were rooted in internal failures in Christian theology in the post-Reformation (and possibly the early modern) periods, notably the reluctance to deploy primary Christian doctrine (Trinity, Christology, pneumatology) in criticism of philosophical teaching, and the assumption that methods of inquiry are content-neutral.

One of the chief aspects of the legacy of these failures has been a widespread belief that positive dogmatics is not and cannot be a critical activity. Dominant strands of modern theology have judged that theology can only be a critical undertaking in so far as – unlike the act of confession – its relation to the object of the church's faith is one of inquiry. In conducting its inquiry, it does not presuppose the truth of the Christian confession but tests its viability against independent criteria. The orientation which has been described so far is obviously incompatible with understanding the Christological task as critical in that way. This does not mean that the task is uncritical; on the contrary, Christology is from start to finish a critical activity. But what makes Christology critical is not conformity to certain methodologies, or a generally suspicious attitude toward received tradition, but its object: Jesus Christ, who as judge is other than any contingent representation. Christology is critical because of that to which it addresses itself and by which it is addressed. It is internally critical, in that it is sharply aware of both the inadequacies of its conceptual apparatus, and its capacity for distorting the object to which it turns itself unless it is ceaselessly and repentantly vigilant. It is externally critical in that at crucial points it begs to differ from the intellectual and spiritual conventions of the culture within which the church makes its confession of Christ, including that culture's conventions of criticism. Sufficient has already been said about the internally critical character of Christology, which derives from the impossibility of any comprehensive rendering of its object, the free, personal self-presentation of the Word made flesh. We now turn to look at the externally critical orientation of the doctrine of the incarnation, that is, its polemical or apologetic edge.

There is no "pure" Christology, no Christology which does not articulate itself with a measure of dependence upon the conventions of its context. But, equally, one test of the adequacy of a Christology will be the vigor with which it prosecutes theological judgments about those conventions, the strength with which it refuses to allow modern challenges to set the terms in which it responds. If Christology allows itself to be transposed into a modern idiom largely without residue, then in some measure its reference to its own object will be obscured. If, on the other hand, it is alert and robust in critical appraisal of the dominant idioms of its culture and refuses their claim to self-evidentness, it may well find itself released from some of the inhibitions under which it has often gone about its work.

A somewhat schematic pathology of modern Christology would identify three such inhibitions: the problem of nominalist treatments of the person and mission of Jesus; the problem of theistic construals of the identity of God; and the problem of the relation of the particularity of Jesus to claims about his universality.

In nominalist Christology, Jesus is illustrative but not constitutive of some reality of ultimate significance.[1] His "name" (that is, his enacted identity as a particular figure) is relative to some supposed ultimate reality, of which it is a contingent expression. That ultimate reality is available under other (though not necessarily more adequate or comprehensive) descriptions. Whether the ultimate reality be conceived in moral terms (as absolute value) or in religious–theological terms (as divine being) matters little; the consequence for an account of incarnation is much the same. Jesus Christ is no longer irreducibly identified as ingredient within the reality of God. He may indicate God's reality, even paradigmatically and supremely so; but he is not identical with it, and so he cannot be the *inconcussum fundamentum veritatis*. As a distinguished representative of this kind of Christology puts it: "What is central is the transforming event associated with the life and death of Jesus of Nazareth, a transformation that brings about a new way of relating both to God and to other human beings" (McFague 1983:333).

Two particular features of such Christologies deserve comment. First, the incomparability of Jesus Christ is de-emphasized, since his identity is rendered in relative terms. As Hans Frei put it, on this model the description of Jesus's identity

> involves comparative reference to the characteristics, conditions, or destinies of some other persons or of all mankind as they may be viewed from the standpoint of a given cultural or social framework. . . . [T]he comparative reference is usually to the common qualities of estrangement, self-alienation, or some other basically divisive conflict that may appear within the self, between the self and its society, or between social forces.   (Frei 1975:89)

The effect of this move is to suggest that Jesus is somehow transcended by some other context, which provides the ultimate ground for understanding him and his actions, in such a way that other persons and actions could be substituted for Jesus without irreparable loss. "Jesus" names not only a person but qualities enacted by or associated with that person.

Second, accordingly, Jesus becomes "archetypal," with a couple of consequences. One is that it does not matter very much whether Jesus is a present, operative figure – in effect, it does not matter whether he is risen from the dead. What endures is not necessarily Jesus himself but that which he instantiates or symbolizes. Nominalist Christologies are thus irresistibly drawn to concentrate upon Jesus's moral and religious teaching, or his enactment of a radically challenging style of human relations, since it is here that his transparency to an ultimate reality can be most clearly discerned. And they are also drawn to exemplarist accounts of the saving significance of Jesus. He saves, not by undertaking a unique mission of which he alone can be the agent, but by acting out and recommending attitudes and commitments which ought to characterize all persons. Within such moralist and exemplarist Christologies, what matters is not that Jesus *is*, but that he *was*. His "presence" is the persistence of an ideal; it is imperative rather than indicative.

A second consequence is that in Christologies in which Jesus functions as archetype, human action threatens to become the real center of gravity. The divine act of incarnation quickly becomes mere mythic representation of work which needs to be undertaken by human persons themselves. Kant, for example, argues that

> It is our universal human duty to *elevate* ourselves to this ideal of moral perfection, i.e. to the prototype of moral disposition in its entire purity, and for this the very idea, which is presented to us by reason for emulation, can give us force. But, precisely because we are not its authors but the idea has rather established itself in the human being without our comprehending how human nature could have even been receptive of it, it is better to say that that *prototype* has *come down* to us from heaven, that it has taken up humanity. . . . This union with us may therefore be regarded as a state of *abasement* of the Son of God if we represent to ourselves this God-like human being, our prototype, in such a way that, though himself holy and hence not bound to submit to sufferings, he nonetheless takes these upon himself in the fullest measure for the sake of promoting the world's greatest good.   (Kant 1996:104)

Faith in Jesus Christ is thus *"practical faith in this Son of God"* (ibid.), a mode of conduct stimulated by him rather than an affirmation or acknowledgment of what he is.

Such Christological constructs shatter the logic of incarnation. At best, Jesus is a (the?) symbolic intensification of the divine; at worst, he is merely ornamental. But he is not God enfleshed. He is, perhaps, a mode of the divine self-manifestation, an instrument in the divine pedagogy; but, in the end, he is not the *content* of the divine instruction.

Undergirding this nominalism are two further features of modern Christologies: theism, and a bifurcation of the universal and the particular.

A good deal of theology in modernity has been theistic, in that the specifics of Christian conviction have not generally been considered constitutive either of the process of coming to believe in God or of the content of such belief.[2] In effect, Christian doctrine concerning the Trinity, the incarnation, and the work of the Holy Spirit in the church have been relegated to merely contingent status, interpreted as refinements of or particular positive variants upon more basic theistic belief, into which they can be rendered without loss of anything essential. The authority of theism is the result of the coming together of a number of factors. One is the rise of prolegomena to theology in the early modern period, in which basic belief in "a god" was considered determinable by philosophical reason without reference to the experience of faith. Another is modernity's unease about revelatory divine action in history, which presses theology to construct its account of the identity of God out of metaphysical resources independent of the religious experience of Israel and the church. A third is modernity's preference for natural over positive religion, largely driven by distaste for the contentious claims of specific traditions and the desire to replace them by rational defense of the plausibility of belief in God as the foundation for moral consensus (such sentiments are still the backcloth for a good deal of contemporary Christian theorizing about the relation of Christianity to other world faiths).

In the case of the doctrine of the incarnation, the authority of theism both rein- ˋ forces and is reinforced by the nominalism of modern theology. Christological nominalism presupposes an ontological separation of Jesus and God, with the result that the content of the term "God" is filled out by appeal to all manner of resources which are not Christologically shaped: *theos* and *Christos* are not mutually determinative. Once this bifurcation is allowed, then the doctrine of the incarnation is immediately unworkable, for that doctrine claims an ontological unity between God and the human career of the man Jesus, a unity not conceivable within the terms of the metaphysics of theism. Divinity, defined *remoto Christo*, cannot exist in union with humanity. And so the claim of the doctrine of the incarnation – that the end of the ways and works of God is to take flesh – comes to be rejected. Within the terms of a theistic understanding of God, there *can be* no hypostatic union, and so Christian theology must restrict itself to a Christology which is non-incarnational (and therefore non-trinitarian) and to a Christology in which Jesus manifests the divine character with singular potency but without ontological entailments.

This is linked, finally, to an antinomy between universal and particular, ultimate and historical. Modern theology was and continues to be deeply shaped by the disappearance of a conviction which shaped Western culture in the premodern period, namely the conviction of "the inextricable tie of all that is ultimately meaningful to Jesus Christ as a particular person" (Marshall 1987:2). The conviction was eclipsed by a metaphysical principle which separated the sensible and supra-sensible realms, and which considered that historical accidentals cannot be the bearers of non-contingent truths. This divorce of historical specificity from the absolute had a clearly devastating effect on incarnational doctrine: time, space, the body are other than that which is ultimate, and so Jesus's spatio-temporal and embodied existence cannot be identified with the being of God.

In the face of this legacy, there are at least three ways of reorienting a theological account of the incarnation. One is a form of accommodation, in which Christian theology accepts in some measure the constraints imposed upon it by the forms of its wider cultural environment, and seeks to develop a plausible account of the Christian confession within the limits imposed by those forms. If Christologies of this type are theologically deficient, it is not only because they often produce accounts whose resemblance to the family of Christian orthodoxy is hard to discern, but also because they are intellectually conservative. These Christologies characteristically exhibit considerable deference to external cultural conventions, and a reluctance to make use of Christian resources in the critical evaluation of intellectual traditions. A second response is apologetic: the general theistic framework is presupposed, but room is carved out for Christian theological conviction by demonstrating that Christian beliefs about the incarnation are a necessary corollary of (or at least are not incompatible with) the metaphysics of God. Again, if accounts of this type are deficient, it is because they may underestimate the critical impact of the Christian confession on philosophical conviction. A third option – adopted here – follows a strategy of combining dogmatic criticism with what might be called archaeology. As dogmatic criticism, it evaluates cultural and philosophical customs (including customary teaching about God) in terms of their compatibility with the church's confession, doing so on the basis of the metaphysical and epistemological priority of the church's confession of the gospel over the world's denial of it. As archaeology, it is especially concerned to unearth how contemporary theological conscience may be held to ransom by scruples which properly ought to have no authority over it.

> If we are to understand, we must look, not at the universe, but at one particular; we must not seek first, within the historical series, universal laws of its development in terms of which we can, so to speak, interpret the fact of Christ; we must not seek to bring him within the terms of our thinking, but rather to recast the whole of our intellectual frame of reference by constant recollection of his particularity. (MacKinnon 1940:45)

What ought to have authority over the theological conscience, is the gospel as confessed by the church. At the heart of the gospel is the joyful and awed affirmation that the Word became flesh – that, as the Niceno-Constantinopolitan Creed puts it, there is one Lord, Jesus Christ, the only begotten Son, begotten from his Father before all ages, light from light, God from God, true God from true God, begotten not made, of one substance with the Father; that it was through this one that all things were made; that for us and for our salvation he came down from heaven and was incarnate by the Holy Spirit of the Virgin Mary, and was made man. We turn to a more extended exposition of this confession.

Exposition

Although the formal Nicene conceptuality may make it initially hard for us to see the point, that confession is an attempt to respond to questions which are lodged in the primitive Christian accounts of Jesus: "What is this?" "Why does this man speak thus? ... who can forgive sins but God alone?" "Who then is this?" (Mark 1:27, 2:7, 4:41). Very little headway can be made in understanding that confession unless we rid ourselves of the lingering suspicion that it is a *suppression* of those primary questions, most of all by offering a definitive and comprehensive answer to them. In reality, a theological answer to a question such as "Who then is this?" is nothing other than a restatement of the question. The disorientation and wonder which come to expression in the question are permanent; there is no "solution," and certainly not a conceptual, theological solution. All that theology can do is lay out its concepts in such a way as to attest the identity of that which lies at the heart of the disorientation.

The Word became flesh

Word   Christian faith describes what takes place in the life, death, resurrection, and glorification of Jesus of Nazareth by saying that "the Word became flesh." That is, the one whom we encounter in the history of Jesus, the subject of this sequence of acts and sufferings, is the Word or Son of God. As such, this "one" participates fully and unreservedly in the divine nature and majesty. He is "true God from true God": whatever is confessed of the dignity, worth and glory of God is confessed of this one also, who with Father and Spirit is one of the three co-essential and co-eternal persons or modes of the triune being of God. The Christological clause of the Nicene Creed establishes this at the beginning by describing the subject of the incarnation as "one Lord." To speak of Jesus Christ as "Lord" is to indicate that he is infinitely superior in majesty to those who confess (or fail to confess) who he is; he *is* (and is not merely considered to be) Lord, for his lordship is antecedent to any evaluation of him or ascription of properties to him. Confession of lordship is therefore properly not a speculative undertaking, but something which the church and therefore theology, is *forced* to make. Put differently: theology *begins* here; it does not reach this point as a conclusion of a speculative or evaluative process, a process (for example) in which his deity serves as an explanation for certain religious impressions or effects which are generated by consideration of Jesus. Because his divinity is truly *divinity*, it is not contingent but basic. The lordship of the incarnate one is axiomatic rather than derivative, "in the same factual and self-evident and indisputable way as Yahweh was of old Israel's God" (Barth 1975:405). And as such, he can only be "one" Lord, incomparably greater than and categorically different from all other putative lords. That is, his uniqueness is not relational but absolute.

"Relational" uniqueness is often proposed by those urging the compatibility of Christianity and other faith traditions, since it seems to maintain the status of Jesus Christ in Christian conviction, but in a non-exclusive fashion.[3] The uniqueness of Jesus is his unique status as an object of Christian devotion, but is not such as to exclude other possible objects of devotion. But to talk in such terms is to confuse confession and ascription. Moreover, uniqueness is not predicated of Christian conviction but acknowledged in the object of confession, who, as Lord, is absolutely unique. Thus Christian theology speaks of *the* incarnation, of the *one* Lord. We may certainly in some cases speak of comparative uniqueness, uniqueness with reference to other realities. But "is this uniqueness . . . the uniqueness which according to traditional Christian theology there has been in the Incarnation of the Word of God? . . . [T]he answer is surely *no*" (MacKinnon 1987:172). In short: the uniqueness of Jesus Christ is not an ascription of value but his ontological singularity as the one incarnate Lord. In this respect there is, therefore, a strict equivalence between the first clause of the Nicene definition ("I believe in one God") and the second, Christological, clause ("and in one Lord Jesus Christ"). Belief in the "one Lord Jesus Christ" is not a supplement to belief in one God but rather a precise statement of the content of such belief, in which it is an ingredient.

It is for this reason that the Nicene confession lays considerable emphasis on the fact that Jesus Christ is antecedently the Son of God. He is the "only begotten Son, begotten of his Father before all worlds." The exclusive particle – "*only* begotten" – is intended to prevent the assimilation of Jesus Christ into the ranks of creatures. The phrase "begotten of his Father before all worlds" indicates that his coming into being is not after the manner of creatures or within the contingencies of created history, but is an event within God's eternal life ("before all worlds"). "Begotten" is primarily a negative rather than a positive term, distinguishing the origin of the Son from that of creaturely ("made") reality, so indicating that the Son is a reiteration within the being of God. To be "begotten" in this sense is to be "light of light," "very God of very God," ingredient within the eternal and effulgent completeness of the being of God.

This Word, this one Lord Jesus Christ, is the *subject* of the event of incarnation. He is not its "object," in that he is not passive or inert but active. The incarnation is therefore not a further instance of a process of becoming, of which the divine life and activity are also part. Nor is the incarnation a creaturely movement; it is free, gratuitous and *ex nihilo*, the exercise of the divine good pleasure and not a necessary consequence of any state of affairs beyond the loving will and purpose of the Father who sends and the free, active obedience of the Son or Word. God is the acting subject; the statement "the Word became flesh" is in no way reversible, and does not entail any intrinsic creaturely capacity or one that cooperates or coordinates itself with the action of Father and Word to make the incarnation possible. That action is unilateral and unidirectional, the majestic downward movement of God to the creature.

Became   That movement is the history of Jesus Christ; the history of Jesus Christ is that movement. Most generally described, it is the movement in which the Word *became* flesh, or in which the Son of God came down from heaven and was made man. What is to be said of this "becoming"?

The becoming to which reference is made is a specific divine action, not a modification of a more general ontology of flux. In formal terms, this means that this "becoming" is defined by its subject ("the Word"). Ontological categories are strictly subordinate to the unique and irreducible event which they try to depict. "It is not a matter of a 'God who becomes'. God's being is not identified with God's becoming; rather, God's being is ontologically located" (Jüngel 2001:xxv). In material terms, this means that "becoming" is not a matter of augmentation or diminution, but rather of that movement in which the being of God in all its fullness is fully achieved:

> The fact that in the incarnation God became man without ceasing to be God, tells us that his nature is characterised by both repose and movement, and that his eternal Being is also a divine *Becoming*. This does not mean that God ever becomes other than he eternally is or that he passes over from becoming into being something else, but rather that he continues unceasingly to be what he always is and ever will be in the living movement of his eternal Being. His Becoming is not a becoming on the way toward being or toward a fullness of being, but is the eternal fullness and the overflowing of his eternal unlimited Being. Becoming expresses the dynamic nature of his Being. His Becoming is, as it were, the other side of his Being, and his Being is the other side of his Becoming. His Becoming is his Being in movement and his Being in movement is his Becoming.   (Torrance 1996:242)

The act of incarnation is a history. Theological talk of the Word made flesh is not a matter of notional arrangement of two static entities (deity and humanity), but a reference to a complex event: "it came to pass. . . ." Through the doctrine, we seek to conceptualize the divine dramatics, the movement of the mission of God in condescension. It cannot be emphasized too strongly that the concepts of the doctrine must therefore be governed by the primacy of what Jean Galot calls "la démarche divine" (Galot 1971:50). However, in its dynamism, the event of the divine procession in the incarnation of the Word is an act of the immutable freedom of God. Some recent incarnational theology has been keen to give great weight to the processive nature of the divine being, and above all to the culmination of that procession at the cross. Sometimes such accounts are made for apologetic reasons, particularly when an incarnational theory of divine passibility is deployed as part of a theodicy. At other times, the motivation may be more strictly dogmatic, in that an incarnational Christology is used as a critical lever against theistic assumptions of the removal of God from historical contingency. But in all cases, considerable vigilance is required if the genuine desire to affirm the procession of God in the Word's becoming flesh is not to threaten divine aseity. Whatever else may be said about God's becoming, that becoming must be understood as a mode of his sovereign self-possession, an aspect of his inexhaustible plenitude.

Thus, for a theological construal of the incarnational "becoming" to succeed, it must not allow itself to be dominated by apologetic concerns but must stick closely to the event of incarnation itself, as it presents itself, without attempting to display any particular "usefulness" of the doctrine. And it must resist the pressure of *a priori* generic concepts, exercising maximal creativity in adapting and reordering conceptual materials to suit its particular purpose. Above all, it must offer as full and rich a description as it is able of the incarnation as divine condescension, describing ἐγένετο as free *act* and *free* act. The Word *became* flesh; there is genuine newness here, yet a newness which is rooted in the mysterious freedom of God. "Becoming flesh" involves no abandonment of deity; the Word does not cease to be entirely himself, but rather takes over, "assumes," that which is not himself, taking it to its own being. The "humiliation" of the Word is thus by no means the contradiction of his exaltation; it is, rather, the chosen mode of his exaltation. If the Lord is servant, it is as Lord that he serves.

One way in which the freedom of the Word's becoming flesh can be given conceptual form is by the language of *anhypostasis* and *enhypostasis*. These concepts are a way of stating, first, that the man Jesus has no personal center of subsistence ("hypostasis") in and of himself, so that he is thus "*an*hypostatic"; and secondly, that his hypostasis is "*in*" the Word which assumes flesh, so that he is "*en*hypostatic." The conceptuality has an unfamiliar air, and is liable to promote misunderstanding if taken as a psychological description of Jesus. What it does state is that the Word's assumption of flesh is wholly gratuitous, in no sense the annexation of enlargement of creaturely possibility. The deity of the incarnate one is not natural to his humanity; on the contrary, his humanity is a predicate of the divinity of the Word. His humanity is thus not self-existent, but comes to exist in the event of the Word's "procession." In effect, this reinforces what is secured by speaking of the Word's *assumption* of humanity, namely that – against adoptionism – Jesus Christ is not merely a human being who pre-exists the action of the Word and is subsequently exalted to union with him; rather, he is himself the sheerly creative life-act of the Word or Son of God.

In sum, God's "becoming" is God's determination of himself to be God *in this way*, to take this particular direction which is the fulfillment of his groundless aseity. Self-emptying (*kenosis*) and self-fulfillment (*plerosis*) are not antithetical, but identical. Thus to be what Mark Taylor calls "thoroughly incarnational" (Taylor 1984:103) we do not need to posit the disappearance of God, "the sacrifice of the transcendent Author/Creator/Master who governs from afar" (ibid.). To speak in such terms is to miss the real force of "becoming," for that term retains the permanent tension between transcendence and historical presence which Taylor's language of the "irrevocable erasure" of the transcendent at the incarnation ignores (ibid.). To be thoroughly incarnational we need a doctrine of the triune God – of God the Father who freely wills this act, of

God the Son who is freely obedient and assumes flesh, of God the Spirit through whom God empowers the Son and mediates his incarnate presence. The being of the incarnate God is thus *in* becoming.

Flesh   That which the Word becomes is *flesh*. The Word incarnate participates fully and unreservedly in the same human nature (including, but not limited to, embodiment) that we ourselves have. "Flesh" is not merely an instrument through which an essentially disincarnate Word operates; flesh is that which he is, not that which he merely appears to be.

> Stop your ears, therefore, when anyone speaks to you at variance with Jesus Christ, who was descended from David, and was also of Mary; who was truly born, and did eat and drink. He was truly persecuted under Pontius Pilate; he was truly crucified and [truly] died, in the sight of beings in heaven, and on earth, and under the earth. He was also truly raised from the dead, His Father quickening Him, even as after the same manner His Father will also raise us up who believe in Him by Jesus Christ, apart from whom we do not possess the true life.   (Ignatius, *To the Trallians*, ix)

He is like us. But he is so in utter liberty, and with no renunciation of the deity of the Word. The fact that the Word is ἐνσαρκος does not abolish or disqualify the fact that the Word is equiprimordially ἀσαρκος. But this same Word is truly enfleshed, and enfleshed, therefore, as a particular human being with an inescapably distinct identity: historical, racial, embodied, gendered.

However, this particular human existence has two specific determinations. First, it is what it is by virtue of the divine self-positing, the mutuality of the mission of the Father and the obedience of the Son in the Spirit's power. Fleshly existence is that which the Word assumes and, in assuming, *creates*. The flesh which he becomes is not a free-standing, pre-existent reality added to the Word, for it has no reality other than that which the Word bestows by the act of assumption. Incarnation is not deification of that which exists apart from God. As Augustine puts it, the incarnation is that in which "the grace of God is supremely manifest, commended in grand and visible fashion," for

> what had the human nature in the man Christ merited, that it, and no other, should be assumed into the unity of the Person of the only Son of God? What good will, what zealous strivings, what good works preceded this assumption by which that particular man deserved to become one Person with God? Was he a man before the union, and was this singular grace given to him as to one particularly deserving before God? Of course not! For, from the moment he began to be a man, that man began to be nothing other than God's Son, the only Son, and this because the Word of God assuming him became flesh, yet still assuredly remained God.   (Augustine, *Enchiridion*, xxxvi)

Secondly, this particular human being is of universal scope. That is, what takes place in and as him is definitive of all human persons. His humanity is inclusive, not in the sense that it is not particular, but in the sense that in the assumption of this particular human identity, a divine determination of all human persons is effected. He assumes 'humanity," that which makes all human persons into human persons; in all his specificity he is the new Adam, that act of God in which created human personhood is reoriented by an inclusive act of divine sovereignty. This universal scope presses for *ontological* definition; it is not mere universal pertinence or applicability or even solidarity, but universal effectiveness in which humanity as a whole is re-made.

This re-making takes place as he assumes *sinful* flesh, human existence in repudiation of and rebellion against its ordering by God to find fulfillment in fellowship with God. The Word assumes the full extent of human alienation, taking the place of humanity, existing under the divine condemnation. But his relation to the human alienation which he assumes is not such that he is swallowed up by it. He does not identify with humanity under the curse of sin in such a way that he is himself sinner. He exists at a certain removal from sinful humanity even as he assumes it. It remains utterly foreign, indeed, utterly hateful to him, because it is disoriented, abased, unrighteous, and under God's condemnation. He adopts the condemned human situation without reserve, but with a peculiar distance from our own performance of our humanness. By not following our path, by refusing complicity with the monstrousness of sin, he is and does what we are not and do not do: he is human. In his very estrangement from us as the bearer rather than the perpetrator of sin, he takes our place and heals our corruption. That the Word became *flesh* means that he takes to himself the accursed situation of humanity in sin. But he *takes* it to himself; he does not evacuate himself into our situation. The flesh which the Word becomes is the flesh which *the Word* becomes, and the flesh which the Word *becomes*. In his utter proximity he is utterly distant from the misery of humanity in sin; and only so is he redeemer.

A theological reflection on the fact that "the Word became flesh" thus tries to bear witness to the identity of Jesus, in and as whom God takes creaturely form, in humble majesty acting for us and for our salvation. In the patristic period, the church's intellectual articulation of the faith took shape through the crafting of two seemingly unkerygmatic but in fact crucial dogmas: that of the "consubstantiality" of the Father and the one Lord Jesus Christ, and that of the union of the divine and human natures in the person of the incarnate one. These two dogmas provided the key markers of orthodox Christian teaching until the slow process of erosion began in the post-Reformation period. How are we to approach understanding them?

The proper home of the notions of "substance," "nature," and "person" is the church's dogmatic definition of the gospel. In a culture which identifies intellectual authenticity with spontaneity, inwardness, and free inquiry, "dogma" can only be a set of shackles: regressive, authoritarian, ecclesiastical faith. However, dogma is not merely to be seen under its aspect of intellectual governance; dogma governs only by virtue of the fact that it gives access to the Spirit's presentation of the gospel. When the church speaks dogmatically, it does so under the guiding, converting and sanctifying impulse of the Holy Spirit, in a way which is ostensive before it is definitive and obligatory. Dogma exhibits the authority of the truth of the gospel which it states, and only so can it command the free asset of faith. As "exhibition," dogma is an element in God's self-communication; it is a human statement which offers a normative reading of the source of the church's life in the revelation to which Scripture bears testimony.

Most modern theology disputes such claims. From F. C. Baur onward, the dominant strands of historical theology, especially those with a preference for the priority of natural, "non-dogmatic," religion, have been deeply skeptical about the dogmatic her-

itage of Christianity, and have offered "naturalized" accounts of dogma and its development as contingent (and not always entirely savory) religious and political processes.
It is undeniable that there is something permanently valuable in such critical accounts:
a protest against the pathological abstraction of dogma from the life-processes of the
church, and against the entanglement of church teaching in the politics of suppression. Nevertheless, on theological grounds we may remain in turn skeptical about
whether the natural history of dogma constitutes a sufficient explanation (and therefore refutation) of its claims on the Christian mind and conscience. Rather than his-
toricizing or naturalizing dogma, a more fruitful counter to its pathology will consist in
careful elaboration of the wider framework within which the notion of dogma makes
sense. Crucial to this will be a pneumatological account of the church and its history
(and therefore of the history of dogma), a depiction of the church as the Spirit-
enlivened community in which human thought and speech are bent to the manifestation of the gospel. The viability of dogma, that is, depends upon grasping that – as
Westcott put it – "we cannot understand the history of Christianity unless we recog-
nise the action of the Holy Spirit through the Christian Society" (Westcott 1881:xlix).
To say that is – emphatically – *not* to remove dogma from history or immunize it from
criticism; it is simply to identify that *in* its historicity and contingency, dogma is a
definitive showing of the gospel's truth and a presentation of the gospel's claim. With
this in mind, we move to some remarks on the two primary Christological dogmas.

"Substance"

The Son or Word, the Nicene Creed states, is "of one substance" (*homoousios*) with the
Father. The core of what the notion of substance achieves is to alert us, however clum-
sily, to the fact that the bond between God and Jesus must be ontological and not merely
moral. Substance language helps state that what takes place in the history of Jesus is
in a direct and immediate way a divine act, and not a mere symbolization of a god whose
identity lies elsewhere. "Substance" thus provides a conceptual blockade against sub-
ordinationism, in which the status of Jesus Christ is relegated to that of being first
among creatures. Such subordination strikes at the vital nerve of the doctrine of the
incarnation by radically recasting the interpretation of Jesus: he is no longer the very
actuality of the condescension of God but rather an echo in the sensible realm of the
reality of God, who remains free only in so far as he is locked in an ultimately abstract
and inscrutable transcendence of time and matter. The dogmatic statement that Jesus
Christ is "of one substance with the Father" thus tries to secure the point that "in Christ
we meet that which is *essentially* divine" (Aulén 1954:212): "Where Christ is, there is
God; and where Christ is active, there God is active also. The self-sacrificing and self-
giving love of Christ is the love of God himself, its struggle against evil is God's own
struggle, and its victory is God's own victory. In the deed of Christ God realizes his own
will and love" (1954:213).

Ritschlian theology in the nineteenth century (and well into the twentieth century,
for Ritschl's heirs are many) objected that the language of substance conceives of God's
relation to Jesus in naturalistic or quasi-physical rather than suitably moral terms,

thereby reducing salvation to an almost magical transaction involving special status objects and obscuring the primary idiom of willed moral fellowship between God and his creatures: ontological judgments endanger religious and ethical estimation of Christ. This tradition can justifiably align itself to a long-standing critique of Christological abstraction from Melanchthon to postmodern critics of ontotheology. But, as has already been hinted, the criticism rests on a misapprehension of what ontological language seeks to achieve. In a Christological context, "substance" is the conceptually minimal attempt to indicate what must be confessed of the relation between God and Jesus. It does not carry with it much by way of descriptive metaphysical content, and does not, for example, commit its users to a type of abstract theism or to a docetic Christology. It is, moreover, properly soteriological in intent, pointing to the place where we might most fittingly begin to answer questions of the identity of the agent of salvation by attesting to his unity with the gracious Lord of the covenant. The home of the notion of substance is thus the church's confession of "that revelation which creates the redemptive fellowship between God and man" (1954:214).

This means, therefore, that the notion of substance does not transpose Christology out of an historical register. Quite the opposite: it functions as a key term in thoroughly historical ontology (the interweaving of mythological and metaphysical language in Christology is inevitable).[4] Accordingly, the familiar antithesis of ontology and function will not bear scrutiny, precisely because the task of ontological language is to point out the identity of the person who is here at work. To dispense with ontological concerns about the person of the savior is to threaten to collapse the work of salvation into mere moral incitement, and so to separate Jesus's ministry from the grace of God. On the other hand, to recover the dogma of the *homoousion* may be to gain purchase on the figure of Jesus by making use of "an instrument for advancing our understanding to enable us to see what it is that is at issue in the simpler, more direct, more immediately moving Christological affirmations of the gospel" (MacKinnon 1972:291).

Two Natures, One Person

> Following, then the Holy Fathers, we all with one voice teach that it should be confessed that our Lord Jesus Christ is one and the same Son, the same perfect in Godhead, the same perfect in manhood, truly God and truly man. . . . One and the same Christ, Son, Lord, Only-begotten, made known in two natures [which exist] without confusion, without change, without division, without separation; the differences of the natures having been in no wise taken away by reason of the union, but rather the properties of each being preserved, and [both] concurring into one Person and one *hypostasis* – not parted or divided into two Persons, but one and the same Son and Only-Begotten, the divine Logos, the Lord Jesus Christ.[5]

Like the notion of substance, the Chalcedonian dogma of the hypostatic union (the union of the divine and human natures of Christ in one person) is not a replacement for Jesus's history, but a means of identifying the unique subject and agent of that history. It is thus all-important to note that the center of gravity of the definition is not the natures considered in isolation from each other, but rather the event of their union in the one subject, Jesus. The definition starts from the union of the natures in the one person and hypostasis of which they are predicated, rather than trying to construct a psychologically credible person by first defining and then uniting two distinct natures. Abstract exposition of the natures is excluded; this subject and agent is irreducibly at the center.

Starting from the unitary subject in this way prevents an account of the incarnation from falling into the trap of proceeding as if humanity and divinity were antithetical. At the very least, such a procedure destabilizes the doctrine, leading, for example, to the idea that certain divine attributes have to be suppressed or jettisoned if the integrity of Christ's humanity is to be maintained. Taken to its extreme, it can issue in highly formal accounts of the natures (especially of the deity), defining them in terms of their mutual opposition and fracturing the doctrine entirely. A long strand of criticism of the doctrine of the incarnation, starting with Spinoza and finding late expression in liberal Anglican Christology, has failed at precisely this point: presupposing that God *cannot* be incarnate, and that genuine humanity *must* be violated if assumed by God, it can only see the doctrine of the incarnation as incoherent: "The doctrines . . . such as that God took on himself human nature, I have expressly said that I do not understand; in fact, to speak the truth, they seem to me no less absurd than would a statement that a circle had taken on itself the nature of a square" (Spinoza 1955:353).[6]

Over against this, and on the basis of the particular event of the person of Jesus of Nazareth, the dogma affirms that "the divinity of Christ cannot be correctly grasped where his temporal and material humanity is denied, and that his humanity cannot be properly understood even in its temporal structure and historical reality, if it is not seen as the self-identification of God in the reality of a human life" (Schwöbel 1995:128). How then is personal union to be understood?

The union is utterly unique, an instance of itself, and in no sense a complement, completion, or parallel to any other realities. The hypostatic union is not the most exalted instance of human self-transcendence, of humanity's being "in God" or of the immanence of God in creation. The incarnation cannot be traced either on the trajectory of humanity's capacity to transcend itself and lose itself in God, or on the trajectory of God's indwelling of creaturely reality. These trajectories may or may not have theological validity; but the hypostatic union is categorically different, neither generalizable nor the condensation of more general realities. Like the relations between the persons of the Trinity, the relation of divinity and humanity in the incarnate one defies analogies. The ground for affirming this uniqueness is the fact that the hypostatic union is an utterly free, uncaused, and wholly underivable act of divine omnipotence, and not merely the culmination of a series or the intensification of an ontological principle of wide application. "With a strange, one-sided, self-glorious spontaneity, we have to do here with the work and action of the faithfulness and omnipotence and mercy of God Himself, which has no ground of reality except in Himself, or ground of knowledge except in His self-revelation" (Barth 1958:58f.). The dogma is distinctly *a posteriori*, a description of an act, not a speculative arrangement of *a priori* considerations. All along the line, therefore, grasping the dogma is a matter of deploying concepts in such a way that they display a singular reality which precedes and transcends them. Once again: *person* precedes *natures*.

Two particular determinations of this union of divinity and humanity are emphasized by Chalcedon. First, the union of the natures is "without confusion, without change," for "the difference of the natures" is "in no wise taken away by reason of the union, but rather the properties of each [are] preserved." Though the person, the single ascriptive subject, Jesus is "one and the same," the natures are not. If they were, then both would be obliterated, and Jesus Christ would be neither divine nor human but some nonsensical third reality. Secondly, the union of the natures is "without division, without separation." That is to say, to talk of divinity and humanity is not to distinguish separate aspects of Christ, as if he were part human and part divine, and as if his properties were divisible between divinity and humanity. Jesus Christ is in his entirety divine and in his entirety human. But this does not entail the conversion of divinity into humanity, or vice versa, but simply their concurrence in one person.

"Concurrence" is a reticent term, less vigorous than some might wish. In modern Lutheran Christology it has been common to lay great emphasis upon the indivisibility and inseparability of the two natures, and to prioritize the second set of negatives ("without division, without separation") over the first set ("without confusion, without change"). The usual short-term reason for this is that strong talk of the union of the natures is of considerable advantage if one has other grounds for highlighting the identity of God with the suffering Christ. The deeper justification tends to involve a highly negative evaluation of those aspects of patristic Christology which resisted the confusion of the two natures, and highly positive evaluation of the Lutheran emphasis upon the communication of properties between divinity and humanity – above all, in order to state how God incarnate can be mortal. The kerygmatic cogency of such moves can hardly be doubted. Where they are less secure, however, is in stating the essential presupposition of the union of the natures, namely that divinity *assumed* humanity, that the Word *became* flesh. Unless the dogma of the hypostatic union as a whole is set within the brackets of the *assumptio carnis*, then the union of the natures becomes a *unity*. Over against this, it is vital to retain a firm sense that the hypostatic union is a matter of free grace, and that in an important sense divinity and humanity are asymmetrically related, though without any impugning of the perfection of each nature. Even in union with humanity in Christ, the deity of God remains immutable – directed to the assumption of flesh, by no means a prisoner of its own unchangeableness, but nevertheless unassailably complete in itself.

Conclusion

Such, in brief compass and shorn of its many historical modulations, is the Christian doctrine of the incarnation. The viability of a Christian doctrine of the incarnation rests in part upon its orderly integration with other tracts of Christian teaching. It needs to be set in relation to the wider scope of the church's Christological confession (especially the resurrection of Jesus) and its immediately neighboring doctrines, the doctrines of the Trinity and salvation. Perhaps one of the major reasons for the growth of moralistic and non-incarnational Christologies in the nineteenth century was the dislocation of Christology from the doctrine of the triune being of God: once the Christian doctrine of God has fallen into disrepair and is no longer operative, the doctrine of the incarnation quickly comes to seem a merely arbitrary bit of speculation, leaving theology free to expound the humanity of Jesus as if it could be an abstraction from his identity as divine agent. Integration into the right dogmatic context, on the other hand, prevents the doctrinal disarray which results from the hypertrophy or atrophy of certain doctrines (anthropology waxes, Trinity wanes), or the deployment of one doctrine to do the job properly assigned to another (ecclesiology takes over the tasks of pneumatology). The effects of this kind of misshaping can readily be seen in an essay by an influential con-temporary theologian which suggests that "[t]he gospels can be read, not as the story of Jesus, but as the story of the (re)foundation of a new city, a new kind of human com-munity, Israel-become-the-Church. Jesus figures in this story simply as the founder, the beginning, the first of many. There is nothing that Jesus does that he will not enable the disciples to do" (Milbank 1997:150). The disease which that (baffling) claim purports to diagnose is Christological and soteriological extrinsicism. But the patient does not survive the cure; when Christology is absorbed into ecclesiology, then Jesus and the event of the incarnation have no shape of their own, no contours and edges, no identity other than that afforded in the repetition of that identity in ecclesial process. We are left with "an ecclesiological deduction of the Incarnation" (1997:159). Many of the same fea-tures can be traced in other styles of theology, such as those Protestant soteriologies which make Jesus's identity subservient to his being *pro me*, and which expound that *pro me* through a phenomenology of human experience. What is all-important, by contrast, is that the shape of the whole not be distorted by the dysfunction of any one part.

Dysfunction is corrected by attention to the shapely structure of the confession and its biblical foundation. That confession says – with joy and fear and trembling – that the secret of the man Jesus is the majestic, saving self-communication of God. In that act of God Jesus Christ has its basis. And in that act, too, is the basis on which alone Jesus Christ can be known as who he is. He may be seen by all if they care to look; but he may not be recognized without his self-disclosure. And when they have been of sound mind, church and theology have witnessed to that necessity in dogma and prayer. And so: "Let us grant that God can do something which we confess we cannot fathom. In such matters the whole explanation of the deed is in the power of the Doer" (Augustine, Letter 137.2).

Notes

1   An important recent example would be Haight (1999).
2   For two (rather different) accounts of this, see Buckley (1987) and Jüngel (1983).
3   See, for example, P. Knitter, *No Other Name?* (1975).
4   See D. M. MacKinnon, "Prolegomena to Christology" (1987:185).
5   I follow the translation in R. V. Sellers, *The Council of Chalcedon* (1953:210f.).
6   For a recent example, see Hanson (1975; 1982).

References

Aulén, G. 1954. *The Faith of the Christian Church.* London: SCM Press.
Barth, K. 1956. *Church Dogmatics* I/2. Edinburgh: T. & T. Clark.

Barth, K. 1958. *Church Dogmatics* IV/2. Edinburgh: T. & T. Clark.

Barth, K. 1975. *Church Dogmatics* I/1. Edinburgh: T. & T. Clark.

Bonhoeffer, D. 1978. *Christology*. London: Collins.

Buckley, M. 1987. *At the Origins of Modern Atheism*. New Haven, CT: Yale University Press.

Frei, H. 1975. *The Identity of Jesus Christ: The Hermeneutical Bases of Dogmatic Theology*. Philadelphia, PA: Fortress Press.

Galot, J. 1971. *Vers une nouvelle christologie*. Paris: Gembloux.

Haight, R. 1999. *Jesus: Symbol of God*. New York: Orbis.

Hanson, A. T. 1975. *Grace and Truth*. London: SPCK.

Hanson, A. T. 1982. *The Image of the Invisible God*. London: SCM Press.

Hodgson, P. and King, R. 1983. *Christian Theology: An Introduction to Its Traditions and Tasks*. London: SPCK.

Jüngel, E. 1983. *God as the Mystery of the World*. Grand Rapids, MI: Eerdmans.

Jüngel, E. 2001. *God's Being is in Becoming*. Edinburgh: T. & T. Clark.

Kant, I. 1996. *Religion within the Boundaries of Mere Reason*, in *Religion and Rational Theology*, eds. A. Wood and G. di Giovanni. Cambridge: Cambridge University Press.

Knitter, P. 1975. *No Other Name?* London: SCM Press.

McFague, S. 1983. "An Epilogue: the Christian Paradigm," in *Christian Theology: An Introduction to Its Traditions and Tasks*, eds. P. Hodgson and R. King. London: SPCK.

MacKinnon, D. M. 1940. *God the Living and the True*. London: Dacre.

MacKinnon, D. M. 1972. "Substance in Christology," in *Christ, Faith and History*. Cambridge: Cambridge University Press.

MacKinnon, D. M. 1987. "Prolegomena to Christology," in *Themes in Theology: The Three-fold Cord*. Edinburgh: T. & T. Clark.

Marshall, B. 1987. *Christology and Conflict: The Identity of a Saviour in Rahner and Barth*. Oxford: Blackwell.

Milbank, J. 1997. "The Name of Jesus," in *The Word Made Strange: Theology, Language, Culture*. Oxford: Blackwell.

Schlink, E. 1967. "The Structure of Dogmatic Statements as an Ecumenical Problem," in *The Coming Christ and the Coming Church*. Edinburgh: Oliver and Boyd.

Schwöbel, C. 1995. "Christology and Trinitarian Thought," in *Trinitarian Theology Today*, ed. C. Schwöbel. Edinburgh: T. & T. Clark.

Sellers, R. V. 1953. *The Council of Chalcedon*. London: SPCK.

Spinoza, B. 1955. Letter 36, in *Chief Works*, vol. 2. New York: Dover.

Taylor, M. 1984. *Erring: A Postmodern A/theology*. Chicago, IL: Chicago University Press.

Torrance, T. F. 1965. "Questioning in Christ," in *Theology in Reconstruction*. London: SCM Press.

Torrance, T. F. 1996. *The Christian Doctrine of God*. Edinburgh: T. & T. Clark.

Westcott, B. F. 1881. *A General Survey of the History of the Canon of the New Testament*. London: Macmillan.

Williams, R. 1976. " 'Person' and 'Personality' in Christology," *Downside Review* 94.

Wood, A. and di Giovanni, G. eds. 1996. *Religion and Rational Theology*. Cambridge: Cambridge University Press.

CHAPTER 14
Redemption

Esther D. Reed

Redemption is God's work of love to restore and renew all things. It is God's work of love to restore humankind to its vocation of union and communion with God (II Corinthians 3:18; II Peter 1:4), and to heal and renew the cosmos (Romans 8:21; Revelations 21:5). Redemption is God's means of dealing with sin and its consequences, and of elevating creation to the blessing that was prepared before the fall into sin (Psalms 103:19; Isaiah 64:4; Romans 9:23). Redemption is not yet complete; it is a movement toward the future in which the whole earth will be healed, restored, and transformed (Isaiah 44:24–8; Romans 1:16, 8:23, 13:11; Ephesians 4:30). "His intrinsically perfect work is still moving towards its consummation" (Barth 1961:327). With this in mind, it will be suggested that redemption entails at least three aspects: God's solidarity with humankind and especially those in need; deliverance from all that prevents life being lived to the full; transformation from imperfection to perfection, from loss of potential to its fulfillment.[1] The particular nuances associated with redemption – notably, release (Luke 2:38), ransom (Mark 10:45), and payment of a price in order to free a prisoner or slave (I Peter 1:18–21) – are integral to each aspect.[2] Yet, they are only partially adequate to speak of the costliness of God's work of love. Investigation of the themes of solidarity, deliverance, and transformation is intended to help us avoid overly literal interpretation of images which might hinder rather than help interpretation of the costliness of God's work of love.

Such an investigation will meet many obstacles. The unfamiliar language of "redemption" in everyday discourse (except for the redemption of gift certificates against the cost of a book, or financial bonds from a stock-exchange) creates for us, perhaps, inhibitions as regards interpretation for the present day. The unpalatable association of redemption with "the blood of Christ" and "sacrifice" brings blushes of embarrassment to the cheeks of many believers – not least because of the supposed idealization of victimhood, victory through violent death, and traditional associations with the satisfaction of male honor. The traditional ways in which Christianity has figured its discourse of redemption often alienate hearers from its truth and (heaven forfend!) seem to evoke connections with forms of psychopathology which suggest an unhealthy attitude to life. Julia Kristeva suggests as much in her reflections on Holbein's painting *The Body of the Dead Christ in the Tomb*: "[O]ne should not forget that a whole ascetic, martyrizing, and sacrificial Christian tradition has magnified the victimized aspect of that offering by eroticizing both pain and suffering, physical as well as mental, as much as possible" (Kristeva 1989b:131). Christianity's "tale of love" portrays suffering as a means of access to heaven, and, she argues, now that Christianity's influence is waning, that which survives in popular consciousness is not the deeper meanings of redemption but a burden of melancholy and depression.

The negativity which Kristeva and others associate with redemption points to a gap between the meaning of biblical and traditional language used to describe redemption in various historical and canonical contexts and interpretation within a present-day horizon. Some feminists are dismissive of the redemption and salvation associated with Christ's substitutionary sacrifice because to emphasize what one individual did two thousand years ago seems to detract from consideration of what we, with God, do now (McFague 1987:54).[3] Leading psychologists have dismissed the spiritual evils of sin as being, in their psychological nature, illusions (Freud 1995:706). The hope of a redemption yet to come, in which the whole earth will be healed, restored, and transfigured, sounds faintly absurd to the average person struggling to make a living and reading in a newspaper about the latest natural disaster. What, then, is the meaning and means of redemption to which the bible and tradition bear witness? In what follows, I link the rationale of redemption to a theological anthropology which emphasizes the perfection or completion of humankind in loving communion with God; this is the ontological end or *telos* of humankind. Jesus urges his hearers: "Be perfect, therefore, as your heavenly Father is perfect" (Matthew 5:48). John claims: "Love has been perfected among us in this: that we may have boldness on the day of judgement, because as he is, so are we in this world. . . . perfect love casts out fear" (I John 4:17–18a). These passages suggest that life is worth living because the human destiny is to become Christ-like and, by grace, to enjoy the fullness of God's presence. Thus, our starting point is a positive stance regarding human potential.

This said, our understanding of redemption should not be unduly anthropocentric. Redemption in its fullest and proper sense cannot be conceived only as the liberation from sinfulness of individual persons or even of all humanity. Rather, it is a doctrine which pertains to the destiny of the cosmos (Romans 8:19–24; Colossians 1:15–20) and challenges us to view all creation as called to give glory to God (Psalms 148; Isaiah 42:4, 43:19–21; Luke 19:40). God is God of both creation and redemption; there is no split in the divine economy. Indeed, writes Athanasius, the Word of God who filled all things everywhere at creation became incarnate in order that all things might be turned away from corruption and quickened by his presence: "no part of Creation is left void of Him: He has filled all things everywhere" (Athanasius 1989b:40). In assuming humanity, the Word of God embraced all creation. This same creation recognized that Christ on the cross was God: "For the sun hid His face, and the earth quaked and the mountains were rent" (1989b:46). It would share in the resurrection hope of new life for all things. Indeed, writes Maximus the Confessor, the expected universal consummation will be the time when the unity of humankind with all creation will be revealed: "the man who is ourselves will rise with the world as a part with the whole and the small with the large, having obtained the power of not being subject to further corruption" (Maximus the Confessor 1985:197). We should anticipate, he suggests, the time when creation will be granted its freedom and it will be seen in what manner humankind and the world properly belong together (Romans 8:12–25).

Redemption as God's Solidarity with Humankind

In what sense, therefore, does God's solidarity with humankind in Jesus have redeeming power? Why is God's solidarity with humanity an important aspect of redemption? In addressing these questions, it is helpful to recall that in the Old Testament, the idea of redemption is expressed by two verbs, *ga'al* (גָּאַל) and *padah* (פָּדָה), with their derivatives. The former, *ga'al*, is used in the legal and economic sense of paying a price for one's kin, to redeem them from slavery (Leviticus 25:25), or to buy back the family property or inheritance (Ruth 4:1–12). God is the redeemer *go'el* (גֹּאֵל) who delivers the people from oppression (Exodus 6:6; Isaiah 43:1, 44:22) and displays mighty power in the face of enemies (Psalms 69:18; 107:2). *Padah* is also used of redeeming by paying a price (Exodus 13:13, 34:20) or setting free from servitude (Deuteronomy 7:8; Jeremiah 15:21). Solidarity is integral to redemption in each of these passages. Kinspersons act for the well being of a relative and in solidarity with the family as a whole, and Yahweh is likened to such redeemers (I Chronicles 17:21; Psalms 31:5, 34:22; Isaiah 43:1, 52:9). Yahweh makes deliberate interventions on behalf of those whose future is unprotected, which might involve the figurative "paying of a price." It is worth noting, however, that this image should not be overplayed. Consider, for example, how there is no hint of a sum of money paid by God to Pharaoh in the defining instance of redemption in the Old Testament, namely, the exodus from Egypt. God's redemption was an act of deliberate intervention which flowed from "steadfast love" or mercy (*hesed* חֶסֶד) but there is no sense that Pharaoh had gained a "right" over the people of God. Thus Moses sang:

> In your steadfast love you led the people whom you redeemed (גָּאָלְתָּ; LXX, ἐλυτρωσω);
> you guided them by your strength to your holy abode.   (Exodus 15:13)

The emphasis is upon God's taking the initiative on behalf of needy persons rather than upon Pharaoh's just claim.

The theme of solidarity as an aspect of redemption persists into the New Testament. Jesus's baptism is an astonishing identification with those called to repent (Matthew 3:1–17; Mark 1:1–11; Luke 3:21–2). Indeed, Jesus's solidarity with sinners (*hamartōloi* ἁμαρτωλοι) (Matthew 9:10, 11:19; Mark 2:16; Luke 5:53, 7:34) is one of the most significant features of his ministry. Assuming with E. P. Sanders that such passages speak of Jesus's association with the most disreputable and fringe members of society and not simply those less than scrupulous in observing purity laws, it is arguable that Jesus stood together with those who offended not only the scribes and Pharisees but the ordinarily pious also.[4] He was a "friend of tax collectors and sinners" (Matthew 11:19), ate and drank with the outcast and excluded (Mark 2:16–17; Luke 5:30), and allowed himself to be touched by those regarded as guilty of repeated and extreme wickedness (Luke 7:37–9). The writer(s) of John's Gospel also offer(s) startling examples of Jesus's solidarity with those in need (John 5:1–18, 7:21–4). The pericope presents his body-language as identifying with a woman caught in adultery (John 7:53–8:11). Jesus is recorded as declaring the wrath of God on a world perishing under the weight of its own sin (John 3:16, 36; 8:24; 16:8–10), and as calling individual persons to a renewed relationship with God (John 3:5–8, 4:23, 5:25, 14:1). Paul speaks of Jesus Christ's solidarity with humankind to the extent that he "died for the ungodly" (Romans 5:6) and became accursed for humanity by accepting on our behalf the judgment of the law and being hanged on a tree (Galatians 3:10–13). He emphasizes Jesus Christ's solidarity with humankind in death. However, the polyphony of New Testament witness reminds us that redemption in Jesus Christ is to be associated not with his death alone but with every moment of his life and ministry; his whole life was born of the necessity of love.

Thus, God's solidarity with humanity in Jesus Christ is an important aspect of the incarnation. But why and how does this solidarity have redemptive significance? At least three answers to this question are given by ancient, Eastern Fathers of the Church: the incarnate Christ's solidarity with humankind has healing, restorative, and persuasive effect. Let's consider each in turn. First, Jesus Christ was a "physician" who, being both human and divine, was capable of freeing human souls from death and corruption, healing them from ungodliness, and restoring to health (Ignatius 1993a:52). His was the "medicine of immortality," the antidote to sin which prevents us from dying and protects against evil (1993a:57).[5] Athanasius wrote:

> He "delivered" to Him [the Son] man, that the Word Himself might be made Flesh, and by taking the Flesh, restore it wholly. For to Him, as to a physician, man "was delivered" to heal the bite of the serpent; as to life, to raise what was dead; as to light, to illumine the darkness; and, because He was Word, to renew the rational nature. (Athanasius 1989c:87)

At creation, all things had been moved and given life by the Word of God. At the incarnation, all things were once more filled by the life-giving presence of the Word, and this "filling" had healing effect because humanity was touched with divinity and, thereby, restored to its vocation: "For He was made man that we might be made God" (Athanasius 1989b:65). Similarly, Gregory of Nazianzen affirms: "what is not assumed cannot be healed and what was united to God is saved" (Gregory of Nazianzen 1954: 215–44, esp. p. 218). This healing was manifest practically and immediately in Jesus's ministry: "He lived a holy life, and healed every kind of sickness and disease among the people" (Ignatius 1993b:64). But it also had ontological effect. The incarnation was not merely a "drop in" visit by God. It constituted a re-creation of humanity because, in Christ, humankind became once more a communicant of divine life. Jesus Christ is the new Adam (Romans 5:15) whose life and ministry has healing and restorative effect for the many.

Secondly, the incarnation had this positive effect because humankind was once more enabled to grow in the knowledge and likeness of God; its original vocation had been restored. Thus Gregory of Nazianzen described the gradual dwelling of the Holy Spirit in the apostles after Pentecost as "making perfect their powers" such that their work might be considered worthy of the majesty of God (Gregory of Nazianzen 1989b:326). John of Damascus spoke of the redeemer making it possible for human nature to attain "perfection," which would be characterized by the following properties: "absence of care and distraction and guile, goodness, wisdom, justice, freedom from all vice . . . communion with Himself" (John of Damascus 1989:75). The healing effected by the incarnation did not have mechanical effect that overrides human freedom, but offers to each person the possibility of becoming more like God and, simultaneously, of becoming more fully human. This is because the essence of humankind is not found in the dust from which we were created (Genesis 3:19b) but in the "image of the invisible God" (II Corinthians 4:4) who is Jesus Christ.

Thirdly, God's solidarity with humankind in the incarnation has redemptive effect in so far as it enables us to learn the things of God. Redemption, argues Irenaeus, is not by violent means but "by means of persuasion": "For in no other way could we have learned the things of God, unless our Master, existing as the Word, had become man . . . redeeming us by His own blood in a manner consonant to reason" (Irenaeus of Lyons 1993:526). Arguably, the persuasive effects of the incarnation would have been necessary even without the fall into sin. According to several early Fathers, the weakness of mortal, human nature – even without the intrusion of death – was sufficient to warrant the incarnation in order that humankind might attain knowledge of God. Hence Athanasius's observation concerning how God knew the weakness of human nature, it being created from nothing, and made provision for their knowledge of himself. This provision included the works of creation, the law, and the prophets, and, pre-eminently, the incarnation: "He did not leave them destitute of the knowledge of Himself, lest they should find not profit in existing at all" (Athanasius 1989b:42). If so, then the redeeming effect of the incarnation was "more than necessary"; it was more than necessary to deal with sin and was an act of abundant love in order that humankind might be drawn toward enjoyment of God. Jesus Christ entered into solidarity with humankind that "through Him [they might] get an idea of the Father, and knowing their Maker, live the happy and truly blessed life" (ibid.).

Redemption as God's Deliverance from Sin and Death

Thus, redemption entails God's solidarity with humankind and this is manifest *par excellence* in the incarnation. But Christian witness is that Jesus Christ not only assumed humanity but also bore the sin of the world and provided deliverance from death. As George Florovsky notes, Jesus Christ bore the sin of the world as an act of will (Florovsky 1976:98). He did not assume it by virtue of solidarity with humankind because the humanity he assumed was pure and innocent; "it behoved the Redeemer to be without sin, and not made liable through sin to death" (John of Damascus 1989:45). Rather, his bearing of sin was a further act of compassion and love, the culmination of his solidarity with humankind, which brought deliverance from the victory of death (Romans 8:2; Galatians 5:1; I Corinthians 15:54–5). Jesus Christ was, writes Paul, "put forward as a sacrifice of atonement by his blood' (Romans 3:23). He took upon himself the curse pronounced against humankind in order that it might be removed from us (Galatians 3:13). How, then, are we to speak of redemption as God's deliverance of humankind from sin and death?

Let's start by noting that biblical witness to the experience of redemption is wide and varied. Redemption is synonymous with deliverance (Exodus 6:6). It comprises a deliberate act to save people from political, economic, physical, and spiritual oppression (Deuteronomy 7:8; Psalms 25:22, 49:7–8). Prophetic texts anticipated the coming of the Lord's anointed as redeemer (Isaiah 59:20, 60:16), whose suffering would transform the lives of the oppressed (Isaiah 61:1). Deliverance is also considered in spiritual and ontological terms. Jesus taught about a whole range of evil brought about by sin, and the need for redemption. He spoke of the fires of hell (Matthew 5:22, 29, 30) and their destruction of both soul and body (Matthew 10:28), and of God's judgment against sin (Matthew 11:22; Luke 11:32, 16:19–31). In the fourth gospel, Jesus is recorded as declaring the wrath of God on a world perishing under the weight of its own sin (John 3:16, 36; 8:24; 16:8–10), and as calling individual persons to a renewed relationship with God (John 3:5–8; 4:23; 5:25; 14:1). Paul's emphasis is upon God's gracious act to rescue humankind from death and the costliness of the incarnation as the means necessary for overcoming death. Sin, says Paul, is failing to give glory and thanks to God (Romans 1:21) and, thereby, falling away from God. It is manifest in an absence of kindness, and in deception, cursing, bitterness, and misery (Romans 3:12). He speaks of redemption as release from debt, or payment of a ransom, as borrowed from a quasi-legal context: "For you were bought with a price" (I Corinthians 6:20, 7:23). Yet, he does not emphasize the notion of debt since it is less a debt than a response of thanksgiving that is owed to God who raised Jesus from the dead.[6] Righteousness is not counted like pay or reward ($\mu\iota\sigma\theta\circ\varsigma$) but as a matter of grace (Romans 4:4).

This diverse biblical witness reminds us that the enormity and mystery of God's work of redemption cannot be enclosed in a single description. The several images never harden into a single or complete explanation, yet they imply a costliness which exceeds human imagining. How, then, are we to understand this costliness? Is a ransom paid to the devil as a matter of justice? Gregory of Nyssa is notorious for having suggested that the ransom of Christ's blood was paid to the devil and not to God the Father, as if the devil had rights. Later writers, notably Anselm, made clear that the devil had no claim which required God to act, not least because neither humankind nor the devil existed outside of God's power. Rather, "each and either of them was a thief, since, one persuading the other, each stole himself from his lord" (Anselm 1909:10). To be fair to Gregory of Nyssa, we should note his conviction that it is ultimately God – and not the devil – upon whom all things depend (Gregory of Nyssa 1989:492–4).[7] This said, it cannot be allowed that either sacrifice or ransom were offered to the devil because that would imply that the devil had just claim upon God, thus denying God's sovereignty. Are we to suppose, therefore, that sacrifice and ransom are offered to God? Anselm suggests as much and answers as follows in response to Boso's question "What is the debt we owe to God?"

> This is the debt which angels and men owe to God: paying which, none sins; and which every one who does not pay it, *does* sin. This is uprightness, or rectitude of will, which con-

stitutes the just or upright in heart, that is, in will; this is the sole and whole honour which we owe to God, and which God requires from us. . . . Whoever renders not unto God this due honour, takes away from God that which is His, and does God dishonour: and *this* is sin.   (Anselm 1909:24)

Sin was an outrage to God and an affront to God's honor. Only Christ could satisfy the outrage of this sin and satisfy God's honor. Christ, who is both human and divine, paid the price of his life to meet this cost and to set humans free from slavery to sin. The radically different categories of culture within which this vocabulary of "honor" was used by Anselm, and within which it is heard today, give rise to problems of interpretation. Indeed, one danger is that such an understanding of redemption implies in a present-day context that God required payment in order to maintain the divine status. Anselm makes plain that God could not simply overlook sin because that would not accord with his dignity. Yet, the God who does anything to avoid dishonor seems to our eyes, perhaps, to be more concerned about maintaining the divine integrity than mending the broken relationship with humankind. To be fair to Anselm, we should recognize that his determining questions concern the moral order of the universe and how to bear appropriate witness to all the divine attributes. Also, he knew that humankind is lost if God is dishonored.[8] How, then, are we to avoid such difficulties yet understand the costliness of redemption?

Some clues are found when we locate our questions within a theological anthropology which emphasizes the ontological end or *telos* of humankind. God, we have seen, created humankind for union and communion with himself and to exist "in the image of his own eternity" (Wisdom of Solomon 1:13, 23). Yet, Adam and Eve – representatives of all humanity – turned away from God, the author of their life, and became tragic figures destined to die and liable to corruption.[9] Sin, says Athanasius, is a rejection of the good and the setting up of false gods instead:

For having departed from the consideration of the one and the true, namely God, and from desires of Him, they had thenceforward embarked in diverse lusts . . . whence the soul became subject to cowardice and alarms. . . . she learned to commit murder and wrong. (Athanasius 1989a:5)

Upon turning away from God the human soul becomes debased and fearful. The image of God in humankind becomes distorted and this results in a condition characterized by death and the "inhumanity" of one person to another. The result of sin is death because humankind has turned its back on life. Adam and Eve became mortal and, whilst we do not inherit the guilt of their personal sin, we inherit their death as mortals born from mortals. There is no quasi-genetic transmission of guilt: "all have sinned and fall short of the glory of God" (Romans 3:23). Sin is the peculiar privilege of each person alone, but we have received mortality from our ancestor's sin and are heirs to the corruption of death. We are also born into societies that are influenced by sin. Death (of the body, soul, hope, relationships, etc.) was not inflicted upon humankind by God but resulted from humankind's turning its back on God's life-giving grace. Death resulted in, and is synonymous with, separation from God. It was allowed by God within divine providence as a matter of "consequent will" and as a concession to free will (John of Damascus of 1963: IX, p. 42). It had no origin in God but was allowed as a way of halting the progression of sin and of ensuring that evil would not be victorious: "He condemned us to the corruption of death in order that that which is evil should not be immortal" (John of Damascus 1963:IX, p. 78).

Thus, according to Christian tradition, God allowed death to persist as part of the divine, providential care over created things but was not content with turning evil into a benefit, and made appropriate provision for its defeat. God refused to disregard the fragility of the human condition in the grip of death but reached out in love toward it, in order to enable humankind afresh to fulfill its vocation. Redemption is a negative moment in the divine economy in the sense that Jesus Christ became accursed with death to deliver humankind from sin and its consequences. Yet, its essential meaning is positive and aimed at the elevation of humankind to enjoy union and communion with God. Lowering himself to our level, God revealed in Christ "the mighty ocean of his love to man [sic]" and offered life to those who had spurned it. This is the free gift of grace of which Paul speaks (Romans 3:24). It surpasses the law because the law only exposes sin: "that sin might be shown to be sin" (Romans 5:13). Indeed, this love surpasses the law because it can bring persons right into heaven (John Chrysostom 1989b:489). As Joshua led the Israelites right into the promised land, writes John Chrysostom, so Jesus Christ has the power to bring people into a new state of being. He has this power only because he unites in himself the extremes of humanity and divinity: "[i]t is that the Lord of Glory is said to have been crucified, although His divine nature never endured the Cross" (John of Damascus 1989:48). Redemption in Christ is possible, argues Irenaeus of Lyons, because Christ "summed up in himself the ancient formation of Adam." By so doing he rendered the human body a participator of the resurrection and of immortality, thus becoming for humankind a Savior of the lost and a Light to those dwelling in darkness (Irenaeus of Lyons 1993:529–30). As mediator between God and humanity, Jesus Christ bore the sin and death of the world and became its remedy.

Redemption, therefore, is the efficacy of God's love available without limit to all in need. The costliness of this remedy was something that only God could bear. As John Cassian stated: "it does not lie in the power of a man to redeem his [God's] people from the captivity of sin" (John Cassian 1989:580). Humans could not pay because they are by nature mortal and corruptible; they are created by God from nothing and are not divine. They could not regain or buy back the incorruption for which they were created. Only God could go in search of those who had turned away from communion with God and identify with them. Therefore, God went "into the far country" to seek out those who were dying and offer them life again (Barth 1956:157–210). To cite Gregory of Nazianzen, "He needed flesh for the sake of flesh which had incurred condemnation, and soul for the sake of our soul" (Gregory of Nazianzen 1989c:441). Only by being perfect in divinity and humanity could he unite to himself the sin of humankind and offer to humankind the forgiving grace of God. His tears and sweat and sufferings would have had little redemptive significance, writes Athanasius, without his being both human and divine. Only God from God, Wisdom from the Wise, Being from Being, could pass on to humanity the things of God and serve as mediator between the two.[10] In his humanity, he accepted our death and endured it as a choice of free love. In his divinity, he brought to nothing the power of death and offered humankind to share in his victory (I Corinthians 15:54, 55, 57; I John 5:4). Redemption was effected by *kenosis*: "Christ . . . emptied Himself to take the form of a slave . . . that he might by His own sufferings destroy sin, and by death slay death" (Gregory of Nazianzen 1989a:246).

Redemption as Transformation from Death to Life

Thus, deliverance from death and the power of sin was required as "the negative facet" in the divine plan (Isaiah 43:14–17; Hebrews 9:15; I John 5:4–5).[11] Redemption as deliverance was not a wiping away of sin in the sense that it can be swept aside as insignificant. Nor was it the satisfaction of debt in an overly-literal sense. Jesus Christ's journey into "the far country" in search of those who had chosen death rather than life was not completed by the payment of debt incurred by sin against God. The language of payment can only begin to express the love beyond limit that rendered human persons capable once more of attaining a share in God's own reign and glory (II Corinthians 3:18; I Thessalonians 2:12; I Peter 5:1). Jesus Christ's life and death made possible for humanity: restoration of the life lost through sin; sanctification of the body (Romans 12:1); acquiring of the mind of Christ (I Corinthians 2:16); and the fulfilling of God-given potential to attain maturity in the faith, which is to have the stature of Christ (Ephesians 4:13). But redemption is not yet complete. That which has been performed in his living and dying will be complete when he returns in glory (Romans 1:16; 8:23; 13:11). Until that time, the efficacy of redemption entails a movement *from* imperfection to perfection and *for* fulness of life and participation in the life divine. With this in mind, let us consider three aspects of redemption as transformation from death to life: personal, social, and cosmic.

First, let us consider the personal hope of transformation from death to life, imperfection to perfection. According to some non-Christian theorists, such a hope of transformation is a psychological illusion which enables the expression of discontent at personal insufficiency. The hope of perfection, writes Julia Kristeva, is an illusory blending of a person's "superego" with their own "ideal ego" (Kristeva 1989a:185). Believers derive sadomasochistic pleasure from their suffering awareness of sin and sink into melancholy, like Job who sank into his ashpit, before the imagined face of the "Thing" or "imagined sun" which is their God (Kristeva 1989a:185, also pp. 15, 176). Dispense with God, the "permanent, tyrannical superego," and one will dispense with the dejection and sadness that results from a supposed call to perfection. Humankind, claimed Nietzsche, can bear its own burden of imperfection; it is only because humankind looks into the brilliant mirror "God" that their own nature seems so dismal (Nietzsche 1986:70–1). Nietzsche and Kristeva assert that the very hope of transformation from imperfection to perfection is harmful to the human condition because it results in depression and dependence. To aspire to God-likeness is a denial of one's potential. By contrast, Christian teaching is that to aspire to God-likeness is true fulfillment. Jesus Christ manifested true humanity and revealed deification to be its true norm; to become like God (*theosis*) is to achieve one's potential in Christ (I Corinthians 15:50–7;

Ephesians 4:13; Colossians 2:10; II Peter 1:4). What, then, is the relationship between redemption and perfection? Is the hope of perfection something from which one should seek release?

According to Christian teaching the relationship between redemption and perfection is intimate and concerns the operation of the Holy Spirit in a person's life. Jesus urged his hearers: "Be perfect, therefore, as your heavenly Father is perfect" (Matthew 5:48). Athanasius writes: "For He has become Man, that He might deify us in Himself . . . and that we may become henceforth a holy race, and 'partakers of the Divine Nature'" (Athanasius 1989e:575). Jesus Christ "put on the creature" that he might both recover and consecrate it, consecration being the outcome and instantiation of the divine energies in a person's life. As Clement of Alexandria says of this transformation: "to drink the blood of Jesus, is to become partaker of the Lord's immortality; the Spirit being the energetic principle of the Word, as blood is of flesh" (Clement of Alexandria 1993:242). God's grace does not force persons but invites cooperation (*synergy*) with God as the Holy Spirit makes Jesus Christ's redemption real in the life of the believer (Romans 7:6, 8:14; I Corinthians 2:11; Galatians 5:5; Ephesians 2:18). The relationship between redemption and perfection is dynamic and ongoing as the Holy Spirit enables one's mode-of-being or life-orientation to be turned toward God. Yet, says Kristeva, the relationship between redemption and perfection leads to dejection, citing Job's cry of despair: " 'What is man that you (God) should make so much of him?' . . . 'Turn your eyes away, leave me a little joy'" (Job 7:17; Kristeva 1989a:185). To Job, hope for transformation seems too much to bear. He does not want to be redeemed because he loathes his life and has no desire to live forever (Job 7:16). He is close to committing "suicide of the soul" and has lost all relish for life.[12]

For Kristeva, the believer will always be disappointed by their defects and conscious of the judgment of God; there is no escape from the dialectic of judgment and forgiveness. The hope of perfection drives one to despair – as, indeed, might the physicalist hope for the ideal body; materialist hope for an impressive job or house; or moralist hope for sanctity in the eyes of others or oneself. Yet, writes John:

> There is no fear in love, but perfect love casts out fear; for fear has to do with punishment, and whoever fears has not reached perfection in love. We love because he first loved us.
> (I John 4:18–19)

The perfection to which he bears witness is a perfection of love which takes the believer beyond judgment and into a new boldness about life and its possibilities. Why is this? Because, writes John, God lives in us; "we have known and believe the love that God has for us" (I John 4:16). Of course, the analyst may have a kind of love for the analysand, but this love is paid for its time. God's love is free; it is a different kind of giving. As distinct from Kristeva's representation, God's is a love that desires transformation far more than we are capable of desiring it ourselves. Thus, God's love made up for Job's lack of desire for life and brought him back from despair. As John Chrysostom writes:

> I said you are gods and all of you are the sons and daughters of the Most High. And this is said because you have been born of God. How and in what manner? Through the

washing of regeneration and renewal in the Holy Spirit. (John Chrysostom 1862:59, 93B)

Redemption does not only release from sin but awakens consciousness of the availabil-ity of love which allows persons to be reborn.[13] A gift is not fully given until it has been received. Thankfully, writes Maximus the Confessor, God gives to those who pray not as they ask but as they are able to receive (Maximus the Confessor 1985b:113).

Secondly, let us consider redemption as transformation from death to life in social terms. What does "redemption" look like in social terms? What might it mean for the church to live redemptively in the hope of God's coming reign? These questions may be approached variously. For our purposes, let us concentrate on biblical examples of when and why redemption exceeds earthly conceptions of justice, and ask why and how the church is called to embody a redemptive polity. To address the former question, we need a working definition of justice. Following Agnes Heller, let us suppose that principles of justice can be discussed in two ways: either as constitutive or as regulative ideas, i.e., either as the substance of justice (such as norms and rules which apply to every member of a social grouping), or as the criteria of justice (such as values upon which justice is administered for the good of the state, fraternity, or efficiency) (Heller 1987:25). Consider the difference between the following maxims of justice that might be either constitutive or regulative: "to each the same thing"; "to each according to their need." The former disallows and the latter requires the norm of proportionality. They are irreconcilable and illustrate the difficulty in arriving at a working definition of justice; no norm or rule can cope with the multiplicities of individual and social needs: "Since individual and social needs almost never coincide, and no norm or rule applies to the former, justice stops short of the *singularity* of the person. Individual structures of needs are the limits of *justice*" (Heller 1987:32). Moreover, writes Heller, a sick person requires more than the practice of justice; no "just" society provides the sick with good friends (Heller 1987:33).

The subject requires more consideration than is possible here. Yet we can ask: Does God's redemption exceed the limits of justice as humanly conceived? Was the landowner who hired laborers at different hours in the day, and paid them the same wage, just? (See Matthew 20:1–16.) Was Boaz just when – within the social constraints of the day – he married Ruth rather than merely redeeming the inheritance, in order that her dead husband's name was maintained with the land (Ruth 4:9–10)? Both instances raise issues concerning the relationship between equality of outcome and the ethics of the means whereby an outcome is attained. The landowner exercised correc-tive justice (which Heller terms equity) to modify social norms and rules, such that the singularity of the workers was taken into account in the final outcome; provision was made for the needs of laborers left behind. Boaz perceived needs which required satis-faction and to which the social conventions of redemption did not apply, such as the need for respect for a dead man's name. His actions were governed by an *ethos* which exceeded the prescription of norms. Similarly, the prophet Isaiah implies that God's redemption exceeds human notions of justice when he describes Jacob and Israel as deeply unworthy:

> Do not fear, you worm Jacob, you insect Israel!
> I will help you, says the Lord;
> Your Redeemer is the Holy One of Israel
> (Isaiah 41:14)

This witness to the holiness and covenantal-faithfulness of Yahweh is located between references to Yahweh's judgment and to his justice (Isaiah 41:1–2, 21–4; 42:4). The God who redeems is the God who judges with all justice, but also the God who hears the prayers of the people: "I the Lord will answer them, I the God of Israel will not forsake them" (Isaiah 41:17b). Yahweh's redemption exceeds the absolutes of justice because divine justice includes mercy. God's redemption reaches its limits only in lack of repentance and refusal to show mercy to others (Matthew 6:15, 18:33).

Thus, it would be wrong to imply that there is a bifurcation between justice and redemption because the divine economy includes both (I John 1:9; Revelations 15:3). However, where justice is strict and exact, giving each person their due, redemption goes beyond justice in its benevolence, kindness, and generosity.[14] Thus, when the prophets cry out against injustice, they plead the cause of the needy:

> learn to do good;
> seek justice,
> rescue the oppressed,
> defend the orphan,
> plead for the widow
> (Isaiah 1:17)

The logic of justice, writes A. J. Heschel, may be impersonal and dehumanizing but the concern for justice which is tempered with compassion is an act of love. Thus Amos's plea that the people may "hate evil and love good, and establish justice in the gate" is qualified by the command that they do not "buy the poor for silver" or the "guilty for a pair of sandals" (Amos 8:6). Arguably, it is difficult for the church today to heed the words of the prophets because global, free-market systems mask the real human costs of profit and consumerist desire to accumulate. The "who pays?" question – at least as it refers to working conditions, inferior health and education facilities, and pollution – is rarely heard because those affected do not have buying-power in the market. Yet, the prophetic idea of redemption is never impersonal or atemporal. Whereas justice may be atemporal, the witness of the prophets is that redemption becomes temporalized wherever a neighbor is in need. The challenge to the church today perhaps is little different from that of the prophets to Israel: be a contrast polity; yours is a covenant with life not death (Isaiah 28:18; Hebrews 9:15); fight oppression and defend the helpless. The redemption of personal, singular needs accords with God's mercy; because of this it is beyond justice.[15]

Thirdly, let us consider redemption as transformation from life to death in cosmic terms. By faith the Christian confesses that God created the cosmos. But what might it mean to pray for the redemption of the cosmos? There is, of course, strong witness in Christian tradition that God's witness will include all creation:

The creation, then . . . now groans and travails, waiting itself also for our redemption from the corruption of the body, that, when we have risen and shaken off the mortality of the flesh . . . it also shall be freed from corruption and be subject no longer to vanity, but to righteousness. Isaiah says, too, "For as the new heaven and the new earth which I make, remaineth before me, saith the Lord, so shall your seed and your name be;" . . . For in reality God did not establish the universe in vain, or to no purpose but destruction . . . but to exist, and be inhabited, and continue.   (Methodius 1993:366)

God's redemptive purposes extend as far as creation itself. Athanasius's portrayal of the incarnation includes a vision of the whole of creation filled with the divine presence of the Word (Athanasius 1989a:4). For this reason, it is not possible theologically to participate in Christ's redemption and disparage or remain indifferent to material reality. Some of the great biblical visions of redemption include reference to the created order (Isaiah 32:15–18, 52:7–10; Ezekiel 36:33–8; Amos 9:13–15). The eucharist is a celebration of the unity of all creation and is "a *cosmic liturgy*" in so far as it sums up the life of the world and offers it to God.[16] Yet, it is not easy to imagine what redemption might mean for the whole created order. Jürgen Moltmann urges his readers to ponder these matters with reference to the sabbath laws (e.g. Exodus 23:10–11; Leviticus 25:1–7) because, in allowing fields to lie fallow, the people learn to live in harmony with the land and to celebrate its blessing (Moltmann 1985, ch. XI). To those who live in cities and have no responsibility for fields, he says: "The ecological day of rest should be a day without pollution of the environment – a day when we leave our cars at home, so that nature too can celebrate its sabbath" (1985:296). To hope for the redemption of the cosmos, to pray that God's reign will come *on earth*, might appear to be to hope against hope. It is certainly a hope that we hold in fear and trembling, hearing the words "work out your own salvation" (Philippians 2:12b) with trepidation. We cannot, of course, earn the redemption of the cosmos by our efforts. Rather, the hope is that we might allow the work of God to be active in creation. This is not the time to presume on God's mercy. It may, however, be a time to remember that God has called us "friends" (John 15:15) and invited us to work together (Mark 16:20, *sunergeō*) in anticipation of the coming reign of God.

Conclusion

Thus, redemption is God's work of love to restore and renew all things. It is God's means of abolishing sin and delivering humankind and all creation from the grip of death in its various manifestations. Born of the necessity of love and burning compassion for the oppressed, the Word of God "emptied himself, taking the form of a slave" (Philippians 2:7) and was born in human form. Instead of giving up on humankind, Jesus Christ became incarnate to accomplish the mystery of redemption by his life, death, and resurrection. Death, according to Christian tradition, is being in sin. Redemption is deliverance from sin (John Chrysostom 1989a:228). Jesus Christ rose in the flesh, and we shall rise after his example (Tertullian 1993:581–2). His resurrection gives hope for what John Chrysostom terms "the very sum of all good things," and no aspect of human life and experience is excluded from this hope (John Chrysostom 1989a:226). The mystery of redemption allows all creation to be reborn.

Notes

1   On the themes of solidarity, deliverance, and transformation, see Brueggemann (1997:173–6).
2   In the Old Testament, that which is paid in redemption is referred to as ransom *kopher* (כֹּפֶר) and is rendered by the Latin Vulgate (Psalms 48:9) as *redemptio*. In the New Testament, these ideas are expressed by *agorazō* (ἀγοραζω) meaning to buy or to purchase (Revelations 5:9), and its compound *exagorazō* (ἐξαγοραζω), which is used by Paul of Christ's having acted to free us from the cruse of the law (Galatians 3:13, 4:5) and of redeeming or improving the time (Ephesians 5:16). The verb *lutroo* meaning to release with a price, and its cognates *lutron* (λυτρον) meaning ransom (Mark 10:45) and *apolutrosis* (ἀπολυτρωσις) – which is the special Pauline word for redemption (Romans 3:24, 8:23; I Corinthians 1:30; and also found in Ephesians 1:7, 14; Colossians 1:14; Hebrews 9:15) – convey the sense of something being given in exchange for a life.
3   Mary Grey rethinks redemption in terms of mutuality and the "making of right relation," in *Redeeming the Dream* (1989), *passim*.
4   E. P. Sanders traces the meaning of *'amme ha-arets* in literature from Ben Sira to the close of the Mishnah and maintains they were those who flagrantly and persistently disobeyed the law (1985:174–211, esp. 208–9).
5   See also Irenaeus, "Against Heresies" (1993:539); Tatian, "Address to the Greeks" (1993:73); Justin Martyr, "The First Apology" (1993:179) for citation of Isaiah 53:1–8.
6   This point is made by C. K. Barrett (1957/62:26, 162).
7   Moreover, Gregory speaks of Christ's death as a necessary consequence of his birth: "death is rendered necessary by the birth, and that He who had determined once for all to share the nature of man must pass through all the peculiar conditions of that nature." See also *The Great Catechism* (Gregory of Nyssa 1989:499).
8   I am indebted for this phrase to Professor Stuart Hall, University of St. Andrews.
9   Athanasius writes in a citation from Wisdom 6:18, "God made man for incorruption, and as an image of His own eternity." In "Incarnation of the Word," §§4–5 (1989b:38).
10 For as he takes our infirmities, not being infirm, and hungers not hungering, but sends up what is ours that it may be abolished, so the gifts which come from God instead of our infirmities, doth he too Himself receive, that man, being united to Him, may be able to partake them." Athanasius (1989d:435).
11 This phrase is used by Vladimir Lossky, *Orthodox Theology: An Introduction* (1978:111).
12 I am indebted for this phrase to Jürgen Moltmann in a seminar at St. Mary's College, University of St. Andrews, February 22, 2000.
13 This wording is taken from *Bodily Resurrection* by the Sisters of the Orthodox Monastery of the Transfiguration (California, CA: Conciliar Press, 1997), p. 13.
14 In this paragraph, I paraphrase A. J. Heschel in Heller (1987:55).
15 Paraphrasing Heller (1987:33).
16 This phrase is used by Christos Yannaras, *The Freedom of Morality* (1996:86).

References

Anselm. 1909. *Cur Deus Homo*, bk. I, ch. VII. Edinburgh: John Grant.

Athanasius. 1989a. "Against the Heathen," in *The Nicene and Post-Nicene Fathers*, 2nd series, vol. IV. Edinburgh: T. & T. Clark.

Athanasius. 1989b. "On the Incarnation of the Word," §8, in *The Nicene and Post-Nicene Fathers*, 2nd series, vol. IV. Edinburgh: T. & T. Clark.

Athanasius. 1989c. "On Luke X:22 (Matt. XI:27)," in *The Nicene and Post-Nicene Fathers*, 2nd series, vol. IV. Edinburgh: T. & T. Clark.

Athanasius. 1989d. "Four Discourses against the Arians," Discourse IV, in *The Nicene and Post-Nicene Fathers*, 2nd series, vol. IV. Edinburgh: T. & T. Clark.

Athanasius. 1989e. "To Adelphius" (Letter LX), in *The Nicene and Post-Nicene Fathers*, 2nd series, vol. IV. Edinburgh: T. & T. Clark.

Barrett, C. K. 1957/62. *A Commentary on the Epistle to the Romans*. London: A. & C. Black.

Barth, K. 1956. "The Way of the Son of God into the Far Country," §59, I, in *Church Dogmatics*, IV/1. Edinburgh: T. & T. Clark.

Barth, K. 1961. *Church Dogmatics*, IV/3, 1 §69. Edinburgh: T. & T. Clark.

Brueggemann, W. 1997. *Theology of the Old Testament*. Minneapolis, MN: Fortress Press.

Clement of Alexandria. 1993. "The Instructor," bk. 2, ch. 2, in *The Ante-Nicene Fathers*, vol. II, Edinburgh: T. & T. Clark.

Florovsky, G. 1976. *Creation and Redemption*. Belmont, MA: Nordland.

Freud, S. 1995. "The Future of an Illusion," in *The Freud Reader*, ed. P. Gay. London: Vintage.

Gregory of Nazianzen. 1954. "To Cledonius against Apollinarius" (Ep. 101), in *The Christology of the Later Fathers*, Library of Christian Classics III. London: SCM Press.

Gregory of Nazianzen. 1989a. "On His Father's Silence," in *The Nicene and Post-Nicene Fathers*, 2nd series, vol. VII. Edinburgh: T. & T. Clark.

Gregory of Nazianzen. 1989b. "On the Holy Spirit," chs. XXVI–XXVII, in *The Nicene and Post-Nicene Fathers*, 2nd series, vol. VII. Edinburgh: T. & T. Clark.

Gregory of Nazianzen. 1989c. "To Cledonius the Priest Against Apollinarius" (Letter CI), In *The Nicene and Post-Nicene Fathers*, 2nd series, vol. VII. Edinburgh: T. & T. Clark.

Gregory of Nyssa. 1989. "The Great Catechism," chs. XXII–XXIV, in *The Nicene and Post-Nicene Fathers*, 2nd, series, vol. V. Edinburgh: T. & T. Clark.

Grey, M. 1989. *Redeeming the Dream: Feminism, Redemption and Christian Tradition*. London: SPCK.

Heller, A. 1987. *Beyond Justice*. Oxford: Basil Blackwell.

Ignatius. 1993a. "Epistle to the Ephesians," ch. VII, in *The Ante-Nicene Fathers*. Edinburgh: T. & T. Clark.

Ignatius. 1993b. "Epistle to the Magnesians," in *The Ante-Nicene Fathers*. Edinburgh: T. & T. Clark.

Irenaeus of Lyons. 1993. "Against the Heresies," in *The Ante-Nicene Fathers*, vol. I. Edinburgh: T. & T. Clark.

John Cassian. 1989. "The Seven Books of John Cassian on the Incarnation of the Lord, Against Nestorius," bk. IV, ch. 12, in *The Nicene and Post-Nicene Fathers*, 2nd series, vol. XI. Edinburgh: T. & T. Clark.

John Chrysostom. 1862. "Homily 14: On John's Gospel," in *Patrologiae Graecae*. Paris: J. P. Migne.

John Chrysostom. 1989a. "Homilies on First Corinthians," Homily XXXVIII, in *The Nicene and Post-Nicene Fathers*, 1st series, vol. XII. Edinburgh: T. & T. Clark.

John Chrysostom. 1989b. "Homilies on Hebrews," Homily XXVII, §6, in *The Nicene and Post-Nicene Fathers*, 1st series, vol. XIV. Edinburgh: T. & T. Clark.

John of Damascus. 1963. "Exposition of the Orthodox Faith," in *The Nicene and Post-Nicene Fathers*, 2nd series, vol. IX. Edinburgh: T. & T. Clark.

Justin Martyr. 1993. "The First Apology," in *The Ante-Nicene Fathers*, vol. I. Edinburgh: T. & T. Clark.

Kristeva, J. 1989a. *Black Sun: Depression and Melancholia*, trans. L. S. Roudiez. New York: Columbia University Press.

Kristeva, J. 1989b. "Holbein's Dead Christ," in *Black Sun: Depression and Melancholia*, trans. L. S. Roudiez. New York: Columbia University Press.

Lossky, V. 1978. *Orthodox Theology: An Introduction*. Crestwood, NY: St. Vladimir's Seminary Press.

McFague, S. 1987. *Models of God: Theology for an Ecological, Nuclear Age*. London: SCM Press.

Maximus the Confessor. 1985a. *Maximus the Confessor: Selected Writings*, trans. G. C. Berthold. London: SPCK.

Maximus the Confessor. 1985b. "Commentary on the Our Father," in *Maximus the Confessor: Selected Writings*, trans. G. C. Berthold. London: SPCK.

Methodius. 1993. "From the Discourse on the Resurrection," part I, §8, in *The Ante-Nicene Fathers*, vol. VI. Edinburgh: T. &. T. Clark.

Moltmann, J. 1985. *God in Creation*. London: SCM Press.

Nietzsche, F. 1986. *Human, all too Human: A Book for Free Spirits*. Cambridge: Cambridge University Press.

Sanders, E. P. 1985. *Jesus and Judaism*. London: SCM Press.

Tatian. 1993. "Address to the Greeks," ch. XVIII, in *The Ante-Nicene Fathers*, vol. II. Edinburgh: T. &. T. Clark.

Tertullian. 1993. "On the Resurrection of the Flesh," ch. XLVIII, in *The Ante-Nicene Fathers*, vol. III. Edinburgh: T. &. T. Clark.

Yannaras, C. 1996. *The Freedom of Morality*. Crestwood, NY: St. Vladimir's Seminary Press.

CHAPTER 15
Eschatology

Andrew Chester

Earliest Christianity is overwhelmingly eschatological from its very inception. This is immediately obvious from the Synoptic Gospels' account of Jesus and his message. Diverse material such as the parables, proclamation of the kingdom, miracles, Lord's Prayer and Last Supper all show this strong eschatological dimension. Mark 13 (and the parallels in Matthew 24 and Luke 21) represents a long, sustained eschatological discourse, dealing with the tribulation and suffering of the end times, the shortening of days and the coming of the Son of Man in glory. Especially striking is Mark 13:30, "this generation will not pass away until all these things take place." Outside Mark 13 we find, for example, Mark 9:1, "there are some of you standing here who will not taste of death until you see the kingdom come with power." These and other texts (e.g. Matthew 10:23; Luke 12:39–40, 22:18) point to the coming of the kingdom and the return of Jesus in glory all in the very near future. It was precisely this point that Johannes Weiss and Albert Schweitzer famously focused on, a century or so ago, and in so doing made eschatology a force that had to be reckoned with in Christian theology as a whole. In insisting on the "consistent" or "thoroughgoing" eschatology (in Schweitzer's phrase) of the gospels, they portrayed Jesus as belonging fully within the climate of Jewish apocalyptic expectation of the imminent end. Despite weaknesses in their position, a major strength is that it refuses to explain away these difficult sayings.

This urgent, imminent expectation is not confined to Jesus or the gospels; it is prominent in most of the rest of the New Testament as well. So Paul, for example, speaks of the "day of the Lord coming like a thief in the night" (I Thessalonians 5:8) and of "us, on whom the end of the ages has come" (I Corinthians 10:11). The same emphasis comes in many other passages in Paul and a wide variety of other New Testament writings. Thus, for example, I Peter 4:7, "the end of all things is at hand"; James 5:8, "the coming of the Lord is at hand"; Hebrews 9:26, "he has appeared at the end of the age"; I John 2:18, "children, it is the last hour." The obvious exceptions to this rule are John's Gospel and Acts, although even here there are indications of a similar underlying tradition.

Just as Jesus's message makes sense in a context of Jewish eschatological expectation, so the sharply imminent emphasis of most of the rest of the New Testament is intelligible in the light of this main theme in the gospels, and would indeed be difficult to make sense of otherwise. Throughout the New Testament, however, the final events are not only about to happen; they are already set in motion. Jesus sees the kingdom as already beginning to arrive in what God is doing through his activity, above all his healing and exorcising ministry (e.g. Matthew 12:28; Luke 11:20). The messianic or final age is inaugurated by Jesus, and it is experienced proleptically and in part by the early Christian communities. So, for example, the Spirit is for Paul the pledge of the final age in all its fullness, but again the fulfillment and consummation are still awaited. The tension between present and future, the "now" and the "not yet," pervades almost the whole New Testament.

This represents a necessary qualification of the position of Weiss and Schweitzer on the gospels. That is, the expectation does not belong wholly to the future; the fulfillment of final hope has already begun. Nevertheless, it is important to note that the expectation is still imminent. Too often in scholarly discussion, the "not yet" element stretches into a distant or unspecified future, or an effectively timeless realm. It is instructive to compare modern interpretations of Mark 9:1: "the kingdom come with power" has been understood variously as, for example, the Transfiguration, the Outpouring of the Spirit at Pentecost (as in Acts 2), and the Resurrection. All of these, however, appear to reflect ways of dealing with the acute problem posed by this verse that are already to be found within the New Testament itself. Thus the Transfiguration probably reflects Mark's interpretation, Pentecost that of Luke and Acts, and the Resurrection that of, for example, Matthew (although it is quite possible that in the New Testament more widely, Jesus's prediction of the kingdom is understood as being at least partially fulfilled in his death and resurrection, especially since his prediction of these in Mark 13 is closely linked with the "toils and tribulations" of the final age). Notably, in Luke and Acts the kingdom is effectively shifted from the stage and interpreted in terms of the coming age of the Church and the Spirit. This "age of the Spirit" (or "Church") can then easily be extended timelessly (as comparably can John's distinctive portrayal), so the kingdom barely appears at all, and the presence of Jesus is replaced by that of the Spirit as the focal point for the new relationship that God has brought about. This effectively is what happens in many treatments of the kingdom in New Testament scholarship which use the "now–not yet" schema. There is a related danger with the salvation–historical scheme proposed by Cullmann. He argues strongly for a "now-and-not-yet" model for the kingdom, and for New Testament eschatology more generally, and certainly allows in principle for the coming realization to be set in the near future. Nevertheless, both for Cullmann and especially for those influenced by him, the major emphasis in fact falls on the *past*, completed act of salvation. In both cases, the cutting edge of the imminent eschatological dimension too easily slips from view, and the provocative challenge of the Weiss–Schweitzer position remains unanswered.

It has to be stressed yet again, therefore, that the Synoptic Gospels portray Jesus as looking for the final fulfillment of the kingdom, and his own coming in glory, in the very near future. Hence it is that earliest Christianity can properly be characterized as a millenarian or messianic movement, in terms of anthropological categorization. This does *not*, however (despite Weiss and Schweitzer, and common misconceptions), necessarily entail a sense of an impending cosmic catastrophe. One the contrary, the main emphasis in the gospels is on a positive and powerful vision of a kingdom opened up to the outcasts of society, a world restored, and lives and people transformed. It is a vision also of final victory over the forces of evil.

The kingdom as such features very little in the rest of the New Testament. There are, however, strong echoes of its main themes in Revelation, with its radical rejection of the present reign of evil, which it sees as doomed to destruction, and the final victory of the Lamb; and above all in its urgent expectation of the transformation and renewal of the world, and the climax of the whole work in the vision of the new heaven, new earth, and new Jerusalem. All this represents, clearly, a transformation of what exists at present, but is also in continuity with it. There are at least some glimpses of this vision elsewhere in the New Testament, as for example II Peter 3:13, "we have his promise of new heavens and new earth, where righteousness dwells." Paul in Romans 8:18ff. presents a sublime vision of creation set free from bondage and brought into the glorious, final, liberated state God intends for it, although both here and elsewhere Paul may have a heavenly rather than earthly world in view.

In I Corinthians 15:24–8, Paul portrays Jesus (in terms of a standard Jewish eschatological model) as finally, at the climax of the eschatological events, handing over the (messianic) kingdom to God. This depiction of the nature of the final events is part of a long, sustained treatment in I Corinthians 15 of eschatological issues, above all, resurrection. It is often claimed that Paul presents a contrast between the resurrection of the body and the immortality of the soul, but this is a false dichotomy. Paul has no concept at all of the soul *apart* from the body, and he has a quite striking emphasis on the resurrection of the physical *body*, that is, the whole person. Certainly Paul speaks of a transformation taking place, and the resurrection body taking on quite different characteristics: it will be imperishable, glorious and spiritual, and will assume immortality. Nevertheless, Paul insists on genuine continuity between the present body and that which is taken on at the resurrection. It has also been suggested that I Corinthians 15 (as also I Thessalonians 4), in clearly making the resurrection of the individual part of the general resurrection that takes place at the Parousia, implies a doctrine of the intermediate state. Elsewhere in Paul, however, it is implied that the believer goes to the presence of Christ immediately at death. The questions raised by I Corinthians 15 (and related Pauline passages) assume great importance in subsequent developments in the eschatological tradition, but they in fact receive very little treatment either in Paul or elsewhere in the New Testament. As we have see, the theme that dominates the New Testament is that the final fulfillment of all that God has promised belongs to the very near future.

The eschatological emphasis of earliest Christianity represents a particular development of strong Jewish tradition, where from an early stage a number of important themes are evident. The most prominent is that of *judgment* (e.g. Amos, Isaiah, Ezekiel, Zechariah, Zephaniah, Joel), with its focus both on the coming "Day of the Lord" but also more generally. It cannot simply be assumed that all this is "eschatological" in our sense, even where phrases such as "in the last days" are used, but at the very least there is a threat of "finality" in the sense of the complete destruction of the nation or end of the covenant relationship. There is also a corresponding, although initially less developed, theme of *deliverance* (from the threat of foreign oppression or exile, or from divine wrath and punishment). This positive sense was presumably represented by the popular understanding of the "Day of the Lord," and is certainly substantially evident in the prophetic tradition (e.g. Isaiah, Micah, Jeremiah, and Ezekiel). The themes of the Day of the Lord, judgment, and deliverance are also prominent in post-biblical texts such as I Enoch, Psalms of Solomon, IV Ezra, II Baruch, I QM and I QS. In a number of places we find quite remarkable and powerful *visions of a new age* that God will bring about: thus, for example, the bringing of all nations together in an age of perfect peace (Isaiah 2; Micah 4); God's kingdom established as an age of perfect justice and peace (Isaiah 9; cf. Isaiah 11 and II Baruch 29); liberation for the deprived and oppressed (Isaiah 61); a new heaven, new earth, and new Jerusalem, full of peace and plenty (Isaiah 65–6); a new covenant and true knowledge of God (Jeremiah 31); and a covenant of peace and prosperity (Ezekiel 34 and 37). These visions are spread over a very long period, and are by no means homogeneous; but they are all very much rooted in present reality, however much they represent a transformation of this, or a Utopian resolution of inherent problems.

The concept of individual resurrection or life after death appears only late on, although from an early stage there is clear evidence of the expectation of collective restoration (e.g. Hosea 6; Ezekiel 37) and survival, and of death not simply being the end for individuals – even if not much more than a rather shadowy picture of Sheol is usually portrayed. Both life and death belong fully to God, and that can give clear grounds for hope. The earliest certain reference to individual resurrection (Daniel 12:2) is from the second century BCE, and although the idea is found more frequently in Jewish writings from this time on (e.g. II Maccabees, I Enoch, IV Ezra, II Baruch), it is clear from Josephus and the New Testament that it was not universally accepted (as, for example, by the Sadducees) even well into the first century CE. Daniel is an apocalyptic work, a category strongly represented in Jewish writings of the following few centuries (and important for the work of Weiss and Schweitzer, but to an extent misleadingly portrayed by them, and frequently since). Essentially it is a visionary mode concerned with the unveiling of divine secrets, and shares main eschatological themes with other Jewish writings of the period. These include a strong emphasis on the judgment (and destruction) of the wicked; deliverance from foreign oppression, and a share in the new age (and/or heavenly world) for the righteous; a great battle preceding the final judgment and renewal of the earth (and Jerusalem); and dramatic, final divine intervention, with at times a messianic figure instrumental in the deliverance.

The points of connection between these various elements of Jewish eschatology and what we find in the New Testament are obvious enough. They provided rich resources for the New Testament writers, and together they bequeathed an enduring legacy for subsequent eschatological development in Christian theology.

As Christian eschatological thought emerges beyond the New Testament period, there is clear continuity with and development of biblical themes. To begin with, at least, there is still urgent expectation of the imminent return of Christ and the nearness of the end in general. Christ is seen as returning in glory and as Judge; bound up with this is the general resurrection and final judgment. There also grows up a strong and striking millenarian tradition, that is, of Christ initiating a reign on earth of a thousand years. This derives from Revelation 21, but it also reflects Jewish tradition of the marvelous, Utopian renewal God will bring about. It is represented by, amongst others, Papias, Justin, Irenaeus, Tertullian, Methodius and Lactantius; it persists over several centuries, and clearly has considerable currency at a popular level for a long time. It is hardly surprising, however, that it came eventually to be vehemently denounced and rejected. Certainly some conceptions of it were crudely carnal and materialistic, but it also predicted something all too tangible and obviously not realized. Equally obviously, however, it was bound to be offensive to a more sophisticated, allegorical and spiritualizing tendency. The attacks came from major figures such as Origen, Jerome, and, especially decisively, Augustine. It needs to be noted, however, that despite its limitations, millenarianism represented a continuation or particular form of the vision of the transformation of the world, but still here on earth. What took its place was effectively a spiritualized and otherworldly interpretation of the divine kingdom and divine promises. With these developments, the urgent expectation and strong emphasis on the end as near also inevitably lost their force. A potentially important, and highly ambivalent, development took place with Augustine identifying the kingdom with the elect who are predestined to salvation, but then in places appearing (although certainly not clearly or emphatically so) to make the visible Church itself the point of identification.

By contrast with imminent expectation, the general resurrection and final judgment retained their central place in the eschatological schema throughout the Patristic period. At the final judgment, the righteous were seen to gain their reward, understood above all as eternal life in the heavenly world; as the tradition developed, this was understood to involve, for example, the contemplation and vision of God, likeness to him, and the truly blessed state of knowing and loving God. The fate of the wicked, by contrast, was understood as eternal punishment and torment. A few voices, from Origen onward, suggested ways for the wicked to be purified and repent, but the mainstream view was much more uncompromising.

The question was inevitably raised, especially as the predicted end events did not materialize, of the fate of the individual at the point of death, and of what happened between then and the final judgment. At least as early as Justin the idea developed of a provisional judgment of the individual taking place at death, and of the souls of individuals being taken to a place of waiting until the final resurrection. There was a clear basis for this in Jewish tradition, and the idea of the soul (in some sense at least) was represented in both Judaism and the New Testament. Hence it was natural for the soul to be brought into discussion of the fate of the individual beyond death. It needs to be noted, however, that the Apologists emphasized strongly, over against Gnosticism, that the soul was not the only part of a person that survived. Nor, they argued, did the soul simply progress to its true goal, out of the earthly world, at the moment of death. There is thus strong insistence by the Apologists, and in repeated and developed form after them (as earlier with Paul), that the resurrection of the *body* formed a central part of Christian hope.

Certainly the survival of the *soul* was also seen as central, and especially through Greek, Platonizing influence, it was understood as both spiritual and immortal (as it had been earlier in the more strongly Hellenized forms of Judaism). The general understanding was that, at the point of death, the soul went to a place of waiting until the general resurrection and final judgment. At this point it was reunited with the resurrected body. The intermediate state in which the soul was set was often seen as a place of preparation (and sometimes improvement) for the eternal destiny in store for it. The idea that at death the soul was transferred immediately to the heavenly world (or a place of punishment) was largely held to apply only in a few exceptional cases. The concept of the resurrection of the body became more developed and sophisticated over several centuries, not least in response to Origen's discussion of it. Nevertheless, there remained a very strong insistence that, along with the immortal soul surviving, the physical body was indeed raised at the final resurrection, even though it was often seen as taking on new qualities or being transformed.

Thus by the end of the Patristic period, the main categories were already established that formed the central core of the Christian eschatological tradition for centuries to come. It is easy to see, from this basis, how the doctrine of the four last things (death, judgment, heaven, and hell) could be formulated. In the medieval period especially there were enhanced depictions, for example, of the last judgment and hell, and further developments in the understanding of the fate of the individual. The idea of the immortality of the soul remained central, but it was now held that at death the soul left the body and went straight to either heaven or hell; body and soul were then to be reunited at the general resurrection. This, however, opened up the question of what happened to the body meanwhile. Thus there were developed the ideas of limbo, essentially a neutral concept, as a place of waiting that was occupied by the good who lived before Christ and by children who died too young, and of purgatory, as a place of punishment and correction to produce repentance. The fear of death was thus easily enhanced, and the overriding emphasis came to be on the individual. Nevertheless, there were sporadic outbreaks of millenarian thought and movements, with powerful Utopian visions of a world renewed, as, for example, with Joachim of Fiore and in the Radical Reformation.

For a very long period, then, it was emphasis on the individual, and preoccupation with the fate of the individual, that predominated. This is a tendency that has persisted, especially at a popular level, right down to the present day. It is entirely understandable that this should be so, particularly in an increasingly individualistic age. In the post-Enlightenment period, however, several factors came into play which contributed to a major shift in perspective in Christian theology generally, including of course eschatology. The impact of Newtonian science and Kantian philosophy, with the idea of a rationally ordered universe, played an important part. Above all, the eighteenth and nineteenth centuries were dominated by the concept of historical progress. One obvious effect of this dominant progressive and teleological understanding of history was that any kind of genuinely transcendent, future eschatology was abandoned in favor of an optimistic, positivist portrayal of Christianity, with a strong Kantian component, progressing to its true fulfillment as a natural development of the present order. The position of Liberal Theology by the end of the nineteenth century can be seen in classic and representative form in A. Harnack's *What Is Christianity?* (1957). Here the main focus of Christianity is supposed to correspond to that of Jesus: the kingdom of God, understood as God's reign in each individual human heart; the Fatherhood of God; the infinite value of the human soul; and the love of God and of neighbor, above all as expressed in the Sermon on the Mount. Here, then, scarcely a trace of Jesus's eschatological message remains; its sharp, indeed urgent, eschatological dimension has been lost. The kingdom is instead individualized and internalized, and is to be brought about as a result of human moral endeavor. The idea of the kingdom was thus now collapsed not into that of the Church, as the visible and concrete representation of God's reign on earth, but into the social order that already existed and was gradually being perfected. In general, as far as there was anything that could properly be called "eschatology" within Christian theology, it closely reflected the ideas of secular society. The emphasis throughout was above all on the *continuity* of present and future.

The historical progressivism and ethical perfectibility of this construct of Liberal Theology, as represented by Harnack and others, could not survive the barbaric horror of the First World War, still less the appalling human genocidal and destructive capacity manifested throughout the twentieth century. And just as events rendered this position untenable historically, so also the work of Weiss and Schweitzer especially rendered it untenable theologically. Their basic argument represented a devastating blow to the whole liberal theological construct. Instead of depicting Christianity as fitting comfortably with the picture of a harmonious social order, it portrayed Jesus as an alien figure, belonging to the bizarre world of Jewish apocalyptic, and having a fanatical and frenzied expectation of an imminent end. This stark, uncompromising account has provoked reactions right down to the present day. One famous example is C. H. Dodd (1961), who argued that the kingdom, far from being wholly and imminently future, is wholly and immanently present, fully realized already in Jesus's ministry. Dodd's argument, both in general and in detail, has not been found convincing, but it drew attention to the realized element that was taken up in the consensus position.

From an early stage, at least some of the New Testament discussion spilled out onto the wider theological scene. This is above all the case in the work of Rudolf Bultmann (1957, 1969), the dominant New Testament scholar of the twentieth century. He had written his doctoral dissertation under Johannes Weiss, and found Weiss's portrayal of Jesus fully convincing, but parted company from Harnack, and Liberal Theology also, because he saw their emphasis as falling on the human and horizontal axis at the expense of the divine and vertical. At the same time, he saw an urgent need to rid Christianity of the "mythological" trappings which prevent people in the modern world from being confronted with the true message of the gospel. Hence (with Weiss) he saw Jesus as a Jewish apocalyptic figure proclaiming the imminent arrival of the Reign of God, but at the same time he saw the historical Jesus as having no constitutive significance for Christian faith and theology. The focus for true Christian faith must be that which is both within history and also at the same time beyond history. For Bultmann, this cannot be Jesus's message of the coming kingdom and his own return on the clouds of heaven. These did not happen and will not happen. Instead it is Jesus's crucifixion which is the "eschatological event in and beyond time," an event which is simultaneously historical and eschatological. What Bultmann means by "eschatological event" is that in the proclamation (or kerygma) of the cross is God's final act and final revelation, which confronts each person with the only possibility for self-understanding and authentic existence.

It is easy to miss the main point of Bultmann's position, especially with the existential overlay to his interpretation. In fact what happens is that Bultmann agrees fully with Weiss that Jesus proclaims the imminent Reign of God as God's eschatological Act which brings the old world to an end. But the point now is that the Church's kerygma proclaims not the kingdom but Jesus (and especially his crucifixion) as the eschatological event. The emphasis is shifted from Jesus as the one who proclaims the decisive eschatological event, to Jesus as the one who is proclaimed as this event. This means, however, that the focus now falls not on the imminent expectation of the kingdom, but on the decisive eschatological event that has *already* taken place on the cross. The continuity, but even more the contrast, with the position of Weiss and Schweitzer is immediately obvious. Thus the decisive eschatological point for each individual is in being confronted by the kerygma.

There are clear points of contact between Bultmann's position and that of Barth, despite differences between them. Barth, like Bultmann, sees the event of Jesus's death and resurrection (above all, for Barth, the resurrection) as the point at which time and eternity meet, and the limitations of the human world and time are transcended. Although Barth speaks of it as the supreme "non-historical" event, this clearly denotes a supreme eschatological and transcendent event. As with Bultmann, the eschatological force lies in the fact that in the proclamation, in the Church's kerygma, each individual is called to respond in faith to this final, decisive saving event. For Barth, however, it is not the kerygma, in and of itself, that *is* the eschatological event, but the proclamation of the resurrection as an objective (although "non-historical") reality. It is through the kerygma that the revealed Word of God can bring about faith in a final, saving sense. The differences between Barth and Bultmann are potentially far-reaching, but the fact remains that for Barth, as for Bultmann, the decisive eschatological event has already taken place. The transcendent, eternal dimension has entered human history or, more precisely, is set over against it. It has erupted, as the divine, "vertical" dimension, and has shattered human concepts of time. Barth's understanding of eschatology, especially as developed in the *Church Dogmatics* (1936–74), is more subtle and complex than is sometimes allowed, although it may seem a rather attenuated eschatology (particularly since the full statement of his position, planned for the *Church Dogmatics*, never appeared). He represents a radical challenge not only to Liberal Theology, but also to Weiss and Schweitzer, in that he disallows the limitations of human temporality as a proper category for divine action.

Both Barth and Bultmann, then, present strongly vertical, transcendental accounts of eschatology. They both stress that all theology is eschatological; but the future (as well as the this-worldly) dimensions of eschatology find very little place. Their contemporary Tillich gives more place in his theology to substantial expression of future hope, in terms of the kingdom of God and the transformation of the world. He emphasizes genuine continuity between the present world and that which is to be brought into being, and conveys something of the powerful biblical tradition of a world renewed.

In the last few decades there has been criticism of Barth, especially, and of Bultmann for making the vertical dimension so important that any genuine or substantial future focus of eschatology is effectively removed from the scene. Thus Pannenberg emphasizes the importance for contemporary theology of Jesus's concentration on the future, and the eschatological fulfillment of his message and ministry. That is, Jesus's message of the kingdom as about to arrive is central for Christian theology. Whereas Barth and Bultmann held that the supreme eschatological event belonged to a category altogether different from that of ordinary, mundane history, Pannenberg insists on holding these together, so that the world which God will bring about sets the eschatological perspective for the world that exists and what happens within it.

Similar in some ways to Pannenberg's position, but much more prolifically developed, is that of Moltmann. Most strikingly in his *Theology of Hope* (1967), he sees Christianity as eschatology from beginning to end, and eschatology as the key to the whole of Christian faith. This might be thought mere rhetoric, or simply echoing Barth and Bultmann; but in contrast to them, Moltmann sees Christianity as oriented above all to the future. It is a future world which God will bring about, and it will involve the transformation of the world. But it is very much the present world, and not some otherworldly sphere, that is in view. Moltmann takes very seriously the biblical eschatological tradition, not least the Old Testament theme of promise, which stretches out to include the whole world and the whole future. It also connects closely with the sharply eschatological emphasis of the New Testament, not just in the case of Jesus but above all with Paul. Moltmann's stress on Christianity's transcendent orientation is so strong that he has been seen as promoting this at the expense of doing justice to the present, realized nature of New Testament (or Christian) eschatology. In fact, however, he argues that the eschatological future creates anticipations of itself in the present. Indeed, Moltmann has at times been thought to have been too heavily influenced by the Marxist philosopher Ernst Bloch, in his extraordinary work *The Principle of Hope* (1986). It has been wryly remarked of this that Bloch portrays Christian hope better than most Christian theologians have managed to, and certainly Moltmann owes a great debt to Bloch: for example, like Bloch, he sees the biblical messianic traditions and Utopian future as the true source and object of hope, and as genuinely revolutionary, and critical of the status quo. Yet at the same time his eschatological thinking differs decisively from Bloch's position. Thus for Moltmann the basis for all Christian hope and eschatology is the event of the resurrection of Jesus. Christian hope for the future therefore depends on divine initiative, and neither accepts the present world and status quo as adequate, nor looks for their transformation from within. Hence despite the inspiration Bloch undoubtedly provides, Moltmann clearly stands opposed to attempts to identify the kingdom of God with the Church or in any sense with the world as it is, and equally, radically rejects all otherworldly versions of Christian hope.

Subsequently, Moltmann has developed his understanding of the *individual* in relation to death and resurrection, and also argues strongly for the importance of what he terms a "cosmic eschatology," not least in the light of the threat of ecological and nuclear catastrophe. Here, as elsewhere, Moltmann is open to criticism, and begs questions of theological method, but he at least sets important issues centrally on the eschatological agenda. His work has been influential on some liberation theologians, although Liberation Theology generally has developed its own distinctive perspectives and has looked much more for the realization of the kingdom on earth in the present, and the real transformation of the present world order.

Catholic thought (apart from Liberation Theology) has also engaged substantially with eschatological issues. For example, Karl Rahner has interpreted eschatology above all christologically; eschatology thus becomes the working-out and fulfillment, in its essential future mode, of all that is involved in Christological tradition and statements. For von Balthasar, the perspective of John's Gospel, with its so-called realized eschatology, represents a particularly appropriate expression of what is distinctive in Christian eschatology. That which is decisively important has happened already. It has done so, however, not as a natural progression within human history, but by God, in the person and event of Jesus Christ, dramatically entering the contingent world and dimension of time. As with Rahner, it is thus again Christ who is the supreme focal point of eschatology.

Not surprisingly, in view of the sustained and developed tradition of previous centuries, the doctrines of the immortality of the soul and the intermediate state have loomed large in some recent Catholic debate. Over against the traditional view (which, predictably, has been strongly reaffirmed, for example by Ratzinger), it has been argued that each individual moves, at the moment of death, into the realm of eternity, yet does so not in the sense of an immortal soul but as a whole person. Clearly it is not only the idea of the immortal soul that is set aside here, but also that of both individual and general resurrection in any traditional sense.

This brief sampling of ways in which eschatology has been understood in Christian theology shows something of the sheer diversity of views and lack of consensus, not least within the twentieth century. It is not possible to assess these views in any detail here, but it is worth trying to appraise the main tendencies and trajectories of development. One obvious tendency is that of giving eschatology an essentially *otherworldly* or spiritualizing focus. This is above all evident in the medieval period, with the importance attached to the beatific vision (and related mystical traditions), but also much more generally (and extending far beyond the medieval period) in the focus on the heavenly world. It is, then a widespread tendency, which in many respects originates within the New Testament itself, especially John's Gospel, with its move toward interpreting the kingdom and the sharp focus of eschatology on a different level and in a different mode. With Paul as well, there is a clear tendency toward spiritualizing, in the case of the kingdom at any rate, and these lines of interpretation are developed strongly in the Patristic period, not least in reaction to the millenarian position. Conversely, of course, it is possible to identify a trajectory that can be seen as very much this-worldly and material, as obviously with the millenarian tradition, and frequently in Liberation Theology as well. The virtual identification of the kingdom with the Church (and, indeed, empire) in the medieval period, although constituting a "this-worldly" tendency, is held along with a strongly otherworldly orientation.

Secondly, there is what can be termed a "horizontal" or (more technically) *immanent* tendency. That is, the kingdom, or eschatological consummation, is seen as developing out of the historical process already underway within the world. This is, above all, the case with the progressive and teleological eschatology of the eighteenth and nineteenth centuries, although it has also appeared again in the twentieth century in forms of process theology and especially with Teilhard de Chardin. Again, of course, the opposite tendency can also be detected; that is, there is a very sharp "vertical" or transcendent dimension, evident for example on Barth's eschatology. A transcendent perspective can be found much more widely in eschatological developments, but not in so absolute a form as with Barth. The strong contrast between the Weiss–Schweitzer position and that of Dodd might also seem to belong to this category, but is in fact better represented as that between imminent and immanent, wholly future and wholly present.

A third tendency is to make eschatology predominantly, if not exclusively, *individual*. This is evident in much of the Patristic period and above all in the medieval development, with the strong preoccupation with what happens to each individual at the point of death. The developed idea of the immortality of the soul was obviously of major importance in promoting this. In fact, however, an individualizing tendency runs right through the Christian tradition: it is developed in John's Gospel, and has persisted into the twentieth century, as, for example (albeit atypically), in Bultmann's eschatology. In arguing that the decisive eschatological theme is the moment of crisis as it confronts each individual, he leaves any larger or collective concern out of the picture. Again, the converse can also be seen. That is, there can be such preoccupation with general or cosmic eschatology that the fate of the individual at death largely goes by default. This can at least appear to be the case with millenarian traditions and Liberation Theology, and it is certainly so with immanent, teleological, and progressive interpretation.

To draw attention to these tendencies is not to condemn them, although some certainly seem more damaging to a sustainable eschatological tradition than others. So, for example, a strongly horizontal or immanent perspective not only appears indifferent to the fate of the individual but also seems to treat the historical process as autonomous and to disallow any disjunctive or decisive divine action. The dominant tendency throughout Christian history toward personal or individual eschatology has been at the expense of serious engagement with or concern for the fate of humanity in general or the world order as a whole. A strongly otherworldly or spiritualizing tendency has led not only to indifference concerning the present world, but also to the kind of Christianity which Marx attacked as being merely the "opiate of the people."

Exploring these various tendencies can thus expose the obvious danger that always lurk of producing a skewed or one-sided interpretation of eschatology. It also shows up the natural temptation to use a controlling mode of interpretation that especially suits the particular situation or interpreter. It is essential always to ask, therefore, whether a particular version of eschatology can be seen as an adequate account of Christian eschatology as a whole. The difficulties in constructing such an account go back to the start of the tradition. Thus it is the imminent expectation pervading the New Testament that has helped give rise, already within the New Testament and still more so subsequently, to the kind of reaction that has produced strongly otherworldly and spiritualizing interpretations, which in turn have caused Christian eschatology to lose its hold on reality and the world as it is experienced. As I have noted, it is possible to detect a shift to the personal and individual as the controlling category, already in Paul, and especially in John, and these both provide an obvious basis for developing eschatology in this direction. More generally, the bizarre imagery and lurid emphasis of, for example, Daniel and Revelation can appear inherently problematic. From at least the Patristic period onward, a crudely literalistic reading of these texts has helped cause the main Christian tradition to eschew them. And, thus abandoned, they have been embraced enthusiastically in the modern period especially by pseudo-Christian sects; all of which only serves to exacerbate the problem.

The Christian eschatological tradition more generally can appear just as ambiguous in its effect. This is certainly so in the case of the two major influences on developing Christian eschatology from outside the sphere of biblical tradition, that is, Platonizing philosophy and Enlightenment scientific and philosophical tradition. The former gave considerable impetus (from early in the Patristic period onward) to the spiritualizing, individualizing tendency that, as I have noted above, was underway from a very early stage. It has also meant that the fate of the individual at death, personal (or individual) eschatology and resurrection, and a complex set of doctrines that have developed in relation to these, have all become a prominent, and in many respects problematic, part of the tradition. The latter gave rise especially to progressive, evolutionary, and teleological accounts of Christian eschatology, which have encouraged too easy an acceptance of an immanentist view of the kingdom, as the natural outgrowth of the present order, and have not given proper place to the radically future, disjunctive, and wholly other nature of what can be understood as a genuinely Christian expression of eschatological hope.

All this looks unpromising as far as the prospects are concerned for developing an eschatology that is both genuinely Christian and also sustainable and defensible in a contemporary context. Nevertheless, there is a great deal to be gained both from drawing on the Christian (especially biblical) tradition and also from being open to per-spectives from within contemporary society. There are a number of respects in which the present climate, both intellectual and more general, could be seen as conducive to the formulation of a considered Christian eschatology. Thus, for example, there is an acute awareness, both at a popular level and in academic discussion, of what have been termed (Giddens 1991) the "high-consequence risks" facing humanity as a whole, both of a global kind (the threat of nuclear catastrophe, ecological disaster, and so on), and at an individual level (for example, the threat of contracting AIDS or cancer). These obviously contribute to the clear perception that the fate of the world and the fate of individuals are bound up together. There is common ground here that can encourage the articulation of a distinctively Christian response and Christian hope. It is appropri-ate both to do this and also to share in the work of devising specific strategies to meet such threats. A Christian eschatological perspective may, however, want to take issue with such concepts as "the colonisation of the future" (Giddens 1991), which, in however sophisticated a shape, can appear to be a form of immanentist approach, proposing essentially that humans can work out ways to gain complete control of the future. No doubt an enormous amount of science fiction could be brought into the picture as well here. This should elicit from a Christian eschatology both a critical response and also an insistence on the conviction that the future lies with God and his good purpose.

There are obviously other examples that could be given. For instance, there is con-siderable impetus from perspectives within the physical sciences, philosophy, and social theory to rethink the whole issue of the time–space continuum. There has of course been substantial theological discussion this century of the nature of time, especially, but there is real need and scope for further work which takes proper account of these wider perspectives. Very obviously, for the Christian eschatological tradition, renewed discussion of classical formulations such as "eternal life" and "resurrection of the dead" will be brought onto the agenda. Again, issues concerning the self and personal identity have been sharply raised from within the natural sciences, philosophy, and social and psychological theory. Acute questions concerning the concept of the immortality of the soul are obviously involved here. Despite the robust defense of this, especially in conservative Catholic thought, the case for seeing the individual as a psychosomatic unity appears compelling, not only as doing more justice to a central concept in biblical and Patristic tradition but also as offering a coherent concept in the contemporary context.

It needs to be stressed again, however, that what should be looked for in a Christian eschatological perspective is a critical awareness of and openness to issues raised in contemporary discussion, not a passive acquiescence in their methods or findings. There is still a need for a rigorous and intellectually sustainable account of Christian eschatology. It may seem churlish to complain, at the end of a century generally recognized as having generated more eschatological discussion than any other, and at the start of a new millennium, of a dearth of eschatology. In fact, however, eschatology was never as fully developed, profoundly reflected upon, or given as rigorous and imaginative intellectual probing, as were other areas of Christian theology (for example, Christology and soteriology) from the Patristic period onward. This is indicative partly of the embarrassment and difficulties that eschatology presents, and partly of a necessary concentration elsewhere. It remains true, however, that eschatology still needs further deep and sustained theological reflection, discussion, and development.

It is not just eschatology in isolation that has suffered from this neglect in the past. Christian theology as a whole has been left correspondingly impoverished, and also still needs this kind of serious work to be undertaken. It is important also, therefore, that discussion of eschatology should become central and integrally related to other main areas of Christian theology, including Christology, soteriology, and ethics. Equally, it is important that eschatology should not be too readily collapsed into any of these (as has happened, for instance, with Christology in some discussions), or become merely some kind of "second-order discourse" deriving from them. The asking of ultimate questions is natural and inevitable, and it is clearly crucial that Christian theology can give a substantial account of its distinctive position concerning hope, the future, and ultimate meaning and destiny.

The Christian tradition contains, as I have said, substantial resources for an eschatology that can have contemporary significance. One aspect of this in particular should not be lost sight of: that is, the biblical tradition of a powerful vision of a world renewed and transformed. It may seem to be tempting providence at the turn of the millennium to make special mention of this particular tradition; but it is precisely because elements at least of it have been hijacked so easily and so often that it is important to argue that it should be held onto and integrated fully again into the main development of the eschatological tradition. Over against repeated attempts to predict the end of the world or to summon up a false millennium, it is necessary to insist that this visionary tradition is in no sense concerned with trying to force God's hand and bring the kingdom in, or to find it in some form of society or even the Church as an alternative society.

In contrast, then, to predicting the future (or collapsing it into the present), it is worth recalling that this vision is held, throughout the New Testament, in balance between present and future, now and not yet. Indeed, the biblical tradition overall holds not only present and future but also promise and judgment in creative tension together. This tradition thus represents a vision which refuses simply to accept the world as it has become, but nevertheless sees a deep continuity between the world as it is and the world as it will become, as well as a profound transformation taking place. It is precisely because it represents a powerful vision of the world as God wills it to be, a world and society ordered by true justice and peace, that it can inform critical Christian engagement with society. It is therefore a vision that is deeply rooted in the present world, but with transcendent and transforming perspectives, able to look beyond the constraints and limitations of human society.

What this tradition represents then, is above all a transforming and liberating vision. It is a vision of both cosmic renewal and individual fulfillment, but it involves neither cosmic nor individual dualism. The hope of renewal and resurrection denotes a vision of the transformation *of* the world and the individual (the *whole* person), not escape *from* the world or self. Thus the overriding perspective for Christian eschatology will be the recognition that the whole future and all time are set within God's control and his good purpose, and that this entails his bringing all human life, both individually and collectively, and the whole created order, to its true end, and liberating it from whatever holds it from its true fulfillment.

Bibliography

Allison, D. C. 1985. *The End of the Ages has Come*. Philadelphia, PA: Fortress Press.

Baillie, J. 1934. *And the Life Everlasting*. London: Oxford University Press.

von Balthasar, H. U. 1998. *Theo-drama: Theological Dramatic Theory*, vol. 5: *The Last Act*. trans. G. Harrison. San Francisco, CA: Ignatius Press.

Barth, K. 1933a. *The Epistle to the Romans*, trans. E. C. Hoskyns. London: Oxford University Press.

Barth, K. 1933b. *The Resurrection of the Dead*, trans. H. J. Stenning. London: Hodder & Stoughton.

Barth, K. 1936–74. *Church Dogmatics*, trans. and ed. G. W. Bromiley and T. F. Torrance. Edinburgh: T. & T. Clark.

Bloch, E. 1986. *The Principle of Hope*, 3 vols., trans. N. Plaice, S. Plaice, and P. Knight. Oxford: Basil Blackwell.

Bultmann, R. 1957. *History and Eschatology*. Edinburgh: Edinburgh University Press.

Bultmann, R. 1969. *Faith and Understanding*, trans. Louise Pettibone Smith, ed. R. W. Funk. London: SCM Press.

Carnley, P. 1987. *The Structure of Resurrection Belief*. Oxford: Clarendon Press.

Cohn, N. 1970. *The Pursuit of the Millennium*, 3rd edn. London: Temple Smith.

Cullmann, O. 1962. *Christ and Time*, rev. edn., trans. F. V. Filson. London: SCM Press.

Cullmann, O. 1967. *Salvation in History*, trans. S. G. Sowers. London: SCM Press.

Daley, B. E. 1991. *The Hope of the Early Church: A Handbook of Patristic Eschatology*. Cambridge: Cambridge University Press.

Dodd, C. H. 1961. *The Parables of the Kingdom*, 3rd edn. London: Nisbet.

Fenn, R. K. 1997. *The End of Time*. London: SPCK.

Giddens, A. 1991. *Modernity and Self-Identity*. Cambridge: Polity Press.

Greshake, G. and Lohfink, G. 1986. *Naherwartung – Auferstehung – Unsterblichkeit*, 5th edn. Freiburg: Herder.

Harnack, A. 1957. *What is Christianity?*, trans. T. B. Saunders. New York: Harper & Row.

Hayes, Z. 1989. *Visions of a Future: A Study of Christian Eschatology*. Wilmington, DE: Michael Glazier.

Hebblethwaite, B. 1984. *The Christian Hope*. Basingstoke: Marshall, Morgan & Scott.

Hick, J. 1976. *Death and Eternal Life*. London: Collins.

Metz, J. B. 1969. *The Theology of the World*, trans. W. Glen-Doepel. London: Burns & Oates; New York: Herder & Herder.

Moltmann, J. 1967. *Theology of Hope: On the Ground and Implications of a Christian Eschatology*, trans. J. W. Leitch. London: SCM Press.

Moltmann, J. 1996. *The Coming of God: Christian Eschatology*, trans. M. Kohl. London: SCM Press.

Pannenberg, W. 1969. *Theology and the Kingdom of God*, ed. R. J. Neuhaus. Philadelphia, PA: Westminster Press.

Perkins, P. 1984. *Resurrection: New Testament Witness and Contemporary Reflection*. New York: Doubleday.

Rahner, K. 1966. *Theological Investigations*, vol. 4, trans. K. Smith. Baltimore, MD: Helicon Press; London: Darton, Longman and Todd.

Rahner, K. 1969. *Theological Investigations*, vol. 6, trans. K.-H. and B. Kruger. New York: Seabury Press; London: Darton, Longman and Todd.

Rahner, K. 1965. *On the Theology of Death*, 2nd edn. New York: Herder & Herder.

Ratzinger, J. 1988. *Eschatology: Death and Eternal Life*, trans. M. Waldstein, ed. A. Nichols. Washington, DC: Catholic University of America Press.

Schweitzer, A. 1954. *The Quest of the Historical Jesus*, trans. W. Montgomery, 3rd edn. London: A. & C. Black.

Tillich, P. 1963. *Systematic Theology*, vol. 3. Chicago, IL: University of Chicago Press.

Weiss, J. 1971. *Jesus' Proclamation of the Kingdom of God*, trans. R. H. Hiers and D. L. Holland. London: SCM Press.

CHAPTER 16
Church and Sacraments

Gavin D'Costa

What Are We Talking About?

Placing "church" and "sacraments" together in the title and locating this chapter after "trinity" and "incarnation" already implies at least three interesting and contentious points. First, it implies that the understanding of the church and sacraments should follow that of trinity and incarnation in the normal order of systematic theology. However, following the old saying that belief is shaped by prayer, *lex orandi lex credendi*, it could be argued that trinity and incarnation are only given to us in the communion of the church, celebrating the event of Jesus Christ in its liturgical actions. The shape of Christian belief follows from the liturgical and sacramental history of Christian practice. In this view, the ordering of the chapters should be church and sacraments, followed by trinity and incarnation (Wainwright 1980; Ford and Hardy 1984). This leads to my second observation. Placing the two topics together, "church" and "sacraments," assumes a highly sacramental ecclesiology. For some Christians, greater stress on the bible and preaching would be preferred, while for others, an emphasis on social and political action should characterize the church. These Christians might well be unhappy with an exclusive coupling of what is viewed as two distinct topics – church and sacraments.[1] But running in the other direction, and thirdly, it might be asked why not speak of "liturgy" instead of "sacraments," for it is only within the former that the latter operate? Framing the discussion thus might well avoid the division between Word and Sacrament that was institutionally enacted in the Council of Trent, in the Roman Catholic response to the Reformers.

I have noted these complexities to show that "Church and Sacraments" could be treated in many ways: a historical survey of sacramental theology, a historical survey of ecclesiology, an examination of the thought of Augustine or Aquinas or Luther on the two topics, and so on.[2] However, I want to introduce readers to the topic by giving a highly tradition-specific snapshot: examining two crises in contemporary Roman Catholic sacramental ecclesiology. This specific focus will allow a whole range of issues to surface: ecumenical questions; the relation of different branches of theology to each other (e.g. liturgical, foundational, pastoral); the relation between philosophy and theology; the manner in which different currents in theology construe issues (e.g. liberation, feminist, and postmodern theologies); and the question of Christianity's relation to the modern world. Hence, in the next section, I shall briefly survey some major historical landmarks in the development of Catholic sacramental theology, always remembering that the historical reality is far more complex and contested than surveys convey. Then, in the following section, I turn to two challenges posed by feminist and postmodern theologies. In the fourth and final section, I will draw the discussion together making observations and comments.

The Historical Construction of the Sacraments

The first major sacramental ecclesiology can be attributed to Augustine, who draws heavily on the important North African theologians Tertullian and Cyprian. The word *sacramentum* was possibly used in the early African Latin translations of the New Testament for the word "mystery" (*mystērion*). This is most significant, for the word "mystery" is often employed by Paul to refer to that which is revealed for our salvation: Jesus Christ (see, for example, I Corinthians 2:7, 4:1; Colossians 1:26–7; Ephesians 6:19). Connectedly, the references that relate to baptism and the eucharist/meal sharing, later to be seen as "sacraments," construe these practices in terms of participation in the paschal mystery of Jesus Christ.[3] This tight symbolic interrelation between Christ, the mystery/sacrament of salvation, and the presence of Christ in his community, called the "body of Christ" by Paul, formed an important context for Augustine. One might say that a major sacramental issue was this: Without the tangible coming of Jesus Christ into the world to bring redemption, there could be no redemption. In so much as the church was the tangible sign of Jesus Christ in the world, then it played a role *analogous* to that of Christ. How was this analogous relationship to be articulated? This is the main ecclesiological–sacramental question I will pursue.

Three important influences shaped the later Augustine's articulation of this relationship: neo-Platonic philosophy; Augustine's increasingly biblical–eschatological understanding of time; and the practical context of the North African church being torn apart with the Donatist and Pelagian controversies.[4] The tendency of neo-Platonic dualism between matter and the spiritual was turned around by Augustine (perhaps not always successfully), in an eschatological fashion, to show how it was only under the specific form of matter, sensible signs (*signum*), that God could communicate Himself to His creation (*res, virtus*). In some respects, the neo-Platonic notion of "participation" helped Augustine to shape this Christian reversal, such that he could eventually argue that the very sign itself (water and the appropriate words in baptism) effected the reality that it signified; just as Christ's paschal mystery effected God's salvation in the world. The visible "sign" bridged the distance between God and creation, such that a visible sign, first Christ, then his church after him, mediated an invisible reality: God – although in distinct and asymmetrical ways. With this understanding Augustine was to develop, in the face of the Donatist and Pelagian controversies, the insight that the reality or integrity of the sacrament could not be compromised because of a recipient's bad disposition. In this sense the sacraments shared, with Christ, the characteristic of an unconditional gift, what would later be called an "objective efficacy" or, in Trent's words, reflected the *ex opera operato* nature of the sacrament. The ill-disposition of the recipient meant the effects or fruits of the sacrament would not grow within such a body, be it an individual heretic or a schismatic community. The reason for this was not the lack of integrity in the sacrament, but the lack of charity in the recipient, in precipitating schism in the one body of Christ. Augustine also argued that some sacraments, such as baptism and ordination, had a perduring character, again regardless of the subsequent life of the recipient.

Augustine thereby constructed some of the major trajectories along which discussion of the sacraments and the church would be conducted in the Latin West. One might summarize the above in terms of three major trajectories. First, Augustine provided important symbolic models to explore the crucial link between the body of Jesus Christ and "the body of Christ," the church. Secondly, the sacraments as "signs" bore a similar character to that of Christ, as mediated signs of God in the world. Thirdly, because of the distinction between the visible reality and the fruits of that visible sign, Augustine facilitated the distinctions between the integrity of the sacrament and the different contexts of reception. The fullness of the latter was dependent on the Holy Spirit, who effected the charity that was required for the church to be the "body of Christ," and on the attitude and faith of the recipient.

The next major stage in sacramental construction is to be found in the medieval debates, mainly between the Franciscans and Dominicans.[5] Amidst many profound contributions to the subject, one in particular prevailed: that of Thomas Aquinas (Gilson 1957:79–81; Ganoczy 1984; Davies 1992). Aquinas's understanding underwent many changes between the *Commentary on the Sentences* (1254–6) and the Third Part of the *Summa Theologica* (1272–3). My exposition is based on the latter.[6] Aquinas not only inherited the beliefs of Augustine, and a variety of other Christian traditions, but also worked out his metaphysics in terms of Aristotle. In this respect, two main categories of Aristotelian conceptuality marked his sacramental theology: those of "causality," and "substance."[7] The questions still revolved around the Augustinian constructions. Aquinas wanted to explain how the sacraments effected grace in the world amidst conflicting understandings of causality, framed around Avicenna's and Averroes' mediations of Aristotle. Aristotle's notion of instrumental causality was Christologically interpreted by Aquinas to explain the relation between God and the created order, to show how the sacraments worked. Aristotle's axiom that "the principal cause moves; the instrumental cause, being moved, moves" (*causa principalis movet, causa instumentalis movet mota*) was employed to explain the action of Christ: Jesus's humanity was the instrumental cause of our salvation, through which God (principal cause) acts via Christ's divine nature. Clearly for Aquinas, as for Augustine, there is a difference between Christ and the sacraments. Aquinas distinguishes two kinds of instruments: "a separate instrument such as a staff" and "a united instrument, co-joined to the principal agent such as a hand" (IIIa, q.62, a.5). Christ's human nature is like a hand, cojoined to his divinity, whereas the sacraments are like a staff, depending for their efficacy on Christ. Hence, while the Christological focus of the sacraments is retained, we see the onset of an eclipsing of the Augustinian symbolic-sign model, which disappeared almost entirely in late medieval nominalism.

The Aristotelian category of "substance" was employed by Aquinas to designate the reality of the gift that existed within the sacrament: its objective givenness.[8] This use of substance had a two-fold effect, both unintended by Aquinas. On the one hand it focused attention on the actual species of the consecration, bread and wine, sometimes distancing them from the ecclesiological context of their operation. This eventually led to infrequent eucharistic participation and an increasing emphasis on the miraculous events surrounding the eucharist (Rubin 1991:108–29, 135–9, 147–55; Bynum 1987:48–72, 260–76). The other effect was to focus on the reality of the sacramental substance in a quasi-physicalist manner. At an extreme, the Dominican Peter de La Palu (c.1277–1342) argued that a mouse who had swallowed a consecrated host must be caught and burnt and washed down a *piscina*, the treatment accorded to old vestments, crumbs of the host, and other sacred materials (Rubin 1991:68). Nevertheless, Aquinas's use of this term was employed solely to safeguard the gratuity of God in the conferring of grace via the sacraments, to affirm grace as a reality (substance), not as a pseudo-efficient cause only disposing a person toward God. The genius of Aquinas was in employing Aristotelian metaphysical categories to give a "different" construction from that of Augustine and his neo-Platonic symbolic framework (Duffy 1992:505–34, at p. 520).

The third stage for our reconstruction is that of the Reformation, culminating in the Council of Trent (1545–63). The Reformers quite rightly protested about numerous sacramental practices that emerged and proliferated in the late Middle Ages. Many of these seemed to benefit the rich and powerful (the buying of indulgences, often through the number of Masses said), or sometimes seemed to make the laity a redundant category within the Church (the exclusion of laity from Eucharistic Communion, the sole administration of all the sacraments by priests). If *lex orandi lex credendi*, this is excellently illustrated in the writings of the Reformers. One can see the differing relations between sacraments and ecclesiology in the theologies of Luther, Calvin, and Zwingli, for in so much as they came to question and reinterpret various sacramental practices, so emerged alternative ecclesiologies and doctrinal tenets (Maxwell 1936:72–120, Dix 1945:613–734, Edwards and Tavard 1983:55–69, Ganoczy 1984, Vorgrimler 1992). Amidst all their serious differences, the Reformers had in common the desire to return to biblical categories and themes, and rejected the various scholastic theories of causality and universals. As Regis A. Duffy puts it, "the Reformers sought to dephilosophize sacramental categories and preferred the biblical categories of God's power-filled promise to those who believe" (Duffy 1992).

The Reformation critiques formed the subject matter of the Council of Trent in both a positive and a negative fashion. Positively, there were important liturgical and sacramental reforms instituted (Sessions 9–25) – and a return to scriptural and patristic sources (Jedin 1957). Some of these reforms were reformed at the Second Vatican Council, such as the refusal of the chalice to lay persons (Megivern 1978).[9] Negatively, there was no real attention to sacramental theology as such. The vital Seventh Session with its "Decree on the Sacraments" (DS) (DS 1547) contained a brief foreword, followed by thirteen canons (proclaiming anathema on various Reformation doctrines).

Most important is the famous eighth canon: "If anyone says that through the sacraments of the New Law grace is not conferred by the performance of the rite itself (*ex opere operato*) but that faith alone in the divine promise is sufficient to obtain grace, *anathema* sit" (DS 1608).[10] The historical-sign mediation of the church is again rightly affirmed and established, even though the *ex opere operato* teaching was constantly prone to mechanistic interpretations, perhaps due to the casuistic metaphysics underlying it. Interestingly the Second Vatican Council did not use the *ex opere* term at all, while clearly affirming its intention: the objectivity and gratuity of grace within the sacramental event.

Trent also established (despite very inconclusive biblical exegesis) that there were seven sacraments and all these were "instituted by Jesus Christ" (DS 1601); it reiterated that the sacraments are "necessary for salvation" (DS 1604), even if not all are necessary; and insisted that preaching and sacraments could never be administered by all (DS 1610); and that the intention of the minister to do "what the Church does" is the minimal requirement for effective ritual performance, even if the minister is in a state of mortal sin (DS 1611–12). One might say that Trent consolidated and fixed many of the significant insights of Augustine and Aquinas. However, many of the Reformers also claimed Augustine as their patron. Partly due to some very anti-Protestant popes (Paul IV being pre-eminent) and the growing power of the Jesuits (especially during Sessions 15–25), Luther's and Calvin's desires to return to a more biblical–symbolic understanding of the sacraments were marginalized. Their critiques on this count were more fully and selectively incorporated in the Second Vatican Council.

The final stage leads to the present day and its culmination in the Second Vatican Council (1962–4). The liturgical renewal was seminal in precipitating many of the liturgical changes that took place. It started in Germany, but spread across Europe and the United States, mainly within the middle classes. Thomas F. O'Meara has carefully related this renewal to the rise of German Romantic philosophy, which facilitated an alternative metaphysical framework to articulate the sacramental event whereby the Absolute is mediated within Nature in a symbolic manner (O'Meara 1985:326–42).[11] Not accidentally one of the most influential theologians of the Council came out of this German environment: the Jesuit Karl Rahner. Rahner's thought exemplifies the critical transition between Thomistic metaphysics and modernity, at least in the shape of German Idealism, Romanticism, and existentialism (Heidegger). Through these various influences Rahner advanced a "theology of the symbol" which is critical for understanding modern Catholic sacramental theology (Rahner 1964, 1966:221–52).[12]

In his seminal essay "The Theology of the Symbol" Rahner argues that: "All beings are by their nature symbolic, because they necessarily 'express' themselves in order to attain their own nature" (Rahner 1966:224). This principle is derived in two ways. First, by analogy from intra-trinitarian relations, whereby it is in their expressive relations (Father–Son–Spirit) that the persons are co-constituted. Secondly, following the earlier transcendental Thomism of *Spirit in the World* (English translation, 1968), Rahner returns to Aquinas's principle that the body is the form of the soul, and therefore becomes, properly speaking, the symbol of the soul. This emphasis on the necessity of bodily, and therefore symbolic, mediation is already a Christological axiom. Rahner cites John 14:9: "He that sees me, sees the Father." Hence, Jesus is the prime symbol of God, which then allows us to see all of creation, *in him*, as mediating God. Rahner has attained a magnificent marriage between Augustine's emphasis on the sign–symbol and Aquinas's metaphysical causality. In his own words:

> If the individual reality, by making the all present, also speaks of God – ultimately by its transcendental reference to him as the efficient, exemplary and final cause – this transcendence is made radical, even though only in a way accessible to faith, by the fact that in Christ this reality no longer refers to God merely as its cause: it points to God as to him to whom this reality belongs as his substantial determination or as his own proper environment.   (Rahner 1966:239)

Rahner reinterprets instrumental causality in terms of a necessary symbolic mediation. He clearly states his preference for the neo-Platonic over the Aristotelian, for in the latter, the sign is seen as genuinely distinct from that signified – recall Aquinas's analogy of the staff (sacraments) and hand (Christ). In the former, the "image participates in the reality of the exemplar" and "brings about the real presence of the exemplar which dwells in the image" (Rahner 1966:243).

Of course, other theologians were important in precipitating the changes in Vatican II, such as Otto Semmelroth, Henri de Lubac, and perhaps most especially Edward Schillebeeckx (1963). The "Constitution on the Liturgy," *Sacrosanctum Concilium*, was the first of the sixteen Vatican Council documents (December 4, 1963). As in Trent, no attempt was made to articulate a sacramental theology. The Council was pastorally oriented.[13] For our purpose, two main points need noting. First, the centrality of the liturgical and sacramental life to Christian existence is affirmed in the opening paragraph of the document, and reiterated especially in paragraph 10: "the liturgy is the summit towards which the activity of the Church is directed; at the same time it is the fountain from which all her power flows." Secondly, in endorsing the vernacular, the liturgy and sacramental practices became more accessible to non-clergy. In Aidan Kavanagh's words: "Shifts in language and initiation signalled recovery of a less clerical and more egalitarian view of the Church as the baptized people of God" (Kavanagh 1991:72). One might see the present Vatican direction as generally reversing these egalitarian tendencies within ecclesiology.[14]

Having focused mainly on the question of the metaphysical articulation of the relationship of God to the world, in terms first of Christ and then, analogically, of Christ's relationship to the church and sacraments, it is now time to explore some important questions being directed by Catholic theologians at the very heart of these metaphysical constructions and the groups that construct them.

Hidden Bodies and Constructing Presence: Two Challenges

To venture a generalization, it might be said that since the 1960s four major philosophical alternatives have struggled to constructively replace or complement the dominant Aristotelian and neo-Platonic frameworks within which Western theology has operated: Marxism, feminism, postmodernism, and other religious philosophies, mainly eastern.[15] Since these are all movements in relative infancy, one should not expect fully developed approaches comparable to those they seek to contest, nor should one too quickly essentialize them. I shall focus on two in particular: feminism and postmodernism.

Feminism has often employed categories from Liberation Theology, and in that respect borrows from Marxist categories of analysis, sometimes installing women in the place of the proletariat (Ruether 1983:43–4, Chopp 1997:393–6). Feminists have also sometimes employed the epistemological category of "women's experience," almost as a metaphysical framework.[16] Some of the most interesting philosophical forms of feminism (in my opinion) are developing in conversation with French postmodernist thinkers like Julia Kristeva and Luce Irigaray, in contrast to the predominantly Enlightenment forms of liberal, radical, and socialist feminisms that have developed in the United States.[17] Hence, it is difficult to characterize the various feminist challenges in terms of a single alternative metaphysics, but the near unified critique of *lex orandi* will inevitably develop into a full blown *lex credendi*.

To avoid generalizations, I shall focus on the Catholic theologian Susan A. Ross.[18] Ross outlines the history of the sacraments along the four stages employed above, noting various issues related to her feminist concerns. Regarding the Augustinian synthesis, Ross applauds the symbolic-sign ecclesiological context of Augustine. However, she laments the consolidation of the *administration* of the sacraments as the preserve of the clergy. With the growth of clerical celibacy, we have an emerging context within which an all-male celibate elite both practically control the distribution of the means of grace, and also formulate the theology underlying such practices. Women become institutionally marginalized in the development of sacramental theology and its praxis. Ross notes that the exclusion of women from the priesthood presents only one important issue for feminists, and the Catholic Church's position on the matter (writing prior to the ban on discussion of the question in 1998) will push feminists to address deeper questions of "embodiment and sexuality" and "symbolic representation" (Ross 1993a:186–7).

Ross is, then, particularly critical of Aquinas's use of instrumental causality to replace the symbolic mediation employed by Augustine. This "functional" approach meant that the sacraments "increasingly became disconnected from their personal and ecclesial dimensions" (1993a:188–9). This was in part because of the "abstract" categories employed, and it also had the effect of removing attention from the space occupied by women: the reception of the sacraments within popular piety. Ross suggests that ironically, in piety, many women found "in the Eucharist a confirmation of the sacred significance of the body which, to some extent, ran counter to the denigration of women's embodiment taught by the church" (1993a:189).

Of the Reformation period, Ross notices two particular "hidden" trajectories within Catholic theology, both of which can be seen in terms of lack. The first, emblematic in the retention of the system of indulgences, maintained a basically legalistic and juridical mentality in relation to sacramental theology and ecclesiology. This would also account for the growth of devotional practices and piety outside official sacramental rites, for such practices in "Roman Catholicism (as in all the other major religious traditions of the world) have provided women with some sense of power as well as a preserve of religious piety not dominated by men" (1993a:190). The second lack was

Luther's unwittingly paving the way for the ordination of women by describing both men and women as "priests to one another"; and the Catholic rejection of Luther's ecclesiological insights (1993a:190).

Coming into the modern period, Ross raises various criticisms, many of which relate to issues throughout the history of the church – and therefore touched on already. The first is the male-dominated sacramental administration and theologizing within the Church – which is just the tip of the iceberg regarding the Church's deeply entrenched and underlying patriarchy. This situation has caused post-Christian feminist spiritual-ities to develop, and for those feminists who have remained in the Church, either painful and problematic belonging,[19] or/and the creation of women-church, a space where women (and sometimes like-minded men) can develop their own liturgies, "sacra-ments" and base communities, without desiring schism or separation (Schüssler Fiorenza 1983, Ruether 1985). While such troubled adherence is the lot of mainly middle-class white intelligentsia, the issues are nevertheless real. With Ross I would agree on two points: first, there are finally no good arguments for the exclusion of women to the priesthood, and were women to occupy significant ecclesial positions, theology and praxis *might* look very different.[20] Secondly, the exclusive focus on the ordination question is unhelpful to the long-term influence of feminist theology, partly because patriarchy runs much deeper, right into the doctrine of God and intra-trinitarian relations, into language and symbols.[21]

Through this process of male control and articulation, following Christine E. Gudorf, Ross suggests that sacraments are in fact the celebration of what women do naturally – give birth, feed, and comfort. Because of the male sacramental structure, these natural processes, still reflected in the "natural" symbols employed, have become sacralized, interpreted "spiritually," and removed from their natural organic connec-tions. Instead they are construed as peak experiences undergone by the individual within the context of sacred space: male-shaped sacramental moments. The dualisms of sacred–profane, special–ordinary, peak–process, particularly reflect the embodied alienation of the elite male celibates, and also construct the demarcation of public pow-erful man and private invisible woman.[22] For example, baptism is a birth ritual, accord-ing to Gudorf. In its ancient form, this was even clearer, for the recipient emerged from the baptismal waters as the child emerges from the amniotic waters of the mother's womb, ready to be claimed and identified through bestowal of a name, and nurtured with love into the community (Gudorf 1987). However, since men control and inter-pret the ritual in the church, the natural-body-related symbolism is erased and baptism becomes ritual purification and cleansing from sin, not the birthing and nurturing process of the mother. Ross correlates this with the fact that in the United States the peak initiatory event is enacted by the male priest, while the long process of most cat-echetical activity is carried out by women. Even when the church is symbolized as maternal, caring, and nurturing, often under the figure of Mary, this symbolism can still be within the control of patriarchal encoding, whereby the woman, bride, is sub-ordinate and obedient to the man, Christ, the groom. Such nuptial imagery is also used to argue that only a man can act *in persona Christi* at the altar.[23]

Assuming the correctness of her analysis (although in various details I would raise some questions), Ross wonders: "If Christian sacramentality is, at its heart, expressive of male separation, along with alienation between the sacred and secular dimensions of human life, then a feminist sacramental theology is impossible" (Ross 1993a:197). However, since the sacraments are rightly rooted in God's taking on *human* flesh, then the notion of sacraments can only be theologically viable when "women's flesh," experience, and reflection, are involved in sacramental reconstruction.

There has been no large-scale work developing Catholic feminist theology of the sacraments.[24] However, Ross does offer suggestions about all seven sacraments, while also asking whether it should be fixed at seven. I will look at just one sacrament, as an example. Regarding confession or reconciliation, Ross suggests two areas for revision. First, drawing on Valerie Saiving's influential work she questions the notion of sin as "pride" and "hubris," for Saiving argues (and many since her, with increasing evidence and sophistication) that this "sin" is "more applicable to men than to women who have been encouraged to be self*less*. Women's sin may well lie more in an underdevelopment of the self and a too-great reliance upon the opinion of others" (Saiving 1979:25–42, Ross 1993a:200). Admittedly, woman's "sin" is also the source of her strength within some feminist discourse: her inter-relatedness, and her refusal of the isolated enlightenment self! Ross is aware of these ambiguities within feminist discourse (Ross 1993a:198–9).

Secondly, within the manuals of moral theology, despite the Church's tradition of social teaching, sin is very often related to sexuality, and therefore ethics "within the home and not the wider society" (Ross 1993a:201). This "privatization" and domestication of morality results in careful control over women's lives given their social positioning, and Ross urges a more holistic ethics so that divisions between private and social are erased, and the Church can then be as concerned with structural evils regarding the oppression of the weak and marginalized as with what happens in the bedroom.[25]

From this single example, one can begin to see the profound repercussions of feminist critiques. Even in an aside on the eucharist and the exclusion of women priests, Ross intimates an interesting reconceptualization:

> one could argue that because women have not had the experience of official priestly ministry, women are in a position to have a greater appreciation for the sacrality of the everyday, to be aware of the *real presence* not just in the Eucharist but in the ordinariness of preparing daily meals, to convey a healing touch to a sick child, to do the daily work of reconciling parents and children, spouses and friends.   (Ross 1993a:205, my emphasis)

While this construction ambiguously relies on women being contained within the domestic, it nevertheless indicates the transformational significance of eucharistic "real presence."

In Ross's work we see many challenges that feminism raises for both sacramental and ecclesiological practice and belief. It is premature to make any definitive judgments on this field, and it is difficult to predict future developments. However, it is worth isolating one critical issue: the gendered nature of the symbol. As I have occasionally pointed out while depicting Ross's position, there is a perhaps inevitable ambiguity regarding her gender discourse. While some feminists complain rightly about gender stereotyping, often those same writers will use such "types" in promoting positive images of women. Hence, Gudorf and influential feminist theorists like Nancy Chodorow suggest that once men play domestic roles, gender differences will finally be erased, as will the ambiguities of such discourse (Chodorow 1978, Gudorf 1987). The social construction of gender difference cannot be denied, but its totalizing explanation is contested. Depending on their underlying anthropology, feminist theologies might explore profoundly different trajectories. Some feminists (like Julia Kristeva and Luce Irigaray), not unlike the influential Catholic theologians Pope John Paul II and Cardinal Ratzinger, argue for sexual difference based on the differences of body. However, sexual difference is read by these two groups in very different ways, such that Irigaray is deeply critical of Elisabeth Schüssler Fiorenza, and Kristeva is critical of Nancy Chodorow, while both would also be critical of the Pope and Ratzinger.[26]

Postmodern (not in the nihilist sense) Catholic theology is also an infant movement, and some of the most interesting works center around sacramental practice.[27] This is hardly surprising, because these writers realize most clearly that the question of "presence" (exemplified in the eucharist) is ultimately a metaphysical question, but they are united in their critique of onto-theology and the dominance of Greek metaphysics in shaping "god."

To avoid generalizations, I will focus on Louis-Marie Chauvet's important book *Symbol and Sacrament: A Sacramental Reinterpretation of Christian Existence* (1995). Chauvet questions the representational metaphysical framework of Western thought, which stages the primacy of being over language/signs. As a result, this schema thereby construes language as instrumental, as second to being, such that language also always has an external referent (reality), other than and distinct from itself. Chauvet, critically following Heidegger, wants instead to argue that language is both the site of the disclosure, the presence and the absence of being, and that we do not possess language purely as users, but are also possessed and shaped by language. Chauvet refuses the mediation of Aquinas afforded by Rahner, for in Aquinas he sees a productionist scheme of representation that actually goes back to Plato.[28] For Aquinas, foundational Being (God) is primary cause, which means that inevitably the sacraments must be understood in terms of instrumental efficient causality (remember the staff/hand distinction), but thereby, the sacraments are actually separated from what they mediate in an extrinsicist fashion. Furthermore, this means that despite all the verbal references to the Holy Spirit, in Aquinas there is no active role for the Spirit in the sacramental economy (1995:456–65). This is primarily due to what Chauvet calls Aquinas's Christomonistic tendencies, whereby Aquinas's sacramental schema operates entirely from the fixed point of the dual nature of Christ, a schema that might be represented in the following fashion:

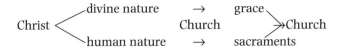

Chauvet wants instead to focus on the *continuing events* inaugurated in the "Pasch of Christ," and the co-joined action of Father and Spirit in the death and resurrection, and the formation of the resurrected body of Christ, the church, in Pentecost (1995:476–90). The scandal of the particularity of Christ is first encountered in the visible church. In this maneuver Chauvet is able to return to the network of relations and signs that inaugurate God's being and becoming within the world. He is also able to develop a more trinitarian sacramental ecclesiology that is facilitated by Aquinas and scholastic theology.

It is important to recall Chauvet's critique of Plato at this juncture, for Chauvet is quite clear about the difference between God and creation, but refuses to think this difference in terms of the dualism between being and language, existence and process. Following Guy Lafon, Chauvet argues that the late dialogues of Plato such as the *Philebus* are typical of denigrating process (*genesis*) as opposed to existence (*ousia*), such that Socrates ultimately reduces the lover–beloved relation to the equivalent of the relation of shipbuilding–boat: process (*genesis*) and outcome (*ousia*). But Chauvet protests: "The boat is a finished product; but the beloved is precisely a product that is *not finished* – and is thus 'infinite' in the sense of 'indefinite', always in process; which is as much as to say that the beloved is *not a 'product' at all. Because the beloved is a 'subject', this person can never be simply reduced to an 'achievement', but always process, development – even a development without end*" (Chauvet 1995:24).[29] Hence, the human subject cannot be understood according to the technical mode of causality, even with a free will. This precisely, according to Chauvet, is "*unthinkable* for Plato and what, in our eyes, characterizes the *metaphysical bent* of Western philosophy: a permanent state of incompleteness defies any logic and destroys any discourse: *any thought which would not come to rest in a final term*, a final significance, a recognizable and ultimate truth for Plato is unthinkable" (1995:24).

Chauvet then locates sacrament within the symbolic network of the church, especially in relation to Word and ethics. His intensely ecumenical insight is the recognition that the sacraments cannot be divorced from the scriptural Word, which forms the liturgy of the church, of which the sacraments are part. Hence, there can be no opposition, even though there is distinction, between the "Liturgy of the Word" and the "Liturgy of the Eucharist" within Mass, for each requires the other for its proper sacramental quality: mediating God through signs, but of differing modality. Chauvet locates Trent as precipitating this divide, reinforced by the Enlightenment, and instead properly suggests that "scripture is sacramental not by derivation but in essence," and cites good patristic precedence such as Origen, for whom the Eucharistic "body" of the Lord can be understood only in relation with both his ecclesial "body" and his scriptural "body" (Chauvet 1995:213–27, Loughlin 1996:64–106, 223–45). Hence, that "the sacraments are always in a sense sacraments of the Word in the Spirit reminds us that their effects are no more automatic or 'magical' than Scripture's" (Chauvet 1995:221).

Regarding ethics, Chauvet argues that cultic practice is the only site whereby Christians learn how to act, for cultic ritual structures Christian existence. Hence, following Irenaeus and Augustine he argues that the eucharist must lead to charity and mercy and new community, for the cult requires a new brotherly and sisterly identity to be learned. In this respect, he attends to both the types of challenges to a sacramental understanding of the church outlined in the opening paragraph of the current chapter: those who want Word and preaching to define church; and those who want liberative ethics to define church. Neither are excluded, finding their place within the sacramental symbolic identity both conferred upon Christians and constructed by them in their becoming the body of Christ.

In many respects Chauvet's project parallels George Lindbeck's cultural–linguistic approach, with two interesting differences. First, following Derrida, because Chauvet locates texts as inscribed within the body, he implicitly pushes Lindbeck's project out of its potential Lutheran Protestant scriptural orbit into one of Word, sacrament, and ethics (as only three elements of a more complex symbolic structuring) such that ecclesiology gains its proper place as the *bodily site* of encountering God.[30] This "body" has a social, historical, and natural/cosmic dimension which allows Chauvet to recover the natural/symbolic sacramental context (with feminists), without uncritically exalting an unmediated "natural" (as do a very small number of feminists and liberation theologians).[31] The second difference is that Chauvet, in contrast to Lindbeck, gives immense weight to the unconscious, repressed, and the hidden within Catholic tradition. This is mainly due to his initially taking French Lacanian semiotic psychoanalysis seriously.[32] As a result he is able to integrate René Girard's discussion of sacrifice extremely creatively, and not uncritically, into his analysis of the eucharist as "sacrifice" (Chauvet 1995:303–11).

An important outcome of Chauvet's argument is his staging of the sacraments in two novel and distinct ways, which both take up traditional teachings and themes, as well as furthering the discussion within this postmodern context. The first involves viewing sacraments as both "instituted" and "instituting." Regarding the former, Chauvet is able to cut through the often bedeviled Catholic discussion concerning the biblical foundations for establishing that Jesus instituted all seven sacraments – following Trent. Instead, he shows that Trent is to be understood symbolically, such that "this institution means nothing else than the identity of the Church as Church *of* Christ, existing only to receive itself from him, as the servant and not the owner of salvation, instituted by an Other and instituting itself, a gift of the grace of the Father through Christ in the Spirit" (Chauvet 1995:381).[33] Regarding the notion of "instituting," Chauvet mediates between what he calls an objectivist schema (productionist, instrumentalist, non-participatory) and a subjectivist schema (grace through faith alone – Barth's synergism, or grace as the sacramental representation of an achievement in life that is already attained – Rahner?). Instead, if language and symbol mediate all reality, then the sacraments are only operative in so much as they are revelatory, and revelatory only in so much as they are operative.

Some Inconclusive Conclusions

Chauvet's achievement is considerable. His critique of onto-theology allows for a recovery of a form of "body theology," which takes the practices of this communal body as the site of identity and formation of the "body of Christ," who is always yet elusive. He takes to their conclusions many of the more timid critiques of Aquinas's causal schema (Rahner and Ross), for finally, the question is one of "representation" and "symbol." His critique disposes of the Greek metaphysical framework underlying Western theology, and in its place is a historicist–symbolic understanding of reality as always mediated, ever anew. The question of representation and symbol was also central to the feminist critique, so a few comments on the interrelationships between feminism and postmodernism are in order, remembering that the "isms" here are chimeric.

In many ways Chauvet's project can be seen as furthering and complementing the feminist critique of Ross, in so much as Chauvet too criticizes the sacraments as peak events located at the altar, focused on proper administration and performance (a view encrusted within instrumental causality), and views them instead as vital parts of the general and slow transformative process of growing into the "body" of Christ, where the process (*genesis*) cannot be distinguished from the result (*ousia*). He regards the recovery of the body – social, historical, and natural – as vital to the reconstruction of sacramental ecclesiology.

It is a shame that there is no real interaction with feminist theology in Chauvet's work, as he remains insensitive to the questions of praxis feminists so poignantly raise. But there is here a more serious failure in Chauvet. That is, while he pays close attention to symbol and language, he never engages with the question of gendered language, despite reading Kristeva.[34] One can only press this criticism because at a vital point in the discussion, Chauvet bases an important part of his trinitarian considerations upon the alleged "neuter" character of the Holy Spirit (Chauvet 1995:511–18). Earlier he sided with Ricoeur in criticizing Heidegger for avoiding the Jewish and focusing too much on the Greek. Now, Chauvet does entirely the same, for in an aside, he notes that the word for Spirit is: "Feminine in Hebrew, it is neuter (*to pneuma*) in Greek, the language that has been most influential in Christian theology" (1995:513). He then carries out the discussion as if the Hebrew never existed, maintaining the neuter character of the Spirit, and in so doing occluding various sorts of symbolic feminizations of the Spirit, such as in the early fourth-century Syrian church (D'Costa 2000:ch.1). Not that such feminizations lead to obvious conclusions, but the occlusion of such feminine symbols within a book on the symbols and sacraments cannot be simply seen as an oversight. It must be pushed, as it might well be on grounds generated by Chauvet, to be a patriarchal occlusion. Given his gender blindness at this crucial point, we can see that Chauvet's project might very well lend itself to a "body theology" that takes differences of bodies seriously at the symbolic level – and might fruitfully complement and further the feminist project. Chauvet's great achievement is to already have done so in an *ad hoc* manner.

Reciprocally, Chauvet's work also illustrates my argument that perhaps some of the most interesting feminist developments might arise from engagement with French postmodern feminism, precisely because it is here that the project of Western logocentric (Derrida) or phallocentric (Irigaray) metaphysics is called into question, and the issue of the symbolic–bodily mediation of all knowledge is brought into view. If patriarchy cannot be eradicated from metaphysics then women priests will only be a change of icing on the same old cake.

Of course, this is to declare my sympathy with both postmodern and feminist concerns, and it would be wise to acknowledge that the possibility of embodied historicist symbolic theology is attainable via other routes, for Aristotle's epistemology certainly requires the priority of the sensible, and the neo-Platonic focuses on the participatory nature of the image with the real, a fusion that Rahner achieves as we saw earlier, and one which facilitates a body theology. While Aquinas adopted Aristotle's assumptions about the form of the body, such that women's bodies were inferior *per se*, Rahner's retrieval of the symbol in terms of the body as the form of the soul, offers an interesting, almost traditional, avenue into body theology if it is prised apart from Aristotle's metaphysical anthropology (Borresen 1981). In fact Rahner's essay on the symbol forms his justification of devotion to the "sacred heart," and he speculates that since single parts of the body always evoke the whole, then different parts might have different powers of expression with regard to their "openness to God" (Rahner 1966:249). Precisely because of this attention to form, Rahner complains against the spiritualizing of natural symbols, fully realizing that their power lies in the natural symbolic force they have (1966:251). However, Rahner never develops his project in terms of sexual difference, or body theology, but neither is it excluded.

Given that the church and sacraments are always dependent on the *embodied* figure of Christ, there are many ways of developing an adequate and full notion of the "body of Christ." But just as the church has often forgotten those first women who proclaimed the good news to the "other" apostles, and sometimes forgotten that it is Christ, no other, who is given in the relations that construct the church, we can perhaps see via these challenges how the task of becoming church always remains unfinished, until the return of its Lord.

Notes

1 Ironically, in Schüssler Fiorenza and Galvin (1992) there is a separate chapter on "Church" which has two chapters dividing it from "Sacraments."

2 For a very good historical survey see Ganoczy (1984); Vorgrimler (1992). On the church, see Avery Dulles's modeling approach: *Models of the Church* (1987), esp. pp. 63–75, locating the novelty of "Church as Sacrament."

3 For a good Roman Catholic account see Schnackenberg (1974) (English translation, 1965); and a quite alternative Protestant account: Schweizer (1961). See also Oscar Cullmann's classic, *Early Christian Worship* (1953:26–32).

4 On Augustine I am indebted to Kelly (1980:412–17); Portalié (1975:230–69); Brown (1967, chs. 19–23); and Ganoczy (1984).

5 For a sense of the complexity and richness of debate see Rubin (1991).

6 See *Summa Theologica* IIIa, qq. 60–90; q. 62 is central here. I have used the Blackfriars edition/translation of 1975. David Bourke's "Introduction" lays much more emphasis on the symbolic than in my exposition (see especially pp. xxi–xxii).

7 Both had entered earlier, with the controversy centered upon Berengar of Tours: see Häring (1948:109–46), and the metaphysical background in Macy (1984).

8 See especially *Summa Theologica*, IIIa, qq. 75, 77; and McCabe and Egner's excellent exchange on the category of substance in *God Matters* (1987:116–64). McCabe suggests a fruitful marriage between Aquinas and Wittgenstein.

9 And see *Sacrosanctum Concilium* 55, 57, and *Lumen Gentium*, 29.

10 All translation in Dupuis and Neuner (1982).

11 See also the good background work of Koenker (1954).

12 Power, *Unsearchable Riches* (1984) locates the main sacramental debate around the question of the symbol (pp. 5–34), and draws heavily on Ricoeur to further the Rahnerian project.

13 See commentary in Vorgrimler, *Commentary on the Documents of Vatican II* (1967; English translation 1966), Commentary by Josef Jungmann, pp. 1–88; Megivern (1978); and Chupungco (1982).

14 The *Catechism of the Catholic Church* (1994) represents an interesting balance between centralist and pluralist tendencies; regarding its liturgical teachings, see Catherine Dooley, "Liturgical Catechesis According to the Catechism," in Marthaler (1994:87–98).

15 To flesh this out, see the essay by Chopp (1997) and the essays by Ward and D'Costa respectively, in Ford, *The Modern Theologians* (1997). John Paul II in *Faith and Reason*, 1998, shows how and why different forms of "authentic" philosophy may be constructively utilized by theology, in faith seeking intelligibility. His definition of postmodernism (paras 90–1) does not cover the type I shall be discussing.

16 See Elisabeth Schüssler Fiorenza's hermeneutical principles at the beginning of her book *In Memory of Her: A Feminist Theological Reconstruction of Christian Origins* (1983). See also Pamela Dickey Young (1990:24–30, 49–69); and Francis Martin's searching questions in *The Feminist Question* (1994, esp. pp. 194–8).

17 See Rebecca Chopp, "From Patriarchy into Freedom" (1993:31–48); and for the latter, Alison M. Jaggar (1983).

18 See Ross, "God's Embodiment and Women," (1993a), in Catherine Mowry LaCugna (1993: 185–209), and her bibliography of further reading on p. 209; see also Ross (1991:345–61); and Ross (1993b:52–64) – and two writers that Ross draws upon heavily: Christine E. Gudorf, "The Power to Create" (1987:296–309), and Rosemary Ruether, *Women-Church* (1985).

19 See, for instance, Hampson (1996), and McEwan (1991).

20 See Swidler, *Women Priests* (1977); and the excellent study by van der Meer, *Women Priests in the Catholic Church?* (1973).

21 LaCugna, *God for Us* (1991) and Johnson, *She Who Is* (1995) have made significant inroads into this question, and see my own *Sexing the Trinity* (2000, chs. 8, 9).

22 See the illuminating analysis of Jean Bethke Elshtain, *Public Man, Private Woman* (1981).

23 See Ross (1991); the Vatican *Congregation for the Doctrine of the Faith*, "Declaration on the Question of the Admission of Women to the Ministerial Priesthood," 1976, uses the "bride = church / groom = Christ = male priesthood" argument: para. 29.

24 But see Ruether (1985); and the Protestant contribution of Marjorie Proctor-Smith, *In Her Own Rite* (1990), who focus mainly on language in preaching.

25 The relation between feminist and liberation theologies has already been noted, and significantly, Ross draws upon Johannes Baptist Metz in this section.

26 See Luce Irigaray on Schüssler Fiorenza: "Equal to Whom?" (1997:198–214); and Kristeva on Chodorow, in *Julia Kristeva Interviews* (1996:113–21). See also Beattie (1997:160–83).

27 See, for example, Jean-Luc Marion, *God without Being* (1991); Gerard Loughlin, *Telling God's Story* (1996); Louis-Marie Chauvet, *Symbol and Sacrament* (1995; English translation 1987).

28 See Chauvet (1995) esp. pp. 7–26, 453–74. Chauvet surely only in effect rejects Rahner's second argument for the "symbol," i.e. Rahner's transcendental anthropology, not Rahner's first argument: the analogy of intra-trinitarian relations.

29 For an entirely different reading of Plato, see Pickstock (1998:3–46).

30 See also Milbank (1990:382–8), for his criticisms of Lindbeck on this count.

31 See Milbank's critique of this in feminist theology, in Milbank (1997:257–67); and my critique of this in Liberation Theology: "Viele Welten – viele Religionen" (1998a:135–52). Also, note Chauvet's recovery of amniotic fluid, etc., within baptism (1995:150–5).

32 See especially the helpful section "Theology and Psychoanalysis" in Chauvet (1995:76–81).
33 This shift away from the historical critical to the symbolic had already been effected by
    Rahner and Schillebeeckx, as indeed had many of Chauvet's other themes, except in so
    much as both their sacramental schemes are fundamentally Thomist. The later Rahner and
    Schillebeeckx both move out of this casuistic framework.
34 There are two references to her, on pp. 77 and 208. Loughlin is the only one of the three
    who attends to gendered language, but surprisingly not once in his actual book, where it
    should occur. See, for example: "Ending Sex," in Davies and Loughlin (1997:205–18).

References

Aquinas, T. 1975. *Summa Theologica*, ed. and trans. D. Bourke. London: Blackfriars.

Beattie, T. 1997. "Carnal Love and Spiritual Imagination: Can Luce Irigaray and John Paul II
Come Together?" *Sex These Days: Essays on Theology, Sexuality and Society*, eds. J. Davies and G.
Loughlin. Sheffield: Sheffield University Press, pp. 160–83.

Borresen, E, 1981. *Subordination and Equivalence: The Nature and Role of Women in Augustine and
Thomas Aquinas*. Lanham, MD: University Press of America.

Brown, P. 1967. *Augustine of Hippo: A Biography*. London: Faber & Faber.

Bynum, C. W. 1987. *Holy Feast and Holy Fast: The Religious Significance of Food to Medieval Women*.
Los Angeles, CA: University of California Press.

Catechism of the Catholic Church. 1994. London: Geoffrey Chapman.

Chauvet, L.-M. 1995. *Symbol and Sacrament: A Sacramental Reinterpretation of Christian Existence*,
trans. P. Madigan, SJ, and M. Beaumont. Collegeville, MN: Liturgical Press.

Chodorow, N. 1978. *The Reproduction of Mothering: Psychoanalysis and the Sociology of Gender*. Los
Angeles, CA: University of California Press.

Chopp, R. 1993. "From Patriarchy into Freedom: a Conversation between American Feminist
Theology and French Feminism," in *Transfigurations: Theology and the French Feminists*, ed.
C. W. M. Kim, S. M. St. Ville and S. Simonaitis. Minneapolis, MN: Fortress Press.

Chopp, R. 1997. "Feminist and Womanist Theologies," in *The Modern Theologians*, ed. D. F. Ford,
2nd edn. Oxford: Blackwell, pp. 389–404.

Chupungco, A. 1982. *Cultural Adaptation of the Liturgy*. New York: Paulist Press.

Cullmann, O. 1953. *Early Christian Worship*, trans. A. S. Todd and J. B. Torrance. London: SCM
Press.

Davies, B. 1992. *The Thought of Thomas Aquinas*. Oxford: Clarendon Press.

Davies, J. and Loughlin, G. eds. 1997. *Sex These Days: Essays on Theology, Sexuality and Society*.
Sheffield: Sheffield University Press.

D'Costa, G. 1997. "Theology of Religions," in *The Modern Theologians*, ed. D. F. Ford, 2nd edn.
Oxford: Blackwell, pp. 626–44.

D'Costa, G. 1999. "Viele Welten – viele Religionen. Warum eine pluralistische Theologie der Religionen in der gegenwärtigen Krise nicht hilfreich ist," in *Pluralistische Theologie der Religionen.
Eine kritische Sichtung*. Frankfurt am Main: Verlag Otto Lembeck.

D'Costa, G. 2000. *Sexing the Trinity*. London: SCM Press.

Dix, D. G. 1945. *The Shape of Liturgy*. Westminster: Dacre Press.

Dooley, C. 1994. "Liturgical Catechesis According to the Catechism," in *Introducing the Catechism
of the Catholic Church*, ed. B. L. Marthaler. London: SPCK.

Duffy, R. A. 1992. "Sacraments in General," in *Systematic Theology: Roman Catholic Perspectives*,
eds. F. Schüssler Fiorenza and J. P. Galvin. Dublin: Gill and Macmillan.

Dulles, A. 1987. *Models of the Church: A Critical Assessment of the Church in All its Aspects*, 2nd edn. Dublin: Gill and Macmillan.

Dupuis, J. and Neuner, J. eds. 1982. *The Christian Faith in the Doctrinal Documents of the Catholic Church*. London: Collins.

Edwards, M. and Tavard, G. 1983. *Luther: A Reformer for the Churches*. Philadelphia, PA: Fortress Press.

Elshtain, J. B. 1981. *Public Man, Private Woman: Women in Social and Political Thought*. Princeton, NJ: Princeton University Press.

Ford, D. F. 1997. *The Modern Theologians*, 2nd edn. Oxford: Blackwell.

Ford, D. F. and Hardy, D. 1984. *Jubilate: Theology in Praise*. London: Darton, Longman and Todd.

Ganoczy, A. 1984. *An Introduction to Catholic Sacramental Theology*. New York: Paulist Press.

Gilson, E. 1957. *The Christian Philosophy of St. Thomas Aquinas*, trans. L. K. Shook. London: Victor Gollancz.

Gudorf, C. E. 1987. "The Power to Create: Sacraments and Men's Need to Birth," *Horizons* 14(2):296–309.

Hampson, D. 1996. *Swallowing a Fishbone? Feminist Theologians Debate Christianity*. London: SPCK.

Häring, N. H. 1948. "Berengar's Definitions of *Sacramentum* and their Influence on Medieval Theology," *Medieval Studies* 10:109–46.

Irigaray, L. 1997. "Equal to Whom?" in *The Postmodern God: A Theological Reader*, ed. G. Ward. Oxford: Blackwell.

Jaggar, A. M. 1983. *Feminist Politics and Human Nature*. Totowa, NJ: Rowman & Allanheld.

Jedin, H. 1957. *History of the Council of Trent*, 2 vols., vol. 2.

John Paul II. 1998. *Faith and Reason*. London: Catholic Truth Society.

Johnson, E. 1995. *She Who Is: The Mystery of God in Feminist Theological Discourse*. New York: Crossroad.

Kavanagh, A. 1991. "Liturgy (*Sacrosanctum Concilium*)," in *Modern Catholicism: Vatican II and After*, ed. A. Hastings. London: SPCK.

Kelly, J. N. D. 1980. *Early Christian Doctrines*. London: A. & C. Black.

Kristeva, J. 1996. *Julia Kristeva Interviews*, ed. R. M. Guberman. New York: Columbia University Press.

Koenker, E. 1954. *The Liturgical Renaissance in the Roman Catholic Church*. Chicago: Chicago University Press.

LaCugna, C. M. 1991. *God for Us: The Trinity and Christian Life*. San Francisco, CA: HarperCollins.

LaCugna, C. M. 1993. *Freeing Theology: The Essentials of Theology in a Feminist Perspective*. San Francisco, CA: HarperCollins.

Loughlin, G. 1996. *Telling God's Story: Bible, Church and Narrative Theology*. Cambridge: Cambridge University Press.

McCabe, H. and Egner, G. 1987. *God Matters*. London: Geoffrey Chapman.

McEwan, D. 1991. *Women Experiencing the Church: A Documentation of Alienation*. Leominster: Gracewing.

Macy, G. 1984. *The Theologies of the Eucharist in the Early Scholastic Period*. Oxford: Clarendon.

Marion, J.-L. 1991. *God without Being: Hors Texte*, trans. T. A. Carlson. Chicago, IL: Chicago University Press.

Martin, F. 1994. *The Feminist Question: Feminist Theology in the Light of Christian Tradition*. Edinburgh: T. & T. Clark.

Maxwell, W. 1936. *An Outline of Christian Worship*. Cambridge: Cambridge University Press.

Megivern, J. 1978. *Worship and Liturgy: Official Catholic Teachings*. Wilmington, NC: McGrath.

Milbank, J. 1990. *Theology and Social Theory: Beyond Secular Reason*. Oxford: Blackwell.

Milbank, J. 1997. *The Word Made Strange: Theology, Language, Culture.* Oxford: Blackwell.

O'Meara, T. F. 1985. "The Origins of the Liturgical Movement and German Romanticism," *Worship* 19:326–42.

Pickstock, C. 1998. *After Writing on the Liturgical Consummation of Philosophy.* Oxford: Blackwell.

Portalié, E. 1975. *A Guide to the Thought of St. Augustine.* Westport, CT: Greenwood Press.

Power, D. N. 1984. *Unsearchable Riches: The Symbolic Nature of Liturgy.* New York: Pueblo.

Proctor-Smith, M. 1990. *In Her Own Rite: Constructing Feminist Liturgical Tradition.* Nashville, TN: Abingdon.

Rahner, K. 1964. *The Church and the Sacraments*, trans. W. J. O'Hara. Freiburg: Herder; London: Nelson.

Rahner, K. 1966. "The Theology of the Symbol," in *Theological Investigations*, vol. 4. London: Darton, Longman and Todd, pp. 221–52.

Ross, S. A. 1991. "The Bride of Christ and the Body Politic: Body and Gender in Pre-Vatican II Marriage Theology," *Journal of Religion* 71:345–61.

Ross, S. A. 1993a. "God's Embodiment and Women," in *Freeing Theology: The Essentials of Theology in a Feminist Perspective*, ed. C. M. LaCugna. San Francisco, CA: HarperCollins.

Ross, S. A. 1993b. "Sacraments and Women's Experience," *Listening* 28:52–64.

Rubin, M. 1991. *Corpus Christi: The Eucharist in Late Medieval Culture.* Cambridge: Cambridge University Press.

Ruether, R. 1983. *Sexism and God Talk.* London: SCM Press.

Ruether, R. 1985. *Women-Church: Theology and Practice of Feminist Liturgical Communities.* San Francisco, CA: Harper & Row.

Saiving, V. 1979. "The Human Situation: a Feminine View" [1960], in *Womanspirit Rising: A Feminist Reader in Religion*, eds. C. Christ and J. Plaskow. San Francisco, CA: Harper & Row.

Schillebeeckx, E. 1963. *Christ the Sacrament of the Encounter with God.* London: Sheed & Ward.

Schnackenberg, R. 1974. *The Church in the New Testament.* London: Burns & Oates.

Schüssler Fiorenza, E. 1983. *In Memory of Her: A Feminist Theological Reconstruction of Christian Origins.* New York: Crossroads.

Schüssler Fiorenza, F. and Galvin, J. P. eds. 1992. *Systematic Theology: Roman Catholic Perspectives.* Dublin: Gill and Macmillan.

Schweizer, E. 1961. *Church Order in the New Testament.* London: SCM Press.

Swidler, L. and Swidler, A. 1977. *Women Priests: A Catholic Commentary on the Vatican Declaration.* New York: Paulist Press.

Van der Meer, H. 1973. *Women Priests in the Catholic Church?* trans. A. and L. Swidler. Philadelphia, PA: Temple University Press.

Vorgrimler, H. 1992. *Sacramental Theology*, trans. Linda M. Maloney. Collegeville, MN: Liturgical Press.

Vorgrimler, H. ed. 1967. *Commentary on the Documents of Vatican II*, vol. 1, trans. L. Adolphus, K. Smyth, and R. Strachan. London: Burns & Oates.

Wainwright, G. 1980. *Doxology: The Praise of God in Worship, Doctrine and Life – A Systematic Theology.* London: Epworth.

Ward, K. 1997. "Postmodern Theology," in *The Modern Theologians*, ed. D. F. Ford, 2nd edn. Oxford: Blackwell, pp. 585–602.

Young, P. D. 1990. *Feminist Theology/Christian Theology: In Search of Method.* Minneapolis, MN: Fortress Press.

PART IV
Key Modern Figures

CHAPTER 17

Kant

Gareth Jones

Introduction

It is a truism to state that Kant's work is central to everything "modern" about modern thought; that his critical philosophy lies at the heart of every *modern* attempt to think through the character and status of knowledge, and consequently – for theologians – faith, too. And yet the claim has substance, because of the abiding strength of Kant's philosophy, and in particular the clarity of his processes of reasoning. It is in this respect – epistemology as a way of thinking through questions and issues – rather than the provision of a self-sustaining system of thought or belief, that Kant remains the pre-eminent philosopher of modernity.

Immanuel Kant was born in Königsberg in East Prussia in 1724. He died there, too, at the beginning of the nineteenth century, having never left the province. His early intellectual work was concerned with the natural sciences, in particular mathematics and physics, fields that remained germane for his later work in philosophy. Kant's life was uneventful, including a lengthy period as a private tutor, before becoming a *Privatdozent* (teaching assistant) at the University of Königsberg in 1755. He remained at the university for the rest of his life, becoming Professor of Logic in 1770, and dying in 1804. Kant never married.

From this basic outline one can see that although Kant started his university teaching career at a reasonably early age, he was 46 before he became a full professor in his discipline. Indeed, Kant's major contributions to modern thought all date from well into his fifties, long after the publication of his professorial dissertation *De Mundi Sensibilis et Intelligibilis Forma* in 1770. It was not until 1781, for example, that Kant published the first edition of his *Critique of Pure Reason*, and 1787 – at the age of 63 – that the second and final edition of this seminal work appeared. If Kant was relatively un-productive in the eleven years immediately following his elevation to his Chair in 1770, however, the period after 1781 was relentlessly fruitful. The year 1783 saw the publi-cation of his *Prolegomena to Any Future Metaphysics*; 1788, the *Critique of Practical*

Reason; 1790, the *Critique of Judgment*; and 1793, his *Religion within the Limits of Reason Alone*.

Kant's final works, including *On Eternal Peace* in 1795 and various other writings related to significant themes in Christianity, are understandably less monumental than the three critiques, but nevertheless are important for any understanding of Kant's contribution to modern theology. One of the most significant of these is Kant's "The End of All Things," a relatively short essay published in the *Berlinische Monatsschrift* in 1794, in which Kant addresses the Christian doctrine of eschatology, otherwise known as the Final Judgment, or the end of the world.

"The End of All Things"

There are two key characteristics to Kant's late works on Christianity, and both of them are to be found in "The End of All Things." First, Kant's thought leads him into conflict with the prevailing orthodox Lutheranism of the Prussian state, which lends a social and political relevance to Kant's ideas that one does not immediately associate with the three critiques. Though historically informative, however, this fact is not lastingly significant. Second, and much more important, Kant turns his mind towards the kind of everyday concern worrying ordinary believers, in order to think through the philosophical deep structure to such issues and thereby make their faith more intelligible and, most important of all, more practicable. Reading an essay like "The End of All Things," therefore, helps us see Kant doing for certain practical issues what his critical philosophy has done for modern theology as a whole, namely, clearing the intellectual ground for a better, for Kant *correct*, understanding of their real significance.

"The End of All Things" starts with a simple proposition: "It is a common expression, particularly in pious talk, to have a dying person say he is *passing from time into eternity*" (Kant 1963:69). As Kant immediately argues, however, it is nonsensical to think of time somehow continuing into eternity, as if they were two parts of one whole. Rather than imagining that somehow we progress out of time, into eternity, we should recognize that we have to think the concept "eternity" *in the midst of time*, because we have no way of thinking it *outside of time*; i.e. in eternity. Kant therefore writes:

> While we now follow up the transition from time to eternity (this idea may or may not have some objective reality regarded theoretically as an enlargement of knowledge), as reason itself makes this transition in a moral respect, we encounter the end of all things considered as beings in time and as objects of possible experience.   (1963:69)

Kant does two interesting things here. First, he inserts the clause in brackets, "this idea may or may not have some objective reality regarded theoretically as an enlargement of knowledge," thereby indicating that any critical discussion of the concept of eternity cannot be bounded by the conditions of cognition (the first *Critique*); for while "eternity" may or may not have objective reality, the *verification* of such a reality is not open to us "as beings in time and as objects of possible experience." Thus – second – Kant concludes that reason thinks through "this transition in a moral respect"; i.e. in terms of the second *Critique*. Thus, Kant concludes:

But since the idea of an end of all things does not originate from reasoning about physical things but from reasoning about the moral course of the world and nothing else, the
moral course of events can be applied only to the supersensible (which is comprehensible
only in relation to the moral).   (1963:70)

This is actually very simply expressed by Kant and, as he indicates a little further on in
his argument, the Ideas (his capitalization) that he is working with are speculative in
so far as they are intended to make sense of the moral way in which human beings
think about their existence. The point of introducing such Ideas, however, and indeed
the entire process of speculative reasoning at this point, is to make intelligible what
otherwise is unintelligible in Christianity; i.e. the Day of Judgment. As Kant writes,
towards the end of his essay:

The rule for the practical use of reason according to this Idea, therefore, intends to express
nothing more than that we must take our maxims as if, in all its changes from good to
better which proceed into the infinite, our moral state, with respect to its disposition (the
homo noumenon, "whose change takes place in heaven"), would not be subjected at all to
temporal change.   (1963:78)

It is this understanding that informs Kant's interpretation of the Christian doctrine that
God is love:

Christianity aims to promote love for the observance of its duty in general and elicits it,
too, because the founder of this religion speaks not in the character of a dictator who
impresses people by a will that demands obedience, but speaks rather in the character of
a humanitarian who brings to the heart of his fellowmen their own well-understood wills,
according to which they would act spontaneously of themselves if they proved themselves
fitting.   (1963:82–3)

And, in a conclusion resonant for all subsequent theology, Kant observes: "It is, therefore, the *liberal* way of thinking – equidistant from both the sense of servitude and
anarchy – whereof Christianity anticipates an effect for its teaching."   (1963:83)

"The End of All Things" is a valuable way into Kant's thought in general, and its significance for modern theology in particular, for three significant reasons. First, it evidences Kant's always consistent emphasis upon critical thinking, the role of reasoning
in meaningful reflection upon human existence. It is this quality, allied to his equally
significant contention that all knowledge requires an ingredient derived from nature
(because all knowledge derives from reflection upon human experience), that makes
Kant's philosophy a break from those that had preceded it. For modern theology, it
reduces creatively to the sense that the authorities for talking about God must be *worldly*
as well as *ecclesial*, something that helps one to understand what Kant means by
"liberal."

Second, Kant places ethical reflection at the heart of his thought about the end of
all things, again creatively reducing the essence of Christianity to a form of moral
conduct that is taught by the founder of Christianity, Jesus of Nazareth. This quality is

linked in Kant's analysis, third, to his argument that the traditional subjects of Christian metaphysics – the ideas of God, freedom, and immortality – are only intelligible in terms of moral reasoning. Kant's conclusion here, that natural theology is an illusion, is something spelled out more clearly in a text closely related to "The End of All Things," Kant's 1793 text *Religion within the Limits of Reason Alone* (Kant 1996).

Religion within the Limits of Reason Alone

Kant's small book is really a collection of four essays on the following subjects: (1) radical evil in human nature; (2) the battle of the good against the evil principle for dominion of humanity; (3) the victory of good over evil, and the foundation of a kingdom of God on earth; (4) religion and priestcraft. The background to the publication of the text is fascinating, leading directly to Kant's problems with and censure by Lutheran Church authorities in Prussia. The essays themselves, however, are quite straightforward, and consistent with the themes already identified in the analysis of "The End of All Things."

   One of the first things the reader of *Religion within the Limits of Reason Alone* is aware of is the somewhat eschatological character of the individual essay titles, and their apparent dualism. As one now expects, however, the language here is indicative of the context of the ideas under scrutiny, rather than their substance; that is, Kant wants us to think about why such ideas might be meaningful, rather than any objective reality they might indicate (which, as something inaccessible to human reason, moral or cognitive, is beyond thought and therefore unintelligible). The first essay, consequently, is really an analysis of human experience of existence, often expressed in somewhat gothic terminology, but reducing down to the reading that humanity is conscious of moral law through its ability to reason morally, "and yet has incorporated into this maxim the (occasional) deviation from it" (1996:79); that is, accepted the option of undermining rather than upholding moral law, and thereby become susceptible to evil. Such evil, writes Kant, is radical because it undermines the philosophical foundation of all moral law, namely that such law is *general* or *universal* and thereby applies equally to all individuals. In essence, what Kant is arguing in this first essay is that humanity's propensity to behave in ways that undermine moral law is characteristic of human nature not because of any supernatural origin, but because of selfish choice.

   Human beings will to be evil, therefore, a circumstance that Kant addresses in his second essay, there relating it to the argument that since we are capable of recognizing moral law, and since moral law is a first principle, rather than a secondary corruption (evil) of a first principle, it is logical to maintain that humanity is predisposed to do good rather than evil. Kant spends more time in this second essay relating his theme to Christianity in particular and religion in general, but the constant theme of his work still holds: the conflict between good and evil is the most fundamental way we have of understanding human conduct, and as such is the only appropriate level on which to discuss all religious questions. Indeed, that is the only way to understand Christian truth claims, within the limits not of an alternative metaphysical system, but of (moral) reason alone:

For here too the principle holds, "It is not essential, and hence not necessary, that every human being know what God does, or has done, for his salvation"; but it is essential to know *what a human being has to do himself* in order to become worthy of this assistance. (1996:96)

Kant's third essay uses this basic definition of religion as moral reasoning to take his argument away from the realm of logic, towards Christian doctrine. Thus, in a series of basic theses Kant moves the argument away from philosophy, towards moral theology as he understands it. Since the philosophical analysis of good and evil concerns the ethical state of nature, therefore, the moral imperative for the religious individual is that he or she leave the state of nature in order to become a member of an ethical community, the concept of an ethical community religiously reducing to that of a people of God under ethical laws, something that is only realizable as a Church: "To found a moral people of God is, therefore, a work whose execution cannot be hoped for from human beings but only from God himself" (1996:135). The requisites for such a Church are universality, purity, freedom, and "the unchangeableness of its constitution," the latter quality being something that Kant argues is established *a priori* in historical revealed faith or "ecclesiastical faith" (1996:136); i.e. a faith based in the Bible.

This is the point at which Kant's analysis becomes ingenious, but also deeply problematic for traditionally orthodox Christianity (like Prussian Lutheranism). The relationship between received ecclesiastical faith, on the one hand, and the universal or pure faith of religion morally prescribed and therefore philosophically established on the other hand, is that the latter is the supreme interpreter of the former. Or, stated another way: moral reasoning renders intelligible the Bible: "There is . . . no norm of ecclesiastical faith except Scripture, and no other expositor of it except the *religion of reason* and *scholarship* (which deals with the historical element of Scripture)" (1996:145). This process of interpretation or exposition, Kant concludes, is the coming of the Kingdom of God, understood in the only way that humanity *can* understand it; i.e. morally. The full potential of this argument, and indeed its inherent difficulty, is laid bare in the following quotation:

It is therefore a necessary consequence of the physical and, at the same time, the moral predisposition in us – the latter being the foundation and at the same time the interpreter of all religion – that in the end religion will gradually be freed of all empirical grounds of determination, of all statutes that rest on history and unite human beings provisionally for the promotion of the good through the intermediary of an ecclesiastical faith. (1996:151)

The rest of Kant's text, both the remainder of the third essay and the whole of the fourth essay, "Of Religion and Priestcraft," is an attempt to work out the implications of this pious hope, both for the character and status of Christian doctrine in general, and ecclesial polity in particular. It contains a surprising amount of engagement with both biblical material and doctrine, and some trenchant criticisms of what is counterfeit and delusory in religion as it is commonly practiced. The really significant dimension of Kant's argument, however, is his working out of the way in which Christianity is a *learned* religion, an emphasis upon the relationship between theology and critical education that has often dominated Protestantism ever since. As Kant wrote, prophetically: "And there still is no foreseeing how many alterations still lie ahead of faith because of this scholarship" (1996:188).

The *Critique of Practical Reason*

One of, if not the, dominant themes of Kant's exposition towards the end of *Religion within the Limits of Reason Alone* is his understanding of conscience as the guiding thread in matters of faith (1996:202). Kant understands conscience as "the moral faculty of judgment," writing that "reason judges itself, whether it has actually undertaken, with all diligence, that examination of actions (whether they are right or wrong), and it calls upon the human being himself to witness *for* or *against* himself whether this has taken place or not" (1996:203). With respect to religion, this translates in the following way:

> The true (moral) service of God, which the faithful must render as subjects belonging to his kingdom but no less also as its citizens (under laws of freedom), is itself just as invisible as the kingdom, i.e. it is a *service of the heart* (in spirit and truth), and can consist only in the disposition of obedience to all true duties as divine commands, not in actions determined exclusively for God.   (1996:208)

The key idea here is "true duties," a synthesis of conscience (duty) and philosophy (truth) that is most fully expressed in Kant's second critique, the *Critique of Practical Reason* (Kant 1993). The *Critique of Practical Reason* is a critique in that its method is synthetic, starting with principles and then proceeding to experiences that it organizes, conceptualizes, and render intelligible. As Lewis White Beck writes:

> Critique is negatively an attack on pretensions to supersensible knowledge, which appear as metaphysical dogmatism and moral fanaticism; affirmatively it establishes the structure, range, use, and validity of concepts like that of cause in the first *Critique*, duty in the second that cannot be objectively valid if derived from experience, but that are essential if science and morals are to "make sense."   (1993:X)

What one finds in the second *Critique*, consequently, is a structural analysis of how the concepts of duty, conscience, and freedom work rationally, which for Kant means logically or purely, so that they are applicable to every individual, in every situation. There is here, therefore, the philosophical deep structure for the religious and theological positions we find in "The End of All Things" and *Religion within the Limits of Reason Alone*, but articulated in terms of the universal analysis established in the *Critique of Pure Reason*. As such, it breaks down into three basic components.

The first part of Kant's argument is a clarification of the doctrine of the elements of pure practical reason. This entails: an analytic of pure practical reason, containing the principles of pure practical reason; the concept of an object of pure practical reason; and the drives of pure practical reason. What this means, in effect, is that Kant proceeds from an analysis of the possibility of practical fundamental principles *a priori*, thereby establishing the conditions of possibility of speaking of pure practical reason at all. In this section Kant identifies freedom and moral law (and hence duty) as the governing maxims for pure practical reason. This allows him to go on and argue, in the second part of this economy, that good and evil and the tension between the two constitute the object of pure practical reason, before concluding in the third part that the drives of pure practical reason arise entirely from the natural respect that human beings feel for moral law, "an object of the greatest respect and thus the ground of a positive feeling which is not of empirical origin." As such, it can be known *a priori*, a quality that is the guiding principle of the analytic of pure practical reason and which leads Kant to conclude: "Respect for the moral law . . . is a feeling produced by an intellectual cause, and this feeling is the only one which we can know completely *a priori* and the necessity of which we can discern" (1993:77).

The second part of Kant's exposition is the dialectic of pure practical reason, which is broken down into two main parts: the dialectic of pure practical reason in general, and the dialectic of pure reason in defining the concept of the highest good. If one remembers that in the first *Critique* Kant uses the dialectic to show that perfect knowledge leads to certain specific metaphysical dogmas, one has a sense of what Kant will attempt in the dialectic of his second *Critique*: a debunking of the hitherto accepted norms of moral philosophy, replacing them with what Kant calls "practical postulates," the ideas of God, freedom, and immortality that are necessary for morality and which, as has been demonstrated, are central to "The End of All Things" and *Religion within the Limits of Reason Alone*. What Kant achieves in the second *Critique*, however, prior to those explicitly religious writings, is to clear the ground for an alternative general theory of how and why people behave ethically. It is, to paraphrase, a philosophical version of the "As if" question of "The End of All Things," only here developed in terms of the critical structures of the first *Critique*. This step allows Kant to understand questions of human freedom in contradistinction from those of natural causation, and thereby to identify a critical differentiation between knowledge and faith that is fundamental to everything he wants to say about how human beings understand reality practically. As Kant observed, most famously, in the first *Critique*: "I have found it necessary to deny *knowledge* in order to make room for *faith*" (1929:XV). As one has seen, however, that faith is not the objective grace of the Lutheran justification by faith alone, but rather the logical possibility that best expresses the free, moral judgment that humans know as their deepest religion.

The *Critique of Pure Reason*

Kant calls the third and final part of the *Critique of Practical Reason* a "Methodology of Pure Practical Reason," on which he writes:

> we understand by methodology the way in which we can secure to the laws of pure practical reason access to the human mind and an influence on its maxims. That is to say, it is the way we can make objectively practical reason also subjectively practical.   (1993:157)

It is the part of the argument in which Kant becomes more specific, moving beyond pure or logical considerations towards a realistic understanding of what all of this means for the ubiquitous "man on the street." One does this, says Kant, in the following way: "The first step is to make judging according to moral laws a natural occupation which accompanies our own free actions as well as our observations of those of others, and to make it, as it were, a habit" (1993:165). If one regards this step as a way of making pure or logical speculations historical, i.e. *experienced*, then one moves back into the world of Kant's first *Critique*; for as Kant wrote in the preface to the first edition, that same relationship between logic and history is central to cognition, albeit approached from the opposite perspective to that of the second *Critique*: "For the chief question is always simply this: what and how much can the understanding and reason know apart from all experience?" (1929:12). Or, to state the matter more prosaically: Kant takes apart reason and experience, better to understand how they fit together, just as in the second *Critique* he took apart freedom and duty, and in *Religion within the Limits of Reason Alone*, he took apart God and faith.

"Taking apart reason and experience" is notoriously difficult, however, and the first *Critique*, though it obeys the same formal structures outlined above with respect to the second *Critique*, is arguably the most difficult philosophical text anyone can attempt to read. Approaching it from the perspective of the religious and ethical writings, however, has the advantage of making several simple moves that help one to understand Kant's larger enterprise. First, however complex the terrain, Kant's goal is simple: to understand how knowledge works logically, in the mind, better to distinguish faith and morality from knowledge. Second, this process will entail an examination of what Kant calls the conditions of possibility of cognition, which again is an analysis of the deep structure of how we come to know what we know. Third, this process is entirely wrapped up with the business of cognizing sense data, of acquiring and sorting knowledge about the natural world, just as ethical or practical reasoning is wrapped up in making clear the objective principles by means of which people can make subjective judgments. It is the same points, again, about logic and experience: remember that and the first *Critique* becomes a lot more manageable.

At root, therefore, the first *Critique* works as follows. Kant, like many of his time, accepted the proven validity of natural science and mathematics as the dominant theoretical vocabulary. Since the physical reality of nature was made up of contingent circumstances, however – and since neither Continental rationalism nor British empiricism could find a plausible language to make related sense of contingent facts – Kant reasoned that the only logical solution was that it was reason itself, understanding (*Verstand*), which prescribed to nature its laws. This in turn meant for Kant that the causality that we see demonstrated in the natural world, that every event has a cause, is not dependent upon some unknown yet posited natural or supernatural principle, but rather in consciousness itself. Thus, Kant reasoned, consciousness itself must be so constituted that it has to interpret the sense data that it receives. What he sets out to achieve in the first *Critique*, therefore, is a systematic analysis of how consciousness works to achieve such a result; the categories that, with sense data, are synthesized intellectually to form knowledge; and the forms of perception, space, and time, that are the mental "formats" under which – or through which – knowledge is received by the understanding.

What we have here, therefore, is in effect Kant's "mapping" of the processes by means of which human beings come to cognize the world around them. It starts from certain basic principles about the causality of the natural order of things, which Kant thinks is demonstrated scientifically and mathematically. It then takes the axiomatic step of assuming that their necessity is logical and universal, rather than physical and particular, thereby requiring the philosopher to find a theoretical solution to a practical question, namely, how do we know what we know about the world? After this step, it is a relatively small additional one to deduce that something else – the categories – is required to "add" to the data we receive via the senses, in order to come up with knowledge as something intellectual "in our minds." The final step – though in a sense the most apparent, for obvious reasons – is to show people how and why time and space are formal qualities, the forms of perception that mind uses to "shape" or configure our knowledge of the world (and without which we would be presented with knowledge with no ability to order it).

Granted Kant's argument about the validity of scientific reasoning, causality, and the role of sense data in cognition – which is surely unarguable – there are really only two big things to understand in Kant, therefore: what are the categories, which synthesize with sense data to form knowledge? And how do time and space "work" as forms of perception? Kant ingeniously answers the second question first in his text, so that the first substantial part of his argument, the "Transcendental Doctrine of Elements," begins with the transcendental aesthetic and the elaboration of time and space as forms of perception. On this work Kant writes, making the fundamental distinction between appearance and reality that is often taken to be the cardinal feature of Kantian epistemology:

> What objects may be in themselves, and apart from all this receptivity of our sensibility, remains completely unknown to us. We know nothing but our mode of perceiving them – a mode which is peculiar to us, and not necessarily shared in by every being, though, certainly, by every human being. With this alone have we any concern. Space and time are its pure forms, and sensation in general its matter.   (1929:82)

Space and time, then, are not conditions of possibility of the reality of things in themselves, as if "space" and "time" were enormous ideal forms, "little bits" of which we bump into as we go about our daily lives. On the contrary – and Kant's use of the word *pure* is the key indicator here – space and time are universal forms, qualities of mind itself, that shape the way we receive knowledge. And, looked at from this perspective, one realizes that Kant is right: in a very sophisticated way, that is exactly what time and space are.

Once this fundamental insight has been achieved, the first *Critique* turns to by far the greater task, which is to elaborate the categories of judgment that mind employs in order to make knowledge out of sense data. As with the second *Critique*, Kant characterizes this work as a transcendental logic, breaking it down into a transcendental analytic and a transcendental dialectic, the former being constructive, the latter largely destructive of bogus or inadequate arguments. The first part, the analytic, is where Kant spends nearly 200 pages identifying and sorting out the transcendental categories which, as the pure concepts of understanding, form the conditions of possibility of the cognition of the appearance of objects in the world. Kant is able to schematize these pure concepts as a table, in the following way:

I
Of Quantity
Unity
Plurality
Totality

II
Of Quality
Reality
Negation
Limitation

III
Of Relation
Inherence and subsistence
Causality and dependence
Community

IV
Of Modality
Possibility–Impossibility
Existence–Non-existence
Necessity–Contingency

Again, the really helpful thing here is to understand this table as a map: Kant is mapping the basic "ingredients" that mind needs to "add" to sense data in order to arrive at knowledge that is intelligible and usable. Most of the rest of the transcendental analytic consists of Kant's attempts to sort out how this mental process occurs, what is and is not involved when cognition occurs, and the errors and wrong turns that philosophy makes when it fails properly to understand the *status* of these pure concepts and the way in which they condition the possibility of the knowledge of the appearance of things. Astonishingly complex and elaborate, Kant's argument is essentially straightforward: without these structures, mind cannot cognize the appearance of things. And for over 200 years philosophers have been trying, unsuccessfully, to prove that Kant is wrong.

There are other significant stages in the development of the transcendental analytic, principally Kant's work on the analogies of experience, but fundamentally these simply continue to elucidate the basic position already considered. As indicated, the second big job in the first *Critique* – again analogous to the *Critique of Practical Reason* – is the transcendental dialectic, the demolition of wrong ideas. Here the key sections concern the antithetic of pure reason, and the ideal of pure reason. On the former, Kant writes: "The antithetic does not . . . deal with one-sided assertions. It treats only of the conflict of the doctrines of reason with one another and the causes of this conflict" (1929:394). In other words, there are *antinomies of reason* – a conflict that appears to run against the logical laws Kant has spelled out – which have to be analyzed skeptically by exposing the way in which they are not really antinomies at all, but rather simply conceptual confusions that transcendental philosophy is designed to remove. The ideal of pure reason, by contrast, is a more positive notion, and works to provide an archetype for understanding the generality of the quality in question. Kant writes:

> By the ideal I understand the idea, not merely *in concreto*, but *in individuo*, that is, as an
> individual thing, determinable or even determined by the idea alone. . . . As the idea gives
> the *rule*, so the ideal . . . serves as the *archetype*. . . . Although we cannot concede to these
> ideals objective reality (existence), they are not therefore to be regarded as figments of the
> brain; they supply reason with a standard which is indispensable to it, providing it, as they
> do, with a concept of that which is entirely complete in its kind, and thereby enabling it to
> estimate and to measure the degree and the defects of the incomplete.   (1929:486–7)

Kant takes the helpful step of differentiating his argument here from Plato's sense of
the ideal, which, as Kant says, was an idea of the divine understanding (1929:486),
but it's already clear how Kant's understanding differs from Plato's and indeed all other
understandings. For Kant, the ideal of pure reason is a way of understanding the
singularity and therefore universality of critical philosophy; it is nothing more nor
less than the archetypal definition of the *genus* of how we all think.

The final section of Kant's first *Critique* is designated the "Transcendental Doctrine
of Method," and as with the methodology section of the second *Critique*, has to do with
how the discipline of pure reason works, its ends or goals. If some of the other parts of
the first *Critique* appear to be a long way from the kind of reflection we considered earlier
in this essay, it is here that Kant's argument comes full circle and we return to the realm
of morality and religion. For, as Kant writes in this section:

> The ultimate aim to which the speculation of reason in its transcendental employment is
> directed concerns three objects: the freedom of the will, the immortality of the soul, and
> the existence of God.   (1929:630)

Critical philosophy, in other words, is logical epistemology; but it is logical epistemology in the service of a wider theological epistemology, defining reason in order to make
room for faith, as Kant so aptly expresses it.

The *Critique of Judgment*

There is one section of the first *Critique*, concerning the distinction of all objects in
general into phenomena and noumena, which allows a useful way into Kant's third
and last major critique, the *Critique of Judgment*. The famous metaphor here is that of
the island of pure understanding, "the land of truth," which is concerned with phenomena, the cognition of the appearance of things (1929:257). Noumena, by contrast,
are things-in-themselves, what we might call the essence of things, as long as "essence"
is not understood concretely. Kant thinks we can understand noumena negatively, as
not an object of our sensible intuition, or positively, *as* an object of a non-sensible intuition, in which case "we thereby presuppose a special mode of intuition, namely, the
intellectual, which is not that which we possess, and of which we cannot comprehend
even the possibility" (1929:268). Kant never did think that pure reason could provide
anything more than a logical sense that noumena must exist, if only because cognition
works by reference to phenomena and phenomena presuppose noumena, however
opaquely "noumena" are defined. He never could quite leave noumena alone, however,

and the closest he came to defining things-in-themselves came in the third *Critique*, albeit in a way that is crucially differentiated from the empirical work of the *Critique of Pure Reason*.

The *Critique of Judgment* is divided into two main parts, the first being Kant's response to esthetics, the second his response to teleology. The "Critique of Esthetic Judgment" is principally concerned with how we arrive at judgments of taste, of the beautiful (in nature and art) and, more opaquely, of the sublime. Judgments of taste are relatively straightforward, because essentially what Kant wants to do is reduce the argument back beyond questions of subjective pleasure, towards an objective quality that we can speak of as beauty. In other words, Kant is interested in the *property* beauty, and as with the first *Critique* he pursues his concern not by asking questions about "inherent" qualities, but rather about qualities of reflection. The key concept here, therefore, is the purposiveness without purpose of the esthetic judgment that constitutes a "pure moment" of esthetic intuition, in which, as Werner Pluhar notes in his Introduction to Kant's *Critique*, Kant appears effectively to equate such purposiveness with something "supersensible," which is where the possibility of an intuition of the noumenal comes in. As Pluhar again notes, Kant is never too clear about exactly what such an intuition might constitute, but the closest he gets is on the matter of the sublime, particularly the work on the sublimity of nature (Kant 1987:lxix). Kant attempts to argue that his analysis retains the argument as a purely mental one, but he is curiously unconvincing (1987:123). Better to appreciate that, in its greatest forms, Kant too succumbs to the conviction that esthetic judgments are the closest people come to a sense and taste for the infinite (the noumenal) which comes to fascinate later generations of Protestant theologians, starting with Schleiermacher in 1799.

Kant and Theology: the Structures of Theological Epistemology

Kant's three *Critiques* constitute the single greatest attempt to define the character and scope of critical thinking in Western philosophy. They embrace critical thinking *per se*, as well as critical moral and esthetic and teleological thinking *per accidens*, and they make room on a number of levels for questions of religious belief. And while it is true that Kant's own understanding of the Christian faith is somewhat attenuated, lacking what would later on be called a thoroughgoing eschatological character, yet there is a complete structure that positions religious belief at its center, and which in turn allows the individual to recognize his or her moral actions in the context of following God, and to determine with relative freedom how they will respond to their confession of belief in the divine.

The century following Kant's death in 1804 is one of great success for Kantian ways of understanding such questions. Notwithstanding Hegel's influence in the 1820s and 1830s – in any case in decline by the time Schelling came to Berlin in 1841 – it was Friedrich Schleiermacher who set the tone for the nineteenth-century appropriation of Kant's thought. This process began in the 1790s, culminating in 1799 with the publication of Schleiermacher's *On Religion: Speeches to its Cultured Despisers* (1996), in which he attempted to provide something like a "Critique of pure religious feeling" in the Kantian vein, taking up Kant's challenge from the first two *Critiques* in general and building upon the third *Critique*'s sense of the sublime in particular. While this tendency was tempered somewhat in Schleiermacher's later *The Christian Faith* of 1821–2, nevertheless that text still betrays Kant's considerable influence, albeit now combined with a greater sense of that pietistic communitarianism that was a large part of Schleiermacher's own roots. Schleiermacher's understanding of the role of Jesus Christ in particular is heavily influenced by Kant's – as evidenced in "The End of All Things" – even if Schleiermacher's interpretation of Christian doctrine goes far beyond anything contemplated by Kant.

The development of neo-Kantianism in the mid nineteenth century, as best exemplified by the work of Albrecht Ritschl, and continuing into the 1930s with the philosophies of Cassirer, Cohen, and Natorp, represents a systematic attempt to raise up Kant's legacy as the dominant moral philosophy of the day. It was very successful, so much so that much of German society and culture was characterized by the same moral and esthetic concerns that are found in Kant's work in the 1790s. That same influence was much felt in German theology from the late nineteenth century onwards, so that figures like Adolf von Harnack and later (though to a lesser extent) Wilhelm Herrmann were influential political figures as well as religious and academic ones. Indeed, one might go as far as to say that the so-called "Culture Protestantism" of the late nineteenth and early twentieth centuries was a particular manifestation of neo-Kantianism. In this later development one sees something of the ambition and scope of Kant's vision, albeit realized in religious and political ways that he himself might not have explicitly envisaged.

One can argue that Kant's influence through neo-Kantianism lasted in Germany until the 1930s, and was only gradually and then abruptly ended by the rise of national socialism. Despite the establishment appeal of neo-Kantianism, however, other philosophies were developing in the late nineteenth century, and after the First World War they became increasingly significant. The work of Kierkegaard and Nietzsche, for example (as well as Hegel), was mediated by the Swiss political thinker Franz Overbeck, whose work had an immediate and lasting effect on the young Karl Barth. Similarly, the "rediscovery" of eschatology in the late nineteenth century, perhaps exemplified by Albert Schweitzer's *Quest of the Historical Jesus* (originally published in 1896; 2000), brought an immediate counterpoint to Kant's reduction of Christ's significance to that of the supreme moral teacher. The theologies of Rudolf Bultmann and Karl Barth emerged out of this collision, and one can trace in their early thought the gradual erosion of faith in neo-Kantian theology, replaced by a different form of critical or *Krisis* thinking. By the 1920s this new "dialectical theology" was established, and though Bultmann and Barth later split from each other, their influence upon the later generation of Pannenberg, Moltmann, and Jungel ensured that no subsequent German theology of any significance could be called "Kantian" – certainly not in the sense that that adjective was used previously.

To a large extent this same situation pertains today: Kant's thought, though respected, is characterized as philosophy, and Barth's influence, with its all too obvious antecedents in Hegel, remains endemic. While it is true, therefore, that the Catholic theologian Karl Rahner remained convinced that tension between general and theological epistemologies was central for critical theology, and therefore Kant remained a key resource for the interpretation of the Christian faith, this conviction is not generally held (and Rahner himself has been eclipsed today by Hans Urs von Balthasar, whose influence is nearly as great as Barth's). To this extent concern with epistemology has been replaced with a concern for ontology in a way that was literally unthinkable to Kant: it would have meant thinking the noumenal, which was unintelligible even conceptually (as he made clear in the third *Critique*). Not just that, but in contemporary theology general ontological reflection has been replaced by theological ontology, which is once again – for the first time in modernity, perhaps – regarded as dominant and *sui generis*. The notion of Christian theology in dialog with general ways of thinking, rather than in combat with them, has largely been eclipsed, and with it much of the credibility of what was once broadly termed "liberal theology."

While it is true that theological liberalism remains an amorphous presence in many church establishments, therefore, explicitly liberal theologies have largely lost their voice.

References

Kant, I. 1929. *Critique of Pure Reason* [1781], trans. N. Kemp Smith. London: Macmillan.

Kant, I. 1963. "The End of All Things" [1794], in *Kant on History*, ed. L. W. Beck. London: Macmillan, pp. 69–84.

Kant, I. 1987. *Critique of Judgment* [1790], trans. W. S. Pluhar. Indianapolis, IN: Hackett.

Kant, I. 1993. *Critique of Practical Reason* [1788], ed. and trans. L. W. Beck. London: Macmillan.

Kant, I. 1996. *Religion within the Limits of Reason Alone* [1793], in *Religion and Rational Theology: The Cambridge Edition of the Works of Immanuel Kant*, eds. A. W. Wood and G. di Giovanni. Cambridge: Cambridge University Press, pp. 39–215.

Schleiermacher, F. D. E. 1996. *On Religion: Speeches to its Cultured Despisers* [1799]. Cambridge: Cambridge University Press.

Schleiermacher, F. D. E. 1999. *The Christian Faith* [1821–2]. Edinburgh: T. & T. Clark.

Schweitzer, A. 2000. *Quest of the Historical Jesus* [1896]. London: SCM Press.

CHAPTER 18
Hegel

Merold Westphal

Hegel got his higher education at the theological seminary in Tübingen, and many of his earliest, unpublished drafts and sketches from Tübingen, Berne, and Frankfurt have come down to us as his "early theological writings" (Hegel 1971a, 1984b). Hegel will abandon much from these experiments, notably the flirtation with a Kantian/Fichtean primacy of practical reason and the hostility toward Christianity. But the mature Hegel of Jena and Berlin remains a theologian out of the deep conviction, stated emphatically at the very outset of his System,[1] that philosophy and religion have the same content, though in different forms.

This is the insight in which the *Phenomenology of Spirit* and the *Philosophy of Spirit* culminate. It is what makes the categories of the Logic into "*metaphysical definitions of God*" (Hegel 1991:¶85; cf.¶24) or "the exposition of God as he is in his eternal essence before the creation of nature and a finite mind" (1969:50; cf. 1969:63; 1984–7, vol. 3:275). It is what makes the philosophy of religion not just "one science within philosophy" but "the *final* one" (1984–7, vol. 1:365). Finally, it is what makes it possible to identify philosophy as *Gottesdienst*, the worship of God.[2]

So when Karl Barth asks, "Why did Hegel not become for the Protestant world something similar to what Thomas Aquinas was for Roman Catholicism?" (1959:268), he points not only to what did not happen but also to what Hegel profoundly desired. He wanted to perform the two tasks of Aquinas's *Summa Theologiae*. First, he wanted to give theology a rational foundation in speculative metaphysics. This is why he introduced his 1821 lectures on the philosophy of religion by saying that they had "the same purpose as the earlier type of metaphysical science, which was called *theologia naturalis*. This term included everything that could be known of God by reason alone, as distinct from a positive, revealed religion, a religion that is known from some source other than reason" (Hegel 1984–7, vol. 1:83). So we should not be surprised to find Hegel defending the proofs for the existence of God throughout his mature work.[3]

But Hegel wants his philosophy of religion to go beyond this task "by treating religion and its knowledge of God as found in *theology in general*" as its object and not "as natural theology had done, God as he is in himself" (Merklinger 1993:3). So, while relating his 1824 lectures to Wolffian *theologia naturalis*, he insists his science has a different goal. Wolff's object was "God as such. Our object, however, is not *just* [emphasis added] God as such; the content of our science is religion." While traditional natural theology was satisfied with "an abstract essence of the understanding," Hegel wants to understand God as spirit, "God *as he is [present] in his community* . . . thus it will be evident that the doctrine of God is to be grasped and taught only as the doctrine of *religion*."[4] Since it will turn out that Christianity is the absolute or consummate religion for Hegel, this means that the philosophy of religion, like the Thomistic *Summa* it seeks to replace, must concern itself ultimately with distinctively Christian doctrines, the "positivity of the Christian religion" that was such a problem for Hegel in his "early theological writings."[5] Hegel is to be a theologian of the Trinity.[6]

It does not follow that Hegel will understand either the traditional proofs or the traditional themes of Christian theology as they have traditionally been understood. In both cases he will find them rational only by radically reinterpreting them. The "heterodox Hegel" will "swerve" away from theistic orthodoxy.[7] His philosophy will take over Christian doctrines, "but only insofar as it can rethink the content in its own terms in the course of obtaining methodically secure knowledge." Christianity is "of interest to Hegel to the extent that he can interpret its doctrines in the context of his philosophy. The Christian religion does not, however, afford a basis for understanding either the terms in which the fundamental principles are formulated or the way in which they are developed in the system."[8]

This hermeneutical violence is justified as the triumph of reason. Hegel claims to be rescuing for reason (*Vernunft*) what has been held captive by the understanding (*Verstand*), in whose thrall mainstream traditions in both natural and revealed theology remained. Unlike Kant and Fichte, the mature Hegel is unwilling to derive theology from practical reason.[9] So his dual project of giving theology a rational foundation presupposes that metaphysics is possible as a science, that conceptual, theoretical, speculative knowledge of God is possible whether discussing the "proofs" or the doctrine of the Trinity, in short that the Kantian critical philosophy has been refuted, along with Jacobi, Schleiermacher, and all the romanticisms that deny reason's power to know God and appeal to some pre-reflective, pre-conceptual immediacy (faith, feeling, intuition) as the foundation of religion.

Thus, as early as 1802, in *Faith and Knowledge*, Hegel launches a critique of "the almighty age and its culture," which assumes that reason cannot free itself from sensibility and therefore cannot know God (1977a:65; translation altered), a critique he will repeat in the introductory materials added to the Berlin versions of the *Encyclopedia*[10] and throughout the Berlin lectures on religion. Specifically targeted are three versions of the claim that God is beyond reason's grasp. First, there is the idea that we can know *that* God is but not *what* God is (Hegel 1991:¶¶ 63, 72–3;1984–7, vol. 1:162, 166–7). Hegel sees this as an open invitation to any content whatever, however arbitrary.

Second is the notion that "philosophy cannot aim at the cognition of God, but only at what is called the cognition of man"(Hegel 1977a:65; cf. 1977a:68, 118). Thus Hegel's undisguised contempt for theologies in which confessional dogmas flee metaphysics in favor of psychological insight or are of interest only as the history of doctrine.[11] In retrospect Hegel says that the path leading from Kant through romanticism ends in Feuerbach's reduction of theology to anthropology.

Finally, as a variation of the second theme, there is the claim "that we can know only our relation to God, not what God himself is. . . . That is why it is that nowadays we merely hear religion talked about but find no investigations into God's nature or what God might be within himself, how God's nature must be defined" (1984–7, vol. 1:163).

Behind all the contemporary attempts to do theology while doing without metaphysics Hegel rightly sees the specter of Kant. But it is not in these polemical reviews, fascinating and instructive as they are, that Hegel rests his claim to have exorcized critical finitism (thereby removing the necessity of romantic appeals to various forms of immediacy). Hegel offers two "refutations" of Kant. One is called *Phenomenology of Spirit*. The other is called *Science of Logic*. No attempt will be made in this essay to summarize the complex argument of these two massive classics. But it is Hegel himself who calls our attention to the fact that his theology stands or falls with the success of those projects. Because philosophy of religion is the *"final"* science within philosophy, "it presupposes the other philosophical disciplines and is therefore a result . . . we are dealing with a result of premises that lie behind us."[12]

Resting on the prior parts of his system, Hegel's *Lectures on the Philosophy of Religion* are the fullest statement of his theology. He gave these in Berlin in 1821, 1824, 1827, and 1831. Of these it is probably the 1827 version that gives us his mature theology in its most complete form.[13] The theology it presents is best described as "Christian" pantheism. This is ironical, for a distinctive feature of the 1827 lectures is the vigorous denial, in response to charges from pietist theologian F. A. G. Tholuck, that his system was pantheistic.[14]

Three pieces of historical background are important for reading the 1827 lectures against the charge of pantheism. Two of these involve public intellectual uproars whose memory had by no means died away; the third concerns Hegel's own development. First there is the *Pantheismusstreit* (pantheism controversy) begun in 1783 when Jacobi told Mendelssohn that Lessing, prior to his death, had confessed to being a Spinozist. Lessing was a hero of the German Enlightenment, and Jacobi hoped by this revelation to discredit both. For pantheism was widely thought to be equivalent to atheism and a threat to both morality and piety. The private correspondence led to a literary debate in 1785 and, ironically, to both a wider interest in and a wider acceptance of Spinoza in German intellectual life. "Nearly all the major figures of the classical *Goethezeit* – Goethe, Novalis, Hölderlin, Herder, F. Schlegel, Hegel, Schleiermacher, and Schelling – became Spinoza enthusiasts in the wake of the controversy. Apparently overnight, Spinoza's reputation changed from a devil into a saint."[15] Thus in one version of his history of philosophy, Hegel says that "to be a follower of Spinoza is the essential commencement of all Philosophy" and "You are either a Spinozist or not a philosopher at all."[16]

The other ruckus was the *Atheismusstreit* (atheism controversy) of 1798–9. Beginning with his 1792 *Critique of All Revelation*, Fichte had been developing a philosophy based on the primacy of practical reason. In 1798 he published an essay, "On the Foundation of Our Belief in a Divine Government of the Universe," in which he argued for a supersensible moral world order above the world of ordinary sense perception and the natural sciences. But he identified God with this moral world order. "I myself, along

with my necessary goal, constitute what is supersensible. . . . This living and effica-
ciously acting moral order is itself God. We require no other God, nor can we grasp any
other . . . the concept of God as a particular substance is impossible and contradictory;
and it is permissible to say this quite openly and to put an end to the idle prattle of the
schools, so that the true religion of joyful right action can make its appearance" (Fichte
1994:147, 151–2).

It turned out not to be permissible to say this openly, and in 1799, just two years
before Hegel joined the faculty at Jena, Fichte was fired from his professorship there.
Pantheism was not the issue, at least not by name, but it was clear that the denial of
God as a personal being distinct from the (human or natural) world as its source could
put a crimp in one's academic career. Hegel thus began his teaching career in a context
where (1) variations on the theme of Spinozistic pantheism were widely influential in
German intellectual life, and (2) it was dangerous in the university to be perceived as
holding to a view incompatible with theism. It was during his Jena years that Hegel
solved this problem with the core principles of his theology, the claim that religion and
philosophy have the same content but in different forms. This view is the key to the
chapter on religion in the *Phenomenology of Spirit* (1807) but it first achieves clear
articulation in the 1805–6 lectures on the Philosophy of Spirit (Hegel 1976:280–3).

The other piece of historical background we need to keep in mind when approaching the lectures of 1827 is Hegel's own pantheistic orientation. This is what made the
problem of reconciling philosophical reason with popular religion and traditional theology at once a political as well as an intellectual problem for Hegel. It is in correspondence with Schelling in 1795 that Hegel's decisive break with theism becomes clear.
This is the year in which the theologian of the Berlin lectures is born. In January
Schelling writes that Fichte's *Wissenschaftslehre* (1794) will deliver philosophy from
"the old superstition of so-called natural religion as well as of positive religion [that]
has in the minds of most already once more been combined with the Kantian letter. It
is fun to see how quickly they can get to the moral proof. Before you can turn around
the *deus ex machina* springs forth, the personal individual Being who sits in Heaven
above!" (Hegel 1984a:29).

In his reply, Hegel indicates his own lack of enthusiasm for orthodoxy's appropriation of Kant. "I believe it would be interesting, however, to disturb as much as possible
the theologians who in their antlike zeal procure *critical* building materials for the
strengthening of their Gothic temple, to make everything more difficult for them, to
block their every escape. . . ." Thus, when he signs off, "May the Kingdom of God come,
and our hands not be idle. . . . Reason and Freedom remain our password, and the Invisible Church our rallying point," he acknowledges that he and his friends (he has just
mentioned Hölderlin's enthusiasm for Fichte) are at odds with the visible Church(es).
Still, with reference to Schelling's scorn for the moral proof "which they know how to
manipulate so that out springs the individual, personal Being," he asks, "Do you really
believe we fail to get so far?" (Hegel 1984a:31–2). Hegel seems less sure of his departure from theism than of his departure from orthodoxy, and in this respect remains
more Kantian than Fichtean.

Early in February, Schelling replies "to your question as to whether I believe we
cannot get to a personal Being by means of the moral proof. I confess the question has

surprised me. I would not have expected it from an intimate of Lessing's. Yet you no doubt asked it only to learn whether the question has been entirely decided *in my own mind*. For you the question has surely long since been decided. For us as well the orthodox concepts of God are no more. My reply is that we get even *further* than a personal Being. I have in the interim become a Spinozist. . . . For Spinoza the world, the object by itself in opposition to the subject, was *everything*. For me it is the *self*." After identifying "the pure, Absolute Self" as both "an infinite sphere of absolute being" and as "*our* [emphasis added] Absolute self," Schelling writes, anticipating Fichte's essay of three years later, "There is no other supersensible world for us than that of the Absolute Self. *God* is nothing but the Absolute Self. . . . Personality arises through the unity of consciousness. Yet consciousness is not possible without an object. But for God – i.e., for the Absolute Self – there is no object *whatsoever*. . . . Consequently there is no personal god. . . ."[17]

In his April reply, Hegel promises to study the *Wissenschaftslehre* over the summer, but already he accepts "the idea of God as the Absolute Self" – with two important comments. First, he expects political benefits from this new philosophy "by which man is being so greatly exalted." Oppression will be overcome by freedom, human dignity, and human rights. On the other hand, he thinks that the idea of "God as the Absolute Self" will need to remain an "esoteric philosophy."[18] Apparently a theistic/Kantian version of the new philosophy will need to gain wide, public currency while the Fichtean/Spinozistic version he now shares with Schelling and Hölderlin will be for the intellectual elite.[19] For himself, the only reservation he has about the latter, expressed in an August letter after the promised study of Fichte and Schelling's own *On the Self as the Principle of Philosophy* and anticipating his own later thought, is whether the category of substance is still appropriately applied to the Absolute Self.[20]

About a year later, Hegel describes his political ideal in a draft we now call the "Earliest System-Program of German Idealism" – "Absolute freedom of all spirits who bear the intellectual world in themselves, and cannot seek either God or immortality outside themselves."[21] The Fichtean overtones of this early pantheism will recede, but Hegel's resistance to any notion of a personal God substantially distinct from human persons remains. It can be traced in "The Spirit of Christianity and Its Fate,"[22] in an 1800 draft of "The Positivity of Christianity" (1971a:176), and in the Jena writings right up to the verge of the *Phenomenology* (see Jaeschke 1990:171–84).

A recurring theme in these texts is the notion that there is nothing ontologically unique about Jesus, but that his sense of being of the same nature as the Father is appropriate to all humans. As this theme emerges, Hegel's early hostility toward Christianity is replaced by the affirmation of a "Christian" pantheism that extends the Nicene claim of being consubstantial with the Father beyond Jesus to humanity as such. It is such a Christianity that is presented in the *Phenomenology* as absolute religion, whose key doctrine is the "incarnation of the divine Being. . . . The divine nature is the same as the human, and it is this unity that is beheld" (Hegel 1977b:459–60). It is a defect of understanding to take this to be a particular truth relating to a single individual rather than a universal truth about human nature as such.[23]

Just before the *Phenomenology*, in the Philosophy of Spirit of 1805–6, Hegel writes about what makes Christianity the consummate religion. "The Absolute religion is this knowledge that God is the depth [*Tiefe*] of self-certain spirit. Thereby he is the self of all [selves]." When this abstraction becomes concrete [*entäussert*], God becomes an actual self. "He is a man who has ordinary spatial and temporal existence. *And this individual is all individuals. The divine nature is not other than human nature*" (1976:280; emphasis added).

Hegel's early theological writings had a Nietzschean hostility toward Christianity. Having abandoned anything like orthodoxy, Hegel joined his friends in abandoning the theism which it presupposed. There is nothing unique in such a story, nor about the turn to pantheism that is part of it. The distinctively Hegelian move, first developed in Jena, is to make this pantheism the key to finding Christianity to be the Absolute Religion so that "all other religions are defective or imperfect [*unvollkommen*]" (Hegel 1976:280).

Turning to the lectures of 1827 we can ask two questions: what is pantheistic about this theology, and what is "Christian"? We can become more precise about the meaning of "pantheism" by beginning with Hegel's adamant denials that his theology should be so designated. In a section entitled "The Concept of God," Hegel gives a four-fold defense.[24] He seeks to counter three misrepresentations of Spinoza, whom for the most part he is willing to identify as a pantheist.[25] Then he seeks to separate himself decisively from Spinoza.

Pantheism could be taken to mean that "this complex of everything existing, these infinitely many individual things – that all this is God . . . not the universality that has being in and for itself but the individual things in their empirical existence." But, Hegel responds, "It has never occurred to anyone to say that everything, all individual things collectively, in their individuality and contingency, are God. . . . No one has ever held that" (1984–7, vol. 1:375; cf. 1971c:¶573). In this crude sense, according to which to buy a pound of coffee is to buy a pound of God, Spinoza is no pantheist.

Secondly, Hegel is aware that the charge of pantheism is often taken to be equivalent to a charge of atheism. He often mentions the two together.[26] But he counters that in the case of Spinoza it is not God who disappears but the world, which disappears into God, who alone remains. This is hardly atheism. Acosmism would be a better description.[27] While defending Spinoza's insistence that finite beings do not have their being in themselves, Hegel worries that Spinoza's acosmism "does not give the principle of difference (or finitude) its due," that his substance as "the universal might of negation – is only the dark, shapeless abyss, so to speak . . . which produces nothing out of itself that has a positive subsistence of its own."[28]

A third charge against Spinoza that Hegel wishes to refute is this: "If everything is one in the way this philosophy asserts, then it asserts with it that good is one with evil, that there is no distinction between good and evil, and therewith all religion is annulled." Hegel points out that for Spinoza as for the theist, "In God there is no evil." But precisely insofar as there is a distinction between the infinite substance and the finite modes there is a sufficient distinction between God and human persons to make it possible for the latter to be either good or evil. "This distinction is not [applicable] within God . . . under this definition as substance. But for human beings there is this distinction."[29]

It is not clear that this defense is compatible either with Spinoza's own text[30] or with Hegel's just-expressed complaint that in his acosmism does not give "difference (or finitude) its due" so that finite things can have a "positive subsistence of [their] own." In what deeper sense must finitude be given its due than to allow finite selves enough subsistence of their own to be evil?

It is clear, however, that Hegel is eager to defend Spinoza, and with him pantheism in general, (1) against the charge of attributing divinity to finite things either individually or in a heap, (2) against the charge of abolishing religion by means of atheism, and (3) against the charge of abolishing religion by abolishing morality. Nevertheless, he wishes to distance himself decisively both from Spinoza and the label of pantheism.

The key to this fourth part of his defense against charges of pantheism (he actually places it first) is found in his notion that the proper movement of philosophical thought is from concepts that are abstract and inadequate to concepts that are increasingly more concrete and more nearly adequate. Concreteness here signifies richer content (though not more sensible content). Thus, to give an example he would welcome, the notion of the animal soul is more concrete than that of the vegetative soul in Aristotle because the former includes and presupposes the latter but places the latter in a subordinate role to the higher activities of the former. The movement from animal soul to rational soul is similarly a move from the (relatively) abstract to the (more) concrete.

The Achilles heel of Spinoza (and of pantheism in general) is that he takes the category of substance to be adequate to the being of God. "The fault of all these modes of thought and systems is that they *stop short* of defining substance as subject and as spirit" (Hegel 1971c:¶573; emphasis added, translation modified). It is true that God is to be conceived as absolute substance. But "we do not stop at that point." Rather, this claim "is part of the presupposition we have made that God is *spirit, absolute spirit, eternally simple spirit, being essentially present to itself*" (Hegel 1984–7, vol. 1:370–1). Just as a human being is a physical object and an organism but essentially so much more, so God is absolute substance but so much more. Along with substance Hegel will identify such categories as being, becoming, life, purpose as appropriate but inadequate "names" for God.[31] Nothing short of the category of spirit will do, a category signifying subjectivity and presence to self. The category of substance "lacks the principle of *personality* – a defect which has been the main cause of hostility to Spinoza's system."[32]

Hegel's defense thus comes down to this: pantheism is not as bad as it is made out to be and in any case he is not a pantheist because, as he puts it in the *Phenomenology*, "everything turns on grasping and expressing the True, not only as *Substance*, but equally as *Subject*" (1977b:10).

It is hard not to suspect Hegel of being disingenuous here. He knows that pantheism is widely seen to be equivalent to atheism, not because it denies that anything deserves to be called God but because it is a-theism, a denial of the theistic conception of God as a personal creator distinct from the world. Theists will have no trouble agreeing that spirit is a more nearly adequate category for speaking about God than substance. But they will want to know whether it is a theistic concept of spirit or a pantheistic concept. For the essence of pantheism, and their problem with Spinoza, was never the category of substance as such but the way it was used to compromise divine transcendence. Hegel's "I'm not a pantheist – I go beyond substance to spirit" is a distraction from this issue, a refusal to address the theist's objection head-on.

For theists transcendence signifies not God's remoteness or absence from the world, in which, they want to insist, God is fully present and active. Rather, it signifies a certain asymmetry. There can be God without the world, but not the world without God. The God relation, namely createdness, belongs both to the being and to the essence of the world, including human persons. But the world does not belong to the being and essence of God. God can be and can be God without the world. Creation is a free and contingent act, not a necessity. Thus, for example, it is not an emanation. The radiation of heat or light from its source is neither a gift nor an act of love. For the theist, creation is both. Creator and creature never dissolve into a single, internally differentiated being. They remain two – two substances, two presences to self, two lovers.

The question is not whether theism or pantheism is true but whether Hegel's philosophy deserves to be classified with Spinoza's as a variety of pantheism in spite of the very real differences between the two systems. That question has already been formulated as the question whether Hegel uses the category of spirit to give an account of divine transcendence substantially at odds with the theistic account. We can ask that question this way. Granted that by means of the category of spirit Hegel's God will have a presence to self apparently missing from Spinoza's, will human consciousness or self-consciousness be an essential means to or locus of that self-presence? Is the human spirit necessary to the being and essence of the divine spirit?

Ironically, it is while seeking to deflect the pantheism charge that Hegel gives us one of the strongest clues that his will be a pantheistic concept of spirit. Chiding those theologians who are blind to the speculative depth of Christian theology, he praises Meister Eckhart for writing as follows: "The eye with which God sees me is the eye with which I see him; my eye and his eye are one and the same. . . . If God did not exist nor would I; if I did not exist nor would he."[33]

Hegel's philosophy of religion culminates in his presentation of Christianity as the absolute or consummate religion. In accordance with Hegel's claim that his philosophy is at once simply the truth and the most adequate expression of the Christian truth, it is clear that we are dealing with Hegel's own theology. Already in the introductory portions of the 1827 version of "Consummate Religion," before we get to the trinitarian exposition, we find two indications that we have before us a version of pantheism.

The first grows out of the seemingly innocent claim that religion is consciousness of God as the absolute essence or being. Consciousness usually distinguishes itself from its object, but this is to render both moments finite. "Thus consciousness [in distinguishing itself from God] knows even the absolute essence only as something finite, not as what is true." The solution to the problem is to reinterpret religious consciousness as self-consciousness, as "consciousness relating itself *to its essence, knowing itself* as its essence and knowing its essence as its own" so that religion is *"essence knowing itself."* This is the meaning of spirit.[34]

The implicit claim here is that theism necessarily renders God finite by understanding religious consciousness as an awareness of something over against itself rather than of itself. The only way God could remain infinite is by being a whole to which all finite beings are internal, which is precisely Spinoza's view (see Hegel 1984–7, vol. 3:263, 281).

Hegel amplifies this self-consciousness motif as he turns to the positivity of Christianity, the particularity of its content that is at least a *prima facie* challenge to the autonomy of philosophical reason. This challenge is especially sharp when Christianity is said to be revealed by God, meaning "that it has come to humanity from without." The irrationality of this givenness could be overcome and we could find it rational only if we can recognize it as "something that is our own . . . the determination of our rationality itself" (1984–7, vol. 3:252–4).

At this point Hegel introduces a theme beloved by the Protestant reformers, the witness of the spirit. For them it was an important part of the story of how God reveals God's nature and will beyond the capacity of our capacities to discover, thus, as Hegel just put it, "from without." On the one hand, God tells us what we need to know in the Bible. But for that to be of any use we need both to recognize the Bible as God's truth and to understand it properly. These two tasks (recognition and understanding) are the work of the indwelling Holy Spirit, the third person of the Trinity, also known as the Spirit of truth because "he will guide you into all the truth" (John 16:13).

For Hegel the problem is not how to recognize a truth that comes "from without" but how to recognize it as "our own" so that it will no longer come "from without." What he needs is a version of Plato's theory of recollection, and the Reformed doctrine of the internal witness of the Holy Spirit to the truth and meaning of the Bible does the job for Hegel – once one "minor" change is introduced. The spirit that witnesses to the truth of Christianity turns out to be "our spirit," which is why we are able to recognize its content as "our own" and as "the determination of our rationality." Thus it is not surprising that the "witness of the spirit in its highest form is that of philosophy, according to which the concept develops the truth purely as such from itself without presuppositions. As it develops, it cognizes – in and through its development it has insight into – the necessity of the truth" (1984–7, vol. 3:353–6).

Philosophical reason, in a particular version to be sure, has been made the criterion of truth and given hermeneutical hegemony over the normative texts and traditions of the Christian religion. This is possible because the human spirit, in the mode of Hegel's system, especially his Logic, has taken on the role of the Holy Spirit. The distinction between the divine and the human has been overcome, which is just what is necessary if religious consciousness is to be self-consciousness.

Hegel makes the same point in a slightly different way while still reflecting on the need for an hermeneutical criterion. On the one hand there is the thought that works with categories of finitude and sees its content as contingent and arbitrary (often as events in a narrative), and thus irredeemably positive. On the other hand philosophy thinks in terms of genuinely conceptual categories that enable it to see the necessity of its content. (In relation to the previous discussion, it is clear that the former, lacking the witness of the spirit, remains at the level of consciousness, while the latter rises to self-consciousness.) One needn't know a great deal of Hegel to see that he is here invoking his standard distinction between Understanding (*Verstand*) and Reason (*Vernunft*), and subsequent passages confirm this explicitly (compare 1984–7, vol. 3:259–61 with vol. 3:280–2 and 347).

Hegel takes over this distinction from Kant. The Understanding, content to deal with the finite and conditioned, is what makes Newtonian physics possible as a science.

Reason, insisting on grasping the Infinite and Unconditioned, is the site where meta-physics, asking questions about God, Freedom, and Immortality, falls into dialectical distress. Both belong to human thought, which Kant sharply distinguishes from divine thought, thereby generating the distinction between appearances and things in themselves, phenomena and noumena.[35]

In claiming to rehabilitate speculative thinking or metaphysics, Hegel naturally makes the counter-claim that Reason can succeed in knowing God, in apprehending the Infinite, the Absolute, the Unconditioned. But what is important here is the further claim he makes at the same time. In moving from the finitude and contingency of the Understanding to the infinity and necessity of Reason, human thought becomes divine thought. That is why, in the original passage distinguishing the two modes of thinking, Hegel says of the Understanding's categories of finitude, that "it is not the divine but the finite spirit that moves in such categories" (1984–7, vol. 3:261). The implication is clear. Philosophy, which thinks in terms of Reason and its Concept, is the divine spirit. This is why its teachings can be identified as the witness of the Holy Spirit.

Hegel has used the distinction between Understanding and Reason to relocate the distinction between the human and divine minds so that it becomes a distinction between two modes of human thinking. We are merely human when our thinking (the-istically) thinks of God and the world, including ourselves, as ontologically distinct. But when it (pantheistically) thinks of the world, including ourselves, as internal distinctions within the divine being, it is divine thought thinking itself.[36] Once again it becomes possible to construe religious consciousness, not in its own terms, but philosophically reinterpreted, as the self-consciousness in which the divine knows itself as human and the human knows itself as divine. Divine transcendence has become the transcendence of Hegelian philosophy and its interpretation of Christianity to all opposing philosophies and interpretations of Christianity.

Finally, we come to the trinitarian exposition of the Christian religion. Hegel repeatedly tells us that he is talking about the Trinity and uses the familiar terms, Father, Son, and Holy Spirit for the three "elements." But reminding us of his earlier claims that religion is for everyone, philosophy only for the few (see note 19, this chapter), and of the distinction between Understanding and Reason, Hegel tells us that the language of Father and Son is only the truth for the many who remain at the level of sense and understanding. Those who rise to the form of the speculative concept have better ways to talk about God (1984–7, vol. 3:283).

For philosophical reason the three moments or elements in the Idea of God are not persons but categories: universality, particularity, and singularity or identity (of universality and particularity) (1984–7, vol. 3:273, 276, 279). We can speak of God the Father as God before the creation of the world, but what that signifies is neither a lover within an actual, immanent Trinity nor the Godhead thought in its unity, but an abstract universality which is not yet anything actual. It is like an Aristotelian form (soul) thought in abstraction from the particular substance apart from which it has no separate reality. Only with creation do we move from concept to reality.[37] In Hegel's system, of course, this is the move from the Logic to the Philosophy of Nature. The idea that in creation we move from an actual cause to an actual effect is dismissed as belonging to the Understanding, below the level of the rational Idea (1984–7, vol. 3:279, 281).

Hegel has very little to say about God the Father. But in the process of denying actuality to God apart from the world, he makes two important points about creation. First, creation is the self-actualizing of God. Nature and finite spirit together are the "*determinate being that God gives himself.* . . . In the absolute idea, in the element of thinking, God is this utterly concrete universal, the *positing of self as other*, but in such a way that the other is immediately defined to be himself, and the distinction is only ideal . . . and does not take on the shape of externality."[38]

The second point is that creation is necessary. "But God is the creator of the world; it belongs to his being, his essence, to be the creator. . . . His creative role is not an *actus* that happened once; [rather], what takes place in the idea is an *eternal* moment, an eternal determination of the idea."[39] These points are much closer to Spinoza than they are to Augustine, Aquinas, Luther, or Calvin.

Turning to God the Son we expect to find a discussion of incarnation and atonement but find ourselves at first in a further discussion of creation that makes clear its inseparability from the fall. If the first element is God before the creation of the world, the second element must be creation. This can come under the heading of the Son because in trinitarian theology the Son represents an otherness within God, while here the world of nature and finite spirit represents that otherness "released as something free and independent." Drawing on Boehme, Hegel suggests that the first other in the divine being "is not the Son but rather the external world." But the world in this "separation or estrangement from God" is fallen and in need of reconciliation (1984–7, vol. 3:292–3). To be created is to be fallen.

Told as a story, the fall is not only distinct from creation but also a transgression, something that should not have happened. But conceptually understood as the flip side of creation, we see that it represents a passage that ought to take place. Innocence can be seen either as evil or as an animal state. In either case, "Humanity ought not to be innocent."[40]

The clue to this surprising move is Hegel's gnosticism. Humankind is "the need for truth . . . the demand to know the absolute truth." As such it is in a "state of untruth" that can only be described as evil. Innocence is the immediacy, the animal state in which the need for truth, so far from having been satisfied, has not yet even been felt. This is a first evil which ought to be transcended by a move, here identified as the fall, to the second evil, the conscious need for truth that calls for a satisfaction Hegel strangely calls reconciliation.[41]

With a straight face Hegel tells us that in this reinterpretation of the story of the fall its content has not been changed, since it is still the case that "the sin consisted in having eaten of the tree of knowledge of good and evil" (1984–7, vol. 3:301). The fact that what the story presents as the transgression of a divine commandment becomes what philosophy requires of us in order to be human suggests not only a generic gnosticism in Hegel's thinking but an affinity with those gnostics who sided with Satan against Yahweh.[42]

Hegel's soteriology revolves around the notion of reconciliation. It begins in his discussion of the Son and culminates in the realm of the Holy Spirit. Both fall and reconciliation are described in ontological rather than moral terms. The antithesis to be overcome is between the divine and the human, but it is not brought about by sin and overcome by atonement and forgiveness. It is rather brought about by finitude and it is brought about by insight. Since the finite is nothing but the self-othering of the Infinite (in Spinoza's language, the modes of the divine Substance), the difference between the two involves no estrangement. Joined inextricably by an ontological bond, the two are eternally reconciled. What is lacking is the awareness by the finite self that it belongs to the Infinite Spirit. Just as the Upanishadic texts tell about Brahman/Atman, eternal, changeless, and unstained, and then say to the pupil, "That art thou," so Hegel describes the eternal, self-actualizing Idea and says to the individual, "Philosophy will help you to see yourself as what you always have been, an integral part of that divine process."

This is what reconciliation is. But what about Jesus of Nazareth, who plays such a crucial role in reconciliation according to Christian scriptures and traditions? In Hegel's theology of the Son, his appearance plays a maieutic role (more like the diagram Socrates draws than like Socrates himself). What needs to be brought about is not reconciliation, which is eternally there, but its recognition by finite selves. So, "the substantiality of the unity of the divine and human nature comes to consciousness for humanity in such a way that a human being appears to consciousness as God." In this event the truth is not attained through philosophical speculation, the only adequate form of truth, but "in the form of *certainty*" (1984–7, vol. 3:312).

Three things are noteworthy here. First, the Jesus event is not the unique occurrence or locus of the unity of the divine and human natures. It is the empirical event through which an eternal and universal truth, which is instantiated in all finite events, becomes known. In its particularity it has no special significance as the truth that is to be understood; it points beyond itself to the necessary and universal truth of which its contingency and particularity are an occurrence.

Second, there is a corresponding emphasis on the epistemic role of the Jesus event, with "certainty" being the key term throughout Hegel's exposition. What Jesus brings to humanity is the certainty of an ontological truth.

Finally, in other places Hegel regularly contrasts certainty with truth (for example, 1977b:104). Certainty is subjective and not in itself a guarantor of truth. Conviction is one thing; insight is another. In general the task of philosophy is to take us from certainty to truth, supplying subjective confidence with a content fully adequate to the real and thus worthy of its trust.

In the present context, the contrast echoes the distinction between faith and reason when faith is conceived Platonically as a lower stage on the divided line at whose top we find pure rational/mystical intuition. A theology, Luther's for example, which finds the certainty of reconciliation in the Jesus event, awaits instruction from speculative philosophy as to the real meaning of its faith. The task of philosophical theology is hermeneutical, not apologetic. It is not to provide certainty in place of doubt but truth (proper interpretation) in place of the certainty which accompanies meanings available to everyone but not up to philosophy's muster.

In Christian orthodoxy, incarnation is closely linked to atonement, so Hegel reinterprets the death of Jesus as well as his deity. As early as *Faith and Knowledge*, while seeking to substitute the "speculative Good Friday" for the "historic Good Friday," Hegel cites the Lutheran hymn according to which "God Himself is dead" (1977a:190–1). Now, repeating that reference, he interprets it to express "an awareness that the human, the finite, the fragile, the weak, the negative are themselves a moment of the divine, that they are within God himself, that finitude, negativity, otherness are not outside of God and do not, as otherness, hinder unity with God . . . finitude . . . is a moment in God himself, although, to be sure, it is a disappearing moment."[43]

This is a double disappearance. The speculative Good Friday is an onto-epistemological event in which the finite "disappears" in the Infinite in the sense that the former is seen to be what it always was, something integral to rather than sepa-rated from the latter and left to itself. On the historic Good Friday Jesus disappears in a rather more literal sense called death by crucifixion. The latter disappearance is impor-tant because it signifies the former, which is also called reconciliation.

Traditionally death is not a hindrance to unity with God, not because it is a moment in God but because (in the words of the Apostles' Creed) of the forgiveness of sins, the resurrection of the body, and the life everlasting. But Hegel anticipates no survival of death for any finite self. Rather, "humanity is immortal only through cognitive knowl-edge, for only in the activity of thinking is its soul pure and free rather than mortal and animal-like" (1984–7, vol. 3:304). So he invokes the speculative Good Friday. Seeing Jesus as divine provides the certainty "that the human is the immediately present God." But this human being, like all others, dies. This death is "the very presentation of the process of what humanity, what spirit is – implicitly both God and dead" (1984–7, vol. 3:326).

As in Nietzsche's doctrine of eternal recurrence, life as we live it here in the cave is to be celebrated rather than repudiated because, in all candor, it just does not get any better than this. Like the original God-man, each human disappears doubly, ontologi-cally in a union that the whole of Hegel's theology has been explicating up to this point, an ontically in a mortality that has nothing penultimate about it. Each of us turns out to be both God and dead.

Once again, with a straight face, Hegel tells us that other interpretations of the death of Jesus "reduce automatically to what has been said here." He specifically mentions the notion of a sacrificial death, according to which "Christ has died for all." The truly ratio-nal meaning of these atonement motifs he finds in his "both God and dead" formula.[44]

Finally, Hegel's doctrine of the Holy Spirit. Taking his cue from the book of Acts, he recognizes the formation of the community (*Gemeinde*, congregation, not *Gesellschaft*) as the outpouring of the Holy Spirit, the point of departure for thinking of God as triune (1984–7, vol. 3:324–8). In keeping with his sustained habit of thinking the human as a dimension of the divine *and vice versa*, Hegel identifies this Holy Spirit as "the spirit that comprehends this [eternal, divine] history spiritually as it is enacted in [the sphere of] appearance, and recognizes the idea of God in it, his life, his movement" (1984–7, vol. 3:328–9).

The Holy Spirit is that thinking spirit that recognizes the eternal idea of God in its historical appearance. In other words, it is that spirit that thinks in terms of Hegelian philosophy. For the original community, and its subsequent theologians, recognized God in the Pentecost event just as they recognized God in the Jesus event, but not as the eternal idea. Remaining stuck in the finite modes of thought characteristic of the Understanding, it was a consciousness of the Holy Spirit as someone other rather than a self-consciousness of itself as the Holy Spirit when and as it rises to the level of spec-ulative thinking. "Thus the community itself is the existing Spirit . . . God existing as community. . . . The third element, then, is this consciousness – God as the Spirit. This spirit as existing and realizing itself is the community" (1984–7, vol. 3:331).

This Holy Spirit is the Invisible Church, of which Hegel wrote so enthusiastically to Schelling in 1795 (see 1984a:31–2). It is not that communion of saints which encompasses both the current members of the institutional churches and their forebears in faith who have already passed on to the heavenly presence of God. It is rather the Hegelian philosophers and their mystical/pantheistic/gnostic forebears who sought and seek their salvation in ontological insight into their own essential divinity.

Of course, the institutional Church continues to exist. Hegel has a good deal to say about its spirituality, its sacraments and its relation to the world. A full account of his theology would have to discuss the ways he seeks to interpret these in keeping with his basic ideas. But beyond what has already been said about the congregation, his ecclesiology does not contribute to this trinitarian theology proper, the foundation in relation to which everything else is superstructure or corollary.

It should now be clear why I speak of Hegel's "Christian" pantheism. What this analysis has tried to show is that Hegel's theology is deeply and robustly pantheistic while only superficially Christian. He uses the same language as the Christian traditions: Father, Son, Holy Spirit, creation, fall, reconciliation, and so forth. But he reinterprets them so that they mean something wildly different from what they mean in the mainstream traditions of Christian theology. On the other hand, he uses language different from Spinoza. Where the latter says *Deus sive natura* and interprets this in terms of the category of substance, Hegel says *Gott oder Geist* and insists on the categorical primacy of spirit over substance. But he uses this different language to make two points more nearly Spinozistic than Christian, namely that the world, including the world of finite selves, is ontologically internal to the being of God as God's self-actualization and that salvation consists in recognizing this fact and accepting its implications. Spinoza calls this the intellectual love of God. At the conclusion of his 1827 lectures, Hegel calls it "the peace of God, which does not 'surpass all reason' [Philippians 4:7], but is rather the peace that *through* reason is first known and thought and is recognized as what is true" (1984–7, vol. 3:347).

It is not simply the form but also the content of Christianity that changes in Hegel's hands. Of course, to show that Hegel's theology is not really Christian, as it claims to be, is not to refute him (except on this claim, to which he is deeply wed). That would require some fairly obvious additional premises which I have obviously not attempted to provide. It may be that pantheistic trinitarianism is a better account of the real than theistic trinitarianism. But in order either to appreciate Hegel's theology in its historical significance or to evaluate its cogency and truth, it is necessary to see as clearly as possible what it is. In this case that goal is served by seeing as clearly as possible what it is not.

Notes

1   See Hegel (1991:¶¶1–6). Cf. Hegel (1984–7, vol. 1:149–53, 396–7; 1971c:¶573).
2   Translated as "service of God" in Hegel (1984–7), *Gottesdienst* is the word for the Sunday morning worship service on church bulletin boards (see 1984–7, vol. 1:84, 153). Cf. vol. 1

(p. 446), where philosophy is described as "a continual cultus." *Cultus* is Hegel's term for the practical enactment of the reconciliation of the divine and human, including devotion and the sacraments. Was Hegel thinking of the time Fichte scheduled his lectures from 10 to 11 o'clock on Sunday morning?

3   Cf. Hegel (1991:¶51, 193; 1969:86–90, 112–13, 442–3, 705–10; 1984–7, vol. 1:414–41; vol. 2:195–206, 404–21, 703–19, 748–52; vol. 3:65–73, 173–84, 351–8).

4   Hegel (1984–7, vol. 1:115–16). But since philosophy and religion have the same content, "Philosophy is only explicating *itself* when it explicates religion . . ." (vol. 1:152–3).

5   See Hegel (1971a:67–301). For detailed analysis of these texts, see Harris (1972).

6   For Hegel on the Trinity, see O'Regan (1994) and Schlitt (1984).

7   In tracing Hegel's "swerves," O'Regan makes it clear that Hegel's heterodoxy is not that of, say, a Lutheran *vis-à-vis* Catholic theology. Rather, in company with Valentinian gnosticism, Boehme, and Eckhart, for examples, he is a revisionist theologian who sets up an alternative to mainstream interpretations, be they Orthodox, Catholic, or Protestant.

8   Jaeschke (1990:332, 287). Cf. p. 206, where Jaeschke notes that Christian dogma does not play "a determining role for Hegel in elaborating his systematic positions. . . ."

9   For Hegel's flirtation with the Kantian/Fichtean attempt to base theology on practical reason, see "The Life of Jesus" (see Hegel 1984b); the correspondence referred to below in Hegel (1984a:29, 31–2, 32–3, 35; 1971a:67–71); and the "Earliest System-Programme of German Idealism" in Harris (1972).

10 Hegel (1991:¶¶37–78). In both versions Kant is tightly linked to British empiricism. In 1802 Jacobi is linked to romanticism, while in Hegel (1991) he is linked to Cartesian intuitionism.

11 Hegel (1984–7, vol. 1:156–8). The question of psychologizing dogma brings the confrontation of Hegel with Schleiermacher to the fore. See Merklinger (1993:chs. 2–4) and Luft (1987).

12 (Hegel 1984–7, vol. 1:365–6). On presupposing the Logic in particular, see vol. 1 (168–76).

13 See Jaeschke (1990:243–7, 296) and Merklinger (1993:113). Hegel (1984–7) includes what is available from all four series. The 1827 lectures are available in a separate paperback edition.

14 On Tholuck, see Hegel (1984–7, vol. 1:7–8, 157 n. 17, 375 n. 20; vol. 3:36); and Merklinger (1993:ch. 5). Hegel refers to him explicitly in the 1827 Preface to the *Encyclopedia* (1991:8 and 13), and in a note to 1971c (¶573).

15 Beiser (1987:44). See chs. 2–4 for a detailed account of the whole controversy. Herder's *God, Some Conversations* (1940) played a major role in this change.

16 Hegel (1963, vol. 3:257, 283). These statements may well be from the Jena version of the lectures in 1805–6, but as they come from Michelet's 1840 version rather than a critical edition, it is not possible to tell. For a similar but less dramatic statement from the lectures of 1825–6, see Hegel (1990, vol. 3:154).

17 Hegel (1984a:32–3). For an almost simultaneous letter describing Hölderlin's synthesis of Fichte and Spinoza, see Hegel (1984a:33).

18 Hegel (1984a:35). Hegel says (1971c:¶573), "The esoteric study of God and identity, as of cognitions, and notions, is philosophy itself."

19 In his 1827 lectures, Hegel will say, "Religion is for everyone. It is not philosophy, which is not for everyone" (1984–7, vol. 1:180).

20 Hegel (1984a:42–3). Just before bemoaning the triumph of orthodoxy over heresy, Hegel expresses his own synthesis of Fichte and Spinoza – "The empirical self arises by self-positing as merely a part of the Absolute Self's reality."

21 Harris (1972:511). I accept the arguments of Pöggeler and Harris that Hegel, rather than Schelling or Hölderlin, is the author of this draft, which is in Hegel's hand.

22   (Hegel 1971a:253, 259–60, 264–9, 278). In a draft associated with this project but not
      included in Hegel (1971a), he presents Jesus as teaching that in him the disciples experi-
      ence a "transubstantiation" so that like him, they are "a modification" of one divine life.
      They are not "substances, utterly separated" from the Father because "there are not two
      substances" (1971b:304).

23   For a detailed interpretation of the *Phenomenology* in these terms, see ch. 7 of my *History
      and Truth* (Westphal 1998).

24   Some or all of these four points are also developed in Hegel (1991); in Hegel (1969:536–40);
      in Hegel (1971c:573); and Hegel (1984–7, vol. 1:344–8) [from the 1824 lectures].

25   Along with Parmenides, certain oriental poetry, Hindu and Muslim, and the identity
      philosophy of Schelling. See Hegel (1971c:305–10; 1991:8–9; 1984–7, vol. 1:374,
      379).

26   Hegel (1991: Remark to ¶50, Addition to ¶151; 1971c:¶573).

27   Hegel (1984–7, vol. 1:376–7). On the origin of this idea in Maimon, see vol. 1 (377 n. 27)
      and cf. Jaeschke (1990:314 n. 54).

28   Hegel (1991: Addition to ¶151). There is an echo of this argument in Hegel (1969:538).

29   Hegel (1984–7, vol. 1:378–9). With explicit reference to Tholuck, he discusses this objec-
      tion in the 1827 Preface to (Hegel 1991:8–10).

30   For example, in a famous letter to Overbeck, Nietzsche lists five points on which he finds
      Spinoza to be his precursor: "He denies the freedom of the will, teleology, the moral world
      order, the unegoistic, and evil" (Kaufmann 1954:92).

31   See Hegel (1991, Remark to ¶50 and Addition to ¶88; 1984–7, vol. 1:344 n. 163).

32   Hegel (1969:537). In Hegel (1991, Addition to ¶151) he suggests that Spinoza's failure to
      reach the notion of personhood is because of his Jewish origins and Oriental intuition. Does
      he mean to suggest that the Yahweh of the Hebrew Bible is absolute substance but not
      absolute person?

33   Hegel (1984–7, vol. 1:347–8 [1824]). The first part of this passage is taken from Sermon
      12, *Qui audit me*, in McGinn (1986:270). Cf. Sermon 10, *In diebus suis* (p. 261), "The close-
      ness of God and the soul admits no difference [between them]. The same knowledge in which
      God knows himself is the knowledge of every detached spirit and nothing else." The second
      part of Hegel's quotation is from Sermon 52, *Beati pauperes spiritu*, in Colledge and McGinn
      (1981:203). In these sermons Eckhart makes other striking claims about being the only-
      begotten Son, about being his own cause and uncreated, and about becoming nothing but
      God himself. No wonder he was condemned by the church, a fact Hegel neglects to mention.

34   Hegel (1984–7, vol. 3:251; italics altered). Already in the *Phenomenology* this reinterpreta-
      tion of religion as self-consciousness is the key to freeing the truth from its inadequate reli-
      gious form for its superior philosophical form. See *History and Truth* (Westphal 1998, chs.
      7–8). There, as here, the claim is that the content remains the same.

35   For the theistic presuppositions of Kant's doctrine of the thing in itself, see "In Defense of
      the Thing in Itself."

36   Hegel's *Encyclopedia* concludes with the quotation from the *Metaphysics*, Book 12, in which
      Aristotle describes God as the thought that thinks itself (Hegel 1971c:315).

37   This is why Schlitt (1984:249) can claim that "Hegel had proposed to establish his trini-
      tarian claim by means of a progression from God to world."

38   Hegel (1984–7, vol. 3:272, 279; emphasis added). Cf. vol. 3 (p. 311): "God is the one who
      as living spirit distinguishes himself from himself, posits an other and in this other remains
      identical with himself, has in this other his identity with himself."

39   Hegel (1984–7, vol. 3:275). Schlitt (1984:46–7) links this question of necessity to the issue
      of the asymmetry mentioned above when he writes: "Yet the basic questions whether or not

Hegel has falsely located the source of any necessity in the relation between infinite and finite within the divine, that is, within infinity, rather than first and foremost within finitude."

40   Hegel (1984–7, vol. 3:298, 307). He gives a very similar account in Addition 3 to ¶24 of Hegel (1991).

41   Hegel (1984–7, vol. 3:295, 297–8). In relation to the will the fall ought to happen because "Innocence means to be without a will."

42   O'Regan traces the links between Hegel and gnosticism throughout his book. On this point see O'Regan (1994:163–4). Cf. Pagels (1979, ch. 2).

43   Hegel (1984–7, vol. 3:326–7). Cf. vol. 3 (p. 332): "For in the idea, the otherness of the Son is a transitory, disappearing moment, not a true, essentially enduring, absolute moment." This is the kind of statement that leads to reading Hegel's trinitarianism as a species of modalism. See O'Regan (1994:126–40).

44   Hegel (1984–7, vol. 3:327–8). Hegel also presents this interpretation of the crucifixion as an interpretation of Christ's death as "the transition to glory" (vol. 3:325).

References

Barth, K. 1959. *Protestant Thought: Rousseau to Ritschl*, trans. B. Cozens. New York: Harper & Row.

Beiser, F. C. 1987. *The Fate of Reason: German Philosophy from Kant to Fichte*. Cambridge, MA: Harvard University Press.

Colledge, E., OSA, and B. McGinn, trans. 1981. *Meister Eckhart: The Essential Sermons*. New York: Paulist Press.

Fichte, J. G. 1978. *Attempt at a Critique of All Revelation*, trans. G. Green. Cambridge: Cambridge University Press.

Fichte, J. G. 1994. "On the Basis of Our Belief in a Divine Governance of the World," in *Introductions to the Wissenschaftslehre and Other Writings*, trans. D. Breazeale. Indianapolis, IN: Hackett.

Harris, H. S. 1972. *Hegel's Development: Toward the Sunlight, 1770–1801*. Oxford: Clarendon Press.

Hegel, G. W. F. 1963. *Hegel's Lectures on the History of Philosophy*, trans. E. S. Haldane and F. H. Simson, 3 vols. London: Routledge & Kegan Paul.

Hegel, G. W. F. 1969. *Science of Logic*, trans. A. V. Miller. London: George Allen & Unwin.

Hegel, G. W. F. 1971a. *Early Theological Writings*, trans. T. M. Knox. Philadelphia, PR. University of Pennsylvania Press.

Hegel, G. W. F. 1971b. *Frühe Schriften*, vol. 1 of *Werke in zwanzig Bänden*. Frankfurt: Suhrkamp.

Hegel, G. W. F. 1971c. *Hegel's Philosophy of Mind*, trans. W. Wallace and A. V. Miller. Oxford: Clarendon Press. [Third part of the *Encyclopedia of the Philosophical Sciences*.]

Hegel, G. W. F. 1976. *Gesammelte Werke*, vol. 8: *Jenaer Systementwürfe III*. Hamburg: Felix Meiner.

Hegel, G. W. F. 1977a. *Faith and Knowledge*, trans. W. Cerf and H. S. Harris. Albany, NY: State University of New York Press.

Hegel, G. W. F. 1977b. *Phenomenology of Spirit*, trans. A. V. Miller. Oxford: Clarendon Press.

Hegel, G. W. F. 1984a. *Hegel: The Letters*, trans. C. Butler and C. Seiler. Bloomington, IN: Indiana University Press.

Hegel, G. W. F. 1984b. *Three Essays, 1793–1795*, trans. P. Fuss and J. Dobbins. Notre Dame, IN: University of Notre Dame Press.

Hegel, G. W. F. 1984–7. *Lectures on the Philosophy of Religion*, trans. R. F. Brown et al., 3 vols. Berkeley, CA: University of California Press.

Hegel, G. W. F. 1990. *Lectures on the History of Philosophy: The Lectures of 1825–26*, vol. 3, trans. R. F. Brown et al. Berkeley, CA: University of California Press.

Hegel, G. W. F. 1991. *The Encyclopedia Logic*, trans. T. F. Geraets et al. Indianapolis, IN: Hackett. [First part of the *Encyclopedia of the Philosophical Sciences*.]

Herder, J. G. 1940. *God, Some Conversations*, trans. F. H. Burkhardt. Indianapolis, IN: Bobbs-Merrill.

Jaeschke, W. 1990. *Reason in Religion: The Foundations of Hegel's Philosophy of Religion*, trans. J. M. Steward and P. C. Hodgson. Berkeley, CA: University of California Press.

Kaufmann, W., ed. 1954. *The Portable Nietzsche*. New York: Viking.

Luft, E. von der ed. and trans. 1987. *Hegel, Hinrichs, and Schleiermacher on Feeling and Reason in Religion*. Lewiston: Edwin Mellen Press.

McGinn, B. ed. 1986. *Meister Eckhart: Teacher and Preacher.* New York: Paulist Press.

Merklinger, P. M. 1993. *Philosophy, Theology, and Hegel's Berlin Philosophy of Religion, 1821–1827*. Albany: SUNY Press.

O'Regan, C. 1994. *The Heterodox Hegel.* Albany: SUNY Press.

Pagels, E. 1979. *The Gnostic Gospels.* New York: Random House.

Schelling, F. W. J. 1980. "On the Self as the Principle of Philosophy," in *The Unconditional in Human Knowledge: Four Essays (1794–96)*, trans. F. Marti. Lewisburg: Bucknell University Press.

Schlitt, Dale, OMI. 1984. *Hegel's Trinitarian Claim: A Critical Reflection.* Leiden: E. J. Brill.

Westphal, M. 1968. "In Defense of the Thing in Itself." *Kant-Studien* 59(1).

Westphal, M. 1998. *History and Truth in Hegel's phenomenology*, 3rd edn. Bloomington, IN: Indiana University Press.

CHAPTER 19
Schleiermacher

Dawn DeVries

A quick glance through the volumes of the nineteenth-century edition of the collected works of Friedrich Daniel Ernst Schleiermacher (1768–1834) says a great deal about the fertile mind of this Reformed pastor, who has been called the father of modern theology. In the first subdivision are works in theological disciplines including New Testament exegesis, hermeneutics, apologetics, dogmatics, theological ethics, church history, homiletics, pastoral care, liturgics, and church order. The second subdivision, consisting of ten fat volumes, is devoted to sermons. The third contains his lectures and writings in "philosophy," broadly construed to include philosophical ethics, esthetics, political theory, pedagogy, the history of philosophy, dialectics, "psychology" or philosophy of mind, and philology. In none of these fields was he a novice or dilettante (despite his own repeated protestations to the contrary). In at least four areas, he made groundbreaking contributions that set the agenda for future discussions in the disciplines: in philosophy of religion, with the famous theory of religion set out in his *On Religion: Speeches to its Cultured Despisers* (1799); in theological studies, with the then innovative curriculum proposed in his *Brief Outline on the Study of Theology* (1811) and with his dogmatic masterpiece, *The Christian Faith Presented as a Coherent Whole According to the Fundamental Principles of the Evangelical Church* (1821–2; 2nd edn. 1830–1); in the theory of interpretation, with his groundbreaking lectures on hermeneutics at the University of Berlin (first published after his death in 1838); and in Plato studies, with his German translation of the complete dialogues of Plato together with textual-critical introductions (a lifelong work published between 1804 and 1828). It is hard to know where to begin in providing an introduction to such a Renaissance man. The sheer scope of his intellectual achievement is awe-inspiring. Even his harshest critics find it hard not to rhapsodize when it comes to Schleiermacher's remarkable achievements. Karl Barth writes, "[With Schleiermacher] [w]e have to do with a hero, the like of which is but seldom bestowed upon theology" (1973:427); Emil Brunner notes, "Nothing speaks more clearly of the historical greatness of a thinker than the necessity to fight with him a hundred years after his death" (1928:7).

In this chapter, I shall follow the suggestion of Martin Kähler (1835–1912) that three things chiefly characterize Schleiermacher's legacy to the discipline of theology: first, a powerful argument for the autonomy of the religious life, its irreducibility to other forms of human experience; second, an unwavering emphasis on the centrality of the person of Christ for the Christian faith; and, finally, resolute refusal to privatize or mystify religion, with an emphasis instead on the socially and historically transformative character of religious life in general and Christianity in particular (Kähler 1962:82). In each of these aspects of his legacy, Schleiermacher was both the heir of Reformed tradition and its translator into a modern idiom, and in this respect he fully deserves Alexander Schweizer's sobriquet "the reviver of the Reformed consciousness in the modern era" (Schweizer 1844–7, vol. 1:91–2).

I

Although his famous *Speeches on Religion* (1799) is most often read as a brilliant apology for religion addressed to the artistic and intellectual elite of Prussian society, it cannot be well understood apart from Schleiermacher's own struggle to understand his faith in the years of his theological education. As a boy, he showed precocious ability in school, especially in the study of languages. His father and mother, however, fearing that he possessed an unseemly pride and an insufficiently pious heart, sent him at the age of 15 to be educated among the Moravian Pietists. Even before his matriculation at their school in Niesky, Schleiermacher notes in his autobiography, he had had a conversion experience (Rowan 1860, vol. 1:6–8). But the years spent in Pietist schools were difficult ones for him. On the one hand, he continued his voracious study habits, now in the company of friends who were also curious about the newest trends in philosophy and literature. But at the same time, perhaps in part because of the strong emphasis his teachers placed on keeping free from the corruptions of the world, he found himself increasingly troubled by doubts about his faith. There was a growing gap between his reading and reflection and the regnant theology in the Moravian community. He poured out his worries in letters to his parents: he was not sure he had the indwelling presence of Christ in his soul, for he still felt himself a sinner; he could not believe that Jesus, who only called himself the Son of man was in fact the true and eternal God; nor could he grasp how God could eternally punish creatures whom He clearly had created not to be perfect but to strive for perfection; finally, he could not accept the death of Jesus as a substitutionary sacrifice for the sins of others, since Jesus himself nowhere claimed that it was (Rowan 1860, vol. 1:46–64). The warfare going on within the soul of the young Schleiermacher and his passionate longing to resolve it in many ways determined the man he was to become: an ardent defender of the compatibility of faith and science. But how could one theoretically ground a pact of non-interference between faith and reason? This was a question that occupied Schleiermacher from his school days through the publication of the *Speeches* and beyond.

For the Protestant orthodox theologians of his day, religion was construed primarily as a set of correct doctrines revealed by God in Scripture and supplementing the knowledge available to unaided human reason. Conflicts between faith and science could best be resolved, according to them, by asserting the superior status of revealed truth and by exposing errors in the discoveries of sinful human minds. For nearly a century before Schleiermacher's time, this view had been subjected to an increasingly devastating critique, first by the English and French Deists, and later by the Rationalist theologians in Germany. Ironically, the most common response of the Deists to traditional views of revelation – their appeal to a universal religion of nature or reason – did little to challenge the orthodox theologians' underlying definition of religion as a form of knowing. Instead of appealing to Scripture as a source of revealed information, the Deists spoke of self-evident religious truths disclosed to enlightened minds across cultures through introspection or the observation of natural law. The core of religion, then, was still a set of doctrines, but for the Deists the list of necessary beliefs was significantly shorter than the list proposed by the Protestant orthodox theologians.

The revolution in epistemology initiated by Immanuel Kant's *Critique of Pure Reason* (1781) presented a serious challenge to the older understanding of religion. Kant argued that reason does not have the competence to gain theoretical knowledge of what lies beyond experience. Things in themselves (or *noumena*) are not grasped by reason apart from the categories imposed by it, such as space and time. All theoretical knowledge is a combination of reason's categories and sensible stimuli, and as such it cannot extend beyond the realm of sense experience. On this basis, Kant dismantled the old theological arguments for the existence of God. The metaphysical foundation of both orthodox and rationalist theologies had been undermined. In its place, Kant spoke of the postulates of practical reason or the moral consciousness (*The Critique of Practical Reason*, 1788): God, freedom, and immortality. While these concepts could not be established by rational proofs, they were presupposed in order to make sense of the universal awareness Kant called the "categorical imperative" – the sense that one ought to do some things and ought not to do others. In order for that feeling not to be an illusion, humans must be free to follow the dictates of conscience, and there must be a moral order established by a righteous lawgiver (God) that will eventually be vindicated (in immortality). Kant's critical philosophy in effect made religion a part of ethics. In his *Religion Within the Limits of Reason Alone* (1793), Kant states it explicitly: "Religion is (subjectively regarded) the recognition of all duties as divine commands" (1934:142).

Schleiermacher first read Kant while at the Moravian seminary in Barby, and continued his thoroughgoing study of the first and second critiques while a student in Halle. From the beginning, he was totally won over by Kant's epistemology which, he claimed, "brings back . . . reason from the desert wastes of metaphysics into its true appointed sphere" (Rowan 1860, vol. 1:68). Many of his early sermons and treatises display strong Kantian overtones – especially the conception of religion as obedience to duty. By the time he was appointed Reformed chaplain at the Charité hospital in Berlin in 1796, however, Schleiermacher had begun to have doubts about Kant's conception of religion, and his association with the circle of intellectuals gathered in the salon of Henriette Herz – especially the charismatic Romantic poet Friedrich Schlegel – only confirmed this new direction in his thinking.

In place of the appeals to reason as the liberator or elevating force of humanity so evident in Enlightenment thinkers, the Romantics called on the power of the imagination to intuit the universe. Instead of the Enlightenment emphasis on abstract universals, the Romantics reveled in the unique particularities of concrete individuals as windows to the Infinite. And in place of the constricting understanding of morality as the grim performance of duty, they substituted the notion of free individual self-cultivation or *Bildung* as the ethical ideal. Schleiermacher found this revolutionary movement intellectually and personally attractive. But he was chagrined that few of his new-found friends could understand why he would work as a pastor in the Church. They were convinced that the dogmas of religion were as stifling of individuality and imagination as had been the dry arguments of rationalist philosophy, and that churchly authority hardly supported the ideal of *Bildung*. Schleiermacher took up the challenge to respond to the intellectual avant-garde of his time by developing a fresh under-standing of the nature of religion itself. He published the result of his efforts anony-mously in 1799 with the title *On Religion: Speeches to Its Cultured Despisers*. Little did he know that his first publication would mark a turning point in the philosophy of religion.

The *Speeches* consists in five dense chapters. In the first, Schleiermacher presents himself as a defender of religion against its contemporary critics. As intellectuals who have made a universe for themselves, he argues, the cultured despisers feel no need of thinking about the Universe that made them. As creators of a richly textured life in this world, they feel no need to contemplate eternity. Schleiermacher challenges the critics not to be content that they have truly understood religion until they learn about it from an expert, and he presents himself as just such an expert. It is not external credentials, however, such as ordination or formal education, that establish one as a virtuoso in the realm of religion. The despisers are right to reserve particular disdain for the clergy and the theologians. The true priests of religion are mediators between finite humanity and the Infinite. They have had the experience of knowing themselves as individuals and as part of the whole, and the power of their religious experience overflows into a need to communicate it to others. If the cultured despisers will only pay attention to such true experts on religion, Schleiermacher argues, they will learn that religion itself is not mortally wounded by the rejection of particular metaphysical doctrines about God or the afterlife.

The second speech presents the heart of Schleiermacher's argument on the nature of religion. The critics define religion either as a particular way of thinking or as a special form of conduct. Schleiermacher notes that the fervent opposition of the despis-ers to religious belief demonstrates that there must be something more to religion than superficial science or conventional morality. Otherwise it would hardly be worth their effort to mount such a strong attack against religion. No, "belief must be something different from a mixture of opinions about God and the world, and of precepts for one life or for two."[1] The first necessary step is not to confuse the essence of religion with its outward manifestations. The sacred scriptures of the religions, for example, are not textbooks of metaphysical and ethical precepts, but rather poetic or rhetorical expres-sions of pious experience. They simply never were intended as primitive science or morality, in spite of the fact that they have been so misused by some people. Religion in its inmost essence, on the contrary, is contemplative. And the object of contemplation is "the universal existence of all finite things, in and through the Infinite, and of all temporal things in and through the Eternal" (Schleiermacher 1894:36). While such contemplation can coexist with reflection and action, it cannot be reduced to either of them, and a correct view of humanity's place in the world requires taking religious experience into account. Schleiermacher writes: "Only when piety takes its place along-side of science and practice, as a necessary, indispensable third, as their natural counterpart, not less in worth and splendor than either, will the common field be altogether occupied and human nature on this side complete" (1894:37–8).

Just as science and morality develop out of particular human faculties, i.e. reason and conscience, so religion has its seat in the human capacities of intuition and feeling (*Anschauung und Gefühl*). "True religion is sense and taste for the Infinite" (1894:39). By "feeling," Schleiermacher does not mean either physical sensations or emotions but rather the moment in consciousness in which one is aware of the self in its unity with all that is – a moment that precedes the split between subject and object. This moment is fleeting, always disappearing from our consciousness and resisting our attempts to grasp it as an object. In a sense we can only have the experience in our reflective self-consciousness as a memory. This profound awareness of the underlying unity in the universe, Schleiermacher argues, is the basis of all religion. He then deftly excises the aspects of conventional religion most objectionable to the cultured despisers. Theological systems and their anthropomorphic descriptions of God are no more essential to religion than any other form of knowledge. Religion is compatible with an endless variety of theologies. Even if the notion of a personal God and belief in immortality are rejected, religion can and does flourish. And without religion it is impossible for an individual to pursue his or her highest calling: to be a self-conscious mirror of Infinity. The cultured despisers already embrace that calling, and with deliberate irony Schleiermacher in Speech Three celebrates them as "however unintentionally, the rescuers and cherishers of religion" (1894:141).

The third speech deals with the concept of self-cultivation or *Bildung* in religion. Because of its inward and contemplative nature, religion cannot be taught or inculcated. Fortunately, all human beings are born with the innate ability to have religious experience, and provided that nothing blocks this religious sense, it will emerge quite naturally. But it is not enough simply to let nature take its course; rather, human beings have the duty to cultivate their religious awareness. While this can occur in an almost infinite variety of ways, Schleiermacher (1894:138) recommends three practices as the most likely means for developing the religious sense: introspection or coming to self-consciousness, exploration of the natural world, and encounters with great art. Each of these avenues of exploration and self-cultivation leads the individual to an encounter with the One-in-All. Religion, therefore, can hardly be the enemy of science and art, for it is precisely through the engagement with them that religious self-consciousness is nourished and deepened.

Up to this point in the text, one could imagine religion as a purely individualistic matter – something to be pursued by persons in the privacy of their own minds. The entire fourth speech is given to a refutation of such a view. Religion, Schleiermacher argues, is by necessity a social phenomenon. Individuals who have had religious experience long both to share that experience with those who have not had it and to communicate with others who have. Thus religion propels people into a community formed and sustained by rhetorical communication. The cultured despisers mistake the institutional Church for true religious society and assume that its hierarchical priesthood and wooden creeds are the marks of the Church. True religious community, on the contrary, is marked by freedom and mutuality: freedom from premature foreclosure on religious communication by creeds or dogmas, and mutuality rather than hierarchy as the organizing social structure.

In the final speech, Schleiermacher turns from the abstract concept of religion to a consideration of concrete religions. Although it is precisely the particularities of the individual religions that most offend the critics, Schleiermacher denies that there is such a thing as a universal or natural religion. "The whole of religion is nothing but the sum of all relations of man to God, apprehended in all the possible ways in which any man can be immediately conscious in his life," Schleiermacher writes, "[Y]et all men will not by any means apprehend them in the same way, but quite differently" (1894:217). Hence, religion is by its very nature pluriform, and the attempt to smooth away the particularities of positive religions with a concept of natural religion is nothing more than an artificial abstraction from true religion. "Resistance to the positive and arbitrary is resistance to the definite and real. If a definite religion may not begin with an original fact, it cannot begin at all" (1894:234). All religious experience takes place within the concrete particularities of specific religions, and anyone who wants to know about religion needs to learn about it from the inside out. "[O]nly those who with their own religion pitch their camp in some such positive form, have any fixed abode, and . . . any well-earned right of citizenship in the religious world . . . and they alone are in the full sense religious persons" (1894:224).

Schleiermacher concludes the fifth speech with an argument that has puzzled many readers since the first appearance of the work.[2] He asserts that Christianity is the highest form of religion yet to appear. If every concrete religion has its own peculiar way of representing the encounter with God, then Christianity's originating idea is "the Universal resistance of finite things to the unity of the Whole, and of the way the Deity treats this resistance. Christianity sees how He reconciles the hostility to Himself, and sets bounds to the ever-increasing alienation by scattering points here and there over the whole that are at once finite and infinite, human and divine" (1894:241). Preeminently in Christ, but also in Scripture and in the ongoing testimony of believers, the Christian Church discovers mediators between God and humanity that reconcile finite being with the Infinite. Such a perspective is more suited to the maturity of the human race than the more childlike religion of Judaism with its atomistic notions of reward and punishment and correspondingly more anthropomorphic image of God. And though it is impossible to rule out the appearance of a superior religion in the future, Schleiermacher assumed that Christianity itself would continue to develop through self-criticism into new and better forms, all the while being tolerant of the other religions that exist alongside it.

Schleiermacher's great achievement in the *Speeches on Religion* was to reanimate discussion on the nature of religion. While the tendency of many eighteenth-century theorists was to explore reductionist strategies for explaining away the intellectually embarrassing and morally ambiguous elements of religion, Schleiermacher provided a strategy for distancing religion from these same elements and preserving its character as a *sui generis* phenomenon. In his insistence on the irreducibility of religion, he set the stage for subsequent explorations in the philosophy of religion that continued well into the twentieth century. And in responding to the criticisms of early reductionists, he opened up an avenue of argument for his successors, who would face the far less friendly reductionisms of Feuerbach, Marx, and Freud. At the same time, Schleiermacher's interest in the *homo religiosus* may be seen as a creative appropriation of John Calvin's arguments in the opening chapters of the *Institutes of the Christian Religion*. According to Calvin, every human being is endowed with the seed of religion and has a "sense of divinity" that drives the person toward worship. The religious sense is neither a particular set of ideas, nor simply the voice of conscience, but rather the intuition of an original relationship with God. The ultimate fate of the human being turns on whether that original religious sense is finally oriented away from idols to recognize the one true God (Calvin 1960, vol. 1:35–74). Despite their differences, it is not difficult to hear the echoes of Calvin in Schleiermacher's impassioned plea for the universality and the significance of the religious life.

II

After a brief stint as Professor of Theology and university preacher at the University of Halle, which was cut short by the French occupation during the Napoleonic wars, in 1809 Schleiermacher was called to Berlin as one of the founding faculty members of the new university. He remained in Berlin for the rest of his life, serving as Professor of Theology in the university and co-pastor with the Lutheran Philip Marheinecke of the Holy Trinity Church. One of the first tasks he set himself was to design a curriculum for the theological faculty, and the results of his efforts were published as the *Brief Outline on the Study of Theology* (Schleiermacher 1966; originally published 1811; 2nd edn. 1830). He argued that the subjects of the theological curriculum find their coherence not in theory but in practice – specifically in the practice of church leadership. All the various skills and disciplines that are to be mastered by theological students are oriented toward skillful leadership in the Church. The ideal theological student possesses both intellectual curiosity and commitment to the Church, and these dispositions are necessary for successful leadership.

Schleiermacher divides the curriculum into three parts: philosophical, historical, and practical theology. The two main branches of philosophical theology – apologetics and polemics – have the tasks of determining the essence of Christianity and protecting it against corrupting influences foreign to the originating witness of the faith. The actual body of the theological curriculum, however, is historical theology, in which he includes not only exegesis and church history but also dogmatics. The primary task of exegetical theology is to determine the canon more exactly – that is, to discriminate through historical criticism what is the normative witness of the New Testament. This kind of criticism requires facility in the biblical languages and knowledge of the general rules of hermeneutics. The task of church history is to trace the total development of Christianity as a historical phenomenon after the age of the apostles. The church historian should attend to both the history of doctrine, which is the religious self-consciousness's developing sense of clarity through time, and the forms of the common life, or the institutional Church's adaptations to the various social and political forces that exist alongside it. A historical grasp of the Church's total career leads to understanding of the present.

Without a doubt the most innovative move that Schleiermacher made in the *Brief Outline* was to define dogmatics as a part of historical theology. To the dogmatician is given the task of interpreting the present condition of Christianity. Dogma, therefore, is no longer seen as the unchanging expression of timeless truths either revealed in Scripture or settled in duly adopted creeds and confessions. Rather, dogmas are the expressions of the religious self-consciousness current in a specific Church in a particular place and time. Schleiermacher argued that the doctrines presented in dogmatics ought to represent the collective faith of a Church and not merely the idiosyncratic opinions of individuals. Moreover, a dogmatic system must always be able to show its coherence with the essence of Christianity through exegesis. But given these boundaries, dogmatics is free to develop new language or conceptual frameworks as more adequate expressions of the Christian way of believing at the present time. This part of historical theology includes not only dogmatics proper but also Christian ethics as the description of the Christian way of acting in the present. Interestingly, Schleiermacher also includes a role for a discipline he called "church statistics" in understanding the present state of Christianity. It is important that dogmatics should be done with a knowledge of the total compass of Christianity throughout the world, "[f]or a proper influence upon one's own Church community is only possible when one works within it as within an organic part of the whole, a part which has to maintain and develop itself vis-à-vis the other parts" (Schleiermacher 1966:85). Church statistics offers such a comprehensive picture of the state of Christianity throughout the world.

Schleiermacher had already lectured on dogmatics during his brief tenure at the University of Halle, but it was during the years in Berlin that his systematic theology was worked out carefully. First published in 1821–2, Schleiermacher's *Christian Faith* or *Glaubenslehre*, as he liked to call it, was a source of controversy and misunderstanding from the beginning. Schleiermacher himself was so disappointed by the critical reviews of the work that he set out to correct them in two "Open Letters" to his friend and colleague Friedrich Lücke, first published in the journal *Theologische Studien und Kritiken* in 1829.[3] This source provides critically important background for understanding the structure and logic of the *Glaubenslehre*.

Because he understood dogmatics as a historical-theological presentation of the Christian faith in the present, Schleiermacher's starting point was not biblical revelation, philosophical first principles, or dogmatic formulas adopted by official church bodies. Rather, in his dogmatics he sought to give an account of the content of Christian experience – specifically, the experience of faith in Jesus as the Redeemer. The criticisms of his method have been consistent. His theology, the critics argue, has no adequate concept of revelation and therefore is really not theology at all but a form of anthropology; as a theology of consciousness, it is only loosely connected with the life of the historical Jesus; and as a system concerned with the coherence of faith and modern science and philosophy, it has sacrificed basic Christian beliefs on the altar of apologetics. Schleiermacher attempted to answer all of these criticisms in the "Open

Letters", but his efforts proved in vain: virtually the same line of criticism was pointed against his theology by Emil Brunner and Karl Barth a hundred years later.

Schleiermacher complained to Lücke that almost none of his critics made it past the introduction to the *Glaubenslehre*, which was not really part of the dogmatics at all but *prolegomena* to it. He blames himself in part for the misunderstanding that his system proceeds from a foundation in general God-consciousness to the specifically Christian beliefs about Jesus. He had toyed with the idea of putting the second part of the system – the part that deals with sin and redemption – first, but had finally decided against it, mainly for stylistic reasons. But he wanted to construct the work "so that at every point the reader would be made aware that the verse John 1 : 14 is the basic text for all theology" (1981:59). At the heart of the Christian faith is a particular determination of God-consciousness that cannot be deduced from anything other than the historical revelation of God in the person of Jesus. Thus, the experience that Christian theology seeks to explicate is nothing other than the mirror of revelation – the subjective correlate to the objectively given revelation. If faith really is the mirror of the revelation of God in Jesus Christ, the theologian cannot afford to be unconcerned with the actual historical events that lie at the origin of faith. Schleiermacher claims always and only to be speaking of the historical Christ in his Christology (1981:37).

The problem of the relationship of faith and science, as we have seen, is one that occupied Schleiermacher from his youth. Throughout the first edition of the *Glaubenslehre* he had revised traditional dogmatic *loci* in ways that made them more coherent with current scientific and philosophical knowledge. In the "Open Letters" he repeatedly denies dependence on any particular philosophical system, although he argues that it is appropriate for the theologian to "borrow" freely from the philosophers if their concepts can help to explicate Christian faith on its own terms. But this is not all he has to say about the relationship between faith and science. Schleiermacher contends that much of what has been previously considered essential to the exposition of Christian faith has come into conflict with the findings of modern science. Specifically, he mentions the doctrine of creation and the miracles of the New Testament. He poses a series of rhetorical questions:

> Do you intend to barricade yourself behind . . . fortifications and cut yourselves off from science? The barrage of ridicule to which you will be subject from time to time causes me no concern, for it will do you little harm once you are resigned to it. But the blockade! The complete starvation from all science, which will follow when, because you have repudiated it, science will be forced to display the flag of unbelief! Shall the tangle of history so unravel that Christianity becomes identified with barbarism and science with unbelief? (Schleiermacher 1981:61)

In answer to his own questions, Schleiermacher asserts that already in the Reformation of the sixteenth century there was the basis for an "eternal covenant between the living Christian faith and completely free, independent scientific inquiry, so that faith does not hinder science and science does not exclude faith" (1981:64). Thus, it is not only possible but necessary to present every dogma that truly represents the Christian religious affections in a manner that "remains free from entanglements with science" (1981:64).

If we were to take our clues about interpreting the various doctrines from Schleiermacher's remarks in the "Open Letters" to Lücke, we might start with the actual heart of the system, the specifically Christian consciousness of sin and grace discussed in Part II of the *Glaubenslehre* (1844–7). But he argues that the specifically Christian consciousness of redemption both presupposes and contains a universal creature consciousness that is thematized in the doctrines of creation and preservation. The content of this creature consciousness, isolated by abstraction from the concrete piety of Christianity, is a feeling of absolute dependence, in which the person intuits his or her immediate existential relationship to God. Unlike the relationship with other finite beings, the relationship with God does not include the give and take of reciprocity. God is the inexhaustible source of all finite existence, yet is in no way dependent upon it. Human beings have relative freedom and dependence in relation to all other finite creatures, but receive their very existence not only at the beginning of life but day by day in utter dependence on God (Schleiermacher 1928:5–26, 131–41).

The doctrine of creation, according to Schleiermacher, posits God as the source of all that is and places God above or outside the web of reciprocity entailed in the nature system. The proper representation of the God–world relation, however, does not entail a defense of the creation narrative of Genesis. A literalistic reading of these texts is ruled out, since God's activity is represented in them as resembling human activity and thus as subject to the antitheses of finite existence. In fact, the doctrine of preservation (or providence) contains in itself everything that needs to be said about the relationship between God and the world. God's activity is present in every part of the created order: God is powerful in everything that occurs, and while divine causality can be distinguished from the natural order (as an infinite, as opposed to a finite, causality), it is equated with it in scope. Consciousness of one's absolute dependence on God coincides with one's awareness of oneself as a part of the nature system. Hence Schleiermacher was able to argue that the interests of piety, rightly understood, are entirely compatible with the interests of the natural sciences (1928:131–56, 170–93).

As an immediate intuition of the God–world relation, the feeling of absolute dependence is a universal endowment of human consciousness. No one, however, has it apart from the particular specification of that feeling within one of the world's religions. In Christianity, the God-consciousness is received in the consciousness of sin and redemption. Once again, Schleiermacher argues that it is not necessary to preserve the notion of a literal fall of the first man and woman at the beginning of history. The narrative of Genesis 3 presents in mythological form the universal possibilities of human existence in relation to God. The "original perfection" of humanity is not a primordial state of innocence at the beginning of time, but rather the possibility for the actualization of God-consciousness both within the human race as a whole and within each individual. Sin is anything that hinders or suppresses the God-consciousness in humanity (1928:238–56, 269–314). "The distinctive feature of Christian piety," Schleiermacher writes, "lies in the fact that whatever alienation from God there is in the phases of our experience, we are conscious of it as an action originating in ourselves, which we call Sin; but whatever fellowship with God there is, we are conscious of it as resting upon a communication from the Redeemer, which we call Grace" (1928:63). For the Christian faith, then, everything is related to the redemption accomplished by Jesus of Nazareth. The centrality of the person of Jesus and the "christo-morphic" shape of Christian faith follow from Schleiermacher's definition of the essence of Christianity.[4]

The heart of the *Glaubenslehre* is its Christology, soteriology, and ecclesiology, for in these doctrines Schleiermacher specifies the content of the Christian consciousness of grace. The actual source of saving faith is the same in all times and places – it is the proclamation of Christ, either his self-proclamation to the first disciples, or the preaching of Christ by the Church. Jesus' own uniquely powerful God-consciousness, which determined every moment of his life on earth, was a true being of God in him, so that in Jesus the ideal for human life has become actual. In the preached "word," Jesus draws his hearers into his own God-consciousness, redeeming them from their alienated sense of God and delivering them to a reconciled consciousness.

Schleiermacher distinguishes between his own understanding of Christ's activity as "mystical" and alternative points of view which he calls "magical" and "empirical." The mystical view is so called because it acknowledges that there can be no proof, strictly speaking, that this influence of Christ on believers takes place: it is a fact of inner experience mediated through the community. The magical view, on the contrary, asserts that Christ can have this inward effect on believers immediately, quite apart from the community of faith. And the empirical view limits Christ's influence to that of teaching and example, and does not acknowledge that he actually communicates his God-consciousness and blessedness to the community of faith (1928:425–38).

Schleiermacher's understanding of sin as subjective alienation from God implies a view of the work of redemption different than those inherited from Protestant scholasticism. The purpose of Christ's work was not to appease the wrath of God kindled by the rebellion of humankind against God's laws. Such a view of God, Schleiermacher thought, is hopelessly anthropomorphic. Rather, Christ's work was directed at the transformation of human consciousness from God-forgetfulness and alienation to acceptance and peace. While it is crucially important for Schleiermacher's understanding of redemption that Christ actualizes the ideal possibilities of the original perfection of human nature, he is critical of Chalcedonian Christology (1928:391–8). Further, he regards the "saving events" recounted in the Catholic creeds (Virgin Birth, Resurrection, Ascension, and Second Coming) as material in no way constitutive of the doctrine of Christ's person, since they do not determine his ability to do the actual work of redemption as Schleiermacher conceives it (1928:398–424). Similarly, he is critical of the Latin tradition on the doctrine of Atonement. The death of Jesus cannot be conceived as a vicarious atonement for human offenses against God. Rather, in his total obedience to the will of God, Christ proclaims the full dominion of the spirit over the flesh and manifests himself as the one through whom God is reconciling the world to himself (1928:451–66). The death of Jesus, then, is the supreme instance of his self-proclamation, to the original disciples and to later believers, so that "the conviction both of His holiness and of His blessedness always comes to us primarily as we lose ourselves in the thought of His suffering" (1928:459).

The redeeming and reconciling work of Christ is subjectively appropriated in the experiences of regeneration and sanctification. Regeneration involves both a changed relationship to God (justification) and a changed manner of life (conversion). Once believers enter into living communion with Christ, more and more they submit their natural abilities to him, and so begin to live a life akin to his in perfection and blessedness, and this is what is meant by sanctification. Schleiermacher lays out his soteriology Christologically: the experience of salvation in each individual takes place in a way analogous to the divine/human union in the person of Christ. In justification and conversion, the human recipient of grace is primarily passive, just as the human Jesus was primarily passive in the "act of union" with the diving being. The divine life alone is active in the first reception of grace. In the "state of union" in which Jesus lived his whole life, every one of his acts was an act of his human nature animated by the divine life. In a similar way, believers in the state of sanctification live their human lives animated by the divine life within (1928:476–524).

The centrality of the person of Jesus in Schleiermacher's understanding of Christian faith is both a material and a formal principle. Materially, there is no Christian faith before the appearance of the Redeemer on earth. His coming into the world is the "miracle of miracles," which could not be predicted or accounted for by anything that came before (Schleiermacher 1981:64). With Jesus something new enters nature and history. The divine decree to send Christ into the world is one with the decree to create the human race, and only with the appearance of Christ is human nature finally perfected. Jesus Christ, therefore, is the beginning, the end, and the center of human history. He is the image of the original perfection of creation and the goal toward which it moves. From the actual human life of Jesus on earth springs forth the new community of grace that counters the old community of sin. Everything circles around him. Formally, Christ's being and work structure the being and life of the new humanity. Just as the individual human's experience of grace is described in analogy to the being of God in Christ, so too the work of the new community – the Church – is described in analogy to the threefold office of Christ as prophet, priest, and king. Schleiermacher's emphasis on the centrality of Jesus carries forward the Reformation principle *solus Christus*. At the same time, it points forward to widely divergent movements in twentieth-century theology. Barth's Christocentrism reflects the structure of Schleiermacher's dogmatics. But no less indebted are the various quests for the historical Jesus. Schleiermacher himself was confident that there was no divergence between the Christ of faith and the Jesus of history, and he tried to demonstrate this in his lectures on the life of Jesus (published posthumously in 1864). Critics of his Christology, including his contemporaries F. C. Baur and David Friedrich Strauss were not so sure, and they accused Schleiermacher of imposing churchly piety on the facts of history. But regardless of how he himself executed the task, Schleiermacher was one of the pioneers in moving modern theology toward a historically grounded Christology.

III

One of the most striking features of the *Glaubenslehre*, from beginning to end, is its emphasis on the group over the individual as the focus of analysis. Although Schleiermacher the Romantic highly valued individuality and its possibility to mirror the divine, his theology was not one that glorified individualism. Already in the *Speeches on Religion* he had argued that at the basis of true religious experience is the discovery of humanity and the universe. Religion reorients the individual from self-absorbed ego-centricity to proper regard of the self as a part of the universe that is the stage of God's creative and redemptive activity. In the *Glaubenslehre*, this theme is developed in specifically Christian language, especially in the doctrines of preservation, original sin, ecclesiology, and eschatology.

As we have seen, Schleiermacher did not consider the doctrine of original sin to be about the fall of Adam and its consequences. In a brilliant reconception of the doctrine, he suggested that original sin is actually the sin which every human "inherits" from his or her participation in structures and social forces that militate against the development of authentic God-consciousness. The sin is "inherited" in the sense that it has its source outside the self and its autonomous actions. And it is not just a tendency to alienation, but "complete incapacity for good, which can be removed only by the influence of Redemption" (1928:282). Because no human being is born in isolation from sinful society, everyone in fact participates in the corporate life of sinfulness: original sin is "not something that pertains severally to each individual and exists in relation to him by himself, but in each the work of all, and in all the work of each; and only in this corporate character . . . can it be properly and fully understood" (1928:288). Sin as a powerful corporate social force, then, cannot be overcome simply by dealing with the guilt of separate individuals. Rather, grace must provide not only healing for the individual and her guilt, but a counter-force to the corporate life of sinfulness. The Christian Church, called into existence by the proclamation of Jesus, is the divinely chosen instrument for combating the social structures of sin and evil.

Schleiermacher's ecclesiology is divided into three main sections: in the first, he describes the origin of the Church through a discussion of the doctrines of election and the communication of the Holy Spirit; in the second, he discusses the nature of the Church as it actually exists in the world, including both its essential and invariable features and its concessions to historical existence; in the third, he describes the "consummation" of the Church, which for him constitutes the real subject matter of eschatology. In each part of his ecclesiology, the focus is on the community of believers – the corporate life of blessedness in opposition to the corporate life of sin – but this emphasis is particularly important in his account of the origin and consummation of the Church.

The community of believers is called into existence by the preaching of Christ, but because the community exists within the laws of the divine government of the world, not everyone can be called at once. Rather, individuals are drawn into the kingdom of God through the proclamation gradually over a long period of time. The doctrine of election, according to Schleiermacher, is an attempt to account for the gradual spread of the gospel in history, and the resultant inequality in its reception among people. The distinction between the "elect" and the "reprobate," he argued, is not a permanent but a vanishing one that accounts for the difference between those who have been taken up into redemptive fellowship with Christ and those who have not yet been incorporated into the Church. Schleiermacher was sharply critical of earlier Reformed understandings of predestination, which he believed wrongly "atomized" the concept, so that the divine decree was taken to be a decision about the fate of each individual independently of others. On the contrary, Schleiermacher maintained, the one divine decree was to redeem humanity in Jesus Christ, and the decree extends to each individual only through his or her participation in the human race. The divine activity is directed primarily toward "totalities" or collective groups of people and should not be understood as ad hoc dealings with individuals (1928:536–60).

The doctrine of the communication of the Holy Spirit describes the vital force of the new corporate life as a "common spirit" of believers created by the union of the Divine Essence with the collective human nature of believers in fellowship with Christ. The divine nature "animates" the life of the Christian fellowship in a way analogous to the way it dwelt within the individual human person Jesus of Nazareth, but now its dwelling place is a community. Each redeemed individual partakes of the indwelling of the Holy Spirit, but he or she does so in common with others (1928:560–81). Thus, Schleiermacher affirms Cyprian's motto "extra ecclesiam nulla salus est": it is impossible to be in communion with Christ apart from the fellowship of the Church. As the corporate dwelling place of the Holy Spirit, the Church is growing into the perfect image of the Redeemer, and within this new corporate life every individual takes an indispensable place as a "subordinate unit in the whole . . . irreplaceable by any other" (1928:580).

The goal of the redemptive activity of God in history – to redeem humanity in Jesus Christ – requires that the Church should overcome the world, for only when it has done so will all humanity possess reconciled God-consciousness in full measure. Thus, the doctrine of last things most properly applies to the perfection of the Church and its final victory over the world, and only in a secondary sense to the fate of individuals after death. Schleiermacher argued that the consummated Church is not a historical possibility but rather the ideal to which the Church ever approximates – an ideal whose realization will constitute the end of history. The redeemed then enter into an eternal state of unchanging blessedness that seems incompatible with the persistence of individual personality as it is commonly conceived. The fullest and most living God-consciousness, traditionally called the "vision of God," implies an unmediated apprehension of God in the consciousness of a creature who wills no longer to retain a separate self-consciousness but to be a vessel for the God who is all and in all (1928:696–722).

Schleiermacher's emphasis on the corporate character of the Christian life and its world-transforming effect can be seen as a faithful appropriation of earlier Reformed theology's emphasis on the divine imperative to shape the structures and institutions of human society according to the Word of God. At the same time, he points forward to the social gospel and liberation theology in his analysis of sin in its corporate and structural dimensions, and in his insistence that preoccupation with the fate of individual souls apart from a new corporate life does little to overcome the reality of sin. While his place in the legacy of Reformed theology has been contested, his greatness as a systematic theologian is undisputed.[5] If a Church Father is one whose articulation of Christian faith is the creative force in a particular era of church history, then Schleiermacher surely deserves to be called the Church Father of the nineteenth century.[6]

Notes

1   Schleiermacher (1894:31). This translation is of the third German edition of Schleiermacher's *Speeches*, which was heavily edited by Schleiermacher himself. For an English translation of the first edition of 1799, see Schleiermacher (1799/1988).

2   Martin Redeker (1973:49) notes that Johann Wolfgang von Goethe, who had read the first part of the *Speeches* with delight, refused to read on when he reached this point in the argument.

3   The text is available in English translation (Schleiermacher 1981).

4   The descriptive term "Christomorphic" is taken from Richard R. Niebuhr's classic study *Schleiermacher on Christ and Religion* (Niebuhr 1964). Schleiermacher's theology is not "Christocentric" in the sense that every doctrine could be deduced from his Christology, but it is "Christomorphic" in the sense that every doctrine is shaped by his doctrine of Christ.

5   Perhaps the most famous critical assessment of Schleiermacher's lineage is Karl Barth's: "Those who accept the thoughts I have brought forward as germane to the essential facts thereby acknowledge themselves descendants of an ancestral line that runs back through *Kierkegaard* to *Luther* and *Calvin*, and so to *Paul* and *Jeremiah*. . . . And to leave nothing unsaid, I might explicitly point out that this ancestral line – which I commend to you – does *not include Schleiermacher*" (Barth 1928:195).

6   The description of Schleiermacher as the "Church Father of the 19th century" was first used in a short work by Christian Lülmann (1907).

References

Barth, K. 1928. *The Word of God and the Word of Man*, trans. D. Horton. London: Hodder & Stoughton.

Barth, K. 1973. *Protestant Theology in the Nineteenth Century: Its Background and History*. Valley Forge, PA: Judson Press.

Brunner, E. 1928. *Die Mystik und das Wort: Der Gegensatz zwischen moderner Religionsauffassung und christlichem Glauben dargestellt an der Theologie Schleiermachers*, 2nd edn. Tübingen: J. C. B. Mohr (Paul Siebeck).

Calvin, J. 1960. *Institutes of the Christian Religion*, trans. F. L. Battles, ed. J. T. McNeill, Library of Christian Classics, vols. 20–1. Philadelphia, PA: Westminster Press.

Kähler, M. 1962. *Geschichte der protestantischen Dogmatik im 19. Jahrhundert*, ed. E. Kähler. Munich: Christian Kaiser Verlag.

Kant, I. 1934. *Religion Within the Limits of Reason Alone*, trans. with intro. and notes T. M. Greene and H. H. Hudson. Reprinted [1960] New York: Harper and Brothers.

Lülmann, C. 1907. *Schleiermacher der Kirchenvater des 19. Jahrhunderts*, in *Sammlung gemeinverständlicher Vorträge und Schriften*, no. 48. Tübingen: J. C. B. Mohr.

Niebuhr, R. R. 1964. *Schleiermacher on Christ and Religion*. New York: Charles Scribner's Sons.

Redeker, M. 1973. *Schleiermacher: Life and Thought*, trans. J. Wallhauser. Philadelphia, PA: Fortress Press.

Rowan, F. trans. 1860. *The Life of Schleiermacher as Unfolded in His Autobiography and Letters*, 2 vols. London: Smith and Elder.

Schleiermacher, F. D. E. 1799/1988. *On Religion: Speeches to Its Cultured Despisers*, trans. of 1st edn. R. Crouter. Cambridge: Cambridge University Press.

Schleiermacher, F. D. E. 1894. *On Religion: Speeches to Its Cultured Despisers*, trans. J. Oman. Reprinted [1958] New York: Harper & Row.

Schleiermacher, F. D. E. 1928. *The Christian Faith*, trans. from the 2nd German edn. H. R. Machkintosh and J. S. Stewart. Reprinted [1999] Edinburgh: T. & T. Clark.

Schleiermacher, F. D. E. 1966. *Brief Outline on the Study of Theology*, trans. T. N. Tice. Richmond, VA: John Knox Press.

Schleiermacher, F. D. E. 1981. *On the Glaubenslehre: Two Letters to Dr Lücke*, trans. J. Duke and F. Fiorenza, American Academy of Religion Texts and Translations Series, vol. 3. Chico, CA: Scholars Press.

Schweizer, A. 1844–7. *Die Glaubenslehre der evangelisch-reformierten Kirche dargestellt und aus den Quellen belegt*, 2 vols. Zurich: Orell, Füssli.

CHAPTER 20

Barth

Mark Lindsay

On December 11, 1968, Eberhard Jüngel told the theological college at the University of Zurich that the task of theology requires a constant re-visitation of "beginnings." Eberhard Busch has remarked similarly that the Church must always be self-reflective, taking stock of its theological heritage by "listen[ing] to the Fathers who have gone before in the faith" (Busch 1994:498). In doing so, it is impossible to go beyond the imposing figure of Karl Barth, who was described by Pope Pius XII as "the greatest theologian since St Thomas Aquinas." The offering of such an accolade from the representative spokesperson of a confessional position which Barth once suspected of being shored up by an "invention of the Antichrist" (*Church Dogmatics* (1936–81) – hereafter *CD*, I/1:xiii) – the *analogia entis* – suggests the legitimacy of what many commentators have long believed; that alongside Aquinas and Anselm, Luther, and Calvin, Karl Barth ranks as pre-eminent among the doctors of the Church. Reflective integrity thus necessitates that in the course of its self-critique, its revisitation of beginnings, the Church needs to come to grips with Barth's theology.

At once, however, the Church is hindered in any attempt to undertake this sort of analytical task. Among the many adjectives that could be used to describe Barth's corpus, arguably the most apt and least controversial is that it is overwhelmingly massive. George Hunsinger has commented that although Barth is frequently honored he is rarely read (Hunsinger 1991:27), but this is hardly surprising when one considers that his *Church Dogmatics* alone is nine times the length of Calvin's *Institutes* and twice as long as Aquinas's *Summa Theologiae*. Barth himself was perhaps not helped by saying that "anyone who does want to talk about me must certainly have read me. Moreover (if he is a serious person . . .), he should have read me completely" (Busch 1994:375). It is precisely the vastness of Barth's legacy, and the necessity of reading the whole in order to understand his "labyrinthine argument" (Hunsinger 1991:3) that makes it so difficult for the Church to integrate his insights into its own program without resorting to simplifications and misinterpretations. *Latet periculum in generabilus* (danger lurks in generalities) was one of Barth's favorite warnings, and it is particularly appropriate in cautioning against simplistic generalizations of Barth's theology which can all too easily result from selective readings of his work. The aim of this chapter, therefore, is to suggest a paradigm of approach that, without expurgating it of its majestic scope, will open up the complexities of Barthian theology and render it more useable for the Church in its own theological task.

Many interpretive models that have been suggested for assessing Barth's work have adopted a narrative approach, according to which Barth's theology can be understood under the rubric of material and formal evolution. In other words, Barth is interpreted as having progressed *from–to*; from liberalism to neo-orthodoxy to evangelical conservatism; or from dialectical to analogical theology; or, perhaps, as T. F. Torrance has put it, from dialectical to dogmatic theology. In most such approaches, emphasis is placed on the mature phase of his development, with earlier stages serving primarily to highlight the brilliance of his later insights. There is nothing wrong with an evolutionary model as far as it goes, as Barth clearly did modify his theology over the course of his career, both formally and materially. Indeed, the title of one of his books, *How I Changed My Mind* (1969), indicates that Barth himself recognized various modifications to his thought over the years. The danger in a developmental paradigm, however, is three-fold; first, there is some difficulty in deciding what Barth developed *from* and what he matured *to*; second, and as hinted above, implicit within this paradigm is the view that Barth's later theology was somehow better than his earlier attempts – a view which may indeed be correct, but which should not be an *a priori* presupposition of analysis; and third, the assumption that Barth's theology is characterized by constant change can ignore the overall coherences that are present within its total structure.

If a narrative evolutionary model is therefore inadequate by itself, how is the serious reader to understand Barth? At this point the qualification should be made that the present chapter neither intends nor pretends to provide a synopsis of the entire *Church Dogmatics*. On the one hand, there is insufficient space to deal here with such a vast topic in a meaningful way. On the other hand, in spite of some scholars' contention that the *Church Dogmatics* is merely an extension of the *Römerbrief*, Barth's work encompasses much more than his Bonn/Basle cycle of dogmatics, and to neglect the other aspects of his corpus would seriously detract from the accuracy of the overall picture. For those who do wish to focus their study on the *Church Dogmatics*, no better book can be recommended than Hunsinger's *How to Read Karl Barth* (1991). This chapter, however, by including but also casting its net wider than the *Church Dogmatics*, will suggest three ways of interpreting Barth, none of which should be used in isolation from the other two but, when used in conjunction with each other, can help assemble a most useful framework within which Barth study can proceed.

The first is the contextual model, in which Barth's life and work are seen within the historical *Sitz im Leben* of early twentieth-century Europe. Ingredient to this approach is the recognition that, whether consciously or not (and even, in spite of one's attempts to avoid it), historico-geographic context impinges upon the theology written within that specific context.

The second is the ecclesial model, according to which Barth is read, not as an isolated figure of theological import, but rather as someone who self-consciously regarded his work as being in direct continuity with his theological predecessors. He certainly deviated at significant points from those who had gone before him. Nonetheless, even in the midst of his divergences, he felt an affinity with them derived from the certainty that he was engaging in the same theological endeavor.

The third model is the dogmatic approach, in which Barth's theology is interpreted as a "rigorous and disciplined inquiry," whose formal determination "arises out of its submission to the Word of God as its norm" and whose "material determination . . . arises out of its attachment to the Word of God as its object . . ." (Torrance 1962:125, 129).

Undoubtedly, the characterization (caricaturization?) of Barth as a "theologian of the Word" may tend to privilege the latter option, and to some degree that privileging would accord with Barth's own self-understanding of who he was and what he did. However, in spite of his avowed rejection of general revelation's legitimacy, the history in which Barth himself was caught up quite clearly had a profound impact upon his work. Thus, the priority of the dogmatic approach cannot be seen in isolation from the contextual and ecclesial paradigms, in the same way that the contextual and ecclesial paradigms cannot be regarded apart from their reference-point of dogmatics. When the three are employed together, however, the shape of Barth's life and theology emerge from the shroud of complexity with which they are veiled, to take on an ultimately more coherent and comprehensible image.

The Contextual Model

Karl Barth was born in Basle on May 10, 1886, and died on December 9, 1968. Within those 82 years, Europe was changed for ever by the cycle of financial depression and boom, the catastrophe of two world wars, the systematic atrocities of the Holocaust, and the dawning of the nuclear age. The Church and its theology reflected the turbulence of these times by swerving first one way and then another; from Ernst Troeltsch's *Religionsgeschichtliche Schule* and Harnack's liberal Protestantism, to Religious Socialism, state-appropriated theological fascism (as exemplified in the Nazi-sponsored *Deutsche Christen*), demythologization and the "death of God" experiment.

Barth was by no means an unmoved observer of these events and movements, adopting a critical stance towards both the diverse theologies and the contexts from which they arose. He was, in fact, the very opposite of the "wholly Other" whose separation from the world and its affairs he supposedly championed in his *Römerbrief*. Just as Europe and the Church were changing, so too was Barth influenced – at times positively, at times negatively – by the course of history around him. Not only were such things as his political affiliation determined by his experiences of the work-a-day world, but his theology was also deeply reflective of his historical context.

The Barth who emerged from his university training in 1909 was a dedicated disciple of "modern theology," particularly in its Herrmannian version. In his own words, he was "second to none among my contemporaries in credulous approval of [it]" (letter to E. Huber, January 14, 1951). Under the tutelage of Martin Rade, Adolf von Harnack, and Wilhelm Herrmann, Barth devoted himself to the dominant theological school of the day which, in continuity with Schleiermacher and Ritschl, understood Christianity to be "on the one hand . . . a historical phenomenon to be subjected to critical examination, and on the other hand . . . a matter of inner experience, of a predominantly moral nature" (Barth 1927:46).

One of the clearest indications of Barth's allegiance to "modern theology" was the argument he set forth in his first published essay, "Moderne Theologie und Reichsgottesarbeit" (1909:317–21). In Barth's eyes, the kernel of modern theology was two-fold; strict religious individualism, both ethically and in terms of one's spiritual awakening, and the insistence on the historical relativity of religion and theology. Both aspects rendered the task of pastoral work more difficult for the students of modern theology than for the conservatives, but the modern road was nonetheless the only viable option. That, at least, was the argument proposed by an enthusiastically "modern" Barth.

Ironically, the experience of pastoral duties in the Aargauer village of Safenwil had for Barth precisely the opposite effect. Far from reinforcing the validity of the modern theological program (as should have been the case according to the "Moderne Theologie" article), parish concerns stimulated the beginnings of a break with Barth's theological teachers. Here, within a small industrial community, Barth first truly grasped the inner link between Christianity and socialism. Under the influence of Werner Sombart's *Sozialismus und Soziale Bewegung*, and the Religious Socialism movement of Herrmann Kutter and Leonhard Ragaz, Barth shifted away from the political conservatism of his mentors and became heavily involved in the local trade unions. In January 1915 he joined the Swiss Social Democratic Party.

It was not only, nor even primarily, at the political level that Barth moved ground. Theologically, his leftist politics correlated to a new vision of the kingdom of God. Barth's signature lecture of this period, "Jesus Christ und die soziale Bewegung"[1] not only contained such provocative statements as "*real* socialism is real Christianity in our time" (Hunsinger 1976:36), but more significantly leveled serious criticisms against Harnack's *What is Christianity?* According to Harnack, Jesus' kingdom was little more than internalized individuality. For Barth, such a view illegitimately separated spirit and matter: "perhaps nowhere else has Christianity fallen farther away from the spirit of her Lord and Master than precisely in this estimation of the relation between spirit and matter, inner and outer, heaven and earth" (Hunsinger 1976:26). Barth's engagement with the realities of economic oppression and class conflict, both of which were defining characteristics of Safenwil life, had thus demonstrated more clearly than any debate with religious conservatives ever could, that "modern theology" simply did not meet the needs of the parishioners. Nor did it necessarily provide an accurate framework into which everyday life could be merged with the kernel of the gospel message.

If the origins of Barth's alienation from his liberal predecessors can be traced to the beginnings of his Safenwil pastorate, the break itself came on October 3, 1915, when "[n]inety-three German intellectuals impressed public opinion by their proclamation in support of the war policy of Wilhelm II . . . Among these intellectuals I discovered to my horror almost all of my theological teachers whom I had greatly venerated" (Barth 1961:12–13). Harnack and Herrmann were both signatories to the manifesto.

For Barth, the entire Safenwil experience was an exercise in learning the inner unity of dogmatics and ethics, of theology and social praxis. The outbreak of World War I provided him with a negative example of this unity. By virtue of the ease with which academic theology had been changed into "intellectual 42 cm cannons" (letter to W. Spoendlin, January 4, 1915), the October manifesto illustrated to him the ethical bankruptcy of liberalism. This failure proved to him that modern theology's "exegetical and dogmatic presuppositions could not be in order" (Barth 1950:4). It was in the face of this shattering disappointment that Barth, along with his friend Eduard Thurneysen, found themselves forced back to a "wholly other" theological foundation. Their mentor this time was neither Schleiermacher, Kant, nor "modern theology," but the Bible itself – and out of this rediscovery of the Bible came the celebrated *Römerbrief* (Barth 1922).

A final word at this point needs to be said about the relationship between the two Romans commentaries and the influence of contemporary politics. Anyone who reads Barth's works from this period cannot fail to be impressed by the frequency with which the "crisis" motif appears. Given the cataclysmic effects that World War I and the Russian Revolution had on the Europe of the day, this seems reasonable. The logical assumption has understandably been that, in the manner of Oswald Spengler's *Decline of the West* and even of Barth's "dialectical" ally Friedrich Gogarten, Barth was employing a term that had come into common currency, as a defining theme of his theological construction. One of the very first English-speaking interpreters of Barth put it this way: "In no other respect does his thought witness to the strain and agony of the War years more than in the stress which he lays on crisis" (Chapman 1931:30). While the connection is most certainly there, it would nonetheless be erroneous to overstate the extent to which Barth depended upon current secular ideas to shape his theology. As McCormack has recently shown, the equation of the postwar socio-political milieu with the Barthian "crisis" is too superficial (McCormack 1995:211–12). For Barth, crisis is more an eschatological realization that occurs when an individual comes under the judging gaze of the cross of Christ and thus knows himself to be an object of divine rejection. It is, in other words, a universal and continual result of revelation that takes place on the receptive side of the grace–judgment dialectic. The cultural and historical understanding of crisis is thus much more limited in scope and effect than that envisaged by Barth. This is not to say that Barth was unaware of or unaffected by the currency of the term "crisis." Rather, it suggests an adoption of it into a theological model that both revolutionized and radicalized it. It is not, to quote from McCormack, that Barth's theology of this period was specifically a "theology *of* crisis . . . [but rather] it was a theology *to* and *for* a time of crisis" (1995:217) in that contemporary attention was directed by Barth away from cultural catastrophe and towards the ultimate judgment that exists in the hearing of the Word of God.

This qualification aside, it can nonetheless be argued that the formative years of Barth's theological development, which culminated in the two Romans commentaries and the appointment to an honorary professorship in Reformed theology in Göttingen, were shaped as much by external historical and political factors as by Barth's personal reflections. The same is surely true of the middle period of his career when, in Bonn and then Basle, his theology was formulated against the backdrop of Nazism, World War II, and genocide.

In 1932, the first part-volume of the *Church Dogmatics* was published. Less than six months later, Hitler's National Socialists had seized power and the entire political, social, and intellectual context of Germany had changed forever. Initially, Barth appears to have been less than overawed by the Nazi *Machtergreifung*. Early in the new year, he wrote to his mother saying that "I don't believe that [Hitler's takeover] will mark the beginning of great novelties in any direction."[2] By June 24, however, he had changed his mind and signaled the about-face with the release of *Theologische Existenz heute!* (1933b; *English Translation Theological Existence Today*). In this landmark publication, Barth laid the foundation for a Christologically driven political ethic that refused to grant legitimacy to the *völkisch* anti-Semitic theology of the "German Christian Movement." He had for a long time been convinced of the error of natural theology and the *Deutsche Christen*, with their attempt to "coordinate" the Evangelical Church into the Nazi state, simply proved to him the political and ethical rightness of his position. From this point on, Barth's theology and theologically conditioned political praxis was decisively directed against Nazism and, not least of all, the genocidal anti-Semitism with which it was permeated.

In 1934, he authored the Barmen Declaration. At the ecclesial level, by recalling the Church to the recognition of Christ as her only Lord and authoritative revelation which she must confess, the declaration became one of the most significant confessional documents since the Heidelberg Catechism and the Westminster Confession of Faith. Politically, the declaration established the Confessing Church as the primary ecclesiastical wing of anti-Nazi resistance.

Shortly after the Barmen Synod, Barth was expelled from Germany for refusing to begin his lectures with the Hitler salute – he preferred prayer! – and so his teaching commitments had to be continued over the border in his home town of Basle. Within the (relative) freedom afforded by Switzerland's neutrality, Barth made use of his opportunities to continue the fight against Nazism. In 1938 – and historically, therefore, in immediate connection with an escalation of the anti-Semitic agenda within Germany – he wrote the pamphlet "Justification and Justice" ("Rechtfertigung und Recht") and co-authored with four of his colleagues the memorandum "Salvation Comes from the Jews". In the first, he rigorously insisted on the internal connection between the theological doctrine of justification and its ethical outworking of social justice. By positing the state as a Christologically-circumscribed entity which has its truest being in providing the Church with space in which to proclaim the gospel, Barth was able to assert that the usurpation by the state of the Church's role – which was manifestly what was happening in Nazi Germany – demanded political resistance as a theological necessity. In such a case, "the fulfilment of political duty [by the Christian] means . . . political action, which may and must also mean political struggle" (Barth 1985:44–5). In the second, Barth championed the cause of Jews generally – not merely Jewish Christians, which was the standard position adopted by most Church statements of the time. They are, he argued, God's anointed to whom He had bound Himself in covenant. The persecution of the Jews, however, "is becoming more horrible day by day." The response? "[R]ise up in the power of the Holy Spirit [and] refrain from letting Christendom be contaminated by Antisemitism."[3]

Nonetheless, important as these pieces were in recalling the Church to an activistic agenda, it was not only in his overt political tracts that Barth exercised his social conscience. The material content of those volumes of the *Church Dogmatics* written during the Nazi era similarly reflect the impact of contemporary events upon his theological formulation.

As early as 1931 when he was preparing the material for *Church Dogmatics*, I/1, Barth was aware of the *völkisch* trend within German society and was determined that it would not corrupt the genuine construction of dogmatic theology. Thus we read that revelation, which is the basis and norm of all theological reflection, is the revelation of *God*. The corollary – particularly apt in the early 1930s – is that the word of the Church must not be "in harmony with the distinctive features and interests of a race, people, nation or state" (*CD* I/1:72). A similar point is made later when, in his discussion of the scriptural mode of revelation, Barth categorically insists that the normative Scriptures come to the Church in the inseparable form of the Old and New Testaments. They are bound together by the unity of the revealing God, Yahweh-Kyrios, who is "a single being," "the one and only Willer and Doer" (*CD* I/1:348; I/2:473–85). The significance of this lies in the recognition that, precisely at the time in which Barth was insisting on the covenantal link between Old and New Testaments on the basis of the one Covenanter who is attested in both, the *Deutsche Christen* were advocating a new Marcionism that would see the Old Testament and all things Jewish radically expunged from the Scriptures and replaced with more genuinely Teutonic material. Clearly, even if the basics of Barth's doctrine of revelation had been obvious to him since his Münster and Göttingen days, the formal presentation of it in the months leading up to the Barmen Synod was intricately connected with the socio-political heresy in the midst of which Barth was forced to work.

Similar examples of Barth's interaction with events around him in the development of his theology can be found in the manner in which he unfolds his doctrine of election. Formulated during the initial period of the "Final Solution," this pivotal article of his dogmatic work presents a dialectically structured defense of the Jew's ongoing covenantal status (*CD* II/2).

Before completing this section, it is necessary to note briefly Barth's theological engagement with postwar history. European politics following 1945 until Barth's death in 1968 were fundamentally predicated upon East–West tensions. More than any other political issue, it was the ability to critique Soviet communism that legitimized a theologian's relevance in Cold War Europe. In this respect, Reinhold Niebuhr and Emil Brunner both criticized Barth's attitude towards communism, particularly in relation to Hungary. Why, they wanted to know, was Barth silent? Why was he not as ferociously anti-communist as he had been anti-Nazi, when Stalinism was surely as totalitarian as the Third Reich? Barth's response was simple. Church political action is case-specific; there is no universal attitude towards statehood that the Church must adopt in every and any situation. Thus, because Nazism and communism are different in nature, so too should the Church response be different.

Primarily, Barth's evaluation of the "Russian question" was informed by the theological recognition that, whereas Nazism had attempted to usurp the place of the Church and impose itself as a pseudo-religion, communism was more ambivalent, even "coldly non-Christian." "It has never committed the basic crime of the Nazis, the removal and replacement of the real Christ by a national Jesus" (Barth 1954:140). In other words, Nazism was a heresy which had to be resisted, while communism was a political attempt to solve the enduring "social problem." Its attempt was certainly tainted by "very dirty and bloody hands" and was not without "totalitarian abomina- tions." Nonetheless, it was the height of hypocrisy for the West to demonize Russian social policy for as long as the West continued to dump its surplus food into the ocean (1954:132, 140). With these remarks, Barth demonstrated that not only was political action firmly embedded in theological existence throughout his career but also, from the other direction, external political events helped mold his theological reflection – in this case, his understanding of statehood and appropriate ecclesial response.

It is clear, therefore, that in spite of his well-known rejection of natural theology and the correlated belief in the superiority of revelation over history in the theological task, Barth's work was not entirely devoid of historical-contextual influences. Two world wars, economic oppression and Nazi idolatry all contributed to a fundamental nexus in Barth's life between theological construction and contemporary events. History was never fully determinative for him – but he nevertheless made sure that the newspaper was always alongside the Bible as he wrote (1969:12).

The Ecclesial Model

Barth's theological program was not only influenced by contemporary history but very much also by church history down the ages, and of which Barth felt intimately a part. As the editors of *From Rousseau to Ritschl* have pointed out, Barth's work can be fully understood only if he is regarded as standing in a line, certainly pointing very clearly forward to such people as Bonhoeffer, Gollwitzer, and Torrance but equally certainly looking back at the work of those like Athanasius, Anselm, and Calvin who came before him in the theological task (Macintyre and McIntyre 1959:9).

This emphasis within Barth's theological construction upon his doctrinal predeces- sors is evident early in his career. During the summer semester of 1922, Barth deliv- ered a series of lectures on Calvin to his Göttingen students, following it up in the winter of 1922–3 with a series on Zwingli, who he regarded as a forerunner to modern liber- alism, and then a series on Schleiermacher in the winter semester of 1923–4. His first academic position was thus clearly delineated by a desire to explore the writings of three seminal figures in theological history. Significantly, while Barth's Reformed sympathies attracted him to much – though not all – of Calvin's theology, he was very much more critical of Schleiermacher. As early as 1921, Thurneysen had reminded Barth of their common realization that they "could no longer share the faith" of this nineteenth- century Protestant giant.[4] Indeed, the Göttingen lectures were designed as the first salvo in what was to be a long-running assault on Schleiermacher (Ritschl 1982:ix). And yet Barth could say at the same time that "Schleiermacher is not dead for us and his theological work has not been transcended. If anyone still speaks today in Protes- tant theology . . . it is Schleiermacher." Insofar as religion, piety, and Christian self- consciousness are concerned, "[w]ho is not at one" with him? (Ritschl 1982:xiii). In other words, suspicion of and sharp divergences from Schleiermacher notwithstand- ing, Barth was nevertheless insistent that theological analysis could not avoid him. Differences in doctrinal conclusions did not in themselves negate the recognition of a

commonality of theological intent. Indeed, at the very end of his life, Barth acknowledged that he had never been able to get away from the great man and that "for all my
opposition . . . I can imagine a very happy reunion with [him] in heaven" (Barth 1968).

The little book on Anselm which Barth published in 1931 gave further proof of his
engagement with doctrinal history, but it was in the preface to the first part-volume of
the *Church Dogmatics* that Barth clarified his position with regard to his theological fore-
runners. "I am now going the way of scholasticism," he said. "Church history no longer
begins for me in 1517. I can quote Anselm and Thomas with no sign of horror [and]
I obviously regard the doctrine of the early Church as in some sense normative" (*CD*
I/1:xiii).

It is quite appropriate, therefore, that Bruce McCormack's brilliant doctoral dissertation on Barth should be entitled *A Scholastic of a Higher Order*. In this major study of
Barth's formative years, McCormack makes the very good point that Barth was not a
scholastic in the traditional sense, because he did not equate allegiance to confessional
statements with allegiance to Scripture. He "violently opposed confessional*ism* which
binds its adherents to a fidelity to the letter of the confession. He was, however, all in
favor of a confessional theology which . . . allowed itself to be guided by the witness of
the church in the past" (McCormack 1989:3).

Thus in Göttingen, when according to McCormack Barth entered a new phase of
dogmatic thinking, he began to insist on the necessity of reading the Bible in the light
of church tradition. "How is it possible to combine a truly serious conviction that God
has a word for the present with disrespect toward and neglect of the past?" (1989:343).
In consequence, dogmatic theology "is the faithful hearing of confessions and Fathers
in the attempt to bring to expression the Word which has been heard under their guidance" (1989:349). In Göttingen, the Fathers to whom Barth paid particular attention
included Polanus, Wollebius, Coccejus, Quenstedt, and Hollaz (1989:344–5) (although
in the *Church Dogmatics* greater emphasis is placed upon Luther, Calvin, and the
Patristic writers).

It is also significant that it was in Göttingen in 1924 that Barth – through the mediation of Heppe and Schmid – adopted the ancient *anhypostatic-enhypostatic* model of
Christology, thus bringing him into line with Cyril and against Nestorius (see also *CD*
IV/2: 49ff). On the one hand, this enabled him to reject all forms of adoptionism, while
on the other hand compelling him positively to affirm the veracity of such orthodox
dogmas as the virgin birth. During the period of Nazism, this modification in his
thought towards a more truly classical Christology reaped other benefits, in that the
anhypostatic pole of the formula retained the distinction between revelation and
history, which both the *Deutsche Christen* and the Nazi Party were wanting to obliter-
ate, while the enhypostatic union gave greater weight to the specifically human – and
thus Jewish – nature of Christ's incarnate existence than would otherwise have been
possible.

Within the *Church Dogmatics* themselves, it has already been suggested that Barth's
treatment of the doctrine of election (*CD* II/2) is perhaps the pivotal point of the entire
corpus, and it is at this place that Barth's indebtedness to and deviation from his theological teachers becomes most obvious. On the one hand, he self-consciously refers to
Calvin as a starting point for his own formulation of the doctrine. The "Calvinist"

notion of "double predestination" – which as Barth shows is not peculiar to Calvin at all (e.g. *CD* II/2: 17), but which has nevertheless become synonymous with his theology – is not at all rebuffed. Election is indeed two-fold in nature. But, and this is where the difference between Barth and Calvin lies, by rejecting the Calvinist *decretum absolutum*, according to which the decision for election is made by Good apart from and outside of Christ, Barth was able to re-configure his understanding of election to make Christ its nodal center. In this way, election remains two-fold – but Jesus Christ is at once the electing God and the elected man, as well as the rejected man. Both the subjective and objective poles of election *and* the subjectively experienced realities of election and rejection find their focus in Christ. He truly becomes the "man for others," to use Bonhoeffer's phrase. As with Schleiermacher, therefore, Calvin's importance for Barth is not to be found in the degree of similarity between them. Barth at times is especially harsh in his condemnation of the Reformer. Calvin's significance for Barth is rather to be found in the face that, in Calvin as much as in Schleiermacher, Barth perceived a fellow theologian, one for whom the task of theology as a witness and service to the Church was as necessary as Barth himself believed it to be. Doctrinal differences aside, dialog could and had to take place precisely because it was in the process of engaging with the insight – even the misguided insight – of previous theologians that the Word of God was mediated appropriately to the contemporary church context.

Thus it can realistically be argued that the Barth of the *Church Dogmatics* had come a long way from the rather more insular Barth of October 1922. At that time, Barth had been as keen to distance himself from those with whom he did not feel an affinity as he was to align himself with those with whom he did. His "ancestral line" ran through "Kierkegaard to Luther and Calvin, and so to Paul and Jeremiah." But it emphatically did not run through "Martensen [or] Erasmus." Barth made the further comment that "this ancestral line – which I commend to you – does not include Schleiermacher" (1978a:195). He was not at this stage willing to consider the value of engagement with those whom he believed to be in the wrong.

It was when he moved to the professorship in Göttingen that he was forced to reconsider. His teaching duties proved to him his "woeful lack of historical breadth" and that he "had only the barest acquaintance with the Reformed tradition" (McCormack 1995:293). By forcing himself to address this deficiency, Barth by necessity came into contact with predecessors from whom he would otherwise quite probably have stayed away. In doing so, he opened himself up to new theological vistas which gave a richness to his own theology that had not previously been apparent, but which, as has been seen, was to become crucial in the shift to dogmatic construction.

The Dogmatic Model

The move to Göttingen did not simply force Barth to acquaint himself more deeply with church, specifically Reformed, history. Precisely because it did this, the shift also compelled him to alter his whole approach to theological thinking. No longer was he free simply to propose a "corrective theology" that served as prophetic critique to contemporary theological trends. Once installed within the university, Barth was required to formulated his theology in a more positive manner. As he wrote to Thurneysen, "Dozens, nay hundreds, want to know where it goes from here and crave to hear from us the B and C that come after A."[5] Practically, this entailed for him a new way of constructing theology, according to which theology was not (only) an individual's confrontation with the revelation of God but, much more properly, was a service performed in the Church and by the Church, to ensure that ecclesial proclamation was an accurate mediation of the Word of God to the world. From the very start of his experimentation with it, therefore, dogmatic thought required from Barth a critical engagement with the word of the Church.

Even in his first tentative attempts at dogmatic construction, Barth clearly understood the context in which dogmatics must occur. In the thesis which begins §1 of the *Göttingen Dogmatics* (Barth 1991; hereafter *GöttDg*), "The Word of God as the Problem of Dogmatics," Barth insists that dogmatics is nothing less than "scientific reflection on the Word of God which is spoken by God in revelation . . . and which now both is and should be proclaimed and heard in Christian preaching" (*GöttDg*: 3). It is neither revelation itself, nor the raw material of preaching – on the contrary, preaching is the raw material of dogmatic enquiry. But because the pulpit is the place "where there is either pure doctrine or not, where there is either room for God's Word or not," dogmatics and preaching – and therefore dogmatics and the Church – are related "in the same way as service at headquarters and at the front. Dogmatics has to serve the Church," by purifying doctrine and thus by purifying the content of Church proclamation (*GöttDg*: 276). An even clearer example of Barth's commitment to the ecclesiastical setting of dogmatics can be found in his recollection of the time spent preparing for this first foray into dogmatics. In applying himself to the study of the post-Reformation theologians, he became excited by the way that they took up the cause of the Reformation while at the same time continuing the doctrinal constructions of the early Church and the Middle Ages. As Barth put it, "I found myself visibly in the realm of the *Church*" (1935:iv).

Barth's next attempt at dogmatics in Münster was not so clear in its determination of context. Certainly, Barth called it a *Christliche Dogmatik*, and its material core was again concerned with the problem of preaching. In the end, however, its title was one of its major drawbacks. Quite aside from the (alleged) reliance within the Münster cycle on existential philosophy which Barth later perceived to be its crucial flaw (*CD* I/1: xiii, 126), the peculiar socio-political climate of 1930s Germany rendered the attachment to something of the adjective "Christian" almost meaningless, because it was hardly descriptive of real content. As far back as 1919, Barth had spoken out against "all those combinations – 'social-Christian,' 'social-evangelical,' 'social-religious' . . ." which made "dangerous short circuits" of the paradoxical "Christ in us" (1978b:276). And again in 1924, he had argued that "in the formula 'Christianity and . . .' lurks the betrayal of Christianity" (1971:52–3). But, by the early 1930s, this both-and syncretism had a more threatening aspect to it due to the Nazified ideology of the German Christian Movement. A "Christian" dogmatics was therefore not necessarily Christian at all. In response, Barth suggested that maybe it would be appropriate to "proceed with caution when we use the adjective 'Christian,' and to use the word in a way quite other than is the vogue in our victorious modern Christendom. . . . Who gives us permission to use this adjective so profusely?" (Barth 1993:37–8). So, when it came time for him to recommence his dogmatics, he felt obliged "to set a good example of restraint in the lighthearted use of the great word 'Christian'" (*CD* I/1: xiii). Christian dogmatics was forced to become *Church* dogmatics. This was not only a practical response to the changing political situation, but was also the reemphasizing of Barth's earlier perception that dogmatics is "bound to the sphere of the Church, where alone it is possible and meaningful" (*CD* I/1: xiii).

If the Church is the only valid context in which dogmatics can be done, what about the method and subject matter with which this science is concerned? The key is to be found in the title of the first part-volume of the *Church Dogmatics*. At its most basic level dogmatics concerns the Word of God, which is that on which dogmatics reflects (*GöttDg*: 14). While dogmatic construction necessarily leads to a positive formulation – or perhaps more accurately, an attempt at re-formulation – of doctrine, the object of enquiry is dogma. As Barth sees it, dogma is not, as Roman Catholicism says, a "truth of revelation as defined by the Church" (*CD* I/1: 265). This would be to equate the word of humanity with the Word of God and thus fall into the same trap of "Titanism," of *Eritus sicut Deus!*, against which he protested so vocally in his *Römerbrief* days. Rather, dogma is the agreement of Church proclamation with the revelation of God as found in the Scriptures, that is, as found in the written Word of God. The task of dogmatics is to enquire into the extent of this agreement (*CD* I/1: 265–7). Consequently, dogmatics also and indeed primarily enquires into the Word of God as the presupposition of all its positive doctrinal constructions. It thus becomes clear why the first volume of the *Church Dogmatics* is a "Prolegomena." Before the engagement with individual doctrines can occur, it is necessary first to explore the basis on which these doctrines are to be built and the norm against which they are to be assessed. According to Barth, the Word of God is this fundamental basis or criterion and thus the Word of God itself requires dogmatic discussion. The prolegomena is not, therefore, an extraneous preface to the real dogmatic task, but is crucial to the development of the whole project.

There is, however, another reason for the necessity of this prolegomena. The prolegomena is as such "an explicit account of the particular way of knowledge taken in dogmatics" (*CD* I/1: 25). It is, in other words, an explication of the dogmatic epistemology. In both the Göttingen and the Bonn dogmatics, however, Barth was perceptive enough to realize that this epistemology was no longer self-evident, as it had been to Lombard, Aquinas, and Zwingli. At fault was not the "modern denial of revelation" that was evident within secular rationalism but the particular understandings of revelation as held by Roman Catholicism and Protestant Modernism. The role of the prolegomena, therefore, was to show "with what inner foundation we stand on the one side and not the other," understanding revelation "not in Roman Catholic or Modernist terms, but in Evangelical terms" (*CD* I/1: 34). That Barth spends the first 1,400 pages of the *Church Dogmatics* in an extended treatment of the Word of God as the criterion of dogmatics – discussing in turn the revelation of God, the Scriptures and the proclamation of the Church – demonstrates the seriousness with which he took the necessity of this prolegomena, and the fact that it was not just a large preface.

Any consideration of the individual *loci* within Barth's dogmatic corpus is premature until his conception of the God who reveals Himself in His Word is explored in greater depth. From at least as early as the first edition of his Romans commentary, Barth was insistent upon the immutable subjectivity of God. God remains Subject even when His revelation becomes objective for us, which occurs most genuinely in the incarnation. This is not to say that Hunsinger and Torrance are wrong to isolate the motif of *objectivism* that recurs throughout the *Church Dogmatics*. For Barth, the knowledge of God certainly does remain grounded in God rather than in human subjectivity (as was argued by Schleiermacher). Similarly, Barth's objectivism is to be found in his understanding of salvation, in which humanity is really and objectively present to God in Christ – soteriological objectivism, in Hunsinger's words.[6] Nonetheless, whatever might accurately be said about the objectivity of Christian revelation insofar as its validity being independent of human perception is concerned, it is impossible in Barth's view to comprehend either the God who comes to humanity in Christ, or the method of God's coming, if we fail to recognize that precisely in this encounter God remains Subject. In fact, it can even be argued that Barth's insistence on the divine subjectivity *in* revelation was designed to maintain the objectivity *of* revelation (McCormack 1995:238). In other words, how can God truly and objectively make Himself known as God, without ceasing to be in control of the divine Self-revelation, or without this revelation ceasing to be the revelation of *God?*

The answer at which Barth first arrived in his *Römerbrief* was the dialectical motif of veiling and unveiling. In the incarnation of Jesus Christ, God becomes known – and knowable – indirectly through the medium of the historical Jesus of Nazareth. At this point, Barth draws a clear distinction between the historical vehicle of revelation and the revelation itself. The "historical Jesus" is not the revelation of God but rather the veil behind which the revelation comes. Nevertheless, God has objectively made Himself known – albeit indirectly – through this veil. The objectivity of revelation is assured as is the subjective unintuitability of God.

In the *Göttingen Dogmatics*, Barth makes the same point by reference to the anhypostatic-enhypostatic Christological paradigm. He begins by exploring the doctrine of the Trinity which is "the recognition of . . . the indestructible subjectivity of God in his revelation" (*GöttDg*: 98). His argument runs somewhat as follows. The Trinity speaks of God's subjectivity. Moreover, only God can reveal God. So, if Jesus reveals God, which is the biblical presupposition, Jesus is God and must therefore be subject. Immediately, there are two subjects – the Revealer (Son) and the Revealed (Father) – but the one God. Finally, if we are to believe that Jesus is God, there must be a third subject – the Holy Spirit – by whom the revelation is received. In all this, God's trinitarian subjectivity is retained, even in revelation. But, and this is crucial, only is this so Christologically.

That God is God, however, means that we cannot know God as He is in Himself, that is, in His subjectivity. "[W]hat organ or capability do we have to grasp him, to penetrate this divine I which alone is God? Woe to us if we confuse our own I with this I" (*GöttDg*: 135). In His revelation, therefore, God remains hidden. Nevertheless, and despite the fact that the content of revelation is *wholly* God, Barth insists that this "non-revelation" is still revelation. That is to say, God in His Godness and in His subjectivity becomes object, to meet us as a human Thou. As Barth puts it, "He would have to be not merely an object but a recognizable I. . . . If non-revelation is to be revelation, everything hinges on God covering his inaccessible divine I-ness with a human I-ness as with a veil so that we can gaze on him as a person" (*GöttDg*: 136). God in His unintuitable subjectivity remains concealed, and yet it is precisely in this veiling that He reveals Himself. By the adoption of the an-/enhypostatic formula, Barth is thus able to affirm that wholly God is revealed in the concealment, or incognito of Jesus Christ, and that His subjectivity remains unassailed in the human objectivity of the form of revelation. Significantly, the immutable subjectivity of God as the basis for a truly objective Self-revelation of God remains critical to Barth throughout his later dogmatics of Münster, Bonn, and Basle. As the triune God, God is and remains the "One who reveals Himself and who is subject, and indeed indissolubly subject, in His revelation" (*CD* I/1: 382).

It is hardly an exaggeration to say that all other dogmatic constructions in which Barth engages are an extension of this one basic epistemological locus. Doctrines of creation, redemption, reconciliation, and their correlative ethics are grounded not just structurally but also formally on the recognition that God is the unintuitable Subject who remains God and never becomes the object of human control – not even, and perhaps *especially* not even in theological discourse! To return to Torrance's earlier remark, it can thus be seen why the Word of God – as the revelation of the divine Subject – is both the norm and the material determination of dogmatic enquiry.

The legacy of Karl Barth's theology goes far beyond the confines of dogmatic exposition. While the massive but incomplete Bonn–Basle cycle of the *Church Dogmatics* provides the reader of Barth with an immeasurably rich seam of theological thought from which one can glean many insights, and has provided the Church with unparalleled leadership that is at once innovative and orthodox, there is far more to him than "simply" 9,000-odd pages of intricate excursus. As has been shown here, as much as Barth was one of the greatest and most prolific theologians since Aquinas and Calvin, he was also a pastor, social advocate on behalf of the oppressed, opponent of Nazism and critically prophetic leader of the German Confessing Church (and, if one can believe Adolf Keller, of the entire ecumenical movement).

His significance cannot, therefore, be measured merely by the formal theology he wrote. Through his political tracts such as "Jesus Christ and the Movement for Social Justice" (1911), *Theological Existence Today*, and "Justification and Justice," he pushed the Church through the barrier of traditional Lutheran acquiescence in state-sanctioned injustices to herald a more ethically active ecclesia. Further, his strongly worded *Nein!* to Emil Brunner in 1934 and the Barmen Declaration of the same year challenged the Church to be more cautious in its willingness to see the movement of God in the ebb and flow of history. And again, his responses to Niebuhr and Brunner illustrated the flexibility of ecclesiastical engagement with the historical and political context of the day.

Perhaps most importantly, however, the Christocentric logic of his theology showed – and shows! – to the Church that, the necessity of social activism notwithstanding, the community of the gospel is defined by its adherence to a Person and not to a program. As he said towards the end of his life, "The last word which I as a theologian and as a politician have to say, is not an idea such as 'grace,' but is a name – Jesus Christ. *He* is grace, and *he* is the last, beyond the world and Church and also beyond theology" (Barth 1970:30–1). Within this name was and is to be found all that Barth strove to proclaim, and all that he believed should form the foundation and essence of the

Church in the world. It is entirely appropriate, therefore, that the three models by which Barth's theology can be approached should finish with the dogmatic paradigm. History and ecclesial context were decisive for Barth's theological formulation. Without his recognition of and encounter with these two factors, his work would have lacked its final richness. Underpinning it all, however, was a commitment to the *Christian* nature of theology. In the midst of continuing challenges to this defining kernel of the Church's gospel, it is perhaps this allegiance which secures Barth's continuing relevance to the task of theological endeavor.

Notes

1   Lecture delivered to the Safenwiler Arbeiterverein, December 17, 1911 trans., "Jesus Christ and the Movement for Social Justice," in Hunsinger (1976:19–37).
2   K. Barth, letter to A.-K. Barth, February 1, 1933, Karl Barth-Archiv, cited in Scholder (1987:221).
3   K. Barth, O. Farner, E. Hurter, W. Vischer, G. Ludwig, "Das Heil kommt von den Juden. Memorandum zur Judenfrage," Die theologische Kommission des schweizerischen evangelischen Hilfswerkes für die Bekennende Kirche in Deutschland, October 1938, p. 1, in the Karl Barth-Archiv.
4   E. Thurneysen, letter to K. Barth, in *Revolutionary Theology in the Making: Barth–Thurneysen Correspondence, 1914–1925*, ed. and trans. J. D. Smart (London: Epworth Press, 1964), p. 75.
5   K. Barth, letter to E. Thurneysen, February 5, 1924, *Revolutionary Theology in the Making*, p. 167.
6   Hunsinger (1991:35–37). See also Torrance, who says that "for Barth the Word of God refers to the most objective reality there is . . ." (1962:96).

References

Balthasar, H. U. von. 1976. *Karl Barth: Darstellung und Deutung seiner Theologie*. Einsiedeln: Johannes Verlag.
Balthasar, H. U. von. 1992. *The Theology of Karl Barth*, trans. E. T. Oakes. San Francisco, CA: Ignatius Press. [Trans. of Balthasar 1976.]
Barth, K. 1909. "Moderne Theologie und Reichsgottesarbeit," *Zeitschrift für Theologie und Kirche* 19:317–21.
Barth, K. 1911. "Jesus Christ und die soziale Bewegung." Lecture given to Safenwiler Arbeiterverein, December 17, 1911 (trans. "Jesus Christ and the Movement for Social Justice," in Hunsinger (1976).
Barth, K. 1922. *Die Roemerbrief, Zweite Fassung*. Munich: Christian Kaiser Verlag.
Barth, K. 1927. *Fakultätsalbum der Evangelisch-theologischen Fakultät Münster*. Cited in Busch 1994.
Barth, K. 1933a. *The Epistle to the Romans*, trans. E. C. Hoskyns. London: Oxford University Press.
Barth, K. 1933b. *Theologische Existen heute!* Munich: Christian Kaiser Verlag.
Barth, K. 1935. "Zum Geleit," in H. Heppe, *Die Dogmatik der evangelisch-reformierten Kirche: Dargestellt und aus den Quellen belegt*, ed. E. Bizer. Neukirchen: Buchhandlung des Erziehungsverein Neukirchen.

Barth, K. 1936–81. *Church Dogmatics, I/1–IV/4*, eds. G. W. Bromiley and T. F. Torrance. Edinburgh: T. & T. Clark.

Barth, K. 1950. "Rückblick," in *Das Wort sie sollen lassen stahn, Festschrift für Professor Albert D. Schädelin*, ed. H. Duerr, A. Frankhauser, and W. Michaehis. Bern.

Barth, K. 1954. "The Church between East and West," in *Against the Stream: Shorter Post-War Writings, 1946–1952*. London: SCM Press.

Barth, K. 1961. *The Humanity of God*. London Collins.

Barth, K. 1965. *Evangelical Theology: An Introduction*. London: Fontana.

Barth, K. 1968. "Nachwort," in *Schleiermacher-Auswahl* (Siebenstern Taschenbuch, 113–14), pp. 297, 310. In Busch 1994, p. 494.

Barth, K. 1969. *How I Changed My Mind, 1886–1968*. Edinburgh: St. Andrew's Press.

Barth, K. 1970. *Letzte Zeugnisse*. Zurich: EVZ-Verlag.

Barth, K. 1971. *The Resurrection of the Dead*, trans. J. M. Stenning. New York: F. H. Revell.

Barth, K. 1978a. "The Word of God and the Task of the Ministry," in *The Word of God and the Word of Man*, trans. D. Horton. Gloucester: Peter Smith.

Barth, K. 1978b. "The Christian's Place in Society," in *The Word of God and the Word of Man*, trans. D. Horton. Gloucester: Peter Smith.

Barth, K. 1985. "Rechtfertigung und Recht," in *Theologische Studien*, eds. E. Jüngel, R. Leuenberger and R. Smend. Zurich: Theologische Verlag.

Barth, K. 1991. *The Göttingen Dogmatics: Instruction in the Christian Religion*, vol. 1, ed. H. Reiffen, trans. G. W. Bromiley. Grand Rapids, MI: Eerdmans.

Barth, K. 1993. "Der heilige Geist und das christlichen Leben" [October 9, 1929], trans. R. B. Hoyle, *The Holy Spirit and the Christian Life: The Theological Basis of Ethics*. Louisville, KY: Westminster Press/John Knox Press.

Busch, E. 1994. *Karl Barth: His life from Letters and Autobiographical Texts*, trans. J. Bowden. Grand Rapids, MI: Eerdmans.

Chapman, J. A. 1931. *The Theology of Karl Barth: A Short Introduction*. London: Epworth Press.

Hunsinger, G. ed. 1976. *Karl Barth and Radical Politics*. Philadelphia, PA: Westminster Press.

Hunsinger, G. 1991. *How to Read Karl Barth: The Shape of his Theology*. New York: Oxford University Press.

McCormack, B. L. 1989. "A Scholastic of a Higher Order: The Development of Karl Barth's Theology, 1921–1931." PhD dissertation, Princeton Theological Seminary, NJ.

McCormack, B. L. 1995. *Karl Barth's Critically Realistic Dialectical Theology: Its Genesis and Development, 1909–1936*. Oxford: Clarendon Press.

Macintyre, A. and McIntyre, J. 1959. "Foreword," in K. Barth, *From Rousseau to Ritschl*. London: SCM Press.

Ritschl, D. 1982. "Foreword," in K. Barth, *The Theology of Schleiermacher*, ed. D. Ritschl, trans. G. W. Bromiley. Edinburgh: T. & T. Clark.

Scholder, K. 1987. *The Churches and the Third Reich*, vol. 1, trans. J. Bowden. London: SCM Press.

Smart, J. D. ed. 1964. *Revolutionary Theology in the Making: Barth–Thurneysen Correspondence, 1914–1925*. London: Epworth Press.

Torrance, T. F. 1962. *Karl Barth: An Introduction to his Early Theology, 1910–1931*. London: SCM Press.

Webster, J. 1998. *Barth's Moral Theology: Human Action in Barth's Thought*. Grand Rapids, MI: Eerdmans.

CHAPTER 21
Rahner

Karen Kilby

Karl Rahner was born in 1904, a year before Hans Urs von Balthasar and 18 years after Karl Barth. He is often paired with one or the other of these figures. In Roman Catholic circles, Rahner and von Balthasar usually figure as the intellectual giants of the twentieth century; in ecumenical contexts, as often as not it is Rahner and Barth. The pairings are never, of course, neutral: von Balthasar and Rahner are taken to represent opposing camps within the Catholic intellectual world; Barth and Rahner stand for fundamentally different options in modern theology.[1]

Exploring the tensions between Rahner's theology and these others has its uses in contributing to a map of the theological scene (and we shall engage in this a little ourselves below), but it can run the risk of offering over-simplified and reductive readings. If the goal is to understand Rahner's theology itself, what is in fact more useful is an examinations of tensions *intrinsic* to Rahner's work.

This can be done on a number of levels. One might for instance explore the tension between the radical and the traditional in Rahner. In spite of the way he is often used, Rahner is not particularly easy to place on a theological spectrum. If one were to ask whether he should be considered conservative or liberal – whether he is for updating the faith or preserving it – the answer could not be straightforward. Rahner cannot simply be placed in one camp or the other, not because he should be located somewhere in the middle, but because he is, or attempts to be, in both camps simultaneously. At his best and most creative Rahner shows that theology is not a zero-sum game, so that the more one is orthodox the less one can rethink the faith in changing circumstances.

If the progressive/conservative tension is something Rahner tries to overcome, one can go a long way toward understanding his theology by examining another tension which he deliberately maintains, even plays with. Running through much of Rahner's work is a concern with the relation of the historical to the universal, with the relation between all that is particular, concrete and changing on the one hand and the (purportedly) changeless structures of human consciousness[2] on the other. The concern to maintain the appropriate kind of tension between, to use his own terms, the "categorical" and the "transcendental," is a key feature of Rahner's understanding of faith, grace, and revelation, of his treatment of the Church and of other religions, of his theology of the sacraments, and of his Christology.

There is yet another kind of tension in Rahner's thought, one which is less widely recognized than those just mentioned, but which is no less important for coming to a balanced understanding of his work, and it is upon this third tension that this essay will focus. Rahner is in many ways a highly systematic thinker. He appears to follow a method, the transcendental method, and advocates that all modern theology ought to do the same. He maintains that there is a universal and changeless structure of human consciousness, one which he is able to characterize (more or less), and which he makes decisive in his understanding of a wide range of theological issues. This systematic, highly confident, one might even say monolithic and totalizing aspect of Rahner's thought is hard to miss, and it becomes even more prominent when Rahner is sum-marized. It is easy to think of Rahner's work simply as a system – especially if one comes to it through *Foundations of Christian Faith* or through secondary literature. Very often in the pages of the *Theological Investigations*, however, something else makes itself felt – a modesty, a tentativeness, a sense of intellectual exploration and creative freedom. These qualities are present, and indeed they are far from peripheral. And yet the sys-tematic side to Rahner's thought cannot be denied. This is the puzzle that is to be explored in this essay.

To get a clearer sense of just how systematic and confident Rahner's theology is, or can seem, we will begin with a brief description of a few of its key features – the *Vor-griff auf esse*, the supernatural existential, the distinction mentioned above between the transcendental and the categorial, and the notion of a divine self-communication.

To begin with, then, the *Vorgriff*. According to Rahner, in all our dealings with the world, we are always at the same time having to do with God. To put it the other way, we always have to do with God, but always through our relations to the world. More particularly, whenever we apprehend some particular object, or will some finite value, Rahner maintains, we never *merely* recognize or choose the particular, but are always at the same time reaching beyond it toward the whole of being, and it is only because of this reaching beyond, or this pre-apprehension (as *Vorgriff* is often translated), that we are able in the first place to recognize or choose the individual finite object. In tech-nical, Kantian terms, the *Vorgriff auf esse* is a transcendental condition of the possibil-ity of all our knowing and willing. And Rahner maintains that in reaching toward, in pre-apprehending, the whole of being, we also reach towards God.

Rahner employs a variety of images in connection with the *Vorgriff*. One is taken from Heidegger: we are aware of infinite being as the *horizon* for our knowledge of finite things. An awareness of being and of God forms the ever-present and necessary back-ground, one might say, for our knowledge of the particular objects that lie in the fore-ground of consciousness.[3] A second image is borrowed from (though not original to) Aquinas: the *Vorgriff* is the *light* which in illumining the individual objects allows our intellect to grasp them. A third image, that of movement, Rahner owes chiefly to Joseph Maréchal, a Belgian Jesuit philosopher from the early part of the century:[4] we have a dynamism toward being and God, so that the mind always moves beyond any particu-lar, never entirely satisfied or at rest. These images, particularly the first two, are intended to point both to an intimate relation between our knowledge of ordinary objects and the *Vorgriff*, and to a profound distinction between the two: we are always aware of things within a horizon, and we do not see without light, and yet the horizon always recedes, and can never become one of the objects that is known within the horizon, and the light is never one of the things which we see, but that *by which* we see. Being and God as given in the *Vorgriff*, then, never can become particular, known, graspable, manipulable objects. The awareness, if one can call it that, that we have of God, is fundamentally of a different kind than that which we have of the objects around us.

The *Vorgriff* is argued for at some length in *Spirit in the World*, Rahner's failed PhD thesis and his first major publication. *Spirit in the World* (1994) is presented as an interpretation (in the light of Kant, Maréchal and Heidegger) of Thomas Aquinas's metaphysics of knowledge, but it is not *merely* an interpretive work – in "reliv[ing] the philosophy [of Thomas] as it unfolds" Rahner is at the same time offering a philosophical argument intended to stand on its own.

The claim about the *Vorgriff* recurs (sometimes under other names) throughout his writings. It is clearly a rather bold assertion: if Rahner is right, then he is able to demonstrate that everyone, whether they describe themselves as agnostic or atheist or indifferent, is actually on some level aware of God. Though Rahner is not involved in proving the existence of God, if he is right no such proof is necessary, since anyone who tries to deny the existence of God is in fact in contradiction with herself. With this notion of the *Vorgriff*, then, Rahner is making a claim about a universal feature of human experience; he is claiming to know better than they do what is really going on in the experience of all kinds of non-theists; and he is doing something *more* than offer a proof of the existence of God, namely, making all such proofs obsolete.[5] Modesty and tentativeness do not, at this stage, seem to be leading characteristics of Rahner's approach.

Closely related to the *Vorgriff*, but at least theoretically to be distinguished from it, is the "supernatural existential." Just as Rahner maintains that there is a universal apprehension of God, so he also holds that there is a universal experience of grace, or at least of grace as offered, and this he calls the supernatural existential.[6] In the theory of the supernatural existential we have another claim of universal scope: it is a theory of the nature of everyone's deepest experience, which is also a theory of the relation of nature to grace, and which is closely linked to Rahner's understanding of revelation, Christology and salvation. It will be helpful to explicate this rather forbidding notion in stages, looking firstly at why it is an "existential," secondly at why Rahner terms it supernatural, and then finally at its relation to the *Vorgriff*.

"Existential" is a term Rahner borrowed from Heidegger, and it refers to a fundamental element in human existence, something which is a constant feature of all our experience rather than one object of experience or one particular experience among others. This is what grace, then, according to Rahner, is like. It is not, or not primarily, something given now and then – the forgiveness of a particular sin, the sudden capacity to overcome a temptation, a particular help in a particular situation, a definitive response to prayer; it is instead an ever-present gift offered to us at such a fundamental and central level that it affects all that we are, and know, and do: "grace," Rahner writes, "always surrounds man, even the sinner and the unbeliever, as the inescapable setting of his existence" (*Theological Investigations*, IV:181).

The supernatural existential is *supernatural* in that it takes us beyond our nature. It is not something which is intrinsically part of what it is to be a human being, not something which humanity can claim as its right. This is a rather delicate point, since on Rahner's account human nature has never in fact existed without this supernatural elevation. Human beings *could*, however, have existed on a merely natural level, and so the supernatural existential is genuinely gratuitous, a second gift from God beyond the basic gift of creation.

The *Vorgriff*, by contrast, Rahner seems to regard as built into our nature as such – not just built into the way we actually find ourselves, our concrete nature, but built into human nature in the abstract theological sense: without it we would not be human beings at all.[7] But how, beyond the fact that one belongs to our nature and one is to be attributed to grace, are we to relate the two? The supernatural existential can be thought of as affecting the way in which the *Vorgriff* is experienced: the supernatural existential alters our relation to our horizon. Because of the supernatural existential, God is not just the infinitely distant goal of all our striving, but the goal which, Rahner says, "draws near" and "gives itself." (The images here, it should perhaps be noted, are not easily pinned down: though the goal may give itself, it does not therefore become a given of our experience, something we can grasp and understand and manipulate like anything else we know.) The horizon, even if it draws near, remains the horizon. Rahner is deliberately paradoxical: grace, he writes, is "the grace of the *nearness* of the *abiding* mystery: it makes God accessible in the form of the holy mystery and presents him thus as the incomprehensible" (*Theological Investigations*, IV:56).

If, then, God had destined us to exist in a merely created, merely natural state, we would still have had a pre-apprehension of infinite being and of God, we would still in fact have been aware, in some sense of the word, of God in all that we know and do, but we would have been aware of God in a different way, as remaining aloof rather than as drawing near and self-giving. As it is, however, we never in fact have an experience of God in this way, but always, in the supernatural existential, we experience God as the one who has drawn near.

Two points must be clarified before we can move on to the next stage of exposition. First of all, Rahner is not, in saying that there is a universal elevation of human nature, *ipso facto* declaring that we are all in a state of sanctifying grace and therefore justified. He wants in fact to steer a rather delicate course between maintaining, on the one hand, that sanctifying grace is universally present, and everyone is in a state of grace (which would be to say too much), and on the other hand that sanctifying grace is universally offered, but *given* only to those who accept the offer (which would be to say too little). His solution is to describe grace as universally present, but present *as offered*. It is, one might say, "there" in all of us, but we have a role[8] in that we accept or reject it, and only if we accept it can we be said to be in a state of sanctifying grace, justified, saved.

The second point is that the supernatural existential can be present, and even present as accepted, without a person being reflexively aware of it. This is because, one might say, it lies so deep within us, because it is an existential, not one distinguishable bit of experience among others, but ever-present, impossible to pin down, easily miss-able. Rahner suggests that his readers should perhaps be able to recognize in their own experience what he is talking about – "If this theological and dogmatic interpretation of [a person's] transcendental experience is offered to him by the history of revelation and by Christianity he can recognize his own experience in it" (1989:131). This is, however, very carefully qualified – the experience itself remains ambiguous and intro-spection on its own would not enable a person to come to such a conclusion. It is impor-tant to emphasize, furthermore, that not only the supernatural existential itself, but also its acceptance (or rejection) is "pre-thematic": it is not a self-conscious, explicit choice to accept which a person makes, and it is perfectly possible, on Rahner's scheme, that many will in fact have accepted the offer of grace in the supernatural existential who if presented with the idea would reject it as nonsense. Indeed, one has to say not only that some might have accepted the supernatural existential without any self-conscious awareness of doing so, but that no one can be completely sure as to what the decision is that they have made or are making in the depths of their consciousness. Here Rahner's insistence on the difference between reflexive awareness and pre-thematic experience and the traditional Roman Catholic rejection of the assurance of salvation meet nicely.

In his later work Rahner frequently frames what he has to say about the *Vorgriff* and the supernatural existential in terms of the more general notion of the human being's transcendence, or of "transcendental experience." To transcend simply means to go beyond; transcendental experience is the experience of going beyond all the things we know and choose and love, even as we are knowing and choosing and loving them. And of course when we go beyond all particular things what we go toward, on Rahner's account, is God.

Just as the awareness of God given in the *Vorgriff* is not ever had on its own, apart from our dealings with the world, and just as the experience of grace is not a separate experience among others but an existential, so transcendental experience is not some-thing that occurs in isolation. It is always given only in an experience of the concrete, the particular, the changing things of the world. Rahner characteristically expresses this point by pairing "transcendental" with either the "categorical" (the realm of that which can be put into categories, that which can be pinned down and grasped by con-cepts) or the "historical." These pairings turn out to be very important to Rahner, and lend themselves to a wide systematic development.[9] Three points are worth mention-ing about the way these pairings work. First, as we have just suggested, the transcen-dental is always experienced through and with the categorical, never "neat." Second, transcendental experience is not a mere accompaniment to the historical and the cat-egorical. It does not merely *happen* to be there, riding along the top, one might say, of our ordinary experience, but is what makes this possible in the first place. This is, it should be noted, little more than the transposition into different terminology of the claim that the *Vorgriff* is a condition of the possibility of our knowing and willing. A third point, however, is one we have not already seen, and it is critically important to much of Rahner's thought: the transcendental, Rahner maintains, always needs somehow to articulate itself, to express itself, in the categorical. By definition, of course, transcendental experience is that realm of experience where language fails: we have language for objects, for distinguishing one thing from another, for putting things in categories, but not for that which cannot in principle be an object, for that which is beyond all categories, for the infinite horizon within which the distinguishing takes place. And yet, insists Rahner, transcendental experience cannot simply remain inarticulate, but always seeks expression in the realm of the categorical. The expression will never be wholly adequate, will always in some way fail, but it must always nevertheless be attempted.

The *Vorgriff*, the supernatural existential and the notion of transcendental experience are all closely related, then. If we mention one more concept, that of divine self-communication, we will be in a position to get a sense of the systematic sweep of Rahner's thought. In connection with the supernatural existential we said that grace is not for Rahner primarily something given now and then, something particular, but an ever-present existential; we could also have said, however, that grace is not in fact some *thing* that God gives us, some particular created gift – grace is actually God's gift of God's self, God's self-communication. In grace God becomes the "innermost constituent element of man"; in grace "The Giver himself is the gift" (1989:116, 120).

Rahner's use of the notion of divine self-communication, furthermore, is not limited to his treatment of grace. In the context of talk of grace it is easy to think in terms of a relationship between God and the individual human being, and so to imagine lots of separate divine self-communications. But more fundamentally Rahner presents God as making a single decision to communicate himself to the world as a whole, to that which is not God. And this single divine self-communication provides the context for understanding not only grace but also revelation, the incarnation, the beatific vision, and even the creation. Just as grace is not primarily about God giving something, but about God giving himself, so revelation has to do most fundamentally not with God's communication of particular propositions, but with God's communication of himself. In the incarnation this divine self-communication reaches a point of absolute definitiveness in history. In the beatific vision it reaches its absolute fulfillment. And this self-communication is the purpose of creation: God creates the world precisely so as to give himself to it; he brings that which is other than himself into being in order to unite himself with it.

We can now begin to indicate how things fit together. God decides to communicate himself to that which is not God. Therefore, he creates the world – he brings that which is other than himself into existence – and he creates a world which reaches its climax in human beings, who are by their nature (i.e. in virtue of the *Vorgriff*) open to him, capable of receiving his self-communication. God then (though it is not a chronologically secondary act) communicates himself to people, and on that level where they are able to receive him, i.e. in the depths of their consciousness, in their transcendental experience. From the human side this self-communication is to be described as the supernatural existential. But transcendental experience by its nature must work itself out in the categorical realm, and in history. So God's self-communication to the world has both a transcendental and a categorical aspect, and so Rahner can speak of both transcendental and categorical revelation. Transcendental revelation is simply God's self-communication in our transcendental experience, i.e. the supernatural existential again; categorical revelation is the gradual self-expression, the attempts at self-interpretation, of transcendental revelation in the religious and cultural history of humanity.[10] Christ, finally, can be seen as the peak both of the transcendental aspect of

God's self-communication – he is the one human being who unambiguously accepts the grace offered in his transcendental experience[11] – and of its categorical aspect: in his life (and particularly death) we have something finite, something in the world which can serve as a categorical expression of the divine self-giving love, but a something in the world which *is also God*, and which therefore becomes the unambiguous and unsurpassable expression of God's self-communication.

This is, in rather sketchy form, the one side of Rahner then – an apparently tightly knit system,[12] vast claims, great intellectual confidence. It is not however, we want to suggest, all that there is to Rahner.

For many the first (or only) encounter with Rahner is in the theory of the anonymous Christian, and at first sight this is simply more of the same – here too, Rahner makes a vast claim (this is a theory which makes all human beings potentially members of the Church in spite of themselves, and which seems to presuppose that Rahner knows better than, say, a Buddhist, what is in fact going on in the depths of her psyche), a claim which is linked with the central "systematic" elements of his thought (especially the supernatural existential, but also his Christology, his theory of revelation and the transcendental/categorical dialectic) and one for which he is regularly accused of insensitivity and arrogance.

A closer examination of Rahner's writings on the subject, however, begins to show a more complicated picture. The first thing to note is that his starting point is never in fact the "system." The article "Anonymous Christians" in *Theological Investigations* (vol. VI), for instance, takes its departure from "the situation in which the believing Christian finds himself" (390), namely that after nearly 2,000 years of missionary efforts much of the world is unconverted, and likely to remain so. In "The Christian Among Unbelieving Relations"[13], Rahner starts from the anguish of Christians whose close relations do not belong to, or whose children have "lapsed" from, the faith. The jumping-off point is not a system, then, but a situation, a problem: here is a difficulty which confronts us – what are we to do about it?

Now the skeptical reader might be unimpressed – just as some preachers like to start their sermons with an ice-breaking story or joke, so perhaps, a speculative thinker like Rahner may begin with a nod toward historical concreteness or pastoral relevance. One might be inclined, in other words, to dismiss the concreteness of Rahner's starting point as extraneous to the heart of his argument. In fact, however, it is not only on the level of presentation, but also in the structure of the argument, that "the system" takes a back seat. The fundamental reason Rahner gives for supposing that there must be anonymous Christians, his basic warrant for the notion, in other words, has no connection to the central systematic elements of his thought – we must speak of anonymous Christians, according to Rahner, not because of the *Vorgriff*, the supernatural existential and the transcendental/categorical distinction, but because Christians believe on the one hand in the universal salvific will of God, and on the other in the necessity of faith in Christ and membership of the Church for salvation.[14] The starting point for the argument, then, is not the conclusions of arguments Rahner has made elsewhere, but certain basic, communally normative "propositions of faith" and the apparent contradiction they generate. The supernatural existential and the rest do of course come into it, as we have already suggested, but they come in only at a second stage, when it is a matter of sketching out how what has to be believed in can in fact be conceived of. Given that something like anonymous Christians *must* be possible, Rahner proposes, here is one way to understand how it *can* be possible.

If a study of the anonymous Christian writings begins to raise questions about the exact role of Rahner's so-called system, an examination of what he has to say about *pluralism* further complicates the situation. In his mature work Rahner repeatedly draws attention to the fact that the intellectual world with all its specializations and divisions has expanded dramatically, so that there is simply too much to know.[15] This poses genuinely new problems, he thinks, for individuals, for the Church and for theology. Not only can no one now be a "Renaissance man," competent in all fields of knowledge, but no one can be competent in all the areas that are relevant to theology and to faith, to "forming a world view." The problem cannot be overcome by working harder as individuals, nor by collective work, since the conclusion of an argument or a line of study is usually of little use to anyone who has not also repeated the process of arriving at it. The situation, Rahner suggests, is radically different from what has held in previous generations, even in the generation to which Rahner's own teachers belonged.

Rahner points to the problem posed by this pluralism in a variety of contexts. How can one responsibly make a decision for, or even responsibly hold, any world view, and in particular the Christian faith, if one cannot possibly in a lifetime come to grips with all the questions and all the information directly relevant to holding this world-view? How can the Church be understood as one and as unified by its single creed if on the one hand there is no getting at this creed in its "purity," apart from some theology, and on the other hand there is a pluralism in theology, or a pluralism *of* theologies, that is not only beyond synthesis but also beyond being schematized? What is the theologian to do about philosophy if on the one hand there is no avoiding philosophizing within theology, and on the other hand there are so many brands of philosophy and so many problems within philosophy that no individual can ever really understand them all?[16]

How, then, one might ask, are we to understand this emphasis on inescapable and irreducible pluralism, including the inescapable and irreducible pluralism of philosophy and theology, in relation to the philosophico-theological "system" outlined above? How, indeed, can Rahner insist on the one hand that there is no getting around pluralism and the historically conditioned nature of our intellectual situation,[17] and on the other advocate a particular theology which makes much of "the changeless a priori structure of the human mind"?[18] Should this recognition of pluralism be regarded as an isolated event which does not affect the core of Rahner's theology – an insight which he fails to integrate with the rest of his thought – or even as something which can be subordinated to this "systematic core"?

The latter option might be tempting to those bent on presenting Rahner's work as a tidy system. They could perhaps argue that all Rahner's talk of pluralism has to be understood as pertinent only to the categorical, historical realm, and that according to Rahner a single transcendental experience *underlies* all that is plural. But it would be quite a strain to defend so tidy a solution, given that Rahner unequivocally includes *philosophy* among those things affected by pluralism. One would have to exempt Rahner's own philosophy from the general rule – or rather, one would have to suppose that all or most of *Spirit in the World* and *Hearer of the Word* (in spite of their context,[19] their complex arguments and a good deal of their language) were not in fact philosophy but something more basic and fundamental, something prior to any and all particular philosophies. It is rather difficult, then, to subordinate Rahner's talk of pluralism to his system.

Should Rahner's recognition of the inescapability and insurmountable nature of pluralism therefore be viewed as something apart from the rest – an isolated event, as we said above, which does not affect the core of his thought? This option, it must be admitted, has something to be said for it. Certainly Rahner devotes little explicit reflection to the significance of pluralism for his own theological proposals. Indeed, in a rather striking series of lectures on theological method[20] he devotes a first lecture to the inescapable problem of pluralism for theology, and the second to the need for all theology to follow what is essentially a single method (the transcendental method), and yet seems to see no need to offer comment on how the two should be understood together.

Though Rahner does not *explicitly* integrate his reflections on theological and philosophical pluralism with his own philosophical and theological proposals, however, it would in fact be a mistake to conclude from this that his recognition of pluralism is indeed an isolated intellectual fact, with no relationship whatsoever to the rest of his thought. The form that his writing takes in the *Theological Investigations* and much of his other work is worth considering in this connection. Rahner's tendency to write short essays should not be seen as *merely* a stylistic matter, a personal preference for a particular genre, or indeed as simply the product of his circumstances. Undoubtedly both individual style and circumstance play a part in Rahner's proclivity for the essay, but this genre must also be understood as a medium for doing theology *in a particular way*. What was said above about the anonymous Christian writings in fact holds true of most of Rahner's essays – his reflections usually begin with a particular problem or situation facing the Church, and although elements from his system very frequently play some role, the "system" as such is almost never the driving force behind the argument. One essay is not a continuation of another, then, nor are the individual essays offered as building blocks for a greater whole. Rahner himself (as distinct from his commentators) does not, usually, choose to present his work as a massive interconnected system, which one must either take as a whole or leave, but as a series of individual proposals relating to individual problems and situations.[21] And in a context of inescapable intellectual pluralism, this is a strategy that makes some sense. To put it rather crudely, larger intellectual structures are likely to be less rather than more persuasive in such a context – they simply multiply the potential grounds for disagreement.[22]

This is not to say that Rahner's use of the essay should be seen as a cynical strategy – in fact it is the strategy of a highly *ecclesial* theologian. Rahner's purpose, we are suggesting, is not to develop, express or promote his own system, but to contribute in a variety of ways to the development of Catholic theology. His ideas may have systematic interconnections, but he only alludes to these insofar as they are helpful in the context of the particular case he is arguing. Indeed, Rahner will sometimes even suppress his own ideas – operating, for instance, with the common, "average" understanding of some concept rather than with his own, if that (the common understading) is all that is needed in some particular case.[23]

Rahner can usefully be contrasted with Karl Barth in this regard, who famously changed the title *Christian Dogmatics* to *Church Dogmatics* precisely in order to underline the ecclesial nature of his undertaking. Certainly Barth's work is "churchly" in his insistence that no standards but those proper to the Church ought to guide it, and in his robust engagement with a host of Church thinkers, both historical and contemporary. But in Barth one does not have the sense, as one does in Rahner, of making contributions to a *common* project. Barth of course understands himself as engaged in the same *kind* of project as other theologians (particularly premodern theologians such as Anselm, Luther, and Calvin), and he works out his own theology in conversation with others, but what he is working out is unquestionably his *own*, his own theology, his own massive and unique version of this project which others may also have attempted. Barth, one might say, is like a man who builds a house – he may indeed build the house in a village among more and less comparable structures, and he may build the house "in conversation" with others, borrowing some features from his neighbors and deliberately rejecting others, but he alone is fundamentally responsible for the construction. Rahner, by contrast, usually writes as one among many involved in a common construction (or reconstruction). He makes proposals, he offers solutions to problems, he seeks to persuade his colleagues that certain ideas, in spite of their novelty and apparent radicality, are compatible with those to which they are already committed. He writes, much of the time, not so much as one who builds a house from the foundations up, but as one who proposes a particular rearrangement of a particular area, or the introduction of a door to join two previously separated rooms, or the removal of a wall which turns out not, after all, to be structurally necessary.

It would be a mistake, then, to suppose that Rahner's "system" is what his theology really is, and that the multiplicity of essays in which it is expressed merely a distracting complication. It would also, however, be a mistake to let "unsystematicness" have the last word. The tension mentioned at the beginning of this essay is a real one. All that has been said in the last few paragraphs needs to be modified with phrases such as "very often" and "for the most part," for at times Rahner did write, and indeed act, like a theologian promoting a unified and unifying program – slogans such as "all theology is anthropology," claims about a "transcendental method" which all theology must follow, and indeed the great effort Rahner spent in editing massive encyclopedias with a "Rahnerian" slant (*Sacramentum Mundi, Handbuch der Pastoraltheologie, Lexicon für Theologie und Kirche*) all point in a rather different direction from what we have been discussing.

This is a tension, I believe, which one should resist the temptation to resolve. Rahner's work really is systematic, monolithic, and totalizing, and it really is tentative, modest, and exploratory, and any attempt to unify the two sides is in danger of suppressing the one or the other. Most often the impulse, by admirers and detractors alike, has been to elevate the systematic side. This is understandable: if one is a critic, it is convenient to be able to pinpoint the fundamental flaw which vitiates the whole, and if one is a sympathetic reader the urge to follow through all the connections, to put the pieces together, and to present to the world the beautifully systematic and coherent whole, is strong. The result, however, is that Rahner's work is seen unduly through the lens of his more programmatic writings (*Spirit in the World*, *Foundations of Christian Faith*) and his more programmatic statements (about the transcendental method, or theological anthropology), and that the connectedness of his ideas is so emphasized as to obscure their context and indeed their purpose. It is also possible, on the other hand, simply to emphasize the unsystematic side of Rahner's thought, and so to ignore or marginalize just those texts such as *Spirit in the World* and *Hearer of the Word* that the other side make so crucial, and thus to sidestep the genuine complexity of Rahner's work.[24]

If the tension ought not be resolved, can it be explained? No doubt a number of accounts are possible: here we will suggest only that it may have had something to do with a change in the broader intellectual milieu in which Rahner worked. Consider, for instance, Rahner's own characterization of the attitude of his generation, in their youth, to philosophy:

> at that time our whole attitude was colored by a belief in *one single* philosophy. Obviously we were aware (as men always have been) of the fact that in practice there were many philosophies. Indeed we studied the history of philosophy and there came to know of a whole range of the most varied systems and theories. And in systematic philosophy we took up a critical attitude towards these systems, deciding what to accept and what to reject in them. But in all this we were, after all, constantly, albeit tacitly, taking as our starting-point the belief that in adopting this approach we were touching more or less upon every-thing in the philosophy of the past and present alike which was of real philosophical importance; that we could and did draw from it into our own system everything that was true and valuable; finally that we were fully justified in rejecting the rest.[25]

He goes on to say, however, that "the situation today is radically and insuperably dif-ferent" – the philosophical confidence of his youth is no longer possible. One way of understanding the tension, then, is to see it as resulting from the *residue* of the youth-ful attitudes in the mature work. Though Rahner may have acknowledged a decisive change, and though by and large his work may have reflected this change, he did not in fact entirely shake off the thought patterns learned in his youth. They continue to intrude, as remnants of another time, into his later theology.

If this central tension in Rahner's work can be put down to something like histori-cal accident, however, this is not to say it is simply regrettable. The tension we have been outlining may well be one of the underlying attractions of Rahner's work. The appeal of any one essay is deepened by the sense that, even though it is a limited piece dealing with a specific question in a particular context, there is a web of interconnected ideas which the reader might, if interested, follow up. The appeal of the whole, on the other hand, is very much dependent on one's awareness that it is not in fact a rigid structure which predetermines all the answers, but that Rahner is in fact always continuing to think. If Rahner were really as systematically unified and tightly integrated as some have supposed, he might have attracted, as for instance Bernard Lonergan has done, a loyal following, a band of students who could endorse every stage of the argument, but he would have had little influence beyond its bounds.

Notes

1   For the contrast with von Balthasar, cf. for instance Williams (1986). For a contrast with Barth, see Marshall (1987).

2   If one were to be fully precise, here and below, one should perhaps not use the word "consciousness," because of its overtones of something that is static and simply *there*. Rahner's focus, as we shall see, is on the unchanging nature of the mind's *activity* in knowing, willing, and so on.

3   The term "background" does not quite, it should be noted, carry the fully connotations of "horizon"; in particular it lacks the sense of something *towards which* one moves.

4   Rahner made a careful study of Maréchal's *Le Point de départ de la métaphysique* during his time as a Jesuit scholastic. Maréchal had an important influence on a number of Catholic thinkers of Rahner's generation, who have come to be known, collectively, as the Transcendental Thomists. ("Transcendental," here, is a reference to Kant's philosophy: the Transcendental Thomists develop a philosophy based on Aquinas, interpreted through the lens of Kant.)

5   Rahner does not, it must be noted, entirely dismiss proofs; there is still a secondary role for them. In *Foundations of Christian Faith* he presents such proofs of the existence of God as the making explicit of the underlying, universal pre-apprehension of God. They have, then, a "thematizing" role.

6   This account is based on Rahner's later writings. The supernatural existential was in fact first introduced, not as grace or even its offer, but as the desire for, and the orientation towards, grace and the beatific vision. It then grew in importance and centrality in Rahner's thought.

7   The supernatural existential may be a *feature* of all our experience, always in some way affecting us, but the *Vorgriff* is a *condition of the possibility* of experience, without which we would be unable to have any experience at all, unable to know or to will or to be aware of ourselves as distinct from other things.

8   Even our acceptance of grace, Rahner is careful to insist, is "borne" by God, made possible by grace itself. This rider may seem to confuse the issue, but without it Rahner would be courting accusations of semi-Pelagianism.

9   It is in *Foundations of Christian Faith* in particular that Rahner harnesses the systematizing potential of the transcendental/categorial distinction.

10   Revelation as it is understood by most Christians – the revelation given in the Old and New Testaments – is simply that part of categorial revelation which has the special standing of being assured by God of its legitimacy (Rahner 1989:155). Note that this does not mean that other attempts to interpret transcendental revelation – other parts of categorial revelation – may not also be legitimate and successful. But they are not *assured* in the same way of their legitimacy.

11   And thereby, it turns out, the one human being who is also divine. Cf. "On the Theology of the Incarnation," *Theological Investigations*, IV.

12   The word "apparently" is important here. Cf. Kilby (1994) for an examination of some of the fissures in the "system."

13   *Theological Investigations*, III. Though the term "anonymous Christian" is not yet in use in this essay (originally published in 1954) the idea is already present.

14   "[W]hen we have to keep in mind both principles together, namely the necessity of Christian faith and the universal salvific will of God's love and omnipotence, we can only reconcile them by saying that somehow all men must be capable of being members of the Church;

and this capacity must not be understood merely in the sense of an abstract and purely logical possibility, but as a real and historically concrete one. But this means in its turn that there must be degrees of membership of the Church, not only in ascending order from being baptised, through the acceptance of the fullness of the Christian faith and the recognition of the visible head of the Church, to the living community of the Eucharist, indeed to the realisation of holiness, but also in descending order from the explicitness of baptism into a non-official and anonymous Christianity which can and should yet be called Christianity in a meaningful sense, even though it itself cannot and would not describe itself as such" ("Anonymous Christians," *Theological Investigations*, IV:391).

15   See, for example, "The Pluralism in Theology and the Unity of the Creed in the Church" (*Theological Investigations*, XI) or "The Faith of the Christian and the Doctrine of the Church" (*Theological Investigations*, XIV).

16   It is worth noting that these claims about "irreducible" pluralism are offered as empirical assertions rather than as a philosophical theory. Rahner does not, then, suggest anything along the lines of an "incommensurability" between different theological or philosophical options. The shortness of life, one might say, rather than the unbridgeability of different languages or conceptual schemes, creates the problem. The problem itself, however, is in the end not very different from that posed by relativism. It is impossible to adjudicate between all conflicting claims, or even to perceive where these *are* conflicting claims, and it is impossible ever to establish any one position as superior to all alternatives: even if we do not live in a relativist's world, then, we live in a world which for many practical purposes might as well be.

17   The theologian "works on the basis of a world of ideas, from certain premises, and with certain philosophical preconceptions as his tools, yet is well aware that these are subject to historical conditions and the limitations of particular epochs. For the first time in the history of theological thought theology is not only conditioned by history, but is also aware of being so conditioned, and besides this is aware of being unable to avoid this conditioning" ("Reflections on Methodology in Theology," in *Theoretical Investigations*, XI:74).

18   This formulation is taken from McCool (1984:xxviii).

19   *Spirit in the World* was written as a doctoral thesis in philosophy, and *Hearer of the Word* originated in philosophy of religion lectures.

20   Published as "Reflections on Methodology in Theology," in *Theological Investigations* XI.

21   J. A. DiNoia's essay on Rahner in *The Modern Theologians* (DiNoia 1997) makes this point forcefully.

22   One could take this line of thinking one step further, and suggest that a recognition of inescapable pluralism calls as well for a particular style of argument in any given piece of writing. One would want to avoid organizing one's argument into a single tightly structured linear form (analogous to a mathematical proof) since then a disagreement at any stage would cause the reader to lose confidence in the whole; one would instead want to present (as Rahner in fact often does) a series of considerations all pointing in the same direction, a cumulative case. Then a disagreement over any one point need not lead to an automatic rejection of the argument as a whole.

23   Note, for example, in "Theology in the New Testament," *Theological Investigations*, V, the fascinating way in which he uses (and gradually transforms the use of) the terms "revelation" and "theology."

24   Two pieces which have particularly underlined the unsystematic side of Rahner are Healy (1992) and DiNoia (1997). It would be unfair, however, to object to one-sidedness in these pieces; there has been such an overwhelming tendency to overplay the systematic side of Rahner that these must be seen as corrective efforts.

25   "On the current relationship between philosophy and theology," *Theological Investigations*, XIII:71.

References

DiNoia, J. A. 1997. "Karl Rahner," in *The Modern Theologians*, ed. D. Ford. Oxford: Blackwell.

Healy, N. 1992. "Indirect Methods in Theology: Karl Rahner as an ad hoc Apologist," *Thomist* 56.

Kilby, K. 1994. "The *Vorgriff auf esse*: a Study in the Relation of Philosophy to Theology in the Thought of Karl Rahner." PhD thesis, Yale University; to be published as *Rahner: Theology and Philosophy*. London: Routledge, forthcoming.

McCool, G. ed. 1984. "Introduction," in *A Rahner Reader*. New York: Crossroad.

Marshall, B. 1987. *Christology in Conflict: The Identity of a Saviour in Rahner and Barth*. Oxford: Basil Blackwell.

Rahner, K. 1961–92. *Theological Investigations*, trans. C. Ernst, K. H. Kruger, B. Kruger, K. Smith, D. Bourke, D. Morland, E. Quinn, H. Riley, and Joseph Donceel: vols. 1–6, Baltimore, MD: Helicon, 1961–9; vols. 7–10, New York: Herder and Herder, 1970–3; vols. 11–14, New York: Seabury, 1974–6; vols. 15–21, New York: Crossroad, 1979–88; vols. 22–3, London: Darton, Longman and Todd, 1991–2.

Rahner, K. 1989. *Foundations of Christian Faith*, trans. W. V. Dych. New York: Crossroad.

Rahner, K. 1994. *Spirit in the World*, trans. W. Dych. New York: Continuum.

Williams, R. 1986. "Balthasar and Rahner," in *The Analogy of Beauty: The Theology of Hans Urs von Balthasar*, ed. J. Riches. Edinburgh: T. & T. Clark.

CHAPTER 22
Bonhoeffer

John W. de Gruchy

Dietrich Bonhoeffer is probably better known beyond the confines of the Church than any other twentieth-century Christian theologian. Two reasons immediately come to mind. The first is his participation in the German conspiracy to assassinate Hitler and his subsequent murder at the hands of the Gestapo. The second is the extent to which his fragmentary theological reflections published posthumously in his *Letters and Papers from Prison* have attracted attention. Within the broader sphere of ecumenical Christianity Bonhoeffer has achieved unofficial canonization as a result of his role in the Church struggle against Nazism and his martyrdom. Several documentary films have been produced on his life,[1] his poetry has been set to music,[2] and he is the subject of an opera.[3] Few theologians, if any, have attracted such attention. Yet his status as a latter-day Protestant saint has not been uncontested.

Indicative of the controversy over Bonhoeffer was the bizarre declaration by the German government in August 1996 that he was no longer regarded as a traitor. This might say more about Germany's legal conservatism than about Bonhoeffer's status. But it also reminds us that the reception of Bonhoeffer in his native land has by no means always been positive. Some who applaud his role in resisting Nazi ideology during the Church struggle (*Kirchenkamp*) draw back from approving his participation in the plot to assassinate Hitler. Reservations have also been expressed about his theology, especially as reflected in the *Letters and Papers from Prison*. As many blame Bonhoeffer for the ills besetting modern theology as those who praise him for helping them to remain Christian in a "world come of age." Yet, however one might assess him or interpret his legacy, it is difficult to ignore him. There is as much scholarly and popular interest in his life and work today as ever before (see de Gruchy 1997, 1999). Indicative of this phenomenon is the recent completion of the new critical edition of his works published in 16 volumes, and the project to translate them all into English (see Floyd 1999).

Bonhoeffer's theological development cannot be understood apart from the context within which he lived and worked. Indeed, it might be said of Bonhoeffer more than any other theologian of the twentieth century that his theology and biography are intrinsically related. This does not mean that his theology cannot be critically evaluated on other grounds, but that it can hardly be understood apart from his life. Hence the need for a brief biographical sketch before we examine Bonhoeffer's theology.[4]

A Fragmentary yet Fulfilled Life

Dietrich was one of eight children born in Breslau in 1906 moments before his twin sister Sabine. His parents came from a long and distinguished line of scholars, theologians, and civic leaders. The family moved to Berlin when Dietrich's father became professor of psychiatry at Berlin University in 1912, and it was this city with its rich cultural heritage, intellectual life, and political activity which became Bonhoeffer's cherished home. The Bonhoeffer family was not overtly religious and seldom attended church. Nonetheless, the twins were influenced by the piety of their Moravian nanny and the less overt piety of their mother. Family hymn singing was a regular and popular event around the piano, reflecting as much the musical talent of the family as it did their Christian heritage. Few who witnessed Dietrich's childhood in the secure and comfortable surroundings of Berlin's upper-class suburbs or the family holiday home in Friedrichsbrunn prior to 1914 could have anticipated how insecure his life was to become. The death of his second eldest brother Walter on the war front in 1918 shattered the tranquility of the home and deeply affected the whole family. By then Dietrich was already sensing a call to become a theologian, not least because he wanted to prove that he could succeed in a different career to those chosen by his brothers. But his choice was much to the chagrin of his father for whom such a vocation was a waste of his youngest son's undoubted talents.

Having started his theological studies at the University of Heidelberg, Bonhoeffer proceeded to the University of Berlin where, at the age of 21, he obtained his doctor's degree. His dissertation, later published as *Sanctorum Communio*, was an unprecedented attempt to integrate theology and sociological theory in the development of an ecclesiology grounded in revelation yet rooted in reality. Deeply influenced by Karl Barth's critique of liberal theology yet sensitive to the expectations of his more liberal and neo-Hegelian teachers and, above all, eagerly seeking ways to make Christian faith socially concrete, Bonhoeffer propounded the thesis that "Christ exists as church-community."[5] The "theology of sociality" which characterizes this early work was developed further in his *Habilitation* published in 1931 as *Act and Being* (1996). Although *Sanctorum Communio* and *Act and Being* have often been neglected by those who have been interested in Bonhoeffer's role in the Church struggle or his theology in prison, they laid the foundations for much which was to follow.

Already during his early student days Bonhoeffer was eager to travel and experience different cultures. This often influenced the direction of his theology. A visit to Rome while he was still studying in Heidelberg led him to focus his attention on the Church as a living community in which Christ is present. After he had completed his studies in Berlin he spent a year working as an assistant pastor in a German-speaking church in Barcelona, Spain. This gave him a fresh perspective on the bourgeois character of so much Protestant Christianity, something reinforced when he returned to Berlin as an assistant lecturer. Then in 1930–1 he was a visiting student fellow at Union Theological Seminary in New York. While he was not impressed by mainline North American theology or preaching, he came to appreciate the concern of his teachers in relating faith and social witness. He also became aware of the racism that permeated American society. This was reinforced through his involvement in the black Abyssinian Baptist church in Harlem. Moreover, as a result of his friendship and discussions with another visiting student, the French pastor Jean Lasserre, Bonhoeffer was challenged to read the Sermon on the Mount more existentially. This was an essential step in his becoming not just a theologian but also a Christian for whom the Bible was far more than a doctrinal or homiletic source book.

Bonhoeffer continued his work at the university after his return to Berlin. He also became a pastor in a working-class parish of the city where he had particular responsibility for the children of the poor and unemployed. This latter experience reinforced his sensitivity to the alienation of the working class from the Church. Meanwhile, his lectures, which conveyed his own deepening commitment to the message of Scripture, soon gained an enthusiastic following. Notable among them were those on "Creation and Sin," later published as Creation and Fall (1997), in which Bonhoeffer demonstrated his ability to interpret the Bible (in this case Genesis 1–3) in a way which spoke directly to his time and context. But it was those on "Christology," subsequently reconstructed from students' notes (Bonhoeffer 1978), which became pivotal for understanding the development and shape of his theology from then on.

The Germany to which Bonhoeffer returned was in crisis. The ill-fated Weimar Republic was in a state of collapse. Adolf Hitler came to power in 1933 and the National Socialist era of totalitarian horror began. Bonhoeffer publicly challenged the claims of absolute authority associated with the "Führer-principle" from the outset.[6] Indeed, even before Hitler's election he was anticipating confrontation with the state. His essay on "The Church and the 'Jewish Question'" published in 1932 clearly expressed the need to resist the state if it failed to fulfill its proper role. In a celebrated passage he declared:

> There are three possible ways in which the church can act towards the state: in the first place it can ask the state whether its actions are legitimate . . . Secondly, it can aid the victims of state action . . . The third possibility is not just to bandage the victims under the wheel, but to put a stake in the wheel itself. Such action would be direct political action, and it is only possible and desirable when the church sees the state fail in its function of creating law and order.   (trans. from Bonhoeffer 1977:225)

Bonhoeffer's attention was dominated, however, by the attempt of the Nazi "German Christians" to take over control of the Evangelical Church (Lutheran and Reformed) and make it subservient to Nazi ideology. Though there were others who agreed with his outspoken position, Bonhoeffer was disappointed by the tendency to compromise on the issues. So during 1933 he accepted an invitation to serve two German congregations in London. In his absence German church opposition to Nazism began to gather momentum and in May 1934 the first Confessing Synod of the Evangelical Church was held at Barmen. This act of defiance against the official *Reichskirche* launched the Confessing Church. The Barmen Declaration, largely drafted by Barth, unequivocally affirmed the Lordship of Jesus Christ over against the ideological claims of Nazism, though it did not speak out on the "Jewish Question." Bonhoeffer, who was in constant contact with the situation in Germany, became an advocate of the Confessing Church within British circles and took a leading role in seeking to isolate the Nazi Christians from the ecumenical Church. His papers and addresses of this period, most notably that on "The Confessing Church and the Ecumenical Movement," demonstrate the clarity of his thought and the incisive way in which he brought theology to bear on the critical issues of the day (1977:326ff).

By 1935 Bonhoeffer was back in Germany as the director of a seminary for ordinands in the Confessing Church located in the remote Baltic village of Finkenwalde. In a remarkable experiment in German Protestant theological formation, Bonhoeffer introduced his students to the unaccustomed discipline of community life centered on Bible study, worship, and prayer. Bonhoeffer and his students also participated fully in the life and witness of the Confessing Church congregations in the vicinity. He was also regularly in touch with events taking place in Berlin. Increasingly under the surveillance of the Gestapo, he was eventually forbidden to teach or preach in Berlin. It was during this period that Bonhoeffer wrote several expositions of biblical texts and themes, including his famous book on *Discipleship*.[7] The Gestapo closed the seminary in 1937, but it continued to function underground for several more months. Bonhoeffer's small but profound book on the nature of Christianity community, *Life Together*, was written at this time, and summed up what he had set out to achieve at Finkenwalde (Bonhoeffer 1996). But perhaps the most significant happening as this phase of his life drew to an end was his engagement to Maria von Wedemeyer, a love story that cannot be told here. Yet it is one which, in hindsight, had considerable influence on Bonhoeffer's closing years and the way in which he began to re-think his theology in prison (Bonhoeffer and Wedemeyer 1994).

In 1939 Bonhoeffer, unwilling to be drafted into the army, had the opportunity to go into exile in New York. After one agonizing month there he decided that he had to return and share in the fate of a Germany on the brink of war. Soon after his return Bonhoeffer joined the conspiracy against Hitler. Several of the leaders of the assassination plot were members of the wider Bonhoeffer family circle and some were in high positions within government and the military. Bonhoeffer himself was made a member of the German Military Intelligence (*Abwehr*) which, ironically, was the center of the conspiracy. Although the Gestapo suspected something was amiss, he was able to use his position to help Jews escape to Switzerland. On a visit to Sweden he also sought, through the mediation of his long-time friend Bishop George Bell of Chichester, to gain the support of Winston Churchill and President Roosevelt for the work of the Resistance. It was also during this period that Bonhoeffer began work on a book on ethics. Although he spent some quality time in the Benedictine monastery in Ettal working on this project, he did not manage to complete it. The posthumously published *Ethics* is composed of several interrelated drafts written at different times and places.[8] Despite this, it remains one of the most important sources for understanding both Bonhoeffer's more mature theology and Christian moral responsibility.

Bonhoeffer was arrested by the Gestapo in April 1943 on suspicion of aiding Jews to escape, and placed in Tegel prison in Berlin. Thus began the final episode of his life that is so well documented in his *Letters and Papers from Prison*. Tragically the attempt to assassinate the Führer on July 20, 1944, failed, and shortly after this all the conspirators were arrested. Information soon came to light implicating Bonhoeffer in the conspiracy. He was then moved from Tegel prison to the Gestapo prison in Berlin, later to the concentration camp in Buchenwald, and finally to Flossenburg where he was executed on April 9, 1945, just a few days before the camp was liberated by the Allies. A year before, Bonhoeffer wrote a letter to his parents in which he reflected on the fragmentary character of life as he and his generation were experiencing it in comparison with that of his parents and previous generations. Their lives, he wrote, "make us particularly aware of the fragmentary and incomplete nature of our own." But Bonhoeffer went on to say: "this fragmentariness may, in fact, point towards a fulfilment beyond the limits of human achievement" (1971:215).

Christ the Center

Many would regard Bonhoeffer's lectures on Christology given in Berlin in 1933 as the pivotal text in his theological development. Hence we will begin our exploration of his theology with these lectures, then take a step back to consider some of the foundations of his thought in his earlier dissertations *Sanctorum Communio* and *Act and Being*, before giving our attention to the theology of the *Ethics* and prison letters.

Christology, Bonhoeffer told his students, is not an attempt to answer the question "how" the eternal Word of God could have become a human being, but to discover "who" this Word is for us today.[9] The mystery of the incarnation is beyond the grasp of human reason, but in the proclamation of Jesus Christ as the crucified "Word made flesh" God addresses us with an immediacy that demands not just the response of the intellect but of the whole person. Christology has to do with this proclamation and its claims. This clearly presupposes the classical affirmation of the Council of Chalcedon (451) that Jesus Christ is "truly God and truly human." Indeed, for Bonhoeffer, Chalcedon sets the parameters for Christology even though it does not answer the contemporary and contextual question "who is Jesus Christ, for us." In seeking to answer this question, Bonhoeffer adapts Martin Luther's "theology of the cross" (*theologia crucis*), insisting that the primary question in Christology is "about the concealment of the God-Man in his humiliation" (Bonhoeffer 1978:54). In Jesus Christ God freely places himself at the service of humanity and the world "for me" and "for us" (*pro me* and *pro nobis*), whether in the cradle or on the cross, whether on the eucharistic altar or in the proclamation of the gospel. It is in and through God's humiliation in Christ that we are redeemed and brought into community. This has far-reaching consequences for what it means to be the Church. For it "is with this humiliated one that the church goes its own way of humiliation. . . . There is here no law or principle which the church has to follow, but simply a fact – put bluntly, it is God's way with the church" (Bonhoeffer 1978:113). Where Christ goes, there the Church must follow.

The question "who is Jesus Christ?" thus leads directly to the question "where is Jesus Christ?" Christ, says Bonhoeffer, is at the center of reality. In other words, Christology does not have to do with a Christ confined to religion or the Church, but with God's presence at the center of the life of the world. Christ is the center of human existence, the center of history and the state, and the center between God and nature. To speak of Christ in this way does, of course, open up the danger of triumphalism on the part of the Church, yet that goes directly contrary to Bonhoeffer's intention. For Christ exists at the center as the "humiliated one." This means that he exists at the center in solidarity with humanity in all its pain and suffering, acting vicariously and redemptively on behalf of the world. If the Church is to follow Christ it must be engaged as a community in solidarity with those who are its victims. It is in this way, says Bonhoeffer, that Christ both challenges the false messianic pretensions of those who exalt in power, and affirms the true messianic hopes of those who long for God's salvation.

Those familiar with the fragments of Bonhoeffer's prison theology will recognize the extent to which so much is already anticipated in these lectures on Christology. But in order to trace the other main trajectories in Bonhoeffer's theological development we now need to take a step back and consider his first two academic treatises *Sanctorum Communio* and *Act and Being*. For while it is true that *Christology* is the pivotal text in his theological development, it is equally true that some of the main concepts which recur and give shape to Bonhoeffer's theology during the Church struggle and especially in his *Ethics* and prison reflections, are already in embryonic form in his dissertations.

A Theology of Sociality

There is a qualitative difference between Bonhoeffer's lively and existentially demanding lectures on Christology and the somewhat dry and densely packed academic dissertations *Sanctorum Communio* (1927) and *Act and Being* (1930–1). The difference can be explained by reference to Bonhoeffer's own personal journey and the historical crisis now facing the church in the year of Hitler's triumph. Bonhoeffer was not trying to impress his academic mentors in order to become part of the theologians' guild; he was concerned about the awesome challenge facing those who wish to follow the "humiliated Christ" at the center of history gone wrong. Yet, despite the differences between the Christology lectures and the dissertations, there are some important continuities which have often been overlooked, not least the fact that at their heart is a Christological assertion which shapes virtually everything which is to follow.

Both *Sanctorum Communio* and *Act and Being* reach their climax with the declaration that "Christ exists as church-community." This not only shows Bonhoeffer's early interest in ecclesiology but how, from the outset, Bonhoeffer's theology was grounded in a social understanding of human existence interpreted in the light of God's revelation in Jesus Christ. Bonhoeffer's theology is, from beginning to end, a theology of sociality (Green 1999). Christ is undeniably *pro me*, yet this existential relationship is always located within a broader framework, for my identity as a human person is inseparable from "the other," and especially the ethical demands which "the other" makes upon me. Bonhoeffer's language reminds one of Martin Buber's *I and Thou*, yet the personalism he affirms is more ethical in character, with "the other" providing the boundary to my existence in such a way that only in responding to him or her do I truly become a person. The fundamental human problem is that "in Adam" community has been destroyed through the alienation of "the other"; it has become "a community of sinners" (*peccatorum communio*).

Bonhoeffer was aware of the dangers of a communalism that denies the place or rights of the person, subjugating him or her to false authority and domination. But he was equally aware of the dangers of a rampant individualism that made the "self" the center. Both were evidence of humanity "in Adam." Only in the "body of Christ" was it possible for the human person to be truly a person in relation to "the other," only through Christ's vicarious action is human community restored. Indeed, the vicarious or representative character (*Stellvertretung*) of Christ's death and resurrection is the "life-principle of the new humanity" (Bonhoeffer 1998:147). "God," writes the young Bonhoeffer, "established the reality of the church, of humanity pardoned in Jesus Christ – not religion, but revelation, *not a religious community, but the church*. This is what the reality of Jesus Christ means" (1998:153). And yet Bonhoeffer refuses to reduce the Church to an event that has no historical reality. After all, his intention was to relate a theology of revelation to social philosophy and thereby to the empirical existence of the Church. So he goes on to say: "yet there is a necessary connection between revelation and religion, as well as between religious community and the church" (1998:153). The Church is not a voluntary society of atomistic individuals but the empirical form of this "new humanity" that Christ has brought into being and of which he is the center. "Christ exists as church-community."

Act and Being, undoubtedly Bonhoeffer's most difficult book, continues his explorations in theological sociality and anthropology, only now in terms of epistemology. Both transcendentalism, with its emphasis on the "act" which breaks into human consciousness from beyond, and ontological systems which posit the continuity of the human self and "being-in-itself," are problematic. The first, as represented by the early Barth (that is, the Barth known to Bonhoeffer), disallows any continuity between the divine and the human and therefore any way whereby human reason can grasp hold of revelation. The second, variously represented by phenomenology, liberal Protestantism's emphasis on religious experience, confessional orthodoxy, or Roman Catholicism (the doctrine of *analogia entis* or "analogy of being"), stresses the continuity between the divine and the human, but in doing so revelation becomes captive to human experience, reason, the confessions, or the Church understood as institution. But, as Bonhoeffer sets out the problem and the way in which he will address it, "the meaning of 'the being of God in revelation' must be interpreted theologically, including how it is known, how faith as act, and revelation as being, are related to one another and, correspondingly, *how human beings stand in light of revelation*" (1996a:27). Bonhoeffer seeks to resolve the problem by reference to the freedom of God for rather than from humanity. The truth of the Christian gospel is that God has freely chosen to become a human being in Jesus Christ, and therefore, while remaining "truly God" has fully bound himself to us. God, in Jesus Christ, has become available for us. This brings Bonhoeffer, in conclusion, back to the sociality of his earlier dissertation, for it is within the Church-community that Christ exists as the one who is God for us. In Christ, understood in this way, humanity is set free from guilt and sin, the true self is restored, and genuine human community is established.

As we previously noted, prior to his 1933 Berlin lectures on Christology, Bonhoeffer taught a course on "Creation and Sin," published as *Creation and Fall* (1997). In many respects, these earlier lectures provide the link between the central theme of his two dissertations, his Christology and his theological ethics. We may balk at Bonhoeffer's Christological interpretation of the Old Testament, but at a time when Nazism demanded the rejection of everything Jewish from the life of the Church and nation, Bonhoeffer's strong affirmation of the Hebrew scriptures as Christian was in itself a firm counter to such anti-Semitic Marcionism. Later, in prison, Bonhoeffer preferred to read the New Testament in the light of the Old, but now his intention was different – and for good reason. Throughout the history of the Church, the downplaying of the Old Testament invariably has led to a Gnostic separation of creation and redemption, and therefore to a dualism which kept body and spirit apart. Such "thinking in two spheres," as he described it in his *Ethics*, meant that the Church no longer took any responsibility for the life of the world and nature, and therefore also eschewed any political responsibility. This was directly related to the Lutheran (but not Luther's) doctrine of the orders of creation which, on the basis of the creation story, gave autonomy to the nation (*das Volk*), the state, the family, and culture. This meant, as some distinguished theologians of the time argued in sympathy with the Nazis, that these were independent of God's revelation in Jesus Christ, and therefore outside the mandate of church responsibility and witness. Over against this, Bonhoeffer argued that, in the light of Christ, these "orders" are for the sake of preserving human life; they do not have the autonomy or authority to develop their own norms and values independent of God's revelation in Jesus Christ. Later, in his *Ethics*, Bonhoeffer revisited this issue, taking his position one step further away from any possible support for autonomous spheres of morality by speaking of God's mandates, for this spoke more clearly of God's demands upon us in Jesus Christ rather than as something inherent within creation.

At the heart of Bonhoeffer's theological exposition of *Creation and Fall* is his Christological interpretation of the meaning of the "image of God" or *imago Dei*. In continuity with his argument in *Act and Being*, Bonhoeffer rejects the notion that this refers to some inherent quality of being which relates the human and divine, just as he rejects any liberal idea that gives autonomy to the human subject. Against the Catholic doctrine of the *analogia entis*, then, he speaks of an *analogia relationis*, or an analogy of relationships. Once again Bonhoeffer's early "theology of sociality" is apparent, but only now more clearly rooted in Scripture, more decisively Christological, and more immediately related to the existential and historical demands of his context. God creates human beings to rule over creation, but their freedom requires responsibility or deputyship (*Stellvertretung*). Sin is the abnegation of such responsibility. Redemption is the recovery of being truly free "for others," and therefore responsible for the world.

Confessing Christ Here and Now

All the theological building blocks were now in place, which were to guide Bonhoeffer's own involvement and reflection in the fateful Church struggle (*Kirchenkampf*) against

Nazism. What remained was the need to speak out clearly and in the most concrete way possible about the meaning of Jesus Christ as Lord against the absolute claims of Nazi ideology. But, for Bonhoeffer, the corollary to confessing Christ was a confessing Church. In a sermon on Peter's confession at Caesarea Philippi (Matthew 16: 13–18) preached at the time of the Church elections in July 1933, Bonhoeffer asked the searching question: where is the Church which is built on the rock against which "the powers of death shall not prevail"? His unequivocal answer was that the true Church of Jesus Christ is the Church that confessed him faithfully. "Church stay a church! But church confess, confess, confess!" he exhorted. And then went on to declare: "The Confessing Church is the eternal church because Christ protects her" (Bonhoeffer 1965:217).

It is beyond the scope of this essay to discuss the many essays and papers which Bonhoeffer wrote or delivered during the Church struggle period. Virtually all the themes we have already mentioned thus far find expression in some form as he takes up the cudgels on behalf of the Confessing Church, the ecumenical search for peace or, however haltingly at first, the Jewish victims of Nazi policy. Confessing Christ concretely meant, for Bonhoeffer, rejecting the compromises of the *Reichskirche*, which had become a "false Church" and following Jesus Christ alone. This uncompromising message lay at the heart of his teaching at Finkenwalde. It also found powerful expression in his book on *Discipleship* (2001) that had been gestating in his heart and mind ever since his encounter with Jean Lasserre at Union Theological Seminary in New York.

Discipleship is divided into two parts, the first being an exposition of the Sermon on the Mount, the second being an interpretation of Paul's theology of justification by faith and ecclesiology. Bonhoeffer undoubtedly wanted to demonstrate that, following Jesus, the suffering Messiah as described in the synoptic gospels was directly related to what it meant to live by faith in Jesus Christ as Lord within the "body of Christ." In this way he was intent on countering the traditionally Lutheran tendency to separate "justification by faith alone" from costly discipleship. Such a separation, he argued, inevitably resulted in the cheapening of grace and the undermining of true evangelical faith and witness. This, Bonhoeffer believed, was at the heart of the problem of the Evangelical Church in Germany. "Like ravens," he wrote, "we have gathered around the carcass of cheap grace. From it we have imbibed the poison which has killed the following of Jesus among us" (2001:53). "Luther's teachings are quoted everywhere, but twisted from their truth into self-delusion" (2001:53). The truth is, "*only the believers obey* and *only the obedient believe*" (2001:63; italics as in original). Believing in the doctrine of "justification by faith alone" was never intended as a substitute for discipleship, on the contrary, without taking the step of obedience through following Christ, faith is not a reality. "Discipleship means adherence to Christ, and, because Christ is the object of that adherence, it must take the form of discipleship. An abstract Christology, a doctrinal system, a general religious knowledge on the subject of grace or on the forgiveness of sins, render discipleship superfluous" (1959:50). By contrast, "when Christ calls a person, he bids him come and die" (1959:79).

That Bonhoeffer practiced what he proclaimed in *Discipleship* is self-evident, and that he sought to ensure the spiritual formation of his students along the same pattern is equally clear from *Life Together*. This remarkable interpretation of Christian community also brought together many of the key themes in Bonhoeffer's earlier theology, notably those of *Sanctorum Communio*. Only now Bonhoeffer wove them into a more explicitly biblical form and practically related them to the daily life of a Church-community intent upon following Christ in the midst of a hostile world. The Christological foundation of Christian community is also evident from the outset. "Christian community means community through Jesus Christ and in Jesus Christ. There is no Christian community that is more than this and none that is less than this. . . . We belong to one another only through and in Jesus Christ" (1996b:31). Such a community is not an ideal to be sought and implemented by like-minded individuals, but a divine reality, a gift, which God brings into being through his Word. Those who turn to *Life Together* for guidance in building community along more "humanistic" or "group therapy" lines soon discover that they have entered a very different ethos. "In the spiritual community the Word of God alone rules; in the emotional, self-centered community the individual who is equipped with exceptional powers, experience, and magical, suggestive abilities rules along with the Word. . . . In the one, all power, honor, and rule are surrendered to the Holy Spirit; in the other, power and personal spheres of influence are sought and cultivated" (1996b:40). Bonhoeffer was fully aware of the strength of his own personality and therefore of the danger in building the "community of brothers" at Finkenwalde around himself. Only Christ could be the true foundation of Christian community, and such community can only be sustained by the Word and the Spirit.

The Ethics of Free Responsibility

Even though, as we have noted, Bonhoeffer was not impressed by the theology he encountered during his year of study at Union Theological Seminary, he soon acknowledged the particular importance which American theologians gave to social ethics and the social witness of the Church. Ten years later, after his second, but very brief sojourn in New York, Bonhoeffer had a sense that American theology was improving under the influence of neo-orthodoxy, and he commented with appreciation on the work of his former teacher and now his colleague, Reinhold Niebuhr. Yet, he still felt that even Niebuhr's theology lacked an adequate Christology. "In American theology," he wrote, "Christianity is still essentially religion and ethics. But because of this, the person and work of Jesus Christ must, for theology, sink into the background and in the long run remain misunderstood, because it is not recognized as the sole ground of radical judgment and radical forgiveness" (1965:115). For Bonhoeffer any notion that Christian ethics, whether personal or social, was a separate discipline with its own norms and methods was alien to his way of doing theology and what it means to confess Jesus Christ in the midst of the world. With this in mind we turn to his *Ethics*.

From Bonhoeffer's perspective, the history of the West from its conversion to Christianity until the Enlightenment could be understood as one in which Christ was shaping the values and norms of society. This inheritance was now squandered. The West had become hostile to Christ, as was blatantly shown in the Nazi persecution of the Jews. Whereas previously Christians knew what God required even if they failed to do it, ethics had now become a matter of finding out what is good on the basis of reason and

then trying to apply such moral principles to life in the world. However, the fundamental point of departure for Christian ethics, and therefore for the reconstruction of
Western society, Bonhoeffer insisted, was not the question "how can we be or do good?"
but rather "how do we know the will of God?" For Bonhoeffer this leads directly to the
reality of God's revelation in Jesus Christ as the point of departure for Christian ethics,
which is quite distinct from philosophical ethics. Yet it is not simply an ethics for the
believer or the Church, for the revelation of God in Jesus Christ irrevocably brings
together the reality of God and the world. It is therefore impossible to experience the
reality of God apart from the reality of the world. Any separation of Christian ethics
from public life is untenable. Such "thinking in two spheres" (1965:188), falsely
assumes that there are areas of life outside the Lordship of Jesus Christ.

By insisting that the will of God is to be discovered in God's revelation in Jesus Christ,
Bonhoeffer also rejects any attempt to base Christian ethics on the "orders of creation"
or on "natural law," though he does begin to express interest in the latter as his *Ethics*
unfolds, relating it to his discussion of the divine mandates (1965:207). But even so
Christian ethics is not a matter of applying certain moral principles to life in the world.
"It is not written," Bonhoeffer emphatically declares, "that God became an idea, a principle, a programme, a universally valid proposition or law, but that God became man"
(1965:85). In other words the starting point for Christian ethics is the incarnation or,
put differently, Christ taking form in the world.

> What matters in the church is not religion but the form of Christ, and its taking form
> amidst a band of men. If we allow ourselves to lose sight of this, even for an instant, we
> inevitably relapse into that programme-planning for the ethical and religious shaping of
> the world, which is where we set out from.   (1965:84)

At one level, Christian ethics is fairly straightforward for it requires that we love God
and our neighbor. The difficulty arises in boundary situations where the only choices
facing one are morally murky. Moral dilemmas abounded in Nazi Germany, where the
traditionally Christian and upright bourgeoisie had capitulated to state immorality.
Questions concerning the right to life were made far more problematic because of the
program to rid society of people who did not measure up to the Nazi model of Aryan
purity and health. Even the question of telling the truth was problematic, for how could
one do so if it meant that the life of a Jewish friend or neighbor was threatened? And,
of course, Bonhoeffer was now part of the German conspiracy. Was it really legitimate
to kill Hitler given the fact that it meant reneging on the oath of loyalty to the Führer
which all German officers had taken; that it ran counter to everything treasured within
patriotic German tradition; and, above all, that it meant disobeying the sixth commandment? This is the background to Bonhoeffer's discussion of "The Structure of
Responsible Life" which lies at the heart of his *Ethics*.

Christian ethics on the boundary, Bonhoeffer argued, required taking the risk of concrete decision. It might be wrong to lie, but that might be the more responsible action
than "telling the truth"; it might be wrong to commit murder, but it was morally irre-
sponsible not to assassinate Hitler. Not to take such a moral risk, not to engage in such
an act of "free responsibility," would, on the basis of the conspirators' analysis of the

situation, lead to many more deaths and increasing devastation. Yet, in taking such a step it was necessary for the conspirators to acknowledge that they were also stepping beyond the boundaries of important and cherished moral norms, and therefore incurring guilt. "When a man takes guilt upon himself in responsibility, and no responsible man can avoid this, he imputes this guilt to himself and to one else; he answers for it; he accepts responsibility for it." Such a person is wholly dependent upon God's grace. "Before other men the man of free responsibility is justified by necessity; before himself he is acquitted by his conscience; but before God he hopes only for mercy" (1965:248). In the end, then, Christian ethics is about the formation of men and women who will act rightly and justly precisely because the incarnate, crucified, and risen One has shaped their lives.

Christianity in a World Come of Age

Bonhoeffer did not complete his *Ethics*. Instead he found himself in prison, where his thoughts began to move in new and unexpected directions even though many of his key prison insights are anticipated in his earlier writings. We cannot explore all of Bonhoeffer's insights as these found expression in his letters to his parents, his fiancée, and especially to his close friend Eberhard Bethge, or in his remarkable poetry. This is a pity for there is so much else that is of interest and significance than just his more controversial comments on Christianity in a "world come of age." Yet it is undoubtedly these latter reflections, starting with those in a letter to Bethge on April 30, 1944, that have attracted most attention.[10] Of course, all that we have is fragmentary in form, for Bonhoeffer was engaged in sharing his thoughts with his close friend and not expecting them to be published, at least not in that form. Yet it is helpful to recall that Bonhoeffer was also engaged in writing a book related to his reflections, and even though all that remains of that project is a tentative outline, this does provide a coherent framework within which to locate his thought. Bonhoeffer had three chapters in mind (1971:380). The first, a "Stocktaking of Christianity," would examine the state of Christianity in a "world come of age"; the second on "The Real Meaning of Christian Faith," would provide a "non-religious interpretation of Christianity"; and the third would discuss the consequences which the preceding discussion would have for the Church.

As we might now expect, the point of departure for Bonhoeffer's reflections was a Christological question. "What is bothering me incessantly," he wrote to Bethge, "is the question what Christianity really is, or indeed who Christ really is, for us today." Yet this question, which weaves his theological development together, now opens up fresh possibilities. Bonhoeffer is no longer primarily concerned about confessing Christ as Lord against Nazi idolatry, nor is he struggling to come to terms with the moral dilemmas of the conspiracy. What is at issue as he reflects on the state of Christianity in anticipation of the post-war period is the fundamental change in the world-view and consciousness of the West that has come about as a result of the Enlightenment, the French Revolution, and the rise of modern science. In the past, Christian proclamation had assumed a human "religious *a priori*," even claiming to be the true religion, but in the meantime the world had become increasingly "religionless." The nineteenth-century critique of religion as a human construction along with Barth's own contention that God's revelation in Jesus Christ was a judgment on all religion, had to be taken seriously. But this was not just a theoretical or philosophical matter. Bonhoeffer was deeply concerned about the fact that both the working class and his secular compatriots in the conspiracy were estranged from both Christianity and the Church, not least because of their well-founded suspicion of religion. Hence the question: "How can Christ become the Lord of the religionless as well?" And, as always for Bonhoeffer, this Christological question immediately raised the further questions: "What do a church, a community, a sermon, a liturgy, a Christian life mean in a religionless world?" (1971:27a).

The phrase "world come of age" relates, of course, to the historical process of secularization in the West. Borrowed from Immanuel Kant and Wilhelm Dilthey, it does not mean that the world has become a more moral place but that it has undergone a fundamental reorientation. With regard to religion, this has meant the withdrawal of Christianity from public life into the private sphere. God himself has been pushed out on to the boundaries of life and become the God of individual piety, bourgeois privilege, and a ghetto Church. In fact, God has been reduced to a *deus ex machina* who is only called upon when everything else has failed. This might be the God of religion, the God affirmed by the pious and rejected by the "religionless," but it is not the God of the Bible. Rather than trying to fit God into the gaps of our experience, Bonhoeffer would "like to speak of God not on the boundaries but at the center, not in weakness but in strength; and therefore not in death and guilt but in the life and goodness of people" (1971:282). Indeed, "God would have us know that we must live as people who manage our lives without him" (1971:360). The transcendence of God has to do with God's presence "in the midst of our life," not some epistemological theory. Thus, what "is above this world is, in the gospel, intended to exist for this world." By this Bonhoeffer does not mean a return to the anthropocentric approach of liberal, mystical, pietistic, or ethical theology, "but in the biblical sense of the creation and of the incarnation, crucifixion, and resurrection of Jesus Christ" (1971:286).

Bonhoeffer's celebrated description of Jesus as the one who "is there only for others" is therefore not reductionist. It refers to our experience of transcendence (1971:381) from the perspective of the cross, and that means from the perspective of the victims of society. The God revealed in Jesus Christ is the God who "lets himself be pushed out of the world on to the cross. He is weak and powerless in the world, and that is precisely the way, the only way, in which he is with us and helps us." The God of the Bible is not the God of religion, but the "suffering God." That, Bonhoeffer declares, "will probably be the starting-point for our secular interpretation" (1971:361). An interpretation undoubtedly influenced by Bonhoeffer's whole life experience, whether in the black ghettos of New York, the slums of Berlin, or more recently in his identification with the plight of the Jews in Nazi Germany. As he told his fellow conspirators shortly before his arrest:

> We have learnt to see the great events of world history from below, from the perspective of the outcast, the suspects, the maltreated, the powerless, the oppressed, the reviled – in short, from the perspective of those who suffer.   (1971:17)

The consequences of this for the Church and for Christian life in the world are far-reaching. Indeed, the words just quoted, perhaps more than any others from Bonhoeffer's whole legacy, have had a remarkable influence on the shaping of theologies of liberation around the world. For what is at stake in Bonhoeffer's "non-religious" interpretation is not apologetics or hermeneutics, but a fundamental reorientation or metanoia which leads to an identification with Christ in his sufferings (1971:361) and therefore to a different way of being the Church-community in the world. If Jesus exists only for others, so too the Church must not seek its own self-preservation but be "open to the world" and in solidarity with others. This does not mean that the Church must surrender its own identity, for that would simply be another example of "cheap grace," or a confusion of the penultimate and the ultimate. Hence the need for the Church to recover the "discipline of the secret" (*disciplina arcanum*), whereby the mysteries of the faith are protected from profanation (1971:286). Prayer, worship, the sacraments, and the creed, remain at the heart of the life of the Church, but they must not be thrust upon the world in some triumphalist manner. In sum, as Bonhoeffer wrote from prison on the occasion of Dietrich Bethge's baptism, "All Christian thinking, speaking, and organizing must be born anew out of [this] prayer and action." He continued:

> It is not for us to prophesy the day (though the day will come) when men will once more be called so to utter the word of God that the world will be changed and renewed by it. It will be a new language, perhaps quite non-religious, but liberating and redeeming – as was Jesus' language; it will shock people and yet overcome them by its power; it will be the language of a new righteousness and truth, proclaiming God's peace with men and the coming of his kingdom."

Notes

1   For example, *Hitler and the Pastor – the Dietrich Bonhoeffer Story*, the Dietrich Bonhoeffer Film Project New York.

2   The Bonhoeffer-Triptychon, by Herman Berlinski, Heinz Werner Zimmermann, and Robert M. Helmschrott, was first performed at Union Theological Seminary in New York by the Dresden Chamber Choir under the direction of Hans-Christoph Rademann, August 12, 1992.

3   *Bonhoeffer*, composed by Ann K. Gebur, premiered at Pennsylvania State University, October 1999.

4   There are several outstanding biographies, but the standard account is Bethge (1970). This is currently being revised and retranslated by Victoria Barnett, and will be published in an unabridged edition by Fortress Press.

5   This is the new translation of "Christus als Gemeinde existierend" in Bonhoeffer (1998).

6   See Bonhoeffer's broadcast on "The Leadership Principle," which the German authorities cut off soon after he began. See Bonhoeffer (1977:190ff).

7   Previously translated in English as *Cost of Discipleship*, and recently republished in 2001 as *Discipleship*, Dietrich Bonhoeffer Works, vol. 4 (Minneapolis, MN: Fortress Press).

8   There has been much debate about the structure of Bonhoeffer's *Ethics*, given the fact that what he left us was not a complete manuscript but several drafts. See the Introduction to Bonhoeffer (forthcoming).

9   English translations are from Bonhoeffer (1978).
10 For a selection of all the relevant passages see de Gruchy (1988:272ff.). For the most recent discussion of the issues from the perspective of a "theology of life," see Wustenberg (1998).
11 "Thoughts on the Day of the Baptism of Dietrich Wilhelm Rudiger Bethge," (see Bonhoeffer 1971:300).

References

Bethge, E. 1970. *Dietrich Bonhoeffer: Theologian, Christian, Contemporary.* London: Collins.

Bonhoeffer, D. 1959. *Creation and Fall: A Theological Exposition of Genesis 7:3*, Dietrich Bonhoeffer Works, vol. 3. Minneapolis, MN: Fortress Press.

Bonhoeffer, D. 1965. *Ethics.* New York: Macmillan.

Bonhoeffer, D. 1971. *Letters and Papers from Prison.* London: SCM Press.

Bonhoeffer, D. 1977. *No Rusty Swords: Letters, Lectures and Notes, 1928–1936. Collected Works of Dietrich Bonhoeffer*, vol. 1. London: Collins.

Bonhoeffer, D. 1978. *Christ the center*, trans. E. H. Robertson. New York: Harper & Row.

Bonhoeffer, D. 1996a. *Act and Being: Transcendental Philosophy and Ontology*, in *Systematic Theology*, Dietrich Bonhoeffer Works, vol. 2. Minneapolis, MN: Fortress Press.

Bonhoeffer, D. 1996b. *Life Together: Prayerbook of the Bible*, trans. D. W. Bloesch and J. H. Burtness, Dietrich Bonhoeffer Works, vol. 5. Minneapolis, MN: Fortress Press.

Bonhoeffer, D. 1997. *Creation and Fall: A Theological Exposition of Genesis 7:3*. Dietrich Bonhoeffer, Works, vol. 3. Minneapolis, MN: Fortress Press.

Bonhoeffer, D. 1998. *Sanctorum Communio: A Theological Study of the Sociology of the Church*, Dietrich Bonhoeffer Works, vol. 1. Minneapolis, MN: Fortress Press.

Bonhoeffer, D. 2001. *Discipleship*, Dietrich Bonhoeffer Works, vol. 4. Minneapolis, MN: Fortress Press.

Bonhoeffer, D. forthcoming. *Ethics*, Dietrich Bonhoeffer Works, vol. 6. Minneapolis, MN: Fortress Press.

Bonhoeffer, D., and Wedemeyer, M. von. 1994. *Love Letters from Cell 92.* London: HarperCollins.

de Gruchy, J. W. 1988. *Dietrich Bonhoeffer: Witness to Jesus Christ.* London: Collins.

de Gruchy, J. W. 1997. "Bonhoeffer. Apartheid and Beyond: the Reception of Bonhoeffer in South Africa," in *Bonhoeffer for a New Day: Theology in a Time of Transition*, ed. J. W. de Gruchy. Grand Rapids, MI: Eerdmans.

de Gruchy, J. W. 1999. *The Cambridge Companion to Dietrich Bonhoeffer.* Cambridge: Cambridge University Press.

Floyd, W. W., Jr. 1999. "Bonhoeffer's Literary Legacy," in *The Cambridge Companion to Dietrich Bonhoeffer*, ed. J. W. de Gruchy. Cambridge: Cambridge University Press.

Green, C. J. 1999. *Bonhoeffer: A Theology of sociality*, rev. edn. Grand Rapids, MI: Eerdmans.

Wüstenberg, R. K. 1998. *Faith as Life: Dietrich Bonhoeffer and the Non-Religious. Interpretation of the Biblical Message.* Grand Rapids, MI: Eerdmans.

CHAPTER 23
Bultmann and Tillich

James M. Byrne

Rudolf Bultmann was born in 1884 in the then Grand Duchy of Oldenburg in northern Germany. His father was a Lutheran pastor, as was his maternal grandfather; his
paternal grandfather was born in Sierra Leone and had been a missionary in West
Africa. Bultmann reported his childhood as a happy one and he was educated at local
schools where he particularly enjoyed the study of Greek. In 1903 he began his theological studies at Tübingen and subsequently spent semesters at Berlin and Marburg,
as is the norm in continental university education. This enabled him to experience the
best available grounding in the theological sub-disciplines as well as encountering some
of the leading German theologians of the day, including Adolf von Harnack (d. 1930)
at Berlin and the influential Wilhelm Hermann (d. 1922) at Marburg. Also at Marburg
was the biblical scholar Johann Weiss (d. 1914) who encouraged the young Bultmann
to pursue his doctoral studies in the field of New Testament.

Bultmann's early research towards his qualification as a lecturer in the German educational system was on *The Style of the Pauline Cynic–Stoic Diatribe* (1910) and *The Exegesis of Theodor of Mopsuestia*. The latter work was completed at Marburg in 1912,
where he remained as a lecturer for four years. Unlike Tillich, Bultmann did not experience World War I directly, being excused service on physical grounds, although his
younger brother was killed on the Western front. In 1916 Bultmann moved to Breslau
and briefly, in 1920, to Giessen as professor, where he succeeded the distinguished
scholar Wilhelm Bousset (d. 1920). In 1921 Bultmann returned to Marburg, where he
remained until his retirement in 1951. He died in 1976, having continued to work and
lecture long after he had retired.

Bultmann's early influences place him firmly within the sphere of nineteenth-
century German liberal theology. The years of his theological education in the first
decade of the new century were those in which the liberal tradition of engagement with
critical post-Kantian philosophy was dominant, even if its greatest achievements were
already behind it and the cracks were beginning to show. The key influence on the development of the liberal tradition was Albrecht Ritschl (d. 1889), whose acceptance into

theology of the Kantian epistemological critique paved the way for what, despite the evident differences between many of the protagonists, can be accurately described as the development of a late nineteenth-century liberal consensus in German Protestant theology. Ritschl and his followers (who were in the ascendant at almost all major German theological faculties) emphasized the historically conditioned nature of all doctrinal and metaphysical formulations, the revelation of God in Jesus' proclamation of the Kingdom, the sheer gratuity of the divine offer of justification and reconciliation, and the moral response of the Christian living historically in church and in society. That this post-Kantian theology which had attempted to meet the Enlightenment critique on its own terms could be later condemned (in the aftermath of war) as the degenerate *Kulturprotestantismus* of imperial Germany was evident to no one at the time; it was the highest point of Protestant engagement with both the Christian message, properly understood, and the critical epistemology of the scientific era.

However, by the turn of the century liberalism had its critics and Bultmann was aware of the reservations about Ritschlian liberalism which were emerging in Germany and elsewhere. In particular, Martin Kähler (d. 1912) and Reinhold Seeberg (d. 1935) criticized the immanentism of liberal thought; they highlighted the difficulty of retaining objective faith in a transcendent God when the emphasis is placed on Jesus as the human moral teacher revealing to us the way to live a good Christian life. Critics of liberalism saw in it the erosion of transcendence, the elision of sin and the consequent reduction of justification to a human act of psychological restoration. Despite his lifelong commitment to the historical-critical method championed by liberalism, this turn-of-the-century critique prepared the way for Bultmann's cautiously positive engagement with the thought of Barth in the 1920s and with dialectical theology's definitive break from the liberal tradition.

Of particular importance in understanding the context of Bultmann's future theological direction is the impact of the "history of religions" movement within liberal theology. From about 1870 onward European scholarship became interested in the study of religion as a social and cultural phenomenon. The possibility of a *Religionswissenschaft* had emerged from the late Enlightenment and early Romantic concern with recognition of the diversity of human culture and had been fostered in the broader sense by a significant increase in knowledge about other cultures and peoples, and in the narrower theological sense by the influence of Hegel and Schleiermacher on the nineteenth century's understanding of what constituted religion as such. The study of religion and religious texts as historical products of human culture allied the scholars of religion with those working in fields such as anthropology and ethnology, set them the goal of providing a general account of religion, and had a profound influence in theology even on those scholars who saw themselves as Christian theologians first of all.

Although German faculties were slow to establish *Religionswissenschaft* as a discrete discipline within the university, through the influence of Max Müller and Cornelius Tiele in the late nineteenth century and Nathan Söderblom and Rudolf Otto in the early twentieth century, Christian theology was presented with a methodological shift toward interpreting Christianity from the same critical perspective as all other religions.[1] Among the biblical scholars influenced by the history of religions approach were Bousset Wilhelm Wrede, Johann Weiss and Hermann Gunkel (the leading figure in the emergence of form criticism); these scholars and others realized that a correct under-standing of biblical history could only be gained through placing the Bible in its social and historical context of the ancient Near East, and interpreting it within the overall framework of parallel mythologies from other cultures. Thus, to take two obvious exam-ples, the story of the flood should be sought for in the memories of other social groups also, and the doctrine of the incarnation could only be correctly understood by placing it within the context of other myths of gods taking human form. The influence of the history of religions approach, particularly that of Bousset, on Bultmann's later project of demythologization is evident, but is already present in his early work before the encounter with dialectical theology.

From among the liberal theologians, however, it is the figure of Wilhelm Hermann who stands out as the decisive influence on Bultmann's later theological development. Hermann's theology was to a great extent influenced by Kant's critique of the power of speculative reason and by Ritschl's subsequent suspicion of metaphysics. But Hermann went beyond Ritschl in his rejection of metaphysical theology, which he saw as unable to grasp the nature of God or of the religious experience in a modern world dominated by the success of science. True religion belonged in a realm free from speculative phi-losophy but also free from interference by science. Correspondingly, for Hermann the autonomy of the scientific method cannot be negated by theology, which has its juris-diction in a sphere of its own. Like many later theologians who struggle with this ques-tion, Hermann responded to the challenge of the scientific world-view by portraying science and religion as addressing two different sets of questions, each belonging in its own sphere.

A consequence of this maneuver for Hermann's theology was that he then had to explain how the personal experience of faith was not merely subjective but could also have objective reference. He did this by claiming that there are two things to which theology can hold firm: the facticity of the inner life of Jesus and the imperative of the moral law (here Hermann is dependent on Kant, although also critical of him). Hermann thought, as Lessing had so vividly argued, that the Christian believer could never cross the "great ugly ditch" separating history from faith and make history the basis of faith. However, while Scripture as a collection of historical texts open to a range of critical interpretations cannot be the basis of Christian faith, in Hermann's estima-tion the gospels were sufficiently reliable as witnesses to the inner life of Jesus to enable the Christian to trust their theological reliability. The Christian's own life of faith is grounded not in the changing opinions of scholars about the historical veracity of the text, but rather in the gospels' witness to the communion of Jesus with God (as evi-denced by the title of Hermann's most important work, *The Communion of the Christian with God*, 1886) and it is the Christian's certainty about the inner life of Jesus which enables faith's own certainty to exist alongside the very different certainties offered by philosophy and science.

From the liberal tradition and Hermann in particular Bultmann inherited: (1) an acceptance of the historical-critical method as the legitimate tool of textual analysis of the Christian scriptures; (2) a recognition of the transformative power of the encounter with the Christ of the gospels which was to allow him to sympathize with Barth's attack on liberalism and provide a key element in his own thought; (3) a concern with the spiritual and "existential" life of the believer in which thought about religion cannot be separated from the life lived; and (4) the premise that we only know God through God's work in us, as we have no philosophical or theological capacity through which we can know God directly. But he also inherited the unresolved tension of Hermann's solution to the problem of faith and history, for Hermann's over-sanguine confidence in the gospels' picture of Jesus is open to the same objection as the liberals themselves posed to theological deductions based on the historically extant texts.[2]

In 1921 Bultmann published *Die Geschichte der synoptischen Tradition* (*The History of the Synoptic Tradition*), one of the high points of form criticism, which traced the origins of much of the synoptic material to its production by discrete early Christian communities. This book was at once both a work of liberal theology within the historical-critical tradition and at the same time a negative judgment on the possibilities of a successful historical reconstruction of the Jesus tradition. Together with the earlier work of Schweitzer and Wrede, the book marked the end of the liberal attempt to reconstruct the historical Jesus. For Bultmann in the early 1920s, therefore, the problems of theology were still the problems of his liberal teachers, but the solutions of liberalism were increasingly unviable; it was only in the encounter with the work of Barth and Gogarten that Bultmann was able to find the independent voice which carried liberal Protestantism's focus on the human religious experience into the new theological context of dialectical theology's concern with the God who is experienced.

Barth's earth-shattering second edition of *The Epistle to the Romans* was published in 1922 and reviewed sympathetically by Bultmann in the same year; it marked the definitive end of the dominance of the old liberal theology in Germany and taught Bultmann that the proper object of theology was not human consciousness, but God who stands over and against humanity. For Barth God is not to be found through the development of the religious character of the individual, nor is the search after the historical Jesus of any theological value. God is the One who addresses us, the utterly transcendent "Other" who is both the origin and the object of theological discourse, and this "Other" is known through our meeting with the risen Christ proclaimed in the kerygma. Liberalism failed because it put its trust in the human moral character, not in God's promise, and the tragedy of World War I had discredited such complacent optimism forever. Through Barth's Copernican revolution in theology, Bultmann was able to cast off the liberal search for religious fulfillment through knowledge and imitation of the historical Jesus; now, the historical criticism which had been at the heart of the liberal search for Jesus and its critique of doctrinal theology is used to reject all historicism as a search for what Barth described as "Christ after the flesh."

The dialectical theology which emerged in the 1920s was a theology which had Scripture at its center. Bultmann agreed with Barth that Scripture had to be allowed to speak with its own voice and that theology was done *with* the biblical authors, and he shared Barth's concern that the theological content which the Scriptures contained be taken seriously and be heard as the kerygmatic proclamation that it is. However, he did not share Barth's theological positivism regarding Scripture as revelation; the texts of Paul or of the evangelists are texts conditioned by the personal and historical circumstances surrounding their production, and are therefore open to critique in theological as well as historical terms.

Bultmann sees the work of the New Testament scholar as a theological task, as not only engaging in exegesis of the content of the text but engaging in critical theological interpretation in the light of other scriptural sources and, indeed, other human knowledge. As dialectical theology was concerned theologically with allowing the proclamation of scripture as the revealed Word of God, it was *a fortiori* a hermeneutical theology. However, there are key differences between Bultmann's hermeneutics and that of Barth, which reveal the major lines of divergence in twentieth-century Protestant theology. Where Barth's hermeneutics was essentially a theological hermeneutics which he saw as a part of dogmatic theology proper, Bultmann saw the hermeneutical process as a philosophical task which came prior to the theologian's engagement with the material of the Scriptures. For Bultmann, we must understand fully what it is that we are going to do before we begin to do it and the way to achieve this is by establishing clearly what are the presuppositions and conditions of the interpretative process; for Barth, this is to sell God's revelation into the "Egyptian bondage" of philosophy, precisely the same situation which he had rejected in liberalism.[3]

Barth's concern was founded on the use which Bultmann made of the existentialist philosophy of Martin Heidegger (1889–1976). The theologian met the philosopher when Heidegger moved to Marburg in 1923 and over a period of five years they held regular discussions, privately and in seminars, in which Bultmann came to see the significance of Heidegger's phenomenology for the New Testament theology with which he was engaged. In particular Bultmann was influenced by Heidegger's treatment in *Sein und Zeit* (*Being and Time*, 1927) of the existential structures of the human being as "Being-in-the-world," structures which allow the theologian to provide an account of the human condition which the gospel message encounters. In *Being and Time* Heidegger provides a phenomenological analysis of what he considers to be the structure of Being-in-the-world: we experience the "thrownness" (*Geworfenheit*) of existence in a world which we have not chosen and which we know that we will leave through death; in this world we may choose to grasp the potentiality which existence offers us or we may hide in the world of the anonymous mass of humanity (*das Man*); to choose the former is to live authentically, to choose the latter – or to allow it to choose us – is to live inauthentically.

In Bultmann's hermeneutical theology, all exegetical theology is interpretation, but presuppositionless interpretation is impossible; therefore before theology as such is undertaken it becomes necessary to delineate the conceptual framework and categories with which one is working. In response to Barth's objection that this is to subject the independence of the gospel revelation to the strictures of the procrustean bed of a philosophical system, Bultmann pointed out that using *some* philosophical system is unavoidable for the theologian and that Barth's own failing lay in his refusal to give adequate critical attention to the conceptual categories which he himself utilized.

Heidegger's *Being and Time* offers a purely formal analysis which conspicuously lacks any ethics or content which would make it useful to the Christian theologian, but paradoxically it is precisely this lack of specific content which allows Bultmann to turn Heidegger to his own theological use. Bultmann always firmly rejected the traditionalist critics who attacked him for directly importing the content of existentialist philosophy into theology, for in Heidegger's phenomenological analysis of the human condition

Bultmann saw no such content. Instead, existentialist analysis offers the theologian the conceptual categories to understand the human condition under which the proclamation of the gospel message is encountered as event. For the exegete as theologian – as Bultmann undoubtedly was – these existential categories themselves can be seen to correspond to many of the theological concepts found in a different linguistic and cultural form in the New Testament, for example in Paul's language of the "old" man and the "new," of "flesh," "world," "body," "soul," "spirit," and so on. In the categories provided by Heideggerian existentialist phenomenology the theologian now has at his disposal a set of conceptual structures which enables the message of the New Testament to be expressed in a way intelligible to an age which no longer shares the language of Paul or John, and which cannot therefore encounter the theological message underlying the mythological language of the scriptures. Texts from the past are not dead letters, but can make a claim on us today.

All of Bultmann's theology subsequent to his extended encounter with Heidegger in the 1920s follows the same pattern, combining the insights of dialectical theology on the relationship of the divine and the human with the existentialist categories which enable the Scriptures to speak to the contemporary person. It is within the framework of this dual focus that Bultmann's "demythologizing" theology must be understood; it emanates from the concerns of hermeneutical theology with the exegesis and interpretation of ancient texts, but these texts require interpretation anew in order to allow their message to be heard clearly again. While there is a gap of understanding separating the horizon of early Christianity from the horizon of the modern scientific world, this is not, for Bultmann, a value judgment on the relative merits of ancient and modern worlds but simply a fact of historical consciousness. This gap can only be overcome by distinguishing the deeper meaning of the New Testament message from the mythological medium in which that message is expressed; we can retain the meaning but abandon the myths. Indeed, Jesus was himself subject to the mythological beliefs of his day and proclaimed in his preaching about the Kingdom of God an immanent apocalyptic end of the world, but as Bultmann put it laconically: "The same world still exists and history continues. The course of history has refuted mythology" (Bultmann 1958:14). Thus we can no longer believe in real places called "heaven" and "hell" or a literal virgin birth, but we must rather ask after the significance of these beliefs for our own religious situation today. Contrary to the critics who saw this as abandoning Christian truth to the spirit of the modern age, Bultmann replied that to demythologize is not to give up on Christianity but to recognize that it is not bound to an obsolete worldview. Christianity is not a theory about the world but a call to humanity to recognize the Word of God and place our trust in God rather than in ourselves or our scientific achievements. When this is understood, Bultmann appears as the quite orthodox Christian theologian that he was, attempting to preserve the core of Christianity while taking seriously the achievements of modern science and the cultural situation in which the modern person finds herself; as the methodological tools of his work he had the historical-critical method, the history of religions approach of his liberal teachers, and the hermeneutical categories of Heidegger, but this methodology was always applied within the framework of dialectical theology and its emphasis on the transcendental God who first of all addresses us and in whom alone true fulfillment can be found.

Bultmann's influence as a New Testament scholar is enormous, but the real significance of his work lies not in the detail of that scholarship itself, much of which has now been superseded, but in the methodological approach as such. In his two major works, *The Gospel of John* (1941) and *The Theology of the New Testament* (2 vols., 1948–53) he applied the demythologizing hermeneutic to great theological effect. His project was the explication through textual analysis of the theological interpretation of the New Testament authors themselves, but in this regard he had something quite restricted in mind. For Bultmann only John and Paul are truly theologians in the strict sense, because the theology of the New Testament only begins with the proclamation of the kerygma. Thus the first paragraph of *The Theology of the New Testament* sets out the key condition under which an explication of New Testament theology is possible: "*The message of Jesus* is a presupposition for the theology of the New Testament rather than a part of that theology itself . . . [and] theological thinking – the theology of the New Testament – begins with the *kerygma* of the earliest church and not before" (Bultmann 1952:1; italics in original). For the study of the message of Jesus as presented by Matthew, Mark, and Luke, Bultmann refers the reader to his earlier work on the Synoptic Gospels, but for theology he can only treat of Christ crucified and risen and proclaimed as such by the Church.

Bultmann's selective isolation of a truly "theological" New Testament is, of course, open to serious questioning on several grounds (which need not concern us here), but it must be recognized as consistent with his pessimism regarding the possibility and value of access to the historical Jesus and also with his theological Lutheranism. Bultmann's treatment of Paul, for example, in chapters 4 and 5 of *The Theology of the New Testament*, utilizes a basic tenet of dialectical theology, namely that theology speaks of God even though it cannot speak of God (this paradox is necessary for Bultmann to avoid any hint of metaphysics or natural theology); but it must nevertheless speak of God if it is not to lapse into silence, so it speaks of God by speaking of man, as we cannot speak of God in himself but only ever of God as significant for us. Bultmann's formulation of his position is precise: "Every assertion about God is simultaneously an assertion about man and vice versa" (1952:191). Paul's theology is both an anthropology and a soteriology, corresponding to the human person before and after the encounter with revelation. But theology is only possible under the conditions of revelation, and revelation as an event of encounter with the God who addresses me can only occur when I recognize myself as the sinner that I am, but at the same time justified by God (Luther's *simul justus et peccator*). Theology is, in the end, a sinful activity.

I do not propose to unravel all the difficulties contained in this understanding of theology, but simply to ask of the value of Bultmann's legacy for us today. All contemporary New Testament scholars are in some respects indebted to Bultmann, and his hermeneutical achievement alone – in placing the question of the analysis of one's pre-understanding of any text at the center of the interpretative endeavor – would place him among the most significant theological thinkers of the twentieth century. The achievement of demythologizing has been enormous in overcoming literalism in theology, but has also been replaced in the study of religion by a more positive appreciation of myth as the bearer of meaning. Biblical scholarship in the past 30 years has changed from a role of service to theology to an interdisciplinary subject which largely

brackets the theological concerns of an earlier generation. Dialectical theology's refusal
to countenance natural theology has issued in the silence it feared, and the demythologizing project which Bultmann saw as part of a constructive theology has itself been
radicalized and has given rise to the death of God theologies. Notwithstanding the limitations of the categories which Bultmann borrowed from Heidegger, the hermeneutics
of the early Heidegger utilized by Bultmann has long been replaced in literary and
textual criticism by a deconstructionist hermeneutics following Heidegger's later work
which, despite its own vacuousness, has served to make Bultmann's work look dated.
A theological context influenced by ecological, liberation, and feminist theologies is no
longer sympathetic to Bultmann's Lutheran theological anthropology based on a per-
sonalistic concept of faith expressed in existentialist categories.

So, although theology today is faced with many of the same questions faced by Bultmann, the mid-twentieth-century solutions now look less and less convincing. While
contemporary theology splits into various forms of reactionary orthodoxy on the one
hand and a growing post-Christian wing on the other, the attempt by Bultmann and
others of his generation to develop a confessional exegetical theology in the service of
the gospel message, but also adequate to the demands of modern scholarship, has taken
its place as an informative part of theology's own history.

The theology of Tillich shares Bultmann's concern with the meaning of the Christian message in the modern world but proceeds from a quite different focal point. As he
himself was well aware, Paul Tillich's theology is intimately bound up with the events
of his life and era. He was born in Germany in 1886, in an area east of Berlin which
was then part of Prussia and is now in Poland. His father was a Lutheran minister who
exhibited a characteristically Prussian authoritarianism and a stern presence, creating
an atmosphere for the young Tillich in which parental and divine authority were inter-
mingled. Despite the kindness and warmth experienced in the family, and his personal
admiration for his father, one of the great breakthroughs of Tillich's life was the struggle to overcome, both intellectually and practically, any external authority, a struggle
which is reflected throughout his work. Tillich's mother was in contrast, and by his own
account, of more lively demeanor and instilled in her son a less authoritarian attitude
and a love of life. She died when he was 17, giving rise to endless speculation later in
his life about the significance of this loss for his well-documented relations with women.

Tillich's education was conventional, but his own independence of thought and
many of the concerns of his later theology are present from an early age. The love of
Greek philosophy which he developed in the *Gymnasium* left him with a concern to
achieve a synthesis between Christianity and Greek thought, rather than an enforced
choice between the two, and is an abiding theme throughout his work. He studied theology at Berlin, Tübingen for a semester, and Halle, where he had Martin Kähler as his
teacher. From Kähler Tillich learned the deeper meaning of Luther's formulation of justification by faith, namely that one is justified while still remaining a sinner and – important for all of Tillich's later work – a doubter. Tillich's later expression of justification
as the capacity "to accept oneself as acceptable in spite of being unacceptable"
(1979:160) – which he took to be an overcoming of the existential condition of guilt
and condemnation – is indebted to this early influence. From Kähler Tillich also gained
an early appreciation of the problem of the relation of theology to culture, which

Kähler was struggling with in the context of his own developing suspicion of some elements of liberal thought. Tillich's own response to this problem was to permeate all his theology and result in some of his most creative and original work. At Halle also, Tillich made his first formal study of the German idealist philosophy of Kant, Fichte, Hegel, and, above all, Schelling, on whom he completed his doctoral thesis at the University of Breslau in 1910. In 1912 he gained his licenciate in theology from Halle and was ordained into the Lutheran Church.

Writing many years later, shortly before his death, Tillich expressed the view that the twentieth century really began on August 1, 1914, with the outbreak of World War I. He served throughout the war as a chaplain, mostly at the front, and experienced the horrors of mass death at first hand. He survived the conflict and two nervous breakdowns to emerge a changed man, and no adequate understanding of Tillich's theology is possible without an appreciation of the effect the war had on him. His youthful respect for the bourgeois world and the military infrastructure was replaced by a political consciousness which was to lead him to socialism and eventually to his emigration from Germany, but more significantly both his personal world-view and his conceptual grasp of Christianity were altered decisively by the war experience and by the attempts of European society to restructure its world in the aftermath, a period which Tillich described as a time of *kairos*.

Tillich's fist public presentation of his own thought came in 1919 when he addressed the Kant Society in Berlin on the topic "On the Idea of a Theology of Culture." This early lecture contains the kernel of his understanding of the balance to be achieved between culture and religion: the religious, correctly understood, is not a separated sphere either inferior or superior to the world of culture, but is the dimension of depth in all of culture. As Tillich developed this idea he came to express it in terms of the dialectical relationship between religion and culture in which neither the reduction of religion to naturalism, nor the suppression of culture by religious supernaturalism is acceptable.

Rejecting both the autonomy of pure naturalism and the heteronomy of religious supernaturalism, Tillich spoke of a "theonomous culture" in which concern for the unconditioned and ultimate is retained (thus "ultimate concern"). But this is not achieved through the heteronomy of religious authority. Rather, human freedom is preserved in the spiritual grounding that both reflects the human concern with the proximate, and transcends the proximate through the expression of an ultimate concern for that which is unconditioned and thereby holy. For Tillich religion itself, in its concrete manifestation as a separate realm from culture, is a sign of the fall, and while the gap between religion and culture may never be overcome in history, a theology of culture is the bridge which can keep the two poles of the dialectic intact.[4]

Throughout the 1920s Tillich developed his own theological ideas at the universities of Berlin, Marburg, Dresden, Leipzig, and eventually Frankfurt, where he was to remain as professor until leaving for the United States in 1933. In this period he widened his engagement with the major artistic movements of the time, particularly German Expressionism, as well as laying down many of the themes which were to come to fuller expression in his English lectures and writings and in the *Systematic Theology*, including the concept of the "demonic" in religion and culture, the elaboration of his own understanding of Protestantism, and the theological principles leading to his endorsement of a "religious socialism."

Also in this period, Tillich formulated his critique of Barth's "dialectical" theology. While his critique of Barth was not particularly influential at the time, it is of considerable significance in the context of the history of twentieth-century theology, for their respective viewpoints represent diametrically opposed theological responses to the challenge posed by the Enlightenment to Christian theology. In accepting fully the Kantian critique of the limits of reason, Barth sought to place theology as a human word always subject to the Word of the God who speaks *to* us, not *through* us. For Barth and his followers, the dialectical nature of all theology is contained in the "impossible possibility" of us being able to speak at all of God, who is utterly removed from us in his transcendence. Tillich saw in Barth the expression of the view that all natural theology, any engagement with culture as theonomous, and the utilization of philosophical ideas in theology, is wholly impossible. His critique of Barth rests on the insight that the Barthian position is ultimately not dialectics at all, but rather paradox, for dialectics involves a "yes" as well as a "no," an affirmation as well as a negation, and this "yes" is absent in Barthianism. In response Tillich defends the early Christian apologists' use of the concept of *Logos*, in which the divine may be encountered in history and in culture; granted, the history of religion is not synonymous with revelation, as the liberal tradition often mistakenly implied, but the radical Barthian corrective results in an answer to the human question which can only be alien to us and, in the end, unintelligible. For Tillich it is only when we transcend ourselves that we encounter the transcendent; but we can never claim to possess the transcendent, as Barth feared, for it is always ahead of us, bringing us forward in a dialectical movement where we are always engaged in both a yes and a no to our experience, our history, and our culture, both secular and religious. Tillich's exposure of the poverty of Barth's dialectic without a "yes" endures, as does his own positive dialectics of an affirmation and a negation, and is an incomparably more rewarding theological canvas to view today than contemporary pale reproductions of the Barthian project.[5]

In 1933 Tillich's *Die sozialistiche Entscheidung* was among the books proscribed by the Nazis and he was removed from his post at Frankfurt. After some agonizing, he left Germany with his family in the autumn of 1933 to take up a post at Union Theological Seminary, New York, at the invitation of Reinhold Niebuhr; he spoke no English and was unknown in the United States, but by the time he left Union in 1955 he was a nationally known figure.

In the postwar period Tillich's conception of culture and of the human predicament changed subtly but importantly. Notwithstanding the methodological emphasis on dialectic, Tillich's work from the 1920s and early 1930s expresses confidence in culture as the positive expression of the human quest for ultimacy; in the period following World War II this gave way to a more differentiated understanding of culture and a concern with the emptiness at the heart of all cultural expressions. Under the shadow of total destruction brought by the threat of the nuclear holocaust there is a void which is expressed in a culture of anxiety and meaninglessness, in which the power of expression of the depth dimension to our culture and religious activity is emptied of significance. Perhaps, thinks the Tillich of this period, it is only the void itself which can open to us the possibility of recognizing our ultimate concern. The culture of anxiety and meaninglessness which is the mark of our age poses a question about the value of human life as such, a question which goes to the heart of the meaning of Christianity and calls for a theological response. This is the meaning of "existential" for Tillich, the expression of a question articulated from the depth of the human condition about the possibility of meaning when meaning is apparently absent. But while the existential dilemmas of existence pose questions, and can even determine the form of the answer, the existential question cannot itself provide the answer but must rely on other traditions which have the symbolic power to provide a response. The task of the Christian theologian is to provide that response through the interpretation of the symbolic power of the Christian message (Tillich 1959:40–51).

Out of this existential question and the resultant task of systematic theology understood as apologetics came Tillich's theological method of correlation; this method of relating the Christian message to the human situation has always been prevalent in Christian theology but must now be consciously and outspokenly articulated to meet the apologetic task of the contemporary situation. Tillich defines the method of correlation as follows: "In using the method of correlation systematic theology proceeds in the following way: it makes an analysis of the human situation out of which the existential questions arise, and it demonstrates that the symbols used in the Christian message are the answers to these questions" (1951:62). Correlation requires an analysis of the human situation which in turn reveals something about the nature of human existence generally, i.e. an "existential" understanding. By "situation" Tillich means "the scientific and artistic, the economic, political and ethical forms in which [individuals and groups] express their interpretation of existence" (1951:3–4). The task of the theologian is then to articulate the symbolic response carried in the Christian message so that the answer to the existential question becomes meaningful in terms of the question itself. This interdependence of existential question and theological answer is the meaning of the term "correlation"; question and answer are correlated insofar as the *content* of the answer is given in the Christian symbol (e.g. Kingdom of God) and the *form* of the answer is given in the question articulated (e.g. what is the meaning of the tragedy and ambiguity of our historical existence?). The advantage of the method of correlation, argues Tillich, is that it enables theology to overcome other, inadequate, methods of Christian theology which gave answers to unasked questions ("supernaturalism"), derived the answer out of the historical religious culture ("naturalism" or "humanism"), or confused the answer with the form of the question ("dualistic" natural theologies).

The method of correlation requires on the part of the theologian – *qua* philosopher – a close analysis of the human situation as a situation of being-in-the-world, in the double sense of the permanent structures of existence as articulated by Heidegger in *Sein und Zeit* (*Being and Time*, 1927), or as a perceptive reading of the issues, questions, and even moods predominant in the artistic, literary, and socio-political culture of the contemporary era. Similarly, as Bultmann also realized in his own way, any Christian theology which would attempt to offer adequate responses to the questions asked by modernity will require a critical reappraisal of the major symbols of the Christian tradition, so that the Christian response is intelligible in terms of the form and context of the questions posed to it.

However, the mutual interdependence of question and answer, which enables theology to articulate answers to real existential questions about the human condition as such, does not for Tillich imply a reciprocal correlation; while the articulation of the question through an analysis of human existence is a properly philosophical task even if done, as it so often is, by a Christian theologian, the response given is always a theological response from within the perspective of Christianity. This should not be misunderstood as a simple fitting of ready-made answers to pre-formed questions, but rather as a complex activity of interpreting the human situation in the context of an ongoing interaction between the message and symbols of the Christian gospel on the one hand and the questions which arise from the human situation on the other. Despite this caveat of the subtleties required in the process of dialogue between Christianity and the contemporary culture, Tillich's restriction of correlation to a question-and-response structure places limits on the extent to which the method as articulated by him could be employed effectively in inter-religious dialogue or interdisciplinary work and, indeed, these issues were not Tillich's main concern. However, his theological heirs, such as Langdon Gilkey, David Tracy, Hans Küng, and others, have developed and expended the method of correlation to involve a reciprocal or mutual correlation which enables a most positive, dynamic, and critical engagement of Christian thought with other religious and cultural traditions in the pluralistic context which characterizes the contemporary situation. Tillich's method of correlation can therefore be rightly acknowledged as a decisive influence on some of the most fruitful theological work achieved in the past half century.

The method of correlation is employed by Tillich throughout the body of his work as a theologian, but comes to full expression in his *Systematic Theology* (3 vols., 1951–63). In formulating his systematic theology, Tillich did not create a system in the way in which that term is sometimes understood in philosophy and theology, namely the rationalistic deduction of a set of truths from more fundamental principles; by "systematic" he meant coherent, interrelated, and consistent of method, for Christian theology is simply "the methodical interpretation of the contents of the Christian faith" (1951:15). In the *Systematic Theology* this interpretation takes place in correlation with philosophy, in particular the existential ontology which for Tillich is fundamental to a theological response to the question of being. The most fundamental theological question is the question of God and the most fundamental ontological question is, by definition, the question implied in being as such; therefore, in terms of the method of correlation, what is required of theology is an analysis of the ontological question as asked by the human condition and a corresponding analysis of the symbol "God," which is theology's answer to this question.

The analysis of the question of being as posed by the human condition involves us in an existential analysis of finitude, for the character of the human encounter with being is that it takes place always in the shadow of the threat of non-being, that is, under the condition of finitude (which may be defined as "being, limited by non-being"). Tillich's analysis here is indebted both to Hegel and to Heidegger (and to a tradition of theology going back before them) for an ontology which is historical rather than static, thus escaping the implied criticism of Sartre and others in the atheistic existentialist tradition which claims that an ontology or theology of the human condition is impossible because it is necessarily dependent upon a static anthropology which denies human freedom. But to be human is to be in and of history, and theology and ontology treat of human nature as historical; the mark of a historical being is finitude and the question of being as asked by us is always the question of how to counter the threat of non-being, whether we encounter it as the threat of the loss of meaning (Sartre) or the loss of being itself in death (Heidegger).

The theological response is the symbol "God." Tillich's concept of God is controversial but greatly influential. He rejected the tradition which thinks of God as the highest being, for this is to place God within the set of things which might or might not exist and to make God subject to the categories of finitude; but God is being-itself, beyond both essence and existence, and to argue for the existence of God as if God were a being among other beings is finally to deny God. The God who is the answer to the question implied in human finitude is the God revealed through the capacity of the finite to assert something about the infinite. This is possible because everything finite participates in being-itself, and this participation is mediated through the power of the religious symbol and experienced through the human concern with the ultimate, which is what we mean when we speak of God. Given that God, for Tillich, can never be the God of classical theism about whose existence or not we may argue, it is perhaps unsurprising that when he stated categorically that "God does not exist" (1951:205), Tillich was understood by some to be advocating atheism. But his concept of God is richer and more profound than such accusations imply; Tillich understood as few others did that under the ontological and epistemological conditions of finitude our religious symbol "God" necessarily involves a dialectical relationship between belief and unbelief, because God can never be an object of our cognition in the way that objects in the world are. In the end, faith in God is only possible through an act of courage which enables us to recognize the God beyond theism as *"the God who appears when God has disappeared in the anxiety of doubt"* (1979:183; italics in original).

This analysis of being and God under the condition of finitude becomes Part 2 of the *Systematic Theology*, and the pivotal point of Tillich's thought. Part 1 of the *Systematic Theology* treats of the epistemological question raised by reason, to which revelation is the symbolic response. While for Tillich ontology is the most fundamental philosophical question, he sees the question of epistemology as contained within the question of being. He therefore treats epistemology first, on the grounds that in situations "where an ontological tradition has become doubtful . . . the question arises whether the tools used in the creation of this tradition are responsible for its failure" (1951:71). Theology, however, always finds itself in the position of having to make explicit its epistemology in anticipation of its ontology because its way of knowing appears so different from the ordinary ways. However, Tillich insists, epistemology can never ground theological truths and any theology adequate to the task must be prepared to explain its epistemology within the framework of an already-existing ontology. The remainder of the system proceeds on this basis: Part 3 of the *Systematic Theology – Existence and the Christ* – contained in volume 2 (1957), and Parts 4 and 5 – *Life and the Spirit* and *History and the Kingdom of God* – contained in volume 3 (1963), each follow the method of correlation by relating an ontological analysis of different aspects of existence to a critical reinterpretation of the appropriate theological symbol. Part 3 analyzes the estrangement of our existence and correlates this with the theological symbol "Jesus who is the Christ"; Part 4 deals with the ambiguous nature of all religion and culture in terms of the Christian theological symbol of "Spirit"; Part 5 treats of the meaning of history in terms of the symbol "Kingdom of God."

Each of these parts of the system merits a full discussion which space here does not permit, but of particular note is Tillich's Christology in Part 3, which is among the most interesting, yet controversial, aspects of his thought. The existentialist analysis of our estrangement from the ground of our own being facilitates a creatively original re-interpretation of traditional theological concepts, including the fall, sin, unbelief, and concupiscence. In response to the estrangement of existence symbolized by these tra-ditional theological categories is correlated the "Christ," the "New Being," which expresses "the universal human expectation of a new reality" (1957:88). The true Christian paradox is contained in the claim that the New Being who achieves the con-quest of estrangement in his own person is Jesus of Nazareth; in the person of Jesus proclaimed as the Christ we encounter the one who brings "salvation," understood by Tillich as "healing," "overcoming the split between God and man, man and his world, man and himself" (1957:166). Thus, for Tillich, "Christology is a function of soteriol-ogy" (1957:150). That is, the question of the possibility of the Christ arises out of the question of the possibility of the healing of a broken – "estranged" – world. Christol-ogy is also the product of ecclesiology, in the sense that the Christ is only the Christ when received as such by the Church; in this regard Tillich shares the emphasis of the "dialectical" mid-century theology on the present experience of the Christ-event over and against any quest after the Jesus of history. Both cross ("a symbol based on a fact") and resurrection ("a symbol and an event") combine elements of history and myth to differing degrees, and taken together are the primary interdependent symbols which express the claim that Jesus is the Christ. However, it is finally only "the certainty of one's own victory over the death of existential estrangement which creates the cer-tainty of the Resurrection of the Christ as event and symbol" (1957:155); this certainty can never be achieved by searching after historical verification or through recourse to extraneous religious authority, biblical or ecclesiastical.

From this it should be clear that how Tillich's theology of the saving event of cross and resurrection is interpreted *vis-à-vis* traditional Christologies and soteriologies will depend in turn on how his concept of "symbol" is read. Put simply, do we read in Tillich's concept of symbol a "deep" interpretation of the underlying truth of the bib-lical and creedal formulations or a "surface" interpretation which empties them of tra-ditional objective reference in favor of an existential resolution within the human person? While unavoidable in the light of his influence and contemporary debates over realism and non-realism, this juxtaposition does not in the end do justice to Tillich's dialectical method which aimed to retain both elements of the polarity. For someone with such a profound sense of paradox, it is fitting that Tillich's formulation of the over-coming of this particular mark of estrangement is sufficiently rich for him to be inter-preted variously as the savior of the classical theology or its destroyer.

Tillich's theological reputation was at its highest during the years preceding his death, and while interest in his work has never waned there are elements of it which, combined with changes in the concerns of our era, make it appear more dated than it actually is. For a generation less attuned to the language of classical ontology, and German idealism in particular, Tillich can appear as adopting unnecessary circumlocutions in getting around to the practical questions of existence (as indeed his American students often pointed out). Further, in an intellectual context in which all metaphysics has suffered the attacks of deconstructionism his work is always in need of sympathetic and philosophically literate defenders for it to be fully appreciated. But as the destructive influence of deconstructionism begins to wane, Tillich's systematics, along with the historical ontology of the early Heidegger, could become one source for a revitalized theological metaphysics. The question of existential estrangement as presented by Tillich also seems not to fit the mood of the present age; existentialism as a historical movement seems to belong to a package of secular salvation myths which have been themselves critiqued (Freudianism, Marxism, capitalist expansionism), and in the light of feminist, liberationist, and ecologist theologies the question of salvation is no longer asked in the same way as it was in Tillich's working life. But far from consigning Tillich to the dustbin of history a new impetus to the central concerns of his work is called for in the new context. His method of correlation as developed by David Tracy and others is of enduring importance in offering a methodology which allows the creative interaction between contemporary culture and the symbols of a religious tradition; his understanding of the nature of the divine offers possibilities beyond the limits of the classical metaphysics and the futile debates over God's existence engendered thereon; his understanding of natural law and its relation to theological ethics, while having its roots in Kant, is an under-explored dimension of his work; and, most importantly, his concern with the theonomous depth of human culture in any age can offer contemporary secular culture in the West the possibility to emerge from its present darkness to regain its lost connection to its religious origin. The tragedy of Western culture since the Enlightenment has been its failure to re-appropriate the symbolic power and depth of its own religious tradition which, in fighting again and again the battles of the past, it has all too easily left in the possession of reactionary forces. Of all modern thinkers Tillich is perhaps the one best placed to offer us creative possibilities for the overcoming of this estrangement.

Notes

1   See Bultmann's *Autobiographical Reflections* in Kegley (1966:xxiv), where he explicitly rejects the position that Christian theology must be thought of in this way.
2   Hermann's position on the relationship between the faith of the Christian believer and the historical Jesus should be read in the light of the exchange with Martin Kähler following the publication of Kähler's *Der sogennante historische Jesus und der geschtichliche, biblische Christus* (1892) which was a defining event in the future of the historical Jesus / Christ of faith debate.
3   Barth (1952:52); trans. Fuller (1962). For a full account of the Barth/Bultmann debate on hermeneutics see Jeanrond (1991:127–48).
4   See both Tillich's essays, "On the Idea of a Theology of Culture" (1919) and "Religion and Secular Culture" (1946) in Taylor (1987:35–54, 119–26).
5   See Tillich (1935). Commentators who see in Tillich and Barth, despite their obvious differences, a close structural similarity in terms of a systematics based on dialectics fail to under-

stand that the profound theological differences are grounded in the very understanding of the nature of dialectic and are not alternative conclusions from the same starting point. This error is made, for example, by Braaten and Jenson (1995), where Barth and Tillich are included together in a chapter titled "New Systematics."

References

Barth, K. 1952. "Rudolf Bultmann: ein Versuch ihn zu verstehen," *Theologische Studien* 34:52 (Zurich).

Braaten, C. E. and Jenson, R. 1995. *A Map of Twentieth-Century Theology: Readings from Karl Barth to Radical Pluralism.* Minneapolis, MN: Fortress Press.

Bultmann, R. 1952. *The Theology of the New Testament,* vol. 1. London: SCM Press.

Bultmann, R. 1958. *Jesus Christ and Mythology.* New York: Charles Scribner's Sons.

Bultmann, R. 1971. *The Gospel of John.* Oxford: Basil Blackwell.

Fuller, R. H. 1962. "Rudolf Bultmann: an Attempt to Understand Him," in *Kerygma and Myth,* 2. London: SPCK.

Jeanrond, W. G. 1991. *Theological Hermeneutics: Development and Significance.* New York: Crossroad.

Kegley, C. W. 1966. *The Theology of Rudolf Bultmann.* London: SCM Press.

Taylor, M. K. 1987. *Paul Tillich: Theologian of the Boundaries.* Glasgow: Collins.

Tillich, P. 1933. *Die Socialistische Entscheidung.* Potsdam: Alfred Prolle. (English translation: *The Socialist Decision,* trans. Franklin Sherman. San Francisco, CA: HarperCollins, 1977.)

Tillich, P. 1935. "What is Wrong with the 'Dialectic' Theology?" *Journal of Religion* 15:127–45.

Tillich, P. 1951. *Systematic Theology,* vol. 1, Chicago: University of Chicago Press.

Tillich, P. 1979. *The Courage to Be* [1952]. Glasgow: Collins.

Tillich, P. 1957. *Systematic Theology,* vol. 2. Chicago: University of Chicago Press.

Tillich, P. 1959. *Theology of Culture.* London: Oxford University Press.

CHAPTER 24
Von Balthasar

Mark McIntosh

Few such major theologians of the modern era have understood their tasks as broadly as Hans Urs von Balthasar (1905–88). Theology in the more academic sense was for him always a collateral enterprise, something he developed in service to his work as a spiritual director, publisher, and leader of a religious community. Von Balthasar chose never to hold an academic teaching position in spite of numerous prestigious invitations over many years.

From the time of his youth he had an enormous love for music and literature, and his doctoral training was in the field of German literary studies. In 1928 he completed his dissertation at the University of Zürich, examining the changing interpretation of human destiny in German literature and philosophy. The following year, after a profound sense of calling during an Ignatian retreat, von Balthasar entered the Jesuit novitiate. After the wide-ranging and interdisciplinary nature of his doctoral work, he found the academic neo-scholasticism of his Jesuit training to be fairly constricting. The theologian-in-making took refuge during this period in a massive revision and extension of his dissertation, later published in three volumes (1937–9) as *The Apocalypse of the German Soul*. This critique of German idealism and its more ominous tendencies was presciently aware of its times; the final volume bore the subtitle *The Divinization of Death*.

As the war began, von Balthasar chose to take up work as a student chaplain in Basle. He had been exposed during his Jesuit training to the efforts of French Roman Catholics to recover and re-appropriate the patristic sources of Christianity. Now he began a similar though even broader task which was to become a lifetime's publishing work, an almost continuous project of translating, editing, and anthologizing Europe's cultural heritage and its Christian roots. Until his death, von Balthasar remained involved in various series of such publications, always seeking to make available to the present the best of the great tradition in literature, drama, poetry, philosophy, and religious thought. Especially notable in this area are his translations of the poets and dramatists Péguy and Claudel and his lengthy books on such novelists and writers as

Georges Bernanos and Reinhold Schneider. The more overtly theological side of this task of exploration and recovery was manifested in his translations and original books on Origen, Gregory of Nyssa, and Maximus the Confessor. Central ideas from each of these thinkers developed into crucial insights in von Balthasar's later work.

During the 1940s a close theological friendship and discussion began to develop between von Balthasar and Karl Barth, fostered perhaps by their mutual love of Mozart. Barth's christocentric impulses were abidingly fruitful in von Balthasar's thought, and while neither thinker converted the other (and von Balthasar was famous for effecting conversions), their respective theologies are perhaps more reciprocally illuminating when studied together than any other pair of twentieth-century theologians. Another encounter, undoubtedly the most significant of von Balthasar's life, also began in this period, namely his spiritual partnership with Adrienne von Speyr, one of the first woman physicians in Switzerland. Her conversion and subsequent baptism by von Balthasar in 1940 was widely noted. Thereafter von Balthasar's role as her spiritual director led him deeply into a life-transforming mission. Her spiritual gifts were authentic and overwhelming in von Balthasar's eyes, and together they founded a religious community and a publishing house as vehicles for sharing and mediating von Speyr's spiritual insights. Von Balthasar spent countless hours recording Adrienne's dictations, eventuating in some sixty volumes of her work. In 1950 von Balthasar took the painful step of leaving the Society of Jesus in order to continue this theological mission with von Speyr. Part of the difficulty stemmed from the Society's concern that it would not be able adequately to support the Community of St John which von Balthasar and Adrienne von Speyr had founded. This community was to remain at the center of his life's work. An institute for laypersons who continued to hold regular secular jobs, the Community is a place of spiritual formation and contemplative mission. Many of the most central themes of von Balthasar's theology are crystalized in von Speyr's thought and in the Community's objectives, which were designed to give concrete form to those insights: in particular one notes the Christological vision of obedience to mission, the silent but often costly readiness to allow the Gospel to become luminous in the world by means of the vehicle of one's own life. Von Balthasar's brief, potent, and lyrical work *The Heart of the World* provides a vital introductory glimpse into the mutual theological vision that continued to shape his life and work long after von Speyr's death in 1967.

The remaining twenty years of von Balthasar's life continued to be hectic and overwhelmingly busy with lectures, retreats, endless correspondence, work for the publishing house and the Community, and a debilitating series of illnesses. Amazingly, it was during this period that his greatest theological work was written: the fifteen-volume trilogy in which theology is orchestrated according the three transcendentals of the beautiful (*The Glory of the Lord*), the good (*Theo-Drama*), and the true (*Theo-Logic*). The Dominican Cornelius Ernst once wrote that "theology is an encounter of Church and world in which the meaning of the gospel becomes articulate as an illumination of the world." This would be a valuable way of understanding von Balthasar's great project. In each "panel" of the triptych, the writer is concerned to show how the most fundamental patterns and structures of human culture are purified, redirected, and consummated in God, how the world is illuminated precisely as it is taken up into a lived exposition of the Gospel.

So, in *The Glory of the Lord*, von Balthasar examines the processes of human esthetic perception in order to lead the reader to an awareness of the enrapturing power of Being; and this is made concrete, visible, and actually achieved in the living, dying, and rising of Christ: the visible form (the Beautiful) of the concrete universal (Being), which can only be perceived in the world we have made as the One who is despised and crucified. Similarly, in *Theo-Drama*, the dramatic structures of human life are exposed to illuminate the real goal and purpose of human freedom, as that becomes enacted precisely in terms of the infinite self-giving of God (the Good) in Christ. Finally in *Theo-Logic*, von Balthasar analyzes the ways in which human understanding and the apprehension of truth are embraced within and transformed by God's speaking and self-understanding (the Truth) in Christ and the Holy Spirit. Or, in his own most lapidary formulation: "A being *appears*, it has an epiphany: in that it is beautiful and makes us marvel. In appearing it *gives* itself, it delivers itself to us: it is good. And in giving itself up, it *speaks* itself, it unveils itself: it is true (in itself, but in the other to which it reveals itself)" (von Balthasar 1993:116).

In the later years of his life von Balthasar reiterated an abiding theme in his work, the intrinsic connection between theology and holiness. In interpretations of mystical figures such as Thérèse of Lisieux and Elizabeth of Dijon, in a variety of theological analyzes of prayer, and in the context of countless retreat presentations and brief essays, von Balthasar stressed the inherently objective, social, and theological significance of Christian spirituality. In an important later work, *The Christian State of Life* (*Christlicher Stand*, 1977; English translation 1983), essentially a theological explication of the theme of vocation, von Balthasar draws on years of work with the *Spiritual Exercises* of Ignatius to free the self from a Cartesian incommunicado and a Kantian disjunction between consciousness and reality. For von Balthasar the unity of the self with the world is guaranteed by the radically relational structure of human selfhood. In his view, human personhood and identity come to fulfillment precisely as the person is called forth into a communal mission in the world – a movement, even an *ekstasis*, that is itself grounded in the trinitarian processions that constitute the Divine Persons. The differences between this perspective and the transcendental analysis of human subjectivity that plays so important a role in the thought of Karl Rahner sometimes led to disagreements between the two sons of Ignatius.

One of von Balthasar's most astute commentators has remarked that "for all their mutual esteem," Rahner and von Balthasar "never understood each other at a really deep level. Rahner's starting point was Kant and scholasticism, while von Balthasar's was Goethe and the Fathers" (Henrici 1991:38). This also helps to explain von Balthasar's concern that theology not understand its present task as necessarily falling into either a grim retreat to bureaucratic pronouncements (he had already argued vigorously against such a trajectory in 1952 with *Razing the Bastions*) or else an overly optimistic accommodation to modernity's most basic tendencies (an option he criticized very sharply in 1966 with *The Moment of Christian Witness*). Instead von Balthasar was tireless in advocating a confident missionary engagement with the world. He frequently approached this task by employing a Goethe-like genealogical taxonomy of cultural forms and ideas, showing how the Christian pattern of life and thought intersected and swept up human history into an utterly unforeseen yet overwhelmingly apt fulfillment.

It is significant for contemporary theology that by adopting this approach von Balthasar offers a phenomenological, cultural, even political alternative to the kind of universalizing metaphysical claims about which postmodern thought has begun to raise many important questions.

Hans Urs von Balthasar died on June 26, 1988, as he was preparing to celebrate daily Mass. Two days later he was to have been elevated as a cardinal.

Theological Habits of Mind

Certain key motifs can be found throughout von Balthasar's thought and a brief survey of them may prove a useful tool in navigating his theology. Generally speaking, these are habits of von Balthasar's theological mind and they tend to shape his approach to most questions, but they should only be taken as pointers toward what is always a lively and flexible approach to theology.

The ever greater

This theme, drawn from von Balthasar's study of Gregory of Nyssa and his Ignatian spiritual heritage, emphasizes the infinity of God's trinitarian life. Because God is an eternal activity of self-giving among the Divine Persons, reality and being are best understood in terms of event and act rather than essence. The eventful character of being is therefore always in motion. Creation, revelation, the Incarnation, are all extensions in time of the ever greater trinitarian activity of self-giving love. What takes place in Christ, for example, is not simply the figural representation of something that is always already everywhere true anyway, so that once having grasped the meaning of the (symbolic) historical event, one might no longer need an actual event in time (Kant). On the contrary, for von Balthasar the *kenosis* of Golgotha is grounded in the eternal mutual *kenosis* of the Divine Persons, and as such has a new, eventful significance even for God; it is a particular, actual unfolding of the infinite possibilities inherent in the trinitarian relationality.

Inclusivity

Since all particular beings are created within the activity of the ever greater trinitarian life, all realities and especially all forms of human relationality are never simply overcome or transcended but can become apt expressions of the divine relationality. Creaturely forms such as culture, language, social solidarity are all natural conversation partners with theology. The ultimate significance of cosmic life and human personhood become apparent as creaturely existence is drawn not into a completed, static divine silence that negates the creaturely, but precisely as the creaturely is included within the divine trinitarian super-expressivity which is the mutual life of the Divine Persons. In this way the creaturely becomes more alive, more itself, by being embraced and included as an element, a "part of speech," within the "speaking" that is God's own life.

The objectivity of form

Human understanding of God is not primarily a correlate of innate human insight or a supposed transcendental quality to human knowing and willing. Rather is it the response to the concrete and objectively present forms of God's self-disclosure. Von Balthasar is uniformly suspicious of any reading of human interiority that might tend to isolate it from the other and especially to ignore the power of objective form to shape and even enrapture the knower. The process of human understanding is therefore irreducibly relational and social. Thus both contemplation and action in the world are forms of attentiveness to Christ; they are not the search for an inner truth but the means of interiorizing and apprehending by personal interpretation the public truth of God's work in the cosmos. Hence for von Balthasar human growth and knowledge emerge as one places oneself at the disposal of the other, above all in loving obedience to Christ. The objectivity of the divine self-disclosure is not less objective for being unfolded and interpreted organically in the life of believers.

Calling and mission

Von Balthasar understands the call to participation in the divine life as fundamental to creaturely existence. Central to his theology is his vision of the trinitarian Persons as constituted precisely by their relational processions. And the particular processions of the Word and Spirit include but are not reducible to their missions in time and human history. For von Balthasar this is what it means to be a person, to be in relational self-giving with the other. And human personhood is itself most consummately achieved as every individual participates uniquely in the trinitarian mission of the Word made flesh. Jesus comes to a full recognition and enactment of his personal identity as God's Beloved as he is drawn to respond to the Father's love by radical availability for the human other. In this sense von Balthasar sees the ever greater call of the human other as the sign and beckoning of the divine Other, and it is by faithful response to this calling that human beings become who they are created to be. This becomes most clearly enacted as the Church fulfills its mission as the Body of Christ, the *Spiel-raum*, the playing space or stage upon which every human life discovers its true meaning and fulfillment through participation in the mission of Christ. Through the process of discerning and following one's call within the mission of the eternal Word, every human person makes the crucial transition from mere role-playing to authentic personhood; and at the same time the meaning of the trinitarian missions becomes luminous in concrete lives of human persons. The openings here for dialog with various forms of phenomenological thought, perhaps that of Levinas in particular, are very intriguing.

Plurality and synthesis

Von Balthasar certainly believes that theology is not simply a reflection upon states of human self-transcendence nor propositional speculation about divine truths. The infinite fruitfulness of the trinitarian life means that theology is always drawn beyond itself into the mystery of God's own life. Because of the infinitely new and unfolding expressions of self-giving in the Trinity, the creaturely apprehension of trinitarian fecundity is quite naturally plural and variously concrete. The participations of the saints and mystics in the interior mystery of Christ are not to be overlooked in the task of theology. Theology's goal is not to reduce this plurality of silence by a process of rational abstraction but rather to render all the concrete forms translucent to their ever greater and ever ungraspable synthesis in God. Rational coherence is not the only "logic" for theology, which must always point toward a multidimensional and pluralistic synthesis of faith and action, form and content, truth and obedience, all converging in the primordial concreteness and self-giving of the trinitarian life.

The Trinitarian Ground of Being

By now it will be clear how entirely von Balthasar's trinitarian vision permeates his thought. His trinitarian theology is, however, rooted in his understanding of Christ; it is not speculative but an attempt to take seriously the historical events of Jesus's ministry, death, and resurrection for our understanding of God. He regularly criticizes what he sees as gnosticizing tendencies in theology that make so much of the eternal heavenly reality that the historical events of Jesus's life seem only pale reflections (e.g. von Balthasar 1990a:34 and 94).

Von Balthasar analyzes the radical self-giving of Jesus to his neighbors and so finally to God, and he sees this *kenosis* as both freely given and constitutive of Jesus's identity. It is the momentum that seems to carry him through his whole ministry and reaches consummation on the cross and the realized public form of that self-bestowal in the Resurrection and Pentecost. Drawing importantly on his study of Maximus and on his Ignatian concept of mission, von Balthasar arrives at a crucial sequence of conclusions: the personal identity of Jesus is given in and with his mission, his mission is defined by a radical relationality and self-giving toward the other, the ultimacy of this self-giving is nothing less than the expression in human history of God's trinitarian relationality. Jesus's life, death, and resurrection become the interpretive key to understanding both who he is (doctrine of the Incarnation) and what the condition for the possibility of his appearing is (doctrine of the Trinity).

First the Incarnation. Von Balthasar adopts a strongly Chalcedonian Christology, emphasizing that the union of the divine and human in Christ is not according to the order of nature or essence (as though the divine "essence" were simply another kind of essence that had somehow to be filtered into the human version of it). Rather, the union of divine and human in Christ is according to the order of person. Jesus is a fully human being with all the psychological and biological characteristics consistent with humanity, but the identity that he enacts (the personhood that constitutes *who* he is) is realized in the concrete shape of his mission. And this mission is to be the Word of God, to enter completely into what is most other than the Father and speak the divine love even there, something that can only be accomplished by bearing the fearful separation of the creature from God and resting in utter solidarity with those who have come to be most alienated from God (descent into hell). Doing this is who Jesus is, and it is a personal identity so radically in relationship to the Father that the earliest Christians were, in von Balthasar's view, quite justified in coming to understand Jesus's identity, his personhood, as nothing less than the enactment in time of a divine pattern of existence. By the time of the Cappadocians, this perception, which had been aroused by Christ, has been further specified: "God" is no longer captive to a divine essence, but is recognized as being an infinitely living event of personal self-giving. In other words, the vulnerable human obedience and love which the church has met in Christ comes to be understood as the speaking in time of an aspect, a Person, of God.

Von Balthasar's interpretation of Christology highlights what he takes to be the most remarkable feature of the early Church's experience, namely that the only conceivable condition for the possibility of what has happened in Jesus is itself God's own life. Nevertheless, von Balthasar is keen to avoid any hint that Christianity's new understanding of God thus subjects God to a new kind of necessity: "Even if it is true that the coming to light of the inner-trinitarian mystery in the dispensation of salvation lets us see something of the law of the immanent Trinity, it is nevertheless impossible to deduce from the inner law that this going-forth [of the Incarnation] was necessary" (von Balthasar 1990a:215). So just as Jesus freely chooses to give himself away to the other, the divine ground of this self-giving must be understood as super-eminently a free act. The divine act of existence is, in von Balthasar's view, constrained by no putative laws of "divine essence" but rather the divine essence is itself the eternally constituted event of the free, mutual self-giving of the Divine Persons. God is "free to do what he will with his own nature. That is, he can surrender himself; as Father, he can share his Godhead with the Son. . . . In generating the Son, the Father does not 'lose' himself to someone else in order thereby to 'regain' himself; for he *is always* himself by giving himself. . . . (Without grasping this there is no escape from the machinery of Hegelian dialectic)" (von Balthasar 1990b:256).

It is precisely this divine self-bestowal, this "othering" which is God's life, and it is also this that makes possible a created other, and even the possibility that creatures may share in the divine life without losing their creaturely reality and freedom: there is room within the event of God's "othering" (trinitarian) life for the creature's own kind of otherness. In fact, von Balthasar argues that it is precisely the divine delight in the trinitarian communion of Persons that assures the distinctness of the Persons and a respect for their mutual otherness: "Something like infinite 'duration' and infinite 'space' must be attributed to the acts of reciprocal love so that the life of the *communio*, of fellowship, can develop" (von Balthasar 1990b:257). This holding open a place for the genuinely other in God is not some kind of cosmic individualism but exists precisely for the sake of a real event of love, an eternal overcoming and delighting in infinite otherness. This is the very basis of the divine life and, in von Balthasar's view, it is this "room" for otherness, expectation, and fulfillment in God that grounds genuine creaturely participation – as an other in the Other – in the trinitarian *perichoresis*.

Here, then, we can see the basis for the union of the divine and human in the eternal Person of the Word. If the basis for union were simply divine essence *per se*, Jesus's human existence would inevitably slide toward an absorption into the divine, to the loss of his real humanity. By contrast von Balthasar suggests that Christ's radical and perfectly human self-giving has made it possible for the church to recognize, as the ground of Jesus's existence, an infinite self-giving in God. This is a self-giving so free, so constitutive of life that it can only be understood as "personal," as having a hypostatic existence quite beyond the inexorable requirements of any essence or nature. Jesus's humanity is "personalized" and enters into life according to the particular pattern of divine self-giving which we call the Word or Son of God.

Indeed von Balthasar argues that as the church comes to participate more and more profoundly in Jesus's mission, a deeper and deeper apprehension of the inner trinitarian life becomes possible. There is this unmistakable reciprocal motion in Balthasar's thought: the historical impact of Jesus opens up within the church a sensibility for what God's life must really be, and the more this life is participated in, the more its patterns and fruitfulness are recognized, in the form of Christ, as the very ground of all creaturely existence. In his early study of Gregory of Nyssa (1942; von Balthasar 1995), von Balthasar had already noted the Cappadocian's significant break with Origen in stressing the infinity and incomprehensibility of God. And what most struck von Balthasar about Gregory's conception of the divine infinity was its complete rootedness in God's triunity. God's infinity does not lie, in other words, in an absolute divine essence lying somehow beyond the historical missions of the Word and Spirit. Rather, the radical incomprehensibility of God is itself an aspect of the infinitely mysterious and fruitful self-bestowal of the trinitarian Persons.

Von Balthasar sees this new apprehension of God as emerging in the church's encounter with Christ. The concrete actuality of the cross, especially, confronts the usual religious and metaphysical aspirations of humankind, arresting humanity's ever ascending inner quest for God as the purest form of an imagined common being. The crucifixion jolts humanity out of this natural religious quest; instead, von Balthasar sees the church's life being constituted by the ever new event of the radical personal freedom of Christ, and by the ground of Christ's freedom in the free decision of the divine Persons to exist and to exist precisely by a mutual self-giving. This opens for the church an awareness of reality beyond nature/essence, namely the radical freedom of the Divine Persons' mutual bestowal of existence: the act of existing comes to be seen as a new thing, an event that is not simply another necessary manifestation of nature but something that is ontologically ecstatic, personal, free, and yet irreducibly social and relational. It is this new awareness that, in von Balthasar's view, has even now still to be completely unfolded in the church's life and thought:

> This is the immense revelation that has been granted to us by the Incarnation: God is Life. Most certainly he had appeared to us, from the time our desire had its first awakening, as that Ocean of Being that our thought would never be in a position to capture. . . . we believed that becoming and Being were opposites. . . . Through the Incarnation we learn that all the unsatisfied movement of becoming is itself only repose and fixity when compared to that immense movement of love inside God: Being is a Super-Becoming. (von Balthasar 1995:153)

The implications of this insight from his early patristic studies would continue to be worked out throughout the Balthasarian *oeuvre*. Not only does the infinite vivacity of this *trinitarian* "giving place" to the other make room for a real *creaturely* freedom and becoming, it would also become for von Balthasar the condition for the possibility of the Incarnation and redemption. The complete abandonment of the Divine Persons one to another in love and freedom represents a divine form of "powerlessness" which includes within itself all possible earthly manifestations:

> We shall never know how to express the abyss-like depths of the Father's self-giving, that Father who, in an eternal "super-kenosis", makes himself "destitute" of all that he is and can be so as to bring forth a consubstantial divinity, the Son. Everything that can be thought and imagined where God is concerned is, in advance, included and transcended in this self-destitution which constitutes the person of the Father, and, at the same time, those of the Son and the Spirit. God as the "gulf" (Eckhart: *Un-Grund*) of absolute Love contains in advance, eternally, all the modalities of love, of compassion, and even of a "separation" motivated by love and founded on the infinite distinction between the hypostases – modalities which may manifest themselves in the course of a history of salvation involving sinful humankind.   (von Balthasar 1990a:viii–ix)

Several points need unfolding in this very important passage. It is clear that for von Balthasar the divine reliability, or, to use the older terminology, the divine immutability, is grounded not in some unchanging divine essence (which would need to be kept pristinely secure from the variability of earthly life) but in the activity of the trinitarian processions of self-giving love. This makes it possible for von Balthasar to conceive of the deepest possible interaction of God in Christ with the suffering and transformation of the world. The sinful brokenness of the world and its alienation from God is capable of being embraced within the ever greater relationality of the Divine Persons. The infinity of mutual trinitarian self-abandonment is an eternally ecstatic giving of love, but when this same pattern of "othering" is enacted within the fragmented life of *our* world it takes the form of the dereliction of Golgotha and, in the resurrection, the declaration by the Spirit of the super-abundance of the divine loving. "God, then, has no need to 'change' when he makes a reality of the wonders of his charity. . . . All the contingent 'abasements' of God in the economy of salvation are forever included and outstripped in the eternal event of Love" (von Balthasar 1990a:ix).

So von Balthasar does not accept anything like a Process account of divine reality. God does not in any way need the universe in order to become more completely God through some process of temporal development. And yet, for all that, von Balthasar is able to envisage a real "becoming" in the ever more of the trinitarian relational life, and this fruitfulness can include the participation of the creatures in the historical missions of the Word and Spirit. But how, exactly, can von Balthasar hold that these creaturely participations are non-necessary to God and yet also represent a real gift with real significance in the unfolding of the Trinity?

We have already noted how von Balthasar learned from Gregory of Nyssa a new conception of divine perfection which is not a philosophical vision of static being but a Christologically-centered apprehension of God's infinite vivacity, a "super-becoming" which is the ever greater unfolding of the mysterious personal event of love. This is especially significant because it highlights the central role played by trinitarian personhood in von Balthasar's thought, not only as the explanation of the ever more in God's life, but as the ground and basis for all human personhood. In other words, God is God precisely in the mystery of personal loving, always full of yet more surprise, expectation, and richness in the unfolding of the personal relations by which God's reality as Love is constituted. Quoting, significantly, from the work of Adrienne von Speyr, von Balthasar writes:

> We can say that, if human love is enlivened by the element of surprise, something analogous to it cannot be excluded from the divine love. It is as if the Son born of the Father "from the outset surpasses the Father's wildest expectations". God loves despite his omniscience, constantly allowing himself to be surpassed and surprised by the Beloved.   (von Balthasar 1998:79)

The more the Divine Persons abandon themselves to one another, the more they unfold and delight in the mutual giving. There is no end to the giving away, because the act of this divine giving is itself not constrained by a prior divine essence but is purely the free personal decision of the Divine Persons to exist in no other way than by giving place to the other. Perhaps the simplest analysis of this complex of ideas in von Balthasar lies in his conviction that what is principally revealed in Christ is Love itself, divine life as the freely chosen loving of one another by the Divine Persons. The pure gratuity of this personal love grounds both the divine existence and also the non-necessary existence of the universe. But this personal freedom also means that there is "room" in God's life for an infinite unfolding of "gifts" as the modes by which the Divine Persons *are* eternally by being *for* one another. There is a kind of blissful playfulness in von Balthasar's conception the Divine Persons' infinite mutual expectations and fulfillments. God's activity in creation and redemption can be seen as utterly gratuitous, but thereby also of real significance in the mutual divine delighting of the trinitarian Persons: "the inner participation of creatures in the life of the Trinity becomes an internal gift from each Divine Person to the Other" (von Balthasar 1998:507).

In a sense we could say that the universe is, in von Balthasar's view, God's way of dramatizing God's love for God. The wonderfully various and freely existing life of creatures is a particular mode of trinitarian delighting and self-giving. And this is nowhere more so than when in Christ the reconciliation of the world to God becomes itself an endlessly costly and cherishable self-offering of God:

> It is not a pale image of heavenly truth that is acted out on earth; it is the heavenly reality itself, translated into earthly language. When the Servant here below falls to the ground tired and spent from the burden of his day's labor, when his head touches the earth to adore his God, this poor gesture captures in itself all of the uncreated Son's homage before his Father's throne. And the gesture forever adds to this eternal perfection the laborious, painful, inconspicuous, lusterless perfection of a human being's humility.   (von Balthasar 1979:50)

The inclusion of humanity in the trinitarian self-giving is not necessary to God, nor does it complete God in some way, yet because we are talking about God not in terms of a fixed divine essence but as the event of triune love there is a sense in which creaturely participation in triune life "adds" something to God: it is a new expression of the continually unfolding desire of the Persons to be *for* One Another. Consider an analogy.

If someone gives her beloved a gift, this does not exactly mean they have more love than before, but it *is* a significant expression of their love and a new manifestation of their ever unfolding relationship. "Infinite richness is rich in freedom and can enrich others (and hence itself) in ways that are ever new; all the more so, since absolute richness lies precisely in the gratuitousness of giving, which presupposes a will to be 'poor', both so that it may receive and so that it may expropriate itself" (von Balthasar 1998:509). In von Balthasar's view we catch a glimpse of this poverty of the Divine Persons, this divine desire to live completely from and for the Other, in the poverty and helplessness of Bethlehem and Calvary. And for that reason the only authentic revelation of God's trinitarian self-abandonment for the Other must take place in a way that elicits this pattern of existence in creaturely terms. That is why the divine self-communication takes the form of vulnerability, in order to awaken a corresponding love within the crea-turely life: in this way God's self-giving life is "spoken" and becomes incarnate as Jesus, precisely as humanity is drawn forth into an answering self-giving love. This human participation in God's life is a real event of God's self-communication and self-sharing. It is a concrete unfolding in time of the infinite possibility of love among the Divine Persons, expressed as the rescuing embrace of the creature's lost existence.

Holiness and Truth

The ever more of the trinitarian richness has of course very definite implications for anthropology, the work of theology, and the human journey towards the truth. If the divine existence and unity are not simply a necessary given, but rather, in von Balthasar's view, the eternally delighted achieving of the Divine Persons' self-giving, then humankind created in the divine image is going to bear the trace of a similar momentum toward the other. Furthermore, the process by which the human commu-nity comes to understand something of God's life and to move toward an ever greater apprehension of truth is also going to be marked by a profoundly concrete and exis-tential calling, a lived availability for truth. The world will come to understand the truth of reality only as it "is able to take the divine things it has received from God, together with the gift of being created, and return them to God as a divine gift" (von Balthasar 1998:521). In this sense von Balthasar's anthropology and epistemology are markedly "eucharistic," shaped and fulfilled by participation in the historical self-giving of the Word to the Father in their Spirit. Far from thinking that knowledge and faith are sep-arate, let alone opposed, faculties of human life, von Balthasar is convinced that worldly knowledge comes to its own proper fulfillment in faith. The broken and isolated shards of the world's being are rendered luminous in their true meaning as they are assem-bled by faith in the light of God's absolute self-giving in Christ, as they are made once more into an offering, a participation in the divine dialog.

We noted above how for von Balthasar every human being comes to the fullness of life not in a solipsistic way but exactly by means of availability and obedience to the call of the other. This mission and obedience awakens a human being from sheer biologi-cal persistence into the freedom and ever greater mystery of true personhood, in direct created analogy to the constitutive mutual self-giving of the Divine Persons. While there is a receptivity to the other inherent in being for the other, there is also a sense of worth and dignity, of having been entrusted with that which is unfathomably significant to God. There is an awakening of mobility, strength, and personal freedom as one's commitment to mission begins to turn into the discovery of one's authentic personhood and identity.

For example, in his treatment of Thérèse of Lisieux, von Balthasar explicates her active self-surrender in terms of this new growth in freedom and authority: "The result is something far removed from passivity which slackly waits on the turn of events, or resignation which bows its head in advance to whatever is to come. Her attitude remains intensely active; she is ready to plunge into the fray. . . . Surrender, *abandon*, is a human act, the highest of human acts since it passes over into the omnipotence of God" (von Balthasar 1954:242). Importantly, obedience for von Balthasar must always be characterized by freedom and love, and apart from these it degenerates into dangerous forms of oppression. Love alone makes obedience authentic, for it transforms what might have been merely an external obligation or demand into a free choice, because the desire of the beloved becomes also the desire of the lover.

This growing access of personal freedom and responsibility reflects the spiritual transition that von Balthasar likens to the shift from mere role-playing to mission, from an artificial kind of play-acting to a new apprehension of one's true identity and authenticity. And for von Balthasar this transition is possible, as human beings are aroused by the calling of the Word, by the concrete participation in the mission of Jesus. Obedience to this mission is no alien passivity because it is in the image of the Word (i.e., the Word's relationality to the Divine Other) that every human being is created. Thus the individual awakening into personhood has begun to sense that the Word is "the truth of me and about me; the word which reveals me and gives me to myself. For we have been created in this word, and so it contains our entire truth, the whole concept of each of us, a concept so unimaginably great and beatific that we would never have thought it possible" (von Balthasar 1986:26).

Already we can see here important implications for von Balthasar's understanding of truth. Humankind in its creaturely nature is accustomed to knowing things that are graspable, items of finite nature. When this tendency comes into play with respect to the Truth, who is ultimately the free, personal God, then conceptual knowledge is indistinguishable from idolatry – all the more sinister for being so metaphysically refined. Human knowing of the divine, then, is most authentically apophatic and is far more appropriately undertaken in terms of continuing personal conversion and obedience to the call of God. And because the mission into which God calls the human is its own truth and freedom as a person, human knowledge of God is most likely to be apprehended not in terms of objective knowledge of certain truths about "something" but in terms of a developing sense of one's own personal identity in God. The human being's personhood, discovered in mission, is itself the language by which God speaks to him or her.

In a real sense the entire theological aesthetics (*Glory of the Lord*) is an analysis of the event whereby the truth of divine existence shows itself in the veiling of earthly form; in this process the human only comes to know the truth as it enraptures the knower and arouses interiorly a new way of living. This is a knowing of truth by means of a following in which the knower is literally "in-formed" by the truth, recognizing it through the apophasis of one's own life of discipleship. The final segment of von Balthasar's trilogy, *Theo-Logic*, begins by considering the habits by which humankind knows truth and the kinds of truths humans know, observing how the truth-knowing capacities of the world are ripe for transfiguration. This is only possible, however, if the convertibility of beauty, goodness, and truth with being itself is kept in mind. "The reduction of a knowledge of the truth to a purely theoretical kind of evidence from which all living, personal, and ethical decisions have been carefully excluded entails such a palpable narrowing of the field of truth that it is already thereby robbed of its universality" (von Balthasar 2000:18). But (in *Theo-Logic* II) human patterns of knowing are reintegrated with all three transcendental determinants of being, for they are taken up and transfigured in the Incarnation of the Logos. Human speaking and acting become in Christ the vocabulary within which the divine Word can come to expression in the words of a human life. And finally (in vol. III) the pneumatological process is explored, by which God the Spirit arouses the human spirit toward the personal journey into truth by participation in the mission of Christ.

The point in all this is that just as absolute truth is, in God, not a static thing, but an unfolding event of triune personal giving, so human apprehension of truth can only be something that "takes place" in the personal self-sharing of a faithful life. So the pursuit of truth draws one into an ever deeper personal encounter with God and yet arouses all the more wonder at the divine mystery:

> Where there is genuine personal love between two people, there is simultaneous growth in intimacy and in respect for the other person's freedom. So God cannot be simply the "Wholly Other" (and hence the Unknowable), but neither can the "revealed religion" become "religion unveiled", transmuted into some kind of absolute information about God. (von Balthasar 1990b:120)

The simultaneity of ever greater intimacy with ever greater mystery that marks personal knowing is a vital characteristic of truth. This self-surrendering quality of absolute truth is, in von Balthasar's view, indispensable to the world's own freedom and wholeness. For if worldly knowledge is cut off from the habit of self-giving love that is intrinsic to faith then it tends always to become a dominating utilitarian "knowledge." In such cases knowledge becomes merely manipulable, productive, and "the springs and forces of love immanent in the world are overpowered and suffocated." The result is "a world in which power and the profit-margin are the sole criteria, where the disinterested, the useless, the purposeless is despised, persecuted and in the end exterminated" (von Balthasar 1968:115). For the sake of the world, the world's own tendencies to reductive and impersonal knowledge need to be immersed in the habit of self-giving love. The inter-personal, trinitarian, ground of truth means that knowing and understanding always include personal involvement and transformation, delight in the illimitable richness of life, and reverence for the humility and availability to the other that mark authentic participation in truth.

Perhaps in this sense von Balthasar may be said to provide a measure for the adequacy and intelligibility of his own theological work: it is true insofar as it awakens in his readers real wonder, and real delight in expropriating oneself for the sake of understanding and loving the other.

References and selected further reading

Works by Hans Urs von Balthasar

1951. *Karl Barth. Darstellung und Deutung seiner Theologie.* Einsiedeln: Johannes Verlag. (*The Theology of Karl Barth: Exposition and Interpretation,* trans. E. T. Oakes, SJ, Communio Books. San Francisco, CA: Ignatius Press, 1992.) (Perhaps von Balthasar's best known work, a controversial and illuminating reading of his greatest Protestant interlocutor.)

1954. *Thérèse of Lisieux: The Story of a Mission,* trans. D. Nichols. New York: Sheed and Ward. (Originally published as *Thérèse von Lisieux: Geschichte einer Sendung,* 1950; reprinted with *Elisabeth von Dijon und ihre geistliche Sendung* [1952], in *Schwestern im Geist.* Einsiedeln: Johannes Verlag, 1970; English translation, 1992.) (With the work on Elizabeth, this is a prime example of von Balthasar's concern to rediscover the objective ecclesial and theological patterns disclosed in the supposedly "subjective" realm of the saints and mystics.)

1968. *Love Alone: The Way of Revelation.* London: Sheed & Ward. (Originally published as *Glaubhaft is nur Liebe.* Einsiedeln: Johannes Verlag, 1963.) (Though highly compressed, this is an excellent preliminary survey of the entire range of the trilogy; it could be complemented by the author's *Epilogue* (English translation, 1992), written as he concluded the last of the trilogy.)

1979. *Heart of the World,* trans. E. S. Leiva. San Francisco, CA: Ignatius Press. (Originally published as *Das Herz der Welt.* Zurich: Arche, 1945.) [A lyrical meditation on the Incarnation and Redemption, capturing already much of von Balthasar's sense of the drama and poignancy of the history of salvation. For an excellent introduction to this work, see the essay by A. Louth in Riches 1986.]

1982. *The Glory of the Lord: A Theological Aesthetics,* vol. I, *Seeing the Form,* trans. E. Leiva-Merikakis. Edinburgh: T. & T. Clark. See also vols. II–VII. San Francisco, CA: Ignatius Press, 1984–91. (Originally published as *Herrlichkeit. Eine theologische Ästhetik,* vols. I; II.1, II.2; III/1.1, III/1.2, III/2.1, III/2.2. Einsiedeln: Johannes Verlag, 1961–84.) (The first segment of the trilogy, according to the transcendental of beauty, containing a vast array of Old and New Testament interpretations as well as studies of major Balthasarian conversation partners and fascinating reflections on the relations between aesthetics, metaphysics, and theology.)

1983. *The Christian State of Life,* trans. Sister Mary Frances McCarthy. San Francisco, CA: Ignatius Press. (Originally published as *Christlicher Stand.* Einsiedeln: Johannes Verlag, 1977.) [A reading of central themes in the *Spiritual Exercises* of Ignatius of Loyola; an important elucidation of the spiritual underpinnings of much Balthasarian theology.]

1986. *Prayer,* trans. G. Harrison. San Francisco, CA: Ignatius Press. (Originally published as *Das Betrachtende Gebet.* Einsiedeln: Johannes Verlag, 1955.) (A theological study of contemplation written for members of the various religious groups founded by von Balthasar; exemplifies the integration of theology and spirituality in his thought.)

1990a. *Mysterium Paschale,* trans. A. Nichols, OP. Edinburgh: T. & T. Clark. (Originally published as *Theologie der drei Tage.* Einsiedeln: Benziger, 1969.) (A polyphonous interpretation of the events of Holy Week and Easter in which the integrity of Christ's mission and the church's life is explored from within.)

1990b. *Theo-Drama: Theological Dramatic Theory,* vol. II, *The Dramatic Personae: Man in God,* trans. G. Harrison. San Francisco, CA: Ignatius Press. See also *Theo-Drama,* vols. I–IV. San Francisco, CA: Ignatius Press, 1988–94. (Originally published as *Theodramatik,* vols. I; II.1, II.2; III; IV. Einsiedeln: Johannes Verlag, 1973–83.) (The *Theo-Drama* was regarded by von Balthasar as the most important part of the trilogy and contains his sustained treatments of anthropology, Christology, soteriology, ecclesiology, trinitarian thought, and eschatology.)

1993.   "Retrospective 1998," in *My Work: In Retrospect*, Communio Books. San Francisco, CA: Ignatius Press. (Originally published as *Mein Werk – Durchblick*. Einsiedeln: Johannes Verlag, 1990.) (Useful collection of essays by von Balthasar, attempting at five different points in his life to offer a synopsis of his concerns and work.)

1995.   *Presence and Thought: An Essay on the Religious Philosophy of Gregory of Nyssa*, trans. Mark Sebanc, a Communio Books. San Francisco, CA: Ignatius Press. (Originally published as *Présence et pensée: Essai sur la philosophie religieuse de Grégoire de Nysse*. Paris: Beauchesne, 1942.) (A fascinating early glimpse of crucial themes.)

1998.   *Theo-Drama: Theological Dramatic Theory*, vol. V, *The Last Act*, trans. Graham Harrison. San Francisco, CA: Ignatius Press. (See 1990b above.)

2000.   *Theo-Logic*, vol. 1: *The Truth of the World*, trans. A. J. Walker. San Francisco, CA: Ignatious Press. Originally published as *Theologik*, vol. I, *Wahrheit der Welt*. Einsiedeln: Johannes Verlag. See also vols. II and III. Einsiedeln: Johannes Verlag, 1985–7. (The final segment of von Balthasar's trilogy, according to the transcendental of truth; the second volume comprises a Christological interpretation of truth, and the third a pneumatology.)

2003.   *Cosmic Liturgy: The Universe According to Maximus the Confessor*, trans. B. E. Daley. San Francisco, CA: Ignatius Press. (Originally published 1941, as *Kosmische Liturgie: Höhe und Krise des griechischen Weltbilds bei Maximus Confessor.* Freiburg: Herder.) (Perhaps, as a single volume, one of von Balthasar's greatest works; crucial Christological and trinitarian insights carefully revised in the later 3rd edition, and centrally significant throughout his work.)

Secondary literature

de Schrijver, G. 1983. *Le Merveilleux Accord de l'homme et de Dieu, Étude de l'analogie de l'être chez Hans Urs von Balthasar*. Leuven: Leuven University Press.

Gawronski, R. 1995. *Word and Silence: Hans Urs von Balthasar and the Spiritual Encounter between East and West*. Edinburgh: T. & T. Clark.

Heinz, H.-P. 1979. *Der Gott des Je-mehr: der christologische Ansatz Hans Urs von Balthasar*. Berne: Herbert Lang.

Henrici, P, SJ. 1991. "Hans Urs von Balthasar: a Sketch of His Life," in *Hans Urs von Balthasar: His Life and Work*, ed. D. L. Schindler, Communio Books. San Francisco, CA: Ignatius Press.

Krenski, Rudolf. 1990. *Passio Caritatis: trinitarische Passiologie im Werk Hans Urs von Balthasars*. Einsiedeln: Johannes Verlag.

Lochbrunner, M. 1981. *Analogia Caritatis*. Freiburg im Briesgau: Herder.

McIntosh, M. A. 1996. *Christology from Within: Spirituality and the Incarnation in Hans Urs von Balthasar*. Notre Dame, IN: University of Notre Dame Press.

Oakes, E. T. 1994. *Pattern of Redemption: The Theology of Hans Urs von Balthasar*. New York: Continuum.

O'Donnell, J. 1992. *Hans Urs von Balthasar*. Collegeville, MN: Liturgical Press.

O'Hanlon, G. F. 1990. *The Immutability of God in the Theology of Hans Urs von Balthasar.* Cambridge: Cambridge University Press.

Riches, J. ed. 1986. *The Analogy of Beauty: The Theology of Hans Urs von Balthasar.* Edinburgh: T. & T. Clark. (See especially Rowan Williams, "Balthasar and Rahner.")

Scola, A. 1995. *Hans urs von Balthasar: A Theological Style*. Grand Rapids, MI: William B. Eerdmans.

PART V

Contemporary Issues

CHAPTER 25
Christianity and Other Religions

Ian Markham

Religious diversity has always caused strife for Christians, from the very beginning, and in this respect it is in line with Old Testament precedents. Ancient Israel had long been preoccupied, so the sources say, with the assertion of exclusive rightness for its devotion to Yahweh, and his Law, and the documents are full of attacks on those of other – i.e. false – religious allegiance. In the New Testament, there is both a confirmation of the rejection of pagan cults as idolatrous and a many-sided controversy about the question of the newness of the Christian faith. How far was it in conformity with Judaism? Had there been a radical break, or was there substantial continuity – and if the latter, then in what respects? In other words, was the faith that centered on Jesus a new dispensation or in some ways (what ways?) in continuity with the faith to be found in the Jewish scriptures?

As the Western Church developed, relations between the developing Christian tradition and other religions became more complex. Generally a commitment to the truth revealed in Christianity meant that those who disagreed needed to be confronted with their error. So the tradition is rich in vehement denunciations of Judaism.[1] However, this attitude also ran parallel with a willingness (whether deliberate or almost unconscious) to learn from and often build upon the insights of other traditions. Christianity was born into a Jewish culture which was strongly influenced by Hellenism (i.e. Greek culture). Plato and Stoicism are two leading schools of Greek thought that significantly influenced the Christian faith. The fifth-century Bishop of Hippo Augustine explicitly acknowledges in *The Confessions* his debt to the Neo-Platonists. Much later, in the thirteenth century, the Dominican Friar Thomas Aquinas helped to reintroduce Aristotelian philosophy into the Church as a result of his wide reading of Islamic thinkers. For many Christian thinkers, the Church has constantly much to learn from non-Christian thinkers, as these two examples illustrate. The indebtedness has of course sometimes been conscious, sometimes virtually unconscious.

The combination of hostility combined with occasional accommodation and mutual influence probably characterized the Christian attitude to other religions right up until the start of the twentieth century. It was at this point that certain distinctively modern questions came to the fore.

Other Religions as a Problem

The twentieth century saw a significant change in Christian attitudes to other religions. This was the century when "Religious Studies" as opposed to "Theology" became popular. (Convention uses the word "Theology" to denote the study of Christian theology, while Religious Studies refers to the study of a range of religions.) Instead of simply judging other traditions by the central doctrines of Christianity, the first task is understanding. Other faith traditions must be understood on their own terms. This tendency opened up a further set of problems. The ancient religions of India (rather inappropriately subsumed under the label "Hinduism") suddenly became more attractive: where the West had insisted for centuries that the world was a relatively recent creation, Hinduism found itself vindicated by contemporary science in believing that the world is millions of years old; and for all sorts of reasons the insistence in the West that a baby dying at two has enjoyed the same unique life as the person dying at seventy makes much less sense than reincarnation. When a religion comes to be treated on its own terms, it is no longer manifestly false or foolish.

So the first factor in shaping the problem of "other religions" was understanding the other on its own terms. The second factor was more philosophical; many Westerners, including Christians, had come to feel that they did not know for sure whether Christianity was the truth; in short there was a problem about epistemology (theory of knowledge). For the West it was chiefly the Scottish philosopher David Hume who created the problem. The argument was simple: a condition of knowledge is that we know with some certainty that something is true. Given that we know virtually nothing with that sort of certainty, we should stop using the category of "knowledge." Immanuel Kant talked about David Hume as "shattering his slumbers." For Hume, especially, knowledge of God was particularly problematic. How can you know whether it is a triune God or an Allah or a Hindu Brahman underpinning everything?

The problem with epistemology can be brought home forcefully with the following thought exercise: imagine that there is an agnostic sitting in the middle of a room. Imagine further that representatives of the major traditions are sitting around the room to present their faith. Let us further imagine that each representative is equally eloquent and clear. Having listened to each presentation in turn, you then turn to the agnostic and ask him or her to determine which religious tradition has the truth. Is it possible for the agnostic to decide?

With the reliability of Scripture being tested by the critical study of the texts and with the reliability of the Church being undermined by a critical study of history, the Church seemed to many to be no longer sure how best to justify faith with authority. This in itself created a further problem: if Christianity is true, then why did God not make it more obvious? Were the old authorities (Scripture, Church decisions, papacy) capable of exercising their traditional weight? The problem of epistemology became more acute when set alongside religious diversity. There are so many options: it is not obvious which one is the truth at all.

The third factor which shaped the problem for Christianity was internal to Christian doctrine. Traditionally Christians believe not simply that they hold a true description of the way ultimate reality is, but also that such knowledge is essential for salvation. In short one will be condemned to hell unless one is a Christian. However, although the Christian religion is the largest religion in the world, it still leaves at least 68 percent of the population who are not Christians. Is a loving God really going to condemn the majority of people to hell? Christianity here had an internal problem – in terms of reconciling some of its long-held but contradictory tenets and traditions.

The traditional response has been to insist that the Church should preach the Gospel to these other cultures and that people should be encouraged to convert. Studies have shown that only a small minority of people convert from one tradition to another. Religion is closely linked in with cultural identity; converting from one tradition to another is often interpreted as an act of betrayal. To put it crudely, a devout Roman Catholic grandmother of traditional outlook may understand the lapsed grandson who is "rebelling" against the Church, but will be deeply upset if he converts to Anglicanism or, even worse, Islam. It is because we feel committed to our families and cultural communities that conversion is so difficult – unless there has been some kind of cultural liberation.

So there are three factors which have come to pose the problem of religious diversity in a particularly acute form, namely, (a) a growth in our understanding of other traditions, (b) a belief that it is difficult to know for sure which tradition has the truth, and (c) the problem of a loving God who is presented traditionally as condemning large numbers of people to hell simply because of their commitment to their culture and faith.

The Christian theology of other religions has become, in recent decades especially, a well-established branch of Christian systematic theology. Any theological account must provide some explanation within the Christian schema of the role and status of the majority of the human race. The recent debate has been shaped by the British philosopher John Hick, whose student Alan Race (Race 1983), created the taxonomy that has come to be dominant. This taxonomy suggested three different Christian responses: pluralism, which insists that all religions are equally salvific (i.e. able to save); inclusivism, which believes that Christianity is the true religion, yet other religions are discovering the truths of Christianity without realizing it; and exclusivism, which insists that conscious knowledge of and commitment to Christianity is essential for salvation.

These three options will now be considered in detail.

The Pluralist Hypothesis

John Hick started formulating his pluralist hypothesis as a direct result of his encounter with other faith traditions. It was as the H. G. Wood Professor at the University of

Birmingham that he started developing links with the local faith communities. In *God Has Many Names* he compares various prayers taken from the Sikh, Hindu, Islamic, and Christian traditions. He notes the striking similarities and then argues that it is unlikely that only one tradition has effective prayers or that there is a different recipient for the prayers of each tradition. Given this, the best explanation is that each tradition is praying to the one true God using the resources and language of that tradition (see Hick 1980, ch. 4).

This is the heart of the pluralist hypothesis – a single reality that is accessed and partially revealed in all the major religions of the world. Over the next twenty years, Hick clarified the details.

To start with, Hick was advocating a "theistic pluralism." A single God, who was loving and good, was underpinning all the major faith traditions. He makes much in his earlier work of a contradiction embedded in Christianity: I Timothy 2:6 describes a God who "desires the salvation of all people," while John 14:6 insists that Jesus is the only way to salvation. If only one religion is salvific, then it cannot be true that God *effectively* desires the salvation of all people. The only way to overcome this contradiction is to believe that all religions are salvific.

"Theistic pluralism" works reasonably well for the Abrahamic faiths (i.e. Judaism, Islam, and Christianity). It might even, in certain ways, extend towards Hinduism, but it completely fails to cope with Buddhism. Buddhism takes innumerable different forms, but there are significant strands that hardly talk about "God" at all. God hardly figures in the four Noble Truths, which are the central teaching of the Buddha. So in Hick's Gifford Lectures, published as *An Interpretation of Religion*, Hick argues for a "Real," which no tradition can describe or claim to know exactly. In this way, the significance of Nirvana in Buddhism can be accommodated in the experience of the Real.

To explain this shift, Hick turns to the Kantian distinction between the noumenal and the phenomenal. The noumenal is knowledge of the divine as "it is in itself." The phenomenal is knowledge of the divine as "it appears to mind." The noumenal is inaccessible. All we know is that each culture is interpreting an "objective" experience of the Real in its own language and concepts. We cannot claim that any particular culture is more or less right, because none of us can transcend our own culture and find out exactly what the Real really is like.

Now there are a whole host of obvious questions facing Hick, which to his credit he confronts with complete clarity. The first is: how does Hick know that the major world faiths are all viable means of accessing the Real? He starts by acknowledging that the best explanation for the global phenomenon of religious experience is to assume that there is an objective reality which is being accessed (see Hick 1989, ch. 13). In addition, he suggests that if only one tradition was effective in accessing the Real, then presumably that tradition would be more effective in producing saints (i.e. for Hick, persons who are ego-transcending Reality centered; see Hick 1989:303). Empirically this does not seem to be the case. Insofar as one can judge, most traditions have been both deeply damaging and at the same time effective in saint production. Christianity is the tradition responsible for both the Crusades and the spirituality of St Francis of Assisi. So, argues Hick, it looks as if all world religions are equally able to produce saints and therefore are vehicles for the transforming power of the Real.

This flows into the second issue. On what criteria does Hick exclude traditions? Can witchcraft or the Branch Davidians become vehicles for the Real? Hick is careful here. Traditions that can be shown to be ethically destructive are not vehicles of the Real; so Nazism, insofar as it has certain similarities with a religion, is excluded on the grounds that it arrived at conclusions that are fundamentally opposed to the growing awareness of ethical insight in the major world faiths.

But he provides a further argument that appeals to the longevity of, at least, the big five (Hinduism, Buddhism, Judaism, Christianity, and Islam). He makes use of Karl Jaspers' concept of the "axial period"; a golden age (starting c.800BCE) when in different parts of the world, at about the same time, a common discovery about objective moral obligations that are grounded in the transcendent confronts humanity. The combination of Socrates in Ancient Greece, the Upanishads in India, Confucius in China, and the eighth-century prophets of Israel, gave birth to the main traditions that shaped the major world faiths. For Hick, it is likely that traditions emerging out of this period are likely to be valid vehicles of the Real.

The third issue is the status of distinctive doctrines within each religion: so Judaism believes that Yahweh gave a chosen people a land; Islam believes that the Qur'an is the final and definitive revelation from God; and Christians insist that Jesus is the incarnation of God. What is the status of these doctrines in Hick's scheme? His position is simple: any distinctive doctrine that conflicts with the pluralist hypothesis must now be interpreted differently from its traditional ways. As a Christian minister, he has attempted to offer alternative interpretations of certain key Christian doctrines. He was the editor of *The Myth of God Incarnate* (1977). This volume formulates a range of arguments, some emerging from Biblical criticism (many New Testament scholars think it unlikely that Jesus claimed to be God or that the earliest texts about Jesus thought of him in such a way), but others stressing rather more the implications of certain other doctrines and insights. It is the latter point that Hick makes central. He writes, "[W]e have to present Jesus and the Christian life in a way compatible with our new recognition of the validity of the other great world faiths as being also, at their best, ways of salvation. We must therefore not insist upon Jesus being always portrayed within the interpretative framework built around him by centuries of Western thought" (Hick 1977:182). For Hick, the pluralist hypothesis requires that we think of Jesus as a person who *shows us* God rather than who *is* God: what Keith Ward, in *A Vision to Pursue*, calls a "functional" Christology rather than an "Ontological" one. Paul Knitter, who develops Hick's arguments, suggests that the "exclusive" claims made for Jesus reflect the enthusiasm of Christians – it is analogous to the love language used between lovers (Knitter 1985). "My partner is the most beautiful person in the world" is rarely meant literally, nor is it always (over?)verifiable; for most of us, it simply means "my love for this person is so significant that I feel that my partner is very beautiful and the overwhelming object of my attention and devotion."

John Hick sets forth his hypothesis with commendable clarity. It offers an account of religious experience and religious diversity that makes sense of many puzzling features. However, it is interesting to note that the academy (not to mention the churches!) has tended to be suspicious of his position. So we turn now to consider the "exclusivist" alternative.

Exclusivism

Exclusivism is characteristic of most conservative forms of religion. Amongst Christians, the strongest defenders are found amongst conservative evangelicals. They almost always start with a commitment to (a) truth, and (b) revelation. Truth is important because they reject the tendency of pluralists to insist that contradictory religions can all be vehicles of the Real. Muslims believe that Jesus was (no more than) a prophet of Allah; Christians insist he is the Incarnation of God. If you accept the correspondence theory of truth (namely, that a correspondence with "reality" determines the truth or falsity of a statement), then these two assertions cannot both be true. One must be true and the other false.

If one decides that there are good reasons to believe in the Incarnation, then pluralism is not an option. The claim that in "reality" God became human in Jesus means that at least in one respect Christianity has knowledge of the Real which is both distinctive and superior. This links to the second commitment made by exclusivists. Knowledge of God, as opposed to guesswork or speculation, as Karl Barth explains, depends on "revelation." Humans can guess about the Real as much as they like, but it does not become knowledge unless the Real breaks in and reveals its nature to us. All religions base their claims for knowledge on revelation; in most cases, this takes the form of an authoritative text. The point is that unless there is some form of authoritative revelation, one cannot make a claim to knowledge.

One problem facing Hick is that he doesn't reckon to know very much about the "Real." To accommodate Buddhism, he cannot know whether the Real is personal or non-personal. All Hick has is an "objective" something, which is applying global pressure that generates religious experience; for many it seems tantamount to agnosticism.

But how does one know which revelation is the truth? Different exclusivists provide different answers. Some attempt to offer criteria to distinguish between different positions. For example, Harold Netland sets out ten principles that provide criteria to distinguish between different religions. He lists those principles as follows, where p stands for Principle and R stands for a particular religion:

P1:   If a defining belief p of a religion R is self-contradictory then p is false.

P2:   If two or more defining beliefs of R are mutually contradictory at least one of them must be false.

P3:   If a defining belief p of R is self-defeating it cannot reasonably be accepted as true.

P4:   If the defining beliefs of R are not coherent in the sense of providing a unified perspective on the world, then R cannot plausibly be regarded as true.

P5:   Any religious world-view which is unable to account for fundamental phenomena associated with a religious orientation or which cannot provide adequate answers to central questions in religion should not be accepted as true.

P6:   If a defining belief p of R contradicts well-established conclusions in other domains, and if R cannot justify doing so, then p should be rejected as probably false.

P7:   If a defining belief p of R depends upon a belief in another domain (e.g. history) which there is good reason to reject as false, then there is good reason to reject p as probably false.

P8:   If one or more defining beliefs of R are incompatible with widely accepted and well-
      established moral values and principles; or if R includes among its essential practices
      or rites activities which are incompatible with basic moral values and practices, then
      there is good reason for rejecting R as false.

P9:   If the defining beliefs of R entail the denial of the objectivity of basic moral values
      and principles; or if they entail the denial of the objective distinction between right
      and wrong, good and evil, then there is good reason for rejecting R as false.

P10: If R is unable to provide adequate answers to basic questions about the phenomena
      of moral awareness this provides good reasons for rejecting R as false.   (Netland
      1991:192–3)[2]

Having provided this extensive set of criteria, which includes coherence, and historical
and ethical principles, Netland then concludes triumphantly: "I should state that the
reason I believe one is justified in accepting the Christian faith as true is because it is
the only world-view that satisfies the requirements of all the above criteria" (Netland
1991:193).

Most contemporary theologians are not persuaded by this approach. The problem
with criteria is that the choice of them will depend on the tradition you are in. There
is a danger of creating a mutually affirming circle. Therefore most academic exclusivists
prefer the route suggested by Lindbeck. In his highly influential book *The Nature of
Doctrine*, Lindbeck argues for the "cultural–linguistic" approach to religion, where
"emphasis is placed on those respects in which religions resemble languages together with their correlative forms of life and are thus similar to cultures" (Lindbeck
1984:17–18). He sets this approach against experiential expressivism, which is very
similar to Hick's pluralism, and cognitive propositionalism, which is very similar
to Netland's exclusivism. For him, this approach comes into its own when it
comes to making sense of other religions. On the unsurpassability of a tradition, the
experiential-expressivist is able to claim "that there is only one religion which has the
concepts and categories that enable it to refer to the religious object, i.e., to whatever
in fact is more important than anything else in the universe" (1984:50), although he
does note that, on this view, traditions will almost certainly embody both true and false
claims about the nature of the religious object. On interfaith dialog, there are reasons
internal to the Christian tradition which justify it. For example, writes Lindbeck, "it can
be argued in a variety of ways that Christian churches are called upon to imitate their
Lord by selfless service to neighbors quite apart from the question of whether this promotes conversions" (1984:54). And on the salvation of other religious traditions, Lindbeck suggests the following:

> The proposal is that dying itself be pictured as the point at which every human being is
> ultimately and expressly confronted by the gospel, by the crucified and risen Lord. It is only
> then that the final decision is made for or against Christ; and this is true, not only of unbe-
> lievers but also of believers. All previous decisions, whether for faith or against faith, are
> preliminary.   (Lindbeck 1984:59)

Lindbeck is a highly sophisticated "exclusivist." Religious schemes are analogous
to "cultures." One learns the language and the form of life. The cosmic claims within

a tradition need to be taken seriously. One accommodates other religious traditions by recognizing that, for example, sharing the commandment to love your neighbor should be sufficient to compel dialog; and the decision for or against Christ is ultimately made at the moment of death.

Many conservative evangelicals consider the maneuvering of Lindbeck unnecessary. They start with "truth" and "revelation," and then work out the implications. The Biblical witness, they insist, teaches the following about religious diversity. First, many alternative traditions are guilty of idolatry, and are perhaps even inspired by a force of evil. Secondly, the Christian obligation is to preach the Gospel and attempt to convert those of other traditions. Thirdly, apart from our confidence that the judge of the earth shall do right, we should not try to speculate on matters that are not revealed; so we do not know exactly what will happen to those who have not heard, though Scripture certainly points us in certain directions.

Inclusivism

It is partly out of a sensitivity to the problem of the ignorant that many Christians are attracted to the third option. Inclusivism is the view that even though salvation is exclusively in Christ, faithful adherents of another faith tradition may be saved through Christ, even though they do not realize it in this world.

The best known exponent of Inclusivism is the Roman Catholic theologian Karl Rahner. He was enormously influential on Vatican II, which took his line. Rahner proposed four theses, of which the first three are the most significant. Rahner writes:

> 1ST THESIS: We must begin with the thesis which follows, because it certainly represents the basis in the Christian faith of the theological understanding of other religions. This thesis states that Christianity understands itself as the absolute religion, intended for all men, which cannot recognise any other religion beside itself as of equal right. . . .

> 2ND THESIS: Until the moment when the gospel really enters into the historical situation of an individual, a non-Christian religion (even outside the Mosaic religion) does not merely contain elements of a natural knowledge of God, elements, moreover, mixed up with human depravity which is the result of original sin and later aberrations. It contains also supernatural elements arising out of the grace which is given to men as a gratuitous gift on account of Christ. For this reason a non-Christian religion can be recognised as a lawful religion (although only in different degrees) without thereby denying the error and depravity contained in it. . . .

> 3RD THESIS: If the second thesis is correct, then Christianity does not simply confront the member of an extra-Christian religion as a mere non-Christian but as someone who can and must already be regarded in this or that respect as an anonymous Christian.   (Rahner 1966: V:118, 121–5, 127, 131–2)

Rahner is attempting to "make sense" of the phenomenon of religious diversity. The first thesis stresses that it is part of Christian self-identification that we believe that Christianity is true. But then, given that Christians believe that God is active in the whole world, we must believe that God is active in all religious traditions. Granted this runs parallel with much error, sin, and self-deception, supernatural elements of those traditions are still not excluded. As it is therefore possible for a tradition to be "lawful," then it must be possible for such a tradition to be a means of salvation.

The use of the term "lawful" is deliberately drawing attention to the status of the Hebrew religion in the Old Testament. Christians who insist that salvation is only possible through conscious acknowledgment of Christ have a problem with all those in the Hebrew Bible. Abraham, Jacob, David, the prophets are all clearly "saved," despite not consciously acknowledging Christ during their lives. One traditional response to this problem is to follow the traditional interpretation of I Peter 3:19 in suggesting that between his death and resurrection, Jesus descended into hell and preached the gospel to the Old Testament patriarchs. One problem with this is that the passage in I Peter probably did not carry this sense. It is better to suggest that God's salvific power in the Cross extends beyond time to reach many lives without their realizing it. The traditional doctrine of Christ as God's eternal Word suggests a mission extending throughout time and space.

The strongest argument for inclusivism, then, is that it is already embedded within the Christian tradition. When we try to make sense of the millions who have never heard of Christianity and all those who pre-date Christianity, we are led to postulate that God is able to save men and women without their realizing it.

Inclusivism represents the position of most more liberal Christians today. In the reply to John Hick's and Paul Knitter's influential book *The Myth of Christian Uniqueness* (1987), called *Christian Uniqueness Reconsidered: The Myth of a Pluralist Theology of Religion* (D'Costa 1990a), almost all the contributors are inclusivists. Gavin D'Costa suggests in his own five theses that inclusivism is the natural expression of a trinitarian world-view. D'Costa's five theses are:

THESIS ONE: A trinitarian Christology guards against exclusivism and pluralism by dialectically relating the universal and the particular.

THESIS TWO: Pneumatology allows the particularity of Christ to be related to the universal activity of God in the history of humankind.

THESIS THREE: A Christocentric trinitarianism discloses loving relationship as the proper mode of being. Hence love of neighbor (which includes Hindus, Buddhists, and others) is an imperative for all Christians.

THESIS FOUR: The normativity of Christ involves the normativity of crucified self-giving love. Praxis and dialog.

THESIS FIVE: The church stands under the judgment of the Holy Spirit, and if the Holy Spirit is active in the world religions, then the world religions are vital to Christian faithfulness.   (D'Costa 1990b:16–26)

D'Costa's position is simple: exclusivists make much of Jesus (the second person of the Trinity), though not much of Jesus as Logos, but lose sight of the Father and the Spirit: the Father who creates and sustains the whole world, and the Spirit who "blows where it wills." Pluralists have a God (a Father) at the heart of the universe and sustaining everything that is, but have no revelation or knowledge of that God (in effect, God the Son and God the Holy Spirit are missing). What we need is a trinitarian understanding of God, which provides both an account of the nature of the love that we should demonstrate to others and a way of seeing how God interacts with other religions.

Critical of the Categories

Many theologians have found the categories that have dominated the debate problematic. Some have pointed out that they conflate a variety of different issues. On the one hand, the central question is soteriological: are those outside the Christian religion saved? On the other hand, that question cannot be answered without considering a whole range of related matters: which religion is true, and how do you know which one is true or where and whether truth resides in the various great faiths? What about the status and significance of Natural Theology? What sort of knowledge of God is possible outside revelation?[3]

Consider, for example, the issue of truth. Anyone committed to the Correspondence Theory of truth will find themselves forced to a version of inclusivism. The correspondence theory states that "x is true if and only if x corresponds to the way things are in reality." So if Christians really believe that God, the creator of the universe, is a trinity, Father, Son, and Holy Spirit, then the trinitarian description of God must be better and more accurate than any other description of God. And if that is the case, then worshippers of other faith traditions might imagine that they are encountering Brahman or Allah or whatever, but in point of fact their encounter is with the Triune God. This is a form of inclusivism.

Even a pluralist, at this point, operates as an inclusivist. Pluralists insist that religious believers may imagine that they are encountering a particular God, described in their tradition as, say, a Trinity, but in point of fact they are encountering a Real which transcends all particular descriptions. If the pluralist hypothesis is true, then it means that the vast majority of adherents of most religions are mistaken and the "symbol system" (i.e. the vocabulary embedded within a particular world-view) of pluralism is what the orthodox are really discovering. A commitment to the truth of pluralism, ironically, makes the pluralist a kind of inclusivist.

Granted the inclusivism of pluralism only applies to "truth" and not to "soteriology," nevertheless Hick does provide a description of the way things are (albeit a highly attenuated one) which he believes is more accurate (corresponds more closely) than alternative accounts (i.e. those held by orthodox believers within each tradition).

Once one sees that the debate obscures a range of technical questions, then there are other options. Keith Ward has suggested a "soft pluralism" at the heart of his "open orthodoxy." Ward is unhappy with Hick's pluralism because it seems to rest on a "pragmatic theory of truth" (Ward 1994:310). Instead Ward wants to talk about more or less adequate accounts of ultimate reality and to say that all traditions contain some false beliefs. He rejects the label "inclusivist" because an inclusivist assumes that his or her tradition includes the best of other traditions, while a soft pluralist believes that other traditions have insights not known (or perhaps not known sufficiently well) within one's own. This is similar to the argument of the Roman Catholic theologian J. A. DiNoia (1992).

There are others who have suggested that the traditional paradigm is much more problematic than has been held. Kenneth Surin, in a brilliantly provocative article, suggests that pluralism is analogous to the infamous McDonald's hamburger. In much the same way that McDonald's sweeps the world, eradicating difference, and offering the same bland global food, so Hick's pluralism does the same thing. So Surin writes,

> The McDonald's hamburger is the first universal food, but the people – be they from La Paz, Bombay, Cairo or Brisbane – who eat the McDonald's hamburger also consume the American way of life with it. Equally, the adherents of the world ecumenism canvassed by the religious pluralists align themselves with a movement that is universal, but they too consume a certain way of life. Not quite the American way of life itself . . . but a single, overarching way of life which has become so pervasive that the American way of life is today simply its most prominent and developed manifestation: namely, the life of a world administered by global media and information networks, international agencies and multinational corporations.   (Surin 1990:20)

For Surin the whole question requires location. It represents the triumph of the Western values of tolerance and imperialism. Instead of imposing a pluralist description of other faiths on the rest of the world, we should listen and politically empower other faith traditions and free them from the tyranny of American power. The theological problem, argues Surin, needs to be eased out of our line of vision: the political problem is much more significant. We need to become "post-pluralistic" (Surin 1990:209).

Two other writers have challenged the traditional taxonomy and developed the debate in interesting ways. The first is K. P. Aleaz, from Bishops' College, Calcutta. He notes the dominance of European and American theologians in the debate and argues that these theologians need to learn to assimilate the insights of other religious traditions into Christianity. Christians in India have been using Hindu insights to shape their understanding of the Trinity and Incarnation. He calls this position "Pluralistic Inclusivism"(Aleaz 1998). The second is Mark Heim who, in two remarkable books, argued that God will realize many of the different and contrasting goals of the different religions. For Heim, the implication of the doctrine of the Trinity is that God intended religious diversity. In addition, we can expect that different lives after death will be realized for different religious traditions (Heim 1995, 2001). So, presumably, Buddhists, Muslims etc., will relate to the divine in the life to come in a different way from the Christians. This book has deservedly provoked considerable discussion as one can see from Paul Knitter's latest textbook introduction to the Christian theology of other religions debate (Knitter 2002).

Moving the Debate Forward

The taxonomy of "pluralism, inclusivism, and exclusivism" remains a useful introduction to the issues. Pluralism is a problem for most religious traditions. The particular truth claims made within each tradition are central to its identity. The Qur'an is central to Islamic identity; and the Qur'an certainly does not teach Hick-type pluralism! The Incarnation and Trinity are key to the Christian understanding of God; and no Church is planning to surrender such key doctrines.

Inclusivism is not popular in Interfaith circles. Bilal Sambur – a Muslim – is typical when he writes about Rahner's concept of the "anonymous Christian": "This concept does not have any contribution to interfaith relations, because people have freely chosen religion as their independent religious identity. Furthermore, that concept includes the disrespectful approach to human freedom and humiliates the religion of the other" (Sambur 1990:30). What Sambur ignores is that the equivalent of Rahner's concept is found in the Islamic doctrine of "people of the book." When the Qur'an affirms Christianity and Judaism as traditions of the book, it means that although Islam has the complete truth, Christianity and Judaism have a partial insight into that truth.

Given that any commitment to the truth of a tradition will entail some form of inclusivism to explain the phenomenon of disagreement, it is not surprising that such devices are found in all the major world faiths. The *Bhagavad Gita*, for example, is explicit: the followers of other gods are really discovering Krishna. Judaism talks about the Noachide Laws, which provide a mechanism for gentiles to have a covenantal relationship with their creator. Islam, as we have noted, has the "people of the book," while Christians have come to talk about "anonymous Christians" and formerly saw Christ the eternal Logos as having inspired both prophets and Greek philosophers.

However, inclusivism is inclined to suggest that we are all simply trapped in our traditions. It does assume that a tradition "includes" or "embraces" the other. Ward's "soft pluralism" is helpful here. Our growing historical and philosophical sensitivity has made us much more aware of the diversity within traditions. For example, there are strands within the Christian tradition which affirm panentheism, which has striking similarities with certain Hindu strands. Broadly "liberal" strands, those that take seriously the achievement of the Enlightenment, have more in common with liberals in other traditions than with the conservatives in their own tradition. Liberal Christians and Jews often find much common ground.

Our historical sensitivity makes us realize that all traditions have been influenced by other traditions. Christianity was born out of a combination of Hellenistic influences and Judaism. St. Thomas Aquinas in the thirteenth century learnt about Aristotle from Islamic thinkers and writers. Buddhism is clearly linked to Hinduism. And Sikhism emerged out of the clash between Hindu and Islamic cultures.

Learning of God from the other has always characterized our traditions, however little people like to recognize it. Continuing to do so is a social and political necessity. As Hans Küng (1991) repeatedly reminds us: there is no peace in the world without peace between the religions.

Notes

1   See Dan Cohn-Sherbok for a comprehensive survey of Christian anti-Semitism (1992).

2   Keith Yandell is another philosopher who has suggested a slightly different list of rational criteria which can be used to evaluate religions. See Yandell (1984), For a good discussion of this approach see Brad Stetson (1994).

3   This is theme of my article called "Creating Options: Shattering the 'Exclusivist, Inclusivist, and Pluralist' Paradigm" (Markham 1993:33–40). See also Gavin D'Costa's reply to my article, which follows that article.

References

Aleaz, K. P. *Theology of Religions: Birmingham Papers and Other Essays*. Calcutta: Moumita Publishers.

Cohn-Sherbok, D. 1992. *The Crucified Jew*. London: Fount.

D'Costa, G. ed. 1990a. *Christian Uniqueness Reconsidered: The Myth of a Pluralistic Theology of Religions*. Maryknoll, NY: Orbis.

D'Costa, G. 1990b. "Christ, the Trinity, and Religious Plurality," in *Christian Uniqueness Reconsidered: The Myth of a Pluralistic Theology of Religions*, ed. G. D'Costa. Maryknoll, NY: Orbis.

DiNoia, J. A. 1992. *The Diversity of Religions: A Christian Perspective*. Washington, DC: The Catholic University of America Press.

Heim, M. 1995. *Salvation: Truth and Difference in Religions*. Maryknoll, NY: Orbis.

Heim, M. 2001. *The Depth of Riches: A Trinitarian Theology of Religious Ends*. Grand Rapids, MI: Eerdmans.

Hick, J. 1977. "Jesus and the World Religions," in *The Myth of God Incarnate*, ed. J. Hick. London: SCM Press.

Hick, J. 1980. *God Has Many Names*. Basingstoke: Macmillan.

Hick, J. 1989. *An Interpretation of Religion*. Basingstoke: Macmillan.

Hick, J. and Knitter, P. eds. 1987. *The Myth of Christian Uniqueness*. London: SCM Press.

Knitter, P. 1985. *No Other Name? A Critical Study of Christian Attitudes to Other Religions*. London: SCM Press.

Knitter, P. 2002. *Introducing Theologies of Religions*. Maryknoll, NY: Orbis.

Kung, H. 1991. *Global Responsibility*. London: SCM Press.

Lindbeck, G. 1984. *The Nature of Doctrine: Religion and Theology in a Postliberal Age*. London: SPCK.

Markham, I. 1993. "Creating Options: 'Exclusivist, Inclusivist, and Pluralist' Paradigm," *New Blackfriars* 74 (January):33–40.

Netland, H. 1991. *Dissonant Voices: Religious Pluralism*. Grand Rapids, MI, and Leicester: Eerdmans and Apollos.

Race, A. 1983. *Christian and Religious Pluralism*. London: SCM.

Rahner, K. 1966. *Theological Investigations*, vol. 5. London: Darton, Longman and Todd.

Sambur, B. 1990. "Is Interfaith Prayer Possible?" *World Faiths Encounter* 23 (July).

Stetson, B. 1994. *Pluralism and Particularity in Religious Belief*. Westport, CT: Praeger.

Surin, K. 1990. "A 'Politics of Speech': Religious Pluralism in the Age of the McDonald's Hamburger," in *Christian Uniqueness Reconsidered: The Myth of a Pluralistic Theology of Religions*, ed. G. D'Costa. Maryknoll, NY: Orbis.

Ward, K. 1991. *A Vision to Pursue*. London: SCM Press.

Ward, K. 1994. *Religion and Revelation*. Oxford: Clarendon Press.

Yandell, K. 1984. *Christianity and Philosophy*. Grand Rapids, MI: Eerdmans.

CHAPTER 26
Economics and Social Justice

Martyn Percy

How are Christians supposed to engage with the world when they are, in truth, expecting a new world that is yet to come? Why bother with the temporal when minds and hearts are meant to be fixed on the eternal? What can theology offer the churches to help Christians of all persuasions maintain their poise and prophetic witness within a public and plural world? These questions pepper the pages of the New Testament as much as they have absorbed Christians for two millennia. On the one hand, Christians are called out of the world, and are to no longer regard themselves as belonging to it. On the other hand, they are to be engaged with the world in all its complexities and ambiguities as fully as possible, being salt, light and yeast in society, incarnating the life of Christ into the hubris of humanity. The apparent dilemma is expressed by one early Christian writer in this way:

> Christians . . . reside in their respective countries, but only as aliens. They take part in everything as citizens and put up with everything as foreigners. Every foreign land is their home, and every home a foreign land. . . . In a word: what the soul is in the body, that Christians are in the world. The soul is spread through all the members of the body, and the Christians throughout all the cities of the world. The soul dwells in the body, but is not part and parcel of the body; so Christians dwell in the world, but are not part and parcel of the world.   (Kleist 1948:139)

The unknown author of the late second-century *Epistle to Diognetus* expresses a paradox that is at the heart of Christian engagement with social ordering, the political sphere, and public life. He or she speaks for the first generation of Christians as much as for those of the twenty-first, by formulating the sense of divided loyalties that can sometimes threaten the very identity of the Church, and the place of Christians within the world.

Yet this tension – with all its possibilities and problems – is at the heart of the Christian gospel. The ministry of Jesus was inherently political in character as much as it was "otherworldly." The Gospel of John presents the reader with a Christ who calls

Christians out of the world, but at the same time leaves them in it (see John 15:19, 17:14, 18:36, etc.). In the same way, the radical words and actions of Jesus appear (at first sight) to point in opposite directions.

For example, consider the miracles of Jesus. Whatever significance may be attached to their historicity, it is the social and political implications that flow from these narratives that are the more compelling. Jesus seems to go out of his way to embrace the "untouchables" of society – lepers, the poor, the unclean, people of other faiths, and those who are marginalized because of their creed or color (Percy 1998:29). Jesus tends not to heal those who already possess significant social, moral, religious, or political status. Instead, much of his healing activity appears to question boundaries and taboos, theologies of taint and forms of social exclusion. Invariably, the healings question the social forces that divide society between the pure and the contagious, between the righteous and the sinner. Jesus, in other words, acts as an alternative boundary keeper, and his healing miracles (like many of his parables) fundamentally question the values that underpin the social ordering of his day, suggesting, or demanding, a radical reordering.

Yet to only understand Jesus as a radical interferer within the social order of first-century Palestine would be to ignore another dimension of his agenda: the Kingdom of God which is to come. The radical discipleship demanded by Jesus may be said to dwell less on reform and more on revolution. Employment and families are to be forsaken for the kingdom – the ushering in of the new reign of God. Even the dead can be left unburied (see Matthew 8:22; Luke 9:57–62). Moreover, the disciples are not to anticipate reward or rule in this life; all recognition of costly service and devotion is postponed until the *eschaton*, where the wheat will be separated from the chaff, and the righteous rewarded (Matthew 6:19–21). (In very early Christian tradition, the apparent imminence of the Kingdom of God led some to give up work, and others to lead a life of celibacy. But by the time the later documents of the New Testament were being written, Christians were being urged to respect and work with temporal authorities, get on with their ordinary labors, and begin to apply gospel principles to this life rather than speculating about the actual date of the *parousia*.)

These two distinct traditions within early Christian teaching are, of course, closely related. Each act of service (hospitality, charity, etc.), the extension of costly love (such as turning the other cheek, loving your enemies), and of vicarious sacrifice, points towards the kingdom that is to come. Within Christian tradition, the kingdom is the place where society is reordered; captives are liberated, the lame walk, and the blind are restored to sight (Luke 4:18–19). It is also the place where the poor inherit the kingdom, the mourners are comforted, the meek and the peacemakers rewarded, and the persecuted redeemed (Matthew 5:3–11). In other words, Christian social teaching anticipates the rule of God in prayer and action: "your kingdom come, your will be done, on earth as it is in heaven" (Matthew 6:9–13).

This tradition and teaching is reflected in the very first Christian communities. Stephen, the first Christian martyr, is a deacon with special responsibility for the daily distribution of alms to widows and orphans (Acts 6:1–3), reflecting the commitment to charity and service that is advocated in the Gospels. In character, the first churches, although diverse in practice and belief, appear nevertheless to have exhibited a radical openness to questions of parity and inclusion. The term for "church" is the simple Greek word *ekklesia*, meaning the "assembly of the people," who belong to but are called out of their community. All over the Mediterranean world, assemblies determined the politics, polity, and civic ordering of communities and cities. But they were usually only open to citizens, and the power to speak and vote was normally confined to men. The assemblies of the New Testament Church – the deliberate adoption of the more internationalist term must have caused confusion to potential converts, as well as making a point – were, in contrast, inclusive if alternative. In these *ekklesia*, women were admitted, as were slaves (see Paul's Letter to Philemon), children, foreigners, and other visitors. In other words, the character of the New Testament *ekklesia* represented and embodied a different kind of spiritual and social ordering that eschewed discrimination on grounds of race, gender, and other criteria.

Closely allied to the notion of *ekklesia* is its apparent antithesis, the *enclasia* – an idea developed by Coleridge (amongst others) to specify that Christians may not (only) be called out of the world, but are also called into it. Coleridge (1839) regarded the idea of *enclasia* as a gospel mandate. Christians were called to be a light to the world, the salt of the earth, and the leaven in the lump. Correspondingly, churches, for Coleridge, rather than being separatist and alternative bodies within their broader communities, were to be deeply embedded within the civic, social, and moral ordering of society, contributing to the overall commonwealth. The theological approach led Coleridge to justify the Church and State being closely interrelated for the sake of the common good.

From this brief introduction, it should already be clear that Christianity was, from the outset, an inherently political and social faith. Its expression always challenges the present world order, but is, at the same time, prepared to work within it, regarding nothing as being beyond redemption. It is incarnate, and yet also prophetic. At the same time, Christianity exhibits a typical feature of many world religions – etymologically, the desire to *bind* spirituality to life, and to make a difference to the present in anticipation of God's future. To consider the social and political character of Christianity further, the remainder of the discussion is grouped under three (somewhat arbitrary) headings: social order, political spheres, and public life. The categories are not exhaustive, and in an essay of this size it will only be possible to outline the dimensions of Christian thought within each arena. A conclusion will explore why theology and the churches continue to need more tenacity, acuity, and wisdom in their engagement with the contemporary world.

Social Order

It is a little-known fact that part of the Edict of Milan (313), which was an agreement between the emperors Licinius and Constantine to recognize the legal personality of churches, to treat all religions equally, and to restore lands and property confiscated under persecution, also made provision for donkeys. According to the agreement, Christians, calling on all others of good will, were to see that beasts of burden were not abused in transporting heavy loads uphill. Such concerns may seem trivial to modern readers, but the Edict provides an early piece of evidence to support the view that the

Christian faith had extensive interests in contributing to social order – even in the minutiae of everyday life. Generations of Christians would follow suit on other issues where prevailing standards and constructions of reality had to be undermined and cast aside if justice was to be done. The emancipation of slaves (Samuel Wilberforce), equality for blacks (Martin Luther King), or the alleviation of poverty (William Booth) are but a few examples.

The Edict of Milan is widely regarded as the point at which the foundation for established Christianity was first laid, although the Edict did not establish Christianity in the formal sense. The emerging Constantinian settlement did, however, provide a paradigm that was to influence much of Europe as it embraced Christianity. This was to link civic governance, religion, and the economy in the interests of providing sustainable patterns of social ordering that were of benefit to communities (such as the prohibition on usury). In England, for example, the relationship between a parish and its church was intrinsic to the identity of a place. Communities that were economically and socially viable were able to sustain a church and the ministry that issued from it, which in turn guaranteed a certain level of moral welfare, social improvement, and pastoral provision (including the availability of the sacraments). Or, put another way, the very existence of a parish church within a community confirmed the identity of the place, conferring it with recognizable significance that invited a form of social ordering in which (amongst other things) the needs of the poor and other matters of moral concern could be addressed on behalf of the community (Pounds 2001).

Similarly, many hospitals, schools, hospices, and other agencies for welfare (adoption, fostering, etc.) began their life as an extension of the pastoral provision of the churches, intended for the common good. Throughout Christian history, there have been many movements and individuals whose faith has spawned something particular that has directly contributed to the reordering of society. Christianity has been especially prominent in health care, welfare, and education, but has taken no less interest in the moral well being of society, most often manifest in areas related to sexuality and procreation, and in various arenas of censorship.

Readers with a more secular outlook on life might wonder at (and perhaps flinch away from?) a faith that aspires to shape society. How can one credo help order societies where there are many beliefs, and none? Are the interests of society not better protected by faith remaining private, and keeping out of the public arena? The fear of fundamentalism (or of religious oppression through the state) is what drives many secularist critics to distinguish sharply between church and society, and to maintain their separateness. Some secularists fear the advent of a theocratic hegemony, like the Republic of Gilead in Margaret Atwood's apocalyptic *The Handmaid's Tale*, the establishment of religion over and against all competing frames of reference (Atwood 1985). Equally, the fear of taint and dilution is what motivates a handful of Christian denominations to withdraw from the world in the interests of maintaining their purity and distinctiveness. In both world-views, religion and society do not mix, and should be kept apart where possible.

For the majority of the world's population, though, religion and society are inseparable; they mix, are mixed, and are not easily extracted one from another, or capable of being told apart. The shaping and ordering of societies invariably has a religious character to it; sometimes seen explicitly, it is more often than not implicit within many aspects of polity. Yet theologically, the ordering of society is a contentious arena. What sources and authorities are to be brought to bear upon pressing social issues? To what extent is a Christian world-view (assuming that this could even be agreed upon) possible in the complexity of the political sphere? What exactly is a Christian government? And what would the City of God look like? (From Augustine to Calvin and through to Milbank, the idea is seldom as attractive as it first appears.) There are many examples of types of Christian social ordering, but space permits only three to be discussed here for our immediate purposes. The theological outlooks to be briefly considered are social justice, social intervention, and social advancement.

The modern notion of social justice can be traced to nineteenth-century Christian Socialism in Britain, and the more dispersed notion of Social Christianity in the USA. (Liberation Theology is discussed as a separate approach in the second section of this essay, "Political Spheres".) The birth of Christian Socialism in Britain can be dated precisely: April 10, 1848. F. D. Maurice, John Ludlow, and Charles Kingsley, three theologians who were already prominent, met to consider a response to the Chartist demonstration that had petitioned in London for political reform. Motivated by a concern for the conditions of "working men" as much as they were motivated to relate the gospel to contemporary culture, Maurice, Ludlow, and Kingsley produced a series of tracts that were to have a significant impact on the social and ideological landscape of Britain (Atherton 1994:1–49).

The presuppositions of the early Christian Socialist movement were comparatively simple, and perhaps to modern minds, obvious. Taking their cue from an emphasis on incarnational theology, they held that as all were in Christ, so was God, in Christ, bound up in the *material* of humanity as much as its spirituality. This meant that the agenda of the kingdom of God was closely related to the concerns of the world, and most especially where suffering and injustice could be located and experienced. Correspondingly, an interest in the extension of suffrage, the relation of capitalism to the laboring poor, and addressing and alleviating the conditions of poverty, became primary arenas for debate, and for developing a Christian perspective. And yet an ideological shift would not be enough for the protagonists. To be sure, Christian Socialism fundamentally challenged the prevailing and complacent views about the scope of theology and the place of the church in society. In effect, the dominant otherworldly piety of Evangelicals and Anglo-Catholics, which had been so strong in the early nineteenth century (a mainly spiritual response to massive social and cultural upheaval, including the rise of industrialization at the expense of agrarian communities), was undermined by the incarnational emphasis Christian Socialists placed on social action and solidarity with the working classes. Initiatives such as the Working Men's College, founded in 1854 to enable adult education, were simply the practical Christian extension of the theological presuppositions that underpinned Christian Socialism.

This emerging tradition of social justice – championed by the early Christian Socialists – evolved steadily throughout the nineteenth and twentieth centuries. Stewart Headlam took the conflation of the secular and the sacred (implicit in Maurice's incarnational theology) and helped to develop the Fabian Society and its championing of collectivism. This outlook, which espoused a kind of organic society and humanity, was directly opposed to the *laissez-faire* capitalism of the same era, which had championed individualism, competition, and the freedom of the markets (and which was to be repeated under Thatcherism in the late twentieth century).

The aspirations of social justice that had begun with theologians such as Maurice were to be further developed and enhanced by the commitment to social intervention and reform that emerged in the first half of the twentieth century. The nurturing context for the possibility of radicalism cannot be overemphasized. Just as Maurice, Ludlow, and Kingsley had responded to and fed off the work of the Chartists, so were the Christian Socialists now able to situate their work in relation to the rise of Communism in Russia and Europe, the poverty wreaked by two world wars, and the stark economic depressions of the 1930s. The new heirs of Christian Socialism in the twentieth century included R. H. Tawney (his 1926 critique of the acquisitive society in *Religion and the Rise of Capitalism* is a classic work of modern theology, blending social theory with ethics and history), Ronald Preston (who espoused middle axioms in dealing with the ambiguities of capitalism and socialism), and William Temple.

Temple's *Christianity and Social Order* (1942) reflects the extent to which the established Church had now adopted the agenda of social(ist) radicalism, and was prepared to argue for reform and intervention. Temple's work – written when he was Archbishop of Canterbury, giving it even more of an edge – argued for a church that would not only point out Christian principles (especially where they conflicted with existing social order), but also help to reshape the existing order so that it more closely conformed with Christian principles. Again, this may not sound radical to modern ears, but the impact of Temple's work at the time should not be underestimated, for it situated the church firmly within the arena of political and social debates, giving it a role of social advocacy. *Christianity and Social Order* is therefore less than circumspect in arguing that "every child should find itself a member of a family housed with decency and dignity, so that it may grow up . . . in a happy fellowship unspoilt by under-feeding, over-crowding, by dirty and drab surroundings or by mechanical monotony." The primacy of human dignity emerges as a key, as Temple goes on to press for access to free education, fair income, representation, and advocacy in employment, leisure, and liberty.

This theological program was, as Temple acknowledged, mildly Utopian. The aim of his Christian social order is "the fullest possible development of the individual personality in the widest and deepest possible fellowship." In turn, this order was founded upon the conviction that the resources of God's earth should be used as God's gifts to the whole of humanity. Not all politicians were impressed with the attempts by English bishops to bring Christian principles to bear upon the political, social, and economic order. in 1926 a group of bishops had attempted to bring the government, coal industry, and miners together to end the disastrous strike. Stanley Baldwin, then Prime Minister, asked how the bishops would like it if he passed the Athanasian Creed to the Iron and Steel Federation for revision (Atherton 1994:90). The controversy over *Faith in the City* (1985) in England simply continues the tradition of Church–government antipathy on issues of social and economic justice.

Lastly, social advancement may take a variety of forms. Perhaps the first thing to say is that the commitment to justice and intervention is usually a form of advancement in its own right, and it should not be implied otherwise. However, in exploring social advancement, it is useful for our purposes here to single out two distinct schools of thought: the social gospel movement (largely confined to the USA) and that of Christian Conservatism.

The social gospel movement in the USA arose in response to the industrialization and urbanization of America from the 1860s, rather like the emergence of Christian Socialism in England; church leaders became concerned at the massive inequalities that were produced by a booming economy, and sought to address the needs of workers. That mode of address required the reformulation of Christian tradition in order to engage with the complexity of the economy. According to Atherton, this involved the rejection of *laissez-faire* Protestantism on the one hand, and on the other, a recognition that the world of work was treated seriously as God's arena of activity, which was underpinned by a liberal theological stress on the solidarity of Jesus within social situations. The movement took a serious step forward with the work of Walter Rauschenbusch (1861–1918 – Rauschenbusch's thought was to significantly influence the theological development of Martin Luther King), whose *Christianizing the Social Order* (1912) offered a radical critique of capitalist society, and advocated a social order organized according to the will of God.

Yet in spite of the promise of the social gospel movement, the agenda began to flounder in the mid-1920s. The liberal theology underpinning the movement began to wane, and its critics argued that the social gospel movement had overestimated the prospect of changing society (bringing about the kingdom on earth), and had underestimated the forces of self-interest and sin that were endemic within all classes and races, which in turn challenged the collaborative ethos that supposed that people would work together for the common good.

What began to emerge in place of the social gospel movement was an altogether more pragmatic approach to the problems posed by the market to theology, churches, and society, with scholars such as Reinhold Niebuhr (1892–1971) leading the field. Niebuhr is a pivotal figure in the history of theological engagement with the economy in the USA, since he held a critical perspective on the idea of the social gospel and its possibilities: he called for "more radical political orientation and more conservative religious convictions" (Atherton 1994:31) to comprehend the culture of his day. The fusion of the radical with the conservative was to pave the way for the emergence of a neo-Christian Conservatism, which would lay stress on the capacity of markets to increase prosperity, improve life, and empower people. Its champions have included Michael Novak in the USA and Brian Griffiths in Britain ,who have argued that faith in the market might be said to open up a pathway to social and individual liberation.

Political Spheres

All of the approaches discussed above – and these are only a tiny representative sample – can be understood as critically empathetic theological approaches to the ordering of society. Each tradition is securely based on a theological presupposition (e.g., solidarity, freedom) that aspires to shape society in relation to market forces, capitalism, industrialization, and the common good. Although politically active, the traditions may be generally characterized as reforming rather than revolutionary. Christian Socialism and Christian Conservatism, even at their most radical, posed no substantial threat to the existing social order of their time. The former may be said to place its main emphasis on sharing wealth as the pathway to creating a fairer and just society, and valuing the commonality of humanity. The latter tradition concentrates on creating wealth as a primary means of generating social and moral improvement. Both traditions share a commitment to social justice, intervention (which would include withdrawal – the practice of non-intervention championed by Thatcherites), and advancement through their particular theological outlook; liberty, dignity, and a God-fearing society remain common goals. It is only the methods of achieving these ends that separate the parties.

The approaches to social ordering outlined so far have assumed that Christianity, theology, and the churches have a certain place within society, and are respected within their various political contexts. William Temple's theological views gain their prominence partly because of his position as Archbishop of Canterbury, within a Church that is established, which gives bishops in the Church of England a role in the affairs of the state at all levels (from membership of the House of Lords to territorial representation of all the peoples within their dioceses). In the USA, although there are no ties between church and state, the character and influence of the churches, coupled to the status of theology within the public sphere, constantly creates the potential for Christianity to involve itself in social and political life – which society mostly welcomes.

However, there have been, and are, situations in which theological discourse and the practice of the churches are seen by the state and (perhaps) by society to be essentially undermining of the status quo, and potentially threatening to the prevailing social order. Here, the shape of theology can be characterized as one of resistance rather than critical compliance. Consider, for example, a well-known twentieth-century example: Dietrich Bonhoeffer. Bonhoeffer was a Lutheran pastor and theologian who witnessed the rise of the Third Reich at first hand. He was fundamentally opposed to the philosophy of Nazism, and was one of the leaders of the breakaway Confessing Church that dissented from offering religious support to Hitler's state. He was quickly banned from teaching, and generally harassed by the Nazis. When war broke out, Bonhoeffer was actually on a lecture tour of the USA. Electing to return to Germany he carried on the fight against Nazism from the inside. He was arrested in 1943, and executed at Flossenburg concentration camp, on April 9, 1945. His ground-breaking *The Cost of Discipleship* had already been published (1937), in which he had meditated on demands of the Christian life in an oppressive political situation. (But perhaps his most famous work remains *Letters and Papers from Prison*, published posthumously.)

Similarly, Martin Luther King's dream of justice and racial equality for blacks was birthed within quite particular contextual contingencies and essentialist theological foundations: a prophetic appeal for equality, calling for an end to oppression and injustice. King's theological vision was partly resourced by the great liberation dramas of the Old Testament, especially the Exodus. He also drew inspiration from the non-violent stance of Mohandas Gandhi, and from theologians such as Rauschenbusch. But for King, a trained Baptist pastor with a PhD in theology from Boston University, the bedrock of his theological and political life emerged not only from his intellectual grooming, but also from his own experiences of powerlessness. The urban decay and poverty that King witnessed at first hand, coupled to his experience of states "sweltering with the heat of oppression," were key motivators in his call for freedom and justice:

> one day on the red hills of Georgia sons of former slave owners will be able to sit down together at the table of brotherhood. . . . I have a dream that my four little children will one day live in a nation where they will not be judged by the color of their skin but by the content of their character . . . that one day, right there in Alabama, little black boys and black girls will be able to join hands with white boys and white girls as sisters and brothers [King, speaking at Washington, DC, in 1963].   (Oates 1982:261)

King's commitment to reconciliation is perhaps surprising. Why should the powerless preach forgiveness of the oppressor in the face of ongoing injustice? King's answer was that the restoration of fractured communities depended on further sacrificial acts: "In our quest to make neighborly love a reality, we have, in addition to the inspiring example of the Good Samaritan, the magnanimous life of our Christ to guide us . . . his altruism was excessive, for he chose to die on Calvary" (King 1963:35). It is interesting to note that King did not see emancipation for the black community coming through any particular ideology, from capitalism or even through some kind of general political liberation: true freedom lay in reconciliation. For King, it was love that was at the center of the reconciling community – but it was also closely linked to justice. In fact for King the two were inseparable: power at its best was love implementing the demands of justice, and justice at its best was power correcting everything that stands against love.

Martin Luther King is only one of a number of examples, drawn from the twentieth century, who have paid specific attention to the relationship between theological concepts of power (e.g., the reign and kingdom of God), and the actual experience of powerlessness that may be common to certain social or political contexts. In common with other figures (such as Desmond Tutu in relation to Apartheid) and movements (such as Liberation Theology), he links the two together. The love, power, and justice of God are not only eschatological concepts; they are also to be worked out in contemporary life, and perhaps most especially through a prophetic social gospel, working alongside political action (including resistance) and appropriate civil action.

King's political life and civil action cannot be understood without reference to his religious convictions, which determined the particular stances that he took, as well as influencing the timbre of his stirring and charismatic polemic. King's theological and political methodologies were often "pragmatism based upon principle," in which negotiation and engagement with culture – in King's case, an often hostile and violent white supremacist culture – required imaginative and reflexive responses. King was, in other words, not only a significant black theologian: he can also be claimed as a pre-eminent practical theologian, set within the earliest paradigms of Liberation Theology. King's theology was part of a political struggle, and to succeed, it needed to mobilize believers and non-believers alike to resist the very real alienating social structures and cultures that oppressed them.

This brings us, lastly in this section, to Liberation Theology itself. The term is normally associated with Latin American theologians such as Leonardo Boff, Gustavo Gutiérrez, Ruben Alves, Juan Luis Segundo, Jon Sobrino and Jose Miguez Bonino. In truth, however, Liberation Theology is an umbrella term that embraces a range of approaches to contexts and various sub-disciplines or penumbra within the wider theological compass. At the risk of generalizing, Liberation Theologians work contextually, explicitly addressing social situations that are deemed to engender oppression. The theological interpretations tend to be "inductive" in character – working from concrete facts and experiences of oppression, then reflecting and theorizing, before finally turning to issues of praxis (normally a militant demand for reordering). At the heart of Liberation Theology is an antipathy towards "abstract" theology or private piety, and a radical commitment to justice through interdisciplinarity, utilizing insights from the social sciences in the construction of theological critiques and solutions. Liberation Theology can cover a number of theological initiatives: Black Theology (e.g., James Cone), Feminist Theology (e.g. Mary Grey), Gay and Lesbian theologies, as well as the responses of South African theologians to Apartheid, or the emergent Minjung Theology in South Korea.

The specific features of Latin American Liberation Theology have arguably provided the key contours for recent theological critiques and forms of ecclesial resistance within a number of political spheres. Liberation Theology sets out to be a practical theological discourse of the poor, determining that this is the primary *place* where theology must be done. Looking to the socio-analytical insights of Marxism, Liberation Theology seeks to address the nature and cause of oppression, emphasizing solidarity and political action as a pathway to empowerment and salvation. However, with the collapse of Communism (coupled to the inexorable rise of capitalism), the initial thrall of Liberation Theology appears to have waned over the last decade. As more reflexive liberal social democracies emerge in Latin America, the fundamental antinomies that produced Liberation Theology are now less apparent. Capitalism, instead of becoming the (obvious) enemy of the poor, has emerged as a potential partner in liberation and regeneration, and part of the solution in the ending of economic and political oppression. Whilst solidarity with the suffering continues to be the abiding passion and a fundamental rationale for Liberation Theology, the discipline is nevertheless beginning to gain a new sense of poise: in a globalized economy its praxis now lies somewhere between the participative and the prophetic (Bell 2001). Once again, we see that something that initially began as a principled revolutionary movement has now evolved into a more pragmatic reformist agenda, in which the original sharpness of theological acuity has become widely accepted and dispersed amongst churches and a variety of theological outlooks. Even so, methodologically, Liberation Theology remains one of the most influential movements within twentieth-century theology, and shows every sign of continuing to make a significant contribution to the social and political complexities of the twenty-first century.

Public Life

The distinctive theological contributions outlined in the previous section – characterized by their resistance to the prevailing social consensus and to political oppression – are markedly different from the kinds of theological and ecclesial paradigms to be discussed in this section. Here, we are concerned with how theology and the churches continue to guide and shape society through a critical support for public life and for the state itself. This position is, arguably, the dominant mediating axiom that synthesizes the social ordering and the social resistance discussed in the previous two sections. At the same time, it is arguably the least obvious paradigm, since the "religion" in question is not encountered so much in the intensity of ecclesial communities (where it may obviously still be found), but is, rather, dispersed extensively within the overall shaping of society. Theologians such as Andrew Shanks argue that this is a vital dimension of Christianity: "The innermost essence of Christianity drives it out beyond the Church; it has to seek its embodiment in nothing less than the body which encompasses the entirety of human life, namely the state" (quoted in Shanks 1995: 114).

Whilst Shanks acknowledges that churches need retain their identity as distinctive bodies, independent of the state and the public, if they are to be the yeast and salt of the Kingdom of God, they are also there to help fund civilizing strands within society. But the churches do not own society, and neither do they entirely generate all the moral strands that might guide and make sociality. As Coleridge suggested almost two centuries ago, the Church of the nation is not quite the same as the Church of Christ, yet it is there to secure and improve the moral cultivation of its people, "without which the nation could be neither permanent nor progressive" (Coleridge 1839: 44). The Church is therefore not a world to come, but another world that now is, whose role is to combat political evil, not just institutional defects – but through critical support, rather than separatism.

Similarly, writers such as Jean-Jacques Rousseau (1712–78) argued that religion should play a key part in the legitimization of the state, but at the same time, it does not follow that this leads to a re-established Church. For Rousseau, Christianity was a religion of inward devotion – a spirituality that was vital for individuals, but which had no obvious or organized political shape, except insofar as it could contribute to what he famously dubbed as "civil religion":

> Now, it matters very much to the community that each citizen should have a religion. . . . Each man may have, over and above, what opinions he pleases, without its being the Sovereign's business to take cognisance of them; for, as the Sovereign has no authority in the other world, whatever the lot of its subjects may be in the life to come, that is not its business, provided they are good citizens in this life. . . . The dogmas of civil religion ought to be few, simple and exactly worded, without explanation or commentary. The existence of a mighty, intelligent and beneficent Divinity, possessed of foresight and providence, the life to come, the happiness of the just, the punishment of the wicked, the sanctity of the social contract and the laws: these are its positive dogmas. Its negative dogmas I confine to one, intolerance.   (Rousseau 1973: 307)

These idealized seedlings articulated by Rousseau – of religion embedded in American civil society – find expression in later thinkers. Ernst Troeltsch (1966) argued that liberal democracy is a product of religious forces. Similarly, Talcott Parsons (1956) suggested that liberal American democracy was not a secular creation, but rather the actual institutionalization of Protestant values. Scholars such as George Jellinek (1979) have argued that the American concept of inalienable rights (and toleration) are traceable to the radical religious movements that were expelled from Europe, and were early settlers in America. Again, religion can be seen to have augmented the creation of public life, and its supporting political scaffolding.

However, this picture of almost benign support – civil society and civil religion living off one another in gentle symbiosis – has changed markedly as American culture has rapidly developed in the postwar years. In America, as in other Western European countries, the supposedly inclusive nature of a civil society has been challenged by religious groups that claim their spiritual or cultural rights are not being respected. This may include pressing for legal exemptions in respect of attire (e.g. Muslim girls wearing headscarves in France, or British Sikhs wearing turbans but not crash helmets), to defending female genital circumcision. Far from being benign, religious values are now commodities that are very definitely mobilized in the interests of protecting ethnic identity. Similarly, the New Christian Right has also gained prominence, becoming increasingly active in politics. In recent years, the New Christian Right has become suspicious of "tolerance" as a general principle of civil religion. Indeed, there are now many religious lobbying groups, highly organized and well funded within the USA, which seek to directly influence the shaping of American life as well as foreign policy. We might say that as public space becomes more complex and atomized – in effect, a morass of competing convictions – "public religion" becomes more difficult to articulate. In other words, *which* public might we be talking about? *What* religion? *Whose* faith? There cannot be one univocal answer to these questions.

Robert Bellah noted some time ago how "pluralized" civil religion had become, being now made up of an eclectic mix of symbols, beliefs, and ideals. Granted, these probably performed a similar legitimizing function to the one Rousseau had in mind, insofar as they provided a fairly simple creed that supported civil society (integrity, neighborly regard, decency, truth, etc.). Yet Bellah also observed how the very foundations of postwar American civil religion were now threatened by vapid individualism (Bellah 1975). The present parameters of the debate are perhaps best described by another American theologian, Richard John Neuhaus. On the one hand, Neuhaus maintains that an American civil society cannot exclude religion from shaping public life and discourse. On the other hand, he also argues that religious traditions can only inhabit such space on the condition that they respect the rules of open public debate, and do not themselves become tyrannical and autocratic (Neuhaus 1984: 258).

Mindful of Bellah's championing of civil religion, of Neuhuas's "public philosophy," and of the improbability of recovering Christendom, Ian Markham suggests that there are now just three ways in which religion can properly enable a process of what he describes as "cultural enrichment" within "secular" society:

> Instead of a unitary culture in which one language, one religion, one history and one set of images dominate, we need a diverse culture in which different languages, many religions, and several narratives and images coexist in stimulating tension. . . . Cultural enrichment requires three different processes. First, we must develop the separateness of each community. We should empower communities to create the space for their tradition to be affirmed. . . . The second process within cultural enrichment is that of community engagement, implying dialog, disagreement, and a mutual exploration of truth. . . . The third process is that of faith communities discovering their voice within the public square. Public policy requires a moral dimension. (Markham 1999: 151)

These are fine sentiments, to be sure. Yet it is not difficult to probe and proscribe the limits of this paradigm; even a brief global survey shows how complex the tensions in public life can be. It is not clear, for instance, that all cultures will agree on what constitutes a "freedom of expression." In a liberal climate within the USA or Europe, say, this may appear to be obvious. There are public standards of taste and decency that reflect sensate values. Western cultural assumptions concerning the freedom that the media offers society may, however, be a problem for Islam (all societies may have interests in controlling or policing the media, due to particular cultural, political, or religious reasons). In other states where there is religious tension between competing convictions, the state may also exercise censorship of religious communication. In Nigeria, for example, this may prohibit the practice of tolling church bells, or public calls to prayer broadcast from minarets. The publication of Salman Rushdie's *The Satanic Verses* in 1988 caused a series of international incidents, many of which raised the specter of the antinomy between freedom and religion, especially in European countries where Islam was a minority faith. Even in apparently progressive pluralist countries such as Singapore, where modernity, consumerism, and globalization are bountiful, media censorship abounds.

These developments arguably represent a stage beyond the civil religion in the sense that Rousseau might have originally meant it. "Civil" has now become elided with "public," and in the process, faiths are now more sharply defined and (perhaps) narrower in their outlook. But what does this mean? In essence, it suggests that the very "public spaces" that religion once nestled within are now either deemed to be empty of values, or alternatively, are full of competing convictions that need policing. This may mean, ironically, keeping religion out of the very public spaces that faiths may once have helped to create. Casanova is probably right when he asserts that religion in modern times is differentiated, but not privatized. It continues to have an influence on the public and political landscape, even though it may now only mainly consist of protests – either against secularism, consumerism, or liberalism, or just more generally against the excesses of the modern state (Casanova 1994). Either way, the place of religion in (First World) public life has shifted slowly but surely over the last two centuries. It has moved from a position of relative privilege where it habitually and naturally shaped sociality (what Coleridge quaintly called "the clerisy of the nation" in England), to one where it is one voice amongst a number that may now claim to create, order, and sustain public life. Arguably, this apparently new situation for religion is conditioned as much by pluralism, globalization, and modernity as it is by secularization. In the Conclusion, therefore, we shall briefly explore how theologians and the churches are to face the task of social ordering, political engagement, and the shaping of public life in a more obviously pluralized and atomized future.

Conclusion: the Liberty of Captives

Politics and the ordering of society is a contested arena of debate and praxis. So, for that matter, is theology. So the idea of a political theology is bound to be contentious and is unlikely to achieve consensus. In this essay we have drawn attention to the inherently political character of early Christianity and that of its founders. In turn, this has led to perspectives on how sociality might be ordered, politics engaged with or resisted, and public life shaped. The sequential history (albeit briefly sketched) has hinted that Christianity and its theologians have, over the last two centuries, progressed from advocating justice, to arguing for a state based on common welfare, to finally arguing for social advancement, either through liberal socialism or through conservatism. Yet some theologians continue to deny that Christian theology can have anything to say to politics or society. Edward Norman's *Christianity and World Order* (1997) argues that while theological truths may have derivative *consequences* for the political, the actual truths of Christianity are inherently non-political and transcendent in character. Yet, from our survey, it should be clear that our early contention, namely that Christianity *is* an inherently political and social faith, is a no less defensible theological stance. Perhaps the only matter to discuss is what kinds of sociality and what kinds of politics might arise from Christianity in its many and various contexts.

That said, how are theologians and the churches to engage with politics and society at the dawn of the twenty-first century? The range of forces that bear upon the identity of the church, Christian discourse and praxis, and general theological acuity are bewildering enough in late modernity, without getting further drawn into the shaping of society and its political life. Yet theology, if it is to continue to offer a public voice for the churches in the marketplace of modernity, will need to adapt the tone and content of its discourse to fit the pluralized, globalized, and atomized world in which it speaks. In part, this project would need to recognize that one person's or community's liberation may be another's oppression; theology will need to discover its mediating skills, as well as recovering the prophetic.

Part of the difficulty that theologians now face in addressing politics and society is that much of the "old world order" has vanished, and the shape of the new world order is, well, more liquid than concrete. With the collapse of Communism, and the shrinking powers and influence of many nation states, there are now many fronts on which to engage. Many countries now live in more politically post-ideological phases. Liberal social democracies – delicate reticulate combinations of socialism, capitalism, liberalism, and conservatism (and perhaps infused with other political timbres) – abound all over the world, even on the poorest continents. The hard ideological certainties of Communism or Facism are hard to find, let alone fight. Many of the old antinomies that once provided the fertile soil for some of the germane theological movements and ideas we have been discussing are now no longer apparent. Industrial relations are now more complex than the (apparently simple) "workers versus the owners" paradigm; politics is more multifaceted than simply being the poor against capitalism. In short, the situations of the twenty-first century seem to warrant theological responses that will be more fluid than those of their forebears, perhaps recognizing the "liquid" character of late modernity. Under such conditions, there continues to be a need to recognize the rights and dignity of workers, but this may be extrinsically linked to a notion of market sustainability, adaptation in productivity, and economic viability within the global marketplace. In other words, capitalism may be here to stay: but how can theologians shape it ethically, socially, and responsibly?

In this new world order, Christian prophetic witness and theological critiques have started to turn away from governments and political ideologies, and concentrate on issues and parameters of common concern. This may include such things as a new consciousness about the environment and the sustainability of the earth. Campaigns for justice and equity may now be directed more at businesses and global capitalism than at any one nation. The recent Jubilee 2000 Campaign received widespread Christian support, and achieved substantial results for the poorest of the Earth. Other Christian organizations (Christian Aid, Oxfam, Tear Fund, Traidcraft, etc.) have challenged big business to trade fairly, and in so doing have begun to shape consumer choice, investment policies, and the global economy. On the more local level, churches have become active in community regeneration, employment, debt counseling, housing the homeless, adult education, and more besides. The breadth of reflexive and imaginative work alluded to here is impressive, and serves to remind that as much as Christianity may be involved in the liberty of captives, it also has its eye on the captives of liberty: those who are left behind by an increasingly mobile, prosperous world, and who are excluded from the global marketplace.

In all of this, it is important to stress that few of the recent theological responses to the new world order now seek revolution. In many spheres of Christian engagement, of charity work and relief for the poor, capitalism has emerged as a partner within the framework of the solution, even if it remains part of the problem. It is the recognition that theology and the churches now function within an age of conversation, participation, and negotiation that is the key to envisioning the theological engagements of the future. Here theologians will need poise, reflexivity, and imagination if theology is to contribute to the shaping of public life and the ordering of politics and society. As a discipline, it may yet prove to be even more useful to society in a public and mediating role.

At the same time, the prophetic vocation of theology should not be ignored, and this must be an essential component in any true Christian theological engagement with the reordering of society. The liberty of captives remains a primary focus of concern for the Christian gospel and its witness. Those enslaved by debt, the lack of rights, injustice, sickness, poverty, and discrimination were close to the center of God's concern in the ministry of Jesus, and the church continues to define itself by embodying that same love, care, compassion, and advocacy for those who suffer in the same way two thousand years later.

Of no less concern, however, are those who are captive to the more subtle forces of late modernity, such as the thrall of the media, entertainment, and consumerism. What will Christianity have to say about a saturated visual, sensate culture, in all its plurality and technopolitanism, and yet which leaves humanity increasingly de-sensitized to the sufferings of the Third World? In the new public square (for all its unevenness), theologians and churches will need to continue to develop viable alternatives and critiques of consumerism and media-saturated societies, perhaps even providing some competition for the very things that beguile, seduce, and enslave humanity. What are the alternatives to an acquisitive society going to be, and how might theology offer them in the shaping of public life? As Brueggemann suggests, prophetic ministry will need to continually penetrate the numbness of humanity, and enable people to once again face reality (including its pain and death). And beyond that, prophetic theology might then seek to break through the despair of all communities, and imagine, create, and embrace new futures (Brueggemann 1978: 109). Social ordering, political theology, and the shaping of public life through Christian witness will need to blend together the participative with the prophetic. As we noted at the beginning of this essay, Christianity, working with its theologians, will continue seeking the kingdom that is to come, whilst all the time hoping, praying, and working for encountering the signs of that same kingdom and its values in the here and now.

References

Atherton, J. ed. 1994. *Social Christianity: A Reader*. London: SPCK.

Atwood, M. 1985. *The Handmaid's Tale*. London: Virago.

Bell, D. 2001. *Liberation Theology after the End of History*. New York: Routledge.

Bellah, R. 1975. *The Broken Covenant: American Civil Religion in a Time of Trial*. New York: Seabury Press.

Boff, L. 1978. *Jesus the Liberator*. New York: Orbis.

Bonhoeffer, D. 1959. *The Cost of Discipleship* [1937]. London: SCM Press.

Bonhoeffer, D. 1967. *Letters and Papers from Prison*, ed. E. Bethge. London: SCM Press.

Brueggemann, W. 1978. *The Prophetic Imagination*. Philadelphia, PA: Fortress Press.

Casanova, J. 1994. *Public Religions in the Modern World*. Chicago, IL: Chicago University Press.

Coleridge, S. 1839. *On the Constitution of Church and State*. London: Taylor & Hessey.

Faith in the City. 1985. London: Church House Publishing.

Gutiérrez, G. 1973. *A Theology of Liberation*. New York: Orbis.

Jellinek, G. 1979. *The Declaration of the Rights of Man and of the Citizen*. Westport, CT: Hyperion Press.

King, M. L. 1963. *Strength to Love*. Cleveland, OH: Collins.

Kleist, J. ed. 1948. "Epistle to Diognetus," *The Ancient Christian Writers* 6. New York: Newman Press.

Markham, I. 1999. *Plurality and Christian Ethics*, 2nd edn. New York: Seven Bridges Press.

Neuhaus, R. 1984. *The Naked Public Square: Religion and Democracy in America*. Grand Rapids, MI: Eerdmanns.

Niebuhr, R. 1963. *Moral Man and Immoral Society*. London: SCM Press.

Norman, E. 1997. *Christianity and World Order*. Oxford: Oxford University Press.

Oates, S. 1982. *Let the Trumpet Sound: A Life of Martin Luther King*. New York: HarperCollins.

Parsons, T. 1956. *Structure and Process in Modern Society*. Glencoe, IL: Free Press.

Percy, M. 1998. *Power and the Church: Ecclesiology in an Age of Transition*. London: Cassell.

Pounds, N. 2001. *The History of the English Parish Church*. Oxford: Oxford University Press.

Rauschenbusch, W. 1912. *Christianizing the Social Order*. New York: Macmillan.

Rousseau, J. 1973. *The Social Contract and Discourses*. London: Dent.

Shanks, A. 1995. *Civil Religion, Civil Society*. Oxford: Blackwell.

Tawney, R. H. 1926. *Religion and the Rise of Capitalism*. London: John Murray.

Temple, W. 1942. *Christianity and Social Order*. Harmondsworth: Penguin.

Troeltsch, E. 1966. *Protestantism and Progress*. Boston, MA: Beacon Press.

CHAPTER 27
Feminism

Patricia Daniel

"I shall speak of nothing of which I have no experience either in my own life or in the observation of others or which the Lord has not taught me in prayer," wrote Teresa of Avila in the sixteenth century. Feminist theology has arguably always been with us. Women such as Hildegard of Bingen, Catherine of Sienna, Julian of Norwich, Margery Kempe, as well as Teresa of Avila have been recognized in recent years for their profound theological insights with the revived interest in their work having a well deserved influence on modern theology. A recent pastoral letter from the Bishop to the diocese in which I worship calls on us to reflect on Catherine of Genoa's treatise on purgatory, written in the fifteenth century. The Quaker missionaries to seventeenth- and eighteenth-century America were among the foremothers of feminist theology as well as modern feminism. Although feminist theology has developed to embrace feminist theory in its widest sense, postmodernism, and current trends in philosophy, it remains in essence a theology of women's experiences and their reaction to those experiences. Teresa's comment is still valid for contemporary women as they articulate *their* experiences, both personal and observed, and voice alternative ways of interpreting Scriptures, church practices, and theological thought inspired by their experiences of God or Goddess.

The feminist theology that emerged in the 1960s and 1970s highlighted the inequalities that existed for women within the Christian Church. Women theologians voiced their exclusion from worship and positions within the Church, often linking this with the invisibility of women in the Bible and the androcentric language in which it is written. They questioned the "maleness" of God and offered alternative models that were more inclusive of women. They highlighted the sexism within the language used within the church. They challenged the need for a route to God through Christ, setting in motion the ideas of post-Christian feminist theology and a renewed interest in the Goddess. At the same time, the influence of the French feminists encouraged women to think of how theology influenced them as individual women, divine women, not just as women in unjust societies. This more philosophical approach to feminist theology gave women the freedom of applying feminist theory to theology, making it more relevant to women's lives.

The diversity of contemporary feminist theology reflects the diversities of the women for whom it speaks as well as the women, and occasionally the men, who are actively engaged in its production. It becomes important then to talk not of feminist theology but of the multiplicity of theologies determined by the experiences, reflections, and interests of the women who are doing it. This chapter aims to highlight some of these current approaches as a means of offering possibilities to others who might be approaching *their* feminist theology for the first time, and to consider the ways that such theological analyzes impact not only on women's lives but on church attitudes and practices. I come to feminist theology as a Catholic woman, so this chapter will be written from *my* Christian perspective. My research interest has been to investigate to what extent culture, ethnicity, Christian denomination, and preferred reading of New Testament texts determine women's personal Christologies. How do Christian women sustain their relationship with Christ, and if this becomes impossible, what do they do? Women's personal Christologies are also influenced by the societies in which they live and worship, so cannot be divorced from secular realities. But feminist theology no longer remains within Christianity. Nor is it any longer a white Western response to what is often referred to as malestream theology, as women throughout Africa, Asia, Latin America, and the developing world interpret theology in the context of their own societies and cultures. Interfaith dialog among women, and feminist understandings of other faiths and religious practices, are growing and can be seen to be influencing our understanding of theology. Women of all faiths are questioning their roles within patriarchal societies built on assumed religious truths which render them invisible and silent. In so doing we all constantly negotiate and renegotiate spiritual and theological understandings which meet our own specific needs and experiences.

Theological Responses to Gendered Inequality

Socio-political, or liberationist, approaches to feminist theology provide a means to challenge injustices in societies which continue to marginalize and oppress women and other vulnerable groups. Using patriarchal sacred texts, written and interpreted by men to women's disadvantage for centuries, feminist theology enables a reader to reread the text so that it can be interpreted in a way which empowers and promotes the weak to a position of strength and equality. I hinted at the opening of this chapter that women have been doing this for centuries, so what is new in a modern feminist approach? With the global awareness of inhumanity and inequality, the growth of media and the relative ease with which communication can reach remote communities, women's voices can no longer be as easily dismissed as those of the so-called mystics, seers, and holy women of the past, but must now be acknowledged with the same respect, even if sometimes grudgingly, as those of male theologians.

Feminist theologians engaged in socio-political issues, seek justice from exploitative practices of legal systems based on male interpretations of the main world faiths or from patriarchal religious practices of dominance and exclusion. Developed democratic societies may argue that the discourse in socio-political feminist theology has moved on from the arguments which dominated the latter part of the twentieth century, such as, in Christianity, the question of the ordination of women, patriarchal language used within worship, and sexual abuse; in Islam, the empowerment or disempowerment of the veil, female genital mutilation; divorce and remarriage within Orthodox Judaism; but for some women these debates are alive and well and have a long way to go before they are over.

The Vatican still attempts to silence those who speak in favor of the ordination of women in the Catholic Church, as Lavinia Byrne experienced after publishing *Woman at the Altar* (1994). However, the feminist theologian and Benedictine nun Joan Chittester, addressing the first international conference on Catholic women's ordination (Dublin, 2001) and commenting on the reaction of the Papacy, declared that an order who had been through the Dark Ages and survived the bubonic plague and two world wars, would hardly let a letter from Rome get them down! In talking to women for my own research I found that in some Presbyterian denominations women are only just beginning to raise the issue of who should lead worship and teach in their churches, because to do so calls into question the authority of the Pauline letters. This creates a real dilemma for women who live strict Bible-based lives yet who acknowledge that in secular society women are effective teachers often bringing qualities to teaching which men do not have. They know that women could enhance the teaching within their churches if only they were given the opportunity to do so. Feminist theology offers ways of reinterpreting such restrictive and dismissive texts within the context of the historical background in which they were written.

The Pauline corpus must bear most responsibility for women's silence and inferiority within the Christian Church. In particular, Paul's letters to Timothy and Titus, which deal very much with the structure of the early Church, and his letter to the church in Corinth, are used as evidence for the head of the church to be male, for women to be allowed only to teach other women and children, and for women's silence. Although Pauline authorship of the Pastoral letters to Timothy and Titus is questionable, they are presented to, and received by, the majority of congregations as authoritative. The letters were written at a time when pseudepigraphical letters were common and used not so much to disseminate the view of the supposed author but to project new thought with the authority of that author. By using interpretative techniques of intertextuality, and by referring to extra-canonical texts such as the Acts of Paul and Thecla and other first-century letters, it is possible to bring fresh insights into the debate on women's silence, which are not in conflict with the strict code of Bible-based faith groups. Mary Fulkerson develops an interesting argument for interpreting these texts in the context of communities. The interpretive community of Presbyterian Women has, she argues, extended its boundaries on this issue through a discourse on the text which places women in the world as much as in the domestic sphere. Through images of the community that breaks the bounds of the domestic location, the discourse becomes destabilized, producing essentially a "canon within a canon" (Fulkerson 1998).

In analyzing the relationship between literary theory and reading biblical texts, Mieke Bal (1987) argues that literary readings of the Bible should raise questions concerning the reading rather than the literature itself. Alternative readings of Biblical texts, she suggests, should challenge the dominant, and therefore mostly male, readings in such a way as to reveal the "gaps and failures of realism" (1987:4) through their own consistency. Thus she seeks to promote readings which do not attempt to overturn the male dominance and replace it with a female one, but try to explore the way in which the text reveals and exposes the alternative perspectives on what are considered dominant interpretations of the myth. It is certainly possible and rewarding from a feminist perspective to do this with the Pastoral letters. By exploring the lives of early Christian communities and placing these letters in the context of that time, it is possible to see that the early Christian Church was establishing itself in communities where women were the dominant leaders within the Goddess and Mystery cults, so to be seen as different was therefore important for a church which was promoting an alternative philosophy. The demand for women's silence need be seen then not as an order for all time because they are not up to the role of teacher, but as an order of its day to prevent the infiltration of practices perceived to be more in keeping with paganism than with the new Christianity.

Paul's apparent endorsement of a male Church hierarchy through his insistence that the head of the church should be like the head of the household, and the listing of the twelve male disciples in the Gospels, continues to leave women with an uphill struggle for visibility. In particular the naming of the twelve men is cited as a reason to still deny women active priestly roles in some denominations. Although women have been ordained in the Anglican Church in the UK for ten years now, their progression through the hierarchy is almost non-existent. There is only one dean and the issue of women bishops gets shelved as soon as it is raised. The glass ceiling so often discussed by feminists is referred to in Church circles as stained glass. I feel concrete may be a better description, man-made and difficult to break.

But concrete crumbles and rots with age and so, with persistent vocalization and determination, will the attitude towards women taking on the roles of leadership. Changes in society will gradually force changes in the Church structure and leadership. The growth in numbers of women priests in the Anglican churches will lead to women being accepted into the role of bishop, when women become more widely seen in senior management within secular society. The different leadership styles of women will gradually break down the patriarchal structure of the rigid hierarchy that has developed as a result of Paul's letters opening the doors to alternative hegemonies. The decline in the numbers of men coming forward for training as priests in the Catholic Church will only lead to women being ordained as priests if the Catholic hierarchy can find no alternatives to the current organizational structures, which preserve the role for men. If we must have one "head" of the Church it need not matter if that person is always a man, if women have an equal voice in who that head should be and an equal opportunity to be in that position themselves if they so wish. It matters enormously all the while women are denied such an opportunity, through readings of these letters which assume their validity for contemporary society – a society which has different desires, different needs, and alternative understandings than that of the society to which they were originally addressed.

Feminist readings of the Synoptic Gospels, and Mark's Gospel in particular, overturn the notion that discipleship, and therefore leadership, resides exclusively in the male domain. Structural and literary analyses of the Gospel reveal a writer who was carefully constructing a message which was intended to subvert the social order of the day, determined in part by the existing temple order, to challenge the practices of exclusion and oppression. Close reading of the Gospel reveals a text with recurring themes, repeated telling of similar events and stories broken up by other stories. Mark's use of the open space, and the inclosed space of the house, the crowd, and the small group, are important in revealing the message of discipleship and service. The entire Gospel is a structure of embedded chiasms, intercalations, and related triples, which are used to reveal the theology of the Gospel as much as for their literary effect (Dewey 1980). The central section of any chiastic structure holds the key to its understanding. What is so striking in Mark's Gospel is the number of times that key involves women. In almost every instance these women are either anonymous (the woman who has bled for twelve years, the Syrophoenician woman) or are named through a man (Simon-Peter's mother-in-law, Jairus's daughter), and they are restored so they can serve.

This anonymity has been highlighted and dealt with in many ways. Dina Cormick, a South African artist, "names" these women in her art work, giving them names of women who are significant to her. Margaret Hebblethwaite (1994) in *Six New Gospels* uses a similar technique in her re-telling of Gospel women's stories. I feel, however, that there is real strength in the namelessness of the women in the New Testament. Once they are named they take on heroic status and can act as role models, but as unnamed women they represent all of us. We can all be the woman who has been drained physically and mentally through exclusion (Mark 5:25–34) yet can come from "behind" to face society and be included. We can all be the woman on the margins (Mark 7:24–30) who persists until she is listened to and rewarded because her worth is recognized. Similarly we can all be the daughters who are restored to wholeness.

The theology of Mark's Gospel reveals that restoration is on a much deeper level than regaining health. The writer uses the same word for the "lifting up" of Simon-Peter's mother-in-law (1:31) and the "raising up" of Jairus's daughter (5:41) when detailing the resurrection (16:6) of Jesus, indicating that through the restoration a newness of existence is taking place. It is no coincidence that Jairus's daughter, whose story incloses that of the woman who is hemorrhaging, is around the age of puberty. The stoppage of the woman's excessive flow of blood and the death of Jairus's daughter are both symbolic of the death of the stigma of uncleanness. Here then is woman's restoration to equal status within society, overturning the notion that otherness should be defined by blood or biology. This might seem one of those finished arguments that I referred to earlier, but in many parts of the developing world, women are still considered unclean because they menstruate and give birth. The effects of these excluding practices have serious implications for these women who are struggling to survive poverty and support their communities, but are denied the opportunity to do so because they are seen as polluting. Gabrielle Dietrich (1996) documents how women in Indian fishing communities of Tamil Nadu and Kerala have to deal with this exclusion on a daily basis to ensure the literal survival of their villages in the face of global economic changes.

It is not, however, all good news for Mark's Gospel, which can been criticized for the strong link it makes between suffering and taking up one's cross as a prerequisite to following Jesus. Suffering as victim has been seen as acceptable because the reward will be closeness to God. Thus the cross has been used as a very powerful weapon of oppression for women and other vulnerable groups throughout history. To follow is to deny oneself and if, in the process, that also includes suffering, so much the better, it would seem. In all societies women have been acculturated to do without and to accept marginalization, allowing a culture of legitimate abuse against women to flourish, often condoned by the Church. Feminist theology questions victim status for women as it seeks ways of interpreting self denial in positive rather than negative theological terms.

I recently heard the crucial passage in Mark (8:34) interpreted in a way which at first sight appears to offer much to a feminist understanding of the text. The argument is that illness, or deprivation, is not to be seen as the cross one has to carry because that is part of life; instead the cross is having to accept and live with the consequences of positive action you have taken in following what you know to be the right path for Christ. Suffering then becomes an act involving self-responsibility, which goes some way to recognizing autonomy, rather than heteronomy, which Daphne Hampson (1996) identifies as problematic for feminists who remain within Christianity. But on deeper reflection such actions can still legitimize the oppression of the vulnerable since our actions can rarely be taken in isolation. This line of argument then begs the question: at what point does suffering cease to be what life throws at you, but once again become the result of someone else's interpretation of just action for God? Whose cross is it that we are really carrying? This becomes particularly relevant I feel in the context of mission, globalization, and post-colonialism, as can be seen in the feminist theologies from Africa, Asia, and Latin America which address the legacies of exploitative practices associated with the imposition of non-indigenous cultural and religious praxis. The voices of the theologians engaged in this discourse offer very different perspectives on theology from those of Western women. To draw attention to this difference, black women theologians sometimes refer to their theology as "womanist" or "women's theology" to separate their knowledge from the feminism that often reflects only the white Western woman's experience, and which appears to be almost as excluding and irrelevant to their lives as is male theology. Likewise, Hispanic women prefer to see their experiences expressed through *Mujerista* theology. The global experience of theologians differs depending on which side of the global divide we are writing from.

Much of the work of the early feminist Quaker theologians was to challenge the theological justification of slavery. The slave trade in human labor continues into the twenty-first century with the trafficking of young women to meet the sexual demands of Western men. Many very young women, often still children, in Burma and Thailand are exploited through sex-tourism, while women from the Philippines, Nigeria, and Eastern Europe are sold into the sex industry of America and Western Europe. Poverty throughout Africa and much of Asia, together with the collapse of the communist regimes in Eastern Europe, poses an increased risk to women as the relatively high income from prostitution enables them to provide daily subsistence for their families, or a living for the men who control them. The overland transportation of goods throughout Afica and India leaves men away from their wives for long periods of time. The relative cheapness of buying sex from a woman surviving on the margins means that the spread of the HIV virus has reached epidemic proportions in parts of Southern

Africa and India, with the consequential catastrophic effects on the most vulnerable in these societies. The rapid growth in the number of HIV-positive men and women means that not only is the women's health at risk from sexually transmitted diseases, but their families too are at risk from the HIV virus and from being left orphans if medication to prevent the virus from developing into AIDS is not available.

Prostitution is not the only action of global capitalism that controls and destroys women's bodies. The demand in the affluent West for out-of-season fruit, vegetables, and flowers has created industries in Africa and Latin America in which women work for subsistence wages in poor working conditions. These industries, owned and controlled by large multinational corporations, make extensive use of fertilizers and chemicals banned in America and the UK, to produce quality blooms and vegetables but which leave women at risk from cancers, miscarriage, and damaged hands. The industry response when challenged, is to point to the benefits of outsourcing for the consumer, and the economy of the host country, whilst glossing over the profit margins made for themselves. A recent correspondence I had with a UK supermarket on the policy of outsourcing foods from Southern African countries in the grip of a food crisis advised me of the benefits these nations receive from the policy, including "£50,000 spent on various causes, e.g. schooling and sports facilities for one of our large flower producers near Lake Naivasha in Kenya; environmental protection and educational projects around Lake Naivasha. It is by supporting businesses in the examples given that we are able to make a difference to some of the people in the Third World." The sum of £50,000 may make a more significant change to a community in Kenya than in the UK, but in the true needs of a country with a developing economy, it is almost insignificant.

A theological response to such policies of "outsourcing" may include a rereading of the pericope in Mark in which Jesus demands that the rich man who has met all the criteria for living a good worldly life should give up all he owns so he can inherit eternal life (10:17–22). The demand to "sell what you own" today cannot be taken literally since it is evident that there has never been a society which operates perfectly on the policy of equal ownership. Human greed and enjoyment of power mean that even in the best-intentioned societies some will benefit at the expense of others. What this teaching demands in a modern context is that we assess the disproportionate distribution of resources that exploit so much of the world for the benefit of the rest. This assessment should be undertaken locally within our own experience as well as globally. Behaving as a true disciple entails consideration of the weakest, through recognition that our own needs must not be gained at the expense of others, relinquishing what we can do without, if someone else needs it more – the wider implication of which must be acknowledged as such by governments which support global organizations that exploit the poorest of the poor. But is this an effective response to a company which has such a limited view of shared resources? Heather Eaton (2000), in reviewing the ecofeminist relationship with theology, questions "whether the problem is greater than myopia, and is located in a distortion in method and starting point, interlocutors and a lack of attending to the world." For her, the real concern is that theology has become powerless in the face of globalization. The amount spent by the UK supermarket chain in Kenya might be an indication of just what little influence the church campaign to draw attention to the world debt and the needs of developing nations actually had on the profit conscience of large companies.

Globalization leaves women's bodies as a site of conflict and disease in many societies. Women struggle to live within bodies which cause pain and discomfort, both physical and emotional; with bodies which are disabled, and the consequential marginalization that comes from being hidden in societies unable to live comfortably with what is perceived as deformity; with bodies which do not function in the way that society accepts as the norm; and to manage this struggle within patriarchal theological interpretations that do little to ease the pain. Society now acknowledges that the body as conflict can also be a man's body. Men too, for example in the developing world, have to face the same effects of poverty as women, and increasingly in the West are facing the stresses that inevitably result from trying to meet the ideals of the perfect body image projected as desirable. The number of young men with eating disorders has grown significantly in the last five years. Throughout history, the Christian concept of the body has been that the male is the norm and the female body inferior and in some way flawed. Feminist theory has been incorporated into theology to enable women, and hopefully men, to think differently about their bodies.

Theorizing Theology or Theologizing Theory?

There is an extensive feminist literature on the theory of the body which reflects the rich and diverse discourse that feminists are engaged in. By deconstructing the binaries that characterize embodiment, postmodern discourse of the female body produces a theory of the body which is not determined purely by biology or by power relations. The Augustinian inferior, unstable female body takes on a new fluidity in postmodern feminist thought. Sarah Coakley's "introduction of Judith Butler to Gregory of Nyssa" in her essay on the eschatological body provides an interesting insight into how a "fluid postmodern 'body' can find some sense of completion without losing its mystery, without succumbing again to 'appropriate' or restrictive gender roles" (Coakley 2000). In *Real Bodies*, Mary Evans points to the positive advantages that can be gained for women if the female body is regarded not as "fixed" but as "a complex of attributes that can fluctuate as social norms" (Evans and Lee 2002:2). Such flexibility has enabled women, for example, to use the advances in reproductive technologies to experience birth and motherhood through means which many religions might call unnatural. These developments raise serious questions amongst feminist theologians. If women have the right to control their own bodies, how should the church respond when they do so in ways which attempt to subvert patriarchal control? To return to the question of prostitution, what should be the theological response to women who choose to use their bodies in whatever way they desire, making prostitution a positive choice of labor and financial income?

In all the major world religions prostitution is "deviant" behavior, the prostitute an "unworthy person," and if she is also an adulterer then in some societies even today she has committed an offence which is punishable by stoning to death. The Christian Church translates this deviance into sin, and labels the prostitute a sinner. The New

Testament reveals a Jesus who is "forgiving" of women who are identified as having transgressed sexually; he invites the crowd to cast the first stone at the woman brought before him for judgment on her alleged adultery but he sends her away without condemnation even though he is reported to tell her "not to sin again" (John 8:11). Mary Magdalene is usually portrayed as the prostitute from whom Jesus cast seven demons (Luke 8:2) but are these demons actual evidence that she was a prostitute, and was she subsequently included in the group of followers simply because she was a repentant woman? Intertextual and intratextual readings of the Gospels link Mary of Magdala with Mary of Bethany and the unnamed woman sinner who anointed Jesus with ointment (Luke 7:37–50). Here the sinners become the teachers and perform prophetic acts, because they understand the meaning of the teaching rather than because they are forgiven women.

If Mary were a prostitute this was possibly her chosen means of gaining an income, as there is no evidence from the Gospels that she was coerced or forced into such a role unwillingly. It would seem from the stronger characteristics of Mary which emerge from both the canonical and extra-canonical Gospels, particularly the Gospels of Mary and of Philip, that Jesus chose her not because she was forgiven for her sins but because she was probably the person who most clearly understood his mission. It was Mary whom he entrusted to carry forward the message of the resurrection. The Gospel of Mary, found among the texts at Nag Hammadi, reveals that Jesus shared more knowledge with Mary than with the male disciples. In the Gospel, it falls to Levi to remind Peter, when he challenges Mary over this, that "the Savior knows her very well. That is why he loved her more than us" (Robinson 1996:527), before he encourages Peter and the others to be ashamed of not learning the true depth of the man they have followed from the one who really knows – Mary. A theological response to the woman who argues for the right to choose how she uses her body to earn her income can be seen in Jesus's attitude to Mary – she was a woman whom he loved for the person that she was, with qualities that he recognized and respected. As Jane Schaberg comments "Mary Magdalene traditions focus the issue of changing attitudes toward the vulnerable ambiguous human body" (Schaberg 2002:352).

The number of women who are able to make such positive choices to work within the sex industry are, however, in the minority. The alternative feminist theory on prostitution argues that it is more frequently the outcome of choices made on behalf of the vulnerable woman by someone who thus has a controlling power over her. Many women working within the global sex industry are more likely to fall into this category than to work within the limits of the safe boundaries that they have set for themselves. How might feminist theology provide an insight for these women? Issues of exploitation of sex workers in the Far East have been addressed by a number of feminist theologians, who argue for an holistic approach to restoring self-esteem (King 1996; Brock and Thistlethwaite 1996; Kyung 1991). In their work on prostitution in Asia and America, Rita Nakashima Brock and Susan Brooks Thistlethwaite argue that women should be healed through the liberation of naming their experiences, as does Chung Hyun Kyung, who addresses issues which particularly affect Korean Asian women. In the context of global capitalism, who are the sinners and what is the sin? To label women caught up in prostitution as sinners is to miss the point of the sin. Sex-tourism, militarism, the lucrative trade in child pornography, and internet sex are all contributors to a sin which creates social injustice and feeds the greed of the wealthy at the expense of the poor. The sinner is not the woman but those who perpetuate systems which label women, thus denying them agency. A liberating theology for prostitution in this situation is one which encourages "repentance" among those who create and maintain the institutions and structures (and this must include the Christian Church), which allow the power of masculine hierarchy and the image of the male body as norm to flourish (Brock and Thistlethwaite 1996). Such a theology, which gives women voice to own their experiences and feelings, subverts victimology, replacing it with a wholeness and completeness of spirit.

The difficulty religion has with the sexualized body becomes even greater when that body is also a lesbian body. Not fitting the desired "norms" for the female body, the lesbian poses a double threat to a patriarchal, heterosexually defined social structure. Michel Foucault's social construction of the body in terms of power relations provides a framework for analyzing gender difference which lends itself to alternative appreciations of the lesbian body. Queer theology, which draws extensively on the work of Foucault and others such as Judith Butler (Stuart 1997), provides a forum for all people whose bodies are different from the heterosexual norm, so it speaks for lesbian women, gay men, transgendered as well as bisexual people. Rather than viewing difference as problematic, queer theory regards difference as non-hierarchical, providing an insight into truth. As such it is possible for "queer" people to remain within Christianity and to explore liberating ways of interpreting Scriptures in much the same way as feminist theologians do, since, as Elizabeth Stuart argues, Christianity provides the rules and structures which inform their spiritual lives. What she insists on is that queer theology must reflect the reality and spirituality of those who live queer lives. Theologians such as Carter Heyward and Elizabeth Stuart have done much pioneering work in this field of feminist theology and have laid the foundations for many lesbian women to feel comfortable within a religion which still speaks to them theologically even if its practices leave them at its margins.

The question of the divine body has intrigued feminist theologians for some time. Within the Christian tradition, the male trinity of Father–Son–Spirit appears to leave no room for woman to have a divine image of herself. But if, as Luce Irigaray (1993) argues in "Divine Women" we require divinity to become free and autonomous so as to achieve subjectivity, we need to create a gendered divine symbolic which not only challenges the masculinist symbolic of the divine, but enables women to reclaim the roles that men have created for them in relation to that divine: "to achieve a new social order, women need a religion, a language and a currency of exchange" (Irigaray 1993:79). Grace Jantzen (1998) proposes the binary opposition theism/atheism as a starting point from which to explore possible alternative divinities which go some way to meeting Irigaray's observation that:

> God forces us to do nothing but *become*. The only task, the only obligation laid upon us is to become divine men and women. To become perfectly, to refuse to allow parts of ourselves to shrivel and die that have the potential for growth and fulfillment. (Irigaray 1993:68)

Jantzen's binary recognizes a shared notion of a God, in which one half of the pair believes and the other half disbelieves. This is a God of the masculinist Western ideal, so by deconstructing the binary, a space can be opened up from which new ideas can emerge; ideas, Jantzen suggests, of desire and imagination, female rather than male, and the vulnerable rather than the powerful – ideas which have previously been repressed. The question is, how to use the language and cultural symbolic that surrounds us to create a feminist symbolic out of these ideas? Within the masculinist symbolic, belief is seen as vital for life on earth, and more importantly, for life after death. Salvation in the Judeo-Christian tradition is necessary for entry into an afterlife in the presence of God. Jantzen questions what happens if, instead of locating projection theories in the context of belief, we consider the adequacy of projecting human characteristics onto the divine. Will such projections "best facilitate human becoming . . . and constitute a worthy divine horizon" (1998:89)? The source of these characteristics, she argues, must be women's experience, which should be seen as "a development of transformative suggestions for a new symbolic" (1998:120), which will then be able to draw positively on the diversity of women's lives.

This new symbolic emerges by rejecting the dependence that the Western religious symbolic has on death, accepting instead a symbolic based on natality. Natality has a gendered basis and is more basic than death since to die it is essential to have been born. Moreover everyone must be born of a woman. There can be no disembodied natality, so therefore, an imaginary of natality recognizes the physical and material and thus provides the foundation of a freedom which "emerges from and takes place within bodily existence" (Jantzen 1998:145). Such an imaginary would not promote the position of woman as mother, since not all women aspire to be mothers, but rather would emphasize that as sexuate beings we are all born of woman, and so there is a connectedness to all humanity. By focusing on natality it is possible to broaden relationships to embrace not only human relationships but our relationship to the planet. The obligation to become divine does not imply that we become infinite since that would be to reject our embodied selves. Instead a rejection of the notion that only the infinite can be divine releases us from the dependence on a necrophilic imaginary which assumes that it is only in death that we have any hope of becoming like God and therefore divine.

The emphasis placed by the Christian Church, throughout history, on the sacredness of the virgin body has left women with confusion towards delighting in a sexuate body. The struggle that women have to accept their bodies as a site of pleasure, rather than one of pain, is mirrored theologically in the struggle between the darkness and light of religious experience. Psychoanalytic theory lends itself to feminist theologies which explore understandings of self. Julia Kristeva (1987), for example, argues that to understand self, there is a need for a primary identification with a loving agency, which she suggests Christians celebrate in divine love: "God was the first to love us, is love and demands nothing in return" (1987:25). The light of self-understanding comes through accepting this unconditional gift of God's love: the believer is assured of God's abundant grace and thus a fusion with God, which Kristeva argues is more semiotic than symbolic.

Kristeva defines abjection as a necessary stage in the managing of the split from the semiotic maternal into identification with the symbolic paternal. Thus through this process the child is able to identify with the father of individual pre-history, to encounter a discourse of love as agape, and consequently to become a speaking subject (Anderson 1997:216). Abjection, however, stays with us, and parallels in theological terms the darkness that comes from being distanced from God. Kristeva herself describes abjection as "immoral, sinister, scheming, a terror that dissembles" (1987:4). But the darkness is overtaken by the light of a primary identification with God. Alison Jasper (1998) uses such a Kristevan analysis of abjection and subjectivity to link the divine Word of John's Gospel, which is associated with patriarchal symbolism, with the maternal body. In Christian understanding the Logos is fused with God and temporarily separated from God, as it becomes flesh. By creating heaven and earth in the beginning, Kristeva (1987) argues, God creates the division which is also the mark of God's presence.

Reading John's Gospel alongside the Wisdom literature of the Old Testament also enables a female image of the divine to emerge. Flesh is a heterogeneous concept for Kristeva, pointing both to a body as drive and to a sublimated spiritual body "completely submersed into (divine) speech in order to become beauty and love" (Kristeva 1987:125). The incarnation of the Word in the Prologue to John's Gospel does not therefore need to become flesh through the medium of this unique *other* – whose impregnation comes from sources outside the norm for human creation. The "word of life" that emerges as the message of the Gospel in the human form of Jesus, has no need to emerge from the womb of a virgin mother, instead it emerges from Wisdom (Sophia), who is eternal, in existence before and after historical time. By replacing Sophia with Logos, to meet the cultural norms of the time, the writer of John's Gospel has ensured that the attributes of Wisdom are all attached to the incarnate Jesus through the Word.

Wisdom characteristics are the key to the mission of Jesus, allowing a multiplicity of models of Jesus/Christ to emerge and making it possible to shift away from Jesus's maleness to what happens *in* Christ. The possibility of God as Mother–Sophia–Spirit opens a whole new way of imagining God; a God in which Mother/Father become functional metaphors rather than ontological statements (Johnson 1992). Human Christic images portraying both male and female life experiences are then possible. The female Christa is still a shocking image for many people, in a way in which black or folk male images may not be. Yet they are extremely empowering for some women. Marcella Althaus-Reid's example of the comic Xena in black leather is a clear illustration of a Christic image not just of a woman on the boundaries but of a queer Christ (Althaus-Reid 2001). Such a radicalized, sexualized image of Christ provides, she argues, a starting point for a reflection on queer theologies. Images of a suffering Christa provide healing strength for some women who have been violated and abused, whilst for other women a Christa image is confirmation that they too are made in the image of Christ.

Theology or Thealogy?

In her essay "Equal to Whom?" Luce Irigaray (1997) argues that any Christological investigations should look to earlier periods when women were dominant, and question why these were censored by the phallocratic patriarchy. She reminds us that the Christian Church often disregards the possibility that Jesus is a bridge, preferring to lock him into a phallocratic system which often forgets the fact that Jesus's ministry was a celebration, an "invitation to share with him in the fruits of the earth and continue with this celebration after he had gone" (1997:201). Through the representation of his body and blood with the fruits of the earth, Irigaray suggests that the bridge is through Jesus's body back to older religions who offer women better examples of "the divinity of woman in her own sexual body." She concludes that Christianity "cannot separate Jesus from nature, the divine from the corporeal or the Eucharist from a respect for the earth" (1997:213). Women who live in societies where much older traditional religions celebrate the Goddess, seem able to absorb aspects of these traditions into their Christian practices.

An example of this in Ireland is the figure of Brigid, who is a strong influence in many Catholic women's lives. Brigid crosses hang over the front doors or in the kitchen of many houses to bring health and well being to the family. The cross, usually woven from the ripened corn, is in the form of a swastika, symbolizing that the healing will spread to all corners of the home. The cross is seen as a Christian symbol, but is also a powerful symbol within Paganism. At the feast of Imbolc in early spring (which coincides with the feast of St Brigid on February 1st) a cross is ceremoniously placed in each room of the house with a recitation to new life and blessings to the home. Stories of Brigid are bound up in the imagery, myth, and legends of both Paganism and the early period of Christianity in Ireland. Symbols associated with her as Goddess are reproduced in the Christian images of her as saint. Brigid is both Goddess and saint, revered in ancient times for her resistance to patriarchy and recognized in modern Ireland for being as strong an influence in Christianizing Ireland as was St Patrick. Her healing powers, whether as saint or Goddess, are invoked by contemporary women either through prayers, or by offerings made at Brigid Wells. These holy wells can be found all over Ireland and are natural puddles in a hollow surrounded by trees. The offerings that are tied to the trees are usually small bits of everyday household objects such as yellow dusters, ripped tea towels, dish cloths, handkerchiefs, socks, and even carrier bags or plastic "ice-pole" wrappers.

Belief in alternative healing, involving what might be seen as witchcraft, or Goddess practice, is no doubt strong in all parts of the Christianized world. Women in Africa may include healing practices of Ju-Ju or Orisha, as may African-American women, while women in the Caribbean have been able to keep African roots within their religious practices through incorporating elements of Voudou into their daily lives. But for many women identification with a maternal God, female images of Christ, or incorporation of traditional practices is not enough to enable them to remain within a religion so steeped in patriarchy. They need an alternative space in which to express their spirituality. These women have found feminist thealogy more open to their beliefs, image, and understanding of self.

Thealogy has a rich and diverse tradition of the Goddess on which to draw. Almost every culture can trace spirituality back to a Goddess associated with nature, the earth, and human creation. There is a sacredness of connectivity to the native earth from which the culture has developed. Many women now feel more drawn to theological expression which speaks of Goddess, God/Mother than to a patriarchal theology that speaks of God/Father. The earth as embodiment of the Goddess becomes a powerful symbol of embodied life (Christ 1997) and therefore more relevant an understanding of self for many women. But is the growth in awareness of the Goddess excluding of men in the same way patriarchal religions have been of women? Carol Christ suggests not, instead she proposes that in time it will be possible to create new images of men, the phallus, and fatherhood which are not of domination and rape but which "bring men back in touch with their physicality, reminding them of their participation in the rhythms of death and rebirth within nature" (Christ 1997:94).

In this chapter I have tried to show the diversity of approaches to feminist theology that are currently being used by women throughout the world. This is by no means exhaustive. Each new woman who comes to feminist theology will extend the boundaries even further. And what place is there for men within feminist theology? Clearly men have been, and will continue to be, liberated by the influence of feminist theology. But can men "do" feminist theology? Men certainly can use feminist methodologies within their theology and should be encouraged to do so. But if men wish to be known as feminist theologians then they need to work within the boundaries and parameters set by women, otherwise women's theology will once again become subsumed into malestream theology.

References

Althaus-Reid, M. 2001. "Outing Theology: Thinking Christianity Out of the Closet," *Feminist Theology* 27 (May).

Anderson, P. 1997. "Julia Kristeva (b.1941): Introduction," in *The Postmodern God: A Theological Reader*, ed. G. Ward. Oxford: Blackwell.

Bal, M. 1987. *Lethal Love: Feminist Literal Readings of Biblical Love Stories*. Indianapolis, IN: Indiana Press.

Brock, R. N. and Thistlethwaite, S. B. 1996. *Casting Stones: Prostitution and Liberation in Asia and the USA*. Minneapolis, MN: Fortress Press.

Byrne, L. 1994. *Woman at the Altar: The Ordination of Women in the Roman Catholic Church*. London: Mowbray.

Christ, C. P. 1997. *Rebirth of the Goddess: Finding Meanings in Feminist Spirituality*. London: Routledge.

Coakley, S. 2000. "The Eschatalogical Body: Gender, Transformation and God," *Modern Theology* 16(1) (January).

Deitrich, G. 1996. "The World as the Body of God," in *Women Healing Earth: Third World Women on Ecology, Feminism and Religion*, ed. R. Radford Ruether. London: SCM Press.

Dewey, J. 1980. *Marcan Public Debate Literary Technique: Concentric Structure and Theology in Mark*. Atlanta, GA: Scholars Press.

Eaton, H. 2000. "Ecofeminism and Globalization," *Feminist Theology* 24 (May).

Evans, M. and Lee, E. eds. 2002. *Real Bodies*. Basingstoke: Palgrave.

Fulkerson, M. M. 1998. " 'Is There a (Non-Sexist) Bible in this Church?' A Feminist Case for the Priority of Interpretive Communities," *Modern Theology* 14(2) (April): 225–42.

Hampson, D. ed. 1996. *Swallowing a Fishbone? Feminist Theologians Debate Christianity*. London: SPCK.

Hebblethwaite, M. 1994. *Six New Gospels: New Testament Women Tell their Stories*. London: Geoffrey Chapman.

Irigaray, L. 1993. "Divine Women," in *Sexes and Genealogies*, trans. G. Gill. New York: Columbia University Press.

Irigaray, L. 1997. "Equal to Whom?" in *The Postmodern God: A Theological Reader*, ed. G. Ward. Oxford: Blackwell.

Jantzen, G. M. 1998. *Becoming Divine: Towards a Feminist Philosophy of Religion*. Manchester: Manchester University Press.

Jasper, A. 1998. *The Shining Garment of the Text: Gendered Readings of John's Prologue*. Sheffield: Sheffield Academic Press.

Johnson, E. A. 1992. *She Who Is: The Mystery of God in a Feminist Theological Discourse*. New York: Crossroad.

King, U. ed. 1996. *Feminist Theology from the Third World: A Reader*. London: SPCK.

Kristeva, J. 1987. *In the Beginning was Love: Psychoanalysis and Faith*, trans. A. Goldhammer. New York: Columbia University Press.

Kyung, C. H. 1991. *Struggle to Be the Sum Again: Introducing Asian Women's Theology*. London: SCM Press.

Robinson, J. M. 1996. *The Nag Hammadi Library in English*, 4th rev. edn. Leiden: Brill.

Schaberg, J. 2002. *The Resurrection of Mary Magdalene: Legends, Apocrypha and Christian Testament*. London: Continuum.

Stuart, E. 1997. *Religion is a Queer Thing*. London: Cassell.

CHAPTER 28

Rediscovery of Mysticism

Ralph Norman

Introduction

Mysticism has suddenly become very important for Christian theology. There is more scholarly interest shown in the subject by academic theologians now than there has been for decades. This represents quite a change in fashion: many of the great modern theologians – especially the Protestant ones – were avowedly dismissive of mysticism. This was primarily because it was taken by them to indicate a general phenomenon of human religiosity rather than something specific to the Christian gospel. Although mysticism might have been of great interest to the study of comparative religion and the philosophy of religion, it had little to offer theologians wrestling with the specific problem of understanding faith in Christ. Thus Albrecht Ritschl (1887:27–8) identified mysticism as a phenomenon alien to Christianity, a corrupting infection of the Gospel by pagan neo-Platonism. In his wake followed Adolf von Harnack (1961:271, n. 3) and Wilhelm Herrmann (1906:19–40), who in turn set the agenda for Barth's,[1] Bultmann's (1960:116–19; 1997:117–29), and Brunner's[2] disparagement of all things mystical. If Gnosticism was the over-Hellenizing of Christianity, then mysticism was certainly (in their opinion) its over-Platonizing; it owed more to Proclus and Plotinus than it did to Peter or Paul. Given that such figures as Barth and Bultmann still today have such an influence over academic theology, some account needs to be given for the renewal of theological excitement about this subject. For mysticism is back in business, not just in comparative religion and the philosophy of religion, but also in the task of seeking to understand the Christian gospel itself.

The root cause of this renewed interest is the fact that theological understandings of mysticism have changed in the last decade. The basic characteristics of this shift in understanding may be summarized as follows:

Mysticism used to be of interest because:

1 It was classed as a form of religious experience that could be analyzed by philosophers and phenomenologists of religion. This seemed meaningful in a context of
   inter-religious dialogue since it suggested there were common spiritual experiences that were manifested in different religious traditions independent of the
   specific teaching of those religions.
2 It was suggested that such experiences were private and individualistic. This
   seemed meaningful in a context of skepticism about traditional, organized
   Christian dogma.

Mysticism is now of interest because:

1 Historical theologians have located Christian mystics in their own context of
   patristic and medieval belief and practice. This is of interest because it deepens
   understanding of wider issues and problems of Christian doctrine.
2 Mystical denials of Christian knowledge of God are of interest in a postmodern
   context where issues of absence, otherness, and difference are often seen to be
   more interesting than affirmations.

In this chapter I will pay attention to all of these themes. I will describe definitions of
mysticism and how the change in theological interest in mysticism came about. This
will involve sketching earlier views of mysticism and comparing them with contemporary ones. I will then locate mysticism within its patristic and medieval contexts and
argue that it is best understood with reference to specific historic Christian doctrines.
Following this, I will explore the relationship of the Christian mystical tradition to the
postmodern, showing why this topic has taken on a wider philosophical significance
today. Finally, I will consider some of the criticisms that have been leveled at the mystical tradition from modern theologians.

Changing Definitions of Mysticism

What is mysticism? I have already said that understandings of mysticism have changed
and that this creates a problem when describing it, for what was meant by "mysticism"
20 years ago differs from current usage of the word. This is exacerbated by the fact that
the older definitions of mysticism typically correspond to the way in which the word is
popularly used. Mysticism, popularly defined (according to many of my students), is
esoteric or exotic religious experience of union with God. Most of us are familiar with
this meaning of the word, and may imagine that a mystic is a spiritual virtuoso, an
especially gifted religious genius who has risen above the common stock of religious
practice. This figure is set apart, the recipient of a special insight that cannot be communicated to the masses because they have not reached the purified state necessary to
grasp it. The mystic gains an intuitive and immediate knowledge of ultimate reality or
God through a personal experience. This may be a state of mind beyond normal human

understanding, beyond the categories of space and time, beyond normal emotions. The mystic is thus separated from creaturely desires and passions and escapes the bonds of the material universe. She may attain a complete understanding of selflessness as she attains union with God, or a sense of joy at the harmony of all things in union with one another and the ultimate reality.

This, at least, is a popular understanding of mysticism. Many of us will also be familiar with how such states of esoteric religious experience have been represented on film: the mystic is clad in white, has a bright light shining on her, moves in slow-motion, and typically lacks a sound-track. (I think that such gross modification of realistic representation is supposed to portray her removal from the material world into a sort of Platonic rapture.) Such portrayals are certainly stock elements in popular culture, and are fine as far as they go. For better or worse, there is a fascination with individuals who have transcended the boundaries of their own identity to gain – perhaps – a psychological adaptability that allows extraordinary artistic or religious invention, or an insight into life and the world that others lack. It is very cool, very counter-culture, very 60s, and has led to the writing of books with titles to get the hearts of intellectual junkies everywhere pounding. Who could resist *Zen, Drugs, and Mysticism* (Zaehner 1972) if it were suggested reading on a college course bibliography?

Lying behind the pop image of the mystic, there is something important that needs to be treated much more seriously. It must be respected and it does not deserve to be joked about. This is the massive and peculiarly modern intellectual project that has attempted to understand mystical experience as a phenomenon that lies behind and unites the world's diverse religious traditions. It is said to be something that Vedantic Hinduism shares with Mahayana Buddhism; that Kabbalistic Judaism shares with Sufi Islam; that Christian mysticism shares with neo-Platonism (see Dupré 1987). William James has been particularly influential in establishing this view, and his definitions of the mystical in his *The Varieties of Religious Experience* are still as commonly accepted as any. Two aspects of James's understanding of mysticism need be noted here. First of all it should be seen (as his title suggests) that the mystical is something *experienced*. Further, as James explains in the text, *ineffability* stamps home the isolated, individualistic, and therefore indescribable and unutterable quality of the mystical experience. The mystic has experienced something extraordinary that ordinary language cannot adequately capture, and which therefore cannot be communicated to non-mystics who have not shared the experience.

Since James, this basic understanding of mysticism has been developed by important and prominent figures like Mircea Eliade to form an understanding of mysticism as immediate spiritual union with ultimate reality, which forms the basis of genuine religiosity in any of its guises. Since mysticism was seen as a form of spirituality that spanned different religions, as a kind of pure religious experience independent of the doctrines that divide the traditions, it was thought to be a useful locus for exploring spirituality in general whilst simultaneously suggesting that doctrine is ultimately less important than experience. It has been a pervasive idea and one that received much attention in the fields of psychology and comparative religion.

This understanding of mysticism as ineffable religious experience was also an important topic of discussion for the philosophy of religion. Here interest focused on

epistemological problems that arise from reports of experiences that are by very definition private and incommunicable. To what extent can mystical experiences be classed
together at all if it is impossible to say what they are? If whatever the mystical is is concealed from the many and known only to the few it would seem to follow that those
who have known mystical experiences cannot tell others about them. If this is the case
then further questions need to be raised, namely, can mysticism be studied at all by the
normal scholarly methods? Can ineffable experiences be analyzed? Philosophers were
(and still are) eager to know whether mystical experiences are evidence of a unique way
of knowing reality, whether they verify the truth claims of various religions, whether
mystical experiences are all the same or different, whether they are shaped and molded
by the intellectual or religious tradition to which the mystic belongs.

Eventually the way mysticism was studied began to change. Although the philosophical debates about the subject had become increasingly sophisticated, the primary
sources – many of them medieval – that were held to describe mystical experiences were
often relegated to a supporting role. Take, for example, the collection of essays edited
by Steven Katz, *Mysticism and Philosophical Analysis* (1978). This book contains ten
excellent essays on the philosophical problems caused by mysticism (in the sense of
"ineffable experience"), but no detailed and extended analysis of a single primary text
within its original context. There are more references in the text to William James and
W. T. Stace than there are to Dionysius the Areopagite, John of the Cross, Meister
Eckhart, the Kabbalah, and the Buddha together. In short, the debate had become peculiarly unhistorical, and mystical writings had been torn from their contexts to support
the agenda of modern scholarship. The scholars appear to be far more interested
in forcing the mystical writers to conform to the modern scholars' own philosophical
and religious agendas than they are in trying to understand what the mystics were
actually saying.

To remedy this, attention turned in the 1990s to the historical and cultural setting
of mystical literature, and scholars began the process of interpreting these texts within
their historical philosophical and theological contexts. The most influential work in this
regard remains Bernard McGinn's series, *The Presence of God: A History of Western
Christian Mysticism* (1992). Following McGinn's work something startling emerged: *the
whole modern debate about mysticism would have been unrecognizable to the great writers of
classical Christian mysticism*. The issue boils down to this: if mysticism is defined (by
James and Eliade, for instance) as a psychologistic experience of union with God, then
Augustine, Dionysius the Areopagite, Bonaventure, Meister Eckhart, the author of *The
Cloud of Unknowing*, Julian of Norwich, and John of the Cross (amongst others) are not
mystics at all. If, however, one defines mysticism in accordance with the teaching and
writings of these Christian mystical theologians something very different comes into
view.

Contemporary scholarship on specifically Christian mysticism (mysticism here
located, it is important to note, within a specific cultural and theological tradition, and
hence *Christian* mysticism rather than mysticism in general) is, then, very, very different from much twentieth-century literature on the subject. Important work by Denys
Turner has demonstrated that the classical Christian mystics were not describing esoteric religious experiences at all; rather, they are meditations on the central Christian
doctrine of the mysteriousness of God. Mystical theology meant something very dif-

ferent in the ancient and the medieval traditions of Christianity than it does to those who typically refer to it today. In his *The Darkness of God*, he describes his position very clearly: "At its boldest, my hypothesis is that modern interpretation has invented 'mysticism' and that we persist in reading back the terms of that conception upon a stock of mediaeval authorities who knew of no such thing – or, when they knew of it, decisively rejected it" (Turner 1995:7).

The great thing about Turner's thesis is not just that it is exciting and challenging; more importantly, it is convincing in terms of historical theology. Turner, like McGinn, holds the opinion that the popular view of mysticism as esoteric religious experience is thoroughly misleading and is the product of nineteenth-century scholarship. The process that led to this misreading can be pieced together as follows. The noun "mysticism" – as opposed to the earlier theological adjectives "mystic" and "mystical" – was first coined in French in the seventeenth century. Following this, sustained academic investigation of this newly coined mysticism began in the early 1800s. These early discussions, it is important to note, took place initially in the context of German Romanticism and absorbed the general Romantic ideals of restoring unity between the self and nature in a harmony that overcomes the disenchantment caused by modernity (McGinn 1992:421, n. 8). This explains why discussions of mysticism (I am thinking of, for instance, the entry by Louis Dupré in the *Encyclopaedia of Religion*, edited by Eliade – see Dupré 1987:247) included references to Romantic writers like William Wordsworth. The point is that descriptions of such Romantic poets seem to express so well the modern understanding of "mysticism": a lonely poetic genius, separated from society in a lonely landscape, writing of his esoteric experiences of a sense of awe at the beauty and harmony of nature, a delicate soul misunderstood by those around him. In effect, Romanticism set the agenda for the interpretation of mystical texts and rendered them unrecognizable. The interpretation became so strained that the meaning of mysticism was utterly changed. The Romantic interpretation of mysticism became so influential that it was presupposed by later writers like Dean Inge and Evelyn Underhill, and via them this meaning of the word was adopted by William James and others. But this meant that mysticism was not mysticism at all – in the sense that Dionysius the Areopagite or Meister Eckhart would have understood it – but a form of religious Romanticism concentrated on the themes of individual subjectivity and heightened emotional or psychological states.

But if mysticism is not the Romantic mysticism of esoteric experiences, what is it? What has been rediscovered in the literature of Christian mysticism? First of all is the notion that these texts can be analyzed in theological and philosophical terms. What emerges is the fact that they are not esoteric, pietistic, or emotively "foggy" expressions of religious feeling, but deliberate, sophisticated, and hard-headed expressions of theological reflection that only make sense within the context of Christian doctrine. As such, anyone reading the mystics' texts with an eye to their intellectual context will be disappointed if they are looking for evidence of subjective and psychologistic religious experiences. This may well not be a view of the mystics that will appeal to students of "spirituality" or "mysticism" in the modern sense, but it is an accurate one. As Turner writes, it is necessary to "rescue [the mystics] from a contemporary 'experientialist' misreading and therefore . . . make them more valuable to us. . . . For as read adequately, they challenge much in contemporary thought and spirituality, in particular they

challenge a certain positivism of religious experience. . . . I am afraid it is more important to dislike these authors, if we must, for what they are than to like them for what
they are not" (1995:5).

So if the Christian mystics are not advocates of a form of religious Romanticism,
what are they? Fundamentally, they are theologians reflecting upon the Christian doctrine of the hiddenness of God. God, say the mystics, is beyond human understanding.
God is a mystery; a concept that can only be formed negatively. We do not know what
God is, only what God is not. This position is typically described as negative theology,
that is, Christian talk about what God is not, rather than what God is. Thus God is not
finite, but infinite; God is not changeable, but unchangeable; God is not comprehensible, but incomprehensible; God is not material, but immaterial. None of these classical
terms for God tell us what God is; all they do is deny something of God. Such Christian
unknowing of God is appropriate because God is understood to be a reality greater than
the capacity of the human mind to think God. For finite human beings, the infinite God
is, as the Prophet Isaiah proclaims, truly a hidden God (Isaiah 45:15). Or, as Augustine
states, the Christian is jubilant when he or she praises "that which cannot be uttered"
(Augustine 1989, "On the Psalms" C.5).

This means that the mystics are not describing ineffable experiences; rather they are
describing the Christian doctrine that God is ineffable. To this extent, there is nothing
really unusual about the mystics: they are, purely and simply, Christian theologians
engaged in an intellectual project, not an experiential one. Whereas modern notions of
mysticism tend to be based on the idea that there is some kind of parting of ways
between mystics and serious theologians, in an ancient or medieval context there is no
difference between the two (Von Balthasar 1984:5). Meister Eckhart was, after all,
Master of Theology at the University of Paris and he defended his theological teaching
by claiming that he was following the doctrine of Augustine and Thomas Aquinas. This
is nothing unusual for a Dominican. Indeed, if mystics are correctly defined as negative theologians, then Thomas Aquinas is arguably one of the greatest mystics Christianity has produced.

Mysticism as Negative Theology

We have seen that "mysticism" is a notoriously slippery word that has been given a wide
range of meanings, some of them, one suspects, deliberately foggy and obscure (Dean
Inge listed 25 different definitions). Why then equate mystical theology with negative
theology in particular? The word *mystikos* is derived from the Greek verb *myo*, which
means "to close," especially when indicating the closure of the eyes. The mystical, then,
refers to that which is hidden, unseen, veiled, or secret. As such, when the shadowy
Dionysius the Areopagite wrote his influential *Mystical Theology* in the fifth or sixth
century – the chief influence on later Christian use of the word "mystical" – he meant
by "Mystical Theology" theology of the hidden or secret God (see Bouyer 1980).
According to Dionysius, acknowledging that one does not know what God is always
takes precedence over any ideas about God that one might hold. What may surprise is
just how radical Dionysius is in his views. If we only truly know what God is not, then

all things must be denied of God. Some of the things that are to be denied of God sound straightforward: God is not material, has no shape, quality, quantity, and weight. God is not in a place and cannot be seen nor touched. God is not perceptible or changeable. Such denials sound fine. But Dionysius goes beyond this to say that God is also not soul nor mind, nor greatness, nor power, nor light, nor life, nor truth, nor oneness. God is not even divinity or goodness. Indeed, God does not even exist.

Moreover, the logic of mysticism is so far-reaching that it is suitable for the Pseudo-Dionysius to say that God is even beyond what is denied of God. That is to say, the denials are also denied. So God is not immaterial, not shapeless, not placeless, not soulless nor mindless nor lifeless nor non-existent. Dionysius is deliberately using language to undermine itself, to express that which is, strictly speaking, beyond language. To do this he makes use of language to subvert itself in oxymorons and paradoxes. That God cannot be placed within the structure of language creates specific problems for a theological philosophy of language, which Dionysius explores. The language draws attention to its own failure. This involves what Graham Ward has described as "a technical manipulation of . . . words in order to mark the new way in which they were being used" (Ward 2002:164). This is an attempt to use language to point outside of language to the Christian God who is "above every name that is named" (Ephesians 1:21).

So mysticism concentrates on the doctrine that God is unknown rather than known, or, to be more precise, is known only as unknown – that is, is known negatively. And one of the tactics mystics use to show just how much they do not know God is a strategy of manipulating language that pushes language to breaking point in order to show that God is ineffable. God is beyond language itself. This, as will be shown, is of great interest in terms of Christian engagement with some postmodern theory. More immediately, however, some explanation need be given of the origins of Christian mysticism. This is because I want to establish that this Christian mysticism is not an expression of a general religious phenomenon, but is, rather, something that thrives within a context of doctrines specific to Christianity. It is a genuine expression of the tradition and is, indeed, inseparable from it.

Origins of Mysticism

I have already mentioned that the nineteenth-century liberal rejection of mysticism that influenced (amongst others) Barth and Brunner focused largely on the supposition that mysticism was not genuinely Christian, but an import from pagan and especially Platonic and neo-Platonic thought. Today, however, it is increasingly clear that Christian mysticism has roots in doctrines unique to the tradition. As such, I argue that the old criticism no longer stands, and Christian mysticism has emerged as a specifically Christian discourse.

Amongst the many different things that may be found in the Bible are a great many statements about the unknowability of God. God is a hidden God (Isaiah 45:15), his face cannot be seen (Exodus 33:20), and he dwells in a thick darkness (Exodus 20:21). God can be compared to nothing and has no likeness (Isaiah 40:18–26), for he transcends all human thought (Isaiah 55:8–9). "It is he alone who has immortality and dwells in unapproachable light, whom no one has ever seen or can see; to him be honour and eternal dominion. Amen" (I Timothy 6:16). More important, however, than selecting a number of verses from the Scriptures is to note the general theme of anti-idolatry that runs through the Hebrew Scriptures and Jewish practice. The strictly Semitic notion of anti-idolatry is not only a ban on attempts to represent the divine with physical objects; the ban also applies to attempts to confuse human *ideas* about God with the divinity himself. God is not to be *imagined* for "we ought not to think that the deity is like . . . an image formed by the art and imagination of mortals" (Acts 17:29). It is simple to see how these themes can be expanded to support the case that the one thing that God reveals is that God is unknown. The divine essence is unthinkable because there is no accurate image of God that can be thought by the human mind. In other words, the one thing spoken of God is a silence.

The insistence that God is unimaginable was reinforced in the early Church by the development of the Christian doctrine of creation from nothing. God, say Christians, is the cause of all reality, the source of everything that has being. This is because an omnipotent God of monotheism needs no assistance when creating the universe, no building-blocks of pre-existent formless matter, no secondary principle, no lesser helper: everything that is, is created by God alone. Before the universe was, there was nothing, and God created the universe out of nothing; "the worlds were prepared by the word of God, so that what is seen was made from things that are not visible" (Hebrews 11:3). God calls into existence things that did not previously exist (Romans 4:17).[3]

The doctrine of creation from nothing was utterly unknown in Greek philosophy and is one of the things that separates ancient Christian and ancient pagan thought. The neo-Platonists, for instance, did not think that the world had been created but that it had emanated from the One, like rays from the sun. One of the consequences of this is that the world is thought of as some kind of extension, or overflowing, of the very being of God, and because of this it is correct to see that the pagan philosophy of emanation is tied up with a panentheistic view that the universe is part of God. In this way God and the world are, for the neo-Platonist, linked together. This means that the possibility is always present to the neo-Platonist that one may somehow – through contemplation or spiritual purification perhaps – find a way up, through the world that emanates from the One, to the One itself. The world acts as a kind of ladder up to God, and knowledge of God may reasonably be expected to be gained in the world that flows out from the One because this world is part of God.

The Christian doctrine of creation from nothing is quite different from the pagan philosophy of emanation because it tears apart the links between God and the universe. The universe is not a part of God. Instead it has a reality that has been caused by God and yet is separated from God because it has not overflowed from God's being but has come into being from precisely nothing at all. This means that the Christian cannot grasp the essence of God from reflecting upon this world, because the essence of the universe is not the essence of God. Christians cannot, therefore, gain knowledge of God in the same way that neo-Platonists seek to; rather they are aware that their very being is distinct from God's being and that it is impossible to gain knowledge of God from this universe of things that exist. Moreover, since human knowledge is not only shaped and formed by the universe around us, but is indeed a constituent part of the universe itself, the early Christians realized that they knew very little about God – less, certainly, than the neo-Platonists claimed to, and very probably nothing at all. Such was the consequence of teaching that God had created from nothing. Basil the Great states very clearly that it is because God is the creator of the universe that God is unknown. All human knowledge is restricted to this universe and cannot pass beyond the beginning of the world to contemplate the essence of the creator:

> The superior remoteness of the Father is really inconceivable, in that thought and intelligence are wholly impotent to go beyond the generation of the Lord; and St John has admirably confined the conception within circumscribed boundaries by two words, "In the *beginning was* the Word." For thought cannot travel outside "*was*," nor imagination beyond "*beginning*." Let your thought travel ever so far backward you cannot get beyond the "*was*," and however you may strain and strive to see what is beyond the Son, you will find it impossible to get further than the "*beginning*."   (Basil the Great 1989:8–9)

Human thought is restricted to things within the universe and cannot penetrate to the unimaginable cause of the universe. If one attempts to imagine what there was "before" the universe came into being one has to think of nothing at all, nothing that has existence, no color, no shape, no form, no duration. One might mistakenly imagine a swirling gray mist, but a swirling gray mist *is something*. One might think of darkness, but darkness *is something*. Whenever one thinks of anything, one thinks of this or that which has some quantity, perhaps, or quality, or spatial extension, or duration, or feeling, or whatever *it* might be. But when one thinks about whatever caused this universe one cannot identify any *it* at all because any *it* is *something*, and all thought is of *something*. Whatever lies behind the universe is strictly unthinkable because thought is restricted to the universe. But God is the creator of the universe and so God is unthinkable and imageless.

God, therefore, is incomprehensible because God is not a part of the universe that human beings comprehend. This means that the Christian God is more incomprehensible than the neo-Platonic One. Gregory of Nazianzus therefore found it necessary to surpass Plato in his ignorance of God. Plato taught (in the *Timaeus* 28e) that it is difficult to conceive of God and that to define God is impossible; Gregory taught that it is impossible to define God and *even more* impossible to conceive of God.[4]

Thus whatever negative theology there is in ancient pagan thought is of a different kind from Christian negative theology; it is of a different degree and has a different intellectual source. The source of Christian negative theology is the doctrine of creation from nothing, unknown to pagan philosophy. Indeed, negative theology is woven into the fabric of Christian doctrine. To take two examples, *ignorance* of God was perhaps the chief factor in the development of the doctrines of the Incarnation and the Trinity. In the case of the Incarnation, it is important to look closely at the arguments Athanasius employed against the Arians. The Arian position – as far, at least, as Athanasius understood it – failed partly because they did not share his "radical distinction between the Creator and everything created out of nothing" (Young 1983:75). For the Arians, God could not be in Christ because that would be rather like fitting a mountain into a sardine tin. But for Athanasius, God should not be thought of as a mountain or any other created thing, not even something of vast dimensions and power: "what sort of resemblance is there between things which are from nothing and the one who rendered the things which are nothing into being?"[5] He continues: "God is not as man . . . they should not think of him in human terms."[6] Now, since God is incomprehensible and not a part of the universe, Athanasius sees that the Incarnation does not involve imagining that one very big thing (God) is linked to the man Jesus; rather, in Jesus is an incomprehensible mystery that is distinct from anything created.

It is because Athanasius can deny that God is like anything we can imagine in the universe that he is also able to argue that the incomprehensible mystery is incarnate in Christ. For how could one deny that something one cannot identify is *not* in Christ. The logic of the Incarnation therefore depended in part on negative theology. And, as Athanasius shows, this negative theology is a result of reflection on the doctrine of creation *ex nihilo*:

> The Word is Christ, "for there is one God the Father, from whom are all things; we are for him, and one Lord Jesus Christ, through whom are all things, and we are through him" [I Corinthians 8:6]. If all things are through him, he himself should not be counted with the all things. He who dares to say that he, through whom are all things, is one of the all things will have the same opinion about God, from whom are all things. If anyone flees from this as absurd and distinguishes God as different from all things, it would follow that even the only-begotten Son, since he is peculiar to the Father's substance, is different from all things. If he is not one of the "all thing," it is not right to say about him "There was once when he was not" and "He was not before he was begotten." Such terms are fittingly said about creatures, but the Son himself is such a one as is the Father, of whose substance he is a peculiar offspring, Word and Wisdom. This is peculiar to the Son in relation to the Father, and this shows that the Father is peculiar to the Son.

Whatever the relationship of the divine nature to the human nature of Christ is, it is certainly a different sort of relationship from any between two created things. Not knowing what God is, neither can one say what this sort of relationship is. And if one does not know what the relationship involves, neither can one deny it. Athanasius does not tell us what the substance of God is: it is an unknown "whatever it is."[7]

This same logic was used by the Cappadocian Fathers to justify the doctrine of the Trinity. The Trinity is not to be viewed as three conceivable things in communion, for that would imply tritheism. Rather, it is precisely because God is not known and therefore not restricted to human concepts like number that the Trinity does not lead to any logical or mathematical absurdity. It is not possible to think of the Trinity as one thing plus another thing plus another thing because God is not any kind of thing. Unknown infinity plus unknown infinity plus unknown infinity equals unknown infinity. It is no surprise therefore that the Cappadocian Fathers are amongst the leading proponents of negative theology in the patristic period. It is certainly the case that Gregory of Nyssa had an especial influence on the Pseudo-Dionysius. Neither is it any accident that later formal Trintarian dogma made special appeal to negative theology. The Athanasian Creed provides a particularly striking example of this: *the Father incomprehensible, the Son incomprehensible, the Holy Spirit incomprehensible.*

The Unutterable Otherness of God and Mystical Union

The witness of the Church, then, is a witness to a God who is wholly other to the universe. But this otherness of God is not an otherness of the sort that is found within the universe, where objects, concepts, and the like can be distinguished from one another. We can see how the component parts of the world are distinguished on the basis of their finite boundaries and the distinction that they have from other things. Thus we can identify red because it is not green, a table because it is not a chair, chalk because it is not cheese, and Jill because she is not Jack. All of these distinctions are made within the universe; but since God transcends the universe and therefore also transcends our ability to recognize distinctions it is impossible for us to know how different from the universe God is. For, to know how God is different from the world we would first have to know what God is. Thus Augustine states:

> Whatever man thinks to the contrary, that which was made is not like Him who made it. Except God, whatever else there is in the universe was made by God. What a difference there is between Him who made, and that which was made, who can worthily imagine? Therefore this man said, "there is none like unto Thee, O Lord: there is not one that can do as thou doest." But how much God is unlike them he said not, because it cannot be said. Let your Charity attend: God is ineffable: we more easily think what He is not than what He is. . . . What is He then? I could only tell thee, what He is not. Askest thou what He is? What "the eye hath not seen, nor the ear heard, nor has risen up in the heart of man." (St. Augustine 1989:413–14; "On the Psalms" 84.11)

Not knowing God, we do not know whether she differs from the universe to a great degree or a small degree. We do not know how different God is at all. God is not different from the universe as a carpenter is to a chair, or as a hand is to a foot, or the sea is to land. God's difference is unutterable. This is not to say that God differs differently from the way things differ in the universe; more precisely, as Meister Eckhart recognized, God is distinct by being indistinct. That is to say, it is impossible to imagine what the difference between God and the world actually is. Not knowing what God is we do not know what God is not. This is the root of mystics' talk of union with God. Far from describing the idea that someone has had a psychologistic experience of being at one with God, the mystics are merely saying that if you cannot consciously recognize that God is different from something then you *have* to say that she is one with something, for union takes place where things are not distinguished by language and thought. If the mystics' know that they cannot distinguish God from the world, then they know *through this unknowing* that they are united with God. As Dionysius explains:

> renouncing all that the mind may conceive, wrapped entirely in the intangible and the invisible, [one] belongs completely to him who is beyond everything. Here, being neither oneself nor someone else, one is supremely united to the completely unknown by an inactivity of all knowledge, and knows beyond the mind by knowing nothing.[8]

Or, as Augustine has it, God is nearer to you than you are to yourself (St. Augustine, *Confessions*, 1991a). Paradoxical language indeed – until it is recognized that God is not distinguishable from yourself and is therefore one with yourself.

The one distinction that mystics are keen on holding onto is the distinction between Creator and creature, but precisely because it is *this* distinction of all distinctions, the distinction between the universe and the unknowable, mysterious whatever-it-is that lies behind the universe, *this* distinction is, of course, not itself known. This distinction is the distinction that makes God indistinguishable from the universe, and it is therefore unlike any other distinction or difference *in* the universe: it is a distinction that cannot be conceptualized, or, as Julian of Norwich says, it cannot be seen. It is an invisible distinction (Julian of Norwich 1987).

Apophaticism, Language, and the Postmodern

Now if God is beyond distinctions, God is also beyond language. This explains the mystics' playful use of language to subvert itself. Dionysius delights in linguistic paradoxes and oxymorons to show that labels cannot be applied to God because she ruptures and breaks apart the capacity of human language to label her. This is the root of that brand of negative theology known as apophaticism, where "*apophasis* is a Greek neologism for the breakdown of *speech*, which, in face of the unknowability of God, falls infinitely short of the mark" (Turner 1995:120). Dionysius takes this so far that – as I described above – at the very end of the *Mystical Theology* he even negates the negations of negative theology itself:

> It is beyond assertion and denial. We make assertions and denials of what is next to it, but never of it, for it is both beyond every assertion, being the perfect and unique cause of all things, and, by virtue of its preeminently simple and absolute nature, free of every limitation, beyond every limitation; it is also beyond every denial.[9]

Whichever way language is used, God is not named by it. It does not matter if language is used only to deny things of God for these denials always fall short of the mark and have *themselves* to be denied. Thus apophaticism creates room for a great deal of affirmative language about God (as long as it is remembered that these affirmations also fall short of the unknowable God). This explains why some Christian mystics, whilst holding fast to the principles of negative theology, nevertheless provide us with a superabundance of seemingly positive images of the divine. These images – illustrated in the works of Julian of Norwich or Teresa of Avila, for instance – in their very superabundance show that none of them encapsulates the reality of God, and therefore underline the fact that God is unknowable. Metaphors are constructed that undermine themselves: "In our *Mother* Christ we grow and develop; in *his* mercy *he* reforms and restores us" (Julian of Norwich 1987:157). As Turner says, "affirmative and negative metaphors are equally metaphors . . . affirmation and negation are equally *language* . . . the 'mystical' is characterised by its transcendence of both affirmation and negation" (Turner 1999:150–1). This position is clearly evidenced in Augustine:

> If thou regardest things visible, neither is God bread, nor is God water, nor is God this light, nor is he garment or house. For all these things are things visible, and single separate things. What bread is, water is not; and what a garment is, a house is not; and what these

things are, God is not, for they are visible things. God is all this to thee; if thou thirstest, He is water to thee; if thou art in darkness, He is light to thee: for he remains incorruptible. If thou art naked, He is a garment of immortality to thee. . . . All things can be said of God, and nothing is worthily said of God. Nothing is wider than this poverty of expression. Thou seekest a fitting name for Him, thou canst not find it; thou seekest to speak of Him in any way soever, thou findest that he is all. What likeness have the lamb and the lion? Both is said of Christ. "Behold the Lamb of God!" How a lion? "The Lion of the tribe of Judah hath prevailed."   (St. Augustine 1991b:88–9)

Predictably, the mystics' recognition that God ruptures language has been of great interest for postmodern philosophers. This is partly because of the mystics' subversive playfulness with language, partly because they are nevertheless concerned with unsaying the foundation of language that is the foundation of all – God the creator who is outside the universe, indistinct from all that is, and therefore one with it. As the Structuralists, like Saussure, have told us, language depends upon recognizing differences, is conceived as a system of differences within a structure: "in the linguistic system there are only differences, *without positive terms*" (Saussure 1960:120). In the hands of a poststructuralist like Derrida this means that in the linguistic system "there are only, everywhere, differences and traces of differences" (Derrida 1981:26). Derrida recognizes that the foundation of the system cannot be identified within the structure of language. Language is therefore arbitrary, a system of infinite referral of difference to difference without any beginning, middle, or end that can serve as a metalinguistic Ur-difference. In other words, the foundation that makes the world meaningful is hidden; all that remains is an endless deferral of meaning.

Some of this is tantalizingly close to the Christian mystical tradition. Tantalizingly close enough, at least, to make it desirable for some Christian theologians who seek to engage with postmodern thought to do so on the basis of the mystical tradition, for, as Davies and Turner have noted, "negative theology can be used creatively to explore affinities with an intellectual environment in which negation – as difference, absence, otherness – is frequently judged to be more interesting than affirmation" (Davies and Turner 2002). Tantalizingly close enough, also, to explain Derrida's own interest in mysticism, which can be found in essays like "Violence and Metaphysics" (Derrida 2001:97–192) and "How to Avoid Speaking: Denials" (Derrida 1992), and in his book *On the Name* (Derrida 1995). Derrida's own opinion is that his project of deconstruction has an uneasy relationship with the *via negativa*. He describes descriptions of his own philosophy as negative theology as precipitous (Derrida 1991:273). This may be colored by his own understanding that the Christian mystics must yet still be thinking about a God who is in some sense really out there, even though whether this is actually the case is a matter of debate. If Dionysius says that God is utterly non-existent, what are the grounds for not taking him at his word?

Nevertheless, there is ground for fruitful dialogue here. Perhaps the most significant difference between the Christian mystical tradition and Derrida's thought lies in their respective understandings of how the unnameable foundation is understood. Certainly, for Derrida the absence of the foundation indicates that it is irrelevant, and this means that we are left hovering in a shifting, fluid deferral of meaning in which all signs are arbitrary and perhaps – in the eyes of some of his interpreters, at least – absurd. On the other hand, in the mystical tradition the absence of the foundation is not taken to mean that it is irrelevant even if we can never perceive it. If God is unknown – indistinct – from the world because God is the creator of the world *ex nihilo*, then *this* unknown can be interpreted more positively and more optimistically not as an absurdity, but as a mystery – and, moreover, as a mystery of love.

This disagreement is between two different ways of apprehending the fact that we do not know what the foundation of the universe is. Although there is agreement that we are ignorant of the foundation, and that the universe is therefore *just given*, nevertheless this *just given* can be taken in two different ways. The phrase *just given* can mean that something is the case, i.e., the world just is the way it is. But for a Christian mystic, working with the doctrine of creation *ex nihilo*, it is necessary to emphasize that the givenness of the universe implies that it is a gift. Since God is incomprehensible it is of course impossible to perceive what reason God had in making the universe. God has just given the universe to us for no reason. And it is possible – just about – to interpret this gift as therefore a gift given because of love.

Seeing the world as a gift freely given for nothing but love distinguishes the Christian world-view from some others; it also coincides with Jesus's teaching that the law and the prophets can be summarized in the command to love one another. This, however, raises a problem for the tradition of negative theology, for if mysticism emphasizes the unknowability and hiddenness of God, what then is to be made of the revelation in Christ? Christianity is, after all, a religion with a revelation in which God speaks: how then can the mystical concealment of God be squared with God's revealed Word?

Concealment and Revelation

This problem is not without solutions. First of all it should be noted that for many mystics revelation itself serves the function of making it known that God is unknown. After all, one has to be told that one does not know something; otherwise one is completely unaware that there is something that one does not know. Thus the Pseudo-Dionysius speaks of God being *hidden* by revelation:

> The transcendent has put aside its own hiddenness and has revealed itself to us by becoming a human being. But he is hidden even after this revelation, or, if I may speak in a more divine fashion, is hidden even amid revelation. For this mystery Jesus remains hidden and can be drawn out by no word or mind. What is to be said of it remains unsayable; what is to be understood of it remains unknowable.

Maximus the Confessor confirms Dionysius's opinion:

> For having become man . . . he himself remains completely incomprehensible, and shows his own Incarnation, which has been granted a generation beyond being, to be more incomprehensible than any mystery. The more he becomes comprehensible through it, so much the more through it is he known to be incomprehensible. . . . What could do more to demonstrate the proof of the divine transcendence of being than this: *revelation shows that it is hidden*, reason that it is unspeakable, and intellect that it is transcendently unknowable.   (Maximus the Confessor 1996)

This, too, is the position held by Aquinas. "Man's utmost knowledge of God is to know that we do not know him," says Thomas. Ironically, revelation does not reveal any knowledge of God; it simply shows that God is hidden from human knowing: revelation simply shows that humanity knows nothing about God. "In this life what God is is unknown to us by the revelation of grace; and so [by revelation] we are joined to him as to something unknown." God is revealed as a purely negative concept. True knowledge of God, proposed by revelation, is the knowledge that God is unknown:

> For then alone do we know God truly, when we believe that he is far above all that man can possibly think of God . . . by the fact that certain things about God are proposed to man, which surpass his reason, he is strengthened in his opinion that God is far above what he is able to think.   (Aquinas 1998: *Summa Contra Gentiles*, 1.5.3)

The content of revelation – the doctrine of the Trinity for instance – surpasses human reason and is incomprehensible. Thus revelation confirms the knowledge that God cannot be known. Thomas therefore conceives of revelation as a *negative* revelation. God's Word shows humanity that God cannot be known.

None of this seems particularly Christocentric and that is because it is not. If Christ is incomprehensible then Christ cannot be placed at the center of Christian thought as a discrete and positive object. But Christ cannot be located within our sphere of knowing: "You will search for me, but you will not find me; and where I am, you cannot come" (John 7:34). According to traditional doctrine, Christ has ascended into heaven, and heaven is a realm invisible to us. Christ has ascended, therefore, above the sphere of human comprehension and is henceforth *hidden* in the cloud that received him from the Mount of Olives.

Aquinas clarifies that the doctrine of the ascension is ultimately a negative theology (or more precisely, a negative Christology) because Christ has ascended above "every name that is named" (Ephesians 1:21):

> Christ, as man, is exalted above all . . . above every name that is named. . . . [He surpasses] everything capable of being named.
>
> For it should be recognized that a name is given to understand the object [referred to]; it signifies the object's substance when what the name designates is the precise intelligibility of the object. In asserting every name that is named he [Paul] lets us know that the exaltation is above every substance which can be known and comprehended by a name . . . [above] those realities of which the Apostle says in 2 Corinthians 12 (4), that "he heard secret words which it is not granted to man to utter." Yet Christ is even exalted above these. "He hath given him a name which is above all names" (Philippians 2:9).   (Aquinas 1966:78–9)

A name that is above any other name is an unnameable name. Christ has ascended to a place that we cannot comprehend. There are no human words that can express where Christ has gone: heaven is strictly mysterious and utterly transcendent. Christ has departed beyond the epistemological horizons of human knowledge. Thus, by his ascension, the Word of God is hidden, leaving behind a God that is known only negatively.

Conclusion

Mysticism, then, is a fundamental aspect of the Christian tradition. I have shown how it is intimately linked with a number of historic Christian doctrines, and how a re-appreciation of mysticism can lead to fruitful and creative insights into central Christian doctrines like the Trinity, Incarnation and Ascension that pose a challenge to much modern theologizing. Further, I have shown how the Christian mystical tradition creates a useful locus for theological exploration of the postmodern. If Christian doctrine is to interact with contemporary thought, then this is certainly an area that needs further investigation. Perhaps most importantly, my description of the transformation of the definition of mysticism in recent years reminds modern theology of the useful-ness of historical theology. All too often contemporary theology looks back on earlier periods through the lenses of received opinions that can be shown to be faulty. And yet, when the tradition is revisited, one discovers there a basis which informs the most up-to-date thought. Perhaps, after all, the premodern and postmodern are peculiarly alike, and if theology is to find a way through the thought of a Derrida or Deleuze, its best bet is to re-adopt the insights of the Christian mystical tradition.

Notes

1   On Barth's and Brunner's rejection of mysticism, see B. McGinn (1992:421, n. 21).
2   Ibid.
3   For critical discussions of this doctrine, see Frances Young, "Creatio ex Nihilo" (1991:139ff; and Gerhard May, *Creatio ex Nihilo*, 1994).
4   See Gregory of Nazianzus, "Second Theological Oration," 4, in Hardy (1954:138).
5   See Athanasius, *Orations against the Arians*, 1.21, in Rusch (1980:84).
6   See ibid., 1.28, in Rusch (1980:91).
7   See ibid., 1.18, in Rusch (1980:78).
8   Dionysius the Areopagite, *Mystical Theology* 1001A, in Rorem (1987:137).
9   Ibid., 1048B, in Rorem (1987:14).

References

Aquinas, T. 1966. *Commentary on St. Paul's Epistle to the Ephesians*, trans. M. L. Lamb. Albany, NY: Magi Books.

Aquinas, T. 1998. *Thomas Aquinas: Selected Writing*, trans. R. McInery. Harmondsworth: Penguin.

Athanasius. 1980. *Orations against the Arians*, in *The Trinitarian Controversy*, ed. W. G. Rusch. Philadelphia, PA: Fortress Press.

Augustine, St. 1989. "On the Psalms" 84.11, in *The Nicene and Post-Nicene Fathers*, 1st series, vol. VIII. Edinburgh: T. & T. Clark.

Augustine, St. 1991a. *Confessions*, trans. H. Chadwick. Oxford: Oxford University Press.

Augustine, St. 1991b. "On the Gospel of St John," Tractate XIII.5, in *The Nicene and Post-Nicene Fathers*, vol. VII. Edinburgh, T. & T. Clark.

Basil the Great. 1989. "On the Holy Spirit," in *The Nicene and Post-Nicene Fathers*, 2nd series, vol. VIII. Edinburgh: T. & T. Clark.

Bouyer, L. 1980. "Mysticism: an Essay on the History of the Word," in R. Woods (ed.), *Understanding Mysticism*. London: Athlone Press, pp. 42–55.

Bultmann, R. 1960. *Primitive Christianity in its Contemporary Setting*. London: Fontana.

Bultmann, R. 1997. *What is Theology?* Minneapolis, MN: Fortress Press.

Davies, O. and Turner, D. eds. 2002. *Silence and the Word: Negative Theology and Incarnation*. Cambridge: Cambridge University Press.

Derrida, J. 1981. *Positions*. Chicago, IL: Chicago University Press.

Derrida, J. 1991. "Letter to a Japanese Friend," in *A Derrida Reader: Between the Blinds*, ed. P. Kamuf. Hemel Hempstead: Harvester Wheatsheaf.

Derrida, J. 1992. "How to Avoid Speaking: Denials," trans. K. Frieden, in *Derrida and Negative Theology*, eds. H. Coward and T. Foshay. New York: State University of New York Press.

Derrida, J. 1995. *On the Name*. Stanford, CA: Stanford University Press.

Derrida, J. 2001. "Violence and Metaphysics," in *Writing and Difference*. London: Routledge, pp. 97–192.

Dupré, L. 1987. "Mysticism," in M. Eliade (ed.), *The Encyclopaedia of Religion*. New York: Macmillan.

Gregory of Nazianzus. 1954. "Second Theological Oration," in *Christology of the Later Fathers*, ed. E. Hardy. Philadelphia, PA: Westminster Press.

Hardy, E. ed. 1954. *Christology of the Later Fathers*. Philadelphia, PA: Westminster Press.

Herrmann, W. 1906. *The Communion of the Christian with God*. London: Williams and Norgate.

James, W. 1985. *The Varieties of Religious Experience*. Harmondsworth: Penguin.

Julian of Norwich. 1987. *Revelations of Divine Love*. Harmondsworth: Penguin.

Katz, S. T. ed. 1978. *Mysticism and Philosophical Analysis*. London: Sheldon Press.

McGinn, B. 1992. *The Foundations of Mysticism: Origins to the Fifth Century, in The Presence of God: A History of Western Christian Mysticism* series. London: SCM Press.

Maximus the Confessor. 1996. *Ambigua 5*, trans. A. Louth, in *Maximus the Confessor*. London: Routledge.

May, G. 1994. *Creatio ex Nihilo: The Doctrine of "Creation out of Nothing" in Early Christian Thought*. Edinburgh: T. & T. Clark.

Ritschl, A. 1887. *Theologie und Metaphysik*. Bonn: Marcus.

Rorem, L. ed. 1987. *Pseudo-Dionysius: The Complete Works*, trans. C. Luibheid. New York: Paulist Press.

Rusch, W. G. ed. 1980. *The Trinitarian Controversy*. Philadelphia, PA: Fortress Press.

Saussure, F. 1960. *Course in General Linguistics*. London: Peter Owen.

Turner, D. 1995. *The Darkness of God: Negativity in Christian Mysticism*. Cambridge: Cambridge University Press.

Turner, D. 1999. "Negative Theology and Eucharistic Presence," *Modern Theology* (April).

Von Balthasar, H. U. 1984. *The Glory of the Lord: A Theological Aesthetics*, vol. 2. Edinburgh: T. & T. Clark.

Von Harnack, A. 1961. *History of Dogma*, vol. 4. New York: Dover.

Ward, G. 2002. "'In the Daylight Forever?' Language and Silence," in *Silence and the Word: Negative Theology and Incarnation*, eds. O. Davies and D. Turner. Cambridge: Cambridge University Press, pp. 159–84.

Young, F. 1983. *From Nicaea to Chalcedon*. London: SCM Press.

Young, F. 1991. "Creatio ex Nihilo: a Context for the Emergence of the Christian Doctrine of Creation," *Scottish Journal of Theology* 44:139ff.

Zaehner, R. C. 1972. *Zen, Drugs, and Mysticism*. New York: Pantheon.

CHAPTER 29
The Context of Eco-theology

Laurel Kearns

The phrase "I'm a tree-hugging Jesus freak," a self-description uttered recently by a Pentecostal environmentalist, demonstrates the complexity of contemporary eco-theology and religious ecological activism. For the past two decades or more, the combination of these two identities seemed unthinkable, for Christians were still struggling to articulate a response, much less a response that would appeal to Pentecostals, usually viewed as un-ecological. This chapter examines many of the historical and more contemporary contexts that shape what is now a rich eco-theological conversation. Although the chapter tries to give a broad international sense of the movement, it draws heavily upon the US context where a diverse and multi-faceted conversation about eco-theology has been going on for over three decades. Furthermore, while there are now ecological voices within all the major religious traditions, this chapter will primarily focus on Christianity as the context of eco-theology.

While there are many historical precedents that one could acknowledge leading into the contemporary environmental movement, such as Aldo Leopold's *Sand Country Almanac* (1949), most scholars agree it began in the 1960s, marked by a variety of publications that brought attention to the issues at hand. In fact, many historians of the movement date the birth of the modern environmental movement to Rachel Carson's 1962 paradigm-changing book *Silent Spring*, which detailed the damage wrought by pesticides throughout the ecological web. Garrett Hardin's "Tragedy of the Commons" (1968), a doomsday scenario about population growth, was published toward the end of the decade. Taken together, these two works exemplify the dominant concerns of the early movement – pesticides, pollution, and population. Also in the late sixties, Lynn White's infamous article "The Historical Roots of Our Ecological Crisis" appeared in *Science* (White 1967), in which White concluded that "Christianity bears a huge burden of guilt for the ecologic crisis." Certainly there were plenty more forces in the sixties that shaped the environmental movement, and to this we will return, but ideas alone do not produce social movements. It was in the sixties, however, that widespread activist and scholarly concern coalesced, and the response from Christian thinkers started to appear.[1] Before tracing some of the subsequent development of the movement, it is helpful to look back at the history of the concept of nature in Western thought, for it is the various religious/philosophical understandings of "nature" in the development of the Western world-view that shape the contemporary religious conversation about environmental issues.

The Western World-view and Nature

As did White, much scholarly attention focuses on certain biblical concepts such as to have dominion, to subdue, and the ideal relationship of humanity to nature, and on the corresponding interpretive issues that reappear again and again in theological and philosophical thought. It is in the two contradictory and contrasting Genesis creation stories that we can see the roots of very different understandings of the human/nature relationship. The priestly or P account in Genesis 1 presents a remote God who appears to create *ex nihilo*.[2] As the crowning point of Creation, God creates male and female in "their" image (as you can imagine, there is much debate over the plural pronoun for God). It is in Genesis 1:28 that the crucial verbs "subdue" and "have dominion" are found, and these which have occasioned a great deal of scholarship over their correct interpretation and application (Habel and Warst 2000).

> Be fruitful and multiply, and fill the earth and subdue it; and have dominion over the fish
> of the sea and the birds of the air and over every living thing that moves upon the earth
> (RSV)

The second chapter of Genesis contains the Yahwist, or J, account. In this creation story, God is no longer remote but forms *adam*, or human–earth creature, out of adamah, the dust and clay of the earth, before there are plants and other living things. As one scholar phrases it, here is a God that gets "her" hands dirty.[3] In this second account, the animals are created as helpmates to Adam, and when that is insufficient, Eve is created out of Adam's rib. The order of creation and its implications are quite different between the two stories. The first represents creation as insufficient until humans are created at the top of the hierarchy; the second shows Adam as insufficient until he is joined both by the living beings, from plants to animals, and then by Eve, or woman. In the third chapter, which contains the curse (Genesis 3:14–19) that accompanies the expulsion from the Garden, other aspects of the human/nature relationship are presented: the land may be hostile and humans will struggle to obtain food, women and animals are separated and against each other, and the very physical nature of women present in the birthing/creation of life will include punishment and pain. There are many interpretive conflicts over these texts and this summary is necessarily only a first-order treatment.

For many, the term "dominion over all the earth" sums up the religious roots of a destructive, anti-ecological, Western world-view that, as White (1967) charged, "insisted that it is God's will that man exploit nature for his proper ends." In response to such charges, many scholars and religious ecologists point out that dominion is more accurately interpreted as stewardship, or the caring and keeping of the earth, because it is the Lord's (DeWitt 1987, Granberg-Michaelson 1987, Hessel 1992). Other scholars de-emphasize the importance of this text by emphasizing the instructions in Genesis 2 to keep and till the Garden of Eden. They see the combined texts in covenantal terms, that is, that humans are to till and keep the land responsibly in return for God's blessing enabling them to be fruitful and multiply. In this same vein, many point out that this stewardship theme runs throughout the Hebrew Scriptures, and is explicit in the numerous commandments regarding agricultural and dietary laws in the care both for the land and for animals (Brueggemann 1977). Ecologically oriented scholars go on to find much merit in the "land ethic" of the Hebrew Scriptures and the idea of a Sabbath for all, animals and the land included. Although it may seem to be more difficult to find ecological messages in the Christian New Testament, scholars point to Jesus's constant illustrations from nature to demonstrate aspects of God, including the affirmation that God loves humans in a comparable manner to God's love for the sparrows and lilies.

White's argument was far more nuanced and complex than merely placing the blame on the Genesis texts, for what he really argues is that it is the anthropocentrism (human-centeredness) of Judaism and Christianity, reflected in the creation story, that poses a major problem. To counter this view, he holds up St. Francis of Assisi as a model of the equality of all creatures, including humans. As tired as many today are of hearing White's thesis, its role in stimulating a flood of historical, philosophical, theological writing and religious activism on the subject of Christianity and ecology cannot be underestimated. Even without White's provocation, eco-theologians have to address the claims that human exceptionalism and anthropocentrism are at the core of the tradition. While White's thesis is the best known of many efforts to identify the sources of the modern view of nature, many scholars object to his emphasis on the Judeo-Christian[4] tradition as the primary source of our world-view. They argue for the diversity and complexity of Western thought on the subject of the human–nature relationship and the multitude of interpretations that competed for ideological dominance in different historical periods. Or, they argue that White places too much emphasis on the role of ideas in social change.[5] But many, even his critics, agree with White's ending conclusion that we must either "rethink our old religion" or create a new one, for religious and moral systems must address the ecological crisis.

Ian Barbour, in *Western Man and Environmental Ethics* (1973), a text that introduced the White essay to a broad audience, made the argument for the important influence of Greek and classical influences (as did Clarence Glacken in *Traces on the Rhodian Shore: Nature and Culture in Western Thought from Ancient Times to the End of the Eighteenth Century*, 1967). Barbour cites Aristotle's view that plant and animal life exist solely for humans; the Stoic view that since animals are non-rational one need not respect them; and the Gnostic and Manichean philosophy that nature is a realm of evil from which humans must escape. In response, the Nicene Creed's emphasis on God as creator, and the emphasis on the goodness of creation in the work of many early Christian theologians, counter the view of nature as evil or entrapping. Creation as good versus creation as corrupt would continue to bedevil Christian thought throughout its history. Many scholars, such as Rosemary Ruether (1992), point to the dualism of Platonic thought, especially seen in a spirit/body, mind/matter division, which privileges reason, spirit, and men over emotion, matter[6] or this-world, women, and animals, which continues to be present in Western thinking.

The influence of Aristotelian and Platonic thought can be seen in the medieval emphasis on the Great Chain of Being, or the hierarchy of creation, as well as in Aquinas's articulation of natural theology. And as White pointed out, many still look to St. Francis (1182–1226) of Assisi as an exemplar of Christian ecology, to the point that Pope John Paul II named him the patron saint of ecologists. Most scholars, however, view the scientific, industrial, theological, and cultural revolutions of the period 1500–1700 as particularly crucial in understanding the modern world-view. Carolyn Merchant's influential treatise *The Death of Nature* (1980) argues that the result of this wide scope of change was the disintegration of a more immanent and organic view of nature, and the ascendancy of the modern, mechanistic world-view that sees nature as dead, or inert, and atomized.

Merchant surveys the various conceptions and organic metaphors for nature, humanity, and human society that shaped medieval and Renaissance thought, and she argues that these restrained invasive human activity, as is seen even in the implications of the concept of "Mother Earth." It was in this period that the revival of Greek thought introduced competing philosophical concepts to the domination of religious thinking, so that religious and philosophical views are no longer intertwined. Merchant is careful to examine more than just ideas, for, during this period, a great many events shaped the dominant world-view. Increasing population pressure and land capabilities (in part due to the "rest" provided by the earlier decimation of the population by the plague) necessitated changed agricultural and extraction practices. Innovations in these techniques led to greater production capabilities and to expanding manufacturing and marketing opportunities, which then created greater demand for goods, etc. All of these social and economic changes in turn contributed to attempts to expand and justify greater land and resource usage, or, in the metaphoric language of the day, greater efforts to "tame" nature. The new scientific discoveries of Copernicus, Galileo, and Kepler challenged the reigning/philosophical cosmology and produced a great sense of unease and disorder about what was seen to be a stable and harmonious, and to some, static, cosmos. The Reformation brought a wide variety of religious challenges to the Catholic and Renaissance world-views and reinforced the growing sense of chaos and disorder in the world. Finally, in the search for economic expansion through new trade and new sources of raw materials, the discovery of "new worlds" and new animals, plants, trade goods, and "heathen" indigenous peoples heightened the dichotomy of orderly, civilized culture back home versus disorderly, chaotic "wild" nature over "there."[7]

As a complex result of these changes, the view of nature as disorderly and threatening, whether as wilderness or as human "nature," became dominant. For instance, in the witch trials, the view of women as weak and passive by nature in the face of stronger natural forces (such as their own alleged insatiable sexuality) was linked with the increasing view that nature had a darker side that could be manipulated by witches. This dual denigration of both internal and external nature contributed to the justification of increased male domination both of women's bodies and of Mother Earth's body. The commentary of Francis Bacon aptly illustrates this connection:

> For you have but to follow and as it were hound nature in her wanderings, and you will
> be able when you like to lead and drive her afterward to the same place again. . . . Neither
> ought a man to make scruple of entering and penetrating into these holes and corners,
> when the inquisition of truth is his whole object.   (As quoted in Merchant 1980:168)

Bacon is also an apt demonstration of how the term "dominion" came to be understood
and applied, for he states that the most noble ambition is "to endeavor to establish and
extend the power and dominion of the human race," so that "the human race [can]
recover the right over nature which belongs to it by divine bequest" (as quoted in
Merchant 1980:172).

Coupled with the growth of scientific understandings of the world, many scholars
suggest that the Protestant Reformation continued the disenchantment of the world,
or the removal of a sense of the sacred in this world, begun by Catholicism's attempt
to eradicate the more nature-oriented indigenous religious traditions of various parts
of Europe.[8] Obviously, a figure such as St. Francis points to a plurality of Catholic views,
and it is important to recognize that both Catholicism and Protestantism held mixed
messages about nature, as Paul Santmire (1985), in *The Travail of Nature*, traces in the
thought of key Christian thinkers throughout history. Although, as Santmire and other
scholars now point out, Calvinism had a mixed message with regard to nature, the
dominant Reformation understanding saw this material world as fallen and corrupt,
needing to be subdued. As the sociologist Max Weber argues ([1904/5] 1958), the
Protestant God became radically transcendent. This "removal" of God or the sacred
from the world, already present in the history of the religious world views of the
Israelites and early Christianity, opened the way for the scientific exploration of the
natural world and widened an already present matter–spirit dualism present in
Christianity. Continuing the mixed attitude toward nature: even though God was no
longer in the world, nature had a positive value because it could reveal, through close
study, the mind of God – this is similar to the natural-law theology of the Cathlolic
Thomistic tradition. In a similar paradox, as Weber argues, the uncertain nature of salvation within Calvinism, a result of the belief in predestination, also fueled the search
for revelations of God's will in the natural world. Although nature could reveal God, it
did not have value in and of itself. Furthermore, in the effort to prove one's salvation
by acting to further the glory of God, this uncertainty led to the desire to order and
control the "fallen" chaos of nature (a seeming contradiction to the idea of studying
nature in order to reveal the orderly mind of God), an impulse seen in the Calvinist
Dutch efforts to rein in their swampy lands by turning them into cultivated fields.[9]

In the developing realms of science, the cultural view of nature as chaos was
balanced by an increasingly mechanized view of the natural world as dead and inert.
In this view, discoverable laws governed the realm of nature. These laws could then be
used to "probe" and "utilize" nature's secrets. The new mechanistic view of nature
was of dead, inert particles governed by laws that could be discovered and used to
manipulate it for human gain. With this new market-oriented interest in the natural
world came the beginnings of the removal of scientific understandings of the world
from commonplace knowledge. In the ensuing centuries, science, in its bid to replace
the role of religion as an ultimate authority, wrapped itself in a cloak of elite discourse,

so that the full implications of new scientific and technological developments were not expected to be understood, and thus were not a part of the everyday understanding of the world.[10]

The assumption of universal, "natural" laws, stemming from the Catholic quest for a natural theology and the Protestant search for the mind of God revealed in nature, also played a key role in Enlightenment thought. The Enlightenment, for all of its exclusive understandings of humanity, stemmed from a desire to think more "scientifically" and search for universals and "inalienable rights" instead of being governed by historical particularities that seemed to cause such strife and chaos.[11] Thus the embrace of reason (and rejection of religion and superstition) replicated the dualistic privileging of mind/matter, spirit/body, reason/emotion, rationality/sexuality, culture/nature, etc. Nature was valued as a revelation of these universal laws, while at the same time being seen in contrast to, or as a hindrance of, the human pursuit of reason. The latter furthered the devaluing of those humans seen as "irrational" or governed in some way by their "nature" – women, children, indigenous peoples, subject or colonized peoples, those of different religious understandings – as opposed to those in possession of the "rational mind," so that the definition of "human" reflected the norms and characteristics of European men. Influenced by the prevailing Christian denunciation of the religious traditions of the peoples encountered in other lands, and its own pursuit of reason over faith, Enlightenment thought is filled with the dismissal of religion as superstitious and irrational, in contrast to Reason, often viewed as the divine spark of God in humans. True religion followed the dictates of reason.

Romanticism presented the major philosophical challenge to the Enlightenment desire to be freed from the yoke of nature through the exercise of human reason. Rather, Romanticism viewed nature as inherently good and as the source of truth. Romantics too talked of Reason, but meant by it access to knowledge through personal experience and intuition, often fostered by solitary experience/contemplation of nature. This romantic sense of truth as a vehicle for revelation and self-understanding differed greatly from the Enlightenment sense of truth in terms of laws regulating the universe. In reaction to the Enlightenment disengagement from nature, and in distress over the results of technological innovation and industrialization, Romanticism sought reunification with nature as a way to religious inspiration, harmony, and community. Today we are as much heirs of the mystical Romantic conception of nature as of the rational Enlightenment view of a mechanistic universe.

For many in the environmental movement, nature romanticism, as embodied in the American figures of Henry David Thoreau and John Muir, represented a source of resistance both to the dominant strains of Christianity, and also to the dominant culture's embrace of science, technology, and progress and the quest for ever-increasing control of and escape from natural constraints. This aspect especially continued to grow in religious importance as varying forms of individual mysticism became accepted. Nature as a source of revelation would become the most important and nuanced response to the disenchantment brought on by much of Protestantism and science.

The notion of nature as a source of revelation remained prominent in many popular streams of Protestantism. Grounded in both the Hebrew and Christian Scriptures, Catholics and Protestants alike had long, as in many religions, interpreted natural phenomena as reflective of divine blessing or punishment. Nature's bounty in the form of natural resources was God's blessing for the settlers in the new lands, and to be good stewards was to use this bounty for the furtherance of Christianity and human benefit. This was particularly true in some of the colonized lands such as the Americas and Australia. Attention to nature as revelatory was also influential on the development of science and in the dedication to the observation of the details of nature emphasized by so many gentlemen (for the vast majority were upper-class men who observed nature as a hobby) "naturalists," for through the observation of the natural world, the mind of God was glimpsed. Yet nature as a source of revelation, especially in Romanticism's understanding, ultimately came to be seen as heretical by many Christians for it eclipsed the authority of institutional religion. On the individual level, nature as revelation provided an avenue to the divine outside of the Church and its control. On the societal scale, the sense that the scientific study of nature or of the material world could reveal the truths of the universe, stripped of any overlay of the mind of God, grew to reach almost deterministic proportions. This was particularly centered on the challenges represented in Darwin, who came to be viewed as a threat, by some, to religious Truth. Science, and not religion, came to be viewed as the final source of truth and authority.[12] In many ways, religion as the basis for understanding the world became subservient to a scientific understanding.[13] The role of Western religion, instead, became primarily to provide meaning and a larger context for the findings of science. Liberal Protestants in particular became "captives of Science" because the "ability of man to have dominion over nature (and his own fate) depended so heavily on his knowledge of God's scientific laws" (McLoughlin 1978:158).

Today, all of these understandings still play into the complex world of both scholarly and popular, practiced ecological theology, and its acceptance or rejection. For many conservative Christians, and "secularists," nature is still a realm to be conquered, tamed, or utilized for human betterment. Nature is viewed as a backdrop to the unfolding of a linear movement of progress, whether it is toward a human world freed from any natural constraints (including age, disease, and "pests") or toward a history of God's salvific action in the world that solely concerns humans (including the dismissal of a need for ecological care because, in the triumph of God's reign, there will be a "new heaven and earth"). Evangelical and conservative Christians are still warned against nature as a source of revealed religious knowledge because it might eclipse the only recognized source of religious knowledge – the Bible. In current-day Christian creationism we see a response to the "battle" between religion and science for understandings of the nature of "Nature." For more typical, mainstream Christians, nature reflects God's bounty and blessing, and scientific and technological progress are part of the civilizing of the world. Although the explicit belief in God's action in the world to restore the natural order is subdued, the faith in science and technology to "fix" all problems remains strong. Both forms remain focused on human salvation, understood in a variety of ways, and human affairs, replicating a strong distinction between humans and nature. These complex views form the heritage of the contemporary movement as participants try to articulate a range of sacred, ecological perspectives. The religious ecology movement is also shaped by many strands and perspectives within the contemporary environmental movement.

Return to the Contemporary Environmental Movement

At the dawn of the contemporary movement, the US and Western European nations were emerging from the most intense period of the Cold War, and the period of recovery from World War II. Major technological innovations spurred economic growth, as did a peacetime population boom that came of age in the 1960s. For huge numbers, television, birth control and commercial air flight all opened up new worlds that contrasted with the world of their parents. Higher education, hailed as a response to the dangerous "irrationality" and bias of the war, was sought by a wide array of youth who could afford the luxury of studying for more than a job. Reaction and disenchantment over the development, and use, of the nuclear bomb provided a descant to the forties' and fifties' song of the triumph of progress and technology, followed by the environmental laments of the sixties – pollution and the limits to growth posed by an expanding population. These voices of critique and disbelief in the salvific abilities of science have significantly shaped the development of religious eco-logical voices, for the ability of science to pave the way to a brighter future was dethroned, creating a space for religious voices whose heritage was the liberal theo-logical acceptance of a separate-spheres[14] policy that gave science purview over the natural world. Many became critical of institutional religion while at the same time adopting a new sense of self, freed from previous social strictures and open to experi-ence and revelation from a variety of sources, including nature and other religions. To understand the religious or spiritual strands within the environmental movement is to recognize this two-pronged shift away from the authority of science and religion regarding "nature."

One significant and symbolic event that shaped the environmental movement in a multitude of ways was the view of Earth from space, and the subsequent 1969 landing on the moon. It is worth pausing a moment to consider the various ways that the "space race" symbolizes different contemporary viewpoints. For many, the human entry into space demolished the last sense of limits on humans, for we were no longer bound by such an elemental force as gravity; we had escaped the *limitations* of Earth. This escape echoes the Greek and Christian desire of "spirit" or the soul to be freed from the con-fines of matter and this-world. The "conquering" of space, as it is often called, aptly demonstrates the triumphal belief that science and technology, as the extension of human reason, can overcome any obstacle; the corollary to this is often the secure belief that any environmental wrongs done, such as global warming, can be undone by science and technology, so we should quit worrying and plunge ahead. For others, the hubris of this view stands in stunning opposition to the humility they feel as a result of having seen the planet as a whole. In this reaction, the picture of Earth from space demonstrates the artificiality of political borders and the fragile interconnectedness of all on the planet, and becomes a powerful symbol for the need to recognize that eco-systems, and the effects of environmental degradation, go beyond often arbitrary political boundaries. The Earth becomes the symbol and source of a mystical insight into oneness and plurality (we are all in this together), so that it became the symbol of one environmental slogan: "Think globally, act locally." The view of the Earth also symbolizes the changing scientific paradigm, from the atomistic approach to "dead and inert" matter that characterized Newtonian and Baconian science to the recognition of the ecological web and the intricate interdependency of a very alive nature seen in ecology, evolutionary cosmology, and other aspects of the new science, such as chaos theory.

One obvious heritage of the 1960s is the legacy of the youth counter-culture in general and the social protest and social movements in particular that characterized the era. Dominated by the civil rights and the anti-war movements, social protest was also directed at concern over race and ethnicity, ecology, peace, the rights of women, gays and lesbians, and the disabled, and human rights in general. Some who study these movements often point out the strong religious influence/motivation of activists involved, as well as a range of religiously motivated or inspired prophets, but scholars tend to emphasize the secular nature of these movements. Many in the "Church" admit that it is often ten years behind the movements of secular society, and in the case of environmentalism, it took a decade for a rich scholarly conversation to emerge (although the Faith, Man, and Nature project of the National Council of Churches of the USA had already begun the conversation in the 1960s). John Cobb's theological call *Is It Too Late?* (1972) reflected the doomsday mood of publications such as the Club of Rome 1972 report (Meadows et al. 1972) on the *Limits to Growth*, predicting resource depletion and economic collapse. Eco-feminist thought took form, and Rosemary Ruether's *New Woman, New Earth* (1975) stimulated the development of Christian eco-feminism. And many, varied responses to Lynn White's essay appeared, along with some early Church/denominational statements on the basis for environmental concern. At the same time, a call for more bio-centric thinking was articulated by philosopher Arne Naess's description (1989) of shallow and deep ecology, as well as chemist James Lovelock's Gaia hypothesis (1979) that the Earth is a living, self-regulating entity. John Passmore's contrasting eco-philosophy in *Man's Responsibility for Nature* also came out in the mid-1970s.

By the 1980s, religious and philosophical ecological voices had become many. For some, the interconnectedness of issues of the unequal construction of society with environmental concern was subsumed by a growing focus on scientific analysis and solutions for environmental problems. Environmental concerns focused on global issues such as acid rain, the ozone hole, the greenhouse effect, rapid deforestation and with it, increasing desertification. Many of the inspired youths of the environmental movements of the sixties had turned into respected scientists and technocrats seeking government recognition and support for their research and proposed solutions, and the movement had grown well beyond its grassroots beginnings. The World Wildlife Fund (now the World-Wide Fund for Nature), host to a significant meeting of world religions on ecology, at Assisi in Italy, boasted over a million members by the end of the decade; Greenpeace claimed over 2 million.

As the organizational aspect of the movement gained access to the centers of societies, it lost much of its moral imperative, or at least the ability to couch it in such terms. In this absence, theologians and philosophers, politicians, religious leaders, and grassroots spirituality groups found there was an audience for their message. The World Council of Churches' theme in the 1980s was "Justice, Peace and the Integrity of

Creation," linking together three of the important social movements of the seventies. Political Green Parties began to play a role in elections. Radical eco-resistance movements such as Earth First!, inspired by the grassroots movement in Australia to oppose the damming of the Franklin River in Tasmania, grew up on the fringe of the movement. The principles of deep ecology were given a wider audience by Devall and Sessions in *Deep Ecology: Living as if Nature Mattered* in 1985. Many Protestant eco-theological and eco-ethical works appeared in the eighties, such as Jürgen Moltmann's *God and Creation* (1985), as well as Catholic voices such as the popular then-Catholic theologian Matthew Fox's *The Coming of the Cosmic Christ*[15] and the work of Thomas Berry, who calls himself a Catholic geo-logian. Berry's work was made widely available in *The Dream of the Earth* (1988), sort of a spiritual deep ecology, stunning its publisher Sierra Club Books by going through seven printings in six years.

Environmental ethics emerged as a distinct discipline, as seen in the work of Holmes Rolston III (1986) or Baird Callicott (1987), as well as in the growth of the animal liberation movement and a distinct discourse on ethics and animal rights. At the end of the decade, John Cobb and Herman Daly, a lead economist with the World Bank, published *For the Common Good* in 1989, a theological and ethical call for attention to the deep ecological problems of capitalist economics and the need for a vision of a sustainable society. Ironically, conservative Pentecostal Christian James Watt, Secretary of the Interior under US President Ronald Reagan, inadvertently alerted many to the need for a responsible religious ethic, when he told Congress not be concerned with the long-term future of natural resources policy because "I do not know how many future generations we can count on before the Lord returns" (Martin 1982). For US secular and religious environmental groups, the anti-environmental Reagan era of the 1980s galvanized people into action.

One important development in the US was the United Church of Christ's publication of *Toxic Wastes and Race* (Lee 1987). The study looked for common factors in the placement of hazardous and toxic waste sites throughout the nation and concluded that race and low income were statistically significant factors in the placement of these sites. This study helped launch a new movement, often critical of the whiteness of the main organizations of the environmental movement, termed "environmental justice," which in the churches became a part of the broader rubric of eco-justice (see below). Since many working on religious eco-justice had come to the movement through concerns over civil rights and economic justice, the articulation of environmental racism continued these concerns. The environmental justice movement is very significant as an organizing and empowering force for indigenous peoples and people of color, long left out of the mainstream movement, and has helped move the religious environmental movement away from being a predominantly white movement.

Earth Day of 1990 dawned with the environment seemingly on everyone's mind. *Time Magazine*, in 1989, had made the planet Earth its "person" of the year in the news. In January of 1990, the well-known physicist Carl Sagan, along with others, issued a call for the cooperation of religious leaders and scientists, stating that "problems of such magnitude and solutions demanding so broad a perspective, must be recognized from the outset as having a religious as well as a scientific dimension" (*New York Times*, January 20, 1990). Pope John Paul II, in his January 1990 World Day of Peace address, pronounced that the "ecological crisis is a moral issue" and reminded Catholics that they have "a serious obligation to care for all of creation." By 1992, both soon-to-be US Vice-President Gore's *The Earth in Balance* and Rosemary Ruether's *Gaia and God* appeared, each very influential in reaching a wide audience in their own way. These works, along with others, demonstrate the parallel global social- and environmental-justice concerns of major eco-theologians during the 1990s, such as the various books by John Cobb critiquing the current economic model and calling for a more sustainable and just economic model, Larry Rasmussen's *Earth Community, Earth Ethics* (1996), Ivonne Gerbara (1999), Leonardo Boff's (1995) works connecting ecology and liberation theology, and the edited volumes of *Women Healing Earth: Third World Women on Ecology, Feminism, and Religion* (Ruether 1996) or *Ecotheology: Voices from South and North* (Hallman 1994). In order to think more globally – a key theme of the 1990s under the specter of global warming – theology groped for metaphors, such as the earth as God's body, found in the work of feminist eco-theologian Sally McFague in her *The Body of God: An Ecological Theology* (1993), or apocalypse: Catherine Keller, in *Apocalypse Now and Then* (1996), took on the symbolism and debilitating thinking of the apocalypse, which loomed large for many with the end of the second millennium approaching.

During the eighties, theologians and religious groups alike had spent time articulating particular viewpoints; by the nineties, a plethora of religious voices and organizations could be found, and various ecumenical efforts flourished. Perhaps the most important was the global religious, indigenous, and NGO (non-governmental organization) effort to be heard at, and to influence, the 1992 United Nations Conference on Environment and Development (UNCED) in Rio de Janeiro, Brazil, and the subsequent Kyoto Conference on global climate change (see Wesley Granberg-Michaelson's *Redeeming the Creation: The Rio Earth Summit – Challenges for the Churches*, published by the World Council of Churches, a major presence at Rio, in 1992). From an environmental standpoint, little good happened at these conferences, dominated by corporate interests and an uncooperative US government presence that refused to sign anything with any teeth to it. Despite strong efforts by the US and multinational corporations to undermine the 1997 Kyoto treaty on global climate change, by the 2002 Johannesburg South Africa UN Summit on Sustainability, enough nations had signed on, including China, to mean that the standards of the treaty for reducing carbon-dioxide emissions will have some impact. Another large, global cooperative effort, in many ways the result of the conference at Rio, was the Earth Charter. This document, which thousands contributed to in hearings and meetings around the globe, was finalized and presented at the UN Summit in Johannesburg. The Earth Charter, as well as the religious and NGO presence at the UN conferences, was an effort to make sure that the voices of those most affected by economic development and environmental degradation – the indigenous, the poor, and developing countries – were heard, and to demonstrate that a new, global, ecological, and morally just vision was needed to guide Earth's citizens. Religious groups have joined this effort wholeheartedly, as illustrated in the following profile of the spectrum of activism, based on US religious groups, but applicable beyond.

Contemporary Ecological Christian Activism

As this brief decade-by-decade overview has shown, there are many who are dissenters from the dominant Western world-view, some from an ecological philosophical viewpoint such as deep ecology, others from indigenous or more pagan religious worldviews, from feminist, womanist (African-American feminism), and *mujerista* (Latina feminism) points of view, new age or nature spirituality, and all the major religious traditions. These many, varied ecological voices are not just theologians, but are emerging from a variety of activist and church-related organizations, for it is in this range that the immense and rich variety of eco-theology is translated into action and problem-solving. In other words, it is at the level of activism that the purpose of eco-theology – that is, to change the way Christians think about ecology – can bear fruit in terms of changing the way people and institutional actors behave. There are many levels of this response, from theological, institutional, and activist organizations.

On the basis of nearly twenty years of research, I group Christian ecological activism into roughly three categories, with a wide range of overlap, exceptions, or variety (see Kearns 1996, 1997, for more detail). These categories do not work neatly for the plethora of theological views nor for neat denominational categories; rather, they are the voices of the "pews" and the no-longer-in-the pews who are still influenced by Christian thought. Following sociologist Max Weber's notion of ideal types, I term these three categories or "ethics": Christian stewardship, eco-justice, and Creation spirituality. By "ethic" I mean to include both world-view and ethos, such as understandings of how the world is and how it should be, what is ideal, and how an individual should act in order to be good. Eco-feminism, the linkage between the treatment of women and of nature, influences all three, particularly the latter two, but there are many within eco-justice and creation spirituality that do not think primarily through an eco-feminist lens, and there are many, many eco-feminists who reject Christianity. All three ethics are critical of science, especially scientific technology, while at the same time embracing it as a valuable and necessary source of knowledge about the world.

Briefly, Christian stewardship is most appealing to those Christians with a more evangelical and Bible-centered theology.[16] They interpret the key "dominion" passage in terms of the sense of dominion given an Israelite king such as David. Kings were responsible to God for their "keeping" of the kingdom, and as such, held accountable. Thus, for many Christian stewards, to be a good Christian is to care responsibly for the earth. Christian stewardship is still anthropocentric, or human-centered, but believes that God calls Christians to be good stewards of the creation, and to till and keep the creation (referring to the Genesis passages). Much of their time and effort is spent trying to dissuade conservative Christians from an otherworldly, or personal-salvation only emphasis (this is eloquently seen in the work of a key figure, Calvin DeWitt). They do this by seeking to thoroughly ground "saving the creation" in biblical texts. Christian stewardship is an important voice countering a widespread strain of conservative Christianity that is anti-science with "creationist" overtones, or is anti-environmental, claiming that environmentalism is a direct threat to Christianity, or in more apocalyptic scenarios, that it is the agent of the anti-Christ. In addition to countering the dismissal of science as an authority, Christian stewardship also must negotiate conservative Christianity's fears of pantheism or "worshiping the creation," harkening back to ancient Israelite fears of their "pagan nature-worshiping" neighbors, or Christian fears of the religious world-views of the conquered peoples. Two examples of more overt Christian stewardship activism are a 1996 campaign to preserve the Endangered Species Act from being gutted by conservative Republicans in the US Congress (who were actively supported by the evangelical, anti-environmental New Christian Right) and a 2002 campaign, in part sponsored by the Evangelical Environmental Network, about fuel-efficient vehicles, asking "What would Jesus drive?" – a take-off on a common conservative Christian phrase and bumper-sticker asking "What Would Jesus Do?" (WWJD). The WWJDrive campaign related driving fuel-inefficient cars such as SUVs (sports utility vehicles) to the unjust treatment of one's "neighbor," acknowledging that pollution and environmental degradation make us all neighbors in a new way.

Eco-justice advocates represent more mainstream and liberal Protestant and Catholic social-justice understandings of Christianity in which God's *kindom* (many would not use the more hierarchical term "kingdom") of just relations between humans and with the realm of creation is to be worked for here on Earth by righting social wrongs. Here the source of authority is the example of Jesus and the Social Gospel tradition. They aptly demonstrate that environmental problems are also justice issues with strong adverse effects on those already excluded – people of color, the poor, women and children. To this end, many eco-justice advocates, such as the World Council of Churches and its constituent members, have worked to expose environmental injustices in the dumping of hazardous and toxic wastes and the enormous health consequences, especially for women, or the shortened lives of children caused by air pollution, arguing that the Christian principle of the just treatment of one's neighbor is applicable to the question of who pays the hidden costs for wastes and pollution. Another major concern has been those who will suffer, and perhaps already are suffering, from global climate, rising waters, failing crops due to erratic and often violent weather, and so on.

Finally, Creation spirituality focuses on the wonder of the universe, and the cosmological story of its evolution, which reveals that humans are but a small part of the "universe story," yet now have the capacity to interrupt the workings of the universe. Proponents often come from the most liberal Protestant and Catholic groups, and are the most open to a wide array of spiritual traditions, deep ecology, mysticism, feminist goddess spirituality, indigenous and "pagan" traditions of earth centeredness, etc. While in the first two, the Bible is either the main or an important source of authority and inspiration, in Creation spirituality, the revelations of the universe supersede the knowledge of most religious traditions (clear in the work of Thomas Berry), and many find themselves creating a collage of spiritual sources that recognizes the need, or incorporates the viewpoint, that humans are but one part of a larger ecological web of beings that need to be acknowledged. They embrace a numinous or immanental sense of the sacred in the world, and while highly critical of the atomistic, Enlightenment scientific world-view, Creation spirituality incorporates the more "mystical" new physics that talks about infinitesimal sub-atomic spaces or the interconnections even found in chaos theory. Creation spirituality advocates work to return a sense of the sacred to everyday life, emphasizing the necessity of combining art, dance, and all the senses in ritual (as advocated by Matthew Fox), or the interconnectedness of humans and Earth represented in bio-dynamic and permaculture agricultural practices, as demonstrated at the Genesis Farm, founded by the Dominican Sisters of Caldwell, New Jersey, a working farm and eco-community that draws people, especially Catholic religious sisters, from all over the globe to study and learn.

Challenges to Eco-Theology

This review of the history of the Western world-view of nature and of the environmental and religious ecological movements reveals many of the challenges still facing eco-theology. The deep-seated dualism of human/nature continues to undermine efforts to think about humans in, with, and as a part of nature. This dualism still haunts eco-theology as it tries to overcome the entrenched notion of God as radically other and outside of this world, and the related this-world/other-world, matter/spirit, body/mind, emotion/rationality, religion/science, or religious/secular binaries that continue to shape much of Christianity. The bifurcation between the worlds of religious concerns and scientific concerns bedevils the attempts of many to get Christians to pay any attention to what are deemed matters of science, such as the environment.

There are a variety of global issues that will shape eco-theological voices – issues that some clearly acknowledge while others try to ignore. Chief among these are the issue of population and consumption, the need for access to and religious legitimation of birth control, and the need to curb an almost religious fervor for consumption that has become the standard for measuring happiness and success in the West. The dueling future-disaster scenarios of over-population and over-consumption and the resulting scarce resources have proven extremely difficult for religious groups to face head on, and they are subsequently addressed in more subtle, covert ways. Issues of population and scarce resources point to the very difficult ethical territory ahead; territory in which religious, ecological, and ethical voices must be heard.

The problem of over-consumption by the "developed" countries points to another critical challenge – the global dominance of a capitalist economic system which values everything only in relation to profit margins, so that natural resources either have economic value for consumption, or have no value. The skewed value system of capitalism with regard to the Earth and its peoples is horrifically demonstrated in a leaked World Bank memo that stated that Africa was under-polluted and African lives worth less, therefore hazardous and toxic wastes, as well as highly polluting industries, should be exported to Africa.[17] Further demonstration of the inherent value system of capitalism is manifest in various free trade agreements and the World Trade Organization, where environmental protection regulations are viewed as barriers to trade and thus seen as being against the terms of free trade agreements. Obviously, the variety of practitioners of capitalism is great, but there is an inherent value system in the "free" market that any eco-theological conversation must at some time address. The struggle over endorsement of the Kyoto Global Climate Treaty, in which religious actors have been vociferous and numerous, is another demonstration of the clash of ecology and economics.[18]

The struggle of religious voices to respond to global warming is indicative of how the subject of pending environmental crisis and disaster, with apocalyptic overtones, often creates numbness and despair. Whereas, from a sociological point of view, religious systems provide meaning in the face of threatening chaos, many who are religious either ignore the sense of crisis, or when faced with the growing feeling of global environmental degradation and breakdown, often turn their gaze elsewhere to find comfort. Since, in most scenarios, any response to numerous global environmental problems will entail sacrifice or asceticism – a seeming "natural" for religious systems – it is notable that many in Christianity prefer to turn their attention to a "health and wealth" gospel of God's blessing in material terms, or to spirituality as a form of personal therapy. Elsewhere, the growing threats of military conflict and violence over scarce resources such as oil and water, or of various scenarios of economic collapse, take even the most concerned minds away from the larger ecological needs of the Earth.

Many of the other challenges to eco-theology have been mentioned in the course of this chapter: dualistic thinking and the persistence of viewing humans and nature as separate; transcendent theocentric, or God-centered, theologies that fear embodiment and the earth, and the related fear of paganism or immanental understandings of God; the tensions between religion and science; the lack of scientific literacy in general, and the distrust and yet reliance on science for knowledge and problem-solving; the connection of nature with threat, darkness, and irrationality, or the romanticization of nature into the cute and cuddly; and the huge gap between changing how we think and changing how we then act.

The very questions of what Christianity is, who is Christian, or who is the audience for eco-theology, present a very large challenge, as Christians of the North Atlantic countries become the minority in global Christianity. With this change has come the growth of certain forms of Christianity, on the right and left, that focus on personal salvation and individual religiosity/spirituality to the detriment of notions of the common good, communal responsibility, or the Kindom of God. Claims to Christian exclusivism that fear other religious claims to truth, or those Christians that await an apocalypse, undermine the absolutely necessary collaboration and cooperation of all in the sinking "lifeboat" of planet Earth. The sense of portability seen in the missionary impulse of Christianity, so that Christianity is a "placeless" or "transitory" religion (as opposed to non-proselytizing religions that are place-based, such as indigenous traditions), means that Christians must develop a sense of place and rootedness that can lead to a care for the land and place. At the same time, there are many who have left Christianity, claiming its anthropocentric (human-centered) bias is irredeemable, and others who have sought to merge parts of Christianity with the insights of other traditions in the search for an ecological spirituality. In the latter, there is the risk of the very well-meaning appropriation of other more nature-centered traditions such as those of Native Americans and Australian Aborigines, which replicates past colonialism. For other people around the globe, and for people of color and women in the "first world," the struggle has been to convince us/them that the religion of the colonizers and oppressors has something to say, or that eco-theology is more than a white "luxury" topic affordable when economic necessity no longer governs one's life. Perhaps, they suggest, it is time the so-called first world starts listening to them.

Finally,[19] eco-theology has slowly moved into a multi-voiced, multi-faced complexity in which a range of theological, geographic and demographic voices are trying to be heard, so that the dominant discourse is not only by white Euro-Americans. This success is also the challenge it faces, for the message will take on a multitude of forms, many that disagree with each other, and can disintegrate into either academic parrying and wound-licking, open conflict, or mutual listening as Christian theology struggles to transcend the many limitations and embrace the many possibilities of its past complex and often ambivalent views of humanity, God, and nature.

Notes

1   There are, of course, scattered precursors. In 1939, in an address on Jerusalem Radio, Walter Lowdermilk outlined an Eleventh Commandment: "Thou shalt inherit the holy earth as a faithful steward, conserving its resources and productivity from generation to generation" (as quoted in Nash 1989:97). The commandment then calls for stewards to avoid overgrazing, soil erosion, "waters drying up," and "the desolation of forest." Joseph Sittler also was an early influential voice.

2   The notion of *ex nihilo*, or "out of nothing," is a much later Christian reading back into the text and thus is not found in most Jewish readings of the text. See Keller (2003).

3   The "her" pronoun for God here refers to the fact that many, many creation stories are about mother goddesses and birth scenarios. Scholars, such as Ruether (1992), point out that one striking aspect about the Jewish creation stories is that creation is not through birthing, but through breath and through artifice, or the molding of dirt/clay.

4   Many scholars now avoid the term Judeo-Christianity for it sees Judaism through the gaze of Christianity and erases the distinctiveness of the ongoing Jewish tradition and thinking about nature. See Silk (1988).

5   In the larger corpus of White's work, he is actually careful about giving too much credence to the role of ideas, and does talk about changing social and technological factors.

6   Note that matter and "mater," or mother, have the same root.

7   Christian missionary texts of the time are full of references to indigenous natives that are "animal-like" or "bestial." Protestant settlers of the Americas thought the indigenous peoples already there were in league with the devil because of their ability to live off the land without seeming to cultivate it. Another glimpse of the colonial view of uncultivated land is found in Nathaniel Hawthorne's *Scarlet Letter* (1850), where Hester Prynne is banished, as punishment, from civilization to the woods for giving in to her lustful, sexual "nature."

8   Lynn White comments that "by destroying pagan animism, Christianity made it possible to exploit nature in a mood of indifference to the feelings of natural objects."

9   The ending to Goethe's *Faust* portrays the restless Dr. Faust finally content as he surveys the damming and diking, or as we might say, "reclamation," of swampy land, to be cultivated, or rescued from its "unproductive" and "disorderly" state.

10   This trend continues today, so that the general populace, according to survey after survey, do not understand even basic scientific principles, such as that chemicals and hazardous

materials don't disappear, or have no effect, just because you can't see them (buried or dumped) anymore.

11   The Enlightenment desire to uncover universal principles led to the evolution of the various social sciences, which studied culture, society, or "irrationality" (psychology) in contrast to the physical sciences, which studied the natural world. This split mirrored an inherent dualism that contrasted society and culture with nature.

12   This tension is very clear in Creationism, or the movement to posit that evolution is no more plausible than the Creation account in Genesis. Some creationists argue that evolution is wrong and should not be taught, while others argue that both "theories" should be.

13   This tension is very clear in Creationism, or the movement to posit that evolution is no more plausible than the Creation account in Genesis. Some creationists argue that evolution is wrong and should not be taught, while others argue that both "theories" should be taught in public schools.

14   The separate-spheres policy gave science domain over the material world, and religion domain over the soul, the unseen, and realms of meaning. Science is about "facts," whereas religion is about "beliefs." Beliefs can be changed; facts cannot be.

15   Fox was later silenced by the Vatican, in part for his theology and in part for his association with Starhawk, a wiccan or "white-witch," who taught, and is still teaching, at Fox's Institute (now University) of Creation Spirituality. Fox has since left the Catholic Church and is an Episcopalian (Anglican).

16   Although not usually viewed as Bible-centered, many Eastern Orthodox Christians would fall under this group, as would many Catholics. The "green" Patriarch Bartholomew of Constantinople has been very active within Orthodoxy and in joint projects with Roman Catholicism.

17   As cited in Rasmussen (1996:78).

18   Ecology and economy both stem from the same Greek root, *oikos* or "household." In that sense, they are about interrelated but distinctly different rules for governing the household of Earth.

19   My colleague Catherine Keller adds to this list of challenges the effect of the cutting-edge deconstruction of "the natural," i.e. that much that is called "natural" and by implication "necessary" is in fact cultural construction. This discourse of deconstruction "has so far distracted more than critically enriched eco-theological work."

References

Barbour, I. G. 1973. *Western Man and Environmental Ethics: Attitudes towards Nature and Technology.* Reading, MA: Addison-Wesley.

Berry, T. 1988. *The Dream of the Earth.* San Francisco, CA: Sierra Club Books.

Boff, L. 1995. *Ecology and Liberation: A New Paradigm,* trans. J. Cumming. Maryknoll, NY: Orbis.

Brueggemann, W. 1977. *The Land: Place as Gift, Promise, and Challenge in Biblical Faith.* Philadelphia, PA: Fortress Press.

Callicott, J. Baird ed. 1987. *Companion to "A Sand County Almanac": Interpretive and Critical Essays.* Madison, WI: University of Wisconsin Press.

Carson, R. 1962. *Silent Spring.* Boston, MA: Houghton Mifflin.

Cobb, J. B. 1972. *Is It Too Late? A Theology of Ecology.* Beverly Hills, CA: Bruce.

Cobb, J. B. and Daly, H. 1989. *For the Common Good: Redirecting the Economy toward Community, the Environment, and a Sustainable Future.* Boston, MA: Beacon Press.

Cooper, D. and Joy A. Palmer. 1988. *Spirit of the Environment.* London: Routledge.

Devall, B. and Sessions, G. 1985. *Deep Ecology: Living as if Nature Mattered.* Salt Lake City, UT: Gibbs Smith.

DeWitt, C. B. 1987. *A Sustainable Earth: Religion and Ecology in the Western Hemisphere.* Mancelona, MI: AuSable Institute.

Fox, M. 1988. *The Coming of the Cosmic Christ: The Healing of Mother Earth and the Birth of a Global Renaissance.* San Francisco, CA: Harper & Row.

Gerbara, I. 1999. *Longing for Running Water: Ecofeminism and Liberation.* Minneapolis, MN: Fortress Press.

Glacken, C. J. 1967. *Traces on the Rhodian Shore: Nature and Culture in Western Thought from Ancient Times to the End of the Eighteenth Century.* Berkeley, CA: University of California Press.

Goethe, J. W. Von. 1994. *Faust I & II (Goethe, The Collected Works,* vol. 2, ed. Stuart Atkins. Princeton, NJ: Princeton University Press.

Gore, A. 1992. *The Earth in the Balance: Ecology and the Human Spirit.* Boston, MA: Houghton Mifflin.

Granberg-Michaelson, W. 1992. *Redeeming the Creation: The Rio Earth Summit – Challenges for the Churches.* Geneva: WCC Publications.

Granberg-Michaelson, W. ed. 1987. *Tending the Garden: Essays on the Gospel and the Earth.* Grand Rapids, MI: Eerdmans.

Habel, N. and Wurst, S. eds. 2000. *The Earth Story in Genesis.* Sheffield: Sheffield Academic Press; Cleveland, OH: Pilgrim Press.

Hallman, D. 1994. *Ecotheology: Voices from South and North.* Maryknoll, NY: Orbis.

Hardin, G. 1968. "The Tragedy of the Commons," *Science* 162:1243–8.

Hawthorne, N. ([1850] 1981). *The Scarlet Letter.* Englewood Cliffs, NJ: Prentice-Hall.

Hessel, D. T. (ed.) 1992. *After Nature's Revolt: Eco-Justice and Theology.* Minneapolis, MN: Fortress Press.

Hessel, D. T. and Ruether, R. eds. 2000. *Christianity and Ecology: Seeking the Well-Being of Earth and Humans (Religions of the World and Ecology, 3).* Cambridge, MA: Harvard University Press.

Kearns, L. 1996. "Saving the Creation: Christian Environmentalism in the United States," *Sociology of Religion* 57(1):55–70.

Kearns, L. 1997, "Noah's Ark Goes to Washington: a Profile of Evangelical Environmentalism," *Social Compass* 44(3):349–66.

Keller, C. 1996. *Apocalypse Now and Then: A Feminist Guide to the End of the World.* Boston, MA: Beacon Press.

Keller, C. 2003. *Face of the Deep: A Theology of Becoming.* London: Routledge.

Lee, C. 1987. *Toxic Wastes and Race.* Cleveland, OH: United Church of Christ Press.

Leopold, A. 1949. *Sand Country Almanac.* New York: Oxford University Press.

Lovelock, J. 1979. *Gaia: A New Look at Life on Earth.* New York: Oxford University Press.

McFague, S. 1993. *The Body of God: An Ecological Theology.* Minneapolis, MN: Fortress Press.

McLoughlin, W. G. 1978. *Revivals, Awakenings, and Reform.* Chicago, IL: University of Chicago Press.

Martin, W. 1982. "Waiting of the End," *Atlantic Monthly* 249(June): 31–7.

Meadows, D. S. et al. 1972. *Limits to Growth: A Report for the Club of Rome's Project on the Predicament of Mankind.* New York: Universal Books.

Merchant, C. 1980. *The Death of Nature: Women, Ecology, and the Scientific Revolution.* New York: Harper & Row.

Moltmann, J. 1985. *God and Creation: A New Theology of Creation and the Spirit of God,* trans. M. Kohl. San Franciso, CA: Harper & Row.

Naess, Arne. 1989. *Ecology, Community and Lifestyle*, trans. D. Rothenberg. Cambridge: Cambridge University Press.

Nash, R. 1989. *Rights of Nature: A History of Environmental Ethics*. Madison, WI: University of Wisconsin Press.

Passmore, J. 1974. *Man's Responsibility for Nature: Ecological Problems and Western Tradition*. New York: Charles Scribner's Sons.

Rasmussen, L. L. 1996. *Earth Community, Earth Ethics*. Maryknoll, NY: Orbis.

Rolston, Holmes III. 1986. *Philosophy Gone Wild: Essays in Environmental Ethics*. Buffalo, NY: Prometheus Books.

Ruether, R. 1975. *New Woman, New Earth: Sexist Ideologies and Human Liberation*. New York: Seabury Press.

Ruether, R. 1992. *Gaia and God: An Ecofeminist Theology of Earth Healing*. San Francisco, CA: HarperSanFrancisco.

Ruether, R. ed. 1996. *Women Healing Earth: Third World Women on Ecology, Feminism, and Religion*. Maryknoll, NY: Orbis.

Sagan, C. 1990. *New York Times*, January 20.

Santmire, Paul. 1985. *The Travail of Nature: The Ambiguous Ecological Promise of Christian Theology*. Philadelphia, PA: Fortress Press.

Silk, M. 1988. *Spiritual Politics: Religion in America Since World War II*. New York: Simon & Schuster.

Weber, M. [1904/5] 1958. *The Protestant Ethic and the Spirit of Capitalism*, trans. Talcott Parsons. New York: Charles Scribner's Sons.

White, Lynn, Jr. 1967. "The Historical Roots of Our Ecological Crisis," *Science* 155: 1203–7.

CHAPTER 30

Drama, Film, and Postmodernity

Richard Arrandale

Introduction

At the end of the film *The Truman Show*, the central character (Truman), having realized that his entire life was a construction, and his entire geography was an enclosed film set, takes the bold step of walking out through the door at the end of the film set. His move is one from controlled certainty, into the unknown and the uncertain. Even though it was a construction, the world that Truman thought he knew was safe and predictable, even down to the greeting he gave every morning when leaving his house for work. Everything seemed real and certain and yet, as we the viewers knew from the very beginning, it was all made up. Truman's realization of the nature of his world is painful, and his leap into the unknown and uncertain world outside is a brave and anxious step. Truman's step outside his film set into the unknown mirrors the steps we take into our postmodern world. Like Truman, the world we thought we knew, with all its certainties, beliefs, geographies, and ideologies is put into question, and we are left to open the door at the end of our film sets to peer outside into the unknown.

Clive Marsh (see Marsh and Ortiz 1997:21–34), following a typology from H. Richard Niebuhr, suggests three possible ways of understanding the theology–culture dialectic, and thus three possible ways in which film and theology could work together. The three possibilities are: theology against culture, which he identifies as having resonances with Barth; theology immersed in culture, which he sees as an extreme postmodern model in which theology loses any privilege as a narrative; and finally, theology in critical dialogue with culture. It is this final position that Marsh takes as his model. What this means, according to David John Graham, is that theologians will "use the motifs and messages in film as a source of theological reflection" (Marsh and Ortiz 1997:36). By extension the same would be true of theologians engaging with drama.

For the purposes of this chapter I want to suggest using another of Marsh's possibilities. It is not that I necessarily disagree with his position; rather, I think there could be even richer resources if one adopts the second option, of theology being immersed in culture. This will mean that theology will lose any privileged status, and will have to compete on equal terms with all other discourses, but I would argue that it is only with such a loss, as happens in postmodernity, that theology may discover new possibilities. Therefore, in this chapter I want to consider film and drama as theological "texts" or activities in themselves, considering what theology can learn from such sister discourses. Although this will bear similarities to Marsh's third option, there is an important methodological difference; namely, that such a dethroning of theology is only the dethroning of a particular method of doing theology. In other words, what is lost is the privilege of theology as a written discourse, and what is gained are the new possibilities that are opened up by allowing theology to be done in other ways.

Theories of the postmodern abound, with a range of contested ideas as to what it is and from where it stems. Moreover there are a range of excellent overviews and analyses of such ideas (see, for example, Ward 1997 and Connor 1997) and I do not need to replicate such material here. Within the multiplicity of approaches I would suggest that there is a common element, identified by Jean-François Lyotard, that the condition of postmodernity involves having an incredulity toward metanarratives.

In the chapter that follows, I want to use the basic idea above as a metaphor for the condition of postmodernity, and consider the role of film and drama as theological reflection. Furthermore, I do not want to discuss the nature of modernity in film and drama in order to be able to label something "postmodern" – an activity always fraught with danger. Rather, I want to suggest that being incredulous toward metanarratives involves being suspicious of traditional discourses used for theology, and suggest that other new discourses may be seen as examples of new ways of doing theology. In each of the sections that follow, I want to offer examples of such possibilities. Therefore, what follows is not meant to be canonical, nor a survey of recent positions; rather it is an example of what can be done, and a prompt to the reader to do it for herself. I am suggesting, therefore, a move away from two of the ways in which theology has tended to engage with film (and by extension drama): either to view it as a resource to plunder, or as something akin to a religious experience in itself. My suggestion is that we treat film and drama as theology in themselves, and see where we are led.

Film

Jean Baudrillard, in one of his reflections on the treatment of history in film, suggests that what marks the postmodern period, and is also its "great trauma," is the "decline of strong referentials" (Baudrillard 1994:43). History itself has become a great myth and one of those lost referentials. For Baudrillard, one of the effects of this lost referential is the privileging of a bygone age, and in particular the attempt to "resurrect the period when at least there was history" (Baudrillard 1994:44). For Baudrillard this can be seen in the retro fashion in film, where simulacras of history are created. From our uncertain postmodern perspective, we create a version of the past that is safe in order to construct a place of refuge. We can see such an activity in the first film I shall look at, *Pleasantville*, which, when seen as a theological text, highlights some dangers of certain trends in modern theology.

Pleasantville: *against nostalgia in theology*

Pleasantville is a film in the same genre as *The Truman Show* in that it is about a character trapped in a film set that becomes "real life." In the film, the two central characters, a brother and sister called David and Jen in the 1990s, get trapped in a 1950s TV soap (*Pleasantville*), with their names changing to Bud and Mary-Sue when they enter this earlier era. The opening scenes make it clear that the late 1990s, with its unemployment, impending ecological catastrophes, plagues of incurable illnesses and so forth, is a dangerous, uncertain, and scary place. This is juxtaposed against the 1950s soap world, in which there is certainty, values, and a sense of what is good and nice; all of which is typified by the fact that it always seems to be sunny at a regular 72°F. The contrast is achieved visually by the fact that, initially, the 1990s is in color and the 1950s is in black-and-white.

There are, in this film, some fairly obvious theological motifs to do with ideas of sin and temptation; of a fall in which knowledge (of sexuality in the initial phase) is gained and eyes are opened. There are also rather simplistic renderings of issues to do with racism (as characters turn from black and white into color, the "no coloreds" signs go up from the conservative, and still black and white, characters) and censorship (in the attempt to ban paintings and the new paint colors that are now becoming available). However, what I think the film really deals with, which is where it is most interesting theologically, is its exploration of the idea of nostalgia.

It was Hans-Georg Gadamer who noted that in times of crisis, interpretation matters. When that crisis is one of meaning and certainty, especially in ethics and values, it appears, as Baudrillard has highlighted, that one strategy is to imagine a past in which things were more certain: people knew wrong from right; everyone knew what they believed in; life, meaning, and everything was more certain. Such a strategy often comes in the form of certain types of literalism and fundamentalism. In theology, this appears in terms of certain groups trying to reassert some lost orthodoxy, some common meaning, or the idea of trying to think, believe, and behave as those (mythical) early Christians.

And so it is with *Pleasantville*. There is, on the part of David, a desire to be in a world away from the uncertainty and pain of his current situation. It is a desire for a world in which regularity appears to be security, something that he longs for from his position in fragmented postmodern times. Of course, as the film progresses, he learns that what appears to be security is of course a prison; it is a world in which once regularity is gone, to borrow a phrase from Heidegger, "everyday familiarity collapses."

What is interesting about both characters is that they both learn something from the experience of nostalgia. David, as Bud, learns that nostalgia can be a prison in which freedom of thought, expression, desires, and longings are thwarted. But Jen, who is portrayed as the "typical" 1990s girl (concerned with dating the most eligible boys, image, and all that is deemed to be superficial), also learns from this nostalgic world. As she is freed from the responsibility of being the 1990s girl she encounters possibilities that she initially thought of as dorkish. Her awakening comes through reading, and she is suddenly exposed to a new world. In both characters, nostalgia has stopped them from accepting fixed worlds (whether as the dork in search of certainty, or in the world of the prom queen), and shown them worlds that are not fixed but contain possibilities.

When interpretation matters, and when truth is challenged, the retreat into nostalgia must, in the end, be seen for what it is: the return to a fictitious world that never existed. Any reading of the history of the early Church, and especially the doctrinal controversies of the Patristic era or the Reformation, will show you that theological meaning has always been contested and unstable. It will show, as one sees the further working out of the implications of one Ecumenical Council to another, or one Reformer to another, that theological truth is something ongoing, and always done in the face of the eschaton. As Pannenberg (1991) has shown, this pushes final meaning away from us, and Truth is no longer something to be grasped or possessed, rather it is something essentially deferred, and can only be explored.

Like the characters in *Pleasantville*, theologians can learn that the retreat into a nostalgic world is just a simulacrum, but like Jen and David, we can learn something about the nature of theology and truth from that simulacrum. *Pleasantville*, when not trying to be overtly theological, offers theology a glimpse of the implications of not accepting that theological truth is unstable, and the dangers of any approach that rests on a nostalgia that things were better, more certain, or simpler in times gone by. Any form of theology, however apparently radical or apparently literalist, that chooses to reside in this nostalgic world will simply end up living in a theological *Pleasantville*. If familiarity breeds contempt, then nostalgia in theology breeds paralysis, and, to borrow a phrase from Baudrillard, "It only resurrects ghosts, and it itself is lost therein" (Baudrillard 1994:48).

So, like those characters at the end of the film, as they discuss the question of what is going to happen next in their now uncertain and liberated *Pleasantville*, and with smiles and laughter they announce that they do not know, so too, in its epistemological quest, theology must look to its eschatological future and in response to the question "Do you know the truth?" it must answer, with smiles and laughter, "No, not yet."

Fahrenheit 451: *the end of the book and the beginning of writing*

Truffaut's brilliant film of Ray Bradbury's haunting science-fiction novel offers us a vision of an Orwellian world in which books are banned and when found, are burnt. The title of the film, we learn, is the temperature at which books catch fire and burn.

From the opening sequence of the film the viewer realizes that the world we encounter is strange and destabilizing. The film begins with a fire engine going to an emergency and we very quickly learn that in this world the job of the fireman is not to put out fires, but to set light to things, namely books. The fireman's job (and they are all men) is to hunt out and destroy the remaining books. As the fire chief tells us, books are "sheer perversity" and have "nothing to say." Novels are about people who never existed, and simply put before us lives which we can never attain; biographies are nothing more than "stories of the dead"; and worst of all, for the fire chief, is philosophy, which is nothing more than mere fashion, like the changing lengths of skirts. It consists of thinkers, each of them saying that all the others are idiots and wrong, whilst asserting that only they are correct. In this world, books make people unhappy, disturbed, and anti-social.

The film maps the story of a fireman, Montag, who discovers books, and in turn discovers a new life. This new life, however, means the collapse of his parallel "normal" life as a fireman. The world we come across in this film is a brutal world that seems only to have a relentless passion for hunting out and destroying books in ways that have no boundaries. A scene in a park, full of mothers with children, shows us firemen doing on-the-spot searches in a way that invades personal space (the frisking of a pregnant woman as a matter of course) and treats all people, including babies in pushchairs or prams, as perpetual suspects. But it is in this brutal book-burning world, to which we are exposed, that we can discover some interesting and important theological issues; and they center on the idea of the book and the text.

The work of any theologian is centered on text and writing. Essentially this center is the Word of God, incarnate and as revealed in Scripture. It will also include the Creeds, the work of other key theologians, and the contribution other disciplines can make. In some senses, then, *Fahrenheit 451* can seem to offer nothing to the theologian but a rather vague and somewhat apocalyptic warning about the importance of books, history, tradition, and free speech. The important thing about the world in this film is that with the disappearance of books comes also the disappearance of "the remembrance of things past." However, what I want to suggest is that it is in the conclusion of the film that the most profound theological lesson is learnt.

As Montag discovers books and reads them, his life is turned upside down. His wife discovers him reading and pleads with him to get rid of the books, but he cannot. In the end she reports him to the fire service and on the day that Montag finally realizes he must leave the fire service, he does his last call, which is to his own house. Montag now knows that he must escape. During the film Montag has met another woman, called Claris, who is also a reader, and she tells him about the Book People, which is where she escapes to. Montag makes his escape, follows Claris's instructions, and searches to find the Book People.

The Book People are made up of those who have disappeared, been arrested and escaped, or have simply rebelled against society. They live on the very edges (both geographically and socially) of society and each of them devotes his or her life to learning one book. They become a huge, human "inward library" and, as one of the characters says, are a minority "crying out in the wilderness." But they are the small, dim lights ready to become brighter when this age of darkness passes. The point about the Book People is that they are a (holy?) remnant; they are the precious resource that contains all human knowledge and history; but much more than this is the fact that they actually become the books they remember. This is not a simple act of memory and repetition, but involves an approach to human existence in which each member of the community becomes their book. This is not a living book museum to honor what has died, but is the first sign of the textual resurrection they all hope for. To become the book is to be ready to commit it back to writing when times have changed. What is important here, for the theologian, are two things: first the idea of the wilderness in which the Book People live, and secondly the idea of being a book.

The wilderness has always had a special place in the Christian tradition. It is a place of temptation and renewal; it is a place of self-discovery and reliance on God; it is a place of spiritual growth; and for the early desert fathers, it is a place where wisdom can be sought, for those who live in the desert are transformed and grow in knowledge. What is important, as Andrew Louth (1991) has shown, is that the wilderness can be both a literal place and a metaphorical place: but whichever of these it is, it is still a wilderness and a site of transformation and renewal.

In the film, the wilderness is a resource, full of desert mothers and fathers who are ready to play their role of spiritual and epistemological mothers and fathers when the time comes. In the film, this wilderness (which, as in the Russian tradition, is a forest) will be the place from which new growth will come. It is a harsh place in many respects, but it is also a place of hope and resurrection. In the film it is only such a place because of the aspirations of the Book People who live there, and this leads me on to my second point about becoming or being the book.

Theology is not simply an activity that one does, and is certainly not simply an activity that is only done in one's head and on paper. Theology is also about *doxa* and *praxis*, worship and action. Our response to God needs a serious intellectual dimension, but should also be a lived experience. To take up one's cross and follow Christ is something that does need thought and exploration, but it is also something that is lived out in one's daily life and pursued through one's worship. In other words, like the Book People, to be theologians must entail becoming our texts, and living in a way that conforms to the Word, which is the Text that we need to inscribe on our hearts. This is not merely a pious sentiment, but is, rather, the sort of theology that has had to happen, in the face of suffering and oppression, in Latin America. It is also the sort of theology that has had to be done by women who felt oppressed and suppressed by the patriarchal character of Christianity.

It is true that Truffaut's film warns us about censorship and the importance of text, but much more than this, it points to the fact that theology itself is a lived experience. The idea of becoming like the Book People is a rich theological idea worth exploring much further than I can do in this chapter.

Drama

While there is a developing industry when it comes to theology and film, the same cannot be said for the relationship between theology and drama. The obvious and most significant exception to this is Hans Urs von Balthasar's monumental *Theo-Drama*. Even though one of the most significant theologians of the twentieth century chose to engage with drama as a model for theological interpretation, it would appear that no one has developed this project or taken it forward in any significant way.

Von Balthasar's key insight in the *Theo-Drama* is the understanding of the Christian story in terms of an unfolding, and as yet unfinished, drama in which we are involved. Indeed, what Jesus Christ offers on the cross (or even achieves on the cross) is the invitation to become central characters in the unfolding drama of God and His creation. More than this, however, and more importantly for this current project, von Balthasar paves the way for theology to engage with drama and dramatic theory in order to see what it can offer or teach the theologian in her practice of theology, and it is this that I want to take from von Balthasar, rather than engaging with him. In the section that follows, I still want to work with Marsh's second option, in which theology is only one discourse among many, and as with film, that drama is treated as something theological in itself.

The two areas of drama I want to explore are Antonin Artaud's concept of "Theater of Cruelty" and some aspects of what is known as the "Theater of the Absurd," for in these approaches to theater lie some interesting theological possibilities. Indeed, at some level I would want to argue that unless one considers these approaches to theater as theologies one actually misses the point of what it is they offer. The most important point then is the engagement with dramatists as theologians in their own right, rather than as something essentially non-theological that theologians can utilize. In this regard I profoundly disagree with Richard Eyre and Nicholas Wright, who claim that "Playwrights don't have a 'set of beliefs'; they are not theologians" (Eyre and Wright 2000:21). Theologians do not (should not) have a static set of beliefs but, like playwrights, who can be and are theologians, they explore what belief might mean.

Artaud and the Theater of Cruelty

Artaud was born in Marseilles on September 4, 1896, and died at a clinic in Ivry on March 4, 1948. He is a complex and fascinating figure whose life was punctuated by failure in that all of his projects (literary, theatrical, artistic, and filmic) were failures in his lifetime. This was exacerbated by the fact that he suffered from periods of extreme mental illness. Although I think it is possible to develop a general aesthetic through engaging with all of Artaud's work, especially in his various theatrical experimentations such as Théâtre Alfred Jarry, in this chapter I simply want to highlight some key elements that led to his development of the Theater of Cruelty.

In August 1931, Artaud saw a group of Balinese dancers, which was an experience that had profound effects on him. In essence, what Artaud saw in these dancers was the possibility of a type of theater that consisted of physical signs and athletic gestures, and was not, like most theater, utterly dependent on script. In these dancers, Artaud saw a revelation of a "physical idea of theatre where drama is encompassed within the limits of everything that can happen on stage, independently of a written script" (Artaud 1970:50). In the same year, Artaud also came across a fifteenth-century painting in the Louvre called *The Daughters of Lot*, by the artist Van Leyden. Artaud saw connections between the experience of seeing this painting and the one he had had on seeing the Balinese dancers, especially in the sense that the painting appeared to him to have elements of the theatrical spectacle about it. In short, the "mental drama" that Artaud saw as being present in this painting has, for him, a "concrete effect" on us (Artaud 1970:26). The effect of the painting, like that of the dancers, causes Artaud to conceive of a theater where words will not dominate, and where theater becomes a spectacle that affects us.

In order to do this, Artaud realized that he must develop a new language of the theater. Moreover, this new language would mean breaking away from theater's subjugation to the text, because such dialogic, speech-centered theater primarily addresses the mind, whereas Artaud wanted theater to appeal to the senses in the first instance. What is important here is to note that Artaud had no wish to ignore, destroy, or do without spoken language in the theater, but he did want to dethrone speech in order for other elements of the theatrical language to gain ascendancy. What Artaud maintains is that "the stage is a tangible, physical place that needs to be filled and it ought to be allowed to speak its own concrete language" (Artaud 1970:27), and that he wanted what he called a "spatial poetry" to take place on the stage, rather than a merely spoken poetry of traditional drama.

Artaud wanted to create an approach to theater that restored it to what he saw as its true goal. For Artaud, myths and stories have a deep power that cloaks what he calls "pure forces," and these pure forces (which are the messages of myths) are damaged or even ruined by a theater designed to attract the mind only. This type of theater reveals nothing; neither does it directly affect us. For Artaud the point is that:

> Theatre will stop being a game and an entertaining way of passing an evening and will become a kind of useful act, restored to the status of therapy, to which the mob in ancient times used to flock to regain a taste for life and the strength to resist the blows of fate. (Artaud 1999:151)

A key principle for Artaud in all of this is that each production must be unique and unrepeatable, for if it could be repeated it would become another example of theater as representation. Moreover, we must understand what Artaud meant by the term "cruelty." What he did not mean was a theatrical version of the video-nasty. For Artaud, cruelty is an approach to theatrical experience which makes the theater, to use Artaud's own, powerful phrase, "a believable reality inflicting [a] kind of . . . laceration" (Artaud 1970:65), thereby having the effect of shocking and transforming us.

Artaud himself described his theater as "holy theatre," and for him the theater was a sacred place designed to effect a kind of salvation on those present. It is through unrepeatable spectacles that shock and lacerate us, in which we move from being spectators to being part of the drama itself, that we engage with the cruelty and suffering of life and overcome it. Although some writers have seized on Artaud's gnostic influences, there is also a more straightforward Christian idea operating here: namely that what has not been assumed cannot be redeemed. For Artaud, the point of theater is that we would assume all the suffering and cruelty of life in order to be redeemed from it.

Artaud's failed theatrical project has much potential when seen as an exercise in theology and in terms of its soteriological intent. Artaud's theater, as a spectacle that engages with myths in an attempt to lacerate and transform us by making us part of the action, has much potential when employed as a liturgical idea. Moreover, his emphasis on a total language of theater, where speech is dethroned and other elements are allowed to speak, can also be seen to have liturgical implications. Finally, his insistence on unrepeatable theatrical events, and his deep suspicion of theater as representation, has much to offer theology in its attempt to represent what in the end is unrepresentable, namely, the divine. The point is, and I have only scratched the surface here, to read Artaud as a theologian and not as a failed dramatist.

The Theater of the Absurd

It is simply not possible to talk about the Theater of the Absurd without mentioning Martin Esslin's seminal work, *The Theatre of the Absurd*. Esslin begins his book with a description of a production of Samuel Beckett's *Waiting for Godot* that was put on in San Quentin penitentiary in November 1957. The audience consisted of fourteen hundred maximum security prisoners. The actors and the director (the very famous Herbert Blau) were extremely nervous, for what they were doing was putting on one of the strangest plays, and possibly one of the more obscure and intellectual plays of this tradition of theater, in a prison.

The point of this story is that this production of *Godot* was an amazing success. Perhaps in the very best traditions of the absurd, Beckett's esoteric and avant-garde play, put on in such absurd surroundings, spoke to those very people so often excluded from society, and so often labeled as uneducated or unthinking. A play that many intellectuals failed to appreciate was seen as powerful and moving by the very people that the critical elite would normally not even consider as the theater-going public. As Esslin powerfully comments, plays such as absurdist dramas, which are "so often superciliously dismissed as nonsense or mystification, *have* something to say" (Esslin 1991:21).

Drama in this tradition is never easy to watch. It often doesn't have a central story (or if it does it is interrupted by strange actions in the play); it often involves seemingly pointless things happening – such as a stage with empty chairs, or people turning into rhinoceroses, or waiting for someone called Godot to appear who never comes.

What these playwrights, loosely associated under the absurdist banner, represent is a serious attempt at religious and theological reflection. They explore the very questions that we all appear to want to explore, and that theology continually engages with, namely those deep existential questions of meaning and purpose, although this does not begin to describe the richness of this tradition.

What the Theater of the Absurd attempts to do is to expose us to the absurdity, even the grossness, of the human condition. Moreover, in some sense it can be seen to owe something to the ideals of Greek theater (especially tragedy) but does so without reference to clearly defined narratives or stories, or, where there are stories, they appear to be, at first sight, nonsensical. This lack of narrative structure can be understood in terms of two postmodern ideas. First, the idea, espoused by thinkers such as Foucault and Barthes, of the death of the author. If modernism celebrated the death of the story, it still celebrated the technical skill and resources of the author. In postmodernity the text is now freed from the restrictions of the author, and a focus on their skill or genius, and we as readers are allowed to engage with texts on our own terms. Secondly, and we have already mentioned this, is the idea in Lyotard that postmodernism can be defined as having "incredulity towards metanarratives."

It is important, as with many areas that we label, that although we use "the Theater of the Absurd" as a kind of shorthand, we don't fall into the trap of believing that what it represents is some unified approach with unified aims; and there are significant differences. At a superficial level, I think one can see Pinter almost as a philosopher of religion, posing questions about the apparent nakedness and absurdity of our situation; one can see in the work of Ionesco a dramatist who tries to use drama as a way of confronting the absurdity and attempting to present a pathway of liberation; and one can see that Beckett presents us with a complex engagement with the question of nothingness.

Some thinkers have tried to liken the effect of the Theater of the Absurd to a mystical experience. Esslin, in his seminal book, talks about this aspect. For Esslin, because the Theatre of the Absurd confronts us with the limits of human experience (with absurdity, with nothingness, with questions about epistemology and what we think we might know) – i.e. the absurd nature of human existence – it means that it can be seen to have similarities with mystics, who also confront the very limits of human experience, spirituality, and knowledge of God. Esslin says: "As the mystics report poetic images, so does the Theatre of the Absurd" (Esslin 1991:428). However, what Esslin, and all other commentators who begin to explore the religious dimension of theater, fail to do is develop this idea in any substantial way.

Harold Pinter

In Harold Pinter's plays what we see is "man trying to stake out a modest place for himself in the cold and darkness that envelops him" (Esslin 1991:401–2). In his early plays, such as *The Caretaker*, *The Dumb Waiter*, and *The Birthday Party*, Pinter creates strange and disturbing scenes full of odd happenings, silences, and painful examples of ruptured communication. Such things conspire to make us feel uneasy, feel the absurdity of what we do, what we say, and how we live. Quite simply, in these early plays, we are confronted with the potential absurdity of our own lives as we try to create meaning. We are confronted with the difficulties and ruptures in our communication, theological and otherwise. We are also confronted with the ways in which we try to cover up for such inadequacies, and are not allowed to get away with it.

Many of Pinter's early plays seem to take place in some form of enclosed space – either a room or a house. The outside world is not engaged with, and seems to be a place that is potentially dangerous and threatening. For example, the entire action of *The Caretaker* is set inside a house, and essentially one room. Outside this safe haven is the dark and threatening world where, for Davies, the "blacks" are. In this play, the blacks become a metaphor, in Davies life, for all that is unfair and threatening. Even in the claustrophobic safety of the room, he is worried about the "blacks" somehow permeating this safe space. This may, in a perverse sense, seem funny at first, but it very soon becomes disturbing, perhaps even frightening. However, what begins as humor soon implicates us, and theologically. Davies's demonization of the "blacks" becomes a powerful cipher for all those who have been demonized in and through theology, as well as making us aware of the very thin basis for such judgments.

The confined space in which *The Birthday Party* takes place is a very safe place; the beginning of the play, though comic, sees Meg and Peaty going about their everyday business in their boarding house in a supremely comic and organized way. Everyone knows what he or she thinks, what they should do and who they should be. Stanley, one of the other central characters, lives in this safe and secure world, and it allows him to develop the fantasy of who he would like to be. As the play develops, two unexpected visitors, Goldberg and McCann, come to the house, and the security and stability are suddenly threatened. In their terrifying interrogation of Stanley, for no apparent reason, one sees, in these two characters, the "outside world" come into this secure place and challenge and break it down.

The questions McGann and Goldberg put to Stanley make no sense, and thus can't be understood – in just the same way that so many religious questions in the modern era must remain unanswered, or even unanswerable. We may, through our religious narratives, construct a security for ourselves, but it is illusory and when questioned it can easily shatter. The absurd situation Pinter creates can be seen to mirror this idea. Indeed, far more disturbingly, in the interrogation, based on such ruptured communication, is a profound lesson for all who try to impose any monolithic account of religiosity or theology on another.

Eugene Ionesco

For many people Ionesco is the quintessential absurdist. On the surface, his plays seem to be about either terrifying situations that appear to make little sense, or ridiculous subjects that also make no apparent sense. But, much like Artaud, for Ionesco theater is a serious thing that has a religious or sacred significance. Whether through terror or the seemingly absurd, Ionesco's drama takes us to the very center of the despair that he thinks molds and shapes our lives. It would, at a superficial level, be easy to think that Ionesco does this simply because he is a born pessimist and wants to share his pessimism with the rest of us. However, nothing could be further from the truth.

For Ionesco, life involves pain and anxiety, especially the anxiety we all face through fear of death. Death is, unless we take our own life, a random certainty. We all know that we are going to die, but none of us knows when this will be or how it will be; and as Heidegger rightly understood, there is an aloneness about death in that no one else can do our dying for us. In the face of an uncertain future, a certain death, Ionesco sees that life can easily be rendered meaningless. For him, then, drama, in taking us to the heart of our anxiety and despair, which for Ionesco are part of the mystery of life, should become a vehicle that shows us possible paths of liberation from that despair. I want to look briefly at Ionesco's famous play *Rhinoceros*, to explore his theological contribution.

The play is about a small provincial town in which all the people begin to turn into rhinoceroses. The central character, Berenger, is appalled by this phenomenon and, although toward the end of the play he nearly capitulates by wanting to become a rhinoceros too, he ends up as the only living thing that has not turned into a rhino, and remains human. His final monologue, a combination of despair, confusion, and near capitulation, ends with the defiant and passionate cry of a man who does not capitulate and turn into a rhinoceros. As a lone individual, Berenger, whilst acknowledging that those who "[t]ry to hang on to their individuality always come to a bad end," resolves to stand fast, be brave, and face his lonely existence; as the last man left he is going to stay "that way until the end." He will not capitulate (*Rhinoceros*, act III; Ionesco 1962:124).

Esslin, as we have seen, says that the absurdists used poetic images on stage in the same way that (Christian) mystics did in their writings. Throughout the history of Christian mysticism, mystics have used a wide variety of poetic metaphors to explore and explain their experience and theology. Examples can be seen in the mystical epistemology explored through the "cloud of unknowing," through Teresa's exploration of the layers of the soul as an interior castle, and through John of the Cross's analysis of his mystical experiences through a dark night and the ascent of a mountain. The list could easily go on. The point of these metaphors is that they provide a way to explore and explain what, because it operates on the very boundaries of thought, language, and experience, normally resists explanation.

In one sense, this may appear an easy play to understand, especially in terms of a political reading to do with the problem of totalitarian states. Ionesco, though he did not directly write the play with this in mind, was appalled by what he saw Nazis do, as well as by his friends who, though initially sharing his anti-Nazi stance, quickly capitulated and joined the movement. He was equally suspicious of any left-wing version of totalitarianism as, for him, such totalitarian states strip one of individuality and rob one of any spirituality. It is through a more conscious religious reading that we can truly understand the depth of this play, for it is a parable about spirtual authenticity in the face of religious totalitarianism. As Martin Luther King learnt, to his cost, there are times when, because of spiritual convictions, one has to stand alone and speak out and resist becoming part of that debilitating totalitarianism. Ionesco achieves this, not through any overt political message, but through mystical and poetic images that are seemingly absurd. To see the full impact of this play it is important to read the stage directions, which make clear how this will be achieved on stage.

Conclusion

I want to end with a brief consideration of Disney's *The Lion King*, which of course has been both a film and a stage production. This may seem an odd place to end, given the caliber of drama I have considered, *The Lion King* being, as it is, an essentially crass story about male supremacy, and in typical Disney style, an over-simplistic morality tale. For some, lamenting that nostalgic bygone age (that olde worlde religion), such drama (for it is the dramatic production I really want to focus on) may well operate as a signifier for all that the world was and should return to. I have already made some comments about the danger of such nostalgia, especially apt in this case, as the nostalgia involves a strong male hunter juxtaposed against a submissive female who simply mourns the loss, and awaits the return, of her hero. However, there is far more we can learn from the stage production itself. If Julie Taymor, the director of the stage version of *The Lion King*, can develop this poor story into a theatrical event of this caliber, how much more can theologians do with a story that is anything but crass.

Artaud, Ionesco, and Pinter, although very different, do share various levels of a desire to challenge the essentially linguistic basis of much drama. For Artaud and Ionesco this involved trying to present drama in which images, staging, lighting, and decor "speak" as much as any actor. Pinter expresses as much linguistically, through silence, as well as showing not so much the impossibility, but certainly the rupture present in verbal communication. All of this is profoundly theological, and more traditionally textual-based theologians can learn a great deal from these stage experiments.

In terms of theology this is about performativity, which in Christian praxis is the two-edged sword of liturgy and life; of ritual and action. Taymor, who herself has come from an extremely radical theatrical background, has staged a version of *The Lion King* that teaches us something about the production of dramatic action that is powerful, moving, and embracing. Indeed the experience of watching this production is one of forgetting the story, as you become taken over by the sheer power of the dramatic spectacle that unfolds in front of you. If Christian liturgy could learn from this, then perhaps, like Artaud's Theater of Cruelty, it would help to transform the audience from spectators to actors, and like Ionesco, begin to use images that speak more powerfully of liberation. But the point of all of this is not to be a liturgical–dramatic end in itself; rather, it should provoke, lacerate, and inspire us to act – to become the text(s) we proclaim, and live them out on the boundaries of a suffering world that is surely in need of messages of hope and liberation.

Film and drama, whether they can be described as postmodern in themselves or not, allow theologians in postmodernity another type of discourse. What I hope to have shown in this chapter are some examples of where such exploration may lead, but the job is far from complete. Postmodernity allows us to begin to explore the subjugated voices in theology, and by extension allows us to explore new discourses. Like Artaud's theater, I am not suggesting the death of written theology – for this is what I am doing in this chapter – but I am suggesting that we can allow other languages of theology to be heard or even created. This means that we cannot simply plunder like pirates the images or experiences that film and drama give, and label them religious or spiritual; rather, it means that we need to take a much bolder step and see them as theology in themselves, and read/watch them accordingly.

In his work on the spiritual nature of art, Wassily Kandinsky saw that in our materialist world there has been a loss of the spiritual. He says that:

> The nightmare of materialism, which turned life into an evil, senseless game, is not yet passed; it still darkens the awakening soul. Only a feeble light glimmers, a tiny point in an immense circle of darkness.   (Kandinsky 1996:4)

Theology can only gain by seeing that, among the arts, film and drama offer rich theologies and thus can be seen as a tiny light that glimmers, offering visions of life that attempt to engage with why, from the point of view of theology, in the end, life cannot be seen as a senseless game. This will entail looking at film and drama in a different way, but that is the possibility that you, as readers, have in your hands.

Bibliography and Further Reading

Artaud, A. 1970. *The Theatre and its Double*, trans. V. Corti. London: John Calder.

Artaud, A. 1978. *Collected Works*, vol. 4, trans. V. Corti. London: John Calder. Originally published as *Antonin Artaud: Oeuvres Completes*, vol. 4. Paris: Gallimard, 1964. This volume contains all the documents of *The Theatre and its Double*.

Artaud, A. 1999. *Collected Works*, vol. 2, trans. V. Corti. London: John Calder. Originally published as *Antonin Artaud: Oeuvres Completes*, vol. 2. Paris: Gallimard, 1961.

Barber, S. 1993. *Antonin Artaud: Blows and Bombs*. London: Faber & Faber.

Baudrillard, J. 1994. *Simulacra and Simulation*, trans. S. F. Glaser. Ann Arbor, MI: University of Michigan Press. Originally published as *Simulacres et simulation*. Paris: Editions Galilee, 1981.

Beckett, S. 1965. *Waiting for Godot*. London: Faber & Faber.

Bentley, E. ed. 1992. *The Theory of the Modern Stage*. London: Penguin.

Bermel, A. 2001. *Artaud's Theatre of Cruelty*. London: Methuen.

Connor, S. 1997. *Postmodernist Culture: An Introduction to Theories of the Contemporary*, 2nd edn. Oxford: Blackwell.

Esslin, M. 1976. *Antonin Artaud: The Man and his Work*. London: John Calder.

Esslin, M. 1991. *The Theatre of the Absurd*. Harmondsworth: Penguin.

Eyre, R. and Wright, N. 2000. *Changing Stages: A View of British Theatre in the Twentieth Century*. London: Bloomsbury.

Fortier, M. 1997. *Theory/Theatre: An Introduction*. London and New York: Routledge.

Fraser, P. 1998. *Images of the Passion: The Sacramental Mode in Film*. Trowbridge: Flicks Books.

Goodall, J. 1994. *Artaud and the Gnostic Drama*. Oxford: Clarendon Press.

Ionesco, E. 1962. *Rhinoceros, The Chairs, The Lesson*. Harmondsworth: Penguin.

Ionesco, E. 1968. *Fragments of a Journal*, trans. J. Stewart. London: Faber & Faber. Originally published as *Journal en Miettes*. Paris: Mercure de France, 1967.

Kandinsky, W. 1996. "Concerning the Spiritual in Art", in *Art, Creativity and the Sacred: An Anthology in Religion and Art*, ed. D. Apostolos-Cappadona. New York: Continuum.

Louth, A. 1991. *The Wilderness of God*. London: Darton, Longman & Todd.

Marsh, C. and Ortiz, G. W. eds. 1997. *Explorations in Theology and Film*. Oxford: Blackwell.

Martin, J. W. and Ostwalt, C. E. Jr. eds. 1995. *Religion, Myth and Ideology in Popular American Film*. Boulder, CO: Westview Press.

May, J. R. and Bird, M. eds. 1982. *Religion in Film*. Knoxville, TN: University of Tennessee Press.

Pannenberg, W. 1991. *An Introduction to Systematic Theology*. Edinburgh: T. & T. Clark.

Pinter, H. 1991a. *The Birthday Party*. London: Faber & Faber.

Pinter, H. 1991b. *The Caretaker*. London: Faber & Faber.

Stam, R. 1999. *Film Theory: An Introduction*. Oxford: Blackwell.

Von Balthasar, H.-U. 1998. *Theo-Drama*, trans. G. Harrison. San Francisco, CA: Ignatius Press.

Ward, G. ed. 1997. *The Postmodern God: A Theological Reader*. Oxford: Blackwell.

Wiles, T. J. 1980. *The Theater Event: Modern Theories of Performance*. Chicago and London: University of Chicago Press.

CHAPTER 31
Race

M. Shawn Copeland

The capacity to live with difference is, in my view, the coming question of the twenty-first century.

(Stuart Hall 1996)

All of us must finally bury the elitism of race superiority / the elitism of sexual superiority / the elitism of economic superiority / the elitism of religious superiority.

(Sonia Sanchez 1995)

Introduction

One hundred years ago, W. E. B. Du Bois wrote: "The problem of the twentieth century is the problem of the color-line, – the relation of the darker to the lighter races of men [*sic*] in Asia and Africa, in America and the islands of the sea" (Du Bois 2003:15). Even the most cursory review of the geo-political and cultural landscape of the past fifty years confirms Du Bois's prescience. Consider, for instance, that the racial make-up of US prisons challenges the undeniable claim of racial progress in the United States, or that surges of xenophobia and anti-Semitism cheapen European assertions of multi-racial inclusiveness, or that investigations of terrorism manipulate race to ambush the basic human rights of Arabs and Muslims. These examples underscore not only the persistence of the color-line but the "continuing significance and changing meaning of race" and racism (Omi and Winant 1993:3).

This chapter takes race and racism seriously. It begins by treating the concept of race, because in order to oppose racism, it is crucial to understand the continuing signifi-cance and changing meanings of race. Thus, the first section explores conceptions, definitions, and theories of race. The idea that the meaning of race or racial identity can change is a relatively new one. Even as recently as forty years ago, race was deemed a fixed concept. Race denoted a group of persons connected by common origin and sharing distinct physical characteristics. Race implied something natural, immutable, an essential category or phenomenon characterizing, even determining, the person. However, during the past twenty-five years or so, a body of theoretical analysis has developed to destabilize and problematize the concept of race.

This section discusses three definitions and theories of the concept of race: race as an ideological construct, as an objective condition, and as a social construct or racial-formation process. This last provides the most comprehensive explanatory capacity and is a variant of what, arguably, is the most dynamic rethinking of race, *critical race theory*. Critical race theory, or CRT, got its start among academic lawyers in the mid-1970s. It probes, unmasks, and "challenges the practices of subordination facilitated and permitted by legal discourse and legal institutions" (Harris 2001:xx). Early theorists who grasped racism's penchant for subtle camouflage include Derrick Bell, Alan Freeman, and Richard Delgado. These thinkers drew inspiration from the reservoir of intellectual energy, imagination, and courage created by African liberation struggles, resistance to anti-Semitism, the modern US civil rights movement, and opposition to colonialism. CRT spread to many disciplines, including education, cultural studies, English, sociology, political science, history, and anthropology.

The chapter's second section provides a definition of racism and reviews ways in which the practice of racism exploits the limitations of the concept of race as an ideology and an objective condition. Racism is a complex and opportunistic social phenomenon that ambiguously marks everyday experience: while the casual outing may risk nothing more than boredom, the probability of random, xenophobic violence is real, and concrete experience has a way of betraying theory.

For the past thirty-five years, critical theologies for human liberation, including African, Asian, black, feminist, Latin American, Latino/a, minjung, mujerista, Native American, and womanist, have protested against racism as social oppression. In particular, black and womanist theologies in the US, Britain, and South Africa stand out for their vigorous resistance. Yet, standing against racism is not necessarily synonymous with standing against race. Only in a few instances do these theologies explicitly interrogate race-thinking. The chapter's third section examines race as a theological category.

Defining and Theorizing Race

In their path-breaking and influential essay *Racial Formation in the United States*, Michael Omi and Howard Winant define race as "a concept which signifies and symbolizes social conflicts and interests by referring to different types of human bodies" (Omi and Winant 1994:55). This compact heuristic contests the major conceptualizations or theoretical understandings of race – either race is an ideological construct or it is an objective condition. Rather, Omi and Winant contend that race is "an element of social structure rather than an irregularity within it . . . a dimension of human representation rather than an illusion." The position that they advocate proposes to understand race as socially constructed (1994:55). In this section we first review the major conceptualizations of race, then turn to the clarification of race as a product of social construction or racial formation.

To explain race as an *ideological construct* or the result of biased thinking (what Marx called "false consciousness") is to render race an illusion. Proponents of this view refer to race as unscientific, as fictitious. Should we display the results and effects of race-thinking, these thinkers are likely to declare that race takes on a life of its own. But if race is an illusion, pure ideology, it does not exist and, therefore, has no life-stuff of its own by which to extend itself. While proponents of this position take on a smug expression, a curious and pathetic set of syllogisms emerges: if race is an illusion, then racial prejudice and racism are illusions. If race is an illusion, then those who "suffered definition" (Spivak 2000:65) along with their memories and narratives can only be illusory. If race is an illusion, then those who oppose racism unwittingly perpetuate race-thinking. Yet, what are we to do with the brutal social facts of racism and racial prejudice? What are we to do with suddenly falsified accounts of conquest, colonialism, and empire? What are we to do with the witness of memories, cemeteries, and decaying ovens? When such a position fails to expunge histories of violence and barbarism, it sanitizes, homogenizes, and reframes these conflicting perspectives into a Utopian, but flat and evasive, narrative. Such a position dodges the field of experience, which is the ground of good theory, and suppresses questioning, the most basic act of human intelligence.

We can conclude that race as an ideological construct holds little if any explanatory value and dissatisfies on two accounts. First, it fails to address the "longevity," resilience, geographic irreverence, as well as the effects produced by "race-thinking and race-acting" (Omi and Winant 1993:5). Secondly, as an illusion race cannot connect to human experience, to human bodies and their locations in particular social or historical circumstances. But, as Omi and Winant argue so trenchantly, our societies are "so thoroughly racialized that to be without racial identity is to be in danger of having no identity. To be raceless is akin to being genderless. Indeed, when one cannot identify another's race, a microsociological 'crisis of interpretation' results" (1993:5).

To attempt to explain *race as an objective condition* seems highly problematic. With its allusion to scientific objectivity, such a definition admits biological racial and eugenicist theories. This approach can be traced through the empirical taxonomies of the eighteenth-century physician François Bernier and naturalist Carolus Linnaeus, to nineteenth-century proponents of so-called scientific racism such as Louis Agassiz and Paul Broca, to Charles Yerkes and Lewis Terman in the early twentieth century (Gossett 1997), up to Richard Herrnstein and Charles Murray's *The Bell Curve* (1994). In the name of scientific objectivity, these thinkers detached race from social and historical conditions and treated it as "an independent variable" (Omi and Winant 1993:6). Because race-thinking took on the mantle of objectivity, race came to function as a universal evaluative tool to measure human hierarchy – whites placed at the top of the scale, blacks at the lowest rung, and brown, yellow, and red women and men ranked in between. In Europe, right into the mid-twentieth century, this racial scale was used to exclude and represent Jews and Irish as inferior others (Miles 1989; MacMaster 2001). In the US, this scale "was combined with an argument that human intelligence was a fixed and hereditary characteristic" that allowed not only the measurement of enslaved Africans and their descendants but also a chart of "acceptable and unacceptable immigrants" (Miles 1989:36).

If the allusion to objectivity makes a convincing appeal to so-called conservatives, it also works well with so-called liberals. Liberals reject the biological argument, but fall short of grasping the "variability and historically contingent character" of race and racial meanings. Their arguments fail to problematize an individual's relation to his or her racial group identity and likewise ignore the "constantly shifting parameters through which race is understood, group interests are assigned, statuses are ascribed, agency is attained, and roles performed" (Omi and Winant 1993:6).

Race as an objective condition also fails as an explanatory strategy. Inasmuch as this approach accepts as objective fact that *one is one's race*, it remains ahistorical. This position endorses, however unwittingly, a notion of "fixed" racial identity and thereby subordinates that identity to criteria that depart from human experience. In other words, although there is a performative dimension to race, no performance need be fixed or prescribed. One way to get at this is to ask, "What does it mean *to act* white or *to act* black?" To interrogate this issue, we might ask, "Does *acting* white in the Southern United States mean the same thing at present as it did in 1937?" And, to complexify the issue, we could ask, "Does *acting* German mean the same thing at present as it did in 1940?" To treat race as an objective condition fails to appreciate the "historicity and social comprehensiveness of the race concept" (Omi and Winant 1993:6).

Further, race as an objective condition fails to appreciate the way in which individuals and groups are pressed to work out "incoherent and conflictual racial meanings and identities in everyday life" (Omi and Winant 1993:6). To concretize this point, we might try a few thought experiments: We might imagine a young woman whose parents are of different races: How should she identify her racial heritage? Or we might puzzle over Paul Gilroy's memorable phrase, "There ain't no Black in the Union Jack." What sort of statement is it? Is it literal or metaphorical, a cultural tag or a political slogan, or some combination of these? Finally, we might conjecture the dilemmas that the race concept posed for individuals and groups who endured and participated in ethnic cleansing in the Balkans or genocide in Rwanda. The differing textures and densities of these experiments lead us to engage a third definition and approach to theorizing race – that is, race as a social construct, or racial formation.

Omi and Winant use the sociological term *racial formation* to denote the complex, historically situated process by which human bodies and social structures are represented and arranged, and how race is linked to the way in which society is organized and ruled. From this perspective, "race is a matter of both social structure and cultural representation." Racial-formation process accounts for a cluster of problems regarding race, including the dilemmas of racial identity and the relation of race to other forms of difference such as gender and nationality; and it clarifies the nature of racism and its relation to social oppression as this is expressed, even in so-called "first world" or developed nations, as economic exploitation, marginalization, powerlessness, cultural imperialism, and systemic as well as random violence (Young 1990:41–59). While this perspective grasps the brutality of race on global and personal levels, it discredits the romanticization of race as essence and its misrepresentation as illusion. Thus, racial-formation process maintains that race is not a deviation within a given social structure, but a constant feature embedded within it.

The racial-formation process thematizes the "sociohistorical process by which racial categories are created, inhabited, transformed, and destroyed" (Omi and Winant

1994:55–6) and its explanatory capacity meets both the macro- and micro-levels. On the *macro-level*, the racial-formation process adequately interprets contemporary social (that is, political, economic, and technological) relations, the shifting "meanings and salience" of race in a global context as well as "across historical time." Here, race as a social construct demonstrates considerable flexibility. Given the increasingly complex and globalized concept of race, the racial-formation process manages the "competing *racial projects*" or "efforts to institutionalize racial meanings and identities in particular social structures, notably those of individual, family, community, and state" (Omi and Winant 1993:7). The desire of women and men of mixed racial parentage to name themselves, the struggles of egalitarian movements against racial backlash, the post-colonial interrogations of empire, the decentering of powerful binary logics – for example, white/black, colonizer/colonized, as well as the sly concealment of discourses and exercises of racial domination: these sometimes contradictory enterprises reinforce the protean character of race (see Rodríguez 2002, Wu 2002). Moreover, these enterprises generate both new forms of social oppression and responses that deploy race not only to expose its toxic limitations, but also to re-imagine and reconfigure social matrices to evoke the achievement and flourishing of authentic humanity (Eze 2001).

Yet, even as race as a social construct admits of what Emmanuel Eze calls a "postracial future" (Eze 2001), that same process charts the terrain of everyday lived experience or the *micro-level*. Here, racial formation spells out how the most mundane as well as the most important tasks can be grasped as racial projects – shopping, banking, walking through a park, registering for school, inquiring about church membership, using public transportation, hailing a taxicab. We have been taught to *see* race, and we do. Race is one of the first things that we notice about people (along with their sex) when we meet them. Further, the ability to read race accurately, to categorize people (black or white, red or brown, Mexican or Indian, Chinese or Vietnamese) has become crucial for social behavior and comfort. The inability to identify accurately a person's race can incite a crisis. Even as we question such interpretation, we continue to analyze and interpret our experience in racial terms. As Omi and Winant observe, "We expect differences in skin color, or other racially coded characteristics, to explain social differences" (Omi and Winant 1994:60). This affects not only our relations to various social institutions, cultural activities, religious rites and rituals, but our relationships with other human persons as well as the constitution of our own identities. The very stereotypes we profess to abhor and repudiate break in on our encounters or our racial apprehensions of a bank teller, baseball player, rap artist, or physician. We work to press down preconceived notions of the black bank teller, the Japanese baseball player, the white rap artist, and the Indian physician. However, critical interrogation of the racial-formation process can uncover social conditioning for what it is – a set of learned behaviors and practices. At the same time, that critical interrogation can identify and support strategies to overcome the debilitating legacy of race.

Race and Racism

Although race is not an ideology, racism certainly is. Because the racial-formation process accords critical attention both to social structures and to social signification, it can account for racism as ideology. Racism is the product of biased thinking, an ideology that willfully justifies, advances, and maintains the systemic domination of a certain race or races by another race. Racism goes beyond prejudice (feeling or opinion formed without concrete experience or knowledge) or even bigotry (doctrinaire intolerance) by joining these feelings or attitudes to the putative exercise of legitimate power in a society; in this way, racism never relies on the choices or actions of a few individuals, but is *institutionalized*.

Racialized subjects sustain and transmit racism as an ideology through their uncritical acceptance of standards, symbols, habits, assumptions, reactions, and practices rooted in racial differentiation and racially assigned privilege. The intent is not to blame but rather to shake us from our drowsing. Racism penetrates the development and transmission of culture, including education and access to it, literary and artistic expression, forms of communication, representation, and leisure; participation in and contribution to the common good, including opportunities to work, or to engage in meaningful political and economic activity; the promotion of human flourishing, including intellectual, psychological, sexual, and spiritual growth; and the embrace of religion, including membership and leadership, catechesis and spirituality, ritual, doctrine, and theology. Thus, as James Boggs comments, racism permeates every sphere of social relations (Boggs 1970:147–8, Goldberg 1993).

As an ideology, racism envelops the "normal" and "ordinary" social set-up and spawns a negatively charged context in which flesh-and-blood human beings live out their daily lives and struggle to constitute themselves as persons. Racism is no mere problem to be solved, but a "way of life" through which we define reality. The racial-formation process alerts us to the fact that racism is not something *out-there* for us to solve, rather it is in *our* consciousness, shapes *our* discourse and practices. Hence, Frantz Fanon's chilling indictment: "The racist in a culture with racism is . . . normal" (Fanon 1967a:40).

To speak about a culture with racism, or *racist culture*, is to grasp culture as "both, and interrelatedly, a signifying system and a system of material production" (Goldberg 1993:8). Although race cannot be explained as an objective condition, in racist culture this idea obtains. Insisting on the empirical aspect of race, racist culture requires racial apprehension, conception, and judgment of each human being. Each human being is reduced to biological physiognomy: innocuous physical traits – skin color, hair texture, shape of body, head, facial features, blood traits – are identified, ordered, exaggerated, evaluated. Each human being is assigned a racial designation that orders her or his relations to other women and men of the same and of different races. Finally, in this arrangement one racial group is contrived as "the measure of human being" and deemed normative. For meanings and values have been embedded in those differences so as to favor the group that has been contrived as "the measure of human being." Virtue, morality, and goodness are assigned to that racial group, while vice, immorality, and evil are assigned to the others. Entitlement, power, and privilege are accorded that racial group, while dispossession, powerlessness, and disadvantage define others.

Racist culture or a culture based on racial privilege and preference absolutizes racial differences "by generalizing from them and claiming that they are final." When the difference is totalized, it "penetrates the flesh, the blood and the genes of the victim . . . it is transformed into fate, destiny, heredity" (Memi 1968:185, 189). When the difference is transformed into fate or destiny or heredity, then that constructed difference is *naturalized*. Whatever the difference, it is made to penetrate profoundly and collectively; it is final, complete, and inescapable. Thus, those who are racially different diverge not only from a set of norms, but from what it means to be a human being, and, hence, diverge from being human.

In a racist culture, definition and displacement, control and mastery, violence and power obtain. For racism will not allow us to overlook race, it demands that we see race and see it in specified and fixed ways. For example, raw reactions of various individuals to a fifty-year-old black man sitting in a tavern will vary certainly, but we cannot predict the outcome of such an ordinary racialized encounter. At the same time, that man's father or grandmother, having endured racial threat and suffered racial assault, quite probably can anticipate a range of scenarios, one of which might well include the risk of death. But, in spite of the enervating irrationality and unpredictability of random violence in racist cultures, marginalized and excluded individuals and groups continue to struggle with integrity against invisibility, indifference, and resignation. For, despite racism's seeming permanence, Fanon inspires us when he says racism is never a constant of the human spirit.

Theology, Race, and Racism

Beginning in the late 1960s, critical theologies for human liberation broke out across the globe in contexts of social (that is, political, economic, and technological) oppression. By naming themselves African, Asian, black, feminist, Latin American, Latino/a, minjung, mujerista, Native American, and womanist, these theologies made explicit a profound concern for the lives of human subjects whose experiences had been neglected in large measure by the prevailing streams of Christian theology (Gutiérrez 1988, Canon 1988, Cone 1997). Although differing from one another in cultural and religious formation, these theologies represented a basic "turn to the other" in compassionate solidarity (Sobrino 1994). At the same time, critical theologies for human liberation contested the role of Christianity in legitimating social oppression and uncovered the Gospel-rooted commitment to a radical love of neighbor (Tinker, 1993). They moved this commitment to the foreground of Christian cognitive and social praxis and, thereby, repudiated the Church's complicity in ideologies of domination and oppression. Critical theologies for human liberation made a fundamental option for the reign of God rather than the reign of the Church (Boff 1985).

Latin American, minjung, Asian, Latino/a, and certain formulations of African theologies thematized a "turn to the other" as a turn to the poor. These theologies made an option *for* the poor, an option that "insert[ed] itself into an option *of* the poor for their own liberation" (Leatt et al. 1986:294). The thrust of such a project carried the seeds of human liberation *for all* – release, development, flourishing, transcendence – and the creation of a just society (Bonino 1975, Gutiérrez 1983). By interrogating the nexus of religion, spirituality, and culture, Native American, Latino/a, and mujerista theologies mapped the inner lives of "the other" and opened a window on the spirituality and religious imagination of poor, excluded, and marginalized peoples (Deloria 1993). These theologies traced the animating work of the Spirit in the lives of those whose experiences made them most receptive to the voice of God (Elizondo 1988, Goizueta 1995, Espín 1997, Rodríguez 2002). Nor did these formulations neglect social oppression, particularly its impact on women (Aquino 1993, Isasi-Díaz 1993). Yet prophetic, dynamic, and critical as these theologies may be, heretofore they have accorded scant attention to race and racism.

The situation is somewhat different with black and womanist theologies in Britain, the Caribbean, South Africa, and the United States. These theologies share not only a racial marker, African heritage, and Pan-African commitment, but a 500-year-old tradition of struggle for the very existence of black human creatures. Even during the most repressive periods of enslavement and apartheid, lynching, detainment, and torture, bantustanization, banning, and segregation, discrimination, and random assault, black theologies and black Christian churches defended black humanity, advocated the unity of all humanity under God (the black Christian principle), and sustained the demands of justice. These theologies know the bone-crushing impact of racism; with the black oppressed they underwent racialized time. Yet, when it comes to the deployment of race, commonalities as well as differences emerge within the family of black theologies.

In the Caribbean, the function of race in theological reflection has proved quite thorny. To begin with, the region's racial and cultural–ethnic diversity was brought about through European (white) colonial force. For example, in Jamaica, black discourse tends to define "African" in terms of color or race; hence, the word "African" or "Jamaican" denotes a dark-skinned person. But only when this homogenizing propensity is problematized can "other" racial–cultural groups, such as the Chinese and Indians, assert their historical presence and identities (Chisholm 1997:75–6, L. Williams 1999:2). Hence, until recently, Caribbean theology defined race in essentialist terms; however, this may shift once the critique of colonial experience is absorbed sufficiently. The Antiguan philosopher Paget Henry has begun such a critique by foregrounding "the need to rethink the problem of the self" in the context of the region's layered, racial, cultural–ethnic criss-crossing (Henry 2000:274). His project calls upon philosophers and theologians to appropriate the discursive heritage generated by the historic struggle of Caribbean peoples against slavery, colonialism, and racism, and to resist regional "othering" practices such as intra-racial color discrimination and ethnic polarization. Such appropriation and resistance can set the stage for authentic engagement with the problems of humanity.

In apartheid South Africa, race was omnipotent, for apartheid South Africa *was* racist culture. Racial identities were assigned at birth, permanently fixed, and hierarchized – whites (Afrikaner, British), coloreds, Indians, blacks. Black life was cheap, disposable, and interchangeable. The black of blackness carried a negative charge that corroded black self-esteem and spawned contempt for "others" – coloreds and Indians. In such a racially repressive context, the very existence of black theology constituted a cry for life, its authenticity rested on adamant refusal to lend any approbation whatsoever to the apartheid system. On the one hand, black theology had to embrace and nurture the blackness of black South Africans whose bodies had been reduced to line items in the household economy, whose beauty had been battered, whose being was deemed disposable. On the other hand, black theology was Christian theology. It exposed apartheid as a sin against human life as God's creation and a heresy that replaced God with the idol of race (whiteness). Thus, theologians such as Manas Buthelezi, Simon Maimela, and Allan Boesak argued that only Christian love, or *agape*, possessed the power to transform "strange neighbors into loving brothers" and sisters (Buthelezi 1973:4). Moreover, agapic love was the responsibility of both blacks and whites, but Boesak and Maimela emphasized the intimate connection between agapic love and justice (Maimela 1981, Boesak 1981). Arguably, this position was possible because of the strenuous work of the Black Consciousness Movement (BCM). Under the leadership of Steve Biko, BCM exposed the racism of so-called "color-free" partnerships as attempts by white liberals to control black liberation, to think and speak for blacks, in other words, to sustain the subjugation of black humanity. In order to bring about the de-racialization of South Africa, Biko proposed to situate despised black identity as a locus of solidarity for creative and humane action across the races (Biko 1998).

During the period of apartheid, race in South African black theology functioned, sometimes simultaneously, in several ways – as essentialist, as an objective condition, as a brutal fact and, perhaps, even as romantic. In the post-apartheid period, black theology in South Africa would do well to problematize current racial meanings in the service of the poor black masses whose deteriorating social condition intimates a collusion between "capitalism and colonialism" and cannot but foreshadow a new struggle (Kunnie 2000:252).

In the United States in the years between 1964 and 1969, blacks began to recognize the limitations and contradictions in civil rights legislation and the shape-shifting ability of racism. Thwarted, broken-hearted, and angry black women and men, and especially youth, rebelled 329 times in 257 US cities. These uprisings were put down with violence, and treated with grudging paternalism and palliative programs. Black life, blackness, black racial life was cheap. At the same time, black cultural nationalists worked out a definition of "blackness" as color, culture, and consciousness that began a break with the prevailing notion of race as essentialist or as an objective condition. These theorists agitated for the rejection of "white" mental and cultural conditioning and, in its place, they proposed the appropriation of African culture. This turn to Africa was uncritical and ambiguous, indulging, in rhapsodic and romantic forms, particularly with regard to the sexist treatment of black women by black men. At the end of those five years of violence and against the backdrop of cultural and racial interrogation, James Cone wrote *Black Theology and Black Power* (1969 [1997]). The intellectual work that grew from his effort, including womanist reflection, accorded the "blackness" of the black human subject a primary place on the theological agendas.

Yet, standing against racism may not be identical with standing against race as ideology, as essential. Cone's earliest treatment of black humanity was steeped in Sartrean existentialism, and Cornel West perceptively has caught its "blues" notes played in an eschatological key (West 1999). For Cone, black humanity was a project; hence, blackness was a project, a becoming human in freedom and struggle against the racist absurd (Cone 1970). Like that of his South African colleagues Buthelezi, Maimela, and Boesak, Cone's theology is a Christian theology. Sin is both communal and personal and involves the idolization of whiteness as well as the repudiation or loss of blackness. Race in Cone's theological program functioned ambiguously – sometimes as an objective condition, sometimes as an essential attribute.

In *Sisters in the Wilderness* (1993), womanist theologian Delores Williams intended to insinuate a paradigm shift in Christian theology by bringing "black women's experience into the discourses of all Christian theology" (1993:xiv). By centering this experience, but never ignoring racism, Williams sought to interrogate what Elisabeth Schüssler Fiorenza has called "kyriarchy" or mimetic patriarchal rule. Williams discovered an "androcentric bias" in the biblical interpretation and constructive work of black male liberation theologians (D. S. Williams 1993:1). This bias betrayed the black community's way of reading the Bible "in such a way that black women's experience figured just as eminently as black men's in the community's memory" (1993:2). Williams recognized that although racism is to be condemned, that condemnation covers over and supersedes the sexism in the black community. Blackness is affirmed in its maleness; blackness is disaffirmed in its femaleness. Black women are erased in the articulation and praxis of black liberation theology. It is possible to read Williams as a racial essentialist, but womanist hermeneutics seeks to problematize not only (white) feminist hermeneutics or black (male) liberation hermeneutics, but any ahistorical, amorphous, essentialist apprehension of black women.

The sharpest criticisms of black and womanist theologies' ambiguous approach toward the meaning and significance of race have come from cultural critics bell hooks (hooks 1992) and Victor Anderson (1995). They have been relentless (hooks, in particular) in exposing the consequences and limitations of arguing racial identity as essentialist. Anderson and hooks push for a move beyond ontological blackness – that is, experiencing black life as bound by truncated, "unresolved binary dialectics of slavery and freedom, Negro and citizen, insider and outsider, black and white, struggle and survival," with no possibility of transcending or mediating these fruitfully (Anderson 1995:14).

Black theology in Britain grew up just as racial identities became increasingly fluid, just as critical race theory emerged. While critical race theory can never account for this theology's defense of personhood in the context of racism, its tools and resources have made a contribution to black British theology's struggle with race and racism. For instance, Robert Beckford's point of departure in black theology is the rich and thickly textured matrix of black expressive culture (Beckford 1998:137). Beckford problematizes the identities of those who inhabit and are responsible for that culture by querying both history and the neo-colonial situation of the immigrant as subject, and attending to differences of class, sexuality, gender, age, ethnicity, economics, and political consciousness (Beckford 1998:138, 140, Beckford 1999:53).

Critical theologies for human liberation insist upon the thick, yet ever ambiguous, particularity that acknowledgment of race provides, for such acknowledgment celebrates the "concrete universal" that the human subject is (Lonergan 1992:764). These theologies name racism for the persistent, yet never absolute, sin that it is. Yet, they humbly envisage subversive incarnations of grace within broken social orders and agitate not merely for fruitful intersubjective, inter-racial, and intra-racial encounters, but the self-transcendence of loving embrace.

References and Bibliography

Anderson, V. 1995. *Beyond Ontological Blackness: An Essay on African American Religious and Cultural Criticism.* New York: Continuum Books.

Appiah, K. A. and Gutman, A. 1996. *Color Conscious: The Political Morality of Race.* Princeton, NJ: Princeton University Press.

Aquino, M. A. 1993. *Our Cry for Life: Feminist Theology from Latin America,* trans. D. Livingstone. Maryknoll, NY: Orbis.

Back, L. and Solomos, J. ed. 2000. *Theories of Race and Racism: A Reader.* New York: Routledge.

Balibar, E. and Wallerstein, I. 1991. *Race, Nation, Class: Ambiguous Identities* [1988]. London: Verso.

Bauman, Z. 1995. *Life in Fragments: Essays in Postmodern Morality.* Oxford: Blackwell.

Beckford, R. 1998. *Jesus is Dread: Black Theology and Black Culture in Britain.* London: Darton, Longman and Todd.

Beckford, R. 1999. "Black Pentecostals and Black Politics," *Pentecostals after a Century: Global Perspectives on a Movement in Transition,* eds. A. Anderson and W. Hollenweger. Sheffield: Sheffield Academic Press.

Beckford, R. 2001. *God of the Rahtid: Redeeming Rage.* London: Darton, Longman and Todd.

Bell, D. 1992. *Faces at the Bottom of the Well: The Permanence of Racism.* New York: Basic Books.

Biko, S. 1998. *I Write What I Like* [1978], ed. A. Stubbs. New York: Harper & Row.

Boesak, A. 1981. *Farewell to Innocence.* Maryknoll, NY: Orbis.

Boesak, W. 1995. *God's Wrathful Children: Political Oppression and Christian Ethics.* Grand Rapids, MI: Eerdmans.

Boff, L. 1985. *Church: Charism and Power: Liberation Theology and the Institutional Church.* New York: Crossroad.

Boggs, J. 1970. *Racism and the Class Struggle.* New York: Monthly Review Press.

Bonino, J. M. 1975. *Doing Theology in a Revolutionary Situation.* Philadelphia, PA: Fortress Press.

Buthelezi, M. 1973. "Christianity in South Africa," *Pro Veritate* 12(2).

Canon K. G. 1988. *Black Womanist Ethics.* Atlanta, GA: Scholars Press.

Chisholm, C. A. 1997. *A Matter of Principle.* Spanish Town: Autos Books.

Cone, J. 1997. *Black Theology and Black Power* [1969]. Maryknoll, NY: Orbis.

Cone, J. 1970. *A Black Theology of Liberation.* Philadelphia, PA: Lippincott.

Cone, J. 1975. *God of the Oppressed.* New York: Seabury Press.

Crenshaw, C. et al. eds. 1995. *Critical Race Theory: The Key Writings that Formed the Movement.* New York: New Press.

Davis, K. 1990. *Emancipation Still Comin': Explorations in Caribbean Emancipatory Theology.* Maryknoll, NY: Orbis Books.

Deloria, V. 1993. *God is Red: A Native View of Religion* [1972]. Golden, CO: Fulcrum Books.

Du Bois, W. E. B. 2003. 1990. *The Souls of Black Folk* [1903]. New York: Modern Library.

Elizondo, V. 1988. *The Future is Mestizo: Life where Cultures Meet.* Bloomington, IN: Meyer-Stone Books.

Espín, O. 1997. *The Faith of the People: Theological Reflections on Popular Catholicism.* Maryknoll, NY: Orbis.

Eze, E. C. 2001. *Achieving our Humanity: The Idea of the Postracial Future.* New York: Routledge.

Fanon, F. 1967a. "Racism and Culture" [1964], *in Toward the African Revolution: Political Essays.* New York: Grove.

Fanon, F. 1967b. *Black Skins, White Masks* [1952]. New York: Grove.

Gilroy, P. 1991. *"There Ain't No Black in the Union Jack": The Cultural Politics of Race and Nation* [1987]. Chicago, IL: University of Chicago Press.

Gilroy, P. 2000. *Against Race: Imagining Political Culture Beyond the Color Line.* Cambridge, MA: Belknap Press.

Goizueta, R. S. 1995. *Caminemos con Jesús: Toward a Hispanic/Latino Theology of Accompaniment.* Maryknoll, NY: Orbis.

Goldberg, D. T. 1993. *Racist Culture: Philosophy and the Politics of Meaning.* New York: Routledge.

Gordon, L. R. 1997. *Her Majesty's Other Children: Sketches of Racism from a Neocolonial Age.* Lanham, MD: Rowan & Littlefield.

Gossett, T. F. 1997. *Race: The History of an Idea in America* [1963]. Oxford: Oxford University Press.

Gutiérrez, G. 1983. *The Power of the Poor in History.* Maryknoll, NY: Orbis.

Gutiérrez, G. 1988. *A Theology of Liberation: History, Politics, and Salvation* [1973]. Maryknoll, NY: Orbis.

Hall, S. 1996. "New Ethnicities" [1989], in *Stuart Hall: Critical Dialogues in Cultural Studies,* eds. D. Morley and K.-H. Chen. London and New York: Routledge, pp. 441–9.

Harris, A. 2001. "Foreword," *Critical Race Theory: An Introduction,* ed. R. Delgado and J. Stefancic. New York: New York University Press.

Henry, P. 2000. *Caliban's Reason: Introducing Afro-Caribbean Philosophy.* New York: Routledge.

Herrnstein, R. J. and Murray, C. 1994. *The Bell Curve: Intelligence and Class Structure in American Life.* New York: Fress Press.

hooks, b. 1992. *Black Looks: Race and Representation.* Boston, MA: South End Press.

hooks, b. 1994. *Outlaw Culture: Resisting Representation.* New York: Routledge.

hooks, b. 1995. *Killing Rage: Ending Racism.* New York: Henry Holt.

Isasi-Díaz, A. M. 1993. *"En la lucha" (In the Struggle): A Hispanic Women's Liberation Theology.* Minneapolis, MN: Fortress Press.

Kunnie, J. 2000. *Is Apartheid Really Dead? Pan-Africanist Working-Class Cultural Critical Perspectives.* Oxford: Westview Press.

Leatt, J. et al. eds. 1986. *Contending Ideologies in South Africa.* Grand Rapids, MI: W. B. Eerdmans.

Lonergan, B. J. F. 1992. *Insight: A Study of Human Understanding,* eds. F. E. Crowe and R. M. Doran. Toronto: University of Toronto Press.

MacMaster, N. 2001. *Racism in Europe, 1870–2000.* Basingstoke and New York: Palgrave.

Maimela, S. 1981. "Man in 'White' Theology," *Journal of Theology for South Africa* 36(3).

Memi, A. 1968. *Dominated Man.* Boston, MA: Beacon Press.

Memi, A. 1967. *Colonizer and the Colonized* [1957]. Boston, MA: Beacon Press.

Miles, R. 1989. *Racism.* London and New York: Routledge.

Mills, C. 1999. *The Racial Contract* [1997]. Ithaca, NY: Cornell University Press.

Omi, M. and Winant, H. 1993. "On the Theoretical Status of the Concept of Race," in *Race, Identity, and Representation in Education,* eds. C. McCarthy and W. Crichlow. New York and London: Routledge.

Omi, M. and Winant, H. 1994. *Racial Formation in the United States, from the 1960s to the 1990s* [1986], 2nd edn. New York and London: Routledge.

Roberts, J. D. 1971. *Liberation and Reconciliation: A Black Theology.* Philadelphia, PA: Westminster Press.

Roberts, J. D. 1974. *A Black Political Theology.* Philadelphia, PA: Westminster, Press.

Rodríguez, R. 2002. *Brown: The Last Discovery of America.* New York: Viking.

Sanchez, S. 1995. "Poem for July 4, 1994," in *Wounded in the House of a Friend.* Boston, MA: Beacon Press.

San Juan, E. 1992. *Racial Formations / Critical Transformations: Articulations of Power in Ethnic and Racial Studies in the United States.* Atlantic Highlands, NJ: Humanities Press.

Sobrino, J. 1994. *The Principle of Mercy: Taking the Crucified People from the Cross.* Maryknoll, NY: Orbis.

Spivak, G. 2000. "Race before Racism: The Disappearance of the American," in *Edward Said and the Work of the Critic: Speaking Truth to Power,* ed. P. Bové. Durham, NC: Duke University Press, pp. 51–65.

Tinker, G. E. 1993. *Missionary Conquest: The Gospel and Native American Cultural Genocide.* Minneapolis, MN: Fortress Press.

West, C. 1982. *Prophecy Deliverance! An Afro-American Revolutionary Christianity.* Philadelphia, PA: Westminster Press.

West, C. 1988. *Prophetic Fragments.* Trenton, NJ: Africa World Press, and Grand Rapids, MI: Eerdmans.

West, C. 1993. *Race Matters.* Boston, MA: Beacon Press.

West, C. 1999. "Black Theology and Human Identity," in *Black Faith and Public Talk: Essays in Honor of James H. Cone's "Black Theology and Black Power,"* ed. D. Hopkins. Maryknoll, NY: Orbis, pp. 11–19.

Williams, D. S. 1993. *Sisters in the Wilderness: The Challenge of Womanist God-Talk.* Maryknoll, NY: Orbis.

Williams, L. 1994. *Caribbean Theology.* New York: Peter Lang.

Williams, L. 1999. Editorial, *Caribbean Journal of Religious Studies* 20.

Williams, P. J. 1991. *The Alchemy of Race and Rights.* Cambridge, MA: Harvard University Press.

Winant, H. 1994. *Racial Conditions: Politics, Theory, Comparisons.* Minneapolis, MN: University of Minnesota.

Wing, A. K. ed. 1997. *Critical Race Feminism: A Reader.* New York: New York University Press.

Wood, F. G. 1990. *The Arrogance of Faith: Christianity and Race in America from the Colonial Era to the Twentieth Century.* Boston, MA: Northeastern University Press.

Wu, F. H. 2002. *Yellow: Race in America Beyond Black and White.* New York: Basic Books.

Young, I. M. 1990. *Justice and the Politics of Difference.* Princeton, NJ: Princeton University Press.

CHAPTER 32
Science

Robert John Russell and
Kirk Wegter-McNelly

Introduction

In 1996 Elizabeth A. Johnson, then President of the Catholic Theological Society of America, called for a re-engagement with the sciences which would entail a "return to cosmology, in order to restore fullness of vision and get theology back on the track from which it fell off a few hundred years ago" (1996b:5). This chapter examines such a "re-engagement" by surveying the rapidly growing interdisciplinary field[1] of "theology and science." The immediate historical roots of this field lie in the 1960s, when major movements in the secular disciplines of philosophy of science, philosophy of religion, new theories and discoveries in the natural sciences, as well as complex shifts in the Christian theological landscape, made possible constructive interaction between otherwise separate and even hostile intellectual communities.

This survey is divided into sections on methodology, current issues, and new voices. As is customary in "theology and science," its primary focus is on theoretical, philosophical, and foundational issues and secondarily on ethical or spiritual concerns.[2] It is also focused primarily on the interaction between the sciences and the diversity of Christian theologies,[3] where most of the material in the field to date has been developed (but see section III).[4]

I   Methodology in Theology and Science

We begin with the question of methodology: how should we relate theology and science? The past four decades have seen a variety of important methodological proposals which, although differing significantly on key questions, still form a somewhat continuous developmental path leading from early insights to a wide variety of current research proposals.[5] Before exploring this path – critical realism – a brief word about classification is appropriate.

Typologies

A number of typologies have been suggested to classify the relations between science and religion. They bring to light underlying assumptions which strongly shape both public and scholarly conversations.

Ian Barbour's typology (1988, 1990) remains the most widely used in the field. Barbour lists four types of relations, each with subtypes: conflict (scientific materialism, biblical literalism); independence (contrasting methods, differing languages); dialog (boundary questions, methodological parallels); and integration (natural theology, theology of nature, systematic synthesis). Arthur Peacocke published a typology (1981:xiii–xv) listing differences and similarities in the realms, approaches, languages, and attitudes of theology and science. Nancey Murphy applied H. Richard Niebuhr's classic five-fold typology to science and religion, claiming that theology could even be a transformer of science (1985:16–23).

In the 1990s, a variety of new typologies appeared, many responding directly to and augmenting Barbour's work. John Haught (1995, chapter 1) includes conflict, contrast, contact, and confirmation, the last of which highlights the philosophical and theological assumptions underlying science. Willem B. Drees (1996:39–53) offers nine ways in which scientific knowledge, philosophy of science, and attitudes toward nature can influence religious cognitive claims, experiences, and traditions. Philip Hefner (unpublished) includes the infusion of religious wisdom into scientific concepts and the evangelical reaffirmation of traditional religious rationality. Anne Clifford (1991) speaks of continuity, separation, and interaction. Ted Peters (1998b:13–22) distinguishes between atheistic scientific materialists (who reject God) and scientific imperialists (for whom science alone produces genuine knowledge of God). Peters also includes ethical overlap, New Age spirituality, and "hypothetical consonance." Mark Richardson (1994) illuminates the broad difference in literary genre between intellectual/rational texts, romantic/affective and esthetic/mystical texts, and tradition-centered texts.[6]

Critical realism

In his ground-breaking publication *Issues in Science and Religion* (1966), Barbour developed what he called "critical realism"[7] through a series of well-crafted arguments regarding issues in epistemology (what kind of knowledge is involved?), language (how is it expressed?), and methodology (how is it obtained and justified?). Together these arguments provided the initial "bridge"[8] between science and religion. Barbour understood critical realism as an alternative to three predominant philosophical views: (1) classical or "naïve" realism: scientific theories provide a "photographic" representation of the world; (2) instrumentalism: scientific theories are mere calculative devices; and (3) idealism: scientific theories depict reality as primarily mental. Instead, according to critical realism, scientific theories yield partial, revisable, and abstract knowledge of the world. Scientific theories are expressed through "metaphor" – open-ended analogies whose meaning cannot be reduced to, or replaced by, a set of literal statements – and through their systematic development into models.

For methodology, Barbour turned to such philosophers of science as Carl Hempel, Michael Polanyi, N. R. Hanson, Thomas Kuhn, and Imre Lakatos. He began with Hempel's "hypothetico-deductive" understanding of the construction and testing of theories.[9] From Hanson, Kuhn, Lakatos, and others, he drew insights regarding the historicist and contextualist elements of the scientific enterprise. These include the "theory-ladenness of data," the intersubjective rather than strictly objective nature of scientific rationality, the role of paradigms and their revolutions in the history of science, the presence of metaphysical assumptions about nature in scientific paradigms, and the role of esthetics and values in theory choice. Barbour offered four criteria for theory choice: agreement with data, coherence, scope, and fertility. He also offered a critical-realist theory of truth, emphasizing correspondence, coherence, and usefulness. For Barbour, then, intelligibility and explanatory power, and not just predictive success, encourage our confidence in the referential capacity of scientific theories.

Barbour's crucial "bridging" insight concerns the *similarity* between these arguments in the philosophy of science, and parallel arguments in the philosophy of religion. Both science and religion make cognitive claims about the world using a hypothetico-deductive method within a contextualist and historicist framework.[10] Both communities organize observation and experience through models that are analogical, extensible, coherent, symbolic, and expressed through metaphors. He also notes, however, important *differences* between them. The type of "data" found in religion differs from that found in science. Religion serves non-cognitive functions missing in science, such as eliciting attitudes, personal involvement, and transformation. It also contains elements not found in science, including story, ritual, and historical revelation. Lower-level laws are not found in religion as they are in science, and the emergence of consensus in religion seems an unrealizable goal. It is the acknowledgment of both similarities and differences and the dynamic tension between them that makes Barbour's approach so fruitful.

Even while Barbour was developing his position, scientific realism was being challenged in a number of ways.[11] Though Kuhn had focused primarily on factors *internal* to the scientific community, sociologists in the 1970s explored the social construction of science. These *externalist* accounts emphasized social, political, and economic influences on science.[12] Barbour's recent assessment is that externalist accounts provide a valuable corrective to the internalist view, particularly regarding the context of discovery. However, the appeal to interests underestimates the degree to which empirical methods reduce distortions.

Barbour's arguments have been developed by a variety of scholars. While acknowledging the diversity of scientific-realist views, Peacocke (1993b) argues for a "common core" of claims: scientific change is progressive and the aim of science is to depict reality. He makes a similar case for critical realism in theology. According to John Polkinghorne (1994), critical realism is the best explanation of the success of science and the view most congenial to scientists themselves. Wentzel van Huyssteen, in earlier writings, viewed theology from a realist perspective, describing theological language about God as "reality depiction" (1989:162). Thomas F. Torrance (1969) defended the scientific character of theology: theology, like science, must adopt a method which is determined by its object – in this case, God as known through revelation. Sallie McFague (1982) described similar and different roles played by models in theology and in science: for example, models provide order in theology but stimulate new discoveries in science. In her study of metaphor in religious and scientific language, Janet Soskice (1985, 1988) emphasized the distinction between metaphor and model, and vigorously defended theological realism, while stressing the social and contextual nature of scientific realism.

Ernan McMullin (1981) introduced the theme of "consonance" between theology and science: a coherent but ever shifting world-view to which all forms of human knowing can make tentative and revisable contributions. Russell (1989) later combined McMullin's idea with McFague's epistemic claim about the "is and is not" structure of metaphor to discuss both consonance and dissonance between scientific and theological theories. Ted Peters (see Peters 1988:274–6; Pannenberg 1993:5) advocated a "hypothetical" view of consonance: theologians should treat their assertions as subject to disconfirmation as well as to confirmation.

Further developments

According to Wolfhart Pannenberg (1976), the truth of Christianity is intimately tied to the claim that theology is a science (*Wissenschaft*). Pannenberg brought to theology Popper's understanding of theories as revisable hypotheses, though he ultimately rejected Popperian falsificationism, arguing instead that theories in the natural and human sciences are to be judged by the criteria of coherence, parsimony, and accuracy. The most adequate theory, for Pannenberg, is the one that can incorporate its competitor.[13]

Nancey Murphy (1990b, chapters 2–3) criticized Pannenberg's methodology: since the Humean challenge to theological rationality is incommensurable with Pannenberg's view, it cannot be incorporated into Pannenberg's own system as his methodology requires. Instead she recommended using Imre Lakatos's methodology of scientific research programs with their central core and surrounding belt of auxiliary hypotheses. According to Lakatos, we should judge the relative progress or degeneration of research programs by their ability to predict and corroborate novel facts (Murphy 1990b:58–61). Murphy provides, through a crucial modification of Lakatos's conception of a "novel fact," a method for deciding which theological programs are empirically progressive (1990b:68).[14] Her approach[15] has been implemented in her own discussion of cosmological fine-tuning (1993), in theological anthropology by Philip Hefner (1993), in Karl Peters's pragmatic evaluation of religion (1997), and in Russell's theological interpretation of cosmology (1993).[16]

Philip Clayton (1989) also urges theologians to use Lakatosian methodology. Clayton views "explanation" as the key concept embracing the natural sciences, the social sciences, and theology. In the natural sciences, where one interprets physical data, the truth of an explanation is pivotal. In the social sciences, however, where one interprets the actions of actor-subjects who are themselves engaged in interpreting the world (the "double hermeneutic"), explanation means "understanding" (*Verstehen*).

Theological explanations, then, are subject to validation not by verificationist or foundationalist standards, but by intersubjective testability and universalizability as performed by the disciplinary community.

Anti-reductionism

1   Three types of reductionism   Francisco Ayala (1974) has distinguished three types of reductionism: (1) methodological reductionism is a research strategy for studying wholes in terms of their parts and a process for applying successful theories in one area to others; (2) epistemological reductionism is the claim that processes, properties, laws, or theories at higher levels of complexity can be derived entirely from those at lower levels; (3) ontological reductionism is the view that higher-level entities are nothing but complex organizations of simpler entities. In a recent essay, Nancey Murphy (1998) has added two additional types: (4) causal reductionism asserts that all causes are "bottom-up," i.e. the processes of the parts entirely determine those of the whole; (5) reductive materialism insists that "[only] the entities at the lowest level are *really* real." Murphy rejects reductive materialism by arguing that higher-level entities are "as real as" the entities that compose them, but accepts ontological reductionism's rejection of vitalism and other ontological dualisms.

2   A non-reducible hierarchy of the sciences   Most scholars in theology and science, while accepting methodological reductionism, view other forms of reductionism as undercutting the credibility of higher-level disciplines. To counter this, they typically argue that the academic disciplines form a non-reducible hierarchy, starting from physics at the bottom and moving upwards through chemistry, biology, physiology, and the neurosciences, to the behavioral, psychological, and social sciences.[17] Lower levels place *constraints* on upper levels while allowing for genuine *emergence* of upper-level laws, processes, and properties. Peacocke (1979, Appendix C; 1993b, chapter 12, esp. fig. 3, p. 216) developed this hierarchy in two dimensions: vertically it contains levels of increasing complexity (the physical world, living organisms, their behavior, and human culture) while horizontally it orders systems by part-to-whole hierarchies (e.g., in biology: macro-molecules, organelles, cells, organs, individual organisms, populations, ecosystems).

Peacocke's analysis reflects the broad consensus of the scientific community. A key issue, though, is the place and role of theology in the hierarchy of disciplines. Peacocke places it at the top, since theology seeks to integrate the totality of knowledge and must be maximally constrained by the rest of the hierarchy. Murphy and Ellis (1996, chapter 4) have argued that this gives theology an essential role in the system: it completes all the lower levels by offering answers to fundamental questions raised by them.[18]

Ontological implications

We now face the most challenging question: What is an appropriate ontology for these epistemic schemes? Most writers in theology and science avoid two extreme positions:

monism (either reductive materialism or absolute idealism) and dualism (either vitalism or Cartesianism).[19] The three most prominent options are:

1   Emergentist monism (non-reductive physicalism): there are genuinely new proper-
    ties and processes at higher levels of organization, but the world is still composed
    strictly of "matter" as described by physics.
2   Ontological emergence: the new properties and processes that emerge at higher
    levels of organization indicate that the ontology of the world, though monistic,
    cannot be reduced to physical descriptions alone. The ontological unity of com-
    plex phenomena is thus intrinsically differentiated (as sometimes suggested by the
    term "dipolarity").
3   Organicism (panexperientialism/process metaphysics): every real event or "actual
    occasion" includes the capacity for experience ("prehension"), and thus a mental
    "pole."[20] Panexperientialists frequently reject "emergence," arguing that the
    mental cannot emerge from the physical, and thereby sharpen the difference
    between this approach and the preceding two (Birch 1995, Griffin 1988).

One can find scholars in theology and science who endorse different combinations of these approaches to epistemology and ontology. Peacocke, Polkinghorne, and Barbour, for example, accept the hierarchy of the disciplines though they differ over its ontolog-ical implications (emergentist monism, dipolar monism, and panexperientialism, respectively). Murphy and Russell work with non-foundationalist epistemologies, with Murphy preferring non-reductive physicalism and Russell favoring ontological emer-gence. On the other hand, theists such as Richard Swinburne and Sir John Eccles continue to support epistemic and ontological dualism. These differences are minor, though, when compared with the views of atheists such as Richard Dawkins and Peter Atkins who view science and religion in conflict and who defend epistemic reduction-ism and reductive materialism.

The role of philosophy in the dialogue

Philosophy typically functions in one of two ways in the conversations between theology and science. On the one hand, it can provide an overarching metaphysical framework for all fields of knowledge, as it does in Stoeger's use of neo-Thomism or Barbour's use of process philosophy. The difficulty comes when the system no longer suits changes in scientific theories, for a metaphysical system is not usually open to a "quick fix."

On the other hand, philosophy can serve the more limited goal of providing definitions or clarifications of specific terms and concepts shared by differing discip-lines. Examples include Peacocke's use of "law and chance" in biological evolution and the doctrine of creation, and Polkinghorne's use of "openness" in chaos theory and divine action. Without a single overall and unifying system, however, broad ques-tions underlying the entire relationship between theology and science may remain unaddressed.

Summary

Over the past four decades, the predominant school of thought among scholars in theology and science has been "critical realism." It has provided the crucial "bridge" between theology and science, making possible real dialog and growing integration between theology and science. It continues to be presupposed by most working scientists and many theologians, and is operative in much of the public discourse about science and religion.

During these four decades, however, elements of this approach have come under criticism. Some scholars have stressed the difficulties facing a realist interpretation of specific scientific theories, such as quantum mechanics (Russell 1988b), as well as key theological concepts such as "God" (Drees 1996:130–49). Others have pointed to the diversity of realist positions taken by philosophers, the continuing challenge to realism by sociologists of knowledge, and the variety of competing models of rationality and their relative appropriateness for "science and religion" (Stenmark 1995). Still others have moved to a non-foundationalist epistemology (Clayton 1989, Murphy 1996a). Finally, some scholars place themselves at increasing distances from critical realism by drawing on feminist critiques of both science and theology and on Continental as well as Anglo-American postmodernism (see section III).

On balance, though, critical realism remains enduringly important to theology and science, both for its crucial role in the historical developments of the past decades and as a point of departure for current research. Whatever directions are taken in the future, critical realism constitutes the key contribution by the "first generation" to the ongoing discussion.

II   Current Issues in Theology and Science

God and nature

The diversity of views within contemporary Christian theology regarding the relationship between God and nature is reflected in the past four decades of discussions about "theology and science," including such perspectives as evangelical, dipolar theist, kenotic, liberationist, neo-Thomist, process panentheist, and trinitarian. Some (Ellis 1998) challenge atheists who co-opt science to attack religion (Dawkins 1987, Weinberg 1992) or who seek a new "science-based" religion (Sagan 1980). Others revise the traditional "arguments for God" in light of contemporary science (Hartshorne 1991; Craig and Smith 1993). Some introduce specific scientific issues into constructive theology via metaphors (McFague 1993 – the world as God's body) or via theories (Nancey Murphy 1995, Thomas Tracy 1995 – quantum mechanics, Polkinghorne 1996a, Denis Edwards 1995a – chaos theory, Hefner 1993, Peacocke 1986 – evolution, Rosemary Radford Ruether 1992 – ecology). Others focus on important themes arising in both theology and science, such as temporality and relationality (Jürgen Moltmann 1985, Johnson 1993).

The relationship between time and eternity and the concept of divine action are two important issues that illustrate the subtle way in which twentieth-century science both challenges and reshapes the God–nature problematic.

1   Time and Eternity   Within the vast literature on this subject, we will touch on a widely held assumption among theologians, namely, the flowing nature of time and its significance for concepts of eternity. For example, in twentieth-century trinitarian theology eternity is no longer regarded as either timelessness or unending time. Instead, God as eternal is the supra-temporal source of the world's temporality (Barth 1960, esp. pp. 520–30) and its eschatological future (Pannenberg 1991). Process theologians (Hartshorne 1948, Suchocki 1982) argue that the world is experienced temporally by God through God's "consequent nature." British natural theologians (e.g. Polkinghorne 1994) stress that God is eternally transcendent to and temporally immanent within the world. The future does not yet exist even for God (Peacocke 1993a). All of these views, while differing in important ways theologically, presuppose the notion of time's flow as based on both ordinary experience and classical physics. However, Einstein's theory of special relativity ("SR" c.1905) directly challenges this view by undercutting the notion of a universal present and the assumption of a uniform rate of time's passage.[21] Because of these and other implications of SR, some have argued that the flow of time is an illusion, proposing instead a "block universe" interpretation of SR in which all events are equally present. Because of this, Hartshorne wrote that SR poses "the most puzzling [challenge] of all" to the classical theistic notion of a universal flowing present (1967:92–3).

Actually, the theological implications of SR depend crucially on its philosophical interpretation and not directly on SR itself. In a recent debate, Polkinghorne defended a subtle "flowing time" interpretation of SR, arguing that the downfall of the present is an epistemic rather than an ontological issue, and that SR does not commit us to a deterministic view of the future or a timeless view of nature. Isham defended a "block universe" view, asking whether its opponents seek merely to *reinterpret* the existing theories of physics or whether they make the "stronger claim that their metaphysical views can be sustained only by *changing* the [scientific] theories" (Isham and Polkinghorne 1993).[22] Barbour stresses that SR points to a universe both "dynamic and interconnected" and yet suggestive, through its lightcone structure, of "a new form of separateness and isolation" (1990:112). John Lucas argues for a divine "frame of reference" (1989:216–21) by which God experiences the real temporal flow of the universe even if such a view challenges SR. Russell (2000) suggests we integrate an "event/worldline" interpretation of SR into a trinitarian understanding of eternity, and taking up Isham's challenge, he suggested that this might have empirical implications for science.

2   Divine action   The relation between divine and natural causality also highlights the challenge twentieth-century science poses for the God–nature problematic. "Divine action"[23] is an issue in philosophical theology that underlies the entire scope of systematic theology from creation to redemption and surfaces explicitly in discussions of creation, special providence and miracles.

According to creation theology, God gives the world its rational, intelligible structure as described by the laws of nature through the transcendent and eternal act of bringing the world as a whole into existence from nothing (*ex nihilo*). As immanent creator, God also continues to create (*creatio continua*) and providentially direct processes and events in general towards their consummation in the eschaton. In acts of "special" providence, God works through particular events and processes with special intentions. Miracles are events which cohere with an overall theological understanding of God's intentions but which seem to fall outside what nature "on its own" might be sufficient to cause (Polkinghorne 1989, chapters 3–4).

Following the rise of modern science and the Enlightenment, theological conservatives and liberals split over the meaning of "special providence." Newtonian physics led to a mechanistic philosophy of nature such that in order to act in particular events God would have to intervene in the causal order by either breaking or suspending the laws of nature. Conservatives maintained that God acts objectively, but accepted the cost of an interventionist account. Liberals rejected interventionism but reduced the notion of special divine action to our subjective response to ordinary natural events.[24] Neither twentieth-century Protestant neo-orthodoxy nor biblical theology was able to overcome this deep divide convincingly.[25]

Remarkably, even as science played a key role in creating this division, it may now play a pivotal role in overcoming it. Wide-ranging developments from quantum physics to evolutionary biology may move us beyond Newtonian mechanism and make possible new approaches to divine action in nature. Such approaches seek to recombine crucial elements of liberal and conservative positions, yielding a non-interventionist, objective view of special divine acts. These approaches divide into three strategies – top–down, whole–part constraint, and bottom–up – with most scholars insisting that a combination of these approaches will eventually be needed for an adequate account of non-interventionist, objective, special divine action in the context of life and mental agency. However, these approaches generally presuppose an incompatibilist view of divine action in nature.[26]

In "top–down" approaches, processes at higher levels of complexity affect those at lower levels. Peacocke (1993b, 1995) explores models involving top–down causality in light of Big Bang cosmology with God acting on the "world-as-a-whole." Nancey Murphy (1999), Clayton (1999), Peacocke (1999), and Meyering (1999) discuss top-down divine action in light of the neurosciences. The challenge for this approach is to show how God's action can bring about actual changes in the processes at lower levels if they are still governed by classical, deterministic physics.

The "whole–part constraint" approach stays within one level of complexity and focuses on the effects a system as a whole has on its parts. Drawing on non-equilibrium thermodynamics,[27] Peacocke (1979, 1993b) views God as bringing about special events by interacting with thermodynamic systems open to their environment. Polkinghorne (1994, 1995) interprets chaos theory[28] as pointing to nature's openness and thus to the possibility of God acting in nature without intervening. Still, thermodynamics and chaos theory are part of classical physics and are thus fully deterministic, so that God's action on them as a whole, or on their boundaries, would seem to be interventionist. (It is possible, as Polkinghorne suggests (1996a), that chaotic systems may be the downward limit of 'holistic chaotic systems' suggestive of ontological indeterminism at the classical level. Thus Polkinghorne's program is actually a search for new physics suggested by his theological convictions.[29]

In the "bottom–up" approach, God acts at a lower level of complexity to influence the processes and properties at a higher level. A number of scholars, including Karl Heim (1953) and William Pollard (1958), Mary Hesse (1975), Donald MacKay (1978), Nancey Murphy (1995), Thomas Tracy (1995), George Ellis (1995), Mark Worthing (1996, esp. pp. 130–46), Christopher Mooney (1996, esp. chapter 3), Philip Clayton (1997a, esp. chapters 7–8), and Robert Russell (1998a, 2001), have interpreted quantum mechanics[30] as supporting an indeterministic ontology at the subatomic level.[31] This would allow God to act at this level by providing the necessary conditions lacking in nature. The challenge here is that quantum physics can also be interpreted in terms of ontological determinism (e.g., David Bohm) and that all such interpretations raise tremendously complex, and as yet unresolved, philosophical and scientific problems.[32]

Alternative models of divine agency draw on the analogy of embodiment – God:world::mind:body. McFague (1993) combines metaphors of agency and organism in light of evolution and develops procreational–emanationist models of the world as God's body. In Grace Jentzen's view (1984), God is immediately aware of all events in nature (God's body) and acts both universally throughout nature and particularly in unique events.

Other approaches to divine agency rely on fully-developed metaphysical systems. Process theologians (Barbour 1990, Birch 1998, Cobb and Griffin 1976, Haught 1998b) contend that every actual occasion involves the divine subjective lure, the prehension of past occasions, and spontaneous, intrinsic novelty. Process theology thus offers a non-interventionist view of God participating intrinsically in every event in nature without entirely determining the outcome. Neo-Thomists such as Stoeger (1995), Johnson (1996a), and Rahner (1978) view God as the primary cause of the world and understand science as limited to studying secondary causes. Drawing on evolution (Moltmann 1985, Johnson 1990) and physics and cosmology (Pannenberg 1993, Ted Peters 1989), trinitarians use the identity of the Immanent and Economic Trinity (Rahner's Rule) to discuss God's work in nature and history. The challenge to all these approaches is to show how God brings about novelty where science describes nature deterministically. Moreover, all proponents of divine action must respond to SR's challenge to the global present and to the theological challenge of theodicy (why doesn't God act to thwart evil).

Creation and cosmology

The doctrine of creation has been explored fruitfully in light of contemporary physical cosmology in various ways over the past four decades. In this section we focus on *creatio ex nihilo* (creation out of nothing), leaving *creatio continua* (continuous creation) to the discussion of evolution.

1   *The Big Bang*   Creatio ex nihilo has been placed in relation to two particular features of the standard Big Bang cosmology:[33] "$t = 0$," which represents the beginning of time;

and the anthropic principle (AP), which points to the striking correspondence between the fundamental physical constants and laws of nature and the necessary conditions for the possibility of the evolution of life.

Is $t = 0$ relevant to the doctrine of creation *ex nihilo?* Some say "Yes": the scientific discovery of an absolute beginning of all things (including time) is empirical confirmation, or even proof, of divine creation. Pope Pius XII supported this in 1951,[34] as did astronomer Robert Jastrow (1978). Craig (Craig and Smith 1993) has developed a sophisticated argument for God based on $t = 0$.[35] Others say "No": Peacocke (1979:78–9) and William Carroll (1998) hold that *creatio ex nihilo* is a strictly philosophical issue regarding the contingent existence of the universe, for which empirical evidence of any sort is irrelevant.

Still other scholars, including McMullin (1981:39), Howard van Till (1990), Worthing (1996:85–90), and Russell (1989, 1993, 1996), argue for the indirect relevance of $t = 0$ to *creatio ex nihilo*. According to Russell, *creatio ex nihilo* implies that the universe is contingent, and one form of temporal contingency is "$t = 0$." Thus "$t = 0$" can play a helpful, if indirect role, for it gives concrete empirical content to the more general notion of contingency at work in these theologies. It is important to remember, however, that the infinities in size and future of some Big Bang models weigh against the contingency of the universe and challenge our view of eschatology (see below).

The "anthropic principle" (AP)[36] focuses our attention on the stunning fact that the values of the fundamental constants of nature (e.g., the speed of light, Planck's constant) and the form of the fundamental physical laws are precisely what is needed for the possibility of the evolution of life as we know it. If these values had differed from their actual values by as little as one part per million, life could not have evolved in the universe (Leslie 1988b, 1989).

To some, this remarkable fact suggests that the universe is "fine-tuned" for life and thus designed by God. Opponents typically combine Humean criticisms of design with arguments for the existence of many (sub-)universes, each with different values of the natural constants, perhaps even different physical laws.[37] Though not a supporter of the design argument, William Stoeger (1993) has noted that the "many-worlds" argument involves a leap from the mathematical formalism of multiple universes to their actual existence. According to John Leslie, "while the multiple worlds hypothesis [is] impressively strong, the God hypothesis is a viable alternative to it" (1988a:297). McMullin (1981:40–52, 1990), however, asks whether the AP is really an "explanation" even within the context of Christian presuppositions. Worthing (1996, chapter 2, esp. p. 47) and Barbour (1990:25–6) both caution that evidence of cosmic design need not lead us to the God of theism, since either a divine demiurge or an emerging divinity would fit the empirical evidence as well.

George Ellis (1993b, 1994) has developed a "Christian Anthropic Principle," combining design perspectives with a theology drawn from William Temple. For Ellis, fine-tuning is a consequence of what we mean by God as the creator of life. Nancey Murphy (1993) reframed Ellis's argument in Lakatosian terms, arguing that cosmological fine-tuning can serve as a "novel fact" in an argument for the existence of God.

Russell (1988a) stresses that contingency and necessity arise dialectically on both sides of the "design vs. many-worlds" debate; the AP is at best, then, an ambiguous argument for God. It can, however, illuminate constructive theology's inner meaning regarding God as creator and suggest otherwise unrecognized connections between theological topics such as creation and theological anthropology.[38]

2 *Inflationary Big Bang and quantum cosmologies*   Since the 1970s, a variety of technical problems in the standard Big Bang model have led scientists to pursue inflationary Big Bang models and, beyond that, quantum cosmology.[39] Given their speculative status, the theological focus has for the most part remained on Big Bang cosmology. Some scholars, though, have asked what effects quantum cosmology might have on their theology of creation.

Lucas (1993) has defended the temporality of God against the difficulties raised by quantum cosmology. Ted Peters (1993a:163–6, 1993b) recognizes the "anti-theological" implications of Hawking's quantum cosmology, but draws on Isham's argument that, even without an initial singularity, God is present at and active in all events in the universe. Russell (1993) has argued that the Hawking/Hartle model reminds us that the concept of finitude need not entail a boundary, leading to new ways to describe the universe as God's creation. However, Drees (1993) suggests that the challenge from special relativity to the notion of God's involvement in "flowing time" is more severe than anything stemming from the lack of $t = 0$ in quantum cosmology.

The "cosmic Darwinism" depicted by the endless infinity of quantum universes threatens to strip the AP–design argument of its force. Still, defenders of the AP stress the speculative status and the technical and philosophical problems with inflation and quantum cosmology while appealing to Occam's Razor in support of the Big Bang, and in turn God, as the simplest explanation of fine-tuning.

Perhaps the most important result to emerge from shifts in cosmology over the past decades is that, regardless of the status of $t = 0$ in these changing cosmologies, the emergence of the hot Big Bang as a "permanent" description of *our* universe from the Planck time ($t = 10^{-43}$ s), some 12 billion to 15 billion years ago, to the present. Hence, the time is ripe for a renewed theological focus on the universe in which we have evolved, its 15-billion-year history, the evolution of life on planet Earth, and perhaps on countless other planetary systems as well, and a setting aside of what previously were interesting issues surrounding $t = 0$.

Creation and evolution

Christian theologians have developed a diversity of positive responses[40] to Darwin's theory of evolution over the past 140 years, which by and large assume that what science describes in terms of evolutionary biology[41] is what theology sees as God's action in the world. Simply put, evolution is God's way of creating life, a view frequently called "theistic evolution." Scholars taking this approach typically employ concepts such as continuous creation (*creatio continua*) and panentheism.

Since the 1970s, Arthur Peacocke (1979, 1984, 1993a, 1993b, 1994, 1998b)[42] has argued that chance events, from genetic variation to environmental alterations, do not mitigate against God's creative purposes or point to a fundamental irrationality in the world, as Jacques Monod argued. Instead, God is the ground and source of both chance and law, which together serve as God's means of continuously creating physical, chemical, and biological complexity in a world thus characterized by continuity and emergence, temporality and open-endedness. Peacocke likens God to an improviser of unsurpassed ingenuity who gives birth to the world "within herself."

From the process perspective of Barbour (1990:174–6, 260–2) and Haught (1995:68–9, 1998a), God is an immanent source of order and novelty, acting within each physical and biological system as a top–down cause. God is continuously, preeminently, but not all-powerfully, active in evolution, influencing events through persuasive love but not controlling them unilaterally. According to Birch and Cobb, God is immanent in the world as the "lifegiving principle" and "the supreme and perfect exemplification of the ecological model of life." Moreover, life is purposeful, not sheer blind "ongoingness" but "the cosmic aim for value" (Birch and Cobb 1981:195–7; see also Birch 1990, 1998).

Evolution and ecology provide the primary context for McFague's panentheistic and feminist theology (1987, esp. pp. 69–78, 1993). Her metaphors of the world as God's body and of God as mother, lover, and friend emphasize mutuality, interdependence, caring, and responsiveness within a procreational–emanationist perspective (1982, 1987, 1988). Clifford (1998) proposes we replace Darwin's metaphor of "natural selection" with that of nature as a mother giving birth. This metaphor brings into dynamic tension the reproductive, evolutionary character of nature and the biblical doctrine of God as creator.

Trinitarian theologians have also found rich resources in biological evolution and ecology. According to Ted Peters (1993a), the inter-relationality and interconnection of all life on the earth are suggestive of recent models of God as "divine-persons-in-relation" much more than of the substantialist models of classical theism. Moltmann places evolution within a trinitarian account of continuous creation and argues that "the 'crown of creation' is God's sabbath still to come" (1985:190–214, esp. pp. 196–7, 206, 212). Edwards believes that a relational account of God as Trinity provides the foundation for an evolutionary theology in which "creation is the free overflow of (the) divine fecundity" (1995b:116). Russell (1998a) has also argued that, since genetic mutations are a key to biological evolution, and since they involve quantum processes, from a theological perspective God can be thought of in non-interventionist terms as acting within evolution.[43]

Evolutionary biology presents yet another domain for the debate between reductionism and holism. As Barbour (1990:165–6) and others stress, population genetics and ecology deal with organisms as a whole, even though methodological reductionism has been fruitful in molecular biology. For Ernst Mayr (1985), evolutionary biology is best treated as historical narrative. As Ayala (1985) points out, there are biological functions and concepts, including "fitness," "adaptation," and "organ," which cannot be defined in purely chemical and physical terms.

Evolutionary biology also reopens the question of teleology. Can nature be given a limited teleological explanation while avoiding both purposelessness and a detailed, preconceived design? According to Ayala's functionalist interpretation (1998a, section 6), biological structures, organs, and behaviors are teleological if they are adaptations which increase reproductive success. Such teleological explanations are fully compatible with efficient causal explanations, and in some cases both are required. Stoeger (1998) argues for directionality in evolution as well as in cosmology, astronomy, and self-organization. Peacocke (1998a) argues that nature exhibits "propensities" toward complexity and information-processing. Wesley Wildman (1998), however, draws attention to the significant challenges facing teleological arguments that move from functional or apparent ends in nature to a metaphysical system that manifests genuine teleological principles.

Theological anthropology, evolution, and neuroscience

How are we to think about human nature and origins, including the *imago dei* and sin, in light of evolutionary biology, socio-biology, behavioral genetics, and neuroscience?[44] In 1996 Pope John Paul II (1998) questioned the traditional, dualist split[45] between body and soul; instead, he referred to the "spiritual" aspects of humanity, including self-awareness, moral conscience, and freedom. Commenting on the Pope's view, George Coyne (1998) proposed thinking of God as participating through love in the process of evolution, an approach which can preserve what is special about the emergence of spirit without resort to interventionism. Karl Rahner (1978:181–3) has systematically developed the concept of spirit in light of evolution as self-consciousness and consciousness of God. Edwards (1991:27–31) takes up the idea that "evolution is the universe's way of becoming conscious of itself" and sets it in a Rahnerian context: evolution is a development of matter toward spirit through God's continuous, immanent, and creative impulse, in which nature becomes conscious of itself in humanity.

Another approach to theological anthropology starts with the biblical concept of the human person as a "psychosomatic unity."[46] According to Peacocke (1993b:226), Christian anthropology assumes the psychosomatic unity of the person "rooted in materiality," while the sciences shed increasing light on the multi-leveled character and evolutionary history of this unity. Peacocke has proposed an "emergentist–monist" account of the personal as an emergent level above the purely biological, and attributes mental properties to the "human-brain-in-the-body-in-social-relations" (1999). He stresses that we have much to learn from socio-biology. He is, however, sharply critical of its incipient reductionism, especially regarding moral reasoning. Human behavior is both a product of evolution and a system of feedback which actually shapes human evolution by shaping our environment.[47]

According to Michael Ruse (1986a, 1986b, 1994, 1999),[48] however, altruism in humans neither has an objective reference nor can it be justified rationally. Instead, it is a biological adaptation rooted in our genes to help our species compete. Peacocke's response (1979:160–4, 1986, chapter 8) is that the content of moral reasoning cannot be determined by evolution, even if it is shaped in accordance with evolutionary history.

Philip Hefner's theological anthropology (1993) is driven by his interpretation of the *imago dei* as "created co-creator": our purpose is to help birth the future that is most wholesome for all of nature. Drawing on Ralph Burhoe[49] (1976, 1979) and Solomon Katz (1980), Hefner understands *Homo sapiens* as a symbiosis of genes and culture, a creature comprised of two "co-evolving organisms." Though the genetic organism makes culture possible, culture is crucial since myth, ritual, and religion offer guidance for the future.[50]

Nancey Murphy (1999) has developed an approach to the psychosomatic unity of the person based on non-reductive physicalism. She employs both emergence and top–down causation to mitigate against reductive materialism, arguing that emergent supervenient properties are often influenced by their context. William Stoeger (1999) and Theo Meyering (1999) have also discussed mental states as supervenient on brain-states in ways that guard the integrity of neurobiological causality while maintaining a distinctive causal role for mentality. Wesley Wildman and Leslie Brothers (1999) have focused on the challenge posed by the neurosciences to the claim that ultimacy is a causal source of religious experience. Their richly textured interpretation of experiences of the ultimate provides guidelines for characterizing authentic religious experiences. Fraser Watts (1997, 1998, 1999) has argued that theological and neurological explanations of religious experience are complementary, not contradictory.

Yet another approach to theological anthropology comes from process theology. Barbour (1990:194–9) rejects both substance dualism and reductive materialism, opting instead for multi-level theories of the person. The process view is congenial to the biblical perspective, in which humanity is rooted in nature, finitude, creatureliness, and mortality, and yet possesses unparalleled abilities such as language, self-consciousness, and freedom. God is not responsible for suffering in nature; rather, in an evolutionary world, death is necessary for life, and pain comes with sentience. The story of Adam's fall in an evolutionary context thus symbolizes the universal human journey from innocence to responsibility and sin.

Writing as a feminist process theologian, Marjorie Hewitt Suchocki (1994) rejects the Augustinian/Niebuhrian view of sin as rebellion against God, and pride as the core form of sin. Instead, sin is rebellion against creation, expressed as unnecessary violence in the ecological context, which in turn affects the consequent nature of God. But what accounts for the universality of sin in an evolutionary perspective? Suchocki draws on the Irenaean/Schleiermachian view that God-consciousness emerges in all of humankind in tension with an underlying self-centeredness that precedes it and is required for our survival. She also draws on Christoph Wassermann's claim (1989) that the transition from violence to actual sin occurred as early humankind gained the ability to transcend its violent tendencies through empathy, memory, and imagination.

Theological anthropology also has much to gain from genetics research.[51] Ted Peters (1998a) discusses eight issues relating genetics to theological assumptions about God, evolution, and the human person. These include genetic discrimination, an intensification of the abortion controversy, patenting and cloning, genetic determinism and human freedom, the "gay gene," somatic vs. germ-line intervention, and "playing God." The issue of genetic determinism actually involves a contradiction between "puppet determinism," in which genes are thought to determine all our behavior, and "Promethean determinism," in which we assume we can guide our evolutionary future armed with genetic knowledge. Both belong to what Peters calls the "gene myth," and both are dangerously misleading in linking genes, crime, class, and race. As for "playing God," Peters argues against viewing DNA, or any part of creation, as sacred, as Jeremy Rifkin and others have done. With Philip Hefner, he understands humanity as a "created co-creator." As humans, we cannot *not* be creative. The ethical challenge comes in aligning our efforts with the future that God is creating.

One final area to mention is the rapidly growing discussion between theologians and the artificial intelligence (AI)[52] community. Anne Foerst (1998a) has described the construction of Cog, a humanoid robot at MIT, and its implications for the *imago dei*. Discussions of Cog, as an example of embodied AI, lead us to consider a symbolic interpretation of the *imago dei* as performative and relational, and enrich our perception and appreciation of human reality.[53] Noreen Herzfeld (1999) argues that the history of failure in symbolic AI, which was built on a substantialist premise, supports a relational understanding of the *imago dei*.

Redemption, evolution, and cosmology

The point of departure for most theologies of redemption is that God shares in the suffering of the world and heals us through Christ. But this raises fundamental questions. Does nature need to be redeemed? What is God's relation to natural evil (the problem of theodicy)? What is the relation between sin, biological death, and redemption? Does redemption merely include life on earth, or the universe as a whole?[54] Responses can be divided into those that view human sin as a radically new phenomenon with no roots in our evolutionary past, and those that view human sin as emerging within human evolution from a variety of preconditions that fade back indefinitely into the past.

On the first view, sin has an entirely human (personal, social, economic, or political) context. The evolution of life on earth and the natural ecosystems, including biological death and the extinction of species, are seen as unequivocally good, the creation of a loving God. But this position minimizes the problem of "natural evil" by denying that pain, suffering, death, or extinction challenge nature's unequivocal goodness.[55] It offers no explanation of the occurrence of sin in the human species, leaving us radically distinct from an otherwise benign universe and yet intimately connected to it through a common evolutionary history. Moreover, the scope of redemption is limited to the human species and not all of life.

On the second view, natural evil as the precondition entailed by sin can be found in our evolutionary past and traced back to the fundamental character of the laws of nature and their instantiation in cosmology, even while moral sin is restricted to the human species. Creation's "groaning" (Romans 8) suggests that death is both natural and yet something to be overcome in an eschatological transformation of the cosmos. Questions arise with this approach as well. If human sin has roots in the evolutionary and cosmological past, doesn't this implicate God as the creator of the universe? And how can we think about the transformation of the universe into the "new creation" given scientific cosmology (see below)? We will follow the second view here.

The relevance of Christology to evolution depends on whether nature needs redemption. Holmes Rolston writes, "Whatever is in travail needs redemption, whether or not there is any sin to be dealt with." The biological process "anticipates what later becomes paramount. . . . The Garden Earth forebodes the Garden of Gethsemane. Creation is cruciform" (1994:218–21, 1999).[56] Barbour (1990:208–14, 238–42) claims that the human and divine aspects of Jesus Christ are continuous with prehuman evolution, *and yet* both include something genuinely new in nature. Christ is thus the product of God's immanent activity in all of evolutionary history, and yet he is a radically new revelation of God's nature. Similarly, Peacocke (1993b:301) views evolution as characterized by the "paradox" of emergence: the rise of the genuinely new within the continuity of natural processes. Gerd Theissen (1985) raises three key questions: Is Jesus a variant (or "mutation") of human existence? Is Jesus the consummation of the prophetic protest against selection? Is Jesus a permanently valid "structure of adaptation"? His response makes Jesus "the central reality to which all life must adapt itself." Juan Luis Segundo (1988) has also used evolutionary categories to understand the significance of Jesus of Nazareth in "this-worldly" terms. Jesus preserved the supreme evolutionary quality, flexibility. In him evolution bends back on itself to become conscious, and thus human. Ruether (1983, 1992) proposes a "this-worldly" view of redemption commensurate with her understanding of mortality as natural: although redemption is the fullness of life within finite limits, she nonetheless retains a view of Christ as the *cosmic* manifestation of God as both creator and redeemer.[57]

Some scholars have also found that specific scientific theories can illuminate particular Christological issues. In a 1974 review of proposals by John McIntyre (1966) and William Austin (1967), each of whom related the issue of complementarity in quantum mechanics to the two-natured view of the person of Christ, Barbour (1974, chapter 8, section 2) cautioned that complementarity is best employed on the "same logical level."[58] In physics, particle and wave are on the same level; in theology, divinity and humanity are not. Christopher Kaiser (1976) compared Chalcedonian Christology to Bohr's notion of complementarity. He noted that both wave and particle point to the same object, an electron, and that both God and human pertain to the same person, Jesus Christ. In each case, two models are necessary for a complete description of the phenomenon and they are dynamically related to each other. More recently, James E. Loder and W. Jim Neidhardt (1992) have related quantum complementarity to the work of Søren Kierkegaard and Paul Møller.

A defining theme for most Christian theologies is the resurrection of Jesus of Nazareth. How is this miracle to be put in relation to science? Peacocke (1993b) and Polkinghorne (1996b) offer differing responses that illustrate the consequences of prioritizing either theology or science here. Both agree that the resurrection is more than mere psychology, yet Polkinghorne is more committed to an "empty tomb."[59] The resurrection of Jesus also bears on the question of life after death and the general resurrection. According to Ted Peters (1995, 1999), the rejection of body/soul dualism in the cognitive sciences and contemporary philosophy has wrongly been taken to undermine the Christian view of eternal life. Instead, resurrection is not the reunion of a resurrected body with an "immortal soul" – a primarily Greek concept – but rather the eschatological transformation of the complete person as a psychosomatic unity.

Evolution also poses the problem of theodicy, given the billions of years of natural disaster, evolutionary wastefulness, suffering, death, and extinction in nature. Polkinghorne (1989, chapter 5) has developed a "free-process defense" of natural evil analogous to the traditional free-will defense of moral evil. Here the conditions for the evolution of free creatures hinge on the existence of genuine chance in nature. God does not intervene, but grants the world and humans independence. Russell (1984, 1990, 1998b) developed a similar approach by exploring the role entropy plays in processes leading to more complex order and organization (often associated with good-ness), and to dissipation, decay, and death (often associated with natural evil). This ambiguous role of entropy in physics and biology, he argues, prefigures what we under-stand as human sin. Tracy (1992, 1998) has recently argued that "pointless" natural evils are those which do not generate particular goods but are mere by-products of preserving moral freedom and the integrity of nature. They appear unnecessary, but the possibility of a personal relationship with God requires them.

We come now to the doctrine of "last things," or eschatology. Some scholars, such as Ruether and Segundo, discuss eschatology primarily in the context of ecology and liberation. According to Ruether, the biblical view of eschatology, with its incorpora-tion of the Hebraic view of earthly blessedness, was replaced by earthly power in the early Church. Ruether develops an "ecofeminist theocosmology" which includes "the transience of selves, the living interdependency of all things, and the value of the per-sonal in communion" (1992:251). For Segundo (1988:104), the "new earth" suggests a new existence in which all the things that seemed to negate our values and our efforts are done away with. The new earth is the new heaven, in which God is identified with the culmination of the human struggle for meaning.

As our awareness of the vast size and complexity of the cosmos grows, though, limiting the scope of our eschatological reflections and hopes to our own species, or even our own planet, appears less and less justifiable. Should our hope for redemption then be expanded to include the cosmos as a whole? Is all of the universe, as creation, to participate in the new creation? Such a move to enlarge the scope of eschatology to include the entire universe immediately runs into a severe challenge from science. According to Big Bang cosmology, the future of the universe is far from anything like a "new creation." Instead it is "freeze or fry," endless expansion or violent re-collapse. Moreover, all life will be extinguished from the universe long before either far-future scenario is relevant. Can Christian eschatology be made consistent with either of these scenarios or with the universal extinction of life? At first glance, the answer would seem to be an alarming, "No!" John Macquarrie (1977:351–62), Wolfhart Pannenberg (1998, chapter 15), and others have noted that if it were shown that the universe is indeed headed for an all-enveloping death, this could be taken to falsify Christian faith and abolish Christian hope. Is this conclusion avoidable?

Not easily, if we agree to play by the methodological rules adopted so far. Since sci-entific cosmology is part of physics, the "freeze or fry" predictions must be allowed to challenge what theology can claim eschatologically – just as the role of death in evo-lutionary biology challenges the traditional connection between sin and death. No easy appeal to contingency, novelty, unpredictability, emergence, or philosophical cosmol-ogy will solve this problem.

However, Freeman Dyson (1979, 1988) worked out a partial response, at least, by showing how life could survive forever in the open or "freeze" scenario. John Barrow and Frank Tipler (1986) then took up Dyson's arguments and applied them to the "fry" scenario of a closed universe. In both cases, however, these scientists reduce life to mere "information processing," and "eternal life" to the endless processing of new information. In his more recent writings, Tipler (1994) claimed to treat a variety of theological concerns, including God, resurrection, and immortality, in terms of his "Omega point theory." Yet Tipler's scientific claims have been attacked aggressively by other scientists (Choi 1995, Stoeger and Ellis 1995), while both Dyson's and Tipler's theological proposals and their reductionist philosophies have been criticized by a variety of scholars including Polkinghorne (1989:96), Barbour (1990:151–2), Peacocke (1993b:345), Clayton (1997a:132–6), and Worthing (1996, chapter 5).[60]

Instead, Worthing (1996:177–8) suggests we understand the *parousia* as a renewal or transformation of the entire universe. This shifts the discussion from the end of the world to the concept of eternity as the real issue in relating science and theology. According to Ted Peters, what we need is "temporal holism" in which the cosmos as a unity of time and space is both created proleptically from the future and redeemed eschatologically by God's future initiative, which we know in Jesus Christ. Peters is ruthlessly honest about the challenge from science. "Should the final future as forecasted by [scientific cosmology] come to pass . . . then we would have proof that our faith has been in vain. It would turn out to be that there is no God, at least not the God in whom followers of Jesus have put their faith" (1993a:175–6). Russell (1997) suggests that the trinitarian conceptions of time and eternity first need to be reformulated in light of Einstein's special theory of relativity before the assumptions on which scientific cosmology is based can be re-evaluated in light of them. In recent work the challenges cosmology poses to bodily resurrection and eschatology have received very promising responses (Polkinghorne 1994, Polkinghorne and Walker 2000, Polkinghorne 2002, Russell 2002).

III   Challenges and Future Directions

Feminist critiques of science and of theology and science

In the introduction to their anthology, *Feminism and Science* (1996), Evelyn Fox Keller and Helen E. Longino pose a watershed question: Are the sciences neutral to social values, the harm they do coming from their misuse, or is there a more intimate problematic at work? According to their analysis, the roots of this question lie in the 1960s revolution in the philosophy of science. Feminist theory has expanded this revolution through its novel concept of "gender" (the social constitution of masculinity and femininity). While early feminists sought a "gender-free" science by urging greater access for women in science education and research and by retrieving the stories of outstanding women scientists, more recent feminists have used gender analysis to critique the content and practice of science. According to Harding and Hintikka (1983), sexist distortions are rooted in epistemology, metaphysics, methodology, and the philosophy of science.[61]

Feminist theology emerged in roughly this same period. However, as Ann Pederson and Mary Solberg (1999) have stressed, very few women are active today in "theology and science," the number of feminist women (or men) is even fewer, and gender issues clearly continue to affect the field. Lisa Stenmark (1999) argues that since participants in science and religion are mostly "white, male, privileged," they carry the same biases found in science. She urges scholars to listen to the "voices from the margins," to turn to postmodernist views of knowledge, to honor the importance of diversity in community, and to adhere to participatory values.[62]

Historical studies on gender bias in science are also leading to a clearer understanding of gender bias in science and religion. David Noble notes that the clerical ascetic culture that first came to dominance in the High Middle Ages was an exclusively male society. When women entered the academic world in the nineteenth century, they were "confronted by another clerical restoration, in the form of a male scientific professionalism that betrayed the same misogynistic . . . habits of the clerical culture it superseded" (1992, "Introduction"). Margaret Wertheim explores the relation between the marginalization of women in religion and the marginalization of women in physics. "The struggle women have faced to gain entry into science parallels the struggle they have faced to gain entry into the clergy" (1995:8–9, 15).

We believe that a sustained focus on issues surrounding gender will mark an important new development in science and religion. The inclusion of womanist, *mujerista*, and other women's voices in this conversation is crucial, particularly as ecofeminist concerns help relate theoretical issues in science and religion to issues of praxis related to technology, environment, and human values.[63]

Postmodern challenges to science and to theology and science

According to van Huyssteen (1997:276), postmodernism[64] threatens to undercut further advance in theology and science. "Does the pluralism and localization of postmodern discourse throw theologians, philosophers, and scientists . . . into near-complete epistemological incommensurability?" Van Huyssteen's response is two-fold: we should understand postmodernity as a movement within modernity, rather than as modern thought coming to its end, and recognize that cosmology and evolutionary biology can provide the resources for interdisciplinary knowledge without necessarily becoming new ideological metanarratives. Niels Gregersen (1998) also supports the search for a fruitful interdisciplinary dialog in the context of postmodern pluralism. He argues that a "contextual coherence theory" has operated throughout Christian history and can now provide a *via media* between critical realism and a radical pluralism.

Inter-religious dialogue, world spiritualities, and science

Most of the literature in theology and science has focused on Christian theology. However, a rapidly growing diversity of religious voices are entering the conversation.

Religious scholars such as Norbert Samuelson (1994) and Daniel Matt (1996), and scientists such as Joel Primack in cosmology (1995), Carl Feit in biology (forthcoming) and Ken Kendler in genetics and psychiatry (forthcoming), have embarked on serious explorations of the relation of Judaism, both in its philosophical and its mystical forms, to contemporary cosmology, evolutionary biology, and psychology. Muslim dialogue with science is developing through the work of religious scholars such as S. H. Nasr (1980) and Z. Sardar (1989), and scientists such as Muzzafar Iqbal in chemistry (1992), Mehdi Golshani in physics (1997, 1998), and Bruno Guiderdoni in astronomy (1997).[65] Buddhist dialogue with science now includes religious scholars such as Jensine Andresen (1999a, 1999b) in the United States.[66] Native American spirituality in dialog with science is being pursued by biologist Dawn Adams and colleagues in the American Indian Science and Engineering Society.[67]

Recently, issues raised by science have also been introduced into ongoing programs of *inter-religious* dialogue. Ryokoku University, for example, has sponsored discussions between Buddhists and Christians on physics and cosmology (Andresen 1999b, Russell 2000). The "Science and the Spiritual Quest" program has brought together an international team of distinguished scientists who are practicing Jews, Christians, and Muslims for workshops and public conferences.

History of science and religion

The historical study of the interaction between science and religion in the West is rapidly expanding. Careful historical research has thoroughly discredited the claim that the relation between science and religion throughout the nineteenth and twentieth centuries was solely one of "warfare."[68] Claude Welch (1996, 1985:198–208) showed that there were at least three kinds of response to science in the nineteenth century: in addition to "opposition" (Charles Hodge, Edward Cardinal Manning), there was "cautious mediation" or "accommodation" (F. D. Maurice, Charles Kingsley, James McCosh, Benjamin B. Warfield, Frederick Temple), and the "exaltation of evolution" or "assimilation" (*Lux Mundi* authors such as Audrey Moore, J. R. Illingworth, Henry Ward Beecher, Henry Drummond). As John Brooke (1991, 1996, 1998) has argued in great detail, historical research into the religious origins of modern science is suggesting an increasingly complex interplay of factors at work in the historical relations between science and religion. Numerous scholars, including John Dillenberger (1960), Michael Foster (1969), Eugene Klaaren (1977), Gary Deason (1986a, 1986b), David Lindberg and Ronald Numbers (1986), Amos Funkenstein (1986), Bernard Cohen (1990), and Peter Hess (1997), have taken up the broad portrayal of the positive significance of religion for the rise of science.

An interaction model of theology and science

A major challenge continues to be whether science and theology can genuinely *interact* in a mutually constructive way, each offering something of intellectual value to the other.[69]

Russell (2002) has identified eight distinct ways in which this interaction can take place, five involving the influence of science on theology and three the influence of theology on science. Limiting our discussion to physics and cosmology, the first five ways are: (1) Physical theories can act as data which place constraints on theology. For example, a theology of divine action should not violate special relativity. (2) Physical theories can act as data to be incorporated directly into theology. For example, $t = 0$ in Big Bang cosmology may be explained via creation *ex nihilo*; the explanation, though, is part of theology and not of science. (3) Theories in physics, after philosophical analysis, can act indirectly as data in theology. For example, $t = 0$ can be interpreted philosophically as evidence of contingency in the Big Bang universe, and thus as evidence for the existence of God. Quantum mechanics may be interpreted philosophically in terms of ontological indeterminism and incorporated into a theology of non-interventionist divine action. (4) Theories in physics can also act indirectly as theological data when they are incorporated into a fully articulated philosophy of nature, such as temporality and relationality in process philosophy. Finally, (4) theories in physics can function heuristically in the theological context of discovery by providing conceptual, experiential, moral, or aesthetic inspiration.

To complete the genuinely interactive, but asymmetrical, nature of the relations, Russell proposes three paths by which theology can influence physics: (6) Theology has provided key historical assumptions which underlie the development of science, such as the contingency and rationality of nature.[70] (7) Theological theories can act as sources of inspiration in the scientific "context of discovery." An example is the influence of religious ideas on the pioneers of quantum theory, including Planck, Einstein, Bohr, and Schrödinger.[71] Finally, (8) theological theories could provide criteria, alongside empirical adequacy, coherence, scope, and fertility, for theory choice in physics, as seen in the debates between steady state and Big Bang cosmologies in the mid-twentieth century.

Appendix: Centers and Programs

USA

American Association for the Advancement of Science Program on Dialog between
     Science and Religion ⟨www.aaas.org/spp/dser⟩
American Scientific Affiliation (ASA) ⟨www.asa3.org/ASA⟩
Boston University's Graduate Program in Science, Philosophy and Religion
     ⟨people.by.edu/wwildman/weirdwildweb/degphd-spr.htm⟩
Center for Faith and Science Exchange (FASE) ⟨www.ctel.net/~keggi/fase/index.html⟩
Center for Process Studies (CPS) ⟨www.ctr4process.org⟩
Center for Research in Science ⟨www.apu.edu/cris⟩
Center for Theology and the Natural Sciences (CTNS) ⟨www.ctns.org⟩
Center of Theological Inquiry (CTI) ⟨www.ctinquiry.org⟩
Columbia Center for the Study of Science and Religion
     ⟨www.columbia.edu/cu/cssr.html⟩
Counterbalance ⟨www.counterbalance.org⟩
Epic of Creation (program of ZCRS)
FASE ⟨www.bostontheological.org/fase/fase.htm⟩
Institute for Theological Encounter with Science and Technology (ITEST)
     ⟨itest.slu.edu⟩
Institute on Religion in an Age of Science (IRAS) ⟨www.iras.org/home.html⟩
John Templeton Foundation (JTF) ⟨www.templeton.org⟩
Metanexus ⟨www.metanexus.org⟩
Philadelphia Center for Science and Religion (PCSR) ⟨www.pc4rs.org⟩
Science and Religion Course Program Resource ⟨www.ctus.org⟩
Science and the Spiritual Quest Resources ⟨www.ctus.org⟩
Tapestry ⟨www.tapestryweb.org⟩
Vatican Observatory Research Group at Tuscon ⟨clavius.as.arizona.edu/vo/⟩
Zygon (Chicago) Center for Religion and Science (ZCRS) ⟨www.zygoncenter.org⟩

Australia

Australia Center for Theology, Science and Culture
     ⟨www.ehlt.flinders.edu.au/theology/lnstitute.html⟩
Australian Theological Forum ⟨www.atf.org.au⟩

Canada

Canadian Scientific and Christian Affiliation ⟨www.csca.ca/⟩
Pascal Center for Advance Studies in Faith and Science ⟨www.redeemer.on.ca/pascal⟩

Europe

Aarhus Forum for Theology and Science (Denmark)
Center for Science and Religion (England) ⟨www.leeds.ac.uk/trs/csr/⟩
European Society for the Study of Science and Theology (ESSSAT) ⟨www.esssat.org⟩
Science and Religion Forum (SRF – England) ⟨www.srforum.org⟩
Society of Ordained Scientists (SOSc – England)
    ⟨userpages.prexar.com/keggi/SOSc/1SOScx.html⟩
Vatican Observatory (Vatican City State)

South Africa

South African Science and Religion Forum (SASRF)

Journals

[R] = refereed; [I] = extensive indices.

CTNS Bulletin[I]
ITEST Bulletin
PERSPECTIVES on Science and Christian Faith[R] (sponsored by the ASA)
Progress in Theology (sponsored by JTF)
Process Studies (sponsored by CPS)
Religion and Science Forum Book Reviews (sponsored by RSF)
SASRF Journal
Science and Christian Belief[R,I] (sponsored by CISE)
Science and Spirit ⟨www.science-spirit.org⟩
Theology and Science (sponsored by CTNS)
Zygon: Journal of Religion and Science[R,I] ⟨www.zygonjournal.org⟩

Notes

1   One can question whether the term "field" is appropriate for what is arguably an interdis-
    ciplinary relationship between two separate and established fields, namely theology and
    science. We use the term here both in a descriptive sense, since it is often used to describe
    the dialog, and to signal in advance that, in our opinion, scholars working on these issues
    have accomplished sufficient results over the past four decades, primarily in the methodol-
    ogy described here, to warrant considering this a genuine field of study.
2   A clear example of this division is reflected in the way Ian Barbour developed his two series
    of Gifford Lectures, although he makes clear the implications of the first series for the second
    (1990, 1993).

3   We take theology to be the critical analysis of the cognitive content of a living religion whose sources include sacred text, tradition, worship, practice, and personal experience in the context of religion, and of cultural and secular pluralism. Theology is accountable to the intersubjective assessment of religious communities and to the wider public communities in which they live and practice. The term "science and religion" suggests a wider context of interaction than "theology and science."

4   Helpful textbooks and overview articles include those by Ian Barbour (1990, 1997), John Haught (1995), Philip Hefner (1996), James Huchingson (1993), Alister McGrath (1999), Ted Peters (1996, 1997, 1998b), John Polkinghorne (1998), W. Mark Richardson and Wesley Wildman (1996), Christopher Southgate et al. (1999), and Wesley Wildman (1996), Teaching resources have also recently been developed by Philip Clayton (1997b), Clayton and Mark Railey (1998), and William Grassie (1997b).

5   Textbook overviews include Barbour (1997, part 2), Haught (1995, chapter 1), Richardson and Wildman (1996, part II), and Southgate et al. (1999, chapters 1 and 2).

6   Other relevant typologies include those by Richard Bube (1995), Mikael Stenmark (1997), Fraser Watts (1998:1–14), and Mark Worthing (1996: 29–32). The textbook by Southgate et al. (1999) summarizes many of them.

7   Many of the scholars mentioned in this chapter draw on philosophers of science who defend what is more commonly called "scientific realism," though typically using Barbour's term, "critical realism." See Jarrett Leplin (1984) for an overview of scientific realism.

8   For a critique of the "bridge" metaphor, see Richardson and Wildman (1996:xi–xiii).

9   For a memorable description that pre-dates Hempel, see Alfred North Whitehead (1978:5).

10   For Barbour, paradigms in science and in religion display "subjective" as well as "objective" features, though the former are more prominent in religion and the latter in science (1974, chapter 7, esp. pp. 118, 144–5; 1990, chapter 2, esp. p. 65).

11   Realists include Ian Hacking (1983), and Jarrett Leplin (1984). Anti-realists include Bas van Fraassen (1980), Larry Laudan (1977, 1984), and Arthur Fine (1984). For a recent collection of essays, see Ernan McMullin (1988).

12   Helpful analysis of such accounts (Bloor 1976, Rudwick 1981) can be found in Mary Hesse (1988).

13   For an extensive and careful introduction to and critique of Pannenberg's methodology in relation to science, see van Huyssteen (1989, chapter 6).

14   Note that without Murphy's modification the notion of "prediction" might seem to under-cut the applicability of Lakatos to theology. See, for example, Polkinghorne (1994:49) and Niels Gregersen (1998:205–12, esp. pp. 208–9). For a substantive critique of the claim that discernment can yield novel facts, see Drees (1996:143–4).

15   The December 1999 issue of *Zygon* profiles Murphy's work.

16   For additional discussion see Philip Clayton and Steven Knapp (1996a, 1996b), Nicolas Wolterstorff (1996), Nancey Murphy (1996b), and Gregory Peterson (1998).

17   One should clearly note that this is not an ontological, valuative or axiological hierarchy, such as those supporting dominance or patriarchy, but a strictly epistemological hierarchy which supports the argument for non-reducibility.

18   For a recent critique of their views, see Christoph Lameter (1998), Russell (1998b), and Kirk Wegter-McNelly (1998).

19   Most scholars hold that the only theologically valid dualism is God and creation. Within the created world, there can be no further ontological bifurcations.

20   Here this mental aspect leads to consciousness and self-consciousness only when sufficient biological complexity (coherent societies of actual occasions) has evolved.

21   For an introduction to special relativity, see William Burke and Peter Scott (1978), William Burke (1980), Edwin Taylor and John Wheeler (1963). For a short overview, see James Trefil and Robert Hazen (2000, chapter 13). See also the elegant treatment in Charles Misner, Kip Thorne, and John Wheeler (1973). For helpful insights see Hark Worthing (1996:23–6).

22   Numerous articles by scientists and philosophers challenging the block universe view of SR can be found in David R. Griffin (1986).

23   For careful analysis of the contemporary theological literature on divine action, see Owen Thomas (1983, 1990). The more conventional term for divine action is "providence," for which see Michael Jerome Langford (1981). For detailed analysis of the philosophical problems involved, see Keith Ward (1990) and Thomas Tracy (1994).

24   Interesting examples of conservative theologians include Charles Hodge (1891), Donald Bloesch (1994), and Millard Erickson (1983). Liberal theologians include Rudolf Bultmann (1951, 1958), Gordon Kaufman (1978, 1983), and Maurice Wiles (1983, 1986).

25   Langdon Gilkey's penetrating analysis (1961) of the failure of neo-orthodoxy suggests how crucial this problem is.

26   Since 1990 the Center for Theology and the Natural Sciences and the Vatican Observatory have sponsored a series of bi-annual research conferences aimed at gaining a clearer understanding of the relation between contemporary science and a non-interventionist approach to special, objective, divine action. The publications from these conferences can be found in Russell, Murphy, and Isham (1993), Russell, Murphy, and Peacocke (1995), Russell, Stoeger, and Ayala (1998), Russell, Murphy, Meyering, and Arbib (1999), and Russell, Clayton, Wegter-McNelly, and Polkinghorne (2001). This series arose out of a Vatican Observatory conference on theology and science, the results of which appear in Russell, Stoeger, and Coyne (1988). For other helpful analyses of the problem of divine action, see Polkinghorne (1989, chapter 2), Barbour (1990, chapters 8 and 9), Peacocke (1993b, chapter 9), and Clayton (1997a, chapter 7). See also Jitze van der Meer (1996, esp. vol. 4), Steven Crain (1997), and Southgate et al. (1999, chapter 7).

27   For an introduction to thermodynamics see P. W. Bridgman (1961), H. C. van Ness (1969), Peacocke (1983), George Murphy (1991), and Trefil and Hazen (2000, chapters 3 and 4).

28   For an introduction to chaos and complexity theory, see James Crutchfield et al. (1986), James Gleick (1987), Joseph Ford (1989). See Wildman and Russell (1995) for extended references and a philosophical analysis of chaos theory.

29   See also Karl Young (1996).

30   For an introduction to quantum mechanics, see Paul Davies (1984) and Trefil and Hazen (2000, chapters 6–12). More technical, older resources include Eugen Merzbacher (1961), Kurt Gottfried (1966), and the classic by Paul Dirac (1958). A recent work for the general reader is Polkinghorne (1989). For an introduction to the philosophical problems in quantum physics, see Max Jammer (1974), Michael Redhead (1987), James Cushing and Ernan McMullin (1989), Abner Shimony (1989), Chris Isham (1995), and Sheldon Goldstein (1998). For an accessible account see Nick Herbert (1985).

31   This approach has been criticized by a number of scholars including Peacocke (1995:279–81), Polkinghorne (1995:152–3), and Nicholas Saunders (2000).

32   For references to Bohm and other interpretations of quantum mechanics, and a recent discussion of the measurement problem, non-locality/non-separability, and the challenge to classical ontology and critical realism, see Russell, Clayton, Wegter-McNelly and Polkinghorne (2001).

33   For a non-technical introduction, see Trefil and Hazen (2000, chapter 15), Donald Goldsmith (1995, chapters 1–9), Trefil (1983, chapters 1–9), Drees (1990, Appendix 1), Ellis and Stoeger (1993), Stoeger (1996), Southgate et al. (1999:35–9). For a technical

introduction, see J. D. North (1990), Misner, Thorne, and Wheeler (1973, part VI), and Steven Weinberg (1972, part V).

34   According to McMullin (1981), the Pope later refrained from making this claim after being cautioned by Georges Lemaître, a Roman Catholic priest and one of the founders of Big Bang cosmology.

35   For a more direct appropriation of Big Bang cosmology by a conservative Christian, see Hugh Ross (1993).

36   This term was coined by Brandon Carter (1974).

37   For helpful surveys of the various views see John Barrow and Frank Tipler (1986), John Leslie (1990), Ellis (1993a), and Southgate et al. (1999).

38   For a related view, see Christopher Mooney (1996, chapter 2).

39   For a non-technical introduction, see Goldsmith (1995, chapter 10 and following), Trefil (1983, chapter 10 and following), Drees (1990, Appendices 3, 4). For a more technical introduction, see Isham (1988, 1993) and Edward Kolb and Michael Turner (1994).

40   For a view of positions taken in the nineteenth century, see Claude Welch (1985, chapter 6) and Ian Barbour (1971, chapter 4). See also David Lindberg and Ronald Numbers (1986).

41   For a helpful introduction, see Trefil and Hazen (2000, chapters 19–25), Roger Lewin (1997), Neil Campbell (1990). For teaching resources, see Ronald Fox (1997), Ursula Goodenough (1996), and Francisco Ayala (1998b).

42   See also the December 1991 issue of *Zygon* for a profile of Peacocke's work.

43   Several conservative and evangelical theologians have also offered creative interpretations of evolution, including Bernard Ramm (1955), Alister McGrath (1999) and Van Till, Young, and Menninga (1988).

44   For an introduction to socio-biology, see E. O. Wilson (1975, 1978), Richard Dawkins (1976), and Craig Nessan (1998). On cognitive and neuroscience, see Joseph LeDoux (1996, 1999), Peter Hagoort (1999), Marc Jeannerod (1999), Leslie Brothers (1997, 1999), Michael Arbib (1999), Arbib and Hesse (1986), James Ashbrook (1996), and Gregory Peterson (1997).

45   It remains to be seen whether theologians will be able to rid themselves of the "lingering Cartesianism" decried by Fergus Kerr (1999) and Antonio Damasio (1994) without acquiescing to epistemic and causal reductionism.

46   See, for example, Paul's use of the term *soma psychikon* in I Corinthians 15 : 44. For a careful analysis of New Testament views of the person, see Joel Green (1998, 1999).

47   The challenge of human freedom in the context of evolution is discussed from a Teilhardian perspective by Karl Schmitz-Moormann (1987). See also Mooney (1996, chapter 4).

48   Michael Ruse is profiled in the March 1994 issue of *Zygon*.

49   For a discussion of Burhoe's legacy, see the four 1998 issues of *Zygon*. which he founded.

50   For recent critiques of Hefner's proposal, see Don Browning (1992), Langdon Gilkey (1995), and Denis Edwards (1998).

51   Although ethical issues *per se* are not within the scope of this essay, human genetics is one area in particular in which ethics and theology are extraordinarily intertwined. For careful reflection on the Human Genome Project and the much broader scientific and technological context in which it is located, see Roger Shinn (1998), Thomas Shannon (1998), Laurie Zoloth-Dorfman (1998), Karen Lebacqz (1993, 1998), and James Gustafson (1993).

52   For an introduction to artificial intellegence, see Foerst (1996).

53   For reactions to this proposal, see Helmut Reich (1998), Mary Gerhard and Allan Russell (1998), and Foerst (1998b).

54   These questions were already present in the climate of the 1930s to 1950s when Teilhard de Chardin (1975) framed his elegant synthesis of science, theology, and spirituality. Teilhard's work was recently revisited in the March 1995 issue of *Zygon*.

55   For a conservative perspective on evolution and natural evil, see Gary Emberger (1994).

56   See also George Murphy (1991), Judith Scoville (1992), Kurt Richardson (1995).

57   Other scholars who have written on these and similar issues include Ronald Cole-Turner (1993), Vincent Guagliardo (1990), and Nancey Murphy (1990a).

58   For a discussion of the philosophical problems surrounding complementarity, see Edward MacKinnon (1996).

59   For a helpful analysis, see Southgate et al. (1999:264–5).

60   See also the Book Symposium in the June 1995 and September 1995 issues of *Zygon*.

61   For additional resources on these and related issues, see Donna Haraway (1991), Kathryn Pyne Addelson (1983), Carolyn Merchant (1980), Mary Midgley (1994), Michael Gross and Mary Beth Averill (1983), Helen Longino and Ruth Doell (1996), Mary Tiles (1996), Sarah Hrdy (1990), and Alice Kehoe (1990).

62   See also Winnifred Tomm (1990) and William Grassie (1996).

63   For a teaching resource, see Nancy Howell (1997).

64   For a teaching resource, see Grassie (1997a).

65   For a particularly helpful analysis, see Southgate et al. (1999, chapter 9).

66   See also the articles in vols. 11 and 12 (1995) of *The Pacific World: Journal of the Institute of Buddhist Studies*.

67   See also Vine Deloria (1992), Vincent Malmstrom (1997), Gregory Cajete (2000), and the online journal *Winds of Change* ⟨www.aises.org⟩.

68   Claude Welch notes that the language of "conflict" was inspired in part by widely influential books by John Draper (1874) and Andrew Dickson White (1896), which had as their main target the institutional Church, particularly Pope Pius IX's *Syllabus of Erros* of 1864.

69   On the issue of the role played by "external" factors in the formation and choice of scientific theories, including theology and philosophy, see Roy Clouser (1991), James Cushing (1994, 1998), Philip Clayton (1997a:130), Henry Folse (1985), Max Jammer (1966, 1974), and Edward MacKinnon (1982).

70   For example, the view of nature as created *ex nihilo* implies that the universe is contingent and rational. These implications provide two of the fundamental philosophical assumptions on which modern science is based (Foster 1969; Klaaren 1977; Lindberg and Numbers 1986; Deason 1986a, 1986b; Kaiser 1991; Wolterstorff 1976; van der Meer 1996, esp. vols. 2 and 3; and George Murphy 1996).

71   See J. L. Heilbron (1986), Peter Degen (1991), Paul Schilpp (1951), Erwin Schroedinger (1945/1967), and Max Jammer (1999).

References

Addelson, K. P. 1983. "The Man of Professional Wisdom," in *Discovering Reality: Feminist Perspectives on Epistemology, Metaphysics, Methodology, and Philosophy of Science*, ed. S. Harding and M. B. Hintikka. Dordrecht, Holland: D. Reidel.

Andresen, J. 1999a. "Science and Technology in Non-Western Cultures," *Zygon: Journal of Religion and Science* 34(2) (June).

Andresen, J. 1999b. "Tibetan Monks of the Gaden Monastery," *Focus: Journal of the Boston University School of Theology*, Winter/Spring.

Andresen, J. 2000. "Vajrayna Art and Iconography," *Zygon: Journal of Religion and Science* 35(2) (June).

Aquinas, T. 1997. *Aquinas on Creation*, ed. S. E. Baldner and W. E. Carroll. Toronto: Pontifical Institute of Mediaeval Studies.

Arbib, M. A. 1999. "Towards a Neuroscience of the Person," in *Neuroscience and the Person: Scientific Perspectives on Divine Action*, eds. R. J. Russell, N. Murphy, T. C. Meyering, and M. A. Arbib. Vatican City State: Vatican Observatory Publications; Berkeley, CA: Center for Theology and the Natural Sciences.

Arbib, M. A. and Hesse, M. B. 1986. *The Construction of Reality*, Gifford Lectures, 1983. Cambridge: Cambridge University Press.

Ashbrook, J. B. 1996. "Interfacing Religion and the Neurosciences: a Review of Twenty-five Years of Exploration and Reflection," *Zygon: Journal of Religion and Science* 31(4) (December).

Austin, W. 1967. "Waves, Particles and Paradoxes," *Rice University Studies* 53:85 ff.

Ayala, F. J. 1974. "Introduction," in *Studies in the Philosophy of Biology: Reduction and Related Problems*, eds. F. J. Ayala and T. Dobzhansky. Berkeley, CA: University of California Press.

Ayala, F. J. 1985. "Reduction in Biology: a Recent Challenge," in *Evolution at a Crossroads: The New Biology and the New Philosophy of Science*, eds. D. J. Depew and B. H. Weber. Cambridge, MA: MIT Press, pp. 67–78.

Ayala, F. J. 1998a. "Darwin's Devolution: Design without Designer," in *Evolutionary and Molecular Biology: Scientific Perspectives on Divine Action*, eds. R. J. Russell, W. R. Stoeger, and F. J. Ayala. Vatican City State: Vatican Observatory Publications; Berkeley, CA: Center for Theology and the Natural Sciences.

Ayala, F. J. 1998b. "The Evolution of Life: an Overview," in *Evolutionary and Molecular Biology: Scientific Perspectives on Divine Action*, eds. R. J. Russell, W. R. Stoeger, and F. J. Ayala. Vatican City State: Vatican Observatory Publications; Berkeley, CA: Center for Theology and the Natural Sciences.

Barbour, I. G. 1966. *Issues in Science and Religion*. Englewoods Cliffs, NJ: Prentice Hall, Reprinted 1971, New York: Harper & Row.

Barbour, I. G. 1974. *Myths, Models, and Paradigms: A Comparative Study in Science and Religion*. New York: Harper & Row.

Barbour, I. G. 1988. "Ways of Relating Science and Theology," in *Physics, Philosophy, and Theology: A Common Quest for Understanding*, eds. R. J. Russell, W. R. Stoeger, SJ, and G. V. Coyne, SJ. Vatican City State: Vatican Observatory Publications, pp. 21–48.

Barbour, I. G. 1990. *Religion in an Age of Science*, Gifford Lectures, 1989–90. San Francisco, CA: Harper & Row.

Barbour, I. G. 1993. *Ethics in an Age of Technology*, Gifford Lectures, 1989–91. San Francisco, CA: HarperSanFrancisco.

Barbour, I. G. 1997. *Religion and Science: Historical and Contemporary Issues*. San Francisco, CA: HarperSanFrancisco.

Barbour, I. G. 2000. *When Science Meets Religion*. San Francisco: HarperSanFrancisco.

Barrow, J. D. and Tipler, F. J. 1986. *The Anthropic Cosmological Principle*. Oxford: Clarendon Press.

Barth, K. 1960. *Church Dogmatics*, eds. G. W. Bromiley and T. F. Torrance, vol. III, 2: *The Doctrine of Creation*, trans. H. Knight, G. W. Bromiley, J. K. Reid, and R. H. Fuller. Edinburgh: T. & T. Clark.

Birch, C. 1990. *A Purpose for Everything: Religion in a Postmodern Worldview*. Mystic, CT: Twenty-Third Publications.

Birch, C. 1995. *Feelings*. Sydney: University of New South Wales Press.

Birch, C. 1998. "Neo-Darwinism, Self-organization, and Divine Action in Evolution," in *Evolutionary and Molecular Biology: Scientific Perspectives on Divine Action*, eds. R. J. Russell, W. R.

Stoeger, and F. J. Ayala. Vatican City State: Vatican Observatory Publications; Berkeley, CA: Center for Theology and the Natural Sciences.

Birch, C. and Cobb, J. B. Jr. 1981. *The Liberation of Life.* Cambridge: Cambridge University Press.

Bloesch, D. G. 1994. *Holy Scripture: Revelation, Inspiration and Interpretation.* Downers Grove, IL: InterVarsity Press.

Bloor, D. 1976. *Knowledge and Social Imagery.* London: Routledge & Kegan Paul.

Bridgman, P. W. 1961. *The Nature of Thermodynamics.* New York: Harper & Row.

Brooke, J. H. 1991. *Science and Religion: Some Historical Perspectives.* Cambridge: Cambridge University Press.

Brooke, J. H. 1996. "Science and Theology in the Enlightenment," in *Religion and Science: History, Method, Dialog,* eds. W. Mark Richardson and W. J. Wildman. New York: Routledge, pp. 7–28.

Brooke, J. H. 1998. *Reconstructing Nature: The Engagement of Science and Religion.* Edinburgh: T. & T. Clark.

Brothers, L. A. 1997. *Friday's Footprint: How Society Shapes the Human Mind.* New York: Oxford University Press.

Brothers, L. A. 1999. "A Neuroscientific Perspective on Human Sociality," in *Neuroscience and the Person: Scientific Perspectives on Divine Action,* eds. R. J. Russell, N. Murphy, T. C. Meyering, and M. A. Arbib. Vatican City State: Vatican Observatory Publications; Berkeley, CA: Center for Theology and the Natural Sciences.

Browning, D. 1992. "Altruism and Christian Love," *Zygon: Journal of Religion and Science* 27(4) (December).

Bube, R. H. 1995. *Putting it All Together: Seven Patterns for Relating Science and the Christian Faith.* Lanham, MD: University Press of America.

Bultmann, R. 1951. *Theology of the New Testament: Complete in One Volume,* trans. Kendrick Grobel. New York: Charles Scribner's Sons.

Bultmann, R. 1958. *Jesus Christ and Mythology.* New York: Charles Scribner's Sons.

Burhoe, R. 1976. "Religion's Role in the Context of Genetic and Cultural Evolution – Campbell's Hypotheses and some Evaluative Responses: Introduction," *Zygon: Journal of Religion and Science* 11(3) (September).

Burhoe, R. 1979. "Religion's Role in Human Evolution: the Missing Link between Ape-Man's Selfish Genes and Civilized Altruism," *Zygon: Journal of Religion and Science* 14(1) (March).

Burke, W. L. 1980. *Spacetime, Geometry, Cosmology.* Mill Valley, CA: University Science Books.

Burke, W. L. and Scott, P. L. 1978. *Special Relativity Primer.* Santa Cruz, CA, Department of Physics (photocopied manual).

Cajete, G. 2000. *Indigenous Science.* San Francisco, CA: Clear Light.

Campbell, N. A. 1990. *Biology,* 2nd edn. [1987] Redwood City, CA: Benjamin/Cummings.

Carroll, W. E. 1998. "Big Bang Cosmology, Quantum Tunneling from Nothing, and Creation," *Laval théologique et philosophique* 44(1) (February).

Carter, B. 1974. "Large Number Coincidences and the Anthropic Principle in Cosmology," in *Confrontation of Cosmological Theories with Observational Data,* ed. M. S. Longair. Dordrecht: Reidel.

Choi, H. S. 1995. "A Physicist Comments on Tipler's 'The Physics of Immortality,'" *CTNS Bulletin* 15(2) (Spring).

Clayton, P. 1989. *Explanation from Physics to Theology: An Essay in Rationality and Religion.* New Haven, CT: Yale University Press.

Clayton, P. 1997a. *God and Contemporary Science.* Grand Rapids, MI: W. Eerdmans.

Clayton, P. 1997b. "Philosophy of Science: What One Needs to Know," *Zygon: Journal of Religion and Science* 32(1) (March).

Clayton, P. 1999. "Neuroscience, the Person, and God: an Emergentist Account," in *Neuroscience and the Person: Scientific Perspectives on Divine Action,* eds. R. J. Russell, N. Murphy, T. C. Meyering, and M. A. Arbib. Vatican City State: Vatican Observatory Publications; Berkeley, CA: Center for Theology and the Natural Sciences.

Clayton, P. and Knapp, S. 1996a. "Is Holistic Justification Enough?" in *Religion and Science: History, Method, Dialogue*, eds. W. M. Richardson and W. J. Wildman. New York: Routledge, pp. 161–9.

Clayton, P. and Knapp, S. 1996b. "Rationality and Christian Self-conception," in *Religion and Science: History, Method, Dialogue*, eds. W. M. Richardson and W. J. Wildman. New York: Routledge, pp. 131–44.

Clayton, P. and Railey, M. S. 1998. "What Every Teacher of Science and Religion Needs to Know about Pedagogy," *Zygon: Journal of Religion and Science* 33(1) (March):121–30.

Clifford, CSJ, A. M. 1991. "Creation," in *Systematic Theology: Roman Catholic Perspectives*, vol. 1, eds. F. Schüssler Fiorenza and J. P. Galvin. Minneapolis, MN: Fortress Press, pp. 193–248.

Clifford, CSJ, A. M. 1998. "Darwin's Revolution in the Origin of Species: a Hermeneutical Study of the Movement from Natural Theology to Natural Selection," in *Evolutionary and Molecular Biology: Scientific Perspectives on Divine Action*, eds. R. J. Russell, W. R. Stoeger, SJ, and F. J. Ayala. Vatican City State: Vatican Observatory Publications; Berkeley, CA: Center for Theology and the Natural Sciences.

Clouser, R. A. 1991. *The Myth of Religious Neutrality: An Essay on the Hidden Role of Religious Belief in Theories*. Notre Dame, IN: University of Notre Dame Press.

Cobb, J. B., Jr. and Griffin, D. Ray. 1976. *Process Theology: An Introductory Exposition*. Philadelphia, PA: Westminster Press.

Cohen, I. B. ed. 1990. *Puritanism and the Rise of Modern Science: The Merton Thesis*. New Brunswick, NJ: Rutgers University Press.

Cole-Turner, R. 1993. *The New Genesis: Theology and the Genetic Revolution*. Louisville, TN: Westminster/John Knox Press.

Coyne, G. 1998. "Evolution and the Human Person: the Pope in Dialogue," in *Evolutionary and Molecular Biology: Scientific Perspectives on Divine Action*, eds. R. J. Russell, W. R. Stoeger, and F. J. Ayala. Vatican City State: Vatican Observatory Publications; Berkeley, CA: Center for Theology and the Natural Sciences.

Craig, W. L. and Smith, Q. 1993. *Theism, Atheism, and Big Bang Cosmology*. New York: Oxford University Press.

Crain, S. D. 1997. "Divine Action and the Natural Sciences," *Zygon: Journal of Religion and Science* 32(3) (September).

Crutchfield, J. P., Farmer, J. D., Packard, N. H., and Shaw, R. S. 1986. "Chaos," *Scientific American* 225 (December).

Cushing, J. T. 1994. *Quantum Mechanics: Historical Contingency and the Copenhagen Hegemony*. Chicago, IL: University of Chicago Press.

Cushing, J. T. 1998. *Philosophical Concepts in Physics*. Cambridge: Cambridge University Press.

Cushing, J. T. and McMullin, E. eds. 1989. *Philosophical Consequences of Quantum Theory: Reflections on Bell's Theorem*. Notre Dame, IN: University of Notre Dame Press.

Damasio, A. R. 1994. *Descartes' Error: Emotion, Reason, and the Human Brain*. New York: Putnam Books.

Davies, P. 1984. *Quantum Mechanics*. London: Routledge & Kegan Paul.

Dawkins, R. 1976. *The Selfish Gene*. Oxford: Oxford University Press.

Dawkins, R. 1987. *The Blind Watchmaker: Why the Evidence of Evolution Reveals a Universe without Design*. New York: W. W. Norton.

Deason, G. B. 1986a. "Protestant Theology and the Rise of Modern Science: Criticism and Review of the Strong Thesis," *CTNS Bulletin* 6(4) (Autumn).

Deason, G. B. 1986b. "Reformation Theology and the Mechanistic Conception of Nature," in *God and Nature: Historical Essays on the Encounter between Christianity and Science*, eds. D. C. Lindberg and R. L. Numbers. Berkeley, CA: University of California Press, pp. 167–91.

Degen, P. A. 1991. "Einstein's Weltanschauung and its Spinozistic Elements," *CTNS Bulletin* 11(3) (Summer).

Deloria, V. 1992. *God is Red: A Native View of Religion*, 2nd edn. Golden, CO: North American Press.

Dillenberger, J. 1960. *Protestant Thought and Natural Science: A Historical Interpretation*. Nashville, TN: Abingdon Press.

Dirac, P. A. M. 1958. *The Principles of Quantum Mechanics*, revised 4th edn. Oxford: Clarendon Press.

Draper, J. W. 1874. *History of the Conflict between Religion and Science*. London and New York: D. Appleton.

Drees, W. B. 1990. *Beyond the Big Bang: Quantum Cosmologies and God*. La Salle, IL: Open Court.

Drees, W. B. 1993. "A Case against Temporal Critical Realism? Consequences of Quantum Cosmology for Theology," in *Quantum Cosmology and the Laws of Nature: Scientific Perspectives on Divine Action*, eds. R. J. Russell, N. C. Murphy, and C. J. Isham, Scientific Perspectives on Divine Action series. Vatican City State: Vatican Observatory Publications; Berkeley, CA: Center for Theology and the Natural Sciences, pp. 331–66.

Drees, W. B. 1996. *Religion, Science and Naturalism*. Cambridge: Cambridge University Press.

Dyson, F. 1979. "Time without End: Physics and Biology in an Open Universe," *Reviews of Modern Physics* 51:447–60.

Dyson, F. 1988. *Infinite in All Directions*. New York: Harper and Row.

Edwards, D. 1991. *Jesus and the Cosmos*. New York: Paulist Press.

Edwards, D. 1995a. "The Discovery of Chaos and the Retrieval of the Trinity," in *Chaos and Complexity: Scientific Perspectives on Divine Action*, eds. R. J. Russell, N. C. Murphy, and A. R. Peacocke, Scientific Perspectives on Divine Action series. Vatican City State: Vatican Observatory Publications; Berkeley, CA: Center for Theology and the Natural Sciences. pp. 157–76.

Edwards, D. 1995b. *Jesus the Wisdom of God: An Ecological Theology*. Homebush, Australia: St Pauls.

Edwards, D. 1998. "Original Sin and Saving Grace in Evolutionary Context," in *Evolutionary and Molecular Biology: Scientific Perspectives on Divine Action*, eds. R. J. Russell, W. R. Stoeger, SJ, and F. J. Ayala. Vatican City State: Vatican Observatory Publications; Berkeley, CA: Center for Theology and the Natural Sciences.

Ellis, G. F. R. 1993a. *Before the Beginning: Cosmology Explained*. New York: Boyars/Bowerdean.

Ellis, G. F. R. 1993b. "The Theology of the Anthropic Principle," in *Quantum Cosmology and the Laws of Nature: Scientific Perspectives on Divine Action*, eds. R. J. Russell, N. C. Murphy, and C. J. Isham, Scientific Perspectives on Divine Action series. Vatican City State: Vatican Observatory Publications; Berkeley, CA: Center for Theology and the Natural Sciences, pp. 367–406.

Ellis, G. F. R. 1994. "God and the Universe: Kenosis as the Foundation of Being," the 1994 J. K. Russell Fellowship Lecture, *CTNS Bulletin* 14(2) (Spring).

Ellis, G. F. R. 1995. "Ordinary and Extraordinary Divine Action: the Nexus of Interaction," in *Chaos and Complexity: Scientific Perspectives on Divine Action*, eds. R. J. Russell, N. C. Murphy, and Arthur R. Peacocke, Scientific Perspectives on Divine Action series. Vatican City State: Vatican Observatory Publications; Berkeley, CA: Center for Theology and the Natural Sciences, pp. 359–96.

Ellis, G. F. R. 1998. "The Thinking Underlying the New 'Scientific' World-views," in *Evolutionary and Molecular Biology: Scientific Perspectives on Divine Action*, eds. R. J. Russell, W. R. Stoeger, SJ, and F. J. Ayala. Vatican City State: Vatican Observatory Publications; Berkeley, CA: Center for Theology and the Natural Sciences.

Ellis, G. F. R. and Stoeger, SJ, W. R. 1993. "Introduction to General Relativity and Cosmology," in *Quantum Cosmology and the Laws of Nature: Scientific Perspectives on Divine Action*, eds. R. J. Russell, N. C. Murphy, and C. J. Isham, Scientific Perspectives on Divine Action series. Vatican City State: Vatican Observatory Publications; Berkeley, CA: Center for Theology and the Natural Sciences. pp. 33–48.

Emberger, G. 1994. "Theological and Scientific Explanations for the Origin and Purpose of Natural Evil," *Perspectives on Science and Christian Faith* 46(3) (September).

Erickson, M. 1983. *Christian Theology*. Grand Rapids, MI: Baker.

Fine, A. 1984. "The Natural Ontological Attitude," in *Scientific Realism*, ed. Jarrett Leplin. Berkeley, CA: University of California Press.

Foerst, A. 1996. "Artificial Intelligence: Walking the Boundary," *Zygon: Journal of Religion and Science* 31(4) (December).

Foerst, A. 1998a. "Cog, a Humanoid Robot, and the Question of the Image of God," *Zygon: Journal of Religion and Science* 33(1) (March):91–111.

Foerst, A. 1998b. "Embodied AI, Creation, and Cog: a Response," *Zygon: Journal of Religion and Science* 33(3) (September):455–61.

Folse, H. J. 1985. *The Philosophy of Niels Bohr: The Framework of Complementarity*. Amsterdam: North Holland.

Ford, J. 1989. "What is Chaos, that We should be Mindful of it?" in *The New Physics*, ed. Paul Davies. New York: Cambridge University Press.

Foster, M. 1969. "The Christian Doctrine of Creation and the Rise of Modern Science," in *Creation: The Impact of an Idea*, eds. D. O'Connor and F. Oakley. New York: Charles Scribner's Sons.

Fox, R. F. 1997. "The Origins of Life: What One Needs to Know," *Zygon: Journal of Religion and Science* 32(3) (September).

Funkenstein, A. 1986. *Theology and the Scientific Imagination: From the Middle Ages to the Seventeenth Century*. Princeton, NJ: Princeton University Press.

Gerhard, M. and Russell, A. M. 1998. "Cog is to Us What We are to God: a Response to Anne Foerst," *Zygon: Journal of Religion and Science* 33(2) (June):263–9.

Gilkey, L. B. 1961. "Cosmology, Ontology, and the Travail of Biblical Language," *Journal of Religion* 41:194–205.

Gilkey, L. B. 1995. "Evolution, Culture, and Sin: Responding to Philip Hefner's Proposal," *Zygon: Journal of Religion and Science* 30(2) (June).

Gleick, J. 1987. *Chaos: Making a New Science*. New York: Penguin Books.

Goldsmith, D. 1995. *Einstein's Greatest Blunder? The Cosmological Constant and Other Fudge Factors in the Physics of the Universe*. Cambridge, MA: Harvard University Press.

Goldstein, S. 1998. "Quantum Theory without Observers," *Physics Today*, March and April.

Golshani, M. 1997. "How I Understand the Study of Science as a Muslim," *CTNS Bulletin* 17(4) (Fall).

Golshani, M. ed. 1998. *Can Science Dispense with Religion?* Tehran: Institute for Humanities and Cultural Studies.

Goodenough, U. 1996. "Biology: What One Needs to Know," *Zygon: Journal of Religion and Science* 31(4) (December).

Gottfried, K. 1966. *Quantum Mechanics*. New York: W. A. Benjamin.

Grassie, W. 1996. "Donna Haraway's Metatheory of Science and Religion: Cyborgs, Tricksters, and Hermes," *Zygon: Journal of Religion and Science* 31(2) (June).

Grassie, W. 1997a. "Postmodernism: What One Needs to Know," *Zygon: Journal of Religion and Science* 32(1) (March).

Grassie, W. 1997b. "Powerful Pedagogy in the Science-and-Religion Classroom," *Zygon: Journal of Religion and Science* 32(3) (September).

Green, J. B. 1998. "Bodies – That is, Human Lives," in *Whatever Happened to the Soul? Scientific and Theological Portraits of Human Nature*, eds. W. S. Brown, N. Murphy, and H. N. Malony. Minneapolis, MN: Fortress Press.

Green, J. B. 1999. "Restoring the Human Person: New Testament Voices for a Wholistic and Social Anthropology," in *Neuroscience and the Person: Scientific Perspectives on Divine Action*, eds. R. J. Russell, N. Murphy, T. C. Meyering, and M. A. Arbib. Vatican City State: Vatican Observatory Publications; Berkeley, CA: Center for Theology and the Natural Sciences, p. 322.

Gregersen, N. H. 1998. "A Contextual-Coherence Theory for the Theology–Science Dialogue," in *Rethinking Theology and Science: Six Models for the Current Dialogue*, eds. N. H. and J. W. van H. Gregersen. Grand Rapids, MI: William B. Eerdmans.

Griffin, D. R. 1986. *Physics and the Ultimate Significance of Time: Bohm, Prigogine, and Process Philosophy*. Albany, NY: State University of New York Press.

Griffin, D. R. 1988. "On Ian Barbour's 'Issues in Science and Religion,'" *Zygon: Journal of Religion and Science* 23(1) (March).

Gross, M. and Averill, M. B. 1983. "Evolution and Patriarchal Myths of Scarcity and Competition," in *Discovering Reality: Feminist Perspectives on Epistemology, Metaphysics. Methodology, and Philosophy of Science*, eds. S. Harding and M. B. Hintikka. Dordrecht: D. Reidel.

Guagliardo, V. 1990. "Nature and Miracle," *CTNS Bulletin* 10(2) (Spring).

Guiderdoni, B. 1997. "Dibattiti sull'origine del mondo nel medioevo islamico al-Ghazali, Ibn Rushd e Ibn Arabi," in *Scienza, Filosofia e Teologia di Fronte alla Nascita dell'Universo*, eds. P. Eligio, G. Giorello, G. Rigamonti, and E. Sindoni, Como: Edizioni New Press, pp. 287–98.

Gustafson, J. M. 1993. "Where Theologians and Genetics Meet," *CTNS Bulletin* 13(3) (Summer).

Hacking, I. 1983. *Representing and Intervening*. Cambridge: Cambridge University Press.

Hagoort, P. 1999. "The Uniquely Human Capacity for Language Communication: from POPE to [po:P] in Half a Second," in *Neuroscience and the Person: Scientific Perspectives on Divine Action*, eds. R. J. Russell, N. Murphy, T. C. Meyering, and M. A. Arbib. Vatican City State: Vatican Observatory Publications; Berkeley, CA: Center for Theology and the Natural Sciences.

Haraway, D. J. 1991. *Simians, Cyborgs, and Women: The Reinvention of Nature*. New York: Routledge.

Harding, S. and Hintikka, M. B. eds. 1983. *Discovering Reality: Feminist Perspectives on Epistemology, Metaphysics, Methodology, and Philosophy of Science*. Dordrecht: D. Reidel.

Hartshorne, C. 1948. *The Divine Relativity: A Social Conception of God*. New Haven, CT: Yale University Press.

Hartshorne, C. 1967. *A Natural Theology for Our Time*. La Salle, IL: Open Court.

Hartshorne, C. 1991. *Anselm's Discovery: A Re-examination of the Ontological Proof for God's Existence*. La Salle, IL: Open Court.

Haught, J. F. 1995. *Science and Religion: From Conflict to Conversion*. New York: Paulist Press.

Haught, J. F. 1998a. "Evolution, Information and Cosmic Purpose," *CTNS Bulletin* 18(1) (Winter).

Haught, J. F. 1998b. "Science, Religion, and the Role of Metaphysics," *CTNS Bulletin* 18(1) (Winter).

Hefner, P. 1993. *The Human Factor: Evolution, Culture, and Religion*, Theology and the Sciences series. Minneapolis, MN: Fortress Press.

Hefner, P. 1996. "Science-and-Religion and the Search for Meaning," *Zygon: Journal of Religion and Science* 31(2) (June).

Heilbron, J. L. 1986. *The Dilemmas of an Upright Man: Max Planck as Spokesman for German Science*. Berkeley, CA: University of California Press.

Heim, K. 1953. *The Transformation of the Scientific World*. London: SCM Press.

Herbert, N. 1985. *Quantum Reality: Beyond the New Physics*. Garden City, NY: Anchor Press.

Herzfeld, N. 1999. *Imago Dei / Imago Hominis: Artificial Intelligence and the Human Need for Redemption* (GTU doctoral dissertation).

Hess, P. 1997. "Science in the Service of God: the Range of Scientific Sophistication in Seventeenth-Century English Theology," *CTNS Bulletin* 17(1) (Winter).

Hesse, M. 1975. "On the Alleged Incompatibility between Christianity and Science," in *Man and Nature*, ed. H. Montefiore. London: Collins.

Hesse, M. 1988. "Socializing Epistemology," in *Construction and Constraint: The Shaping of Scientific Rationality*, ed. E. McMullin. Notre Dame, IN: University of Notre Dame Press.

Hodge, C. 1891. *Systematic Theology*, 3 vols. New York: Charles Scribner's Sons.

Howell, N. R. 1997. "Ecofeminism: What One Needs to Know," *Zygon: Journal of Religion and Science* 32(2) (June).

Hrdy, S. B. 1990. "Raising Darwin's Consciousness: Females and Evolutionary Theory," *Zygon: Journal of Religion and Science* 25(2) (June).

Huchingson, J. E. 1993. *Religion and the Natural Sciences: The Range of Engagement*. Fort Worth: Harcourt Brace Jovanovich College Publishers.

Iqbal, M. 1992. "Five Eminent Early Muslim Scientists and their Contributions to Islamic Scientific Thought," *Islamic Thought and Scientific Creativity* 3(3) (September).

Isham, C. J. 1988. "Creation of the Universe as a Quantum Process," in *Physics, Philosophy, and Theology: A Common Quest for Understanding*, eds. R. J. Russell, W. R. Stoeger, SJ, and G. V. Coyne, SJ. Vatican City State: Vatican Observatory Publications, pp. 375–408.

Isham, C. J. 1993. "Quantum Theories of the Creation of the Universe," in *Quantum Cosmology and the Laws of Nature: Scientific Perspectives on Divine Action*, eds. R. J. Russell, N. C. Murphy, and C. J. Isham, Scientific Perspectives on Divine Action series. Vatican City State: Vatican Observatory Publications; Berkeley, CA: Center for Theology and the Natural Sciences, pp. 49–90.

Isham, C. J. 1995. *Lectures on Quantum Theory: Mathematical and Structural Foundations*. London: Imperial College Press.

Isham, C. J. and Polkinghorne, J. C. 1993. "The Debate over the Block Universe," in *Quantum Cosmology and the Laws of Nature: Scientific Perspectives on Divine Action*, ed. R. J. Russell, N. C. Murphy, and C. J. Isham. Scientific Perspectives on Divine Action series. Vatican City State: Vatican Observatory Publications; Berkeley, CA: Center for Theology and the Natural Sciences. pp. 134–44.

Jammer, M. 1966. *The Conceptual Development of Quantum Mechanics*. New York: McGraw-Hill.

Jammer, M. 1974. *The Philosophy of Quantum Mechanics: The Interpretations of Quantum Mechanics in Historical Perspective*. New York: John Wiley.

Jammer, M. 1999. *Einstein and Religion*. Princeton, NJ: Princeton University Press.

Jastrow, R. 1978. *God and the Astronomers*. New York: W. W. Norton.

Jeannerod, M. 1999. "The Cognitive Way to Action," in *Neuroscience and the Person: Scientific Perspectives on Divine Action*, ed. R. J. Russell, N. Murphy, T. C. Meyering, and M. A. Arbib. Vatican City State: Vatican Observatory Publications; Berkeley, CA: Center for Theology and the Natural Sciences.

Jantzen, G. 1984. *God's World, God's Body*. Philadelphia, PA: Westminster Press.

John Paul II. 1998. "Message to the Pontifical Academy of Sciences," in *Evolutionary and Molecular Biology: Scientific Perspectives on Divine Action*, ed. R. J. Russell, W. R. Stoeger, and F. J. Ayala. Vatican City State: Vatican Observatory Publications; Berkeley, CA: Center of Theology and the Natural Sciences.

Johnson, E. A. 1990. *Consider Jesus: Waves of Renewal in Christology*. New York: Crossroad.

Johnson, E. A. 1993. *She Who Is: The Mystery of God in Feminist Theological Discourse*. New York: Crossroad.

Johnson, E. A. 1996a. "Does God Play Dice? Divine Providence and Chance," *Theological Studies* 57(1):3–18.

Johnson, E. A. 1996b "Presidential Address: Turn to the Heavens and the Earth," *CTSA Proceedings* 51:1–14.

Kaiser, C. B. 1976. "Christology and Complementarity," *Religious Studies* 12:37–48.

Kaiser, C. B. 1991. *Creation and the History of Science*, History of Christian Theology series, no. 3. Grand Rapids, MI: Eerdmans.

Katz, S. H. 1980. "Biological Evolution and the Is/Ought Relationship," *Zygon* 15 (June):155–68.

Kaufman, G. D. 1978. *Systematic Theology: A Historicist Perspective*. New York: Charles Scribner's Sons.

Kaufman, G. D. 1983. "On the meaning of 'Act of God,'" in *God's Activity in the World: The Contemporary Problem*, ed. Owen Thomas, Studies in Religion series/American Academy of Religion, no. 31. Chico, CA: Scholars Press, pp. 137–62.

Kehoe, A. B. 1990. "Gender is an Organon," *Zygon: Journal of Religion and Science* 25(2) (June).

Keller, E. F. and Longino, H. E. eds. 1996. *Feminism and Science*. Oxford: Oxford University Press.

Kerr, F. 1999. "The Modern Philosophy of Self in Recent Theology," in *Neuroscience and the Person: Scientific Perspectives on Divine Action*, eds. R. J. Russell, N. Murphy, T. C. Meyering, and M. A. Arbib. Vatican City State: Vatican Observatory Publications; Berkeley, CA: Center for Theology and the Natural Sciences.

Klaaren, E. M. 1977. *Religious Origins of Modern Science: Belief in Creation in Seventeenth-Century Thought*. Grand Rapids, MI: William B. Eerdmans.

Kolb, E. W. and Turner, M. S. 1994. *The Early Universe*. Reading, MA: Addison-Wesley.

Lameter, C. 1998. "Cosmology in *On the Moral Nature of the Universe* by Murphy and Ellis," *CTNS Bulletin* 19(4) (Fall).

Langford, M. J. 1981. *Providence*. London: SCM Press.

Laudan, L. 1977. *Progress and its Problems: Toward a Theory of Scientific Growth*. Berkeley, CA: University of California Press.

Laudan, L. 1984. "A Confutation of Convergent Realism," in *Scientific Realism*, ed. J. Leplin. Berkeley, CA: University of California Press.

Lebacqz, K. 1993. "Fair Shares: Is the Genome Project Just?" *CTNS Bulletin* 13(4) (Autumn).

Lebacqz, K. 1998. "Fair Shares: Is the Genome Project Just?" in *Genetics: Issues of Social Justice*, ed. T. Peters. Cleveland, OH: Pilgrim Press, pp. 1–48.

LeDoux, J. E. 1996. *The Emotional Brain: The Mysterious Underpinnings of Emotional Life*. New York: Simon and Schuster.

LeDoux, J. E. 1999. "Emotions: How I've Looked for them in the Brain," in *Neuroscience and the Person: Scientific Perspectives on Divine Action*, eds. R. J. Russell, N. Murphy, T. C. Meyering, and M. A. Arbib. Vatican City State: Vatican Observatory Publications; Berkeley, CA: Center for Theology and the Natural Sciences.

Leplin, J. ed. 1984. *Scientific Realism*. Berkeley, CA: University of California Press.

Leslie, J. 1988a. "How to Draw Conclusions from a Fine-tuned Universe," in *Physics, Philosophy, and Theology: A Common Quest for Understanding*, eds. R. J. Russell, W. R. Stoeger, SJ, and G. V. Coyne, SJ. Vatican City State: Vatican Observatory Publications, pp. 297–312.

Leslie, J. 1988b. "The Prerequisites of Life in Our Universe," in *Newton and the New Direction in Science*, eds. G. V. Coyne, J. Zycinski, and M. Heller. Vatican City State: Vatican Observatory.

Leslie, J. 1989. *Universes*. London: Routledge.

Leslie, J. ed. 1990. *Physical Cosmology and Philosophy*. New York: Macmillan.

Lewin, R. 1997. *Patterns in Evolution: The New Molecular View*. New York: Scientific American Library.

Lindberg, D. C. and Numbers, R. L. eds. 1986. *God and Nature: Historical Essays on the Encounter between Christianity and Science*. Berkeley, CA: University of California Press.

Loder, J. E. and Neidhardt, J. W. 1992. *The Knight's Move: The Relational Logic of the Spirit in Theology and Science*. Colorado Springs, CO: Helmers & Howard.

Longino, H. E. and Doell, R. 1996. "Body, Bias, and Behaviour: a Comparative Analysis of Reasoning in Two Areas of Biological Science," in *Feminism and Science*, eds. E. F. Keller and H. E. Longino. Oxford: Oxford University Press.

Lucas, J. R. 1989. *The Future: An Essay on God, Temporality, and Truth*. Oxford: Basil Blackwell.

Lucas, J. R. 1993. "The Temporality of God," in *Quantum Cosmology and the Laws of Nature: Scientific Perspectives on Divine Action*, eds. R. J. Russell, N. C. Murphy, and C. J. Isham, Scientific Perspectives on Divine Action series. Vatican City State: Vatican Observatory Publications; Berkeley, CA: Center for Theology and the Natural Sciences, pp. 235–46.

McFague, S. 1982. *Metaphorical Theology: Models of God in Religious Language*. Philadelphia, PA: Fortress Press.

McFague, S. 1987. *Models of God: Theology for an Ecological, Nuclear Age*. Philadelphia, PA: Fortress Press.

McFague, S. 1988. "Models of God for an Ecological, Evolutionary Era: God as Mother of the Universe," in *Physics, Philosophy, and Theology: A Common Quest for Understanding*, eds. R. J. Russell, W. R. Stoeger, SJ, and G. V. Coyne, SJ. Vatican City State: Vatican Observatory Publications, pp. 249–72.

McFague, S. 1993. *The Body of God: An Ecological Theology*. Minneapolis, MN: Fortress Press.

McGrath, A. E. 1999. *Science and Religion: An Introduction*. Oxford: Blackwell.

McIntyre, J. 1966. *The Shape of Christology*. London: SCM Press.

MacKay, D. M. 1978. *Chance and Providence*. Oxford: Oxford University Press.

MacKinnon, E. M. 1982. *Scientific Explanation and Atomic Physics*. Chicago, IL: University of Chicago Press.

MacKinnon, E. M. 1996. "Complementarity," in *Religion and Science: History, Method, Dialogue*, eds. W. M. Richardson and W. J. Wildman. New York: Routledge, pp. 255–70.

McMullin, E. 1981. "How should Cosmology Relate to Theology?" in *The Sciences and Theology in the Twentieth Century*, ed. A. R. Peacocke. Notre Dame, IN: University of Notre Dame Press, pp. 299–302.

McMullin, E. ed. 1988. *Construction and Constraint: The Shaping of Scientific Rationality*. Notre Dame, IN: University of Notre Dame Press.

McMullin, E. 1990. "Is Philosophy Relevant to Cosmology?" in *Physical Cosmology and Philosophy*, ed. J. Leslie. New York: Macmillan.

Macquarrie, J. 1977. *Principles of Christian Theology* [1966], 2nd edn. New York: Charles Scribner's Sons.

Malmstrom, V. H. 1997. *Cycles of the Sun, Mysteries of the Moon: The Calendar in Mesoamerican Civilization*. Austin, TX: University of Texas Press.

Matt, D. C. 1996. *God and The Big Bang: Discovering Harmony Between Science and Spirituality*. Woodstock, VT: Jewish Lights Publishing.

Mayr, E. 1985. "How Biology Differs from the Physical Sciences," in *Evolution at a Crossroads: The New Biology and the New Philosophy of Science*, eds. D. J. Depew and B. H. Weber. Cambridge, MA: MIT Press, pp. 67–78.

Merchant, C. 1980. *The Death of Nature: Women, Ecology, and the Scientific Revolution*. New York: Harper & Row.

Merzbacher, E. 1961. *Quantum Mechanics*. New York: John Wiley.

Meyering, T. C. 1999. "Mind Matters: Physicalism and the Autonomy of the Person," in *Neuroscience and the Person: Scientific Perspectives on Divine Action*, eds. R. J. Russell, N. Murphy, T. C.

Meyering, and M. A. Arbib. Vatican City State: Vatican Observatory Publications; Berkeley, CA: Center for Theology and the Natural Sciences.

Midgley, M. 1994. *The Ethical Primate: Humans, Freedom, and Morality.* New York: Routledge.

Misner, C. W., Thorne, K. S., and Wheeler, J. A. 1973. *Gravitation.* San Francisco, CA: W. H. Freeman.

Moltmann, J. 1985. "God in Creation: a New Theology of Creation and the Spirit of God," in *The Gifford Lectures, 1984–1985.* San Francisco, CA: Harper & Row.

Mooney, SJ, C. F. 1996. *Theology and Scientific Knowledge: Changing Models of God's Presence in the World.* Notre Dame, IN: University of Notre Dame Press.

Murphy, G. L. 1991. "Time, Thermodynamics, and Theology," *Zygon: Journal of Religion and Science* 26(3) (September).

Murphy, G. L. 1996. "Possible Influences of Biblical Beliefs upon Physics," *Perspectives on Science and Christian Faith* 48(2) (June).

Murphy, N. 1985. "A Niebuhrian Typology for the Relation of Theology to Science," *Pacific Theological Review* XVIII (3) (Spring):16–23.

Murphy, N. 1990a. "Of Miracles," *CTNS Bulletin* 10(2) (Spring).

Murphy, N. 1990b. *Theology in the Age of Scientific Reasoning.* Ithaca, NY: Cornell University Press.

Murphy, N. 1993. "Evidence of Design in the Fine-tuning of the Universe," in *Quantum Cosmology and the Laws of Nature: Scientific Perspectives on Divine Action,* eds. R. J. Russell, N. C. Murphy, and C. J. Isham, Scientific Perspectives on Divine Action series. Vatican City State: Vatican Observatory Publications; Berkeley, CA: Center for Theology and the Natural Sciences, pp. 407–36.

Murphy, N. 1995. "Divine Action in the Natural Order: Buridan's Ass and Schrodinger's Cat," in *Chaos and Complexity: Scientific Perspectives on Divine Action,* ed. R. J. Russell, N. C. Murphy, and A. R. Peacocke, Scientific Perspectives on Divine Action series. Vatican City State: Vatican Observatory Publications; Berkeley, CA: Center for Theology and the Natural Sciences, pp. 325–58.

Murphy, N. 1996a. *Beyond Liberalism and Fundamentalism: How Modern and Postmodern Philosophy Set the Theological Agenda.* Valley Forge, PA: Trinity Press International.

Murphy, N. 1996b. "On the Nature of Theology," in *Religion and Science: History, Method, Dialogue,* eds. W. M. Richardson and W. J. Wildman. New York: Routledge, pp. 151–60.

Murphy, N. 1998. "Supervenience and the Nonreducibility of Ethics to Biology," in *Evolutionary and Molecular Biology: Scientific Perspectives on Divine Action,* eds. R. J. Russell, W. R. Stoeger, SJ, and F. J. Ayala. Vatican City State: Vatican Observatory Publications; Berkeley, CA: Center for Theology and the Natural Sciences.

Murphy, N. 1999. "Supervenience and the Downward Efficacy of the Mental: a Nonreductive Physicalist Account of Human Action," in *Neuroscience and the Person: Scientific Perspectives on Divine Action,* eds. R. J. Russell, N. Murphy, T. C. Meyering, and M. A. Arbib. Vatican City State: Vatican Observatory Publications; Berkeley, CA: Center for Theology and the Natural Sciences.

Murphy, N. and Ellis, G. F. R. 1996. *On the Moral Nature of the Universe: Theology, Cosmology, and Ethics,* Theology and the Sciences series. Minneapolis, MA: Fortress Press.

Nasr, S. H. 1980. *Living Sufism.* London: Unwin.

Nessan, C. L. 1998. "Sex, Aggression, and Pain: Sociobiological Implications for Theological Anthropology," *Zygon: Journal of Religion and Science* 33(3) (September).

Noble, D. F. 1992. *A World without Women: The Christian Clerical Culture of Western Science.* Oxford: Oxford University Press.

North, J. D. 1990. *The Measure of the Universe: A History of Modern Cosmology* [1965]. New York: Dover Publications.

Pannenberg, W. 1976. *Theology and the Philosophy of Science,* trans. F. McDonagh. Philadelphia, PA: Westminster Press.

Pannenberg, W. 1991. *Systematic Theology*, vol. 1, trans. G. W. Bromiley. Grand Rapids, MI: Eerdmans.

Pannenberg, W. 1993. *Toward a Theology of Nature: Essays on Science and Faith*, ed. T. Peters. Louisville, KY: Westminster/John Knox Press.

Pannenberg, W. 1998. *Systematic Theology*, vol. 3, trans. G. W. Bromiley. Grand Rapids, MI: Eerdmans.

Peacocke, A. 1971. *Science and the Christian Experiment*. London: Oxford University Press.

Peacocke, A. 1979. *Creation and the World of Science: The Bampton Lectures, 1979*. Oxford: Clarendon Press.

Peacocke, A. 1981. *The Sciences and Theology in the Twentieth Century*. Notre Dame, IN: University of Notre Dame Press.

Peacocke, A. 1983. *An Introduction to the Physical Chemistry of Biological Organization*. Oxford: Clarendon Press.

Peacocke, A. 1984. *Intimations of Reality: Critical Realism in Science and Religion: The Mendenhall Lectures, 1983*. Notre Dame, IN: University of Notre Dame Press.

Peacocke, A. 1985. "Intimations of Reality: Critical Realism in Science and Religion," *Religion and Intellectual Life* II (4) (Summer).

Peacocke, A. 1986. *God and the New Biology*. San Francisco: Harper & Row.

Peacocke, A. 1993a. "Science and God the Creator," *Zygon: Journal of Religion and Science* 28(4) (December).

Peacocke, A. 1993b. *Theology for a Scientific Age: Being and Becoming – Natural, Divine and Human*, enlarged edn. Minneapolis: Fortress Press.

Peacocke, A. 1994. "The Religion of a Scientist: Explorations in Reality (*Religio philosophi naturalis*)," *Zygon: Journal of Religion and Science* 29(4) (December).

Peacocke, A. 1995. "God's Interaction with the World: the Implications of Deterministic 'Chaos' and of Interconnected and Interdependent Reality," in *Chaos and Complexity: Scientific Perspectives on Divine Action*, eds. R. J. Russell, N. C. Murphy, and A. R. Peacocke, Scientific Perspectives on Divine Action series. Vatican City State: Vatican Observatory Publications; Berkeley, CA: Center for Theology and the Natural Sciences, pp. 263–88.

Peacocke, A. 1998a. "Biological Evolution – a Positive Theological Appraisal," in *Evolutionary and Molecular Biology: Scientific Perspectives on Divine Action*, eds. R. J. Russell, W. R. Stoeger, SJ, and F. J. Ayala. Vatican City State: Vatican Observatory Publications; Berkeley, CA: Center for Theology and the Natural Sciences.

Peacocke, A. 1998b. "Biology and a Theology of Evolution," *Zygon: Journal of Religion and Science* 33(1) (March): 695–712.

Peacocke, A. 1999. "The Sound of Sheer Silence: How does God Communicate with Humanity?" in *Neuroscience and the Person: Scientific Perspectives on Divine Action*, eds. R. J. Russell, N. Murphy, T. C. Meyering, and M. A. Arbib. Vatican City State: Vatican Observatory Publications; Berkeley, CA: Center for Theology and the Natural Sciences.

Pederson, A. and Solberg, M. 1999. "CyberFlesh: an Embodied Feminist Pedagogy for Science and Religion." Paper given to the Science and Religion group at the AAR Annual Meeting.

Peters, K. E. 1997. "Storytellers and Scenario Spinners: Some Reflections on Religion and Science in Light of a Pragmatic, Evolutionary Theory of Knowledge," *Zygon: Journal of Religion and Science* 32(4) (December).

Peters, T. 1988. "On Creating the Cosmos," in *Physics, Philosophy, and Theology: A Common Quest for Understanding*, eds. R. J. Russell, W. R. Stoeger, SJ, and G. V. Coyne, SJ. Vatican City State: Vatican Observatory Publications, pp. 273–96.

Peters, T. ed. 1989. *Cosmos as Creation: Theology and Science in Consonance*. Nashville, TN: Abingdon Press.

Peters, T. 1993a. *God as Trinity: Relationality and Temporality in the Divine Life*. Louisville, KY: Westminster/John Knox Press.

Peters, T. 1993b. "The Trinity In and Beyond Time," in *Quantum Cosmology and the Laws of Nature: Scientific Perspectives on Divine Action*, eds. R. J. Russell, N. C. Murphy, and C. J. Isham, Scientific Perspectives on Divine Action series. Vatican City State: Vatican Observatory Publications; Berkeley, CA: Center for Theology and the Natural Sciences, pp. 263–92.

Peters, T. 1995. "The Physical Body of Immortality," *CTNS Bulletin* 15(2) (Spring).

Peters, T. 1996. "Theology and Science: Where Are We?" *Zygon: Journal of Religion and Science* 31(2) (June).

Peters, T. 1997. "Theology and the Natural Sciences," in *The Modern Theologians: An Introduction to Christian Theology in the Twentieth Century*, 2nd edn., ed. D. F. Ford. Oxford: Blackwell, pp. 649–68.

Peters, T. 1998a. "Genes, Theology, and Social Ethics: Are we Playing God?" in *Genetics: Issues of Social Justice*, ed. T. Peters. Cleveland, OH: Pilgrim Press, pp. 1–48.

Peters, T. 1998b. *Science and Theology: The New Consonance*. Boulder, CO: Westview Press.

Peters, T. 1999. "Resurrection of the Very Embodied Soul?" in *Neuroscience and the Person: Scientific Perspectives on Divine Action*, eds. R. J. Russell, N. Murphy, T. C. Meyering, and M. A. Arbib. Vatican City State: Vatican Observatory Publications; Berkeley, CA: Center for Theology and the Natural Sciences.

Peterson, G. R. 1997. "Cognitive Science: What One Needs to Know," *Zygon: Journal of Religion and Science* 32(4) (December).

Peterson, G. R. 1998. "The Scientific Status of Theology: Imre Lakatos, Method and Demarcation," *Perspectives on Science and Christian Faith* 50(1) (March).

Polkinghorne, J. C. 1989. *Science and Providence: God's Interaction with the World*, 1st Shambhala edn. Boston, MA: Shambhala Publications.

Polkinghorne, J. C. 1994. *The Faith of a Physicist: Reflections of a Bottom–Up Thinker*, Theology and the Sciences series. Minneapolis, MN: Fortress Press.

Polkinghorne, J. C. 1995. "The Metaphysics of Divine Action," in *Chaos and Complexity: Scientific Perspectives on Divine Action*, eds. R. J. Russell, N. C. Murphy, and A. R. Peacocke, Scientific Perspectives on Divine Action series. Vatican City State: Vatican Observatory Publications; Berkeley, CA: Center for Theology and the Natural Sciences, pp. 147–56.

Polkinghorne, J. C. 1996a. "Chaos Theory and Divine Action," in *Religion and Science: History, Method, Dialogue*, eds. W. M. Richardson and W. J. Wildman. New York: Routledge, pp. 243–54.

Polkinghorne, J. C. 1996b. *Scientists as Theologians: A Comparison of the Writings of Ian Barbour, Arthur Peacocke and John Polkinghorne*. London: SPCK.

Polkinghorne, J. C. 1998. *Science and Theology: An Introduction*. London: SPCK.

Polkinghorne, J. C. 2002. *The God of Hope and the End of the World*. New Haven, CT: Yale University Press.

Polkinghorne, J. C. and Welker, M. eds. 2000. *The End of the World and the End of God*. Harrisburg, PA: Trinity Press International.

Pollard, W. G. 1958. *Chance and Providence: God's Action in a World Governed by Scientific Law*. London: Faber and Faber.

Price, D., Wiester, J. L., and Hearn, W. R. 1986. *Teaching Science in a Climate of Controversy: A View from the American Scientific Affiliation*. Ipswich: American Scientific Affiliation.

Primack, J. R. and Abrams, N. 1995. " 'In a beginning . . .': Quantum Cosmology and Kabbalah," *Tikkun* 10 (Jan.–Feb.):66–73.

Putnam, H. 1975a. *Mathematics, Matter, and Method: Philosophical Papers*, vol. 1. Cambridge: Cambridge University Press.

Putnam, H. 1975b. *Mind, Language, and Reality: Philosophical Papers*, vol. 2. Cambridge: Cambridge University Press.

Rahner, K. 1978. *Foundations of Christian Faith*, trans. William V. Dych. New York: Crossroad.

Ramm, B. 1955. *The Christian View of Science and Scripture*. Grand Rapids, MI: W. B. Eerdmans.

Redhead, M. 1987. *Incompleteness, Nonlocality, and Realism: A Prolegomenon to the Philosophy of Quantum Mechanics*. Oxford: Clarendon Press.

Reich, H. 1998. "Cog and God: a Response to Anne Foerst," *Zygon: Journal of Religion and Science* 33(2) (June).

Richardson, K. A. 1995. "The Naturalness of Creation and Redemptive Interests in Theology, Science, and Technology," *Zygon: Journal of Religion and Science* 30(2) (June).

Richardson, M. 1994. "Research Fellow's Report," *CTNS Bulletin* (Berkeley), 14(3) (Summer). The Center for Theology and the Natural Sciences.

Richardson, W. M. and Wildman, W. J. eds. 1996. *Religion and Science: History, Method, Dialogue*. New York: Routledge. Appendix A includes an extensive bibliography.

Rolston, H. III. 1994. "Does Nature Need to be Redeemed?" *Zygon* 29(2):205–29.

Rolston, H. III. 1999. *Genes, Genesis and God: Values and their Origins in Natural and Human History*. Cambridge: Cambridge University Press.

Ross, H. 1993. *The Creator and the Cosmos: How the Greatest Scientific Discoveries of the Century Reveal God*. Colorado Springs, CO: NavPress Publishing Group.

Rudwick, M. 1981. "Senses of the Natural World and Senses of God: Another Look at the Historical Relation of Science and Religion," in *The Sciences and Theology in the Twentieth Century*, ed. A. R. Peacocke. Notre Dame, IN: University of Notre Dame Press.

Ruether, R. R. 1983. *Sexism and God-Talk: Toward a Feminist Theology*. Boston, MA: Beacon Press.

Ruether, R. R. 1992. *Gaia and God: An Ecofeminist Theology of Earth Healing*. San Francisco, CA: HarperCollins.

Ruse, M. 1986a. "Evolutionary Ethics: a Phoenix Arisen," *Zygon: Journal of Religion and Science* 21(1):95–112.

Ruse, M. 1986b. *Taking Darwin Seriously: A Naturalistic Approach*. Oxford: Basil Blackwell.

Ruse, M. 1994. "Evolutionary Theory and Christian Ethics: Are They in Harmony?" *Zygon: Journal of Religion and Science* 29(1) (March).

Ruse, M. 1999. "Evolutionary Ethics: What can we learn from the Past?" *Zygon: Journal of Religion and Science* 34(3) (September).

Russell, R. J. 1984. "Entropy and Evil," *Zygon: Journal of Religion and Science* 19(4) (December).

Russell, R. J. 1988a. "Contingency in Physics and Cosmology: a Critique of the Theology of Wolfhart Pannenberg," *Zygon: Journal of Religion and Science* 23(1) (March).

Russell, R. J. 1988b. "Quantum Physics in Philosophical and Theological Perspective," in *Physics, Philosophy, and Theology: A Common Quest for Understanding*, eds. R. J. Russell, W. R. Stoeger, SJ, and G. V. Coyne, SJ, Vatican City State: Vatican Observatory Publications, pp. 343–74.

Russell, R. J. 1989. "Cosmology, Creation, and Contingency," in *Cosmos as Creation: Theology and Science in Consonance*, ed. T. Peters. Nashville: Abingdon Press, pp. 177–210.

Russell, R. J. 1990. "The Thermodynamics of 'Natural Evil,'" *CTNS Bulletin* 10(2) (Spring).

Russell, R. J. 1993. "Finite Creation Without a Beginning: the Doctrine of Creation in Relation to Big Bang and Quantum Cosmologies," in *Quantum Cosmology and the Laws of Nature: Scientific Perspectives on Divine Action*, eds. R. J. Russell, N. C. Murphy, and C. J. Isham, Scientific Perspectives on Divine Action series. Vatican City State: Vatican Observatory Publications; Berkeley, CA: Center for Theology and the Natural Sciences.

Russell, R. J. 1996. "T = 0: Is it Theologically Significant?" in *Religion and Science: History, Method, Dialogue*, eds. W. M. Richardson and W. J. Wildman. New York: Routledge, pp. 201–26.

Russell, R. J. 1997. "Philosophy, Theology and Cosmology: a Fresh Look at their Interactions," in *Scienza, Filosofia e Teologia di Fronte alla Nascita dell'Universo*, eds. P. Eligio, G. Giorello, G. Rigamonti, and E. Sindoni. Como: Edizioni New Press, pp. 215–46.

Russell, R. J. 1998a. "Special Providence and Genetic Mutation: a New Defense of Theistic Evolution," in *Evolutionary and Molecular Biology: Scientific Perspectives on Divine Action*, eds. R. J. Russell, W. R. Stoeger, SJ, and F. J. Ayala. Vatican City State: Vatican Observatory Publications; Berkeley, CA: Center for Theology and the Natural Sciences.

Russell, R. J. 1998b. "The Theological Consequences of the Thermodynamics of a Moral Universe: an Appreciative Critique and Extension of the Murphy/Ellis Project," *CTNS Bulletin* 19(4) (Fall).

Russell, R. J. 2000. "Time in Eternity." *Dialog* 39(1) (March).

Russell, R. J. 2001. "Divine Action and Quantum Mechanics: A Fresh Assessment," in *Quantum Mechanics: Scientific Perspectives on Divine Action*, eds. R. J. Russell, P. Clayton, K. Wegter-McNelly, and J. Polkinghorne. Vatican City State: Vatican Observatory Publications.

Russell, R. J. 2002. "Bodily Resurrection, Eschatology, and Scientific Cosmology," in *Resurrection: Theological and Scientific Assessments*, eds. T. Peters, R. J. Russell, and M. Welker. Grand Rapids, MI: W. B. Eerdmans.

Russell, R. J., Stoeger, SJ, W. R., and Coyne, SJ, G. V. eds. 1988. *Physics, Philosophy, and Theology: A Common Quest for Understanding.* Vatican City State: Vatican Observatory Publications.

Russell, R. J., Murphy, N. C., and Isham, C. J. eds. 1993. *Quantum Cosmology and the Laws of Nature: Scientific Perspectives on Divine Action*, Vatican City State: Vatican Observatory Publications; Berkeley, CA: Center for Theology and the Natural Sciences.

Russell, R. J., Murphy, N. C., and Peacocke, A. R. eds. 1995. *Chaos and Complexity: Scientific Perspectives on Divine Action*, Scientific Perspectives on Divine Action series. Vatican City State: Vatican Observatory Publications; Berkeley, CA: Center for Theology and the Natural Sciences.

Russell, R. J., Murphy, N. C., Meyering, T. C., and Arbib, M. A. eds. 1999. *Neuroscience and the Person: Scientific Perspectives on Divine Action.* Vatican City State; Berkeley, CA: Vatican Observatory Publications; Center for Theology and the Natural Sciences.

Russell, R. J., Stoeger, SJ, W. R., and Ayala, F. J. eds. 1998. *Evolutionary and Molecular Biology: Scientific Perspectives on Divine Action*, eds. R. J. Russell, W. R. Stoeger, SJ, and F. J. Ayala. Vatican City State: Vatican Observatory Publications; Berkeley, CA: Center for Theology and the Natural Sciences.

Russell, R. J., Clayton, P., Wegter-McNelly, K., and Polkinghorne, J. eds. 2001. *Quantum Mechanics: Scientific Perspectives on Divine Action.* Vatican City State: Vatican Observatory Publications.

Sagan, C. 1980. *Cosmos.* New York: Random House.

Samuelson, N. M. 1994. *Judaism and the Doctrine of Creation.* Cambridge: Cambridge University Press.

Sardar, Z. 1989. *Explorations in Islamic Science.* London: Mansell.

Saunders, N. T. 2000. " 'Does God Cheat at Dice?' Divine Action and Quantum Possibilities," *Zygon: Journal of Religion and Science* (to appear).

Schilpp, P. A. ed. 1949 (1951). *Albert Einstein: Philosopher–Scientist*, vols. 1 and 2. New York: Harper & Row.

Schmitz-Moormann, K. 1987. "On the Evolution of Human Freedom," *Zygon: Journal of Religion and Science* 22(4) (December).

Schroedinger, E. 1945. *What is Life? Mind and Matter* [1967]. Cambridge: Cambridge University Press.

Scoville, J. 1992. " 'Natural Evil' and God's Action: a Critical Examination," *CTNS Bulletin* 12(3) (Summer).

Segundo, J. L. 1988. *An Evolutionary Approach to Jesus of Nazareth*, trans. John Drury. New York: Orbis.

Shannon, T. A. 1998. "Genetics, Ethics, and Theology: the Roman Catholic Discussion," in *Genetics: Issues of Social Justice*, ed. T. Peters. Cleveland, OH: Pilgrim Press, pp. 144–79.

Shimony, A. 1989. "Conceptual Foundations of Quantum Mechanics," in *The New Physics*, ed. P. Davies. Cambridge: Cambridge University Press.

Shinn, R. L. 1998. "Genetics, Ethics, and Theology: the Ecumenical Discussion," in *Genetics: Issues of Social Justice*, ed. T. Peters. Cleveland, OH: Pilgrim Press, pp. 122–43.

Soskice, J. M. 1985. *Metaphor and Religious Language*. Oxford: Oxford University Press.

Soskice, J. M. 1988. "Knowledge and Experience in Science and Religion: Can we be Realists?" in *Physics, Philosophy, and Theology: A Common Quest for Understanding*, eds. R. J. Russell, W. R. Stoeger, SJ, and G. V. Coyne, SJ. Vatican City State: Vatican Observatory Publications, pp. 173–84.

Southgate, C., Deane-Drummond, C., Murray, P. D., Negus, M. R., Osborn, L., Poole, M., Stewart, J., and Watts, F., eds. 1999. *God, Humanity and the Cosmos: A Textbook in Science and Religion*. Harrisburg: Trinity Press International.

Stenmark, L. L. 1999. "Seeing the Log in our Own Eye: the Social Location of the Science and Religion Discourse." Paper given to the Science and Religion group at the AAR Annual Meeting.

Stenmark, M. 1995. *Rationality in Science, Religion, and Everyday Life: A Critical Evaluation of Four Models of Rationality*. Notre Dame, IN: University of Notre Dame Press.

Stenmark, M. 1997. "An Unfinished Debate: What are the Aims of Religion and Science?" *Zygon: Journal of Religion and Science* 32(4) (December).

Stoeger, SJ, W. R. 1993. "Contemporary Physics and the Ontological Status of the Laws of Nature," in *Quantum Cosmology and the Laws of Nature: Scientific Perspectives on Divine Action*, eds. R. J. Russell, N. C. Murphy, and C. J. Isham, Scientific Perspectives on Divine Action series. Vatican City State: Vatican Observatory Publications; Berkeley, CA: Center for Theology and the Natural Sciences, pp. 209–34.

Stoeger, SJ, W. R. 1995. "Describing God's Action in the World in Light of Scientific Knowledge of Reality," in *Chaos and Complexity: Scientific Perspectives on Divine Action*, eds. R. J. Russell, N. C. Murphy, and A. R. Peacocke, Scientific Perspectives on Divine Action series. Vatican City State: Vatican Observatory Publications; Berkeley, CA: Center for Theology and the Natural Sciences, pp. 239–62.

Stoeger, SJ, W. R. 1996. "Key Developments in Physics Challenging Philosophy and Theology," in *Religion and Science: History, Method, Dialogue*, eds. W. M. Richardson and W. J. Wildman. New York: Routledge, pp. 183–200.

Stoeger, SJ, W. R. 1998. "The Immanent Directionality of the Evolutionary Process, and its Relationship to Theology," in *Evolutionary and Molecular Biology: Scientific Perspectives on Divine Action*, eds. R. J. Russell, W. R. Stoeger, and F. J. Ayala. Vatican City State: Vatican Observatory Publications; Berkeley, CA: Center for Theology and the Natural Sciences.

Stoeger, SJ, W. R. 1999. "The Mind–Brain Problem, the Laws of Nature, and Constitutive Relationships," in *Neuroscience and the Person: Scientific Perspectives on Divine Action*, eds. R. J. Russell, N. Murphy, T. C. Meyering, and M. A. Arbib. Vatican City State: Vatican Observatory Publications; Berkeley, CA: Center for Theology and the Natural Sciences.

Stoeger, SJ, W. R. and Ellis, G. F. R. 1995. "A Response to Tipler's Omega-Point Theory," *Science and Christian Belief* 7(2):163–72.

Suchocki, M. H. 1982. *God, Christ, Church: A Practical Guide to Process Theology*. New York: Crossroad.

Suchocki, M. H. 1994. *The Fall to Violence: Original Sin in Relational Theology*. New York: Continuum.

Taylor, E. F. and Wheeler, J. A. 1963 (revised, 1992). *Spacetime Physics*. San Francisco, CA: W. H. Freeman.

Teilhard de Chardin, P. 1975. *The Phenomenon of Man*, trans. B. Wall. New York: Harper & Row.

Theissen, G. 1985. *Biblical Faith: An Evolutionary Approach*, Philadelphia, PA: Fortress Press.

Thomas, O. ed. 1983. *God's Activity in the World: The Contemporary Problem*, Studies in Religion Series/American Academy of Religion, no. 31. Chico, CA: Scholars Press.

Thomas, O. 1990. "Recent Thought on Divine Agency," in *Divine Action*, ed. B. Hebblethwaite and E. Henderson. Edinburgh: T. & T. Clark.

Tiles, M. 1996. "A Science of Mars or of Venus?" in *Feminism and Science*, eds. E. F. Keller and H. E. Longino. Oxford: Oxford University Press.

Tipler, F. J. 1994. *The Physics of Immortality: Modern Cosmology, God, and the Resurrection of the Dead.* New York: Doubleday.

Tomm, W. A. 1990. "Sexuality, Rationality, and Spirituality," *Zygon: Journal of Religion and Science* 25(2) (June).

Torrance, T. F. 1969. *Theological Science.* London: Oxford University Press.

Tracy, T. F. 1992. "Evil, Human Freedom, and Divine Grace," *CTNS Bulletin* 12(1) (Winter).

Tracy, T. F. ed. 1994. *The God who Acts: Philosophical and Theological Explorations.* University Park, PA: Pennsylvania State University Press.

Tracy, T. F. 1995. "Particular Providence and the God of the Gaps." In *Chaos and Complexity: Scientific Perspectives on Divine Action*, eds. R. J. Russell, N. C. Murphy, and A. R. Peacocke, Scientific Perspectives on Divine Action series. Vatican City State: Vatican Observatory Publications; Berkeley, CA: Center for Theology and the Natural Sciences, pp. 289–324.

Tracy, T. F. 1998. "Evolution, Divine Action, and the Problem of Evil," in *Evolutionary and Molecular Biology: Scientific Perspectives on Divine Action*, eds. R. John Russell, W. R. Stoeger, SJ, and F. J. Ayala. Vatican City State: Vatican Observatory Publications: Berkeley, CA: Center for Theology and the Natural Sciences.

Trefil, J. S. 1983. *The Moment of Creation: Big Bang Physics from Before the First Millisecond to the Present Universe.* New York: Macmillan.

Trefil, J. S. and Hazen, R. M. 2000. *The Sciences: An Integrated Approach*, updated edn. New York: John Wiley.

Van der Meer, J. M., ed. 1996. *Facets of Faith and Science.* 4 vols. Ancaster, Ontario; Lanham, MD: Pascal Center for Advanced Studies in Faith and Science; University Press of America.

Van Fraassen, B. C. 1980. *The Scientific Image*, Clarendon Library of Logic and Philosophy series. Oxford: University Press.

Van Huyssteen, J. W. 1989. *Theology and the Justification of Faith: Constructing Theories in Systematic Theology.* Grand Rapids, MI: Eerdmans.

Van Huyssteen, J. W. 1997. *Essays in Postfoundationalist Theology.* Grand Rapids, MI: W. B. Eerdmans.

Van Ness, H. C. 1969. *Understanding Thermodynamics.* New York: McGraw-Hill.

Van Till, H. J. 1990. *Portraits of Creation: Biblical and Scientific Perspectives on the World's Formation.* Grand Rapids, MI: Eerdmans.

Van Till, H. J., Young, D. A., and Menninga, C. 1988. *Science Held Hostage: What's Wrong with Creation Science and Evolutionism.* Downers Grove, IL: InterVarsity Press.

Ward, K. 1990. *Divine Action.* London: Collins.

Wassermann, C. 1989. "The Evolutionary Understanding of Man and the Problem of Evil," in *Kooperation und Wettbewerb: Zur Ethik und Biologie menschlichen Sozialverhaltens*, ed. H. May. Loccumer Protokolle.

Watts, F. N. 1997. "Psychological and Religious Perspectives on Emotion," *Zygon: Journal of Religion and Science* 32(2) (June).

Watts, F. N. ed. 1998. *Science Meets Faith: Theology and Science in Conversation.* London: SPCK.

Watts, F. N. 1999. "Cognitive Neuroscience and Religious Consciousness," in *Neuroscience and the Person: Scientific Perspectives on Divine Action*, eds. R. J. Russell, N. Murphy, T. C. Meyering, and M. A. Arbib. Vatican City State: Vatican Observatory Publications; Berkeley, CA: Center for Theology and the Natural Sciences.

Wegter-McNelly, K. 1998. "'He Descended into Hell': a Liberation Response to the Kenosis in *On the Moral Nature of the Universe*," *CTNS Bulletin* 19(4) (Fall).

Weinberg, S. 1972. *Gravitation and Cosmology: Principles and Applications of the General Theory of Relativity*. New York: John Wiley.

Weinberg, S. 1992. *Dreams of a Final Theory*. New York: Pantheon.

Welch, C. 1985. *Protestant Thought in the Nineteenth Century*, vol. 2. New Haven, CT: Yale University Press.

Welch, S. 1996. "Dispelling some Myths about the Split between Theology and Science in the Nineteenth Century," in *Religion and Science: History, Method, Dialogue*, eds. W. M. Richardson and W. J. Wildman. New York: Routledge, pp. 29–40.

Wertheim, M. 1995. *Pythagoras' Trousers: God, Physics, and the Gender Wars*. New York: Times Books.

White, A. D. 1896. *A History of the Warfare of Science with Theology in Christendom*. London and New York: D. Appleton.

Whitehead, A. N. 1978. *Process and Reality*, corrected edn, eds. D. R. Griffin and D. W. Sherburne. New York: Free Press.

Wildman, W. J. 1996. "The Quest for Harmony: an Interpretation of Contemporary Theology and Science," in *Religion and Science: History, Method, Dialogue*, eds. W. M. Richardson and W. J. Wildman. New York: Routledge, pp. 40–60.

Wildman, W. J. 1998. "Evaluating the Teleological Argument for Divine Action," in *Evolutionary and Molecular Biology: Scientific Perspectives on Divine Action*, eds. R. J. Russell, W. R. Stoeger, and F. J. Ayala. Vatican City State: Vatican Observatory Publications; Berkeley, CA: Center for Theology and the Natural Sciences.

Wildman, W. J. and Brothers, L. A. 1999. "A Neuropsychological–Semiotic Model of Religious Experiences," in *Neuroscience and the Person: Scientific Perspectives on Divine Action*, eds. R. J. Russell, N. Murphy, T. C. Meyering, and M. A. Arbib. Vatican City State: Vatican Observatory Publicatons; Berkeley, CA: Center for Theology and the Natural Sciences.

Wildman, W. J. and Russell, R. J. 1995. "Chaos: a Mathematical Introduction with Philosophical Reflections," in *Chaos and Complexity: Scientific Perspectives on Divine Action*, eds. R. J. Russell, N. C. Murphy, and A. R. Peacocke, Scientific Perspectives on Divine Action series. Vatican City State: Vatican Observatory Publications; Berkeley CA: Center for Theology and the Natural Sciences, pp. 49–92.

Wiles, M. 1983. "Religious Authority and Divine Action," in *God's Activity in the World: The Contemporary Problem*, ed. O. Thomas, Studies in Religion Series/American Academy of Religion, no. 31. Chico, CA: Scholars Press, pp. 181–94.

Wiles, M. 1986. *God's Action in the World: The Bampton Lectures for 1986*. London: SCM Press.

Wilson, E. O. 1975. *Sociobiology: The New Synthesis*. Cambridge, MA: Belknap Press, Harvard University Press.

Wilson, E. O. 1978. *On Human Nature*. Cambridge, MA: Harvard University Press.

Wolterstorff, N. 1976. *Reason within the Bounds of Religion*. Grand Rapids, MI: Eerdmans.

Wolterstorff, N. 1996. "Entitled Christian Belief," in *Religion and Science: History, Method, Dialogue*, eds. W. M. Richardson and W. J. Wildman. New York: Routledge, pp. 145–50.

Worthing, M. W. 1996. *God, Creation, and Contemporary Physics*, Theology and the Sciences series. Minneapolis, MN: Fortress Press.

Young, K. 1996. "Deterministic Chaos and Quantum Chaology," in *Religion and Science: History, Method, Dialogue*, eds. W. M. Richardson and W. J. Wildman. New York: Routledge, pp. 221–42.

Zoloth-Dorfman, L. 1998. "Mapping the Normal Human Self: the Jew and the Mark of Otherness," in *Genetics: Issues of Social Justice*, ed. T. Peters. Cleveland, OH: Pilgrim Press, pp. 180–204.

Zycinski, J. M. 1996. "Metaphysics and Epistemology in Stephen Hawking's Theory of the Creation of the Universe," *Zygon: Journal of Religion and Science* 31(2) (June).

Index

Note: Page references in **bold** type indicate major references to main topics. Names of contributors to the Handbook are indexed only where cited in chapters other than their own.

Key Reference

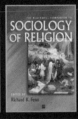

Volumes in
Religion &
Theology

Offering original,
state-of-the-art essays by
internationally recognized
scholars, the Blackwell
Companions to Religion
provide outstanding
reference sources.

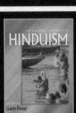
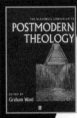
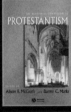
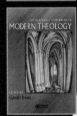

Forthcoming:

For more information on our Companions
to Religion & Theology series, visit
www.blackwellpublishing.com/reference

Blackwell
Publishing